CROSSW

F

DICTIONARY

CROSSWORD PUZZLE DICTIONARY

Unit 5A, 202–208 New North Road,
London N1 7BJ, England

ENGLISH EDITION

PRINTED IN GREAT BRITAIN

A

aa - - - - - - - - - - - - - LAVA
Aaron's associate - - - - - - HUR
abaft - - - AFT, ASTERN, BEHIND
abandon - DESPAIR, FORSAKE, LEAVE, DESOLATE, DESERT
abandoned - - - DERELICT, DESOLATE
abandonment - - - - - - DESERTION
abase - LOWER, DISCREDIT, HUMBLE, DEGRADE, DISHONOUR
abasement - - - - - - - - SHAME
abash - - - SHAME, DISCONCERT, HUMILIATE, CHAGRIN, CONFUSE
abate - LESSEN, DIMINISH, SUBSIDE, DECREASE
abatement (colloq.) - - - - - LETUP
abbe - - - - - - - - - - ABBOT
abbe's estate - - - - - - - ABBACY
abbess - - - - - - - - - - AMMA
abbey superior - - - - - - - ABBOT
abbot - - - - - - - - - - - ABBE
abbreviate - - - - - - - CURTAIL
abdicate - - - DEMIT, RELINQUISH, RENOUNCE
abdominal - - - - - - - VENTRAL
abduct - - - - - - - - - - KIDNAP
abed - - - ASLEEP, SICK, RETIRED
Abelard's wife - - - - - - HELOISE
aberrant - - WANDERING, ABNORMAL
aberration - - - DELIRIUM, LAPSE
Abe's birthplace - - - - - - - - UR
Abe's nephew - - - - - - - - LOT
Abe's wife - - - - - - - - SARAH
abet - AID, ASSIST, URGE, INSTIGATE, EGG, INCITE, ENCOURAGE, PROMOTE, FOMENT, HELP, SANCTION, UPHOLD, SECOND
abhor - - - HATE, DETEST, LOATHE
abide - - WAIT, REMAIN, SOJOURN, DWELL, TARRY, STAY
ability - COMPETENCE, TALENT, POWER, SKILL
abject - - - - - - - SERVILE, BASE
abjure - DISAVOW, RENOUNCE, RECANT
ablaze - - - - - - - - - BURNING
able - COMPETENT, COULD, CLEVER, CAPABLE
able to discharge debts - - - SOLVENT
able to pay - - - - - - - SOLVENT
able to read and write - - - LITERATE
ablution - - - - - - - - - BATH
abnegate - - - - - - - - - DENY
abnormal - ANOMALY, ABERRANT, ODD
aboard ship - - - - - - - - ASEA
abode - - RESIDENCE, LODGE, HOME, HABITATION, HABITAT, LODGING, DWELLING
abode of ancient harp - - - - TARA
abode of the dead - - ARALU, AARU, HADES
abode of first parents - - - - EDEN
abode of the gods - - - - ASGARD
abode of Morgan le Fay - - - AVALON
abode of souls barred from heaven LIMBO
abolish - - - - - - REPEAL, ANNUL
abolishment - - - - - - EXTINCTION
abolition - - - - - - - ANNULMENT
abolitionist - - STEVENS, GARRISON
abominable - - - - - - - - - BAD
abominate - LOATHE, HATE, EXECRATE
abomination - - - - CRIME, VICE
aboreal marsupial - - - - - - KOALA
aboreal rodent - - - SQUIRREL
aboriginal American - - - - - INDIAN
aborigine - - - - - - - - - NATIVE
aborigines of Antilles - - - - INERIS
abortive - - - - - - - FRUITLESS
abound - - - - - TEEM, EXUBERATE
abounding - - - - - REPLETE, RIFE
abounding in a certain fuel - - PEATY
about - OF, ON, ANENT, AROUND, AT
about (abbr.) - - - - - - - - CIRC
about (prefix) - - - - - - - - BE
about this - - - - - - - - HEREOF
above - - - - - - OVER, UP, ATOP
above and in contact with - - - UPON
above (contr.) - - - - - - - O'ER
above the ear - - - - - - - EPIOTIC
above (Latin) - - - - - - - SUPRA
above (poet.) - - - - - - - - O'ER
above (prefix) - - - - - SUPER, SUPRA
above and touching - ONTO, ON, UPON
abra - - - - - - - - - - - DEFILE
abrade - - - - WEAR, GRATE, RASP, EXCORIATE
abrading tool - - - - FILE, GRATER
abrasive material - - EMERY, BORT
abri - - - - - - - - - - SHELTER
abridged and classified - - DIGESTED
abridgment - - - - - - - EPITOME
abridge (var.) - - - - - - - RASEE
abroad - - - - - - OVERSEAS, AFAR
abrogate - REPEAL, RESCIND, ANNUL, CANCEL
abrupt - - - STEEP, SUDDEN, HASTY, UNEXPECTED, SHORT
abscond - - ELOPE, DESERT, ELOIN
absent - - - - - - - - - - AWAY
absent-minded - - - - - - DISTRAIT
absolute - - UTTER, SHEER, STARK, IMPLICIT, MERE, TOTAL, PURE
absolute likeness - - - - - IDENTITY
absolute monarch - - - - - DESPOT
absolute superlative - - - - - ELATIVE
absolve - - - FREE, REMIT, PARDON
absorb - - - - - - MERGE, IMBIBE
absorb into something else - - MERGE
absorb liquid color - - - - - - DYE
absorbed - - - - - - - - - - RAPT
absorbent article - - - - - - SPONGE
absorption - - - - - - - - MERGER
abstain from - - - AVOID, ESCHEW, REFRAIN
abstain from food - - - - - - FAST
abstemious - - - - - - - ASCETIC
abstinent - - - TEMPERATE, SOBER
abstract - - - - - - - RECONDITE
abstract being - - - - - - ENS, ESSE
abstruse - - COMPLEX, RECONDITE, ESOTERIC
absurd - - - - - - - - - - INEPT
abundance - - PLENTITUDE, PLENTY, GALORE, STORE, FLOW
abundant - - - - AMPLE, GALORE, PLENTIFUL, COPIOUS
abundant supply - PLENTY, GRANARY, STORE, MINE
abundantly - - - - - - - - - WELL
abuse - - REVILE, MALTREAT, MAUL, OUTRAGE, MISTREAT
abusive remarks - - - - - - - - MUD
abut - - BORDER, ADJOIN, PROJECT
abutment of arch - - - - - - ALETTE
abyss - - - PIT, CHASM, DEEP, GULF
Abyssinian - - - - - - ETHIOPIAN
Abyssinian herb - - - - - - RAMTIL
Abyssinian title or governor - - RAS, NEGUS

A

academic attainment - - - - DEGREE
academic themes - - - - - THESES
acarid - - - - - - - - MITE, TICK
accede - - CONSENT, AGREE, COMPLY
accent - - STRESS, EMPHASIZE, TONE
accept - - - - - - - - - TAKE
accept as one's own - - - - ADOPT
accept as true - - CREDIT, BELIEVE
accept as valid - - - - - - ADMIT
access - ENTREE, DOOR, ENTRY, ADIT
accessible - - - - - - - - OPEN
accessory - - ADJUNCT, SUBSIDIARY
accident - - - - MISHAP, CHANCE
acclaim - - PRAISE, CLAP, OVATION, APPLAUSE
acclamation - - - - - - APPLAUSE
accolade - - - - - AWARD HONOUR
accommodate - ADAPT, SUIT, PLEASE, OBLIGE
accommodation - - - - - - SPACE
accommodative - - - - - ADAPTABLE
accompany - - - - ESCORT, ATTEND
accompanying - - - - - ATTENDANT
accomplice - - - - - - TOOL, PAL
accomplish - - EXECUTE, DO, REALIZE
accomplishment - - - - - FEAT, DEED
accord - - - - - - - - - UNISON
according to - - - - - - - - ALLA
according to law - - - - - - LEGALLY
accost - - - HAIL, GREET, ASSAIL, ADDRESS
account - - - REPORT, RECITAL, TAB
account (abbr.) - - - - - - - - AC
account book - - - - - - - LEDGER
account entry - - - - - - - ITEM
accountable - - - - - - - LIABLE
accouterments - - - - - TRAPPINGS
accredit - - - - - - AUTHORIZE
accrue - - - - - - - - REDOUND
accumulate - AMASS, STORE, COLLECT, PILE
accumulation - - - - - - GAIN, PILE
accuracy - - - - - - - PRECISION
accurate - - EXACT, CORRECT, TRUE
accusation - - - - - - - CHARGE
accuse - - CENSURE, BLAME, CHARGE ARRAIGN
accuse formally - - - - - - ARRAIGN
accustom (var.) - - - ENURE, INURE
accustomed - - - - - USED, INURED
ace - - - TOP, UNIT, EXPERT, JOT, PARTICLE
ace of clubs - - - - - - - BASTO
acerb - BITTER, HARSH, SOUR, TART, ACID
acerbity - - - - - - - TARTNESS
acetic - - - - - - - - - - SOUR
acetose - - - - - - - - - SOUR
ache - - - - - - - AIL, PAIN, PANG
achieve - WIN, EARN, GAIN, ATTAIN, DO
achievement - - DEED, ACT, RECORD, FEAT, GEST
Achilles' sore spot - - - - - - HEEL
acid - - - - - - - - SOUR, BITING
acid of apples - - - - - - - MALIC
acid berry - - - - - - GOOSEBERRY
acid beverage - - - - - - - - SOUR
acid chemical - - - - - - - - AMIDE
acid condiment - - - - - - - VINEGAR
acid counteractive - - - - - ALKALI
acid (kind) - - - - - - - - - BORIC
acid liquid - - - - - - - - VINEGAR
acid neutralizer - - - - - - ALKALI
acid substance from grape juice - TARTAR
acidity - - - - - - - - - - ACOR

acknowledge - - OWN, ADMIT, AVOW, CONFESS, CONCEDE
acknowledge applause - - - - - BOW
acknowledge openly - - - - - AVOW
acknowledgement - - - - - AVOWAL
acknowledgement of a wrong - APOLOGY
acme - - - - - - - - - APEX, TOP
acolyte - - - - - - - - - NOVICE
aconite - - - - ATIS, MONKSHOOD, WOLFSBANE
acor - - - - - - - - - - ACIDITY
acorns and the like - - - - - - MAST
acquaint - - - - - - - - - APPRISE
acquiesce - - ASSENT, AGREEMENT, CONSENT, AGREE
acquiescence - - - - - - - CONSENT
acquirable - - - - - - - SECURABLE
acquire - GAIN, LEARN, SECURE, WIN, GET, ATTAIN, EARN
acquire beforehand - - - - PREEMPT
acquire knowledge - - - - - - LEARN
acquire by labor - - - - - - - - EARN
acquire with difficulty - - - - - EKE
acquit - - EXONERATE, CLEAR, FREE
acre (1/4) - - - - - - - - - - ROD
acred - - - - - - - - - - - LANDED
acreage for planting - - - - - FARM
acrid - SOUR, BITTER, PUNGENT, TART
acrimonious - - - - - - - - ACRID
acrogen - - - - - - - - - - - FERN
across - - ASTRIDE, OVER, BEYOND
across (poet.) - - - - - - - - O'ER
act - DEED, FEAT, BEHAVE, DO, FEIGN, SIMULATE, LAW
act in agreement - - - - - CONFORM
act of aiding (law) - - - - - - AIDER
act of calculation - - - - - LOGISTIC
act of calling forth - - ELICITATION
act of carrying - - - - - - PORTAGE
act of coming in again - REENTRANCE
act of concealing - - - - SECRETION
act dispiritedly - - - - - - - - MOPE
act of distributing cards in wrong way MISDEAL
act emotionally - - - - - - - EMOTE
act of flying - - - - - - - - FLIGHT
act of following - - - - - - PURSUIT
act of forcing oneself in - - INTRUSION
act of greeting - - - - - - - SALUTE
act hesitatingly - - - - - - - FALTER
act of holding - - - - - - RETENTION
act of incorporation - - - - - CHARTER
act of interment - - - - - - - BURIAL
act jointly - - - - - - - COOPERATE
act of lending - - - - - - - - LOAN
act of lowering - - - - - DEPRESSION
act as mediator - - - - - INTERCEDE
act of migrating - - - - - - - TREK
act of mortification - - - - - PENANCE
act of neglect - - - - - - - OMISSION
act of nourishing - - - - NUTRITION
act of omitting - - - - - - - ELISION
act out of sorts - - - - - - - - MOPE
act of quitting - - - - - - - - EXIT
act of reading - - - - - - - PERUSAL
act of reposing - - - - - - REPOSAL
act in response - - - - - - - REACT
act of retaliation - - - - - REPRISAL
act of retribution - - - - - NEMESIS
act of revending - - - - - - - RESALE
act of selling ecclesiastical preferment SIMONY
act of shunning - - - - - AVOIDANCE
act of splitting into pieces - FISSION
act sullen - - - - - - - MOPE, POUT
act of taking part - - PARTICIPATION

A

act toward - - - - - - - - TREAT
act of turning on an axis - - ROTATION
act of twisting - - - - - - TORSION
act of wearing away - - - EROSION
act wildly - - - - - - - - RAVE
act with dispatch - - - - HUSTLE
act with violence - - - - - RAGE
act of withdrawing - - - SECESSION
action - - - - - - - - DEED, ACT
action (kind of) - - - - - - ACETIC
act in law - - - - - - - - RES, RE
action (pert. to) - - - - - PRACTICAL
action to recover goods - - REPLEVIN
activate - - - - - - - - - LIVEN
active - SPRY, NIMBLE, ALIVE, ASTIR, BRISK, QUICK
active consciousness - - - ATTENTION
active (dial.) - - - - - - - YARE
active place - - - - - - - - HIVE
actor - - - PLAYER, THESPIAN, DOER
actors in a play - - - - - - CAST
actual - - - - - - - - - - REAL
actual being - - - - - - - - ESSE
actuality - - - - - - - - - FACT
actualized - - - - - - - - DONE
actually - - - - - - - - - REALLY
actuate - INCITE, MOVE, AROUSE, IMPEL, URGE
acumen - - - SAGACITY, SHARPNESS
acute - KEEN, INTENSE, POINTED, SHREWD, POIGNANT, TART, CRITICAL
adage - SAW, PROVERB, SAYING, MAXIM, MOTTO
adamant - HARD, FIRM, IMMOVABLE
adamantine - - - - - - IMMOVABLE
Adam's consort - - - - - - - EVE
Adam's grandson - - - - - - ENOS
Adam's son - - - - - - - - SETH
adapt - ADJUST, SUIT, CONFORM, FIT
adapt for acting - - - - DRAMATIZE
adapt to the shape - - - - - - FIT
adapted - FIT, SUITED, TUNED, FITTED
adapted to curling - - - - REMEDIAL
adapted to grinding - - - - - MOLAR
aday - - - - - - - - - - - DAILY
add - APPEND, INCREASE, TOTAL, AUGMENT, ATTACH, ANNEX, AFFIX
add spirits to - - - - - - - LACE
add sugar to - - - - - - - SWEETEN
added - - - - - - - - - APPENDED
addenda - - - - - - - - ADDITION
addicted - - - - - - - - - PRONE
addition - ADDENDA, ALSO, BESIDES, ASIDE, PLUS, YET, MORE, TOO, ELSE, AND
addition to a bill - - - - - - RIDER
addition to a building - - - - - ELL
addition to a document - - - - RIDER
addition to a letter - - - - - - P.S.
addition of a syllable to end of word - PARAGOGE
additional - EXTRA, OTHER, MORE, PLUS
additional allowance - - - - - BONUS
additional breathing sound - - - RALE
additional name - - - - - - - ALIAS
additional publication - - - - REISSUE
address - SERMON, ORATION, TALK, DIRECT, APPLY, ACCOST, GREET
address of greeting - - - - SALUTATORY
address to king - - - - - - - SIRE
adduce - - - - - - - - CITE, ALLEGE
adeem - - - - - - - - - - REVOKE
adept - EXPERT, PROFICIENT, SKILLED
adequate - - FIT, EQUAL, SUFFICIENT
adhere - - - STICK, PERSIST, CLING
adherent - - - - - - - - FOLLOWER
adherent of the crown - - - - - TORY
adherent of (suffix) - - - - - - - ITE
adhesion - - - - - - - ATTACHMENT
adhesive - GLUE, PASTE, MUCILAGE, GUM
adipose - - - - - - - - - FATTY, FAT
adipose tissue - - - - - - - - - FAT
adit - ENTRANCE, ACCESS, APPROACH
adjacent - - - - - CLOSE, ABUTTING
adjective (suffix) - ILE, ENT, IAN, IVE, IC
adjective termination - - - - - - IC
adjoin - - - - - - - - ABUT, TOUCH
adjoining - - - - - - - - - - NEXT
adjourn - - - - - DEFER, PROROGUE
adjudge - OPINE, DEEM, AWARD, DECREE
adjudged unfit for use - CONDEMNED
adjunct - - - - - - - - ACCESSORY
adjunct to bed - - - - - - MATTRESS
adjure - - - - - - - - - - ENTREAT
adjust - ADAPT, SET, ARRANGE, DEEM, REGULATE, FIX, RANGE, FRAME, SETTLE, ALIGN
adjust evenly - - - - - - - - ALIGN
administer - - - - - - - - MANAGE
administer corporal punishment - SPANK
admirable - - - - - - - GOOD, FINE
admire - REVERE, APPROVE, ESTEEM
admission - - - - - ENTREE, ACCESS
admit - CONCEDE, ALLOW, CONFESS, OWN
admit to be true - - - - - - - OWN
admitted fact - - - - - - - DATUM
admonish - - - - WARN, REPRIMAND
ado - - - FUSS, BUSTLE, NOISE, STIR
adolescent years - - - - - - - TEENS
Adonis' slayer - - - - - - - - ARES
adopt - - - - PASS, TAKE, ASSUME
adoration - - - - - - - - WORSHIP
adore - - - - VENERATE, WORSHIP
adorn - GRACE, CREST, DRAPE, ORNAMENT, TRIM, BEDECK, ORNATE, DECORATE, DECK
adorned with nacre - - - - - PEARLED
adorned with sparkling ornaments - SPANGLED
Adriatic island - - - - - ESO, LIDO
Adriatic seaport - - - - - - TRIESTE
Adriatic winter wind - - - - - BORA
adrift - - - - - - - - - - AFLOAT
adroit - - - - SKILLFUL, NEAT, DEFT
adroitness - - - - - - - - - - ART
adulate - - - - - - - - - FLATTER
adulation - - - - - - - - - PRAISE
adult - - - - - - - - - - GROWN
adult form of insect - - - - - IMAGO
adult steer - - - - - - - - - BEEVE
adulterated - - - - - - - - IMPURE
advance - PROMOTE, GAIN, PROGRESS
advance guard - - - - - - - - - VAN
advance notice - - - - - - - WARNING
advanced - - - - - - - - - - - FAR
advanced course of study - - SEMINAR
advancement - PROGRESS, PROMOTION
advantage - STEAD, BEHOOF, PROFIT, GAIN
advantageous - - - - - - STRATEGIC
adventure story (colloq.) - - - - YARN
adventurous - - - - - - - - ERRANT
adversary - - - - FOE, RIVAL, ENEMY
adversary of man - - - - - - SATAN
adverse criticism - - - - - - CENSURE
adversity - - - - - - - - - - - ILL

A

advertising - - - - - - - PUBLICITY
advertising handbill - - - - DODGER
advertising sign - - - - - POSTER
adviser - - - - - - - - ASSESSOR
advocate - PROPONENT, PLEAD, PLEADER
Aeetes's daughter - - - - - MEDEA
Aegean island - PSARA, NIO, IOS, SAMOS, DELOS
aerial - - - - - - - - - - AIRY
aerial maneuver - - - - - - - SPIN
aeriform matter - - - - - - - GAS
aeronaut - - - - - - - - AVIATOR
aeronautics - - - - - - - AVIATION
aery - - - - - - LOFTY, SPIRITUAL
Aesir (one of the) - - - - - LOTHUR
afar - - - - - - DISTANT, ABROAD
affable - - DEBONAIR, MILD, POLITE
affairs - - - - - - - - - - MATTERS
affairs of chance - - - - - LOTTERY
affect - - - - INFLUENCE, CONCERN
affect deeply - - PENETRATE, IMPRESS
affect harshly - - - - - - - - RASP
affect supernaturally - - - - - INSPIRE
affectation - POSE, LOVE, PRETENSION, PRETENSE
affectation of being shocked - - - FIE
affecting an individual - - PERSONAL
affecting many in the community - EPIDEMIC
affection - - - - - - LOVE, ARDOR
affectionate - - - - - - - - - FOND
affects preciseness - - - - - MINCES
affidavit - - - - - - - - - - OATH
affinity - - - - - - - - - - - KIN
affirm - AVER, ALLEGE, ASSERT, DECLARE, ASSEVERATE
affirmative - - - YES, AYE, YEP, YEA
affirmative vote - - - - - - PRO, YEA
affix - - - - - - - - APPEND, ADD
affixed postage - - - - - - STAMPED
affixed signature - - - - - - SIGNED
afflict with ennui - - - - - - BORE
afflicted - - - - - - - - SMITTEN
affliction - ILL, SORE, DISTRESS, PAIN, WOE, SORROW
affluence - - - - - - - - WEALTH
affluent - - - - - - RICH, WEALTHY
afford - SUPPLY, LEND, FURNISH, PROVIDE
afford aid - - - - - - - - - HELP
afford pleasure - - - - - - PLEASE
afforded - - - - - - - - - - LENT
affording aid - - - - - - - HELPFUL
affray - - - - - - - MELEE, FEUD
affright - - - - - - - - - SCARE
affront - - - - INSULT, DISPLEASE
Afghan. coin - - - - - - - AMANIA
Afghan. prince - - - - - AMIR, AMEER
afire - - - EAGER, BLAZING, FLAMING
afloat - - - BUOYED, ADRIFT, AWASH
aforesaid thing - - - - - - - DITTO
aforethought - - - - - - PREPENSE
afraid - TIMOROUS, FEARFUL, SCARED
afresh - - - - - - - - - - ANEW
African - - - - - - - - - NEGRO
African animals - AYEAYES, OKAPI, GIRAFFES
African antelope - GNU, ELAND, ADDAX, PEELE, BONGO
African city - - - - - - - TRIPOLI
African cony - - - - - - DASSIE, DAS
African country - NIGERIA, ETHIOPIA
African desert - - - - - - - - GOBI
African fly - - - - - - - - TSETSE
African gazelle - - - - - ARIEL, CORA
African giraffe - - - - - - - OKAPI
African hartebeest - - - - - - TORA
African hemp - - - - - - - - - IFE
African Hottentot - - - - - - NAMA
African hunting expedition - - SAFARI
African lake - - - - - - CHAD, TANA
African monkey (small) - - - GRIVET
African mountain - - - - - CAMEROON
African native - - - - - - ZULU, IBO
African Negro - - - - - - - - - IBO
African Negro tribe - KABONGA, KREPI, NUBA
African Portuguese territory - ANGOLA
African region - - - - - - - SUDAN
African republic - - - - - - LIBERIA
African river - CONGO, NIGER, BIA, CALABAR, NILE, NUN, SENEGAL
African ruminant - - - - - - CAMEL
African seaport - CASABLANCA, TUNIS
African soup ingredient - - - - LALO
African tree - SHEA, COLA, TARFA, BAOBAB
African tribesman - - - - - - BANTU
African village - - - - - - - STAD
African wild hog - - - - - - WART
African wildcat - - - - - - - SERVAL
African wood - - - - - - - EBONY
African worm - - - - - - - - - LOA
aft - - - - - - - ASTERN, STERN
after - - - - - - - BEHIND, LATER
after awhile - - - - - - ANON, LATER
after charges - - - - - - - - - NET
after the manner of men - - HUMANLY
afternoon - - - - - - - - - - P.M.
afternoon nap - - - - - - - SIESTA
afternoon performance - - - MATINEE
aftersong - - - - - - - - - EPODE
afterward - - - - - - - - - LATER
again - ANEW, OVER, ENCORE, MOREOVER
again (Latin) - - - - - - - ITERUM
again (prefix) - - - - - OB, ANTI, RE
against - - - - - - - - CON, VERSUS
against (prefix) - - - - - - - ANTI
agalloch - - - - - - - AGAR, ALOES
Agamemnon's son - - - - - ORESTES
agape - - - - - - - OPEN, STARING
agar - - - - - - - - - - AGALLOCH
agave - - - - - - - - - - - ALOE
agave fiber - - - - - - - - - ISTLE
age - EPOCH, SENIORITY, ERA, EON, CENTURY, LIFETIME
aged - - - - - - - - - SENILE, OLD
aged (abbr.) - - - - - - - - - AET
ageless - - - - - - - - - TIMELESS
agency (suffix) - - - - - - - - IST
agent - CONSIGNEE, BROKER, FACTOR, DEPUTY, PROMOTER, REPRESENTATIVE, DOER
aggravate - - TEASE, NAG, INTENSIFY
aggregate - - - - - - - - - - SUM
aggregation - - - - - - CONGERIES
aggregation of people - - TRIBE, MASS
aghast - - - - - AMAZED, TERRIFIED
agile - SPRY, NIMBLE, ALERT, LITHE, LIVELY
agio - BROKERAGE, PREMIUM, DISCOUNT
agitate - STIR, ROIL, RILE, FRET, DISTURB, VEX, PERTURB, FLURRY, MOVE
agitated - - - - - - - - EBULLIENT
agitation - - - - - - - - - FLURRY
aglow - - - - - - - ALIT, SHINING
agname - - - - - - - - - NICKNAME
agnate - - - - - - - - - - ALLIED
agnostic - - - - - - - - - SKEPTIC

ago - - - - - PAST, SINCE
ago (poet.) - - - - - - - - AGONE
agog - - - - - - - - - - EAGER
agonize - - - - - - - - - SUFFER
agony - - - PAIN, PANG, SUFFERING
agree - CONSENT, ACCEDE, ASSENT, ACCEPT, COINCIDE, CONCUR, COMPORT, GIBE, HOMOLOGATE, CONFORM
agreeable - - - - - NICE, PLEASANT
agreeable odor - - - - - - - AROMA
agreeableness - - - - - - AMENITY
agreement - COVENANT, YES, PACT, CONSENT, UNITY, ASSENT, TREATY, UNISON, CONTRACT, COINCIDENCE, UNITY
agreement in a design - - - CONCERT
agricultural establishment - - - FARM
agricultural implement - PLOW, MOWER
agricultural Indian - - - - PAWNEE
agriculture - - - AGRARIAN, FARMING
agriculturist - - - FARMER, GARDENER
ahead - - - - - - - ON, FORWARD
ai - - - - - - - - - - - SLOTH
aid - ABET, ASSIST, BEFRIEND, SUSTAIN, SUCCOR
aidance - - - - - - - - - - HELP
aidant - - - - - - - - - HELPING
aide - - - - - - - - - - HELPER
aigret - - - - - - - - - - HERON
ail - - - - - - - SUFFER, BOTHER
ailing - - - - - - - - - - - ILL
ailment - - - - - - - - - MALADY
aim - - - POINT, GOAL, AMBITION, PURPOSE, END, INTENT, IDEAL, OBJECTIVE, ASPIRATION, TARGET, DIRECT, OBJECT
aim at - - - - - - - - - ASPIRE
aim high - - - - - - - - - ASPIRE
aiming at - - - - - - - - - - TO
aimless - - - - - - - DESULTORY
aimless wanderer - - - - MEANDERER
air - - - TONE, ARIA, BREEZE, TUNE, CARRIAGE, MANNER, MIEN, DISPLAY, ATMOSPHERE, SONG, MELODY, VAPOR
air in brisk motion - - - - - - WIND
air (comb. form) - - AERO, AER, AERI
air filled film of liquid - - - BUBBLE
air hero - - - - - - - - - - ACE
air (of the) - - - - - - - - AERIAL
air passage - - - - - - - - - FLUE
air (pert. to) - - - - AURAL, AERIAL
air vehicle - - - - - - - - GLIDER
aircraft - - - - AERI, AERO, BLIMP
aircraft carrier - - - - - - - WASP
aircraft flight record - - - - - LOG
aircraft (pert. to) - - - - - - AERO
aircraft shelter - - NACELLE, HANGAR
aircraft with no engine - - - GLIDER
airing - - - - - - - - - - OUTING
airlike fluid - - - - - - - - - GAS
airplane - - - - - - - - - - AERO
airplane manoeuvre - - - - - - LOOP
airplane operator - - - - - AVIATOR
airplane part - - - - - - - AILERON
airplane shed - - - - - - - HANGAR
airplane stabilizing attachment - - FIN
airplane throttle - - - - - - - GUN
airplane (type) - - - - - - TRIPLANE
airship - - - - PLANE, TRIPLANE, DIRIGIBLE
airy - - ETHEREAL, LIGHT, SPRIGHTLY, AERIAL
aisle - - - - - - - - PASSAGE

ait - - - - - - ISLET, ISLE, ISLAND
akin - - - RELATED, ALIKE, SIMILAR, ALLIED, SIB
Alabama county - - - - - - - LEE
alackaday - - - - - - - - - ALAS
alacrity - - - - - - - BRISKNESS
alar - - - - - - - - - AXILLARY
alarm - - ALERT, AROUSE, FRIGHTEN, STARTLE, SCARE
alarm bell - - - - - - - - - TOCSIN
alarm whistle - - - - - - - - SIREN
alarm whistle (var.) - - - - - SIRENE
alas - - - - - - - - - - - - AY
alas (German) - - - - - - - - ACH
Alaskan auks - - - - - - - ARRIES
Alaskan cape - - - - - - - - NOME
Alaskan capital - - - - - - JUNEAU
Alaskan city - - - - - - - - NOME
Alaskan district - - - - - - - SITKA
Alaskan garment - - - - - - PARKA
Alaskan Mt. - - - ADA, FAIRWEATHER
Alaskan native - - - - - - - ALEUT
Alaskan river - - - - - - - YUKON
alb - - - - - - - - - VESTMENT
Albanian coin - - - - - - - - LEK
Albion - - - - - - - - ENGLAND
albite - - - - - - - - FELDSPAR
alcohol - - - - - - - - - SPIRITS
alcohol-burning vessel - - - - ETNA
alcohol (solid) - - - - - - STEROL
alcoholic beverage - RUM, MEAD, GIN, POSSET, WINE
Alcyone's husband - - - - - - CEYX
alder tree (Scot.) - - - - - - ARN
ale (obs.) - - - - - - - - - EALE
alert - - - READY, AGILE, VIGILANT, PREPARED, NIMBLE, AWAKE, AWARE
alfalfa - - - - - - - - LUCERNE
alga - - SEAWEED, DEMID, DIATOM
Algerian cavalryman - SPAHS, SPAHEE
Algerian city - - - - - - - - ORAN
Algerian governor - - - - - - - DEY
Algerian seaport - - - - ORAN, BONE
Algon. Indian - - CREE, SAC, LENAPE
alias - - - - - - - - - ASSUMED
alidade - - - THEODOLITE, DIOPTER
alien - - - - - - - - - - STRANGE
alienate - - - SEPARATE, ESTRANGE, DISAFFECT, WEAN
alight - - - - - - - - - - - LAND
align - - - - - - - - - - - DRESS
alike - - - EQUALLY, SIMILAR, AKIN, ANALOGOUS, SAME
aliment - - - - - - - - - - FOOD
alimental - - - - - - - NOURISHING
alit - - - - - - - - - - - AGLOW
alive - - - RANK, ACTIVE, ANIMATE, SWARMING
alkali - - - - - - - - - - - SODA
alkaline compound - - - - - - SODA
alkaline solution - - - - - - - LYE
alkaloid in bean - - - - - - ESERIN
alkaloid in tea plant - - - - THEINE
all - ENTIRE, WHOLLY, TOTALLY, TOTAL, EVERY, INDIVIDUALLY, SOLELY, QUITE
all (comb. form) - - - - - PAN, OMNI
all powerful - - - - - - OMNIPOTENT
all two - - - - - - - - - - - BOTH
allay - - - EASE, RELIEVE, MITIGATE, ASSUAGE, MOLLIFY, CALM, QUELL, SLAKE
allege - ADDUCE, AFFIRM, MAINTAIN, ASSERT, AVER, QUOTE, CITE
alleged electric force - - - - ELOD

A

alleged force - OD
alleviate - ALLAY, EASE, MITIGATE, RELIEVE
alleviation - RELIEF
alleviator - ALLAYER
alley - PASSAGE
alliance - TREATY, UNION
alliance (pert. to) - FEDERAL
allied - COGNATE, AGNATE, AKIN
Allied air force - RAF
Allied beachhead, Italy - ANZIO
alligator pear - AVOCADO
allocate - APPORTION
allot - METE, DESTINE, ASSIGN, RATION
allotted place - BERTH
allotted portion - QUOTA
allow - LET, PERMIT, GRANT, ADMIT
allow to remain - LEAVE
allow free use of - LEND
allowable variation - TOLERANCE
allowance - RATION
allowance for changes - MARGIN
allowance for depreciation - AGIO
allowance for past services - PENSION
allowance for waste - TRET, STET, TARE
allowance for weight or wt. of container TARE
allowing that - IF
alloy of copper and zinc - BRASS
alloy for domestic utensils - PEWTER
alloy of gold and silver - ASEM
alloy of iron - STEEL
alloy of tin and zinc - OROIDE
allude to - REFER, MENTION
allure - TEMPT, WIN, ENTICE, LEAD, DECOY
alluring quality - CHARM
allusion - REFERENCE, HINT
alluvia - DELTAS
alluvial deposit - DELTA
ally - HELPER, UNITE
almanac - YEARBOOK, CALENDAR
almighty - OMNIPOTENT
almost - NEARLY
almost (arch.) - ANEAR
almost (prefix) - PENE
alms - DOLE, DOLES, CHARITY
alms box - ARCA
alms dispenser - ALMONER
almsgiving - CHARITY
almshouse - POORHOUSE
alodium - ALOD
aloe - AGAVE
aloft - UP
alone - SOLO, SINGLY, UNIQUE, SOLITARY, ONLY
alone (L.) - SOLUS
along - EVER, ON, FORWARD, ONWARD
alongside - BY
aloof - RESERVED, DISTANT
alosa - SHAD
aloud - ORAL, AUDIBLY
alphabetic character - LETTER, RUNE
alphabetical list of particles CATALOGUE
Alpine primrose - AURICULA
Alps - ALPINE, MOUNTAINS
also - AND, TOO, WITHAL
also (arch.) - EKE
also called - ALIAS
also (poet.) - EKE
alt - ISLE, ISLET, ISLAND
alt (Fr.) - ILE
altar screen - REREDOS
altar slab - MENSA
alter - CHANGE, MODIFY, AMEND, VARY, MUTATE, EMEND
altercation QUARREL, CONTROVERSY
alternate - OTHER, ROTATE
alternated - ROTATED
alternative - OR
alum - STRINGENT, SALT
always - EVER, EVERMORE, AYE
always (cont. or poet.) - E'ER
always (dial.) - ALGATE
ama - CHALICE
amain - FORCIBLY, VIOLENTLY
Amalekite king - AGAG
amalgamate - FUSE, UNITE
amalgamation - UNION
amaryllis plant - AGAVE
amass - HEAP, COLLECT
amateur - DABBLER, DILETTANTE
amative - LOVING
amaze - SURPRISE, ASTOUND, ASTONISH
amazed - AGHAST
amazing event - MIRACLE
Amazon estuary - PARA
Amazon mouth - PARA
ambary - DA
ambassador - LEGATE
amber-coloured substance - ROSIN
ambiguous - DELPHIC, INDEFINITE, ORACULAR
ambit - BOUNDS
ambition - AIM, GOAL, TARGET, ASPIRATION
ambitious soldier - MARINE
amble - PACE
ambling horse - PADNAG
ambrosia - NECTAR
ambrosia plant - RAGWEED
ambrosial - DELICIOUS
ambulant - SHIFTING
ambush - TRAP
amelioration - SOLACE
amen - VERILY, SOBEIT
amend - ALTER, RECTIFY, REPEAL, REVISE, IMPROVE, BETTER
ament - CATKIN, CATTAIL, JUL
amerces - FINES, MULCTS, DEPRIVES
American aborigine - INDIAN
American actor - DREW
American admiral - EVANS, SIMS, DEWEY
American artist - PYLE, PEALE
American author - HARTE, REO, GREY, PAINE, ALDEN, POE
American canal - PANAMA
American capitalist - ASTOR, RASCOB
American cartoonist - ARNO, DORGAN
American cataract - NIAGARA
American clergyman - OLIN
American composer - PAINE, NEVIN, SPEAKS
American critic - AYRES
American cruiser - BOISE
American diplomat - REID, GREW
American divine - OLIN
American editor - BOK
American educator - HUME, FISK, DEWEY
American engineer - EADS
American essayist - MABIE
American expert on internat. law - MOORE
American explorer - PEARY, LEWIS
American feminist - CATT
American financier - BIDDLE
American flycatcher - PHOEBE
American general - OTIS, LEE, ORD
American geologist - DANA
American grapes - NIAGARAS
American herb - SEGO, LEAFCUP

American humorist - ADE, NYE, TWAIN, LARDNER, ARTEMUS, COBB, DAY
American illustrator - - - - NEWELL
American inventor - HOE, MORSE, HOWE
American isthmus - - - - - PANAMA
American journalist - HOLT, BIGELOW, REID
American jurist - - - MOORE, PAINE
American larch - - - - - - TAMARACK
American lawyer - - - PAINE, ELLERY
American lotto - - - - - - - KENO
American machinist - - - - - - HOWE
American monetary unit - - - DOLLAR
American musician - - - - - - PAINE
American novelist - STEELE, HARTE, ROSE
American operatic singer - - FARRAR
American painter - - - - - PETERS
American pathologist - - - - EWING
American patriot - - PAINE, OTIS, ROSS
American philanthropist - - - - RIIS
American pioneer - - - - - - BOONE
American pirate - - - - - - - KIDD
American poet - - POE, RILEY, TATE, LANIER
American quail - - - - - - - COLIN
American railroad magnate - - - REA
American republic (abbr.) - - - U.S.A.
American river - - - - - - - PLATTE
American sculptor and painter - PROCTOR
American socialist leader - - - DEBS
American statesman - - JAY, LOGAN, DAWES, BLAINE
American surgeon - - - - - - LONG
American writer - - - - BOK, PYLE
amiable - - - - - - - PLEASANT
amicable - - - - - - - - FRIENDLY
amical - - - - - - - - FRIENDLY
amid - - - - - - - AMONG, AMIDST
amide (pert. to) - - - - - - - AMIC
amidst - - - AMONGST, AMONG, AMID
amiss - - AWRY, FAULTILY, WRONG, FAULTY, ASTRAY, IMPROPER
ammonia derivative - - AMINE, AMIDE, AMIN, ANILIDE
ammunition for blowgun - - - DART
ammunition wagon - - - - - CAISSON
among - - - IN, AMID, MID, AMIDST
among (poet.) - - - - - MID, AMID
among (pref.) - - - - - - - - - EPI
amongst - - - - - - - - AMIDST
amoret - - - - - - - SWEETHEART
amorous look - - - - - LEER, OGLE
amorphous brittle mass - - - - GUM
amort - - - LIFELESS, SPIRITLESS
amount - - - - - - SUM, QUANTITY
amounts of interest - - - - RENTE
amount lost - - - - - - - - LOSS
amount offered - - - - - - - - BID
amount of money - - - - - - FUND
amount taken in - - - - - - INTAKE
amount which cask lacks of being full ULLAGE
amphibia order - - - - - - - ANURA
amphibian - - - - - - TOAD, FROG
amphibious carnivore - - - - - MINK
amphibole - - - - - - - - EDENITE
Amphion's wife - - - - - - - NIOBE
amphitheater (part of) - - - - ARENA
ample - - PLENTY, ABUNDANT, FULL, PLENTEOUS
ample (poet.) - - - - - - - ENOW
amplify - - - ADD, WIDEN, ENLARGE
amulet - - - - CHARM, TALISMAN
amuse - - - - ENTERTAIN, DIVERT
amusement - - - - - - SPORT, GAME
an - - - - - - - - - - - - - ONE
ana - - - - - - - - - - - - - BITS
anaconda - - - - - - - - - - BOA
anagram - - - - LOGOGRIPH, REBUS
analogous - - - - - - - - - ALIKE
analogic - - - - - - - - SIMILAR
analogy - - - - - - - COMPARISON
analyze grammat. - - - - - - PARSE
Anatole France's novel - - - - THAIS
anarchist - - - - - - - - - - RED
anarchistic - - - - - - - - - RED
anathema - - - - - - - - CURSE
anathematize - - - - - - BAN, CURSE
Anatolian goddess - - - - - - - MA
ancestor - - SIRE, ELDER, FORBEAR, FOREFATHER, FOREBEAR
ancestral - - - - - - - - - AVITAL
anchor - - - - - MOOR, CAT, KEDGE
anchor bill - - - - - - - - - - PEE
anchor (small) - - KEDGE, GRAPNEL
anchor tackle - - - - - - - - - CAT
anchorage for ships (Scot.) - - - RADE
ancient - EARLY, OLDEN, OLD, AGED, ARCHEAN (see also EARLY, OLDEN)
ancient Alexandrian writer - - ORIGEN
ancient alloy - - - - - - - - ASEM
ancient alphabetical character - - RUNE
ancient Anatolian goddess - - - MA
ancient Arabian measure - - - - SAA
ancient Argolis's vale - - - - NEMEA
ancient armed galley - - - - AESC
ancient Aryan - - - - - - - MEDE
ancient Aryan language - - SANSKRIT
ancient ascetic people - - - ESSENE
ancient Asia Minor city - - EPHESUS
ancient Asiatic country - MEDEA, ELAM, EOLIS
ancient Asiatic region - - - - ARIA
ancient Asiatic (S.) country - - ACCAD
ancient British tribesman - - - PICT
ancient Caucasian race - - - ARYANS
ancient Chinese - - - - - - - SERES
ancient city - - - - - NINEVEH, TYRE
ancient copper - - - - - - - - AES
ancient country - - - MEDIA, ARAM
ancient country north of Persia - ELAM
ancient court - - - - - - - - EYRE
ancient Danish legal code - DANELAW
ancient drink - - - - - - - MORAT
ancient Egyptian alloy - - - - ASEM
ancient Egyptian city - - THEBES, NO
ancient Egyptian king - RAMESES, TUT
ancient Egyptian scroll - - - PAPYRI
ancient Egyptian title - - - - SOTER
ancient Egyptian wt. - - - - - - KAT
ancient English court - - - - LEET
ancient English dance - - - MORRIS
ancient English king - - - CANUTE
ancient fine for homicide - - - CRO
ancient firearm - - - - - - - DAG
ancient form for shaping objects - AME
ancient Gaelic capital - - TARA, ERIN
ancient game - - - - - - - MORA
ancient Genoa coin - - - - - - JANE
ancient German tribe - - - TEUTON
ancient German tribesmen - - TEUTONS
ancient gold coin - - - - - - - RIAL
ancient Greek - - - - - - - IONIAN
ancient Greek city - ARGOS, CORINTH, ELIS
ancient Greek city (pert. to) - THEBAN
ancient Greek contest - - - - AGON
ancient Greek country - - EPIRUS, ELI, AEOLIA
ancient Greek invader - - - DORIAN
ancient Greek judge - - - - DICAST
ancient Greek kingdom - - - ATTICA

ancient Greek marker - - - - STELE
ancient Greek platform - - - - BEMA
ancient Greek province - - ACARNANIA
ancient Greek warship - - - TRIREME
ancient hammering form - - - - AME
ancient headdress - - - - - MITER
ancient Hebrew liquid measure - BATH
ancient Hebrew notes on Old Test. - - MASORA
ancient Hebrew ram's horn - - SHOFAR
ancient Hindu scripture - - - VEDA
ancient Hindu scripture (pert. to) - - VEDIC
ancient implement of war - ONAGER, CELT
ancient infantrymen - - - FUSILIERS
ancient instrument of torture - CROSS, RACK
ancient Irish capital - - - - TARA
ancient Irish chieftain - - - TANIST
ancient Irish clan - - - - - SEPT
ancient Irish fort - - - - LIS, LISS
ancient Irish priest - - - - DRUID
ancient ivory horn - - - - OLIPHANT
ancient Jewish cabalistic book - ZOHAR
ancient Jewish high priest articles - - URIM
ancient Jewish measure - - - OMER
ancient Jewish sacred objects - - URIM
ancient Jewish title - - - - ABBA
ancient kings of Peru - - - - INCA
ancient Laconian capital - - - SPARTA
ancient language - PALI, SANSKRIT, LATIN
ancient Latin grammar - - - DONAT
ancient lyre - - - - - - - ASOR
ancient manor court - - - - - LEET
ancient manuscript - - - - CODEX
ancient Media people - - - - MEDES
ancient Mexican - - - - - - AZTEC
ancient military machine - - ONAGER, CATAPULT
ancient money - - - - - - - AES
ancient money unit - - - - TALENT
ancient musical character - - NEUME
ancient musical instrument - - ASOR, ROTA, CITHARA
ancient Norse minstrel - - - SCALD
ancient Norwegian king - - - - OLAF
ancient ointment - - - - - NARD
ancient Palestine city - - - GILEAD
ancient Palestine cry - - - JERICHO
ancient Palestine language - ARAMAIC
ancient Palestine town - - - - BIRE
ancient Palestine village - - - ENDOR
ancient people who invaded India - SAKA
ancient persecutor of Christians - NERO
ancient Persian priests - - - - MAGI
ancient Peruvian title - - - - INCA
ancient pillarlike monument - - STELA
ancient pistol - - - - - - - DAG
ancient playing card - - - - TAROT
ancient race - - - - MEDES, GOTHS
ancient Roman cloaks - - - PLANETAE
ancient Roman deity - - IANUS, JANUS
ancient Roman festivals - - CEREALIA
ancient Roman measure - - - WINS
ancient Roman port - - - - OSTIA
ancient Roman priestess - - - VESTAL
ancient Roman seats - - - - SELLAE
ancient Roman shield - - - CLYPEUS
ancient Roman sock - - - - - UDO
ancient Roman tax gatherer - PUBLICAN
ancient Roman wall - - - - SPINA
ancient Scandinavian (pert. to) - NORSE
ancient Scand. alphabetical character RUNE
ancient Scand. minstrel - - - SCALD
ancient Scot. fine - - - - - CRO
ancient Scot. king - - - - ROBERT
ancient Scot. name - - - - - ALBA
ancient Scot. tax - - - - - - CRO
ancient Semitic god - - - - - BAAL
ancient sepulchral slab - - - STELA
ancient shield - - - - - - - ECU
ancient silk fabric - - - - SAMITE
ancient Span. division - - CATALONIA
ancient spice - - - - - - - STACTE
ancient stone implement - - EOLITH
ancient storyteller - - - - - AESOP
ancient stringed instrument - - LUTE, NEBEL, ASOR, REBEC
ancient Syrian country - - - - ARAM
ancient tax - - - - - - - - CRO
ancient temple - - - - - - NAOS
ancient Toltec capital - - - - TULA
ancient torture instrument - - - RACK
ancient trading vessel - - - - NEF
ancient Troy - ILIAC, TROAS, ILION, ILIUM
ancient Troy region - - - TROAD
ancient vehicle - - - - - CHARIOT
ancient war machine - - - - ONAGER
ancient warship - - - - - GALLEON
ancient weapon - DAG, CELT, LANCE, SLING, SPEAR, PIKE, MACE
ancient weight and money unit - TALENT
ancient wicked city - - - - SODOM
ancient wine pitcher - - - - - OLPE
ancient wine receptacle - - - - AMA
and - - - - - - - - - - - ALSO
and so forth - - - - - ETCETERA
and ten (suffix) - - - - - - TEEN
andiron - - - - - - - FIREDOG
anecdotes - - - - - ANA, TALES
anesthetic - - - - - ETHER, GAS
anet - - - - - - - DILL, DILLSEED
anew - - - - - - AGAIN, AFRESH
anew (prefix) - - - - - - - ANA
angel - - - - SERAPH, SERAPHIM
angel of death - - - - - AZRAEL
angel of light - - - - - - CHERUB
angelic - - - - CHERUBIC, SAINTLY
angelic messenger - - - - GABRIEL
anger - ENRAGE, IRE, WRATH, RAGE, IRRITATE, FURY, CHOLER, EXASPERATE, ANIMOSITY
anger (colloq.) - - - - - - RILE
angle - - - - CORNER, FISH, HOOK
angle iron - - - - - - - LATH
angle of leaf and stem - - - - AXIL
angler - - - - - - - - FISHER
angler's basket - - - - - - CREEL
angler's hope - - - - - - - BITE
Anglo-Indian coin - - - - - ANNA
Anglo-Indian number - - - - CRORE
Anglo-Indian nurse - - - - AMAH
Anglo-Indian title of address - - BABU
Anglo-Indian weight - - - TOLA, SER
Anglo-Saxon coin and money of account ORA
Anglo-Saxon consonant - - ETH, EDH
Anglo-Saxon free servant - - - THANE
angry - - - - - - - IRATE, IREFUL
angry (colloq.) - - - - SORE, MAD
angry stare - - - - - - GLOWER
anguish - PAIN, TRAVAIL, REMORSE, DOLOUR
anguish (poet.) - - - - - - DOLOUR
anile - - INFIRM, FEEBLE, IMBECILE, CHILDISH
animal - BRUTE, BEAST, SLOTH, GENET, CREATURE, BOAR

animal's backbone - - - - - - CHINE
animal's body - - - - - - - SOMA
animal's coat - - HAIR, FUR, PELAGE
animal's disease - - - - - - MANGE
animal doctor - - - - - VETERINARY, VETERINARIAN
animal enclosure - CORRAL, CAGE, PEN, STABLE
animal fat - ADEPS, SUET, WAX, ESTER, LARD, TALLOW, GREASE
animal food - - - - - FLESH, MEAT
animal handler - - - - - - TAMER
animal of mixed breed - - MONGREL
animal mother - - - - - - - - DAM
animal neck hair - - - - - - MANE
animal skin - - - - - - HIDE, FUR
animal sound - - - - - - - SNORT
animal stomach - - - - MAW, CRAW
animal stomach part - - - - - TRIPE
animal thigh - - - - - - - - HAM
animal track - - - - - TRAIL, SPOOR
animal trail - - - - - - RUN, TRACK
animate - LIVEN, ALIVE, INVIGORATE, ENLIVEN
animate person - - - - - - BEING
animated - - - ALIVE, INVIGORATED, VITALIZED, LIVELY, QUICKENED, ENLIVENED, VIVACIOUS, VIGOROUS
animates (slang) - - - - - - PEPS
animating principle - - - - - SOUL
animating spirit - - - - - - GENIUS
animation - - LIFE, PEP, VIVACITY, SPIRIT
animator - - - - - - - ENLIVENER
animosity - - ANGER, SPITE, RANCOR
anise - - - - - - - - - - FLAVOR
anisette - - - - - - - - CORDIAL
ankle - - - - - - - TALUS, TARSUS
ankle bones - - - - - - TALI, TALUS
ankle (of the) - - - - - - - TARSAL
annals - - - - - - - - - HISTORY
Annamese measure - - SAO, QUO, TAO
anneal - - - - - - - TEMPER, FUSE
annealing oven - - - - - - - LEER
annex - - - ADD, ATTACH, SUBJOIN, EXTENSION, JOIN
annihilation - - - EXTERMINATION
annoint - - - - - - - - - ANELE
announce - - - - - - - - - STATE
announce loudly - - - - - - BLARE
announcement - - - - - - NOTICE
annoy - - PESTER, IRK, NAG, HARASS, BLESS, VEX, HARRY, EXASPERATE, DISTURB, IRRITATE, TEASE, MOLEST, PEEVE, NETTLE, RILE
annoyance - - - BORE, PEST, PEEVE
annoying - - - - - - - - - PESKY
annual - - - - - - - - - - YEARLY
annual bean - - - - - - - - - URD
annual produce - - - - - - - CROP
annul - - REVOKE, RESCIND, ELIDE, REPEAL, ABOLISH, NULLIFY, ABROGATE, CANCEL, UNDO
annularly - - - - - - - RINGWISE
annulment - - - - - - - ABOLITION
annum - - - - - - - - - - - YEAR
anoint - - - - - - - - OIL, ANELE
anon - - - LATER, SOON, PRESENTLY
anonymous - - - - - - - NAMELESS
another time - - - - - - - AGAIN
answer - - REPLY, RETORT, RESPOND, RESPONSE, SOLUTION
answer in kind - - RETORT, RESPOND
answer the purpose - - - SERVE, DO
answer sharply - - - - - - RETORT
ant - - - - - - - - EMMET, TERMITE
ant cow - - - - - - - - - - APHID
anta - - - - - - - - - - - - PIER
antagonist - - - - - - - - ENEMY
Antarctic bird - - - - - - PENGUIN
Antarctic sea - - - - - - - - ROSS
ante - - - - - - - - - - - STAKE
antecedent - - - - PRECEDENT, PRIOR
antecedent period - - - - - - PAST
antelope (female) - - - - - - - DOE
antelope (kind) - SEROW, GNU, ADDAX, ELAND, BONGO
antelope (striped) - - - - - - BONGO
antelope (male) - - - - - - - BUCK
antenna - - - - - - - FEELER, AERIAL
anterior - FORWARD, PREVIOUS, PRIOR, BEFORE
anthem - - - - - - - - - - MOTET
anthology - - - - - - - - - - ANA
anthracite refuse - - - - - - CULM
anthropoid animal - - - - - - APE
anthropoid ape - ORANG, ORANGUTAN
antic - - - - - - - - CAPER, DIDO
anticipate - ANTEDATE, HOPE, EXPECT
anticipate with foreboding - - DREAD
anticipation - - - - FORETASTE, HOPE
Antilles island - - - - - - - - CUBA
antipathy - - AVERSION, DISTASTE, DISLIKE
antiquated - - PASSE, OLDISH, OLD
antiquity (arch. and poet.) - - - ELD
antiquity (obs.) - - - - - - - ELDE
antiseptic - - - - - - - - - IODINE
antiseptic oil - - - - - - RETINOL
antitheses - - - - - - ANTIPODES
antitoxic fluid - - - - - - - SERUM
antitoxic lymphs - - - - - - - SERA
antitoxin - SERUM (sing.), SERA (pl.)
antler - - - - - - - - - - - HORN
antlered - - - - - - - - - - SPIKY
antlered animal - STAG, DEER, MOOSE
antler's furry skin - - - - - VELVET
antrum - - - - - - - - - - CAVERN
anvil - - - - - - - - TEEST, INCUS
anxiety - - - - - - CARE, CONCERN
anxious - - - - - EAGER, CONCERNED
any - - - - - - - - - - - - SOME
any person - - - - - - - - ANYONE
any of several stars - - - - - DENEB
any trifle - - - - - - - - NOTHING
anybody - - - - - - - - - - - ONE
anything destructive - - - - - BANE
anything short-lived - - - EPHEMERA
anything strictly true - - - - - FACT
anything of value - - - - - - ASSET
apace - - SWIFTLY, FAST, RAPIDLY, QUICK
apart - ASIDE, SEPARATE, BORDERS, ASUNDER, SEPARATELY
apart (pref.) - - - - - - - - - DIS
apartment - - - - - - - SUITE, FLAT
apartment for females - - - - HAREM
apathetic - - - - - - - INDIFFERENT
apathy - - - - - - - - - LETHARGY
ape - LAR, MIMIC, SIMIAN, SIMULATE, COPY, IMITATE, IMITATOR, GORILLA, MONKEY
apelike - - - - - - - - - - SIMIAN
aper - - - - - - - - - - - MIMIC
aperitif - - - - - - - - APPETIZER
aperture - SLOT, GAP, LEAK, MOUTH, HOLE, VENT, RIMA, STOMA
apex - POINT, ACME, SUMMIT, TOP, VERTEX, ZENITH
aphorism - - - - - - - ADAGE, SAW
Aphrodite's son - - - - - - - - EROS
apiece - - - - - - - - - - - EACH

A

Apocalypse - - - - - REVELATION
Apocryphal book of Bible - - TOBIT
apodal - - - - - - - - FOOTLESS
apogee - - - - - - - - CLIMAX
Apollo's mother - - - - - - - LETO
Apollo's oracle - - - - - - - DELOS
Apollo's sister - - - DIANA, ARTEMIS
Apollo's son - - - - - - IAMUS, ION
apology - - - - - - - - AMEND
apostate - - - - - - - RENEGADE
apostle - PAUL, PETER, MARK, DISCIPLE
apothecaries' wt. - - - - DRAM, GRAIN
appall - - AWE, ASTONISH, HORRIFY, SHOCK, DISMAY, OVERCOME
apparatus to convert paper into pulp MACERATER
apparatus for heating liquids - - ETNA
apparatus to unclose cars - - TIPPLE
apparel - - RAIMENT, GEAR, ATTIRE, GARB
apparent - - EVIDENT, PATENT, PLAIN
apparently - - - - - - SEEMINGLY
apparition - SHAPE, GHOST, IDOLON, SPECTER
apparition (Fr.) - - - - - REVENANT
appeal - PLEAD, REQUEST, ENTREATY, REFER
appeal to for confirmation - - PROTEST
appear - - - - SEEM, ARISE, LOOK
appear again - - - - - - - RECUR
appear melancholy - - - - - - MOPE
appearance - ASPECT, MIEN, GUISE, PHASE, LOOK, AIR
appearing gnawed - - - - - - EROSE
appearing successively - - - SERIAL
appease - PLACATE, ATONE, PROPITIATE, CONCILIATE, PACIFY
appellation - - EPITHET, TITLE, NAME
append - - - - ADD, ATTACH, AFFIX
appendages - TAILS, ADDENDA, TABS, ARISTA, TAGS
appendages at base of leaf - STIPULES
appendages of a crustacean - - ENDITE
appertain - - - - - RELATE, BELONG
appetite - - - STOMACH, LONGING, CRAVING
appetizer - - - CANAPE, APERITIF
applaud - - - - - - CLAP, CHEER
applauder - - - - - - - ROOTER
apple - POME, PIPPIN, CRAB, WINESAP, RUSSET, ESOPUS, SPY
apple acid - - - - - - - - MALIC
apple juice - - - - - - - - CIDER
apple (pert. to) - - - - - - MALIC
apple seed - - - - - - - PIT, PIP
apples crushed by grinding - POMACE
application - USE, TERM, DILIGENCE
applied, be (var.) - - - - - - ENURE
apply - - DEVOTE, ADDRESS, TREAT
apply friction - - - - - - - - RUB
apply habitually - - - - - - ADDICT
apply heat - - - - - - - - WARM
apply liquid medication - - - BATHE
apply oneself to - - - - - - - PLY
apply remedies to - - - - - - TREAT
appoint - - COMMISSION, ORDAIN, DETAIL, ASSIGN, NOMINATE
appoint as agent - - - - - - DEPUTE
appoint as heir - - - - - - ENTAIL
appointed as agent - - - DEPUTED
appointed time - - - - - - - HOUR
appointment - - - - DATE, TRYST
apportion - - METE, DELE, RATION, DEAL, ALLOT, DOLE, LOT, ALLOCATE
apposite - - - RELATIVE, RELEVANT
appraisal - - - - - EVALUATION
appraise - - RATE, EVALUATE, PRICE, ESTIMATE, VALUE, GAUGE
appreciate - - - - - - - - VALUE
apprehend - - NAB, ARREST, GRASP, PERCEIVE
apprehend clearly - - - - - REALIZE
apprehend through the senses - SENSATE
apprehension - - - - - - - FEAR
apprehensive - - - - - - - JUMPY
apprise - - - - - - - - INFORM
appriser - - - - - - - INFORMANT
approach - VERGE, COME, NEAR, ADIT
approach nearer together - CONVERGE
approach stealthily - - - - - STALK
approaching - - - - - - - TOWARD
approaching day - - - - - TOMORROW
appropriate - - PROPER, SUIT, APT, SUITABLE, BECOMING, FIT, MEET
appropriate for one's use - BORROW, USURP
appropriated - - PREEMPTED, TAKEN
approval - ENDORSEMENT, CONSENT, SANCTION, IMPRIMATUR
approval (colloq.) - - - - - - OKAY
approve - - - ADMIRE, PASS, O.K.
approve (colloq.) - - - - - - - O.K.
approvingly - - - - - FAVOURABLY
approximate - - - APPROACH, NEAR
approximately - - - ABOUT, NEARLY
aprenaceous - - - - - - - - SANDY
apron - - - - - - - - PINAFORE
apron (dial.) - - - - - - - BRAT
apron top - - - - - - - - - BIB
apt - - FIT, PAT, LIABLE, TALENTED, CLEVER, TIMELY, SKILLED, DEXTROUS, FITTING
apteral - - - - - - - - WINGLESS
aptitude - - ART, TALENT, BENT, SKILL
aquatic animal - OTTER, FISH, POLYP, NEWT
aquatic bird - DABCHICK, FLAMINGO, GOOSE, GULL, COOT, SWAN, DUCK, SMEW
aquatic mammal - SIRENIAN, WHALE, OTTER, SEAL
aquatic vertebrate - - - - - - FISH
aquatic worm - - - - - - - CADEW
aqueduct - - - - - - - CONDUIT
aquilegia - - - - - - COLUMBINE
ara - - - - - - - - - - MACAW
Arab - SARACEN, TAD, GAMIN, SEMITE, URCHIN, BEDOUIN
Arabia (poet.) - - - - - - - ARABY
Arabian capital - - - - - - - SANA
Arabian chieftain - - - EMIR, EMEER
Arabian city - - - - - - - - ADEN
Arabian cloth - - - - - - - - ABA
Arabian commander - - EMIR, EMEER, AMEER, AMIR
Arabian country - - - - - - YEMEN
Arabian fabulous bird - - - - ROC
Arabian garment - - - - - - - ABA
Arabian gazelle - - - - - - - ARIEL
Arabian gulf - - - - - - - - ADEN
Arabian jasmine - - - - - - - BELA
Arabian judge - - - - - - - CADI
Arabian kingdom - - - IRAK, IRAQ
Arabian language - - - - - - ARABIC
Arabian magistrate - - - - - - CADI
Arabian Moslem - - - - - - WAHABI
Arabian night bird - - - - - - ROC
Arabian nights prince - - - - ASSAD
Arabian peninsula - - - ADEN, SINAI
Arabian prince - - - - - - SHERIF
Arabian river bed - - - - - - WADI

Arabian seaport - ADEN
Arabian shrub - KAT
Arabian state - OMAN
Arabian sultanate - OMAN
Arabian tambourine - TAAR, DAIRA
Arabian title - EMIR
Arabian wind - SIMOON
arable - TILLABLE
arachnid - SPIDER, MITE, ACARUS, TICK
arbiter - JUDGE, UMPIRE, REFEREE
arbitrate - MEDIATE, DECIDE
arbitrator - REFEREE, JUDGE
arbor - BOWER, PERGOLA
arboreal mammal - LEMUR, OPOSSUM, RACCOON
arborization - DENDRITE
arc - BOW, ARCH
arc formed in the sky - RAINBOW
arcade - GALLERY, LOGGIA
arch - CURVE, CHIEF, ARC, BEND, SLY, BOW, SPAN, WAGGISH, ROGUISH, RAINBOW
arch over - COVE, SPAN
arch (pointed) - OGIVE
arch of sky - COPE
archaic article - YE
archaic preposition - UNTO
archaic pronoun - YE, THY, THINE
archangel (one of) - MICHAEL
Archbishop of Canterbury (early) - CRANMER, ANSELM
archean - ANCIENT
arched passageway - ARCADE
archer - BOWMAN
archetype - IDEAL
archfiend - SATAN
architect's drawing - PLAN
architectural column - PILASTER
architectural design - SPANDREL
architectural member - PILASTER
architectural ornament - DENTIL, CORBEIL
architectural pier - ANTA
architectural screen - SPIER
Arctic - POLAR, FRIGID
Arctic dog - SAMOYEDE
Arctic exploration base - ETAH
Arctic explorer - KANE
Arctic goose - BRANT
Arctic lawyer - HYDE
Arctic native - ESKIMO
Arctic treeless plain - TUNDRA
ardent - INTENSE, ZEALOUS, FERVID, EAGER, FIERY, RETHE
ardent partisan - DEVOTEE
ardent person - ENTHUSIAST
ardor - ELAN, FERVOR, AFFECTION, ZEAL
arduous - HARD
area - SPACE, EXTENT, SITE, TRACT, SECTION, RANGE, SCOPE, REGION
area in acres - ACREAGE
area (pert. to) - AREAL
area (small) - AREOLA, PLOT
areal - REGIONAL
arena - OVAL, STADIUM, FIELD, RING
arenaceous - SANDY
arenose - SANDY
Are's sister - ERIS
argali - BIGHORN
argent - A. G., A. R., SILVERY, SILVER
Argentine president - PERON
Argentine timber tree - TALA
argentum - A. G.
Argonaut's leader - JASON
argot - SLANG, DIALECT, JARGON, CANT
argue - DEBATE, REASON, DISPUTE, DISCUSS
argue in court - PLEAD
argument - DEBATE, SPAT, ROW
argument against - CON
argument in favor of - PRO
aria - TUNE, SONG, SOLO
aricular - AURAL
arid - BARREN, WATERLESS, DRY, PARCHED, SERE
arid region - SAHARA
Aries - RAM
arise - EMANATE, ASCEND, ORIGINATE, ISSUE, MOUNT, SPRING
arista - BEARD, AWN
aristate - AWNED
aristocratic (slang) - TONY
Arius's follower - ARIAN
Arizona river - GILA
ark - COFFER
ark's builder (var.) - NOE
ark's landing place - ARARAT
arm - FORTIFY, MIGHT, BRANCH
arm covering - SLEEVE
arm of sea - INLET, BAY, FIRTH, GULF
armadillo - APARA, APAR, PEBA, TATOU
armed band - POSSE
armed conflict - WAR, BATTLE
armed engagement - BATTLE
armed fleet - NAVY
armed force - REGIMENT, ARMY
armed galley of Northmen - AESC
armed guard - SENTRY, SENTINEL
armed merchantman - RAIDER
armed power - ARMAMENT
armed ships (pert. to) - NAVAL
Armenian capital - ERIVAN
Armenian mt. - ARARAT
armhole - SCYE
armies (bib.) - SABAOTH
armistice - TRUCE
armour - MAIL
armour bearer - ESQUIRE, SQUIRE
armour splint - TACE
armour for the thigh - TASLET, TACE
armoured animal - ARMADILLO
armoured vehicle - TANK
armpit - ALA
army - HOST, HORDE
army follower - SUTLER
army meal - MESS
army movable equipment - BAGGAGE
army section - CORPS
army unit - BRIGADE
aroar - RIOTOUS
aroma - FRAGRANCE, ODOUR, SCENT FLAVOUR
aromatic - FRAGRANT, SPICY
aromatic berry - CUBEB
aromatic condiment - SPICE
aromatic gum resin - MYRRH
aromatic herb - ANISE, MINT, THYME, SPEARMINT, CARAWAY
aromatic plant - MINT, NARD, BASIL, HERBY, TANSY, ANGELICA
aromatic principal of violet root - IRONE
aromatic quality - SPICERY
aromatic seasoning - SPICE
aromatic seed - ANISE
aromatic smoke - FUME
aromatic spice - MACE
aromatic tree gum - BALSAM
aromatic wood - CEDAR
arouse - ACTUATE, EXCITE, STIR, ALARM

arouse to action - - - - - - RALLY
arousing aversion - - - REPELLENT
arrow - - - - - - - - STRAIGHT
arraign - - - - INDICT, DENOUNCE
arrange - - PREPARE, ADJUST, PLAN, SETTLE, DISPOSE, PLACE
arrange in battle formation - DEPLOY
arrange beforehand - - - - - PLAN
arrange to bring out differences - - - CONTRAST
arrange compactly - - - - - STOW
arrange for exhibition - - - - STAGE
arrange in folds - - - - - DRAPE
arrange as hangings - - - - DRAPE
arrange in layers - - TIER, LAMINATE
arrange in a line - - - - - ALINE
arrange side by side - - - - APPOSE
arrange in succession - - - SERIATE
arrange in tabular form - - TABULATE
arrange in thin layers - - - LAMINAL
arranged in layers - LAMINATE, LAMINAR
arranged in a row - - - - SERIAL
arranged in a table - - - - TABULAR
arrangement - PLAN, SYSTEM, SETUP, ORDER, DISPOSAL
arrangement of interwoven parts - WEB
arrangement of sails - - - - RIGS
arrant - - - - - - - - ERRANT
arras - - - - - - - - TAPESTRY
array - DRESS, GARB, CLOTHE, DECK, ATTIRE
arrest - - HALT, STEM, CHECK, REIN, HINDER, SEIZURE, DETAIL, RESTRAIN, CAPTURE, STOP, APPREHEND
arrest (slang) - - - - - - PINCH
arret - - - - - - - EDICT, DECREE
arrive - - - - - - - COME, REACH
arrogance - - - - - - - - PRIDE
arrogant - - - - HAUGHTY, PROUD
arrow - - - - - - - DART, BARB
arrow body - - - - - - - - STELE
arrow case - - - - - - - QUIVER
arrow poisoning - - - INEE, CURARE
arrowlike - - - - - - - SAGITTAL
arsenic (comb. form) - - - - ARSENO
arsenic (symbol) - - - - - - - A. S.
art - - KNACK, APTITUDE, SCIENCE, WILE, FACILITY, SKILL
art of controlling - - - MANAGEMENT
art of discourse - - - - RHETORIC
art gallery - - - - - - - - SALON
art of government (pert. to) - POLITICAL
art of horsemanship - - - - - MANEGE
art of flying - - - - - - AVIATION
art of reasoning (pert. to) - DIALECTIC
Artemis's mother - - - - - - LETO
Artemis's twin - - - - - - APOLLO
artery (large) - - - - - - - AORTA
artery (pert. to) - - - - POLITICAL
artful - - - - - - - - - SLY, WILY
artichoke leafstalks - - - - - CHARD
article - - THING, ITEM, AN, A, THE
article of apparel - - - - - - GAITER
article (arch.) - - - - - - - - - YE
article of belief - - - - TENET, CREED
article of commerce - - - - - STAPLE
article in a document - - - - CLAUSE
article of faith - - - - - - - TENET
article of food - - VIAND, FRITTER
article of personal property - CHATTEL
article of trade - - - - - COMMODITY
article of virtu - - - - - - - CURIO
articulated support - - - - - HINGE
artifice - - GUILE, TRICKERY, RUSE, FINESSE, WILE, DODGE, STRATAGEM, ART
artificial - - UNREAL, PASTE, SHAM, FEIGNED, ASSUMED
artificial bait - - - - - - - LURE
artificial butter - - - - - - - OLEO
artificial elevation - - - - - - TEE
artificial fishing fly - - - - - NYMPH
artificial grain - - - - - - - MALT
artificial hill - - - - - - - MOUND
artificial irritant - - - - - - SETON
artificial ivory - - - - - - IVORIDE
artificial as jewels - - - - - PASTE
artificial language - - IDE, IDO, RO, ESPERANTO
artificial light - - - - - - - LAMP
artificial manners - - - - - - AIRS
artificial moat - - - - - - - FOSS
artificial oyster bed - - - - - LAYER
artificial teeth - - - - - - DENTURE
artificial waterway - - CANAL, SLUICE
artisan - - - - - - - OPERATIVE
artist - - - - - - - - - - PAINTER
artistic dance - - - - - - - BALLET
artist's medium - - - - - - - OIL
artist's mixing board - - - - PALETTE
artist's stand - - - - - - - EASEL
artless - - - - - - - NAIVE, NAIF
artless woman - - - - - - INGENUE
artlessness - - - - - - - NAIVETE
arum - - - - - - - - - - - LILY
arum plant - - - ARAD, AROID, LILY
Aryan - - - - - - - - SLAV, MEDE
as - - - - - - - - - - BECAUSE
as before - - - - - - - - - DITTO
as compared with - - - - - - THAN
as far as - - - - - - - - UNTO, TO
as it stands (mus.) - - - - - - STA
as long as - - - - - - - - - WHILE
as well - - - - - - - - ALSO, AND
Asarum camphor - - - - - ASARONE
ascend - - ARISE, MOUNT, UP, CLIMB, SCALE
ascendant - - - - - - - - - RISING
ascending axis - - - - - - - - STEM
ascending in thought or expression - - CLIMATIC
ascent - - - - - - - - RISE, RISING
ascertain - LEARN, SEE, DETERMINE
ascertain the bearings of - - ORIENT
ascertain the duration of - - - TIME
ascertain the volume of - - MEASURE
ascetic - - - STOIC, YOGI, ESSENE
ascribable - - - - - - - - - - DUE
ascribe - REFER, IMPUTE, ATTRIBUTE
asea - - - - - - - - - - MUDDLED
ash - - - - - - - - TIMBER, CINDER
ash solution - - - - - - - - - LYE
ashen - - - - PALE, GREY, ASHY
ashes (Scot.) - - - - - - - - - ASE
ashy - - PALE, WHITE, ASHEN, WAN, LIVID, GREY
Asia Minor island - - - - - - SAMOS
Asia Minor mountain - - - - - - IDA
Asia Minor republic - - - - - SYRIA
Asiatic - ASIAN, TATAR, HUN, KOREAN, TURK
Asiatic animal - RASSE, SEROW, TIGER
Asiatic bean - - - - - - - - - SOY
Asiatic bird - - - - MINIVET, MYNAH
Asiatic climbing pepper - - - - BETEL
Asiatic coast wind - - - - MONSOON
Asiatic country - SIAM, TIBET, IRAN, KOREA, NEPAL, IRAQ, INDIA, ARABIA, RUSSIA, ANAM, BURMA, SYRIA, CHINA
Asiatic country (ancient) - MEDEA, ELAM, EOLIA
Asiatic domestic cattle - - - - - ZOBO

Asiatic gazelle - - - - - CORA, AHU
Asiatic isthmus - - - - - - - KRA
Asiatic kingdom - NEPAL, IRAQ, ANNAM, IRAK, ANAM, SIAM
Asiatic lemur - - - - - - - LORIS
Asiatic leopard - - - - - - PANTHER
Asiatic mink - - - - - - KOLINSKY
Asiatic monkeylike animal - - LORIS
Asiatic mountains - - - - - - ALTAI
Asiatic native - - - - - - - ARAB
Asiatic nomad - - - - - - - ARAB
Asiatic palm - - ARECA, NIPA, BETEL
Asiatic peninsula - - KOREA, ARABIA
Asiatic perennial - - - - - - RAMIE
Asiatic pheasant - - - - - TRAGOPAN
Asiatic plant - - - - - - - - ODAL
Asiatic river - - - AMUR, INDUS, OB, TIGRIS, LENA
Asiatic rolled tea - - - - - - CHA
Asiatic ruminant - - - - CAMEL, YAK
Asiatic Russian city - - - - - URALAK
Asiatic sea - - - - - - - - ARAL
Asiatic tea - - - - - - - - CHA
Asiatic tree - - - - - - SIRIS, DITA
Asiatic tribesman - - - - - - TATAR
Asiatic vine - - - - - - - - BETEL
Asiatic weight - - - - CATTY, TAEL
Asiatic wild ass - - - - - - ONAGER
Asiatic wild sheep - - RASSE, ARGALI
aside - - - APART, AWAY, SEPARATE
asinine - - - - - - SILLY, STUPID
ask - INQUIRE, INVITE, BID, SOLICIT, REQUEST, BEG
ask alms - - - - - - - - - BEG
ask contributions - - - - - SOLICIT
ask for formally - - - - - - - PRAY
ask payment - - - - - - - - DUN
ask (Scot.) - - - - - - - - SPERE
askance - - - - - - - - - - AWRY
askew - WRY, ATILT, AWRY, CROOKED
aslant - - - - - - - - - - ATILT
asleep - - - - - - ABED, DORMANT
aslope - - - - - - - - - - CANTED
asp - - - VIPER, REPTILE, SNAKE
aspect - PHASE, GUISE, APPEARANCE, SIDE, MIEN
aspen - - - - - - POPLAR, SHAKING
asperation - - - - - - - - SLUR
asperity - - - - - - - - - RIGOR
asperse - SLANDER, VILIFY, TRADUCE, CALUMNIATE
aspersion - - - - - SLUR, SLANDER
aspirant - - - CANDIDATE, NOMINEE
aspiration - - AIM, DESIRE, AMBITION
aspire - - PRETEND, DESIRE, SEEK, REACH
aspiring to be artistic - - - - ARTY
ass - - - - - - - - - SIMPLETON
ass (wild) - - - - - - - - ONAGER
assail - - BESET, ATTACK, SCATHE, ASSAULT, ACCOST
assail with missiles - - - - - PELT
assailant - - - - - - - - ATTACKER
Assam silk - - - - - - - - - ERI
Assamese tribe - - - - - - - - AO
assassin - - - - - - - - - KILLER
assault - - ASSAIL, ONSET, ATTACK, RAID, ONSLAUGHT
assay - - - - - - - - - - TEST
assayer - - - - - - - - - TESTER
assaying vessel - - - - - - - CUPEL
assemblage - MEETING, HOST, GROUP
assemble - - MEET, CONVENE, MASS, CONVOKE, CONGREGATE, MUSTER
assemble as troops - - - - - MUSTER
assembling a body - - - - - SESSION
assembly - - - - - - DIET, AGORA
assembly of delegates - - - - - DIET
assent - AGREE, AGREEMENT, CONSENT, CONCUR, SANCTION
assert - STATE, AVER, ALLEGE, ATTEST, AVOW, PREDICATE, AFFIRM, MAINTAIN, AVOUCH, DECLARE, CONTEND, PRONOUNCE
assert earnestly - - - - - PROTEST
assert as fact - - - - - - - - POSIT
assertion - STATEMENT, AFFIRMATION
assertion of a fact - - - - - CLAIM
assess - - - TAX, LEVY, ESTIMATE
assessment - - - - - - - TAX, STENT
assessment rating - - - - - - RATAL
assessor - - - - - LEVIER, ADVISER
asset - - - - - - - - - - ESTATE
asseverate - - - AFFIRM, VOW, AVER
asseveration - - - - - - - - - VOW
assign - - - - - RELEGATE, AWARD, DESIGNATE, LABEL, APPOINT, ALLOT
assign parts - - - - - - - - CAST
assign to a post - - - - - STATION
assign time to - - - - - - - DATE
assign to - - - - - - REFER, CLASS
assigned service - - - - - - - DUTY
assignment - - - - - - - - - TASK
assimilate - - - - - DIGEST, ABSORB
assimilate mentally - - - - - LEARN
assimilation - - - - - - DIGESTION
assimilative - - - - - - DIGESTIVE
assist - BEFRIEND, AID, HELP, ABET
assistance - - - - - HELP, SUCCOR
assistance (be of) - - - - - - AVAIL
assistant - - HELPER, AIDER, AIDE, AUXILIARY
assistant chairman - - - - CROUPIER
assistant to curate - - - - - - VICAR
assistant pastor - - - - - - CURATE
associate - PARTNER, FELLOW, ALLY, MIX, HERD, CONSORT
associate familiarly - - - - - HOBNOB
associated - - - - - - - CONJOINT
associated surroundings - - - CONTEXT
assort - - - - - - - - - CLASSIFY
assuage - RELIEVE, SLAKE, MITIGATE, ALLAY
assuasive - - - - - - - - LENITIVE
assume - DON, WEAR, SUPPOSE, ADOPT, PRETEND, FEIGN
assume an attitude - - - - - - POSE
assume as fact - - - - - - - POSIT
assume a reverent posture - - - KNEEL
assume a role - - - - - - - - ACT
assume unrightfully - - - - - USURP
assumed biological units - - - IDANTS
assumed character - - - - - - ROLE
assumed function - - - - - - ROLE
assumed manner - - - - - - - - AIR
assumed name - - - - - - - ALIAS
assumption - - PRETENCE, PRETENSE
assurance - - - - - - - - APLOMB
assure - CONVINCE, VOUCH, CONFIRM
assure dowry to - - - - - - ENDOW
assuredly - - - - - - - DECIDEDLY
Assyrian capital - - - - - - NINEVEH
Assyrian deity - - - - - ASHUR, IRA
astare - - - - - - - - - - GAZING
Aztec god of sowing - - - - - - XIPE
aster plant - - - - - - TANSY, OXEYE
asteraceous plant - - - - - - DAISY
asterisk - - - - - - - - - - STAR
astern - AFT, ABAFT, BACKWARD, BEHIND
asteroid - - - - - - - - - - EROS
astir - - - - - - - - AGOG, ACTIVE

A

astonish - - - - AWE, APPAL, AMAZE, SURPRISE
astonishment - - - - - SURPRISE
astound - - - - AMAZE, AWE, STUN
astounded (colloq.) - - FLABBERGASTED
astraddle - - - - - - - - ASTRIDE
astral - - - - - STARRY, STELLAR
astral body - - - - - - - - STAR
astray - - - - - - - - - - AMISS
astride - - - - - - - - ASTRADDLE
astringent - - - - - ALUM, TANNIN
astringent salt - - - - - - - ALUM
astrologer - - - - - - - STARGAZER
astronomical - - - - - - - URANIAN
astronomical arc - - - - - - AZIMUTH
astronomical instrument - - - ORRERY
astronomical phenomenon - - NEBULA
astronomical unit of measure - SIRIOMETE
astute - - - SHREWD, CRAFTY, SLY, CUNNING
asunder - - - - - - - - - - APART
asunder (prefix) - - - - - - - DIS
asylum - - - - - - - - - SHELTER
at - - NEAR, BY, ABOUT, DURING, IN
at all - - - - - - - - - - - EVER
at all events - - - - - - - - - SO
at all times - - - - - - - - - EVER
at all times (poet.) - - - - - E'ER
at any time - - - - - - - - - EVER
at a distance - - - AFAR, OFF, ALOOF
at ease - - - - - - - - INACTIVE
at an end (poet.) - - - - - - O'ER
at hand - - - - - - - - - NEAR, BY
at the highest (comb. form) - - ACRO
at large - - - - - - - - - ABROAD
at least - - - - - - - - LEASTWISE
at no time - - NEVER, NE'ER, (POET.)
at odds - - - - - - - - - - - OUT
at once - - - - - - - NOW, PRONTO
at proper time - - - - - - - DULY
at some past time - - - - - - ONCE
at that place - - - - - - - YONDER
at that time - - - - - - - - - THEN
at this time - - - - - - - - - NOW
at the top - - - - - - - - - APICAL
at which - - - - - - - - - WHEREAT
at work - - - - - - - - - - - BUSY
atelier - - - - WORKSHOP, STUDIO
Athama's wife - - - - - - - - - INO
Athena - - - - - - - - ALEA, PALEA
Athens lawgiver - - - - - - SOLON
Athens statesman - - - - - PERICLES
Athens temple - - - - - PARTHENON
Athens title - - - - - - - - - ALEA
athlete's crown - - - - - - LAUREL
athletic field - - - - - - - - OVAL
athletic game - - - - - - - SPORT
athirst - - - - - - - - - - EAGER
athwart - - ASLANT, ACROSS, AGAINST
Atilla's follower - - - - - - - HUN
atilt - - - ASKEW, ASLANT, SLANTING
atis - - - - - - - - - - ACONITE
atmosphere - - - - AURA, AIR, ETHER
atmospheric - - - - - - AERIAL, AIRY
atmospheric conditions - - - - CLIMATE
atmospheric disturbance - STORM, FOG
atmospheric optical illusion - - MIRAGE
atmospheric pressure (pert. to) - BARIC
atom - PARTICLE, IOTA, JOT, PROTON, ION
atom bomb particle - - - - - PROTON
atom constituent - - - - - ELECTRON
atom part - - - - - - - - - - ION
atomic - - - - - - - - - - - TINY
atone - - EXPIATE, APPEASE, REDEEM, RECONCILE
atoned for - - - - - - - - REDEEMED
atonement - - - - - - - REPARATION
atop - - - - - - - - - ABOVE, UPON
atrocity - - - - - - - - - ENORMITY
attach - ANNEX, APPEND, ADD, FASTEN, LINK
attached - - - - - - - - - - - FOND
attached to the branch - - - SESSILE
attached the lure - - - - - - BAITED
attachment - ADHERENCE, DEVOTION, ADHESION
attack - - ASSAIL, ASSAULT, ONSET, ONSLAUGHT, RAID
attack violently - - - - - - STORM
attack warning - - - - - - - ALERT
attacker - - - - - - - - ASSAILANT
attain - GAIN, ACHIEVE, REACH, EARN, COMPASS, ACQUIRE
attain success - - - - - ARRIVE, WIN
attainment - - - - - - - SUCCESS
attaint - - - - - CORRUPT, DISGRACE
attempt - - - - TRIAL, EFFORT, ESSAY, STRIVE, TRY, ENDEAVOUR, STAB
attempt (colloq.) - - - - - GO, STAB
attempt (Scot.) - - - - - - - - ETTLE
attend - - - AWAIT, ESCORT, WAIT, MINISTER
attend to - - - HEED, LISTEN, NURSE
attendant - AIDE, HELPER, MINISTERING, CLERK, SERVER
attendant on a lord - - - - - THANE
attent - - - - - - - - - HEEDFUL
attention - - - - - EAR, DILIGENCE, OBSERVANCE, HEED, CONSIDERATION
attentive - - - OBSERVANT, HEEDFUL
attentive consideration - - - - EAR
attentive to unimportant details - - - MINUTIOSE
attenuated - RAREFIED, THIN, DILUTED, WEAKENED
attest - ASSERT, WITNESS, CONFIRM, TESTIFY, CERTIFY
attestation of the truth - - - - OATH
attic - - - - - - - - GARRET, LOFT
attire - - - GARB, DRESS, RAIMENT, EQUIP, RIG, ROBE, HABIT, ARRAY
attitude - - - - POSE, MIEN, POSTURE
attitudinize - - - - - - - - - POSE
attract - DRAW, ALLURE, CHARM, LURE
attractive - - - - TAKING, ENGAGING
attractive as a child - - - - - CUTE
attractive (colloq.) - - - - - - CUTE
attractiveness - - - - - - - CHARM
attribute - - - - - REFER, ASCRIBE
attune - - - - - - - - HARMONIZE
auction - - - - - - - - - - - SALE
audacious - - - - - - - - - BOLD
audacity - - - - - - - NERVE, CHEEK
audibly - - - - - - - - - - ALOUD
audience - - - - - - - - - - - EAR
audition - - - - - - - - - HEARING
auditor - - - - - - LISTENER, HEARER
auditory - - - - - - - - - - - OTIC
augment - - - - - - - - - EKE, ADD
augmentation (her.) - - - - ADDITION
augur - - BODE, PORTEND, FORBODE
augury - - - - - - - - - - - OMEN
august - - - - - GRAND, VENERABLE
auk - - - - - - - - - - - - MURRE
aunt (S. Afr.) - - - - - - - - TANTA
aunt (Sp.) - - - - - - - - - - TIA
aural - - - - - - - ARICULAR, OTIC
aureate - - - - - - - - - GOLDEN
aureola - - - - - - - - - - - HALO
aureole - - - - - - - - - - - HALO
auricle - - - - - - - - EAR, PINNA

auricle of the ear - - - - - - PINNA
auricular - - - - - - OTIC, AURAL
auriculate - - - - - - - - EARED
auriferous - - - - - - - - GOLDEN
aurora - - - - - - - - DAWN, EOS
auroral - - - - - - - - - - EOAN
auspices - - - - - - - - - - EGIS
austere - SEVERE, GRANITIC, STERN, HARD, FROSTY
austerity of manner - - - - - FROST
Australian aborigine - - - - - - MARA
Australian badger - - - - - WOMBAT
Australian bear - - - - - - - KOALA
Australian bird - - - - - - - EMU
Australian boomerang - - - - - KYLIE
Australian brushwood - - - - MALLEE
Australian canvas shoe - - PLIMSOLL
Australian cape - - - - - - - HOWE
Australian city - - - - - - - PERTH
Australian clover fern - - - NARDOO
Australian insect - - - - - - - LERP
Australian lake - - - - - - - EYRE
Australian marsupial - - TAIT, KOALA
Australian ostrich - - - - - - - EMU
Australian parrot - - - - - LORIKEET
Australian resin - - - - - - DAMAR
Australian seaport - - - - - BRISBANE
Australian soldier - - - - - - ANZAC
Australian tree - - - - - - - BILLA
Australian tribe - - - - - - - MARA
Australian wild dog - - - - - DINGO
Austrian botanist - - - - - MENDEL
Austrian capital - - - - - - VIENNA
Austrian coin - - - - - - FLORIN
Austrian composer - - - - - MOZART
Austrian province - - - TIROL, TYROL
Austrian province (pert. to) - TYROLESE
Austrian war club - - - - - LEEANGLE
Austrian weight - - - - - - - SAUM
authentic - - - - - - - REAL, TRUE
authenticate - - - - - - - - - SEAL
author - - - - - - WRITER, CREATOR
authoritative - - ASSERTIVE, OFFICIAL
authoritative answer - - - - - ORACLE
authoritative command - - - - - FIAT
authoritative decree - - - - - ARRET
authoritative requirement - - MANDATE
authoritive - - OFFICIAL, CANONICAL
authoritive decree - - - - - - EDICT
authoritive permission - - - - LICENSE
authority - - - EXPERT, DOMINANCE, DOMINION
authorize - - - ACCREDIT, DELEGATE, LICENSE
authorize to receive - - - - - ENTITLE
authorizing - - - - - - - LICENSING
authorizing letter - - - - - - BREVE
auto - - - - - - - - - - - CAR
auto cover - - - - - - - - HOOD
autocrat - - - - - - DESPOT, MOGUL
automatic fuel (colloq.) - - - - GAS
automatic recorder - - - - - - METER
automaton - - - - - ROBOT, GOLEM
automobile - - - - - - - - - SEDAN
automobile adjunct - - - - - STARTER
automobile body - TONNEAU, SEDANET
automobile operator - - - - - DRIVER
automobile speed - - - - - REVERSE
automotive vehicle - - - - - - MOTOR
autonomous republic (E. Russ.) - TARTAR
auxiliary - - ANCILLARY, ALLY, ALAR, HELPING, ASSISTANT
auxiliary verb - - - - - - - SHALL
avail - STEAD, BENEFIT, PROFIT, USE, BOOT
available money - - - - - - - CASH

avalanche - - - - - - - - - SLIDE
avarice - GREED, CUPIDITY, GRASPING
avaricious - - - - GREEDY, COVETOUS
avaricious money lender - - - USURER
avenaceous - - - - - - - - - OATEN
avenge - REVENGE, RETALIATE, REQUITE
avenger - - - - - NEMESIS, PUNISHER
avenging deity - - - - - - - ERINYS
avenging spirit - - - - - ATE, ERINYS
avenue - - - - - - - - - - - MALL
aver - STATE, VERIFY, ASSERT, ALLEGE, AFFIRM, AVOUCH, DECLARE, VOUCH, SAY
average - - MEAN, ORDINARY, USUAL, MEDIUM, MEDIAL
averse - RELUCTANT, LOATH, OPPOSED, INIMICAL, UNWILLING
aversion - DISLIKE, DISTASTE, HATE, HATRED
avert - - - - - - - PREVENT, AVOID
aviation - - - - - - - - - - FLIGHT
aviator - - ACE, PILOT, FLIER, FLYER, AERONAUT
avid - - - - - - - - EAGER, GREEDY
avifauna - - - - - - - - - - ORNIS
avital - - - - - - - - - ANCESTRAL
avocation - - - - - - - - - HOBBY
avoid - SHUN, SHIRK, EVADE, AVERT, ELUDE, SIDESTEP, ESCAPE, ESCHEW, BEWARE
avoid (old word) - - - - - - EVITATE
avouch - - - - - - - - AVER, ASSERT
avow - AVER, ACKNOWLEDGE, ASSERT, TESTIFY, OWN, CONFESS, PROFESS
await - - - - - EXPECT, ATTEND, BIDE
await settlement - - - - - - - PEND
awaited adjustment - - - - - PENDED
awake - - - - - - - VIGILANT, ALERT
awaken - - - - - - - ROUSE, AROUSE
award - METE, ASSIGN, BESTOW, PRIZE, GRANT
award of valor - - - - - - - MEDAL
aware - - - - COGNIZANT, INFORMED, KNOWING, ALERT, KNOW, VIGILANT
awash - - - - - - - - - - AFLOAT

B

Babbitt's author - - - - - - LEWIS
babble - - PRATTLE, PRATE, JABBER, BLATHER
babe - - - - - - - - - - INFANT
Babylonian abode of the dead - ARALU
Babylonian chief priest - - - - - EN
Babylonian god - EL, EA, BEL, ANU, ADAD, HEA, BAAL
Babylonian god (var.) - - - - - - IRA
Babylonian goddess - - - - - - AYA
Babylonian hero - - - - - - - ETANA
Babylonian numeral - - - - - - SAR
Babylonian storm god - - - - - ADAD
baby - - - - - - - - INFANT, HUMOR
baby ailment - - - - - - - - CROUP
baby carriage - - - - STROLLER, PRAM, GOCART
bac - - - - - - - - - CISTERN, VAT
Baccal. degree - - - - - - - B.A., A.B.
Bacchanal cry - - - - - - - - EVOE
back - REAR, FRO, SUPPORT, UPHOLD
back of animal - - - - - - DORSUM
back debt - - - - - - - - - ARREAR
back gate - - - - - - - - POSTERN
back (in the) - - - - - - - - AREAR
back of neck - - - - - - - - NAPE
back payment - - - - - - - - ARREAR

B

back (pert. to) - - - - - - DORSAL
back (prefix) - - - - - - - UN, ANA
back of skull (pert. to) - - OCCIPITAL
back streets - - - - - - - - ALLEYS
back (to) - - - - - - - - SPONSOR
backbone - - - - - - - - - - SPINE
backbone of animal - - - - - CHINE
backer - - - - - - - - - SPONSOR
backless seat - - - - - - - - STOOL
backward - - - - - - ASTERN, AREAR
backward bend - - - - - - RETORTION
bacon cut - - - - - - - - - RASHER
bacteria culture - - - - - - - AGAR
bacteria dissolver - - - - - - LYSIN
bacteriological culture - - - - - AGAR
bacteriological wire - - - - - - OESE
bad - - SPOILED, HARMFUL, BALEFUL, INFERIOR, ILL, POOR, FAULTY
bad habits - - - - - - - - - - VICE
badge - - - - - - - - - PIN, TOKEN
badge of honour - - - - - - - MEDAL
badge of mourning - - - - - - CREPE
badger - - - - - - - - PERSECUTE
badgerlike mammal - - - - - - RATEL
badinage - - - - - - - - - BANTER
badly - - - - - - - - - - - ILLY
badly (prefix) - - - - - - - - - MAL
baffle - - - ELUDE, EVADE, THWART
baffling - - - - - - ELUSIVE, EVASIVE
baffling question - - - - - - - POSER
bag - SACK, POUCH, SATCHEL, VALISE, ENTRAP, CAPTURE
bag floating in air - - - - - BALLOON
bagpipe - - - - - - - - - - DRONE
Bahama Islands capital - - - NASSAU
Bahama Islands group - - - - BIMINI
Bahrein Islands capital - - MANAMEH
bail - LADE, SECURITY, REPLEVIN, HOOP
bailing a person (act of) - - REPLEVINS
bait - LURE, HARASS, TORMENT, WORRY
bake - - - - - - - - - - - ROAST
baked clay - - - - - - - - - - TILE
baked clay pot - - - - - - - - OLLA
baker's implement - - - - - - - PEEL
baking dish - - - - - - - RAMEKIN
baking soda - - - - - - SALERATUS
Balaam's steed - - - - - - - - ASS
balance - SCALES, POISE, REMAINDER, PAR, EVEN
balance which remains due - ARREARS
balcony - - - - - - - - - TERRACE
bald - - - - - - - HAIRLESS, BARE
balderdash - - - - - - - - PALAVER
baleful - - - - - - - - - - - - BAD
balk - - - - - - - - - - - - - JIB
balk as a horse (Scot.) - - - - REEST
Balkan country - - - - - - BULGARIA
ball - - - - DANCE, GLOBE, PELLET
ball of thread or yarn - - - - - CLEW
ball used in tenpins - - - - - BOWL
ballad - - - - - - SONG, LAY, DERRY
ballet dancer - - - - - - - BALLERINA
ballet by Delibes - - - - - - - NAILA
balloon basket - - - - - - - - - CAR
balloon car - - - - - - - - BASKET
ballot - - - - - - - - - - - - VOTE
balm - - - - - - - - - - - BALSAM
balmy - - - - - - - - - - - BLAND
balsa - - - - - - - - - CORKWOOD
balsam (kind) - - - - - - TOLU, BALM
balsamic resin - - - - - - - - BALM
Baltic Sea island - - - - OSSEL, OESEL
Baltic seaport - - - - - - - - - KIEL
baluster - - - - - - - - - BANISTER
balustrade - - - - - - - - - RAILING
bamboo shoot - - - - - - - - ACHAR
ban - - - FORBID, CURSE, EXCLUDE
banal - - - - - - - - TRITE, TRIVIAL
band - BELT, COMPANY, GROUP, STRIP, STRAP, TROOP, GIRDLE, CREW, FETTER, UNITE, STRIPE
band across an escutcheon - - - FESS
band for the carpus - - - - WRISTLET
band of colour - - - - - - - - STRIPE
band for hair - - - - - - - - FILLET
band of leather - - - - - - - - STRAP
band of retainers - - - - - - - ROUT
bandage - - - - - - - - - - LIGATE
bandit - - - - - - - - - - BRIGAND
bandy - - - - - - - EXCHANGE, CART
bane - HARM, POISON, RUIN, MISCHIEF, WOE
baneful - - - - - - - - - - ILL, BAD
bang - - - - - - - - - SLAM, THUMP
banish - EXILE, DEPORT, OUST, EVICT, EXPEL, EXPATRIATE
banishment - - - - - - - - - - EXILE
banister - - - - - - - - - BALUSTER
bank - - TIER, BRINK, RIDGE, MOUND
bank customer - - - - - DEPOSITOR
bank note - - - - - - - - - - - BILL
bank officer - - - - - - - - - TELLER
bank of river - - - - - - - - - RIPA
bankrupt - - - - - - - - - - - RUIN
bankruptcy - - - - - - - - FAILURE
banner - - - - FLAG, ENSIGN, PENNON
banquet - - - - - - - - - - - FEAST
banteng - - - - - - - - - - - TSINE
banter - BADINAGE, RAILLERY, CHAFF, WIT, PLEASANTRY
Bantu language - - - - - ILA, RONGA
Bantu tribesman - - - - - - - - ZULU
baptismal vessel - - - - - - - - FONT
baptismal water - - - - - - - - LAVER
bar - - EXCLUDE, CAKE, EXCEPT, RAIL, STRIPE, ESTOP
bar of balance - - - - - - - - BEAM
bar of cast metal - - - - - - - INGOT
bar legally - - - - - - - - - ESTOP
bar in a loom - - - - - - - - EASER
bar one's self - - - - - - - - ESTOP
bar of a soap frame - - - - - - - SESS
bar to slacken thread in a loom - EASER
bar suspended by two ropes - - TRAPEZE
bar to transmit force - - - - - LEVER
bar used with fulcrum - - - - - LEVER
bar on which a wheel revolves - - AXLE
bar of wood or metal - - - - - - RAIL
barb - - - - - - - - - DART, ARROW
barbarian - - - - - - - - HUN, GOTH
barbarity - - - - - SAVAGERY, FERITY
barbed appendage - - - - - - - AWN
barbed implement - HARPOON, SPEAR
barbed spear - - - - - - - - - GAFF
bard - - - - - - - - POET, MINSTREL
bare - OPEN, PLAIN, EXPOSED, EXPOSE, MERE, MEAGER, STARK, DENUDE, NUDE, STRIP, BALD, BLANK, NAKED
bare rock standing alone - - - - - SCAR
bargain - - - - - - - - - DEAL, SALE
barge - - - - - - - - - TOW, SCOW
bargemen - - - - - - - - BURGEES
barium oxide - - - - - - - - BARYTA
bark - YAP, YELP, BAY, CLAMOR, RIND
bark cloth - - - - - - - - - - TAPA
bark exterior - - - - - - - - - ROSS
bark of paper mulberry - - - - - TAPA
bark shrilly - - - - - - - - - - YELP
bark shrilly (colloq.) - - - - - - YIP
barley beard - - - - - - - - - AWN
barley let germinate - - - - - - MALT
barn - - - - - - - - - - - STABLE

barometer (kind) - - - - - ANEROID
baron - - - - - - - - - - NOBLE
baronet's title - - - - - - - - SIR
baronet's wife - - - - - - - DAME
barracks - - - - - - ETAPE, CASERN
barracuda - - - - - - - - - - SPET
barrel - - - - - - CASK, KEG, TUN
barrel hook, side piece and slat - STAVE
barrel maker - - - - - - - COOPER
barrel stave - - - - - - - - - LAG
barrel support - - - - - - - STAVE
barren - STERILE, FALLOW, ARID, EFFETE
barricade - - - - - - - - - BARRIER
barrier - - DAM, HEDGE, BARRICADE, HURDLE
barrier of fire - - - - - - BARRAGE
barrier to be surmounted - - - HURDLE
barrister - - - - - - - - - LAWYER
barter - SELL, TRADE, EXCHANGE, TRUCK
base - LOW, MEAN, SORDID, STATION, BED, PEDESTAL, IGNOBLE, ABJECT, VILE, ESTABLISH, SNIDE
base of column - - - - - - PLINTH
base of decimal system - - - - TEN
base of felled tree - - - - - STUMP
base forming element - - - - METAL
base for a statue - - - - - PLINTH
baseball gloves - - - - - - MITTS
baseball inning - - - - - - FRAME
baseball term - - - - BUNT, LINER
baseboard decoration - - - - DADO
baseless - - - - - - - GROUNDLESS
bashful - - - - - - - - SHY, COY
bashful person - - - - - - SHEEP
basic element - - - - - - - METAL
basin - - - - - - - VESSEL, LAVER
basis - - - - - - - - - - - ROOT
basis of an argument - - - PREMISE
basis of assessment - - - - - RATAL
basis of a conclusion - - - - PREMISE
basis for discussion - - - - - DATA
basis of fruit jellies - - - - PECTIN
basis of quartz - - - - - - SILICA
basket - - - - - - - - - HAMPER
basket of balloon - - - - - - CAR
basket to carry load on back - PANNIER
basketry filling - - - - - - SLEWING
Basque cap - - - - - - - - BERET
bass horn - - - - - - - - - TUBA
basswood - - - - - - - - LINDEN
bast - - - - - - - - - - - FIBER
bast fiber - - - - - - - - CATENA
baste - - - - - - - - - - TACK
Bastogne hero - - - - - McAULIFFE
bat - - - - - - - - CUDGEL, CLUB
bate - - RESTRAIN, REDUCE, LOWER, LESSEN, MODERATE
bath - - - - - - - - - ABLUTION
bath house (Sp.) - - - - - - CABANA
bathe - - - - - - - - - - LAVE
batten - - - - - - - - - - THRIVE
batter - - - RAM, BRUISE, BOMBARD, HITTER
battering instrument - - - - - RAM
battery plate - - - - - - - - GRID
battle - - - - FIGHT, CONFLICT, WAR
battlefront (part) - - - - - - SECTOR
battleground - - - - - - - TERRAIN
battlement - - - - - - - - - CRENEL
battleship - - - - - - - - OREGON
bauble - - - - - - TRINKET, GEWGAW
bawl - - - - - - - - - - - SHOUT
bawl out - - - - - - BERATE, SCOLD
bay - - - COVE, SINUS, INLET, BARK
bay-like recess - - - - - - - COVE
bay of Naples island - - - - CAPRI
bay (Scot.) - - - - - - - - LOCH
bay of sea - - - - - - - - - SINUS
bay tree - - - - - - - - - LAUREL
bay window - - - - ORIEL, MIRADOR
bayou - - - - - - - - - - CREEK
bazaar - - - - - - - - - - - FAIR
be - - - - - - - - LIVE, EXIST, ARE
be abundant - - - - - - - - TEEM
be affectionate - - - - - - - COO
be available - - - - - - - - ENURE
be deprived of - - - - - - - LOSE
be enough - - - - - - - - - - DO
be expected - - - - - - - NATURAL
be false to - - - - - - - - BELIE
be flooded - - - - - - - - - SWIM
be in harmony - - - - AGREE, CHORD
be indisposed - - - - - - - - AIL
be informed - - - - - - - - HEAR
be lodged - - - - - - - - - BILLET
be motionless - - - - - - STAGNATE
be on one's guard - - - - - - BEWARE
be of the opinion - - - - - - FEEL
be pendent - - - - - - - - - LOP
be present - - - - - - - - ATTEND
be prominent - - - - - - - - STAR
be property of - - - - - - - BELONG
be related - - - - - - - - INHERE
be repeated - - - - - - - - RECUR
be restless - - - - - - - - - TOSS
be ruled by - - - - - - - - OBEY
be situated - - - - - - - - - LIE
be skilled in - - - - - - - - KNOW
be smarter than - - - - - - OUTWIT
be sorry for one's sins - - REPENT, RUE
be in store for - - - - - - - AWAIT
be sufficient - - - - - - - - - DO
be in suspense - - - - - - - PEND
be swallowed up - - - - - - MERGE
be undecided - - - - - DOUBT, PEND
be of use - - - - - - - - - AVAIL
be wanting - - - - - - - - - FAIL
be will of - - - - - - - - PLEASE
beach - - - - STRAND, SAND, SHORE
beach coverings - - - - - - - SAND
beach employee - - - - - LIFESAVER
beach grass - - - - - - - MARRAM
beach (poet.) - - - - - - - STRAND
bead - - - - - - - GLOBULE, DROP
beaded moisture - - - - - - - DEW
beads used as money - - - - - PEAG
beak - - - - - - - NEB, NIB, BILL
beaklike process - - - - - - ROSTEL
beam - RAY, SHINE, RAFTER, RADIATE
beaming - - - - - - - - RADIANT
bean - LEGUME, SOY, SOYA, GOA, LIMA
bear - ENDURE, STAND, CARRY, BRUIN
bear (the) - - - - - - - - - URSA
bear down on - - - - - - - PRESS
bear (female) - - - - - - - - URSA
bear heavily - - - - - - - - PRESS
bear (Latin) - - - - - - - - URSA
bear oneself well - - - - - - BEHAVE
bear up under - - - - - - - ENDURE
bear weapons - - - - - - - - - ARM
bear witness to - - - - ATTEST, DEPONE
bearable - - - - - - - - ENDURABLE
beard - - - - - ARISTA, AWN, GOATEE
beard of grains and grasses - - AWNS, AVELS, ARISTAE
bearded - - - - - - - - - ARISTATE
bearer - - - - - - - - - - CARRIER
bearing - AIR, MIEN, ORLE, CARRIAGE
bearing (her.) - - - - - - - - ENTE
bearing a heraldic device - - CRESTED
bearing spines - - - - - - SPINATE
bearing three flowers - - - TRIFLORAL

B

bearlike - - - - - - - - - URSINE
beast - - - - - - - - - - ANIMAL
beast of burden - ONAGER, ASS, CAMEL, YAK, DONKEY, MULE, LLAMA
beasts of burden - - - - - - - OXEN
beat - THRASH, HAMMER, DEFEAT, LASH, DRUB, FLAY, LAM, BEST, FLOG, PULSATE, SWINGE, PULSATION, PUMMEL, CONQUER, FLAIL, DRUM, SURPASS
beat back - - - - - REPEL, REPULSE
beat down - - - - - - BATTER, BATE
beat hard - - - - - - - - HAMMER
beat it - - - - - - - - - - SCRAM
beat soundly - - - - - - - LARRUP
beat thin - - - - - - - MALLEATE
beat thoroughly - - - - - - - DRUB
beat (var.) - - - - - - - CHASTIZE
beaten - BATTERED, CANED, DEFEATED
beaten path - - - - - - - - TRAIL
beater - - - - - - - - DASHER, RAB
beater for mixing mortar - - - - RAB
beatify - - - - - - - - - - BLESS
beau - - - - - - - DANDY, SUITOR
beautiful girl - - - - - - - BELLE
beautiful handwriting - - CALLIGRAPHY
beautify - - - - - - - - - IDEALIZE
beauty of form or movement - - GRACE
because - - - SINCE, FOR, AS, THAT
beck - - - - - - - NOD, COMMAND
becloud - - - - - - BEDIM, DARKEN
become - GROW, WAX, GET, SUIT, BEFIT
become acid - - - - - - - - SOUR
become apparent - - - - - DEVELOP
become aware of - - SENSE, LEARN, PERCEIVE
become bankrupt - - - - - - - FAIL
become blunt - - - - - - - - DULL
become blurred - - - - - - - - MIST
become brown - - - - - - - - - TAN
become buoyant - - - - - - LEVITATE
become compact - - - - - - - KNIT
become congealed - - - - - - FREEZE
become dim - - - - - - - - - MIST
become dull - - - - - - - - - PALL
become empty - - - - - - - - DRAIN
become entangled - - - - - - FOUL
become exhausted - - - - - - PETER
become grave - - - - - - - SOBER
become happy - - - - - - - - ELATE
become indistinct - - FADE, DIM, BLUR
become insignificant - - - - - - PALE
become insipid - - - - - PALL, STALED
become known - - - - - - TRANSPIRE
become less dense - - - - - - RAREFY
become less severe - - - - - RELENT
become less violent - - - MODERATE
become long and slender - - SPINDLE
become operative - - - INURE, ENURE
become a part of - - - - - - MERGE
become precipitous - - - - - STEEPEN
become ragged - - - - - - - TATTER
become sour - - - - - - - - - TURN
become tangled - - - - - - - SNARL
become of use - - - - - - - AVAIL
become vapid - - - - - STALE, PALL
become visible - - - - - - APPEAR
become void - - - - - - - - - LAPSE
becoming - - - - - - APPROPRIATE
becoming red - - - - - - RUBESCENT
bed - COUCH, MATRIX, STRATUM, BASE
bed canopy and drapery - - - - TESTER
bed coverlet - - - - - QUILT, SPREAD
bed linens - - - - - - - - SHEETS
bed of straw - - - - - - - PALLET
bedaub - - - - - - - - - - SMEAR
bedeck - - - - - - - - - - ADORN
bedew - - - - - - - - - MOISTEN
bedim - - - - - - - BECLOUD, MIST
bedlamite - - - - - - - - LUNATIC
Bedouin - - - - - - - - - NOMAD
bee's house - - - - - - - - APIARY
bee (kind) - - - - - DRONES, APIAN
bee (male) - - - - - - - - - DRONE
beef animal - - - - - - - - - STEER
beef on hoof - - - - - STEER, CATTLE
beehouse - - - - - - - APIARY, HIVE
beer - - - - - - - - - - LAGER, ALE
beer (colloq.) - - - - - - - - - MALT
beer ingredient - - - - - - - - MALT
beer mug - - - - - - - STEIN, SEIDEL
bees - - - - - - - - APIAN, DRONES
bee's pollen brush - - - - - - SCOPA
Beethoven's birthplace - - - - - BONN
beetle - - - - DOR, ELATER, SCARAB, OVERHANG
befall - - - - - - HAPPEN, HAP, TIDE
befit - - - - - - - - BECOME, SUIT
befitting - - - - - PROPER, SUITABLE
befog - - - - - - - - - - CONFUSE
befool - - - - - - - DELUDE, DECEIVE
before - PRE, ERE, ANTE, DI, ANTERIOR, PRIOR, PREVIOUSLY
before all others - - - - - - - FIRST
before (dial.) - - - - - - - - AFORE
before long - PRESENTLY, SOON, ANON
before (naut.) - - - - - - - - AFORE
before now - - - - - - - - - SINCE
before (prefix) - PRO, PRE, ANTE, PRO
before this - - - - - - - - ERE NOW
befriend - - - - - - - - - AID, HELP
befuddle - - - - - - - - - - - ADDLE
beg - - PLEAD, IMPLORE, BESEECH, ENTREAT, PETITION
beget - - - SIRE, FATHER, ENGENDER
beggar - - - - - ROGUE, MENDICANT
begin - - OPEN, START, COMMENCE, INITIATE, LEAD
begin again - - - - - - - - - RENEW
begin to grow - - - - - - - - - BUD
beginner - NOVICE, ENTRANT, NEOPHYTE, TYRO
beginning - ONSET, OPENING, FIRST, ORIGIN, INCEPTIVE, GENESIS, START, OUTSET, DAWN
beginning to develop - - - - NASCENT
begone - - AVAUNT, OUT, OFF, SCAT
begrime - - - - - - - - - - - SOIL
begrudge - - - - - - - - - - - ENVY
beguile - - - - - DELUDE, ENTERTAIN
behalf - - - - - - - - - - - - SAKE
behalf of (in) - - - - - - - - - FOR
behave - - - - ACT, DEMEAN, REACT
behave towards - - - - - - - - - USE
behaviour - - - MANNERS, TREATMENT, DEMEANOR
behead - - - - - - - - DECAPITATE
behest - - - - - - - - - COMMAND
behind - REAR, AFTER, ABAFT, ASTERN
behind (naut.) - - - - - - ABAFT, AFT
behind time - - - - - - - - - SLOW
behind a vessel - - - - ASTERN, AFT
behold - - - - - - - - - - LO, SEE
beige - - - - - - - - - - - - ECRU
being - - - - - ESSE, ENS, EXISTENCE
being in suspension - - - - - ABEYANT
belabor - - - - DRUB, FLOG, THRASH
belate - - - - - - - - - - - DELAY
belay - - - - - - - - - SURROUND
beldam - - - - - - - - - - - - HAG
beleaguer - - - - - - - - - BESIEGE
beleaguerment - - - - - - - - SIEGE

B

Belgian canal - - - - - - - - YSER
Belgian city - ANS, SCHENT, GHENT, ARLON, YPRES, SPA
Belgian coin - - - - - - - - BELGA
Belgian commune - - - - - - - - ANS
Belgian Congo river - - - - - - UELE
Belgian marble - - - - - - - RANCE
Belgian province - - - - - - - NAMUR
Belgian resort - - - - - - - - SPA
Belgian river - - - - - - YSER, LYS
Belgian seaport - - - - - - OSTEND
Belgian town - - - - - - SPA, YPRES
Belgian violinist - - - - - - - YSAYE
Belgrade ruler - - - - - - - - TITO
Belial - - - - - - - - - - SATAN
belie - - - - SLANDER, CALUMNIATE
belief - - ISM, FAITH, CREED, TENET, CREEDENCE, CREDENCE, CREDO, IDEA, TRUST, DOCTRINE
belief in ghosts - - - - - EIDOLISM
believe - - - CREDIT, OPINE, THINK, SUPPOSE
believer in God - - - - - - - DEIST
believing - - - - - - - - CREANT
belittled - - - - DERIDED, DECRIED, DISPARAGED
bell - - - - - - - - - - - GONG
bell call to prayer - - - - - ANGELUS
bell clapper - - - - - - - - TONGUE
bell sounds (obs.) - - - - - - TOLES
bell tower - - - - - - - - - BELFRY
bells (set of) - - - - - - CARILLON
bellicose - - - - - - - BELLIGERENT
belligerent - - - - - - - BELLICOSE
bellow - - - - - - - - ROAR, LOW
belong - - - - APPERTAIN, PERTAIN
belonging to - - - - - - - - - OF
belonging to neither - - - - - NEUTER
belong to order of flightless birds IMFENNATE
belonging to the people - - - - - LAY
belonging to the spring - - - - VERNAL
belongings - - - - - - TRAPS, GEAR
beloved - - - - - - - - - - DEAR
below - - - INFRA, UNDER, BENEATH
below (poet.) - - - - - - - - 'NEATH
belt - GIRDLE, SASH, BAND, ENCIRCLE, ZONIC, STRAP, ZONE, SURROUND
belt material - - - - - - - - BELTING
bemoan - - - LAMENT, BEWAIL, WAIL
bemuddle - - - - - - - - - CONFUSE
bemuse - - - - - - DAZE, CONFUSE
bend - STOOP, TREND, LEAN, CROOK, CURVE, FLEX, NOD, BOW, ARCH, SAG
bend downward - - - - - DROOP, SAG
bend forward - - - - - - - - STOOP
bend in reverence - - - - - - - - BOW
bend from a straight line - - REFRACT
bend in timber - - - - - - - - - SNY
bend upward (shipbldg.) - - - - - SNY
benediction - - - - - - - - BLESSING
bending point in painting - PENNUMBRA
bendlet (her.) - - - - - - - - BATON
beneath - - - - - - BELOW, UNDER
benediction - - - - - - - - BENISON
benefactor - - PATRON, DONOR, GIVER
benefice without cure of souls - - - SINOCURE
beneficent gift - - - - BLESSING, BOON
beneficial - - - - - SALUTARY, GOOD
beneficial fly - - - - - - - - TACHINA
benefit - - - AVAIL, PROFIT, INTEREST
benevolence - - - - - MERCY, CHARITY
benevolent - - - - - - - - - - KIND
benign - - - - - - - - - GRACIOUS
benison - - - - - - - - - BLESSING
Benjamin's son - - - - - - - - - EHI
bent - - - - - TREND, PRONENESS, INCLINATION, APTITUDE, TENDENCY
bequeathed - - DEMISED, LEFT, WILLED
bequeather - - - - - - - - TESTATOR
berate - - - - - SCOLD, RAIL, LASH
bereave - - - - - - - - - - DEPRIVE
bereft - - - - - - - LORN, FORLORN
Bermuda arrowroot - - - - - - ARARAO
berry (botanical) - - - - BOCCA, BACCA
berry (kind) - - - - - - PEPPERCORN
berth (kind) - - - - - UPPER, LOWER
beseech - PRAY, PLEAD, ENTREAT, BEG
beset - - - - HARASS, ASSAIL, SIEGE
beset annoyingly - - - - - - - PESTER
berry with small prickles (var.) - - - ACULEOUS
beside (prefix) - - - - - - PAR, PARA
besides - ALSO, YET, ELSE, MOREOVER, AND
besiege - - - - - BELEAGUER, STORM
besmatter - - - - - - - - - - - DAUB
besmirch - - - - - SOIL, SMEAR, MAR
besmudge - - - - - - - - - - TAINT
besom - - - - - - - - - - - BROOM
besot - - - - - - - - - - - STUPEFY
bespangle - - - - - - - - - - - STAR
bespatter - - - - - - SPLASH, MUDDY
bespeak in advance - - - - - RESERVE
best - - FINEST, OVERCOME, DEFEAT, CREAM
best achievement - - - - - - - RECORD
best of its kind - - - - - - - - ACE
best part - - - - - - - - - - CREAM
bestial - - - - - BRUTISH, DEPRAVED
bestow - GRANT, GIVE, CONFER, RENDER, AWARD, IMPART
bestow approval - - - - - - - - SMILE
bestow as due - - - - - - - - AWARD
bestow income upon - - - - - - ENDOW
bestow profusely - - - - - - - - RAIN
bestower - - - - - - - - - - DONOR
bestrew - - - - - - - - - - SCATTER
bestride - - - - - - - - - STRADDLE
bet - - - - - WAGER, STAKE, GAMBLE
bet in roulette - - - - - - - - - BAS
betake oneself - - - - - - GO, REPAIR
betel - - - - - - - - - - - - - SIRI
betel palm - - - - - - - - - - ARECA
betide - - - - - - HAPPEN, BEFALL
betimes - - - - - - - - - - - EARLY
betoken - FORESHOW, INDICATE, BODE, AUGUR
betray - - - - - - - - - - - - SELL
betray confidences - - - - - - - SPILL
betrayal of one's country - - TREASON
betrayer - - - - - - - - - - TRAITOR
betrothed - - - - - - - - - ENGAGED
betrothed person - - FIANCE, FIANCEE
better - - - - - - - - - - - AMEND
better fitted - - - - - - - - - ABLER
between - - - - - - AMID, BETWIXT
between (prefix) - - INTER, META, DIA
between sunrise and sunset - - DAYTIME
between two extremes - - - - - MESNE
betwixt - - - - - - - - - - BETWEEN
bevel - - - - - - - - SLOPE, SLANT
bevel out - - - - - - - - - - - REAM
beverage - - LAGER, PORTER, DRINK, COCOA, LEMONADE, TEA, ALE
beverage herb - - - - - - - - - TEA
beverage (kind) - - - - - - - - TOKAY
beverage made from molasses - - RUM
bevy - - - - GROUP, FLOCK, GALAXY
bewail - - - LAMENT, BEMOAN, WEEP

B

beware - - - - - - - - - AVOID
beweep - - - - - - - - - LAMENT
bewilder - - DAZE, STUN, FOG, DAZZLE
bewildered - - - - - - - - ASEA
bewitch - - - - - - ENCHANT, HEX
bewitch (local) - - - - - - - HEX
beyond - OVER, ACROSS, FARTHER, PAST
beyond control - - - - - - - OUT
beyond limit of supply - - - - OUT
beyond (prefix) - - - EG, PARA, SUR
beyond in time - - - - - - - PAST
bias - - PLY, INFLUENCE, DIAGONAL, SLANT
biased - - - - PARTIAL, ONESIDED
bib - - - - - - - - - - - NAPKIN
Biblical character - PELEG, BOAZ, NOAH, IR, HAMAN, COZ, ESAU, EZRA, IRI, ELIAS, ER, ENOS, ANUB, JOSIAH, ABEL, CAIN, ATER, ENAN, JONAH, AMOS, NERI, MERED, ADER, EKER, ERI, PILATE, LABAN, TOBIT
Biblical city - AVEN, TYRE, NAIN, IVAH, SIDON, NOB, SODON, SODOM, ONO
Biblical country - EDAM, EDOM, ELAM, OPHIR, SODOM, SEBA, MOAB
Biblical native - - ELAMITE, EDOMITE
Biblical expression - - - - - - SELAH
Biblical food - - - - - - - MANNA
Biblical giant - - - - - - - GOLIATH
Biblical hunter - - - - - - NIMROD
Biblical judge - - - - - - - ELON
Biblical king - ASA, EVI, AMON, AGAG, REBA, HEROD
Biblical kingdom - - - - - - SHEBA
Biblical land - - - - - - TOB, NOD
Biblical mountain - HOREB, ARARAT, OLIVET, PEOR
Biblical name - - CALEB, ERI, ATER, ADAH, LEAH, PELLEG, ARI, IRI
Biblical nation - - - - - - MOABITES
Biblical part (abbr.) - - - - OT, NT
Biblical passage - - - - - - - TEXT
Biblical patriarch - ABRAHAM, ISRAEL, NOAH
Biblical people - - - - - - MOABITE
Biblical plain - - - - - - - SHARON
Biblical pool - - - - - - - SILOAM
Biblical preposition - - - - - UNTO
Biblical priest - - - - - ELI, AARON
Biblical prophet - - - ELISHA, ELIAS
Biblical region - - - - - ENOM, ENON
Biblical region of darkness - - RAHAB
Biblical sign - - - - - - - - SELAH
Biblical site - - - - - - - - OPHIR
Biblical spice - - - - - - - STACTE
Biblical thief - - - - - - BARABBAS
Biblical tower - - - - - EDAR, BABEL
Biblical town - CANA, NAIN, BETHEL, ENDOR
Biblical tribe - - - - - - - AMON
Biblical vessel - - - - - - - - ARK
Biblical weed - - - - - - - - TARE
Biblical wise men - - - - - - MAGI
Biblical word - - - - - SELAH, MENE
Biblicist - - - - - - - - - BIBLIST
bicker - - - - - - - - - WRANGLE
bicycle for two - - - - - - TANDEM
bid - OFFER, SUMMON, ORDER, INVITE, OBEY, ENJOIN, COMMAND
bid in bridge - - - - - - - - SLAM
bid of seven (bridge) - - - - - SLAM
bide - - - TARRY, TOLERATE, AWAIT
big - - - - BULKY, LARGE, GREAT
bighorn - - - - - - - - - ARGALI
bigoted - - - INTOLERANT, NARROW
bilk - - - - - - - - - - - CHEAT
bill - - - - - - - - BEAK, POSTER
bill of fare - - - - - - CARTE, MENU
bill unpaid - - - - - - - - - DEBT
billiard cue - - - - - - - - - MACE
billiard player and writer - - HOPPE
billiard shot - - - - - CAROM, MASSE
billiard stick - - - - - - - - - CUE
billow - - - - - WAVE, SURGE, SEA
billowy - - - - - - - - - SURGING
bin - - - - - - - - - - - - CRIB
binary - - - - - - - - - - DOUBLE
binary compound of oxygen - OXIDE
bind - TAPE, TRUSS, TIE, RESTRAIN, FASTEN, OBLIGATE
bind mouth - - - - - - - - - GAG
bind up tightly - - - - - - SWATHE
biographical fragment - - ANECDOTE
biography - - - - - MEMOIR, LIFE
biological factor - - - - - ID, GENES
biological group - - - - - - SPECIES
biological unit - - - - - - - - - ID
bird - EGRET, DIVER, ARA, MARTIN, IRRISOR, VIREO, WREN, DAW, PEEWIT, EMU, TODY, SANDPIPER, LOON, EAGLE, WOODPECKER, JACKDAW
bird beak - - - - - - - - - - NEB
bird craw - - - - - - - - - - MAW
bird crest - - - - - - - - - - TUFT
bird crop - - - - - - - CRAW, MAW
bird dog - - - - - - - - - - SETTER
bird food - - - - - - - - - - SEED
bird of gull family - - - - - - TERN
bird house - - - - - AVIARY, NEST
bird (large) - - - - - EMU, PELICAN
bird life of a region - - - - - ORNIS
bird note - - - - - - CHIRP, TWEET
bird of paradise - - - - - MANUCODE
bird of peace - - - - - - - - DOVE
bird (pert. to) - - - - AVINE, AVIAN
bird of plumage - - - - - - - HERON
bird of prey - EAGLE, KITE, VULTURE, ERNE, OWL, ELANET, HAWK, ERN
bird of a region - - - - - - - ORNIS
bird (small) - TODY, SERIN, TIT, WREN, PEWEE, FINCH, TOMTIT, VIREO
bird that transported Sinbad - - - ROC
bird wing part - - - - - - - ALULA
bird wing part (pl.) - - - - - ALULAE
birdling - - - - - - - - - NESTLING
birds - - - - - AVES, AVIAN, AVINE
birds (pert. to) - - - - - - - - AVIAN
birds of a region - - - - - - - ORNIS
birth (pert. to) - - - - - - - - NATAL
birthright - - - - - - - - HERITAGE
biscuit - ROLL, BUN, RUSK, CRACKER
Bishop of Calcutta - - - - - - HEBER
Bishop's headdress - - - MITER, MITRE
Bishop's jurisdiction - - - - DIOCESE
Bishop's office - - - - - - - - - SEE
bison - - - - - - - - - - BUFFALO
bit - - - - - SCRAP, MORSEL, PIECE
bite - STING, CHOP, MORSEL, CORRODE, NIP, SNAP
bite of food - - - - - - - - MORSEL
bite impatiently - - - - - - - CHAMP
bite noisily - - - - - GNAW, CHAMP
biting - - SHARP, ACID, SARCASTIC
bits - - - - - - - - - - - - - ANA
bitter - VIRULENT, POIGNANT, GALL, ACERB, ACRID, PAINFUL
bitter cynic - - - - - - - - - TIMON
bitter flavoring agent - - - - ASARUM
bitter herb - - - - - - - RUE, ALOE
bitter nut - - - - - - - - - - COLA

bitter plant - - - - - - - - ALOE
bitter principle of ipecac root - EMETINE
bitter vetch - - - - - - - - - ERS
bitterness - - - - - - - - - MARA
bivalve - - - - - - OYSTER, CLAM
bivouac - - - - - - CAMP, ENCAMP
bizarre - - - - - - - - ODD, OUTRE
Bizet's opera - - - - - - - - CARMEN
black - EBON, MELANIC, INKY, SOOTY, SABLE, JET
black and blue - - - - - - - - LIVID
black bread ingredient - - - - - RYE
black covering - - - - - - - - PALL
black eye (slang) - - - - - - SHINER
black gum - - - - - - - - TUPELO
black kind of garnet - - - - MELANITE
black magic - - - - - - WITCHCRAFT
black mineral - - - - - - - - - JET
black mineral of vegetable origin - COAL
black nightshade - - - - - - - MOREL
black pipe of Otago - - - - - MIRO
black powdery substance - - - - SOOT
black rock - - - - - - - - - BASALT
Black Sea peninsula - - - - - CRIMEA
Black Sea port - - - - - - ODESSA
black substance - - - - - TAR, SOOT
black swan - - - - - - TRUMPETER
black and white mixture - GRAY, GREY
black wood - - - - - - - - - EBONY
blackbird - DAW, CROW, ANI, RAVEN, MERL, STARLING, JACKDAW
blacken - - SOOTY, INK, DENIGRATE
blackface singer - - - - - MINSTREL
blackfish - - - - - - - - - TAUTOG
blacksmith's art - - - - SMITHWORK
blacksmith's tool - - - - - - ANVIL
blacksnake (kind) - - - - - - RACER
blacktail fish - - - - - - - DASSY
blackthorn fruit - - - - - - - SLOE
blade of grass - - - - - - - SPEAR
blame - CENSURE, ACCUSE, REPROACH
blameless - - - - - - - - INNOCENT
blanch - - - - - - PALE, WHITEN
bland - MILD, BALMY, OPEN, GENTLE
blandish - - - - - - - - - FLATTER
blank - - - - - - - - - - - BARE
blanket worn as garment - - - - SERAPE
blankness - - - - - - - - NEGATION
blare - - - - - BLAZON, PROCLAIM
blare of trumpet - - - - - TANTARA
blarney - - - - - - - - - FLATTERY
blase - - - - - - - - BORED, SATED
blaspheme - - - - - - - - - SWEAR
blast - SERE, SEAR, BLIGHT, SHRIVEL
blast furnace - - - - - - SMELTER
blast of horn - - - - - - - - - TOOT
blatant - - - - - - - - - - NOISY
blather - - - - - - BLEAT, BABBLE
blaubok - - - - - - - - - - ETAAC
blaze - - - - - - - - FLAME, FLARE
blazing - - - - - - - - - - AFIRE
blazoned - - - - - - - - - BLARED
bleach - - - - - WHITEN, ETIOLATE
bleach in certain light - - - - - SUN
bleak - - - - DREARY, RAW, DISMAL
blear - - - - - - - - - DIM, BLUR
bleat - - - - - - - - - - - - BAA
blemish - STAIN, MAR, SPOT, SPECK, FAULT, SCAR, TAINT, BLOT
blend - - - - MIX, MINGLE, MERGE
bless - - ANELE. GLORIFY, HALLOW, PROTECT, BEATIFY, CONSECRATE
blessed - - - - - - - - - - - HOLY
blessing - - - - - BENISON, BOON
blest - - - - - - - - - - - HAPPY

blight - - - - - - - - NIP, BLAST
blighting - - - - - - - - BLASTING
blind - - SEEL, SIGHTLESS, SHUTTER
blind the eyes (falconry) - - - - - SEEL
blind fear - - - - - - - - - PANIC
blinder - - - - - - - - - - - SEELER
blinding light - - - - - - - - GLARE
bliss - - - - - - - - - - - - - JOY
blissful - - - - EDENIC, PARADISIAC
blissful state - - - - - - - RAPTUROUS
blister - - - - - - - - - - SCORCH
blithe - GAY, RIANT, CHEERFUL, JOYFUL
blithesome - - - - - - - - - - GAY
blithesomeness - - - - - - - - BLISS
block - DAM, BAR, PREVENT, CHUMP, STOPPAGE
block as base - - - - - - - PLINTH
block to prevent wheel from rolling - TRIG
block up - - - - - - - - OBSTRUCT
blockade - - - - - - - - - - SIEGE
blockhead - - - - - DOLT, OAF, LOUT
blockhead (arch.) - - - - - - - MOME
blood - - - - - - - - - - - - GORE
blood (comb. form) - - - - - - - HEM
blood feud - - - - - - - - VENDETTA
blood of the gods - - - - - - ICHOR
blood kindred - - - - - - - - GENS
blood sucking animal - - - - - LEECH
blood vessel - - - - - ARTERY, VEIN
blood vessel (pert. to) - - - ARTERIAL
blood vessel from heart - - - - ARTERY
bloodhound (her.) - - - - - - - LYME
bloodless - - - - - - - - - - - PALE
bloody - - - - - - - - - - - GORY
bloom - - FLOWER, BLOSSOM, GLOW
blooming - - - - - - - - - - ROSY
blossom - - BUD, FLOWER, BLOOM, FLOURISH
blot - SPOT, SULLY, BLEMISH, STAIN
blot out - - ERASE, DELETE, CANCEL
blotch - MESS, STAIN, MOTTLE, BLOB
blow - - RAP, STROKE, SLAP, THUMP, INFLATE
blow air forcibly through nose - SNORT
blow gently, as a flute - - - - TOOTLE
blow on head - - - - - - - - - - NOB
blow hole in whales - - - - SPIRACLE
blow a horn - - - - - - - - - HONK
blow up - - - - - - - - - - INFLATE
blow upon - - - - - - - - - - - FAN
blow whistle - - - - - - - - - TOOT
blowgun missile - - - - - - - DART
blue - - AZURE, PERSE, DEPRESSED
blue bird - - - - - - - - - - - JAY
blue dye - - - - - - - - - INDIGO
blue grass or bluegrass - - - - - POA
blue mineral - - - - - - - - IOLITE
blue star - - - - - - - - - - VEGA
bluish gray - - MERLE, PEARL, SLATE
bluish red - - - - - MALLOW, RAISIN
bluish white metallic element - ZINC
blunder - - - - ERR, ERROR, MISTAKE
blunder (slang) - - - - - - - BONER
blunt - - DULL, OUTSPOKEN, OBTUSE, DEADEN, HEBETATE
blunt end - - - - - - - - - - STUB
blunt end of ax - - - - - - - - POLL
blur - - - - - - - - - BLEAR, DULL
blush - - - - - - - - - - - REDDEN
blushing - - - - - - - - ROSY, RED
bluster - - - - - - - - - - ROISTER
boa - - - - - - - - - - ANACONDA
board - - - - - - - - - - - PLANK
board a ship - - - - - - - - EMBARK
board a ship (on) - - - - - - - ASEA

B

boarding house - - - - - - PENSION
boast - VAUNT, BRAG, PRAISE, EXTOL
boaster - - - - - - - - BRAGGART
boastful behaviour - - - - - BRAVADO
boastful talk (full of) - - - - - GASSY
boat - - BARGE, SCOW, TUG, PUNT, VESSEL, DORY, FREIGHTER, CANOE, CORACLE, SKIFF
boat marker - - - - - - - - BUOY
boat part - - - - - - - PROW, AFT
boat tiller - - - - - - - - HELM
boated - - - - - - - - - - SAILED
bob - - - - - SHAKE, PENDENT
bobbin - - - - - - - REEL, SPOOL
bode - INDICATE, PORTEND, AUGUR, PRESAGE
bodice - - - - - - - - - - WAIST
bodice posy - - - - - - - CORSAGE
bodies at rest (pert. to) - - - - STATIC
bodily appetite - - - - - - - LUST
bodily manipulation - - - - MASSAGE
bodily secretion - - - - - - - BILE
bodily structure - - - - - - ANATOMY
body - - - - - - - CONSISTENCY
body of advisers - - - - - CABINET
body of armed men - - - - - POSSE
body of assistants - - - - - - STAFF
body bones - - - - - - - - RIBS
body of cavalry - - - - - - - TROOP
body of church - - - - - - - NAVE
body (comb. form) - - - - - - SOMA
body of Jewish law - - TALMUD, TORA
body joint - - - - - - - - KNEE
body of laws - - - - - - - - CODE
body of learning - - - - - - - LORE
body organ - - LUNG, LIVER, GLAND
body (pert. to) - - - - - - - SOMAL
body of printed matter - - - - - TEXT
body of regents - - - - - - REGENCY
body of religious ceremonies - RITUAL
body at rest (pert. to) - - - - STATIC
body of rules - - - - - - - CODE
body servant - - - - - VALET, MAID
body of solar system - - - - PLANET
body of soldiers - PLATOON, CORPS, MILITIA, TROOPS, REGIMENT
body treated for burial - - - - MUMMY
body of tree - - - - - - - - BOLE
body of troops - - - - - - PHALANX
body of water - - - - - - - - POOL
body which attracts iron - - MAGNET
body as a whole (pert. to) - SYSTEMIC
bog - - FEN, MOOR, MIRE, MORASS, MUSKEG, MARSH, SWAMP, SYRT
bog orchid - - - - - - - - CALYPSO
bog substance - - - - - - - PEAT
bogged down - - - - - - STALLED
boggy - - - - - - - - - - MIRY
boggy ground (dial.) - - - - - - SOG
bogus - - - - - - - - - SPURIOUS
Bohemia city - - - - - - - - PILSEN
Bohemia dance - - - - - - - REDOWA
Bohemia religious reformer - - HUSS
Bohemia river - - - - - - - - ISER
boil - - - - STEW, SEETHE, SIMMER
boil on eyelid - - - - - - - - STY
boil slightly - - - - - - - - SIMMER
boisterous outcry - - - - - - ROAR
boisterous play - - - - - - - ROMP
bolar - - - - - - - - - - CLAYEY
bold - - - - - PERT, DARING, STEEP
bold fish - - - - - - - - - - EEL
Bolero composer - - - - - - RAVEL
Bolivian Indian - - URO, URU, ITEN
Bolivian product - - - - - - - TIN
Bolshevist leader - - - - - LENIN
bolster - - - - - - SUPPORT, PROP
bolt - - - RIVET, LOCK, DART, PIN, FASTEN, FASTENER, SIFT
bolt fastener - - - - - - - - - NUT
bomb (kind) - - PETARD, GRENADE, ATOM, SHELL
bombard - - - - - - BATTER, SHELL
bombard fiercely - - - - - - STRAFE
bombast - - - - - - - - RANT, RAVE
bombastic - - - - - - - - INFLATED
bombastic talk - - - - - - - - RANT
Bombay vessel - - - - - - PATAMAR
bomber - - - - - - - - LIBERATOR
bombproof chamber - - - - CASEMATE
bombycid moths - - - - IOS, EGGERS
bond - - TIE, SECURITY, COVENANT, LIGAMENT
bondage - - - - - SERFAGE, SLAVERY
bondman - SLAVE, THRALL, VASSAL, SERF
bone - - - - - - - - OS, RIB, ILIA
bone of ankle - - - - - TALI, TALUS
bone of arm - - - - - - - - - ULNA
bone cavity - - - - - - - ANTRUM
bone (comb. form) - - - - - OSTEO
bone of forearm - - - - ULNA, ULNAR
bone of hard palate - - - - PALATINE
bone of hind limb (pert. to) - FIBULAR
bone of leg - TIBIA, PERONE, FIBULA
bone (prefix) - - - - - - - - - OSTE
bone of thigh - - - - - TIBIA, FEMUR
bones - - - - - - - - - - - OSSA
bonnet - - - - - - - - - - POKE
bony - - - - - - - - OSTEAL, THIN
bony fish - - - - - - - - - TELEOST
bony scale - - - - - - - - - SCUTE
bony shelled reptile - - - - - TURTLE
boo - - - - - - - - - - HISS, JEER
book - - - - - - - - - - - - MO
book of accounts - - - - - LEDGER
book of Apocrypha - - - - - - TOBIT
book of Bible - JONAH, KINGS, AMOS, GENESIS, LEV, TITUS, ROMANS, MICAH, LUKE, PSALMS, HOSEA, EZRA, EXODUS, ACTS, MARK
book of devotions - - - - - - MISSAL
book of few sheets of printed matter PAMPHLET
book of fiction - - - - - - - NOVEL
book of gospel - - - - - - - - MARK
book of Jewish law - - - - - TALMUD
book (large) - - - - - - - - TOME
book of Old Testament - HOSEA, ISAIAH, DANIEL, AMOS, EZRA
book of palm - - - - - - - - TARA
book part - - - - - - - - - LEAF
book of psalms - - - - - - PSALTER
book of runrics - - - - - - - ORDO
book section - - - - - - - - - PAGE
bookbinder's establishment - BINDERY
bookbinding tool - - - - - - - KEY
boom - - - - - - - - - - - ROAR
boon - - - - - - - - - BLESSING
boor - - - - - CHURL, KERN, RUSTIC
boost - - - - - - - - HOIST, RAISE
Boot (the) - - - - - - - - - ITALY
booth - - - - - STALL, LOGE, STAND
boots - - - - KICKS, AVAILS, SHOES
booty - PREY, SWAG, SPOILS, SPOIL, LOOT
border - ABUT, SKIRT, FRINGE, HEM, MARGIN, SIDE, EDGE, BRINK, VERGE
border for a picture - - - - - - MAT

bordering the ocean - - - - SEABOARD
bore - - - - - PALL, DRILL, WEARY
bore into - - - - - - - - - - EAT
boreal - - - - - - - - - NORTHERN
bored - - - - - - - - BLASE, TIRED
boredom - - - - - - - - - ENNUI
boring - - - - - - DULL, TIRESOME
boring tool - AWL, BIT, AUGER, WIMBLE, GIMLET, DRILL
boorish - - - - - - - - - - RUDE
born - - - - - - - - NATURAL, NEE
born again - - - - - - RENASCENT
borne - - - - - - RIDDEN, CARRIED
borne (be) - - - - - - - - - RIDE
Borneo pepper plant - - - - - ARA
boron (of) - - - - - - - - - BORIC
boron with another element - - BORIDE
bosk - - - - - - - - - - THICKET
boss - - - - - - - - - - FOREMAN
Boston suburb - - - - - BRAINTREE
botanical sac - - - - - - - THECA
botch - - - - - - - - - - - MESS
both (comb. form) - - - - - - AMBI
bother - - MOLEST, PESTER, HARASS, TROUBLE, ADO, BORE, FUSS, AIL, PERPLEX
bothered - - - - - - - - - DITHERY
bottle - - - - - - - - - DECANTER
bottle for liquids - - - - - CARBOY
bottle (small) - - - - - - - - VIAL
bottle stopper - - - - - - - - CORK
bottle top - - - - - - - - - - CAP
bottom - - - - - - - - - - - ROOT
bottom of ship - - - - - - - - KEEL
bottomless - - - - - - - - ABYSMAL
bottomless gulf - - - - - - - ABYSS
bough - - - - - - - LIMB, BRANCH
bough of tree - - - - - - - RAMAGE
bound - DART, OBLIGATED, TIED, BASE, LEAP, LIMIT, AMBIT
bound back - - - - - - - - RECOIL
bound (colloq.) - - - - - - - LOLLY
bound by a vow - - - - - - VOTARY
boundary - TERMINUS, LIMIT, METE, LINE, SIDE, MARGIN
boundary line - - METE, PERIPHERY
boundary of plane figure - PERIMETER
boundary (outer) - - - - - PERIMETER
bounder - - - - - - - - - - - CAD
bounding main - - - - - - - - SEA
bounding portion - FRINGE, MARGIN, SIDE
boundless - - - - - - - - INFINITE
boundary of torrid zone - - - - TROPIC
bounds - - - - - - - - - - AMBIT
bountiful - - - - GENEROUS, PROFUSE
bounty (Fr.) - - - - - - - LARGESSE
bouquet - CORSAGE, AROMA, BUNCH, SPRAY, POSY
bout - - - - - - - SET-TO, CONTEST
bovine animal - COW, OX, CATTLE (pl.)
bovine animal (male) - - STEER, BULL
bovine quadrupeds - - - - - - OXEN
bow - - - - NOD, ARC, BEND, PROW, SUBMIT, STOOP, YIELD, CURVE, ARCH
bow like curve - - - - - - - - ARCH
bow of vessel - - - - - - - - PROW
bow of wood - - - - - - - - - YEW
bower - - - - - - - - - - ARBOR
bowfin - - - - - - - - - - - AMIA
bowl out at cricket - - - - - - YORK
bowler - - - - - - - - - - DERBY
bowling alley game - - - - - TENPINS
bowling green part - - - - - - RINK
bowling target - - - - - - - - PIN
bowman - - - - - - - - - - ARCHER
box - - CRATE, SPAR, CASE, CHEST, STOW, LOGE
box for - - - - - - - - - - - DRAB
box for live fish - - - - - - - - CAR
box for packing - - - - - - - - KIT
box of slats - - - - - - - - CRATE
boxing match - - - - - - - - BOUT
boxing (old) - - - - - - - - SAVATE
boxing ring - - - - - - - - - ARENA
boxing term - - - - - - - - - K.O.
boy - - - - - - - - - - LAD, SON
boy attendant - - - - - - - - PAGE
boy (small) - - - - - - - - - TAD
Boy Scout gathering - - - - JAMBOREE
boyhood - - - - - - - - - - YOUTH
brace - PAIR, PROP, SUPPORT, STRUT
braced as a chrysalis - - - - - GIRT
braced framework - - - - - TRESTLE
bracelet for the arm - - - - - ARMLET
bracer - - - - - - - - - - - TONIC
braces - - - - - - - - SUSPENDERS
bracing - - - - - - - - - - - TONIC
bracing medicine - - - - - - - TONIC
brace as a roof - - - - - - TRUSSING
brad - - - - - - - - - - - - NAIL
brag - - - - - CITE, CROW, BOAST
braggart - - - - - - - - - BOASTER
braid - - PLAIT, LACET, CUE, TRESS, INTERLACE, PLAT
brain - - - - - - - INTELLECT, MIND
brain disease - - - - - - - PARESIS
brain (of the) - - - - - - - CEREBRAL
brain passage - - - - - - - - - ITER
brainy - - - - - - - - WISE, SMART
brake - - - - - - - - - - THICKET
brake part - - - - - - - - - - SHOE
brambly - - - - - THORNY, PRICKLY
branch - - - - - BOUGH, LIMB, ARM
branch (having) - - - - - - - RAMOSE
branch of learning - - - - ARTS, ART
branch of mathematics - - CALCULUS
branch of medical science - ETIOLOGY
branch off - - - - - DIVERGE, FORK
branch (pert. to) - - - - - - - RAMAL
branch of postal delivery (abbr.) - RFD
branch railway track - - - - - SIDING
branch (short sharp) - - - - - - SNAG
branch of Tai race - - - - - - - LAO
branch (small) - - - - - SPRIG, TWIG
branch of tine - - - - - - - - - SNAG
branched - - - - - - - - - RAMOSE
branches - - - - - - - - - - - RAMI
branchia - - - - - - - - - - - - GILL
branching ornament - - - - - SPRAY
brand - - - - - - - - STAMP, MARK
brandish - - - - - SWING, FLOURISH
brandy (kind) - - - - - - - COGNAC
brash - - BOLD, BRITTLE, IMPUDENT, SAUCY
brass horn - - - - - - - - - - TUBA
brave - - DARE, INTREPID, VALIANT, SPARTAN, DEFY, STOUT, DARING, HEROIC, GALLANT
brave and enduring person - SPARTAN
brave man - - - - - - - - - HERO
brave woman - - - - - - - HEROINE
bravery - - - - - - - - - - VALOR
brawl - - RIOT, MELEE, ROW, FRACAS
bray - - - - - - - - - - HEEHAW
braying instrument - - - - - PESTLE
Brazil bird - - AGAMI, ARA, SERIEMA
Brazil city - - - - - - - - PARA, RIO
Brazil coin - - - - - - - - - - - REI
Brazil drink - - - - - - - - ASSAI

B

Brazil estuary - - - - - - - PARA
Brazil medicinal plant - - - AYAPANA
Brazil money - - - - - - - - REI
Brazil palm - - - - - - - JUPATI
Brazil parrot - - - - - - - - ARA
Brazil red - - - - - - - - ROSET
Brazil river - - - - - - - ICA, APA
Brazil rubber tree - - - - - - PARA
Brazil seaport - PARA, NATAL, SANTOS
Brazil state - - - - - BAHIA, PARA
Brazil tapir - - - - - ANTA, ANTAE
Brazil tree - - - - - - - ARAROBA
Brazil wood - - - - - - KINGWOOD
breach - - - - - GAP, RENT, STRAND
breach of faith - - - - - - TREASON
bread basket - - - - - - PANNIER
bread boiled in water - - - PANADA
bread maker - - - - - - - BAKER
bread and milk - - - - - - PANADA
bread part - - - - - - - - CRUST
break - - SNAP, FRACTURE, DESTROY, RENT, RIFT, SEVER, REND
break away - - - - - - - ESCAPE
break in continuity - - - - - - GAP
break a hole in - - - - - - STAVE
break in a mesa - - - - - - ABRA
break off - - - - - - - - - - END
break one's word - - - - - RENEGE
break into pieces - SHATTER, CRUMBLE
break into small pieces - - - FRITTER
break suddenly - - - - - - - POP
break in two - - - - - - - - SNAP
break up - - - - - - - DISBAND
break in upon - - - - - INTERRUPT
break violently - - - - - - BURST
break without warning - - - - SNAP
breakage - - - - - - - - BRITTLE
breaking forth - - - - - - ERUPTIVE
breaking waves - - - - - - - SURF
breakwater - - - - PIER, MOLE, COB
bream - - - - - - - - - SUNFISH
breastbone (pert. to) - - - - STERNAL
breastplate - - - - - - - - ARMOR
breastwork - - - - - - - PARAPET
breath - - - - - - - - - - WIND
breathe - - - - - - - - - RESPIRE
breathe convulsively - - - - - GASP
breathe in - - - - - - - - INHALE
breathe noisily - - - - - - SNORT
breathe quickly - - - - - - - PANT
breathe through nose - - - - SNIFF
breathing - - - - - - - - - RALE
breathing orifice - - - - - SPIRACLE
breathing space - - - - - - RESPITE
breech loading rifle - - - CHASSEPOT
breed - - PROGENY, ILK, ORIGINATE, PROPAGATE
breed of cattle - - - - - - DEVON
breed of chickens - SHANGHAI, BANTAM
breed of dog (abbr.) - - - - - - POM
breed of draft horse - - - - SHIRE
breed of pigeons - - - - - - - NUN
breed of Scottish terriers - - - SKYE
breeding ground of seals - - ROOKERY
breeze - - - - - AURA, AIR, ZEPHYR
breezy - - - - - - - AIRY, WINDY
Breton - - - - - - - - - - CELT
brew - - - - - - - ALE, GATHER
brewer's mash tub - - - - - - KEEVE
brewing agent - - - - - - - MALT
bribe - - - - - - - SOP, GREASE
bric-a-brac (object) - - - - - CURIO
bric-a-brac stand - ETAGERE, WHATNOT
brick - - - - - - - - - - - TILE
brick carrier - - - - - - - - HOD
brickbat - - - - - - - - MISSILE
bridge - - - - - - - - - - SPAN
bridge arch - - - - - - - - SPAN
bridge builder - - - - - - PONTIST
bridge (kind) - - - - - CANTILEVER
bridge over gorge - - - - - VIADUCT
bridge part - - - - - - - - SPAN
bridge term - - - - - - - TENACE
bridle - - - - - RESTRAIN, REPRESS
bridle bit without curb - - - SNAFFLE
bridle part - - - - - - - - - BIT
bridle strap - - - - - - - - REIN
brief - - - - SHORT, CURT, CURTAL, TRANSITORY, TERSE
brief expression - - - - - LACONISM
brief extract - - - - - - - SCRAP
brief notice - - - - - - - MENTION
brief period - - - - - - - - SPURT
brief quotation - - - - - - SNIPPET
brief remark - - - - - - - - WORD
brier - - - - - - - - THORN, PIPE
brigand - - - - - - - - - PIRATE
brigantine-like vessel - - - - SCOW
bright - - GARISH, SMART, SUNNY, ROSY, NITID, RIANT, LOUD
bright burning gas - - - ACETYLENE
bright coloured birds - - TANAGERS, ORIOLES
bright flickering light - - - - FLARE
bright saying - - - - - - - - MOT
bright star - - - - - - - - NOVA
brighten - - - - - - - - - LIGHT
brightened - - - - - - - - - - LIT
brightest star - - COR, SUN, LUCIDA
brightly - - - - - - - - - BRISK
brightness - - - SUNNINESS, SHEEN, SUNSHINE
brilliancy of achievement - - - ECLAT
brilliant - - REFULGENT, ILLUSTRIOUS
brilliant stroke - - - - - - - COUP
brilliantly coloured bird - - TANAGER, ORIOLE
brilliantly coloured fish - - - OPAH, CATALINA
brim - - - - - LIP, EDGE, MARGIN
brimless cap - - - - - - TAM, FEZ
brimming - - - - - - - - WATERY
brindle - - - - - - - - - STREAK
bring - - - - - - - - - - FETCH
bring about - - - - - - OCCASION
bring back - - - - - - - RESTORE
bring bad luck (colloq.) - HOODOO, HEX
bring to bear - - - - - - - EXERT
bring charge against - ACCUSE, DELATE
bring to completion - - - - - - - DO
bring down - - - - - - - - LOWER
bring down on oneself - - - - INCUR
bring forth - - - - - - - - - EAN
bring forth (Scot.) - - - - - - EAN
bring forward - - - - - - ADDUCE
bring from foreign source - - IMPORT
bring into being - - - - - - CREATE
bring into conflict - - - - - ENGAGE
bring into court - - - - - ARRAIGN
bring into equilibrium - - - - POISE
bring into exact position - - - TRUE
bring into existence - - - - CREATE
bring into harmony - - - - - ATTUNE
bring into row - - - - ALINE, ALIGN
bring into subjection - - - - - TAME
bring on - - - - - - INDUCE, INCUR
bring to a level - - - - PLANE, GRADE
bring to life again - - - - - REVIVE
bring to light - - - UNEARTH, ELICIT
bring to memory - - REMIND, RECALL
bring to mind - - RECALL, REMEMBER

bring reproach on - - - DISPARAGE
bring to standstill - - - - STALL
bring together - - - - - - COMPILE
bring up - - - - - - - - REAR
bring up by hand - - - - - - CADE
bringer of misfortune - - JONAH, JINX
brink - EDGE, VERGE, BORDER, RIM, BANK
briny - - - - - - - - - - SALTY
briny deep (on) - - - - - - - ASEA
brisk - LIVELY, LIVE, SPRY, SNAPPY, FRESH, ACTIVE, BRIGHTLY
briskly - - LIVELY, SNAPPY, ACTIVELY
briskness - - - - - - - ALACRITY
bristle - SETA, TELA, AWN, (pl.) SETOE
bristle characteristic of grasses - AWN
bristle (comb. form) - - - - SETI
bristle-like appendage - - - ARISTA
bristling - - - - - - - HORRENT
bristly - - - - - - - SETOSE, SETA
British Arabian protectorate - - ADEN
British Arctic navigator - - - - ROSS
British bar - - - - - - - - - PUB
British coins - - - - - - - PENCE
British colony - - - - - - - SHIRE
British colony in Arabia - - - ADEN
British gasoline - - - - - - PETROL
British general - - BYNG, SHRAPNEL
British Indian coin - - - - - ANNA
British Indian district - BANDA, BENGAL
British Indian monetary unit - ANNA, RUPEE
British Indian political leader - GANDHI
British Indian province - SIND, ASSAM
British Indian river - - - - SURMA
British island group - - - BERMUDA
British island near Malay - SINGAPORE
British island stronghold - - - MALTA
British Isle inhabitant - - - - SCOT
British legislature - - - PARLIAMENT
British mining truck - - - - CORF
British oak - - - - - - - - ROBUR
British Parliament members - COMMONS
British principality - - - - WALES
British royal stables - - - - MEWS
British statesmen - EDEN, SIMON, PITT, CLIVE, AMERY
British streetcar - - - - - - TRAM
British territorial division - - SHIRE
British territory in Africa - - NIGERIA
British title - - - - - - LADY, DAME
British weight - - - - - - - STON
British yachtsman - - - - - LIPTON
brittle - - CRISP, BRASH, FRAGILE
brittle limestone (prov. Eng.) - GANIL
broad - - WIDE, SPACIOUS, LIBERAL
broad flat piece in chair back - SPLAT
broad stripe - - - - - - - - BAR
broad thick piece - - - - - - SLAB
broad thin piece - - - - - - SHEET
broad topped hill - - - - - - LOMA
broadcast - - - - - - - - SOW
broaden - - - - - - - - - SPREAD
broiler - - - - - - - - GRILLER
broken down - - - - - - DECREPIT
broken stone - - - - - - - RUBBLE
broker in land - - - - - - REALTOR
brokerage - - - - - - - - AGIO
bronco - - - - - - - - MUSTANG
bronze - - - - - - - - - - TAN
bronze coin - - - - - - - - AES
brood - INCUBATE, SIT, SET, TEAM, PONDER
brood of pheasants - NYES, NIDE, NYE, NID
brood of young fishes - - - - FRY
brook - - - - - - - RUN, STOMACH
brook (small) - RILL, RILLET, RIVULET
broom - - - - - - BESOM, BARSOM
broth - - - - - - - - - - SOUP
broth (thin) - - - - - - - GRUEL
brother - - - - - - - - - - - FRA
brother of the Lord - - - - - JAMES
brotherly - - - - - - - FRATERNAL
brought up by hand - - - - - - CADE
brow of hill (Scot.) - - - - - BRAE
brown - - - - - - - - - - TOAST
brown apple - - - - - - - - RUSSET
brown colour - SEPIA, PABLO, UMBER, TENNE
brown mineral - - - - - - LEDERITE
brown over a fire - - - - - - TOAST
brown (pale) - - - - - - - ECRU
brown seaweed - - - - - - - KELP
"Brownies" creator - - - - - - COX
brownish black - - - - - - - SOOTY
brownish colour - - - - - - - - DUN
brownish purple - - - - - - - PUCE
brownish red dye - - - - - - EOSIN
browse - - - - - - - - - GRAZE
bruin - - - - - - - - - - BEAR
bruise - POMMEL, BATTER, CONTUSE, CONTUSION
bruising implement - - - - - PESTLE
Brunhild's daughter - - - - ASLANGA
brush - - - - - - SWEEP, SKIRMISH
brushwood - - - - - - - - - BRAKE
brushwood (short) - - - - - - COPSE
brusk - - - - - - - - - - - CURT
brute - - - - - - - - - - ANIMAL
brutish - COARSE, BESTIAL, STOLID, GROSS
bryophytic plant - - - - - - MOSS
bubble - - - - - - - - BLEB, BEAD
bubble up - - - - - - - - - BOIL
buccaneer - - - - - - - - - PIRATE
bucket - - - - - - - - - - PAIL
bucket (kind) - - - - - - - - OAKEN
bucket used in mining - - - - - TUB
bucketlike vessel - - - - - - - TUB
buckwheat tree - - - - TITI, TEETEE
bucolic - - - - - - - RUSTIC, RURAL
bud - - SPROUT, SCION, BURGEON, BLOSSOM, CION
Buddhist church in Japan - - - TERA
Buddhist column - - - - - - - LAT
Buddhist dialect - - - - - - - PALI
Buddhist monk - - - - - - - - BO
Buddhist mound - - - - - - STUPA
Buddhist pillar - - - - - - - LAT
Buddhist priest - - - - - LAMA, BO
Buddhist scripture language - - PALI
Buddhist temple approach - - TORAN
buddy - - - - - - - - CRONY, PAL
budge - - - - - - - - - - - MOVE
buffalo - - - - - - - - - - BISON
buffet - - - - - - - - - - TOSS
buffeted - - - - - - - - - SMOTE
buffoon - - MIME, CLOWN, MIMER, DROLL
buffoon (obs.) - - - - - - - - DOR
buffoonery - - - - - - - DROLLERY
bug - - - - - - - - ROACH, INSECT
bugaboo - - - - - - - - SCARECROW
bugle call - - - - - - - - - TAPS
build - ERECT, CREATE, CONSTRUCT
build a nest - - - - - - - - NIDIFY
building - - - - - - ERECTION, EDIFICE
building lot - - - - - - - - - SITE
building to make goods - - FACTORY
building material - MORTAR, CONCRETE, LATERITE

B

C

building part - - - - WING, APSE
building site - - - - - - - - LOT
building to store grain - - ELEVATOR
building used by militia - - ARMORY
built out window - - - - - - ORIEL
bulb shaped stem - - - - - - CORM
bulblike stem (botanical) - - - CORM
bulbous plant - - - - - TUBEROSE
Bulgarian coin - - - - - - - LEV
Bulgarian money unit - - - - LEV
bulging pot - - - - - - - - - OLLA
bulk - - - - - - - - MASS, SIZE
bulkiness - - - - - - - - - MASS
bulky - - - - - - - - BIG, LARGE
bull - - - - - - - TORO, TAURUS
bull fighter - - TOREADOR, MATADOR, TORERO, PICADOR
bull of Hercules - - - - - - CRETAN
bullet - - - - - - - - SHOT, SLUG
bullfighter on foot - - - - - TORERO
bullfinch - - - - - - - - - - OLP
bully - - - - - - - - - - HECTOR
bully tree - - - - - - - - - BALATA
bulrush - - - - - - - - - - - TULE
bulwark - RAMPART, DEFENSE, FENCE
bump - - - - - - - - - - - JOLT
bumper of liquor - - - - - CAROUSE
bumpkin - YAHOO, YOKEL, LOUT, YAP, CLOWN
bumpskins - - - - - - - - - DOLTS
but - - - - YET, SAVE, MERELY, MERE
butcher bird - - - - - - - - SHRIKE
butt - - - - - - - - RAM, TARGET
butt of the joke - - - - - - - - IT
butter substitute - - - - - - OLEO
butterfly - - - - - - - - - - - IO
butterfly (kind) - - DIANA, SKIPPER, URSULA
butting animal - - - - - - - - RAM
button - - - - - - - - - - - STUD
buttress - - - - - - - - - - PROP
buy - - - - - - - - - - PURCHASE
buy back - - - - - - - - - REDEEM
buzz - - - - - - - - DRONE, HUM
by - PER, AT, PAST, ALONGSIDE, NEAR, VIA
by accident - - - - - - - - - HAPLY
by a line - - - - - - - - LINEALLY
by means of - - - - - - - - - PER
by much - - - - - - - - - - - FAR
by oneself (comb. form) - - - - AUT
by passes - - - - - - - - TUNNELS
by way of - - - - - - - - VIA, PER
bye - - - - - - - - - - SECONDARY
bypath - - - - - - - - - - - LANE

C

caama - - - - - - - - - - - ASSE
cab - - - - - HACK, HANSOM, TAXI
cabal - - - - - - - - - - - - PLOT
cabala - - - - - - - - - - MYSTERY
cabbage - - - - - - - - - - - KALE
cabbage like plant - - - - - - COLE
cabbage like plant (var.) - CALE, KALE
cabin - - - - - - - - - HUT, LODGE
cabinet wood - - - - - - ROSEWOOD
cache - - - - - - - - - - - - HIDE
cachet - - - - - - - - - - - SEAL
cactaceous plant - - - - - MESCAL
cactus (small) - - - - - - MESCAL
cad - - - - - - - - - - - BOUNDER
cad (slang) - - - - - - - - - HEEL
Cadamus's daughter - - SEMELE, INO
caddis worm - - - - - - - CADEW
Caddoan Indian - - - - - - - - REE
cadent - - - - - - - - - - FALLING
cadillo - - - - - - - - - - BURDOCK
cadis worm - - - - - - - - - CADEW
cadmium - - - - - - - - - - - C.D.
Cadmus's daughter - - TEMPLE, INO, SEMELE
cadre - - - - - - - - - FRAMEWORK
cafe - - - - - - - - - - - SALOON
cage - - - - - CONFINE, IMPRISON
cage of elevator - - - - - - - CAR
cage for hawks - - - - - - - - MEW
Cain's victim - - - - - - - - ABEL
cajole - - FLATTER, WHEEDLE, COAX
cake - - - - - - - - - SCONE, BAR
cake of bread - - - - - - - - LOAF
cake (kind) - - - - - - - - - LAYER
cake in pipe bowl - - - - - DOTTLE
cake (small) - - - - - - - - - BUN
calabash - - - - - - - - - - GOURD
calamitous - - DIRE, EVIL, TRAGIC, FATAL
calamity - - - - - - - - DISASTER
calcium gypsum - - - - - - PLASTER
calcium oxide - - - - - - - - LIME
calcium sulphate - - - - - PLASTER
calculate - RATE, ESTIMATE, FIGURE, RECKON
calculate means of - - - - AVERAGE
calculating instrument - - - - ABACUS
Caledonian - - - - - - - - - SCOT
calendar - - - - - - - - ALMANAC
calender - - - - - - - - - - ROLL
calf flesh - - - - - - - - - - VEAL
calf of leg (pert. to) - - - - - SURAL
caliber - - - - - - - - - - - BORE
California bulrush - - - - - - TULE
California city - - MORAGA, ALAMEDA, LODI
California holly - - - - - - TOYON
California lake - - - - - - - TAHOE
California laurel - - - - - - MYRTLE
California mountains - - - - SIERRAS
California mountain peak - - SHASTA
California river - - - - - - TRINITY
California rockfish - - RENA, REINA
California town - - - - - - - - ASTI
California tree - - - - - EUCALYPTUS
California volcano - - - - - SHASTA
calk on football shoes - - - - CLEAT
call - - DUB, TERM, NAME, PAGE, ENTITLE, STYLE, SUMMON, DENOMINATE, VISIT
call for aid - - - - - - - - APPEAL
call at an auction - - - - - - - BID
call boy - - - - - - - - - - PAGE
call to excite attention - - - HOA, HO
call forth - - - - - - EVOKE, ELICIT
call loudly - - - - - - - - CRY, HAIL
call for a repetition - - - - ENCORE
call together - - - - - - - CONVOKE
call upon - - - - - - - - - - VISIT
caller - - - - - - - VISITOR, GUEST
calico pony - - - - - - - - - PINTO
calling - - - - - - - - - - METIER
callous - - - - - - - - - - - HARD
calloused - - - - - - - - - HORNY
callow - - - - - - - - - UNFLEDGED
calm - SERENE, MILD, ALLAY, SOOTHE, COMPOSED, COOL, PEACE
calmness (state of) - - - - STARAXY
calorie - - - - - - - - - - THERM
calumniate - - ASPERSE, SLUR, BELIE, SLANDER
calumniator - - - - - - - TRADUCER
calumny - - - - - ASPERSION, LIBEL

calypter - - - - - - - - - ALULA
calyx leaf - - - - - - SEPAL, PETAL
Cambridge University college servant GYP
came to rest - - - - - LIT, ALIT, SAT
camel - - - - - - - - DROMEDARY
camel driver - - - - - - - SARWAN
camel hair cloth - - - - - - - ABA
cameloid ruminant - - - - - - LLAMA
camelopard - - - - - - - GIRAFFE
cameo cutting tool - - - - - - SPADE
camera stand - - - - - - - TRIPOD
Cameroon native - - GARA, SARA, ABO
"Camille" author - - - - - - DUMAS
camp follower - - - - - - - SUTLER
camp out - - - - - - - - - TENT
can - - - - - ABLE, TIN, PRESERVE
Canaanite chief - - - - - - SISERA
Canadian capital - - - - - - OTTAWA
Canadian city - SASKAT, LEVIS, BANFF
Canadian court decree - - - - - ARRET
Canadian emblem - - - - - - MAPLE
Canadian lake - - - - - - REINDEER
Canadian national park - - - - - YOHO
Canadian peninsula - - - - - - GASPE
Canadian physician - - - - - - OSLER
Canadian province - - N.S., ONTARIO, MANITOBA, ALTA
Canadian resort - - - - - - - BANFF
Canadian river - - - - - - - YUKON
canal - - - - - PASSAGE, DUCT, SUEZ
canal zone lake and town - - - - GATUN
canard - - - - - - - - - - - HOAX
cancel - - - DELETE, DELE, REVOKE, RESCIND, REMIT, ERASE, ANNUL
candid - - - - - - - - - - FRANK
candidate - - - ASPIRANT, NOMINEE
candidate list - - - - - - - - SLATE
candle - - - TAPER, LUMINARY, DIP
candle material - - - - - - - - WAX
candlelight (poet.) - - - - - - EVE
candlenut tree - - - - - - - - AMA
candor - - - - - - - - FRANKNESS
candy - - - - - - SWEETS, CARAMEL
candy base - - - - - - - - FONDANT
cane - - - - - - FLOG, RATTAN, FLAY
canine - - - - - - - - - DOG, FOX
canine disease - - - - RABIES, MANGE
canine (kind) - - - - - - - - PUG
cannon - - - - - - - - - - - GUN
cannon (kind) - - - - - - - MORTAR
canny - - - - - - - - - CAUTIOUS
canoe - - - - - - - - - - - PROA
canoe propeller - - - - - - PADDLE
canon - - - - - - - - - - - LAW
canonic - - - - - - - - - REGULAR
canonical hour and offices - - - NONES
canonical law of Islam - - - - - SHERI
canonize - - - - - - - - - - SAINT
canonized person - - - - - - - SAINT
canopy - - - - FINIAL, TESTER, DAIS
canopy over altar - - - - BALDACHIN
cant - SLANT, TIP, TILT, SLOPE, HEEL, ARGOT
cantaloupe - - - - - - - MUSKMELON
canter - - - - - - - - - - - LOPE
canticle - - - - - - - - - - SONG
canvas covering - - - - - - CANOPY
canvas lodge - - - - - - - - - TENT
canvas propeller - - - - - - - - SAIL
canvas vessel - - - - - - - CANOE
canvaslike fabric - - - - - - - WIGAN
canvass for political support - - - - ELECTIONEER
canyon - - - - - - VALLEY, RAVINE
Caoutchouc tree - - - - - - - - ULE

C

cap - BERET, FEZ, TAM, CROWN, COVER, EXCEL, TOP, COIF, COMPLETE
capable - ABLE, COMPETENT, EFFICIENT
capable of being disjoined - SEPARABLE
capable of being divided - - DIVISIBLE
capable of being extended - - TENSILE
capable of being hammered or rolled thin MALLEABLE
capable of being held - - - - TENABLE
capable of being maintained - TENABLE
capable of being protected against loss INSURABLE
capable of being taken out - REMOVABLE
capable of endurance - - - - - WIRY
capable of extension - - - - - TENSILE
capable of perception - - - - SENTIENT
capacious - - - - - - - AMPLE, LARGE
cape - - - - - - - - - - - NESS, RAS
Cape Cod food fish - - - - - - - CERO
Cape Verde Island - - - - - FOGO, SAL
Cape Verde Negro - - - - - - - SERER
capelike garment - - - - - - - DOLMAN
caper - PRANK, ANTIC, PRANCE, DIDO, GAMBOL, FRISK
caper (colloq.) - - - - - - - - DIDO
capital - - - - - CHIEF, PREEMINENT
caprices - - - WHIMSIES, VAGARIES, FANCIES, WHIMS
capsize - - - - - - - - - - - KEEL
capsule - - - - - - - - - - AMPULE
capsule of a plant - - - - - - - BOLL
captain of Absalom - - - - - - AMASA
captain's boat - - - - - - - - - GIG
caption - - - - - - - - - - HEADING
captious objector - - - - - - CAVILER
captivate - ENAMOR, CHARM, ENTHRAL
captive - - - - - - - - - PRISONER
capture - - BAG, TAKE, ARREST, CATCH
capture birds - - - - - - - - - BAG
capture as a fish - - - - - - - LAND
capture by strategem - - - - - - NET
Capuchin monkey - - - - - - - - SAI
car - - - - - - - - - - - - AUTO
caravan - - - - - - - - - - - VAN
caravanlike vehicle - - - - - TRAILER
caravansary - - - - - - SERAI, HOTEL
carbon - - - - - - - - - - - SOOT
carbonized vegetable material - - PEAT
carborundum - - - - - - - - EMERY
card - - - - - - - - - - - CARTE
card above the nine - - - - HONOUR
card combination - - - - - - TENACE
card in faro - - - - - - - - - SODA
card game - - SKAT, WHIST, MONTE, BEZIQUE, LOO, PAM, ECARTE, FARO, VINT, STUSS, LU, HEARTS, PEDRO, CASINO, BRAG, CASSINO, FANTAN, PINOCHLE, NULLO
card game (old) - - - - - - PAM, LOO
card holding - - - - - - - TENACE
card as wool - - - - - TEASE, ROVE
cardinal - - - - - - - - - PRINCIPAL
cardinal numeral - FIVE, TWO, MILLION, ELEVEN, NINE
care - CONCERN, DESIRE, VIGILANCE, WORRY, HEED, MIND, CAUTION, ANXIETY, TEND, FORETHOUGHT
care chiefly for one's interest - SELFISH, REGARD
care for - TEND, ATTEND, MIND, NURSE
careen - - - - - - - - LIST, LURCH
careening - - - - - - - - - - ALIST
career - - - - - - COURSE, VOCATION
careful - - - PROVIDENT, DISCREET
careless - - - - HEEDLESS, REMISS, NEGLECTFUL, SLACK

C

caress - - ENDEARMENT, FONDLE, PET
caretaker - - - - - - - CUSTODIAN
caretaker's house - - - - - LODGE
cargo - - - LOAD, LADING, FREIGHT
cargo cast overboard - - - - JETSAM
caribou - - - - - - - - - REINDEER
caricature - - - - - - - - CARTOON
carmine - - - - - - - - - - - RED
carnelian - - - - - - - - - - SARD
carnivore - CIVET, GENET, RATEL, CAT, LION
carnivorous animal - - - - CAT, LION
carnivorous insect - - - - - MANTIS
carnivorous mammal - - - - MARTEN
carnivorous quadruped - - - - CAT
carnivorous quadruped (small) - - GENET
carol - - - - - - - SING, WARBLE
Caroline Island - - - - - - - YAP
carolla leaf - - - - - - - - PETAL
carom - - - - - - - - - REBOUND
carousal - - - SPREE, REVEL, ORGY
carouse - - - - - - - - - - REVEL
carp - - - - - - - - - - - CAVIL
carp fish - - - - - - - - - DACE
carpenter - - - - - - WOODWORKER
carpenter's tool - - - - - SAW, PLANE
carpentry joint (part) - - - MORTISE
carpet - - - - - - - - - - - MAT
carpet of long pile - - - - - AFGHAN
carplike fish - - - - - - - - DACE
carpus - - - - - - - - - - WRIST
carriage - PHAETON, MIEN, POISE, SHAY, RIG, GIG, AIR, CLARENCE, CHARIOT, BEARING
carriage (light) - - - - - CALASH
carried - - - - - - - - - BORNE
carried on by letters - - - EPISTOLARY
carrier - - - - - - TOTER, BEARER
carrier of bad luck - - - - - JINX
carrotlike plant - - - - - PARSNIP
carry - - - - BEAR, TOTE, SUSTAIN
carry across water - - - - - FERRY
carry away as property - - - - ELOIN
carry on - PROSECUTE, WAGE, TRANSACT
carry on person - - - - - - - WEAR
carry out - - - - - - - - EXECUTE
carry out again - - - - - REENACT
carry through - - - - DO, TRANSACT
carry too far - - - - - - - OVERDO
carry weight - - - - - - - - COUNT
carryall - - - - - - - - - - BUS
carrying case - - - - - - - ETUI
carrying charge - - - - - - CARTAGE
cart - - - WAGON, HAUL, DRAY, VAN
cart (low) - - - - - - - - - DRAY
cart wheel ruts (Scot.) - - - - RITS
cartage - - - - - - - - HAULAGE
carte - - - - - - - - - - - CARD
Carthaginian general - - - HANNIBAL
carting vehicle - - - - - - - VAN
cartoonist - - - - - - - - ARTIST
cartridge - - - - SHUT, SHOT, SHELL
carve - - - - - - - - CUT, SLICE
carved gem and stone - - - - CAMEO
carved images - - STATUARY, STATUES
carving tool - - - - - - - - CHISEL
cascade - - - - - - - WATERFALL
case - - - INSTANCE, CRATE, CHEST, ENCASE, BOX, CONTAINER, EXAMPLE, PLIGHT
case for enclosing a light - - - LIGHT
case for small toiletries - - - - ETUI
cased for shipment - - - - CRATED
casern - - - - - - - - - BARRACKS
cash - - - - - - - SPECIE, MONEY
cash box - - - - - - - - - - TILL
cash register - - - - - - - - TILL
cask (deep) - - - - - - - VAT, TUN
cask (large) - - - TUN, BARREL, KEG, TIERCE, TUB, VAT, BARECA
cask (small) - - - - - - - - TUB
casket for valuables - - - - - COFFER
cassowary (var.) - - - - - - MOORUK
cast - - SHADE, THROW, HEAVE, HOVE
cast aside - - - - - - - - ELIMINATE
cast ballot - - - - - - - - - VOTE
cast down - - - - - - - - - ABASE
cast forth - - - - - - HEAVE, HOVE
cast metal mass - - - - - PIG, INGOT
cast metal (obs.) - - - - - - - YET
cast off - - - - - - - SHED, MOLT
cast off capriciously - - - - - - JILT
cast out - - - - - - - - - - EXPEL
cast sidelong glances - - - - - LEER
castaway - WAIF, DISCARDED, OUTCAST
caste - - - - - - - - - - - CLASS
caster - - - - - - - - - - CRUET
castigate - - - - - - - - - PUNISH
Castilian - - - - - - - - SPANISH
casting mold - - - - - - - - - DIE
castle - - - FORT, PALACE, FORTRESS
Castor and Pollux - - - - - - GEMINI
Castor and Pollux's mother - - - LEDA
casual observation - - - - - REMARK
cat - FELINE, FELID, GRIMALKIN, PUSS, MANX, ANCHOR
cat cry - - - - - - MEW, PUR, PURR
cat (kind) - ANGORA, MALTESE, OCELOT
cat like - - - - - - - - - - FELINE
cat (pet name) - - - - - - - PUSS
catalogue - - - - - - - - - - LIST
catapult (kind) - - - - - - ONAGER
cataract - - - - - - - - WATERFALL
catastrophe - - - - - - - DISASTER
catch - NAB, SNARE, SEIZE, DETENT, HASP, OVERTAKE, TRAP
catch the breath - - - - - - - GASP
catch of game - - - - - - - - BAG
catch for a hook - - - - - - - EYE
catch sight of - - - - - - - - ESPY
catch (slang) - - - - - - - COP, NAB
catch the toe - - - - - - - - STUB
catch unawares - - - - - - - TRAP
catch up with - - - - - - OVERTAKE
catcher's mask - - - - - - - CAGE
catching device - - - - - - - - NET
catchweed - - - - - - - CLEAVERS
catchword - - - - - - CUE, SLOGAN
category - - - - - - - - - - GENRE
catena - - - - - - - - - - CHAIN
cater - - - - - - - - - - PURVEY
cater to base desires - - - - PANDER
caterwaul - - - - - - - - - MIAUL
cathartic - - - LAPACTIC, PURGATIVE
catkin - - - - - - - - - - AMENT
catlike - - - - - - - - - - FELINE
catnip - - - - - - - - - - - NEP
cattails - - - - - - - - - RUSHES
cattle - - - - - - - - KINE, COWS
cattle dealers - - - - - - DROVERS
cattle thief - - - - - - - RUSTLER
catty - - - - - - - - MALICIOUS
Caucasian race (pert. to) - - SEMITIC, OSSET
Caucho tree - - - - - - - - - ULE
caudal appendage - - - - - - TAIL
caught sight of - - - - - - - SPIED
cause - - REASON, PRODUCE, MOTIVE, PROVOKE
cause of action - - - - MAINSPRING
cause to adhere - - - CEMENT, UNITE
cause to branch - - - - - - RAMIFY

cause to coalesce - - - - - - MERGE
cause emotion - - - - - - - EMOTE
cause exhaustion of - - - - - DRAIN
cause of false alarm - - SCARECROW
cause to float gently - - - - - WAFT
cause to flow in a stream - - - POUR
cause to go - - - - - - - - - SEND
cause to heel over - - - - - CAREEN
cause pain - - - - - - - - - - AIL
cause a panic - - - - - - STAMPEDE
cause to remember - - - - - REMIND
cause to revolve - - - - - - TRUNDLE
cause of ruin - - - - - - - - BANE
cause (Scot.) - - - - - - - - GAR
cause to shake - - - - - - - - JAR
cause to sound - - - - - - - BLOW
cause to soar upward - - - - - KITE
cause sudden surprise and fear - STARTLE
causeway - - - - - - - - - - DIKE
causing dislike - - - - - - REPELLENT
causing emotion - - - - - - EMOTIVE
causing laughter - - - - - GELASTIC
caustic - - ACRID, ERODENT, LYE, TART
caustic compound - LYE, ERODENT, LIME
cauterize - - SCAR, SERE, SEAR, BURN
caution - - - WARN, CARE, WARINESS
caution in advance - - - - FOREWARN
cautious - - CAREFUL, WARY, CANNY
cavalier - - - - - - - - - KNIGHT
cavalry arm - - - - - - - - - SABER
cavalry soldier - - - - - - - LANCER
cavalry sword - - - - - - - SABER
cavalryman - - - - TROOPER, UHLAN
cave - - GROTTO, CAVERN, DEN, LAIR
cave (arch.) - - - - - - - - ANTRE
cave formation - - - - - - STALACITE
cavern - GROTTO, CAVE, ANTRUM, DEN
cavernous - - - - - - - - - HOLLOW
cavil - - - - - - - - - - - CARP
caviler - - - - - - - - - - CRITIC
cavities - - - - - - - ATRIA, ANTRA
cavity - SINUE, SAC, ORATER, PIT, HOLE, ATRIUM, ANTRUM
cavity (anat.) - - - - - - - SINUS
cavity (small) - - - - - - - - CELL
cavity for tenon - - - - - - MORTISE
cavort - - - - - - - PLAY, PRANCE
cavorting - - - - - - - CAPERING
cay - - - - - - - - - - - - ISLET
cease - DESIST, CESSATE, PAUSE, STOP, QUIT
cease (former spelling) - - - - - SACE
cease (naut.) - - - - - - - - AVAST
cease work - - - - - - - - - REST
ceaseless - - - ETERNAL, UNENDING
ceaselessly (poet.) - - - - - - E'ER
Caesar's conspirator - - - - - BRUTUS
Caesar's death city - - - - - - NOLA
Caesar's river of decision - - RUBICON
cebine monkey - - - - - - - - SAI
cede - - - - - - - - YIELD, GRANT
cedrat - - - - - - - - - - CITRON
ceiling (arch.) - - - - - - LACUNAR
ceiling of semicircular rooms - - - - SEMIDOMES
celebrate - - - - - - - - - FETE
celebrated - - - - - - - - - NOTED
celebration - - GALA, FESTIVITY, FETE
celebrity - - - - - - - - - - STAR
celerity - - - - - - - - - SPEED
celestial - - - - - - - - - URANIC
celestial beings - - ANGELS, SERAPHS, SERAPHIM
celestial body - - COMET, STAR, SUN, MOON
celestial body (transient) - - - METEOR
celestial phenomenon - - - - NEBULA
celestial region - - - - - - - - SKY
celestial sphere - - - - - - - ORB
celibate - - - - - - - UNMARRIED
cell (biol.) - - - - - - - - - - CYTE
cellulose fiber - - - - - - - RAYON
Celt - - - - - - - - - - BRETON
Celtic - - - - - - - - - - - IRISH
Celtic chieftain - - - - - - - TANIST
Celtic language - GAELIC, ERSE, WELSH, IRISH
Celtic Neptune - - - - - - - - LER
cement - PASTE, LIME, MASTIC, SOLDER, LUTE, UNITE
cense - - - - - - - - - - PERFUME
censer - - - - - - - - - THURIBLE
censorious outpourings - - - TIRADES
censurable - - - - - REPREHENSIBLE
censure - - ASPERSE, SLATE, ACCUSE, TAUNT, BLAME, REPROVE, CONDEMN
census taker - - - - - ENUMERATOR
cent - - - - - - - - - - COPPER
center - - - - - - - - CORE, MIDDLE
center of attention - - - - - TARGET
center of a wheel - - - - - - - HUB
centerpiece - - - - - - - EPERGNE
central - - - EBOE, MID, CHIEF, HUB
Central American Indian - ONA, CARIB, INCA, NAHUA
Central American native - - - CARIB
Central American republic - - PANAMA
Central American rodent - - - - PACA
Central American tree - EBOE, EBO, ULE
Central Asia fox - - - ADIVE, CORSAC
Central Asia ox - - - - - - - - YAK
central boundary terminated line - - - DIAMETER
central cylinder of plants - STELA, STELE
central female character - - HEROINE
central male character - - - - HERO
central part - - - - - - - - - CORE
central part (denoting) - - - - - MID
central part of stems and roots - STELE
central personage - - - - - - - HERO
central point - - - - - - FOCUS, HUB
central point (pert. to) - - - - FOCAL
century - - - - - - - - - - - - AGE
century plant - - - ALOE, AGAVE, PITA
ceorl - - - - - - - - - - - CHURL
cerate - - - - - - - - - - - WAX
ceratoid - - - - - - - - - HORNY
cere - - - - - - - - - - - - WAX
cereal - - - - - - - - - RICE, GRAIN
cereal grass - - - - - - - - - OAT
cereal grass for fodder - - - - - SORGO
cereal husk - - - - - - - - - BRAN
cereal plant (pert. to) - - - - - EAR
cereal seed - - - - - - - - KERNEL
cereal spike - - - - - - - - - EAR
cerebral cortex - - - - - - CORTICAL
cerebrate - - - - - - - - - - THINK
ceremonial - - - - - - - - RITUAL
ceremonial dance - - PAVANE, PAVAN
ceremonial display - - - - - - POMP
ceremonial procession - - - - - PARADE
ceremonially unclean - - - - - - TREF
ceremony - - - - RITE, FETE, POMP
Ceres' mother - - - - - - - - - OPS
cerotic acid - - - - - - - - CERIN
certain - - - - - - - SURE, POSITIVE
certain language (pert. to) - - ROMANIC
certainly (arch.) - - - - - - - - YWIS
certificate - - - - - - - - - SCRIP
certificate of graduation - - DIPLOMA
certificate in lieu of cash - - - SCRIP
certify - - - - - - - - - - ATTEST

C

cess - - - - - - - - - - TAX
cessation - PAUSE, FAILURE, STOP, LULL
cessation of being - - - - - DESITION
cessation of life - - - - - - DEATH
cestus - - - - - - - - - - GIRDLE
cetacean - - - - - - - - - - INIA
Ceylon hill dweller - - - - - - TODA
cha - - - - - - - - - - - - TEA
chafe - FRET, GRATE, RUB, GALL, IRK
chaff - - - - - - - - BANTER, GUY
chaff (colloq.) - - - - - - - - GUY
chaff like bract (botanical) - - - PALEA
chaffer - - - - - - - - - DISPUTE
chaffy part of grain - - BRAIN, BRAN
chagrin - - ABASH, SHAME, VEXATION
chain - - CATENAE, CATENA, FETTER, RESTRAIN
chain part and ring - - - - - - LINK
chain set with precious stones - SAUTOIR
chainlike - - - - - - - - CATENATE
chair - - - - - - - - - - - SEAT
chair back piece - - - - - - - SPLAT
chair state - - - - - - - - - - DAIS
chair supports - - - - - - - - LEGS
chaise (kind) - - - - - - - - - GIG
chalcedony (var.) - - - SARD, AGATE
Chaldea city - - - - - - - - - - UR
chalice - GRAIL, GRILL, AMA, GOBLET
chalice cover - - - - - - - - - PALL
chalk - - - - - - CRAYON, WHITEN
chalky - - - - - - - - - - WHITISH
challenge - DARE, CARTEL, STUMP, DEFY
chamber - - - - - - - - - - ROOM
champagne (kind) - - - - - - - AY
champion - - PALADIN, TITLEHOLDER
champion of the people - - - TRIBUNE
chance - ODD, HAP, RANDOM, FORTUNE, LIKELIHOOD, RISK, VARIATION, HAPPEN, ACCIDENT, LUCK
chance upon - - - - - - - - - FIND
chancel part - - - - - - - - - BEMA
chancel seats for clergy - - - - SEDILIA
change - - - REVISE, ALTER, SHIFT, MUTATION, MUTATE, CONVERT, TRANSMUTE, TRANSFER, EMEND, AMEND, VARY, REVISION
change for the better - REVISE, REVISAL
change (colloq.) - - - - - - - - ALTER
change colour of - - - - - - - - DYE
change course - - - - - - - REVERSE
change direction - - - - VEER, TURN
change form - - - - - - - - REMODEL
change law - - - - - - - - REVERSAL
change to the opposite - - - - REVERSE
change place - - - - - - - - - MOVE
change position - - TRANSFER, MOVE
change residence - - - - - - - MOVE
change the title - - - - - - - RENAME
changeless - - - - - - - - CONSTANT
changeling - - - - - - - - - - - OAF
channel - CHUTE, FLUME, VALE, STRAIT, GAT, WAY, PASSAGE
channel (var.) - - - - - - - - - - GUT
chant - - - INTONE, CHORTLE, SING
chaos - - - - - - - - - - DISORDER
chap - - - - FELLOW, SPLIT, CRACK
chapel - - - - - - - - - - - VESTRY
chaperon - - - - - - - - - DUENNA
chaplet - - - - - - - - - - ANADEM
char - - - - - - - - SCORCH, BURN
character - - ROLE, NATURE, QUALITY, TONE, STAMP
character of a people - - - - - ETHOS
character of primitive alphabet - RUNE
character in romance - - - - RINALDO
character of a sound (pert. to) - TONAL
characteristic - MARK, TRAIT, TYPICAL, FEATURE
characteristic form of expression - IDIOM
characteristic mark - - - - - - - STAMP
characteristic taste - - - - - - - SMACK
characterization - - - - - - - - ROLE
characterize - - - - DESCRIBE, MARK
characterized by excessive floridity - - ASIATIC
characterized by dependence - ANACLITIC
characterized by moderation - TEMPERATE
characterized by union - - - - UNITIVE
characterless - - - - - - - - INANE
charade - - - - - - - - - - - PUZZLE
charge - COST, RATE, LOAD, DEBIT, FEE, ACCUSATION, FARE, RUSH, PRICE, ACCUSE
charge for boat transportation - PORTAGE
charge per unit - - - - - - - - RATE
charge on property - - - - - LIEN, TAX
charge a sum - - - - - - - - - - DEBIT
charge to transport mail - - POSTAGE
charge for using a road - - - - - TOLL
charge with crime - - - - - - - INDICT
charge with gas - - - - - - - AERATE
charged atom - - - - - - - - - - ION
charged with electricity - - ALIVE, LIVE
charger - - - - - - - - - - - STEED
chariot - - - - - - ESSED, CARRIAGE
charioteer - - - - - - - - - - - HUR
charitable gift - - - - - - - - - ALMS
charity - - ALMS, LOVE, BENEVOLENCE
charivari - - - - - - - - - SERENADE
charlatan - - - - - - - - - - QUACK
Charles Dickens - - - - - - - - BOZ
charm - GRACE, ATTRACT, CAPTIVATE, AMULET, TALISMAN, SPELL, ENTRANCE, ENTICE, ENCHANT
chart - - PLAN, MAP, PLOT, GRAPH
charter - - - - - - - - - - - - HIRE
chary - - FRUGAL, SPARING, PRUDENT
chase - - - - PURSUE, FOLLOW, HUNT
chasing tool - - - - - - - - TRACER
chasm - - - - ABYSS, GULF, CLEFT
chaste - - - - - - - PURE, MODEST
chasten - - SMITE, TRAIN, CHASTISE
chastise - BERATE, SWINGE, REPROVE, CHASTEN
chat - - - - - - - TALK, CONVERSE
chat (colloq.) - - - - - - - CONFAB
chatter - - - - PRATE, GAB, GABBLE
chatter idly - - - - - - - - - TATTLE
chatter (slang) - - - - - - - - CHIN
chattering bird - - - - - - - - - PIE
cheap race horse - - - - - - PLATER
cheat - DUPE, COZEN, FRAUD, HOCUS, FLEECE, DEFRAUD, MULCT, FOB, BILK, SWINDLER
cheat (slang) - - WELSH, BAM, STICK
check - REPRESS, STEM, REIN, ARREST, TEST, CURB, INHIBIT, RESTRAIN
check (colloq.) - - - - - - - STICK
check growth - - - - - - STUNT, NIP
check memorandum - - - - - - - STUB
checkered woolen cloth - TARTAN, PLAID
cheek - - - - - - - - - - - - GENA
cheekbone - - - - - - - - - MALAR
cheek (of the) - MOLAR, MALAR, GENAL
cheer - - - GLADDEN, ELATION, RAH, ENCOURAGE, HEARTEN, APPLAUD, INSPIRIT
cheer in trouble - - - - - - SOLACE
cheerful - - GENIAL, BLITHE, JOYFUL, SUNNY
cheerful tune - - - - - - - - - LILT
cheerless - - - - - - - - - DREARY

cheese dish - - - - - - - RAREBIT
cheese (kind) - **EDAM, BRIE, GRUYERE, PARMESAN, CHEDDAR, STILTON**
chef - - - - - - - - - - COOK
chemical agent in photography - - - RESTRAINER
chemical compound - - ESTER, AMINE, WATER, AMIDE, SUCRATE
chemical compound (suffix) - INE, YL, AL, OL, ITE, OSE, OLID
chemical compound from flax - LINEN, ID
chemical vessel - - - - UDELL, ALUDEL
cherish - - - BOSOM, NURSE, FOSTER
cheroot - - - - - - - - - CIGAR
cherry colour - - - - - - - CERISE
cherry (kind) - - - - - - - MORELLO
cherry part - - - - - - - - - PIT
cherubic - - - - - - - - ANGELIC
chess opening - - - - - - - GAMBIT
chess pieces - MEN, PAWNS, ROOKS, CASTLES, KNIGHTS, QUEENS
chess sacrifice - - - - - - - GAMBIT
chess term - - - - - - - - MATE
chessman - - - - - - - - - ROOK
chest - - SAFE, THORAX, CASE, COFFER
chest bone - - - - - - - - - RIB
chest noise - - - - - - - - RALE
chest protection - - - - - - - RIB
chestnut and grey - - - - - - ROAN
chevrotain - - - - - - - - NAPU
chew - - - MANDUCATE, MASTICATE
chew audibly - - - - - - - CRUNCH
chew and swallow - - - - - - - EAT
chewing structure - - - - - - - JAW
chic - - - - - - - MODISH, SMART
chick pea - - - - - - - - - GRAM
chicken (breed) - - - - - WYANDOTTE
chicken enclosure - - - - - - RUNWAY
chicken (small) - - - - - - BANTAM
chickory-like herb - - - - - - ENDIVE
chide - - - SCOLD, BERATE, REBUKE
chide vehemently - - - - - - BERATE
chief - HEADMAN, HEAD, PRINCIPAL, STAPLE, PRIMAL, ARCH, MAIN, PRIME, CAPITAL, PARAMOUNT, FIRST, CENTRAL
chief actor - - - - - - - - STAR
chief Assyrian deity - - - - - ASHUR
chief character - - - - - - - HERO
chief of clan - - - - - - - THANE
chief commodity of region - - - STAPLE
chief events - - - - - - - EPOCHS
chief of evil spirits - - - - - - SATAN
chief of Grail knights - - - TITUREL
chief of the janizaries - - - - - - DEY
chief Olympian deity - - - - - - ZEUS
chief singer - - - - - - - CANTOR
chief of Teutonic gods - - - - - ODIN
chief workman - - - - - - FOREMAN
chief (was) - - - - - - - - - LED
child - - - - - - - - - - - TOT
child (comb. form) - - - - - - PED
child (small) - - - - - - - TOT, TAD
childish - - - - - - PUERILE, ANILE
childish talk - - - - - - - PRATTLE
childish walk - - - - - - - TODDLE
childishness - - - - - - - PUERILITY
childlike - - - - - - - - INFANTILE
children - - - - - - - - - TOTS
child's apron - - - - - - - PINAFORE
child's textbook - - READER, PRIMER
Chile city - - - - - - - TALCA, ARICA
Chile seaport - - - - - - - - ARICA
Chile timber tree - - MUERMO, RAULI
chill - - - ICE, COOL, AGUE, FROST
chills and fever - - - AGUE, MALARIA
chill by formality - - - - - - FROST
chilly - - COLD, RAW, PENETRATING
chimes - - - - - - - - - - BELLS
chimney - - - - - - - - FLUE, STACK
chimney carbon - - - - - - - - SOOT
chimney passage - - - - - - - FLUE
chimney top - - - - - - - - - COW
China (poet.) - - - - - - - - CATHAY
Chinese animal - - - - - - - - RASSE
Chinese antelope - - - - - - TSERIN
Chinese boat - - - - - - - SAMPAN
Chinese building - - - - - - PAGODA
Chinese bushy plant - - - - - - UDO
Chinese card game - - - - - LU, LOO
Chinese cash - - - - - - - - TIAO
Chinese city - AMOY, UDE, NOM, PEKIN
Chinese civet cat - - - - - - RASSE
Chinese coin - - - - TAEL, TSIEN, PU
Chinese (comb. form) - - - - - SINO
Chinese dependency - - - - - TIBET
Chinese dialect - - - - - - - - WU
Chinese diplomat - - - - - - - WU
Chinese dynasty - MING, HAN YIN, TANG
Chinese herb - - - - - GINSENG, TEA
Chinese labourer - - - - - - COOLIE
Chinese measure - TUA, LI, TAEL, TU, RI
Chinese medium of exchange - - SYCEE
Chinese mile - - - - - - - - - LI
Chinese monetary unit - - - - - TAEL
Chinese money - - - - - - - SYCEE
Chinese money of account - - - - TIAO
Chinese obeisance (var.) - - - - SALAM
Chinese official - - - - - MANDARIN
Chinese pagoda - - - - - - - TAA, TA
Chinese philosopher - - - CONFUCIUS
Chinese plant - - - - - - - - - TEA
Chinese port - - - - SHANGHAI, AMOY
Chinese pound - - - - - - - CATTY
Chinese puzzle - - - - - - TANGRAM
Chinese religion - - - - - - TAOISM
Chinese river - - - - PEH, GAN, TUNG
Chinese secret society - - - - - TONG
Chinese shrub - - - - - - - - - TEA
Chinese skiff - - - - - - - - SAMPAN
Chinese statesman - - - - - - - KOO
Chinese string of cash - - - - - TIAO
Chinese tea - - - - - - - - - TSIA
Chinese temple - - - - - - - PAGODA
Chinese treaty port - AMOY, WENCHOW
Chinese unit of value - - - - - TAEL
Chinese unit of weight - - - - - - LI
Chinese wax - - - - - - - - - PELA
Chinese weight - - - LIANG, TSIEN, LI
Chinook Indian - - - - - - FLATHEAD
chip - - - - - - FRAGMENT, FLAKE
Chipewayan Indian group - ATHABASCA
chiropodist - - - - - - - - PEDICURE
chirp - - - - PEEP, TWITTER, TWEET
chirrup - - - - - - - - - TWITTER
chisel to break ore - - - - - - - GAD
chivalrous enterprise - - - - - QUEST
chloroform substance - - - - ACETONE
choice - ELITE, PRIME, BEST, OPTION
choice morsel - - - - - - - - TIDBIT
choicest - - - - - - - - - - BEST
choicest part - - - - - - - MARROW
choir boy - - - - - - - CHORISTER
choir vestments - - - - - - - COTTA
choler - - - - - - - ANGER, IRE, RAGE
choose - SELECT, PREFER, ELECT, OPT
choose for office - - - - - - - SLATE
chooser - - - - - - - - - ELECTOR
chop - HEW, MINCE, LOP, BITE, HACK
chop irregularly - - - - - - - - HACK
chop off - - - - - - - - - - - LOP
chopped meat and vegetables - SALPICON

C

chopper - - - - - - - - - HEWER
chopping tool - - - - - - - AXE, AX
choral composition - - - - - CANTATA
choral vestment - - - - - - - CAPE
chord of three tones - - - - - - TRIAD
chore - - - - - - - - - STINT, TASK
choreographic artist - - - - - DANCER
chortle - - - - - - - LAUGH, CHANT
chosen - - - - - - SELECTED, ELECT
Chosen - - - - - - - - - - - KOREA
Christian era (abbr.) - - - - - - A.D.
Christian Indo Port. half caste - TORAS
Christian love feast - - - - - AGAPE
Christmas - - - - - - - YULE, NOEL
Christmas carol - - - - - - - NOEL
Christmas day - - - - - - NATIVITY
chronicle - - - - - RECORD, ANNAL
chronicler - - - - - - - HISTORIAN
chronological correction - - - - EPACT
chrysalis - - - - - - - PUPA, PUPAE
chthonian - - - - - - - - INFERNAL
chuckle - - - - - - - - - CHORTLE
chum - - - - - FRIEND, CRONY, PAL
chump - - - - - - - - - - - BLOCK
church - - - - - CHAPEL, BASILICA
church bench - - - - - - - - - PEW
church body - - - - - - - - - NAVE
church caretaker - - - - - - SEXTON
church ceremony - - - - - - - MASS
church chancel - - - - - - - - BEMA
church congregation - - - - - SYNAXIS
church council - - - - - - - - SYNOD
church devotion - - - - - - - NOVENA
church dignitary - CANON, PRELATE, POPE
church festival - - - - - - - EASTER
church head - - - - - - - - - POPE
church land - - - - - - - - - GLEBE
church of a monastery - - - - MINSTER
church offerings - - - - - OBLATIONS
church officer - - TRUSTEE, BISHOP, ELDER, SEXTON, PRIEST, PASTOR
church official - ELDER, POPE, DEACON, BEADLE
church position - - - - - - BENEFICE
church part - - APSE, NAVE, CHANCEL, STEEPLE, ALTAR, TRANSEPT, PEW, STALL
church reader - - - - - - - - LECTOR
church recess - - - - - - - - - APSE
church seat - - - - - - - - - - PEW
church service - - - - - - - - MASS
church service book - - - - - MISSAL
church sitting - - - - - - - - - PEW
church vault - - - - - - - - - CRYPT
churl - - - - - - - - - BOOR, CEORL
churned cream - - - - - - - - BUTTER
chyme - - - - - - - - - - - - PULP
cicada - - - - - - - - - - - LOCUST
cicatrix - - - - - - - - - - - SCAR
cigar - PANETELA, CHEROOT, STOGIE, STOGY
cigar box - - - - - - - - HUMIDOR
cigar fish - - - - - - - - - - SCAD
cigar (long) - - - - - - - - CORONA
cigar shape - - - - - - - - CORONA
cigarette (slang) - - - - - - - - FAG
cinch - - - - - - - - - - - - PIPE
cincture - - - - - - - - - - - GIRDLE
cinder - - - - - - - - - - - - ASH
cinder (arch.) - - - - - - - - GLEED
cinnabar - - - - - - - - - SINOPLE
cion - - - - - - SPROUT, TWIG, BUD
cion (hort.) - - - - - - - - - GRAFT
cipher - ZERO, CODE, NULL, NAUGHT
Circe's sister - - - - - - - MEDEA
circle - - - - ARC, RING, ORB, LOOP
circle around the moon - - - - CORONA
circle generating an epicycloid - EPICYCLE
circle of light - - - - - - - - HALO
circle part - - - - - - - - - SECTOR
circlet - - - - - - - RING, WREATH
circling around a center - - - - SPIRAL
circuit - - TOUR, CYCLE, LAP, AMBIT
circuit court - - - - - - - - - EYRE
circuitous course - - - - - - DETOUR
circular - - - - - - - - - - - ROUND
circular band - - - - - - - - - HOOP
circular in cross section - - - TERETE
circular disc - - - - - - - - - PLATE
circular indicator - - - - - - - DIAL
circular plate - - - - - - DISC, DISK
circular tower for fodder - - - - SILO
circulate - - - - - - - - - - - PASS
circumscribed - - - NARROW, LIMITED
circumspect - - - CHARY, PRUDENT
circumstance - - - - - - FACT, EVENT
cistern - - - - - - BAC, TANK, VAT
citadel - - - - TOWER, STRONGHOLD
citadel of Moscow - - - - - KREMLIN
cite - ADDUCE, ALLEGE, QUOTE, SUMMON
citizen - - - - - - - - - RESIDENT
citizens of a state - - - - - - DEMOS
citron - - - - - - - - - - - CEDRAT
city of leaning tower - - - - - - PISA
city official - - - MAYOR, ALDERMAN
city (pert. to) - - - - - CIVIC, URBAN, MUNICIPAL
civet - - - - - - - - - - - - RASSE
civet like animal - - - - - - - GENET
civil - - - - - - - - - - - - POLITE
civil law term - - - - - - - - AVAL
Civil War admiral - - - - - FARRAGUT
Civil War battle - - - - - - - SHILOH
civil wrong - - - - - - - - - - TORT
clad - - - - GARBED, DRESSED, DREST
clad (var.) - - - - - - - - - - DREST
claim - - MAINTAIN, REQUIRE, TITLE, DEMAND, LIEN
claim on property - - - - - - - LIEN
claimant - - - - - - - - PRETENDER
clam (kind) - - - - - - - - - RAZOR
clamber - - - - - - - - - - - CLIMB
clamour - DIN, NOISE, OUTCRY, BARK
clamorous - - - - - - - LOUD, NOISY
clamp - - - - - - - - NIP, FASTENER
clamping device - - - - - - - - VISE
clan - SEPT, TRIBE, SECT, GENS, CLIQUE
clandestine - - - - - - - - - SECRET
clap - - - - - - - - - - - APPLAUD
clarify - - - - - - - - DEFINE, CLEAR
clarity - - - - - - - - - - LUCIDITY
clash - - - - - - - - JAR, CONFLICT
clasp - GRASP, FASTENER, HOLD, HOOK, SEIZE
clasp pin - - - - - - - - - BROOCH
class - - SECT, GRADE, CASTE, GENUS
class jargon - - - - - - - - - ARGOT
classes - - - - - - - - - - - GENERA
classic - - - - - - - - - - STANDARD
classic water jar - - - - - - - HYDRIA
classical Greek - - - - - - - HELLENIC
classical language - - - - - - - LATIN
classified information - - - - - DATA
classify - - - RATE, SORT, ARRANGE, ASSORT, LABEL, GRADE
clatter - - - - - RATTLE, CLACK, DIN
clattering sound - - - - - - - - DIN
clavichord - - - - - - - - - SPINET
claw - - - - - TALON, NAIL, SCRATCH
clawlike process on bird - - - CALCAR

clay - - LOAM, LATERITE, MARL, PUG, EARTH
clay musical instrument - - - OCARINA
clay (pert. to) - - - - - - BOLAR
clay pipe (colloq.) - - - - - - T.D.
clayey - - - - - - BOLAR, LOAMY
clayey earth - - LOESS, LOAM, MARL
clean - PURE, NEAT, SPOTLESS, PURIFY, FAIR, WIPE
clean house - - - - - - - - DUST
clean thoroughly - - RENOVATE, SCOUR
cleanse - BATHE, RINSE, SCRUB, SCOUR, PURIFY, DETERGE
cleanse wool - - - - - - - - CARD
cleanser - - - - - - - RENOVATOR
cleansing - - - - - - - - - BATH
cleansing agent - - - BORAX, SOAP, DETERGENT
cleansing process - - - - - - BATH
clear - PURE, EXONERATE, NET, SERENE, RID, CLARIFY, PLAIN, EVIDENT, CRYSTAL, LUCID, MANIFEST
clear out suddenly - - - - DECAMP
clear out unnecessary things - - WEED
clear profit - - - - - - - - - NET
clear sky - - - - - - - - - ETHER
cleared woods - - - - GROVE, GLADE
clearing - - - - - - - - - GLADE
cleat - - - - - - - - - WEDGE
cleavable rock - - - - - - - SLATE
cleave - CUT, REND, TEAR, RIVE, SPLIT, HEW
cleavers - - - - - - - CATCHWEED
cleft - - - DIVIDED, RIVEN, CHASM, FISSURE, CUT, RIFT, GAP
cleft in rock (Scot.) - - - - - RIVA
clemency - - - - - MERCY, LENIENCY
clement - - - - - MILD, LENIENT
Cleopatra's attendant - - - - - IRAS
Cleopatra's pet - - - - - - - - ASP
cleoresin - - - - - - - - - ELEMI
clergyman - - VICAR, PRIEST, CLERIC, RECTOR, PARSON, MINISTER, CURATE, PASTOR
clergyman's charge - PARISH, PASTORATE
clergyman's enclosed stage - - PULPIT
clergyman's title - - - - - REVEREND
cleric - - - - - - - - - - MINISTER
clerical collar - - - - - - - RABAT
clerical dress - - - - - - VESTMENT
clerical title - REVEREND, ABBA, ABBE
clerical vestment - - - - - - - ALB
clerk - - - - - - - - - ATTENDANT
clerk on passenger vessel - - PURSER
clever - - ASTUTE, SMART, TALENTED, CUTE, APT, ABLE, DEXTEROUS, SHREWD, SLICK
clever retort - - - - - - - REPARTEE
cleverness - - - WIT, SMARTNESS, ART
click beetle - - - - - - ELATER, DOR
cliff - - - - - - - CRAG, PRECIPICE
climate (poet.) - - - - - - - CLIME
climatic conditions - - - - - WEATHER
climax - - - - - APOGEE, TOP, END
climb - - SCALE, ASCEND, RISE, SHIN
climb crawlingly - - - - - CLAMBER
climbing - - - - - - - - SCANDENT
climbing device - - - - - - LADDER
climbing herb - - - - - - HOP, PEA
climbing organ of a vine - - TENDRIL
climbing palm - - - - - - RATTAN
climbing pepper - - - - - - BETEL
climbing plant - VINE, LIANE, LIANA, BINE, CREEPER, IVY
climbing stem - - - - - - - - BINE
climbing vine - - - - - - - - PEA
clime - - - - - - - - - - REGION
clinch - - - - - - - NAIL, GRAPPLE
cling - - - COHERE, ADHERE, HANG
cling with fondness - - - - - - HUG
clinging fish - - - - - - - - REMORA
clingy - - - - - - - - TENACIOUS
clip - SHEAR, SNAP, CURTAIL, SNIP, NIP, MOW
clip (Scot.) - - - - - - - - - COLL
clipped - SHORN, SNAPPED, SNIPPED
clique - COTERIE, SET, FACTION, CLAN
cloak - - - - ROBE, WRAP, MANTLE, DISGUISE, HIDE
clock - - - - - - - - - - - TIME
clock face - - - - - - - - - - DIAL
clock part - - - - - - - PENDULUM
clock in shape of ship - - - - - NEF
clog - - - - - - - - - - - IMPEDE
clog with mid - - - - - - - DAGGLE
cloister - - - - HERMITAGE, PRIORY
close - - END, NEAR, SHUT, DENSE, FINALE, SEAL, NIGH
close associate - - - - - - PARTNER
close bond - - - - - - - - - - TIE
close by - - - - - - - - - - NIGH
close of day - - - EVENTIDE, SUNSET
close of day (poet.) - - - - EEN, EVE
close firmly - - - - - - - - - - BAR
close fitting cap - - - COIF, CLOCHE
close fitting jacket - - - - - REEFER
close hermetically - - - - - - SEAL
close mouthed person (slang) - - CLAM
close (poet.) - - - - - - - - ANEAR
close ties - - - - - - - - - BONDS
close tightly - - - - - - - - - SEAL
close to - - - - - - - - - NEAR, AT
close with click - - - - - - - SNAP
closed curves - - - - - - - ELLIPSES
closed four wheeled carriage - CLARENCE
closely twisted - - - - - - - KINKY
closing chord sequence - - CADENCE
closing part of musical composition CODA
closing part of opera - - - STRETTO
cloth - - DENIM, SERGE, MARL, BAIZE, SATINET, REP, SATIN, MELTON, TWEED, WORSTED, LENO
cloth (cotton) - - - - - - - - LENO
cloth to cover shipboard goods - CAPOT
cloth for drying - - - - - - - TOWEL
cloth fibers - - - - - - - - - - NAP
cloth of flax - - - - - - - - - LINEN
cloth measure - - - - - - - - - ELL
cloth strainer - - - - - - - - TAMIS
cloth used at table - - - - - NAPKIN
cloth with uncut loops - - - - TERRY
clothe (colloq.) - - - - - - - - TOG
clothe richly - - - - - - - ENROBE
clothed - - CLAD, GARBED, ATTIRED, DRESSED, ARRAYED
clothes - - TOGS, APPAREL, TOGGERY
clothes basket - - - - - - HAMPER
clothes brush - - - - - - - - WHISK
clothes dryer - - - - AIRER, WRINGER
clothes moth - - - - - - - - TINEA
clothes rack - - - - - - TREE, AIRER
clothes stand - - - - - - - - - RACK
clothing - - - - - - - - - - GEAR
cloud region - - - - - - - - - SKY
cloud (type) - - - - CUMULUS, CIRRUS
clouded mental condition - - - - HAZE
cloudless - - - - - - - - - - CLEAR
cloudlike mass - - - - - - - NEBULA
cloudy - - NEBULOUS, DIM, NEBULAR
clover - - - - - - - HERB, SAINFOIN
cloverlike plant - - - - - - MELILOT

C

clown - - MIME, BUFFOON, BUMPKIN, JESTER
cloy - - - - - SATE, PALL, SURFEIT
club - - - - - - - - - MACE, BAT
club shaped - - CLAVATE, CLAVIFORM
clue - - - - - - - - - - HINT, TIP
clump - - - - - - - - - - - TUFT
clump of earth - - - - - - - - CLOD
clumsily formed - - - - - - SPLAY
clumsy - - - - - INEPT, AWKWARD
clumsy boat - - - - - - - - - ARK
clumsy fellow - - LOUT, LUBBER, OAF, GAWK
clumsy person - - - - - - - - OX
clumsy work - - - - - - - - BOTCH
Cluny - - - - - - - - - - - LACE
cluster (botanical) - - - - - - SORUS
cluster of spore cases - - SORI, SORUS
cluster of trees - - - THICKET, GROVE
cluster of wool fibers - - - - - - NEP
clutch - GRASP, HOLD, GRAB, SEIZE, GRIP
clutter - - - - - - - - - - LITTER
coach - - - - - - TRAINER, TRAIN
coachman - - - - - - - - - DRIVER
coagulate - - - CLOT, CURDLE, GEL
coal box - - - - - - - - - - HOD
coal digger - - - - - - - - - MINER
coal distillate - - - - - - - - TAR
coal fragment - - - - - - - - EMBER
coal lifter - - - - - - - - - SHOVEL
coal mine shaft - - - - - - - - PIT
coal miner - - - - - - - - COLLIER
coal product - - - - - - - - - TAR
coal shuttle - - - - - - - - - HOD
coal smoke deposit - - - - - - SOOT
coal wagon - - - - - - - - - TRAM
coalesce - - - - - - - - - - UNITE
coalition - - - - - - FUSION, UNION
coarse - - BRUTISH, RIBALD, THICK, CRASS
coarse cloth - - SHROUDING, MANTA, BURLAP, LENO, SCRIM
coarse cotton fabric - - - - - SCRIM
coarse fiber - - - - - - - TOW, ADAD
coarse file - - - - - - - - - RASP
coarse flax fiber - - - - - - - - TOW
coarse flour - - - - - - - - - MEAL
coarse grass - - - - - - - - - SEDGE
coarse ground wheat - - - MIDDLINGS
coarse hemp - - - - - - - - - TOW
coarse hominy - - - - - SAMP, GRITS
coarse lace - - - - - - - MACRAME
coarse linen fabric - - - CRASH, ECRU
coarse matted wool - - - - - - SHAG
coarse outer cereal coat - - - - BRAN
coarse rigid hair - - - SETA, BRISTLE
coarse rustics - - - - - - - - BOORS
coarse woolen blanket - - - - - COTTA
coarse woolen cloth - - - - - KERSEY
coarse woven fabric - - - - - SCRIM
coast - - - SHORE, SLIDE, SEASHORE
coaster waver - - - - - - - - ROLLER
coasting vehicle - - - - - BOB, SLED
coasting vessel (East) - - - - - GRAB
coat - - - - - - - - COVER, LAYER
coat of animal - - - - - FUR, PELAGE
coat of arms - - - - CREST, HERALDIC
coat of certain alloy - - TERN, TERNE
coat of gold - - - - - - - - - GILD
coat with icing - - - - - - - GLACE
coat of metal - - - - - - - - PLATE
coax - - - - - - - TEASE, CAJOLE
cob - - - - - - - - - - - - GULL
cobbler's tool - - - - - - - - - AWL
cocaine (slang) - - - - - - - SNOW
cocked hat and wig - - - - - RAMILLIE
cockfight - - - - - - - - - - SPAR
cocoa (kind) - - - - - - - - BROMA
cocoanut husk fiber - - - - - - COIR
cocoanut juice - - - - - - - - MILK
cocoanut meat - - - - - - - - COPRA
cod like food fish - - - - - - - LING
code - - - - - - - - - CIPHER, LAW
code signal - - - - - - - - - ROGER
coddle - - - - - - - - - - PAMPER
codlike fish - - - - - - - - - LING
coerce - - - - - - - - - - COMPEL
coercive - - - - - - - - COMPELLING
coffee bean - - - - - - - - - - NIB
coffee cake - - - - - - - - STOLLEN
coffee (kind) - - - - - MOCHA, JAVA
coffer - - - - - - - - - CHEST, ARK
coffin - - - - - - - - - - - - BIER
coffin cover - - - - - - - - - PALL
coffin of a saint - - - - - - - - PALL
cog - - - - - - TOOTH, PAWL, GEAR
cog wheel set - - - - - - - - - GEAR
cogent - - - - VALID, CONCLUSIVE, CONVINCING
cogitate - THINK, PONDER, MUSE, MULL
cogitate (colloq.) - - - - - - - MULL
cognate - - - - - - - - - - ALLIED
cognition - - - - - - - - KNOWLEDGE
cognizance - - - - - - - - - - KEN
cognizant - - - - - - - - - AWARE
cognizant of (be) - - - - - LEARNED
cognomen - - - - - - - - - - NAME
cogwheel - - - - - - - - - - - GEAR
cohere - - - - - - - - - - - CLING
coherence of ideas - - - - - - SENSE
coherent - - - - - - - - CONNECTED
coif - - - - - - - - - - - - - CAP
coign - - - - - - - - - - - CORNER
coil - - - TWIST, TWINE, CURL, WIND
coil (comb. form) - - - - - - - SPIRO
coil into a ball - - - - - - - - CLEW
coiled - - - - - - - - - - - SPIRAL
coin - MINT, MONEY, PENCE, ORIGINATE
coincide - - - - AGREE, CORRESPOND
coincidence - - - - - - - AGREEMENT
coincidently - - - - - - - TOGETHER
cold - - ICY, FRIGID, GELID, CHILLY, FROSTY, RESERVED
cold blooded animal - - - - - - FISH
cold dish - - - - - - - - - - SALAD
cold enough - - - - - - - - - ZERO
cold season - - - - - - - - - WINTER
cold weather garment - - - - - PARKA
colin - - - - - - - - - - - - QUAIL
collapse - - - - - - - - - DEFLATE
collapsible - - - - - - - KNOCKDOWN
collar (slang) - - - - - - - - GRAB
collar chain - - - - - - - - TORQUE
collar (kind) - - - - - - - - - ETON
collarbone - - - - - - - - CLAVICLE
colleague - ALLY, PARTNER, CONFRERE
collect - - - GATHER, LEVY, AMASS, GARNER, POOL, ACCUMULATE, COMPACT
collect and keep - - - - - - - HOARD
collect to a point - - - - - - CENTER
collect together - - - COMPILE, POOL
collection - - - - - - - - SET, PACK
collection of animals - - - - - - ZOO
collection of cattle - - - - - DROVE
collection of documents - - - DOSSIER
collection of facts - - - - - - - ANA
collection of implements - - - - KIT
collection of people - - - - - TROOP
collection of walruses - - - - - POD
collective whole - - - - - - - BODY

collector's item - - - - - - CURIO
college campus (colloq.) - - - QUAD
college cheer - - - - - - RAH, YELL
college dance - - - - - - - PROM
college grads - - - - - - - ALUMNI
college officer - - - - - - PROCTOR
college official - - - - - - REGENT
college organization (colloq.) - - FRAT
college session - - - - - SEMINAR
college song - - - - - - - - GLEE
college student - - - SOPHOMORE, FRESHMAN, JUNIOR, SENIOR
college treasurer - - - - - BURSAR
collide with - - - - - - RAM, BUMP
collision - - - IMPACT, PERCUSSION
colloquial affirmative - - - - - YEP
colloquialism - - - - - - - SLANG
collude - - - - - - - - CONSPIRE
collusion - - - - - - - - DECEIT
Colombian Indian - - TAMA, MIRANA
colonial founder - - - - - - PENN
colonist - - - - - SETTLER, PLANTER
colonist greeting to Indian - - NETOP
colonize - - - - - - - - - SETTLE
colour - - TINT, DYE, ROAN, PAINT, STAIN, PUCE, TINGE, BICE, HUE, OLIVE, SEPIA
colour of animal - - - - - BRINDLE
colour of courage in heraldry - - RED
colour lightly - - - - - - - TINGE
colour matter - - - - - - - - DYE
colour of mole's coat - - - - TAUPE
colour quality - - - - - - TONE, HUE
colour variation - - - - - - NUANCE
Colorado county - - OSTERO, OTERO
Colorado Indian - - - - - - - UTE
Colorado mountain - - - OWEN, OSO
Colorado park - - - - - - - ESTES
Colorado resort - - - - - MANITOU
coloured chalk - - - - - - - PASTEL
coloured glass - - - - - - SMALTO
coloured horse - - - - - - - ROAN
colourer - - - - - - - - - DYER
colouring agent - - - - - DYE, PAINT
colourless - - - WAN. PALE, PALLID
colourless crystalline compound RETENE, TROPINE
colourless gaseous element - - NEON
colourless liquid compound - - OLEIN
colourless volatile liquid - - - ETHER
colossal - - - - - - - - - LARGE
colt - - - - - - - - - - FOAL
Columbine - AQUILEGIA, PERENNIAL, DOVELIKE
Columbus's birthplace - - - GENOA
Columbus's ship - NINA, PINTA, SANTA MARIA
column - - - - - PILLAR, PILASTER
column shaft - - - - - - - TRUNK
columnar - - - - - - - - TERETE
coma - - - - - STUPOR, LETHARGY
comate - - - - - - - - - HAIRY
comb - - - - - - - - - HACKLE
comb wool - - - - - - CARD, TEASE
combat - - DUEL, STRUGGLE, FIGHT
combat place - - - - - - - ARENA
combative disposition (of) - MILITANT
combination - - - UNION, MERGER
combination of companies - - MERGER
combination of horizontal moldings - - LEDGMENT
combination of interest - - - POOL
combine - - UNITE, MERGER, MERGE
combine resources - - - - - - POOL
combine with certain gas - - OXIDATE
combined whole - - - - - - - UNIT
combustible heap - - - - - - PYRE
combustion - - - - - - - - - FIRE
combustion product - - SMOKE, SOOT, ASH
come - - ARRIVE, REACH, APPROACH
come ashore - - - - - - - - LAND
come back - - - - - - - RETURN
come back to mind - RECUR, REMEMBER
come before - - - - - - - PRECEDE
come between - - - - - INTERVENE
come closer together - - - CONVERGE
come forth - - - - - EMERGE, ISSUE
come into existence - - - - - ARISE
come into operation - - - - - ENURE
come into view - - APPEAR, EMERGE, LOOM
come out - - - - - EMERGE, ISSUE
come out even - - - - - - - DRAW
come to pass - - TRANSPIRE, BEFALL, HAPPEN
come to perfection - - - - - - RIPEN
come to rest - - - - - LODGE, LIGHT
come short of - - - - - - - MISS
come together - - - CLASH, MEET
come upon - - - - - - - - MEET
comedy - - - - - - - - - FARCE
comely - - - - - - - FAIR, PRETTY
comestible - - - EDIBLE, EATABLE
comet part - - - - - - - - TAIL
comfort - - - EASE, REST, SOLACE, CONSOLE
comfortable - - - - - - - - EASY
comic - - - - - - - FUNNY, DROLL
comic actors in opera - - - BUFFOS
comical - - - - FUNNY, LUDICROUS
comicality - - - - - - - - HUMOR
coming - - - - - - - - ARRIVAL
coming forth - - - - - - EMERGENT
command - - ORDER, BADE, BEHEST, BID, FIAT, BECK, MANDATE, DICTATE, ENJOIN, EDICT
command to a cow - - - - - - SOH
command to a horse - - GEE, WHOA
commander - - - - - LEADER, CHIEF
commemorate - - - - - CELEBRATE
commemoration - - - - - MEMORIAL
commemorative - - - - - MEMORIAL
commemorative disc - - - - - MEDAL
commence - - - - - - OPEN, START
commenced (arch.) - - - - - - GAN
commencement - - BEGINNING, START
commend - - - - - PRAISE, ORDER
comment - - - - - - - - REMARK
comment freely - - - - - - DESCANT
commentator - - - - - - - CRITIC
commerce - - - - - - TRADE, START
commercial - - - - - - MERCANTILE
commercial combination - - - MERGER
commercial dealings - - - - - TRADE
commercial form of iron - - - - STEEL
commercial traveller - - - - SALESMAN
comminuted lava - - - - - - - ASH
commission - - - - - - - - ERRAND
commission (honorary) - - - - BREVET
commit - INTRUST, ENTRUST, CONSIGN
commit depredation - - - - - - PREY
commit to memory - MEMORIZE, LEARN
commit an offense - TRANSGRESS, SIN, ERR
committed theft - - - - - - - STOLE
common - - - - - - - - - USUAL
common fund - - - - - - - - POOL
common gander - - - - - - SOLAN
common (Hawaiian) - - - - - - NOA
common informer - - - - - DELATOR
common level - - - - - - - - PAR

C

common locust - - - - - - CICADA
common people - - DEMOS, POPULACE
common people (pert. to) - PLEBEIAN
common red currant - - - - - RISSEL
common sayings - - - - - - DICTA
common short syllable - - - - MORA
common talk - - - - - - - RUMOR
commonly supposed - - - - PUTATIVE
commonplace - BANAL, TRITE, STALE, USUAL, PROSAIC
commonplace discourse - - - - PROSE
commonplace statement - - BROMIDE
commonwealth - - - - DEMOS, STATE
commotion - - STIR, TODO, NOISE, WELTER, ADO, FRAY
communicate by wire - - - - PHONE
communicating corridors - - PASSAGES
communication - - MESSAGE, WORD
communion cup - - - - - - - - AMA
communion plate - - - - - - PATEN
communion table - - - - - - ALTAR
compact - - TIGHT, SOLID, TERSE, CONDENSE
compact by pounding - - - - - TAMP
compact mass - - - - - - - - WAD
compact in rows - - - - - - SERRY
companion - - - MATE, PLAYMATE, COMRADE, PAL, FRIEND
companionable - - - - - - - MATEY
companionship - - - - - - SOCIETY
company - - - - - - BAND, TROOP
company of females - - - - - - BEVY
company of players - - TEAM, TROUPE
company of seamen - - - - - CREW
comparative - - - - - - RELATIVE
comparative suffix - - - - - - - ER
compare - - - - - LIKEN, CONTRAST
compare critically - - - - - COLLATE
compare with fixed standard - MEASURE
comparison - - - - SIMILE, ANALOGY
compass - - - - - PELORUS, ATTAIN
compassion - - - - - - - - - - PITY
compatible - - - - - - CONSISTENT
compeer - - - - - - - - - - EQUAL
compel - - OBLIGE, FORCE, IMPEL, COERCE, DRIVE
compel attention - - - - - - ARREST
compel forward - - - - - - DRIVE
compel obedience - - - - - ENFORCE
compelled (is) - - - - - - - MUST
compelling - - - - - - - COERCIVE
compendium - - - - - - - - DIGEST
compensate - REDEEM, REQUITE, PAY, REMUNERATE
compensation - - - - FEE, PAYMENT
compensation for loss - - INDEMNITY
compete - - - - - - - - VIE, RACE
competent - - - ABLE, CAPABLE, FIT
competition - - - - - - - CONTEST
competitor - - - - - - - - - RIVAL
compilation - - - - - - - - DIGEST
compile - - - - - - - - - - EDIT
compiler of English word book - ROGET
complacent - - - - - - - - - SMUG
complain - - REPINE, MOAN, GRUNT, GRUMBLE, KICK, WHINE, BEEF, CRAB
complain (slang) - - - - - - BEEF
complaining cry - - - - - - WHINE
complaint - - - - - - - - PROTEST
complement of bolt - - - - - - NUT
complement of a hook - - - - - EYE
complement of a mortise - - - TENON
complement of stars - - - - STRIPES
complete - PLENARY, ENTIRE, FINISH, END, UTTER, PERFECT, FULFILL, TOTAL, WHOLE, EVERY, CAP, INTACT
complete disorder - - - - - - CHAOS
complete electric circuit - - - - LOOP
complete entity - - - - - - INTEGER
complete fullness - - - - - REPLETION
completed - - - - - - - - - OVER
completed (poet.) - - - - - - OER
completely - - - - - - - ALL, QUITE
completely confused - - - - CHAOTIC
completely developed - - - - MATURE
completeness - - - - - - - ENTIRETY
completion - - - - - - ENDING, END
complex - - - ABSTRUSE, INTRICATE
complex device - - - - - APPARATUS
complexion - - - - - - - - - SKIN
compliant - - - - - - WEAK, SUPPLE
complicated - - - - - - INTRICATE
complicated scheme - - - - - - WEB
complicated state of affairs - IMBROGLIO
complication - NODUS, NODE, SNARL
compliment - - - - - - ADULATION
comply - - - ADAPT, OBEY, ACCEDE, CONFORM
comply with the occasion - TEMPORIZE
component - - ELEMENT, MATERIAL, INGREDIENT
component of the atom - - - - PROTON
component of molecule - - - - ATOM
comport - - - - - - AGREE, BEHAVE
compose - - WRITE, FRAME, REPOSE
compose poetry - - - - - - POETIZE
composed - - - - - - - - - CALM
composed of - - - - - - - CONSIST
composed of different parts - COMPOUND
composed of grains - - - - GRANULAR
composed of hackled flax - TOWY, TOURY
composed of two elements - - BINARY
composed in verse - - - - - POETIC
composite - - - - - - - INTEGRAL
composition - - THEME, ESSAY, OPUS
composition for nine - - - - - NONET
composition for two - - - - - DUET
composition in verse - - - - - POEM
compositor - - - - - - - - PRINTER
composure - - - - - - - - - POISE
compound of fruit - - - - - - PECTIN
compound of selenium - - - SELENIDE
compound of silica - - - - - GLASS
comprehend - UNDERSTAND, GRASP, REALIZE, SENSE
comprehensible - - - - - EXOTERIC
comprehension - - - - - KEN, GRASP
comprehensive - - WIDE, PANORAMIC
compress - SQUEEZE, WRING, STUPE
compress in bundles - - - - - BALE
comprise - - - - - - - - EMBRACE
compulsion - - - - DURESS, STRESS
compulsory motives - - - - PRESSURES
compunction - - PENITENCE, REMORSE
compute - ADD, RECKON, CALCULATE
con - PERUSE, STUDY, LEARN, AGAINST
concave - - - - - - - - - HOLLOW
conceal - - HIDE, MASK, VEIL, MEW, SECRETE, PALLIATE
concealment - - - - - - - - AMBUSH
concede - GRANT, HIDE, YIELD, ADMIT
concede as true - - - - - - ADMIT
conceited - OPINIONED, VAIN, PRIDED, EGOTISTIC
conceited nature - - - - - - - EGO
conceited person - - EGOTIST, SNOB
conceive - - IDEATE, IMAGINE, THINK
concent - - - - - - - - CONCORD
concentrate - CENTER, FOCUS, MASS, CONVERGE
concentrated - - - - - - INTENSIVE

concept - - NOTION, IDEA, OPINION
conception - - - - - - - - IDEA
concern - - PERTAIN, CARE, MATTER, ANXIETY, INTEREST
concerning - ANENT, RE, ABOUT, ON, OF
conciliate - - PROPITIATE, APPEASE, MOLLIFY
conciliatory - - - - - - - IRENIC
conciliatory theology - - - IRENICS
concise - - - - - - TERSE, CURT
conclave - - - - - - - - MEETING
conclude - - END, DETERMINE, INFER, TERMINATE
concluded - - - - - OVER, ENDED
concluding - - - TERMINAL, FINAL
concluding passage - CODA, EPILOGUE
conclusion - - END, FINIS, UPSHOT
conclusion of speech - - PERORATION
conclusive - - - COGENT, DECISIVE
concoct - - - - - - BREW, HATCH
concord - - - - - - PEACE, UNISON
concrete - - BETON, SPECIFIC, REAL
concur - - - - - - AGREE, ASSENT
condemn - - - - DOOM, CENSURE, DENOUNCE, SENTENCE
condemnation - - - - - - - DOOM
condense - - - - - - - COMPACT
condensed moisture - - - - - DEW
condensed vapor - - - - - - FOG
condescend - - - - - - - DEIGN
condiment - VINEGAR, CURRY, SPICE, MUSTARD, SALT, PEPPER
condiment cruet - - - - - - CASTER
condiment stand - - - - - - CASTER
condition - - - STATE, STATUS, IF, ESTATE, TERM, SITUATION, FETTLE
conditioned barley - - - - - - MALT
condition of payment - - - - TERMS
condition requiring action - EMERGENCY
conditions - - - - - - - - TERMS
condole - - CONSOLE, SYMPATHIZE
condones - - - - - - - PARDONS
conduce - - - - - - - - - TEND
conduct - LEAD, WAGE, DIRECT, RUN, PRESIDE, TRANSACT, DEPORTMENT, DEMEAN, ESCORT, DEPORT
conduct festivities - - - - - M.C.
conduct oneself - - BEHAVE, DEMEAN
conduct of upstarts - - - SNOBBERY
conduct violating the law - - - CRIME
conductor - MAESTRO, LEADER, GUIDER
conductor of electricity - - - METAL
conductor of heat - - - - - METAL
conductor of newspaper - - - EDITOR
conductor's stick - - - - - BATON
conduit - - - - - - - - - MAIN
cone - - - - - - - - - - - PINE
cone bearing trees - - PINES, FIRS, CONIFERAE
cone shaped - - - - - - - CONIC
conepate - - - - - - - - SKUNK
confection of nut kernels - - PRALINE
confectionary - - - CANDY, SWEETS
confectionary flavouring - - VANILLA
confections - - - SWEETS, CANDIES, PRALINES
confederacy - - - - - - - LEAGUE
confederate - - - - - ALLY, BAND
Confederate general - - BRAGG, LEE
Confederate president - - - - DAVIS
Confederate soldier (colloq.) - - REB
confer upon - - ENDOW, DUB, GRANT, BESTOW
confer with an enemy - - - - PARLEY
conference - - - PARLEY, POWWOW
confess - - - - ADMIT, OWN, AVOW
confession - - - - - - - - - CREED
confession of faith - - CREDO, CREED
confide - - INTRUST, ENTRUST, TRUST
confidence - - SECRET, TRUST, FAITH
confident - - - - SURE, RELIANT
confidential - - - SECRET, ESOTERIC
confine - - STINT, PEND, SEAL, PEN, COOP, MEW, CAGE, RESTRICT, TETHER, LIMIT, IMPRISON, INTERN
confirm - - ASSURE, SEAL, RATIFY, ATTEST
confirmed - - - - - - - ARRANT
conflagration - - - - - - - - FIRE
conflict - - WAR, CLASH, CONTEST, BATTLE
conform - - - - - - - - - AGREE
conform to - - - - ADAPT, COMPLY
conform to the shape - - - - - FIT
conformable - - - - - - ADAPTABLE
conformity to customs - - PROPRIETY
confound (Eng.) - - - - - - - STAM
confront - - - - - - FACE, MEET
confuse - BEFOG, FLUSTER, BEMUDDLE, MUDDLE, DISTRACT, ABASH, OBFUSCATE, BEMUSE
confuse utterly - - - - - BEDEVIL
confused - - - - - - - - CHAOTIC
confused jumble - - - - - - MESS
confused language - - - - JARGON
confused murmur - - - BIZZ, BUZZ
confused noise - - - - - SPLUTTER
confused view - - - - - - - RIOT
confusion - BOTHER, MESS, TURMOIL
confusion (state of) - MESS, TUMULT, MOIL
confusion of voices - - - - BABEL
congeal - - - - - - - FREEZE, SET
congenial - - - - - - - - BOON
congregate - - MASS, MEET, SWARM, ASSEMBLE
congregation (eccl.) - - - SYNAXIS
conic section - - PARABOLA, ELLIPSE
conical roll of thread - - - - - COP
conical tent - - - - - - - TEEPEE
conifer - - - - - - - - FIR, PINE
coniferous tree - - YEW, CEDAR, FIR, PINE
conjecture - OPINE, GUESS, IMAGINE, WEEN, SPECULATE
conjoint - - - - - - ASSOCIATED
conjuration - - - - - NECROMANCY
conjurer - - - - - - - - - MAGE
conjurer's rod - - - - - - WAND
Conlaech's mother - - - - AOIFE
connect - - - - - UNITE, JOIN
connect as links - - - - CATENATE
connect systematically - - CORRELATE
connected - - - - - - COHERENT
connected sequence - - - - SERIES
connected with - - - - - - - OF
connecting body of water - - - STRAIT
connecting link - - - LIAISON, BOND
connecting part - - - - - - - LINK
connecting pipe - - - - - - - TEE
connection - RELATION, LINK, NEXUS
connection from stove to chimney - - STOVEPIPE
connective - - - - - - AND, THAT
connective tissue - - - - TENDON
connive at - - - - - - - - ABET
connoisseur - - - - - - - - JUDGE
connoisseur of food - - - EPICURE
connotation - - - - - - - INTENT

C

connote - - - - - - - PREDICATE
connubial - - - - - - - MARITAL
conquer - MASTER, DEFEAT, OVERCOME, TAME, BEAT, SUBJUGATE
conqueror - - - - - - VICTOR, HERO
Conqueror (the) - - - - - WILLIAM
conquest - - - - - - - - VICTORY
consanguinity - - - - - - KINDRED
conscious (be) - - - - - - - AWARE
consciousness - - - - - - - SENSE
conscript - - - - - - - - DRAFT
consecrate - BLESS, DEVOTE, DEDICATE
consecrated person - - - - - - SAINT
consent - AGREE, ASSENT, APPROVAL, PERMISSION
consequence - - - - - END, RESULT
consequence (of) - - - - - - MATTER
consequent - - - - - - ATTENDANT
consequently - - - SO, HENCE, THUS
conservative - - - - - - - - - TORY
conserve - - - - - - - - - - SAVE
consider - - - RATE, PONDER, DEEM, REGARD, OPINE, ESTEEM, JUDGE, REVIEW, THINK
consider one's own interests - SELFISH
considerable number - SEVERAL, MUCH
considerate - - - - THOUGHTFUL
consideration - - - REASON, PRICE, ATTENTION, REGARD
considered as one - - - CORPORATE
consign - - - RELEGATE, COMMIT
consigned to the scrap heap - RELEGATED
consistency - - - - - - - - BODY
consistent - - - - - - - UNIFORM
consisting of large particles - COARSE
console - SOLACE, COMFORT, CONDOLE
consolidate - - - - - - UNITE, KNIT
consolidated annuity - - - - CONSOL
conspicuous - - - - - - - SALIENT
conspicuous position - - LIMELIGHT
conspiracy - - - - - - PLOT, CABAL
conspire - - PLOT, SCHEME, COLLUDE
constancy - - - - - - - FIDELITY
constant - - CHANGELESS, INVARIANT
constant desire (slang) - - - - ITCH
constant quantity in equation - - - PARAMETER
constantly - - - - - - - - EVER
constantly (poet.) - - - - - - - EER
constellation - - ARIES, LEO, BOOTES, ARA, RAM, ORION, URSA, GEMINA, ARGO, LYRA, DIPPER, DRACO, SIRIUS
constellation on equator - - - ORION
constellation (southern) - - - ARGO, MENSA, ARA, GRUS, ERIDANUS, LEPUS
consternation - - - TERROR, DISMAY
constituent - - - - ELEMENT, PART
constituent of earth's crust - - SILICA
constituent parts - - - - ELEMENTS
constrain - ASTRICT, MANACLE, FORCE, TIE, OBLIGE, IMPEL
constraint - - - - - - - DURESS
constrict - - - - - - - - CRAMP
constrictor - - - - - - - - - BOA
construct - - - BUILD, ERECT, REAR
construct anew - - - - - REBUILD
construe - - TRANSLATE, INTERPRET
consume - - - - - - EAT, DEVOUR
consumer - - - - - - EATER, USER
consummate - - - - END, PERFECT
consummation - - - - - - - END
contact - - - - - - - - - TOUCH
contagion - - - - - - - MIASMA
contagious matter of disease - VIRUS
contain - - - - - HOLD, EMBRACE
contained in oil - - - - - OLEIC
container - - CASE, PAIL, BASKET, CRATE, POT, BOX, HOLDER, URN, SACK, TUB, VAT, CAN
container for documents - - HANAPER
container to mix drinks - - - SHAKER
container with perforated top - SHAKER
containing all possible - - - - FULL
containing iron - - - - - - FERRIC
containing a letter - - - ENVELOPE
containing local allusions - - TOPICAL
containing lumps - - - - - NODULAR
containing maxims - - - - - GNOMIC
containing metallic element - YTTRIC
containing nothing - - - - - EMPTY
containing salt - - - - - - SALINE
contaminate - - - - - DEFILE, TAINT
contaminator - - - - - - - VITIATOR
contemn - - - - - - - - - - SCORN
contemner - - - - - - - - DESPISER
contemplate - - MEDITATE, PONDER
contemptible - - - CHEAP, MEAN, DESPICABLE, BASE
contemptuous - - - - - - - SNEERING
contemptuous (slang) - - - - SNOOTY
contend - - - VIE, COPE, STRIVE, MAINTAIN, MILITATE, ASSERT
contend with - - - - - - - - - DEAL
contended in - - - - - - - - RACED
content - - - - - - FAIN, SATISFY
contented - - - SATISFIED, PLEASED
contention - - - - - - - - STRIFE
contents of an atlas - - - - - - MAP
contest - - - GAME, DISPUTE, RACE, CONFLICT, VIE, ARGUE, STRIFE, BOUT, STRUGGLE
contest judges - - - - - - - JURY
contest law - - - DERAIGN, LITIGATE
contiguous - - - - - - - - - NEAR
continent - - - - - - - - MAINLAND
continental inhabitant - - - - ASIAN
contingency - - - - - EVENT, CASE
contingent - - - - - - DEPENDENT
continual - - - INCESSANT, ENDLESS
continually (poet.) - - - ALWAY, EER
continuation - - - - - - - - SEQUEL
continue - - LAST, RESUME, REMAIN, PERSIST, PROCEED
continued knocking - - - - RATATAT
continued pain - - - - - - - ACHE
continuing for a long time - CHRONIC
continuous drumming - - - TATTOO
continuous outcry - - - - CLAMOR
continuous rolling noise - - RUMBLE
contorted - - WRY, WARPED, TWIST
contour - - SHAPE, LINE, OUTLINE
contract - - - - NARROW, SHRINK, AGREEMENT, KNIT, LEASE, COVENANT, INCUR
contract as the brow - - - - KNIT
contract muscles - - - - - - SPASM
contract for services of - - - - HIRE
contract the shoulders - - - SHRUG
contracted strait - - - - - - GUT
contraction - - - - - - - - - TIS
contradict - NEGATE, BELIE, REBUT, DENY
contradictory statement - - PARADOX
contralto - - - - - - - - - ALTO
contrary - - - - - - - - REVERSE
contrary to rules - - - - - - FOUL
contrary to sound reasoning - ILLOGICAL
contrast - - - - - - - - COMPARE
contribute - REDOUND, RENDER, TEND
contribute to common fund - - POOL
contribution - - - - - - - - SCOT
contrite - - - - PENITENT, SORRY,

REPENTANT, SORROWFUL
contrition - - - - - - - PENITENCE
contrivance - - - - DEVICE, ENGINE
contrivance to wash ore - - - - DOLLY
contrive - DEVISE, INVENT, MANAGE, PLAN, WEAVE
control - REIN, DOMINATE, GOVERN, STEER, MANAGE, DEMEAN
controversial - POLEMIC, POLEMICAL, ERISTICAL, ARGUMENTAL, DISPUTATIVE
controversy - - - - - ALTERCATION
contumely - - - - - - RUDENESS
contuse - - - - - - - - BRUISE
contusion - - - - - - - - BRUISE
conundrum - - - - - - - RIDDLE
convene - - - - - - - MEET, SIT
convenient - - - - - - - - HANDY
conventional - - - - - - - FORMAL
conversant - - - - - - - VERSED
conversation - - SPEECH, TALK, CHAT
converse - - - - - - - TALK, CHAT
conversion to steel - - - ACIERATION
convert - - - CHANGE, PROSELYTE, TRANSMUTE
convex - - - - - - - - GIBBOUS
convex molding - - OVOLO, BOLTEL, TORUS, REED
convey - - SELL, IMPART, REMOVE, BRING, RIDE, BEAR, CARRY, MOVE, TRANSFER, TRANSPORT
convey beyond jurisdiction (law) - ELOIN
convey for consideration - - - SELL
convey by deed - - - - - - REMISE
conveyance - TRANSIT, CAR, VEHICLE
conveyance charge - - - - - - FARE
conveyance for dead - - - - HEARSE
conveyer - - - - - - - - MOVER
conviction - - - - - - - - TENET
convince - - - - - - - - ASSURE
convincing - - - - - - - COGENT
convoke - - - - - - - ASSEMBLE
convoy - - - - - - - - - ESCORT
convulsion - - - - - - SPASM, FIT
convulsive cry - - - - - - - - SOB
convulsive sigh - - - - - - - SOB
cony of Scriptures - - - - - DAMAN
cook - - - - - - - - STEW, CHEF
cook in certain manner - - - SAUTE
cook's delight - - - - - - RECIPES
cook in hot oil - - - - - - - FRY
cook in oven - - - - - - - ROAST
cook with dry heat - - - - - ROAST
cooked sausage filled rolls - RISSOLES
cooking place - - - - - - - RANGE
cooking term - - - - - - - RISSOLE
cooking apparatus - - - - - - STOVE
cooking compound - - - - - - LARD
cooking direction - - CREAM, MINCE, SCALD, DICE, BROWN
cooking formula - - - - - - RECIPE
cooking herb - - - - - - - - CHIVE
cooking pot - - - - - - - - - OLLA
cooking soda - - - - - - SALERATUS
cooking stove - - - - - ETNA, RANGE
cooky - - - - - - - - - - - SNAP
cool - - - ICE, SOBER, CALM, FAN
cooling device - - FAN, REFRIGERANT
coon - - - - - - - - - - RACCOON
coop up - - - PENT, PEN, CORRAL, CONFINE
cooperate secretly - - - - - CONNIVE
coordinate - - - - - - - - - EQUAL
coordinate article - - - - - - - OR
cop - - - - - - - - - - - - HEAD
cope - - - - - - - - - CONTEND
copier - - - - - - - - - - IMITATOR
copious - - - - - - - - ABUNDANT
copper - - - - - C.U., CENT, PENNY
copper coins - - - - - CENTS, PENCE
copper iron sulfide - - - - - BORNITE
copper money - - - - - - - - - AES
coppice - - - - - - - - - - - COPSE
copse - - - - - - COPPICE, THICKET
copy - IMITATE, APE, MIMIC, REPLICA, IMAGE, TRANSCRIBE
copying (pert. to) - - - - IMITATIONAL
copyist (pert. to) - - - - - CLERICAL
copyright - - - - - - - - - PATENT
coquette - - - - - - - - - - - FLIRT
coquettish - - - - - - - - - - - COY
coquettish glance - - - - - - OGLE
coral islands - - ATOLLS, KEYS, ATOLL
cord - - LINE, TWINE, STRING, ROPE
cord to fasten - - - - - - - - LACE
cordage fiber - - - - - - - - COIR
corded cloth - - - - - REP, POPLIN
Cordelia and Regan's father - - LEAR
cordial - - - - - - - - - ANISETTE
core - - - HEART, GIST, PITH, AME
cork - - - - - - STOPPER, SUBERIC
corkwood - - - - - - - - - - BALSA
corn - - - - - - - PICKLE, CALLUS
corn bread - - - - - - - - - - PONE
corn lily - - - - - - - - - - - IXIA
corner - ANGLE, NOOK, TREE, NICHE, COIGN, IN
corner of a snail - - - - - - - CLEW
cornered - - - - - - - - - - TREED
Cornish prefix signifying town - - TRE
cornmeal bread - - - - - - - - PONE
cornmeal mush - - - - - - - ATOLE
cornucopia - - - - - - - - - HORN
Cornwall fish basket - - - - - CAWL
corolla leaf - - - - - - - - - PETAL
coronet - - - - - - - TIARA, CROWN
corporally - - - - - - - - ANIMALLY
corporeal - - - - - - - - MATERIAL
corpulent - - - - - - - FAT, OBESE
correct - - AMEND, EMEND, RIGHT, ACCURATE, FIT, O.K.
correct (colloq.) - - - - - - - - O.K.
correct one's ways - - - - - REFORM
corrected proofs - - - - - REVISIONS
correction - - - - - - EMENDATION
correlative - - - - - - NOR, EITHER
correspond - - - TALLY, COINCIDE, COMMUNICATE
correspond to - - - - - - - PARALLEL
corridor - - - - - - - - - - - HALL
corrode - - BITE, GNAW, RUSH, EAT
corroded - - - - ATE, EATEN, ERODED, RUSTED
corrosion - - - - - - EROSION, RUST
corrosion in metal work - - - PITTING
corrosive - - - - - - - - - - ACRID
corrupt - TAINT, DEGRADE, POISON, DEPRAVE, PERVERT, EVIL, ATTAINT
corrupt officials - - - - - GRAFTERS
corsair - - - - - - PIRATE, PRIVATEER
cortical - - - - - - - - - EXTERNAL
corundum - - - - - - - - - - EMERY
corvine bird - - CROW, RAVEN, ROOK
Cosam's son - - - - - - - - - - ADDI
cosmetic - - - - - - - PAINT, ROUGE
Cossack chief - - - - - - - ATAMAN
cosset - - - - FONDLE, PET, PAMPER
cost - EXPENSE, CHARGE, PRICE, RATE
Costa Rican seaport - - - - - - LIMON
costly - - - - DEAR, EXPENSIVE, HIGH, VALUABLE
costume - - - - - - - ATTIRE, GETUP
cote - - - - - - - - - - - - - SHED

C

coterie - - - - - - - CLIQUE, SET
cottage - - - - - - - - - VILLA
cottager - - - - - - - - COTTER
cotton drilling - - - - - - - DENIM
cotton fabric - PERCALE, DENIM, LENO, PIMA, SURAT, SILESIA, CALICO, SATINET, KHAKI, NAINSOOK, MUSLIN, SCRIM, CRETONNE, GALATEA, LAWN, GINGHAM
cotton gauze - - - - - - - - LENO
cotton seed capsule - - - - - - BOLL
cotton seeding machine - - - - - GIN
couch - - - - BED, DIVAN, SOFA
couch to convey wounded - - - LITTER
couched - - - - - - - - - - ABED
cougar - - - - - - - - - - PUMA
cough to attract attention - - AHEM
counsel - - - - - - - - - ADVISE
counsel (Scot.) - - - - - - - REDE
count - - - - - - - - NUMBER
count over - - - - - - ENUMERATE
countenance - - ABET, FACE, VISAGE
counterfeit - PRETEND, BASE, SHAM, SIMULATE, FAKE, FORGE
counterpart - - - PARALLEL, TWIN
counterweight - - - - - - - TARE
countess - - - - - - - - - LADY
countrified - - - - - - - - RURAL
country - - - LAND, NATION, SOIL
country between India and Tibet - NEPAL
country gallant - - - - - - SWAIN
country home - - - - - - - MANOR
country (of the) - - - - - - RURAL
county - - - - - - - - - - SHIRE
county officer - - - - - - SHERIFF
coup - - - - - - - - - - UPSET
couple - - PAIR, YOKE, TWO, LINK
coupled - - - - - - - - - GEMEL
courage - - VALOR, NERVE, METTLE, DARES, HEART, GRIT, SAND
courage (slang) - - - - - - - SAND
courageous - - - - - BOLD, BRAVE
course - WAY, TRAIL, ROUTE, CAREER, PATH, DIRECTION, TENOR, ROAD
course of action - - TREND, ROUTINE, HABIT
course of eating - - - - - - - DIET
course of operation - - - - - - RUN
course of procedure - - - - PROCESS
course of public life - - - - CAREER
course of running water - - - STREAM
course of travel - - - - - - ROUTE
court - - - WOO, SOLICIT, PATIO
court crier - - - - - - - - BEADLE
court crier's call - - - OYEZ or OYES
court hearings - - - - - - - OYERS
court of appeals - - - - - APPELLATE
court of justice - - - - - - - BAR
court officer - - - - - - - CRIER
court order - - - WRIT, MANDAMUS
court sessions - - - - - - ASSIZES
court woman - - - - - - COURTESAN
courteous - - - - - - - - - POLITE
courtly - - - - - - - - - - AULIC
courtship - - - - - - - - - - SUIT
courtyard - - - - - - - PATIO, AREA
covenant - - PROMISE, TESTAMENT, BOND, CONTRACT
cover - SHEATHE, LID, SCREEN, CAP, COAT, TREE, PRETEXT, ENVELOP, SHELTER, HIDE
cover compactly - - - - - - - PAVE
cover for the face - - - - - - MASK
cover the inside - - - - - - - LINE
cover superficially - - - - - VENEER
cover the top - - - - - - - - CAP
cover the top wall - - - - - - CEIL
cover with asphalt - - - - - - PAVE
cover with cloth - - - - - - DRAPE
cover with dots - - BEDOT, STIPPLE
cover with excuses - - - - - PALLIATE
cover with fabric - - - - - UPHOLSTER
cover with first plain coat - - PRIME
cover with gold - PLATE, GILD, ENGILD
cover with hard coat - - - - INCRUST
cover with hard surface - - - - PAVE
cover with jewels - - - - - - BEGEM
cover with something solid - - INCASE
cover with water - - - - - - FLOOD
covered cloister - - - - - - - STOA
covered colonade - - - - - - STOA
covered garden - - - - - HOTHOUSE
covered part of locomotive - - - CAB
covered stall - - - - - - - BOOTH
covered vehicle - - - - - - - VAN
covered wagon - - - - - - - - VAN
covered walk - - - - - - - ARCADE
covered with asphalt - - - - - PAVE
covered with cloth - - - - - DRAPE
covered with hair - - - - - - PILAR
covered with hoarfrost - - RIME, RIMY
covered with low green plants - MOSSY
covered with small figures - - - SEME
covered with sward - - - - - SODDY
covered with turf - - - - - GRASSED
covered with vine - - - - - - IVIED
covered with water - - - - - AWASH
covered with white of eggs - GLAIREOUS
covering - - - - - - - - - CANOPY
covering for ankle instep - - GAITER
covering of beaches - - - - - SANDS
covering of corn - - - - - - HUSK
covering for face - - - - - - MASK
covering in front - - - - - - FACING
covering of head - - - - - - SCALP
covering of high mountains - - SNOW
covering (outer) - - - - - - - SHELL
covering of the teeth - - - DENTINE
covering of throat - - - - - - BARB
covering of watch dial - - - CRYSTAL
covert - THICKET, SHELTERED, SECRET, HIDDEN
covet - DESIRE, ENVY, CRAVE, WISH
covetous person - - - - - - MISER
covetousness - - - - - - AVARICE
cow - - DAUNT, OVERAWE, CATTLE, KINE
cow barn - - - - - - - - - BYRE
cow headed deity - - - - - - - ISIS
cow (kind) - - - - - - - - JERSEY
cow's plaint - - - - - - - - MOO
cow shed - - - - - - - - - BYRE
coward - - - RECREANT, CRAVEN, DASTARD, SNEAK, POLTROON
cowardly - - - CRAVEN, DASTARDLY
cowardly carnivore - - - - - HYENA
cowardly fellow - - - - - - SNEAK
cowardly spotted animal - - - HYENA
cowboys - - - - - - - - VAQUEROS
cower - - - CRINGE, SHRINK, QUAIL
cowfish - - - - - - - - - - TORO
cowhide - - - - - - - - - LEATHER
coworker - - - - - - - - - - ALLY
coxa - - - - - - - - - - - - HIP
coy - - - SHY, DEMURE, RESERVED, BASHFUL
cozenage - - - - - - - - - DECEIT
cozy - - - - - - - - - - - SNUG
cozy retreat - - - - - - - - NEST
crab (kind) - - - RACER, SHELLFISH
crabbedness - - - - - - ACRIMONY
crack - - - SNAP, FISSURE, CHAP

crackbrained - - - - - - - NUTTY
crack in glacier - - - - - CREVASSE
crack and roughen - - - - - - CHAP
crackle - - - - - SNAP, CREPITATE
craft - ART, TRADE, VESSEL, CUNNING
craftsman in metals - - - - - SMITH
crafty - - - - - - - SLY, ASTUTE
crafty device - - - - - - ARTIFICE
crafty mammal - - - - - - - FOX
crag - - - - - - - - CLIFF, TOR
craggy hill - - - - - - - - - TOR
cram - - - - - WAD, STUFF, CROWD
cramp - RESTRAIN, CONSTRICT, HINDER
craned - - - - - - - - - YEARNED
cranium - - - - - - - - - SKULL
cranny - - - - - - - - - FISSURE
crash - - - - - - - - - - SMASH
crass - - STUPID, OBTUSE, GROSS, DENSE, COARSE
crate - - - - - - - - - - - BOX
cravat - - - - - - - - TIE, ASCOT
crave - SEEK, COVET, DESIRE, LONG, ENTREAT
craven - - - - - COWARD, COWARDLY
craving - - YEN, DESIRING, APPETITE, THIRST, BULIMIA
craw - - - - - - - - - CROP, MAW
crawl along - - - - SLITHER, CREEP
crawling animal - - REPTILE, WORM
crayon - - - - - - - CHALK, PENCIL
crayon picture - - - - - - - PASTEL
craze - MANIA, FAD, DERANGE, FUROR, MADDEN
crazed - - - - DERANGED, MADDENED
crazy - - - - - DAFT, LOCO, LOONY, DEMENTED, DAFFY
crazy person - - - - - - - MANIAC
cream (the) - - - - - - - - - ELITE
creamy white substance - - - - IVORY
crease - - - - WRINKLE, FOLD, RUGA
create - ORIGINATE, GENERATE, MAKE, FORM, PRODUCE, DEVISE
creation - NATURE, UNIVERSE, GENESIS
creative - - - - - - - - PRODUCTIVE
creative force - - - - - - - - NATURE
creator - - - - - - - - - - AUTHOR
creature - - - - - - - - - ANIMAL
credence - - - - - - - - - - BELIEF
credible - - - - - - - - - - LIKELY
credit - - - - TRUST, HONOUR, BELIEVE
creditor - - - - - - - - - - DEBTEE
credo - - - - - - - - CREED, BELIEF
creed - - - - - - - - CREDO, TENET
creek - RIA, STREAM, BAYOU, RIVULET, COVE
creep - - - - - - - - - - - CRAWL
creep away - - - - - - - - - SLINK
creeping - - - - - - - - - - CRAWL
creeping plant - - IPECAC, VINE, LIANA
crenate - - - - - - - - - NOTCHED
crescent shaped - - - - LUNATE, LUNE
crescent shaped marking - - - - LUNULE
crest - - PEAK, TOP, CROWN, PLUME, TUFT, SUMMIT
crest of cock - - - - - - - - - COMB
crest (dial.) - - - - - - - - - - COP
crest of a wave - - - - - - - - COMB
Crete mountain - - - - - - - ADA, IDA
crevice - - - - - - - - - INTERSTICE
crevice in rock - - - - - - - - LODE
crew - - - - - - - - - GANG, BAND
crib for storage - - - - - - - - BIN
cribbage pin - - - - - - - - - - PEG
cribbage score - - - - - - - - - PEG
cribbage term - - - - - - - - - NOB
cricket player - - - - - - - - TWISTER
cricket position - - - - - - - - SLIP
cricket side - - - - - - - - - ELEVEN
cricket sound - - - - - - - - - CHIRP
crime - - - - - - FELONY, INIQUITY
Crimea river - - - - - - - - - - ALMA
criminal - FELON, DESPERADO, CULPRIT
criminal judiciary magistrate - RECORDER
crimp - - - - - - - WRINKLE, CRINKLE
crimson - - - - - - - - - - - - RED
cringe - - - - COWER, GROVEL, FAWN
crinkle - - CRUMPLE, CRIMP, WRINKLE
crinkled material - - - - - - - CREPE
cripple - - - - - - - - - MAIM, LAME
crisp - - - - - - - - - BRITTLE, CURT
crisp biscuit - - - - - - - - CRACKER
crisp cookie - - - - - - - - - - SNAP
criterion - - - - - - TEST, STANDARD
critic - - - - - - - CENSOR, CAVILER
critical - - - - - - - - - - - - ACUTE
critical moment - - - - - - - - CRISIS
critical remark - - - - - - - COMMENT
criticize mercilessly - - - - - - FLAY
criticize officially - - - - - - CENSOR
criticize severely - - - - - - - SCORE
criticize severely (colloq.) - ROAST, PAN, RAP
critique - - - - - - - - - - - REVIEW
croak - - - - - - - - - - - GRUMBLE
Croatian - - - - - - - - - - - CROAT
crochet - - - - - - - - - - - - KINK
crochet stitch - - - - - - TRICOT, LOOP
crock - - - - - - - - - - - - - SMUT
crocodile - - - - - - - MUGGER, GOA
croft (arch.) - - - - - - - - - GARTH
crone - - - - - - - - - - - - - HAG
crony - - PAL, BUDDY, FRIEND, CHUM
crook - - - - - - - - - - CURVE, BEND
crook by straining - - - - - - - BEND
crooked - - AWRY, WRY, BENT, ASKEW
crooked (Scot.) - - - - - - - - - AGEE
crop - - - - SPROUT, CRAW, PRODUCE
croquet (form of) - - - - - - ROQUE
croquet wicket - - - - - - - - - ARCH
cross - TRAVERSE, ROOD, ANGRY, SPAN, INTERSECT, SURLY, PEEVISH
cross question (Scot.) - - - - - TARGE
cross rib in vaulting - - - - - LIERNE
cross shaped - - - - - - - CRUCIATE
cross stroke - - - - - - - - - - SERIF
cross timber in shipbuilding - - - SPALE
cross by wading - - - - - - - - FORD
crossbeam - - - - - - - - - - TRAVE
crossbreed - - - - - - - - - - HYBRID
crosscountry runner - - - - - HARRIER
crosscut logging saw - - - - - BRIAR
crotchety person - - - - - - - CRANK
crow - - EXULT, RAVEN, BRAG, ROOK
crow cry - - - - - - - - - - - - CAW
crowbar - - - - - - - - - - - LEVER
crowd - - MOB, GATHERING, HORDE, SERRY, PRESS, THRONG, CRAM, JAM, PACK, HERD
crowd together - - PACK, HERD, HORDE
crowfoot flower - - ANEMONE, PEONY
crowlike bird - - ORIOLE, ROOK, DAW, JACKDAW, RAVEN
crown - - - - TIARA, CREST, DIADEM, CORONET, CAP, PATE
crown (of a) - - - - - - - CORONARY
crown of the head - - - - - - - PATE
crucial - - - - - - - - - - - SEVERE
crucial time - - - - - - - - - CRISIS
crucifix - - - - - - - - - - - ROOD
crude - - - - - - - - - RAW, CRASS
crude dwelling - - - - - - - - - HUT
crude metal - - - - - - - - - - ORE

C

crude metal casting - - - - - - - PIG
crude native platinum - - - - PLATINA
crude cream of tartar - - - - - ARGOL
cruel - - - PITILESS, ORGISH, MEAN
cruel person - - - - - - - - BEAST
cruet - - - - - - - - - - CASTER
cruise - - - - - - - - - - - SAIL
crumple - - - - - - - - - - MUSS
crus - - - - - - - - SHANK, LEG
crush - - - - - - - MASH, GRIND
crush (colloq.) - - - - - - SCRUNCH
crush under foot - - - - - - TRAMPLE
crush with teeth - - - - - - - BITE
crushing - - - - - - - - - - MOLAR
crust of bread - - - - - - - - HEEL
crustacean - CRAB, PRAWN, LOBSTER, ISOPOD
crustacean's covering - - - - - SHELL
cry - WEEP, MOAN, SNIVEL, SOB, HUE, SHOUT, WAIL
cry of cat - - - - - - - - - - MEW
cry of disapproval - - - CATCALL, BOO
cry of distress - - - - - - - - MOAN
cry joyfully - - - EXCLAIM, SHOUT
cry loudly - - - - - - - ROAR, WAIL
cry out - - - - - - EXCLAIM, CALL
cry of rook - - - - - - - - - - CAW
cry of sorrow - - - - - - - - AY, ALAS
cry weakly - - - - - - - - - SNIVEL
cry of wild goose - - - - - - CRONK
crypt - - - - - - - - - - - VAULT
cryptic - - - - - - - - - - OCCULT
cryptogamous plant - - - - - - MOSS
cryptogamous plant seed - - - SPORE
crystal - - - - - - - - - - CLEAR
crystal gazer - - - - - - - - SEER
crystalized limestone - - - - MARBLE
crystalized rain - - - - - - - SNOW
crystalline compound - - - ELATERIN, ALANINE, PARILLIN
crystalline metallic element - - - ZINC
crystalline mineral - - SPAR, SPINELLE
crystalline salt - - - BORAX, NITER
crystalline sodium carbonate - - TRONA
Cuban capital - - - - - - - HAVANA
Cuban measure - - - - - - - - TAREA
Cuban tobacco - - - - - - - - CAPA
cube - - - - - - - - - DIE, DICE
cube in mosaic - - - - - - TESSERA
cube root of eight - - - - - - - TWO
cubic capacity of merchant vessels TONNAGE
cubic content - - - - - - - VOLUME
cubic decimeter - - - - - - - LITER
cubic measure - - - - - - - - CORD
cubic meter - - - - - - - - STERE
cubical contents - - - - - - CUBAGE
Cuchullin's wife - - - - - - - EMER
cuckoo - - - - - - - - - - - ANI
cuckoopint - - - - - - - - - ARUM
cucumber - - - - - - - - GHERKIN
cud - - - - - - - - - - - RUMEN
cud chewing animal - - - - RUMINANT
cuddle - - - - - - NESTLE, SNUGGLE
cudgel - - - - - - BAT, STAFF, DRUB
cue - - - - - - - - - HINT, BRAID
cuirass - - - - - - - - - - LORICA
culinary art - - - - - - - COOKERY
cull - - - - - SIFT, SORT, ASSORT
culminate - - - - - - - - - - END
culminating point - - - - - - ZENITH
culmination - - CLIMAX, ACME, END, ZENITH
culpability - - - - - - - - - GUILT
culpable - - - - - - - - - GUILTY
culprit - - - - - - - - - CRIMINAL
cult - - - - - - - - - - - - SECT
cultivate - TILL, FARM, GARDEN, FOSTER, HOE
cultivated ground - - - - - - ARADA
cultivated plot - - - - - - GARDEN
cultivating implement - HOE, HARROW, RAKE
cultivator - - - HOE, TILLER, FARMER, GROWER
culture - - - - - - - - REFINEMENT
culture media - - - - - - - AGAR
cultured man - - - - - - GENTLEMAN
cultured woman - - - - - - - - LADY
cumulative wager - - - - - - PARLAY
cuneiform - - - - - - - - - CUNEAL
cunning - SLY, CUTE, CRAFT, ASTUTE, FOXY
cunning person - - - - - - - - FOX
cunning trick - - - - - - - DODGE
cup - - - - - - - - - - - - - MUG
Cupid - - - - - - - - EROS, AMOR
Cupid's first name - - - - - - DAN
Cupid's lover - - - - - - - PSYCHE
cupidity - - - - - - AVARICE, GREED
cuplike spoon - - - - - - - - LADLE
cupola - - - - - - - - DOME, TURRET
cur (var.) - - - - - - - - - - MUT
curate - - - - - - - - CLERGYMAN
curative - - - - - - - - MEDICINAL
curator - - - - - - - - OVERSEER
curb - REPRESS, RESTRAIN, REIN, CHECK
curdle - - - - - - - - - COAGULATE
cure - - HEAL, VULCANIZE, REMEDY, PRESERVE
cure-all - - - - - - PANACEA, ELIXIR
curious (be) - - - - - - - WONDER
curious person - - - - - - - - - PRY
curl - - TRESS, RINGLET, COIL, TWINE
curl around - - - - - - - - - TWINE
curled up at the edges - - CRISPATED
curling mark - - - - - - - - - - TEE
currency - - - - - - - - - - MONEY
current - TIDE, STREAM, RIFE, TORRENT
current of air - - - - - - - - DRAFT
current (comb. form) - - - - - RHEO
current flowing in - - - - - - INTAKE
currently - - - - - - - - - - - NOW
currier - - - - - - - - - - CARDER
curry as a horse - - - - - - - DRESS
currying instrument - - - - - - CARD
curse - - - - OATH, BAN, ANATHEMA
curt - SHORT, BRIEF, CONCISE, BRUSK, CRISP
curtail - - - - - - SHORTEN, CLIP
curtain - - - - - - - DRAPE, VEIL
curtain of fire - - - - - - BARRAGE
curtain material - - - - - - - SCRIM
curtal - - - - - - - - - - - - BRIEF
curve - ARC, BEND, WIND, ARCH, LOOP, BOW
curve parallel to an ellipse - - TOROID
curve sharply - - - - - - - - - VEER
curved - - - - - - - - - - - - BENT
curved structure - - - - - - - ARCH
curved support - - - - - - - - - RIB
curved timber in a ship's frame - - - STEMSON
cushat - - - - - - - - - - - - DOVE
cushion - - - - - - - - - PAD, MAT
cushioned seat - - - - - - - - DIVAN
cusp - - - - - - - - - POINT, PEAK
custom - - USAGE, HABIT, WONT, USE, MANNER
customary - HABITUAL, WONTED, USUAL
customary requirement - - FORMALITY
cut - - CLIP, BOB, SNIP, HEW, SLASH,

GASH, NIP, INCISION, SHEAR, SUNDER, MOW, LOP, SLIT, SAW, CARVE, CLEAVE, LANCE, FELL, INCISE, SHORTEN, SLICE, SEVER, REAP, SNEE, SAWED, CLEFT, MINCE
cut across - - - - - - - INTERSECT
cut after terms with snick - - - SNEE
cut asunder - - - - - - - - SEVER
cut away - - - - - - - - - - LOP
cut deeply - - - - - - - - GASH
cut down - - - - MOW, FELL, REAP
cut expenses - - - - - - - RETRENCH
cut fine - - - - - - - - - - MINCE
cut gem part - - - - - - - - FACET
cut of hair - - - - - - - - - BOB
cut from larger piece - - - - - SLICE
cut lengthwise - - - - SLIT, SLITTED
cut lumber - - - - - - - - - SAW
cut meat - - - - - - - - - CARVE
cut of meat - - LOIN, RUMP, STEAK, SPARERIB
cut off - - - SNIP, NIP, LOP, ELIDE, MUTILATE
cut closely - - - - - - - - SHAVE
cut short - LOP, ELIDE, SNIP, SNIPPED
cut at one stroke - - - - - - SNIP
cut out - - - - - - - ELIDE, EXCIDE
cut at random - - - - - - - SLASH
cut roughly - - - - - - - - HACK
cut short - - - - - - - BOB, CLIP
cut in small cubes - - - - - - DICE
cut in small pieces - MINCE, DICE, HASH
cut thin - - - - - - - - - - SLICE
cut in thin slices - - - - - - SHAVE
cut in thin strips - - - - - - SLICE
cut through - - - - - - INTERSECT
cut top from - - - - - - TRUNCATE
cut in two - - - - - - SEVER, BISECT
cut with ax - - - - - - - - - CHOP
cut with knife - - - - - - - CARVE
cut with scissors - - - - - - - SNIP
cut with toothed tool - - - - - SAW
cut wood - - - - - - - - - SAW
cute - - - - - - - - - - CLEVER
cutting implement - - RAZOR, KNIFE, JACKKNIFE, SCISSORS, SHEARS, MOWER
cutting machine - - - MOWER, SLICER
cutting members of a saw - - - TEETH
cutting of plants - - - - - - - SLIP
cutting off of a vowel - - - ELISION
cutting small faces upon - - - FACETED
cutting sound - - - - - - - - SWISH
cutting tool - SLICER, AX, ADZ, ADZE, KNIFE
cutting wit - - - - - - - - SATIRE
cuttlefish - - - - - SEPIA, SPIRULA
cyanogen compound - - - - - NITRILE
Cyclades Islands - SAMOS, DELOS, SYRA, NIO
Cyclops' mother - - - - - - - - GE
cylinder - SPOOL, ROLLER, ROLL, TUBE
cylinder disk - - - - - - - PISTON
cylinder to hold a ship's rope - CAPSTAN
cylindral - - - - - - - - - TERETE
cylindrical and hollow - - - TUBULAR
Cymbeline's daughter - - - IMOGEN
Cymric - - - - - - - - - - WELSH
Cymric language - - - - - - WELSH
Cymric sun god - - - - - - - LLEU
cyprinoid fish - - - - - - - ID, IDE
Cyrano's author - - - - - - ROSTAND
cyst - - - - - - - - - - - WEN
Czar's daughter - - - - - TSAREVNA
Czar's wife - - - - - - - TSARINA
Czech. coin - - - - - - - - HALER
Czech. president - - - - - - BENES

C

D

D

dab - - - - - - - PECK, FLOUNDER
dabble - - - - - - - - - - - MESS
dabbler - - - - - - - - - AMATEUR
Daedalus's son - - - - - - - ICARUS
daffy - - - - - - - - - - FOOLISH
daft - - - - - - - - - - - IDIOTIC
dagger - - - SNEE, DIRK, STILETTO, PONIARD
dagger handle - - - - - - - - HILT
dagger wound - - - - - - - - STAB
daily - - - - - - - DIURNAL, ADAY
daily fare - - - - - - - - - - DIET
daily food and drink - - - - - FARE
daily record - - - - - - - - DIARY
dainty - - - - - - - - - - - FINE
dairymaid (Scot.) - - - - GOWAN, DEY
dais - - - - - - - - - - - STAGE
daisy (kind) - - - - - - - - OXEYE
daisy (Scot.) - - - - - - - GOWAN
dale - - - - - - - - - GLEN, VALE
dally - - - - - - - - - TRIFLE, TOY
dam - OBSTACLE, MILLPOND, BARRIER, WEIR, RESTRAIN
dam in river - - - - - - - - WEIR
dam up - - - - - - - - - - STEM
damage - LOSS, HURT, MAR, SCATHE, HARM, INJURE, IMPAIR
damaged - - - INJURED, IMPERFECT, IMPAIRED
dame - - - - - - - - - - MATRON
damsel - - - - - - - - - - - GIRL
damp - - - - - - - - MOIST, HUMID
damp and cold - - - - - DANK, RAW
dampen - - WET, DEPRESS, MOISTEN
dampness - - - - - - - - HUMIDITY
damsel - - - - - - - - - - MAIDEN
dance - BALL, FRISK, BALLET, DANDLE
dance (kind) - - - GALOP, JIG, REEL, REDOWA, POLKA, PAVAN
dance like minuet - - - - - - GAVOT
dance (slow) - PAVANE, ADAGIO, MINUET
dance step - - - - - - - - - - PAS
dancing shoes - - - - - - - PUMPS
dandelion peduncle - - - - - SCAPE
dandle - - - - - - - - - - DANCE
dandy - - - - - - DUDE, FOP, NATTY
dandy (English slang) - - - - - TOFF
danger - - PERIL, HARM, HAZARD, RISK
danger signal - - - WARNING, ALARM
dangerous - - - - RISKY, PERILOUS
dangerous to tip - - - - - - CANOE
dangerous woman - - - - - - SIREN
dangerously - - - - - - PERILOUSLY
Danish borough in England - - - BORG
Danish coin - - - - - - ORE, KRONE
Danish composer - - - - - - - GADE
Danish divisions - - - - - - - AMT
Danish island - - - AERO, ALS, FAROE
Danish king - - - - - - - CANUTE
Danish measure - - - - - ALEN, RODE
Danish money - - - - - - - - - ORA
Danish physician - - - - - - - GRAM
Danish weight - - - - - - ESER, LOD
dank - - - - - - - - - - - MOIST
dap - - - - - - - - DIB, DIP, DIBBLE
dapper - - - - - - - - - - SPRUCE
dapple - - - - - - - SPOT, SPOTTING
dappled - - - - - - ROAN, SPOTTED
darb - - - - - - - - - - - - DART
dare (dial.) - - - - - - - - - DAST

D

dared - - - DURST, DEFIED, RISKED, VENTURED, BRAVED
daring - - - FEARLESS, BOLD, BRAVE
daring project - - - - - ENTERPRISE
dark - - DEEP, GLOOMY, UNLIGHTED, DUSKY, EBON
dark coloured - - - - - - - DINGY
dark gray to black rock - - - BASALT
darkened - - - CLOUDED, DEEPENED, BECLOUDED, MURK, OBSCURED, SHADOWED
darkness - - - - - - MURK, GLOOM
darling - - - - - - - - - - DEAR
darn - - - - - - - - - - - - MEND
dart - - FLIT, ARROW, BOLT, SPEAR, BOUND, DARB, BARB, JAVELIN, SHOOT, ROLE
dart (colloq.) - - - - - - - SCOOT
dart forth - - - - - - - - - SPURT
dart suddenly - - - - - - - - DASH
d'Artagnan's friend - ATHOS, ARAMIS
dash - SPIRIT, ELAN, DART, SHATTER, SPRINT
dash against - - - - - - - - LASH
dasher - - - - - - - - - BEATER
dasher of a churn - - - - PLUNGER
dashing - - - - - - - - - SMART
dastard - - - - - - - - COWARD
dastardly - - - - - - - COWARDLY
data - - - - - - - - - - - FACTS
date - - - - - - AGE, APPOINTMENT
date sugar - - - - - - - - - GHOOR
date tree - - - - - - - - - - PALM
dating from birth - - - - - - NATAL
dating machine - - - - - - - DATER
daub - - - - - SMEAR, BLOB, PLASTER
daughter of river god - - - - - IO
daunt - - - - - - - - - - - COW
dauntless - - - - - - - - INTREPID
David Copperfield character - - HEEP, URIAH
David Copperfield's father - - - JESSE
David Copperfield's wife - - - DORA
David's son - - - - - - - SOLOMON
Davis Cup holder - - - AUSTRALIAN
dawdle - - - - - - - POKE, LINGER
dawdler - - - - - - - - - - IDLER
dawn - - - - - DAYBREAK, AURORA
dawn (comb. form) - - - - - - - EO
dawn (pert. to) - - - - - - - EOAN
dawn (poet.) - - - - - - - - MORN
day before - - - - - - - - - - EVE
day lily - - - - - - NIOBES, NIOBE
day (part) - - - - - - - - - - HOUR
day in Roman month - CALENDS, NONES, IDES
daybreak - - - - - - - - DAWN, MORN
daydream - - - - - - - - - REVERIE
days march - - - - - - - - - ETAPE
daze - - - TRANCE, STUN, BEMUSE
dazzle - - - - - - - - - - - GLARE
dazzling light - - - - - - - GLARE
dead - - - - - - EXTINCT, LIFELESS
dead body - - - - - - - - CADAVER
dead flesh - - - - - - - - CARRION
dead person - - - - - - - DECEDENT
deaden - - - - - STUN, BLUNT, MUTE
deadly - LETHAL, FATAL, DESTRUCTIVE
deafen (Scot.) - - - - - - - - DEAVE
deal - - - - - BARGAIN, TRADE, SALE
deal in - - - - - - - - - - - - SELL
deal out - - - - - - - - - - - DOLE
deal with - - HANDLE, TRADE, COPE
dealer - - - - - - - - - - - TRADER
dealer in foodstuffs - - - - - GROCER
dealer in cloth - - - - - - DRAPER
dealer in skins - - - - - - FURRIER
dealer in securities - - - - - BROKER
dear - - BELOVED, DARLING, COSTLY, PRECIOUS, LOVED
dearth - - - - - - - - LACK, FAMINE
death - - - - - - - - - - DECEASE
death notice - - - - - - - - - OBIT
death notice (var.) - - - - - - OBET
debar - - - - PRECLUDE, EXCLUDE
debar temporarily - - - - - SUSPEND
debark - - - - - - - - - - - - LAND
debase - DEMEAN, TRADUCE, DEGRADE, SINK, REDUCE, LOWER, HUMILIATE, DEFILE
debatable - - - - - - - - - - MOOT
debate - - REASON, ARGUE, DISCUSS, DISCUSSION, MOOT, PALAVER
debilitate - - - - ENERVATE, WEAKEN
debility - - - - - - - - - LASSITUDE
debit - - - - - - - - - - - CHARGE
debris - - - RUINS, TRASH, RUBBISH
decade - - - - - - - - - - - - TEN
decant - - - - - - - - - - - - POUR
decapitate - - - - - - - - - BEHEAD
decay - - - - - - ROT, DECOMPOSE
decayed - - - - - - - - - - ROTTEN
decease - - - - - - - - - - DEMISE
deceit - FRAUD, COZENAGE, COLLUSION, GUILE, IMPOSTURE
deceitful - - - EVASIVE, FRAUDULENT
deceive - - BETRAY, DELUDE, DUPE, ENTRAP, MISLEAD, FOOL, BEFOOL, HOODWINK
deceive for sport - - - - - - - HOAX
decency - - - - - - - - - MODESTY
decent - - - - - MODEST, PROPER
deception - - DELUSION, IMPOSTURE
deceptive - - - - - - - - - ILLUSIVE
deceptive appearance - - - - ILLUSION
decibel (abbr.) - - - - - - - - - D.B.
decide - DETERMINE, RESOLVE, SETTLE, OPT, ARBITRATE
decide judicially - - - - - - ADJUDGE
decide upon - - - - - - - - - ELECT
decided taste - - - - - - - PENCHANT
decimal unit - - - - - - - - - - TEN
decipher - - - - - - - - - - DECODE
decisive - - - - - - - - - - - FINAL
deck - - - - - - - - - - - - ADORN
deck out - - - - - - - - TOG, ARRAY
deck out (arch.) - - - - - - BEDIGHT
deck out cheaply - - - - - - BEDIZEN
deck room for cooking (naut.) - CABOOSE
deck with openwork fabric - - BELACE
declaim - - - - - - - - ORATE, RANT
declaim bitterly - - - - - - - INVEIGH
declaim vehemently - - - - - - - RANT
declamation - - - - ORATION, TIRADE
declamatory passage - - - - - TIRADE
declaration - - - - - - - STATEMENT
declare - - - AVER, ASSERT, STATE, PROCLAIM, AVOW, AFFIRM, PRONOUNCE
declare innocent - - - - - - ACQUIT
decline - FALL, DROOP, DETERIORATE, DIE, REFUSE, EBB, DIP, WANE
decline gradually - - - - - - - WANE
decline of life - - - - - - - - - AGE
declining period (poet.) - - - - - EVE
declivity - - - - - - - - SLOPE, SIDE
decode - - - - - - - - - - DECIPHER
decompose - - - - - - - ROT, DECAY
decomposition - - - - - - - - - ROT
decorate - DECK, EMBELLISH, ADORN, FESTOON, ORNATE, TRIM, PAPER,

PAINT
decoration - - - - - - ADORNMENT
decoration for valour - - - - MEDAL
decorative - - - - - - ORNAMENTAL
decorative earthenware - - - FAIENCE
decorative ensemble - - - - DECOR
decorative house plant - - - - CALLA
decorative plant - - - - - - FERN
decorative ribbons - - - - RIBANDS
decorous - DECENT, DEMURE, PROPER, MODEST
decoy - ENTRAP, LURE, ENTICE, ALLURE
decrease - LOWER, WANE, DEATH, EBB, EASE
decree - TENET, ORDAIN, LAW, UKASE, ENACT, FIAT, ADJUDGE, RESCRIPT, EDICT, ARRET
decree of Moslem ruler - - - IRADE
decreed - - - - - - - - WILLED
dedicate - - - DEVOTE, INSCRIBE, CONSECRATE
dedicated by a vow - - - - VOTIVE
deduce - - - INFER, DERIVE, EVOLVE
deduct - - BATE, REBATE, SUBTRACT
deduction - - REBATE, SUBTRACTION, INFERENCE
deed - - ACT, FEAT, ACTION, EVENT, REMISE, ESCROW, EXPLOIT
deem - - CONSIDER, REGARD, THINK, JUDGE
deep - - DARK, PROFOUND, OBSCURE, HIDDEN
deep bow - - - - - - - OBEISANCE
deep covered dish - - - - - TUREEN
deep gorge - - - - - - - RAVINE
deep hole - - - - - - - - PIT
deep-seated - - - - - - ROOTED
deep sleep - - - - - - - SOPOR
deep valley - - - - - - - CANYON
deep waters - - - - - - - - SEA
deepen - - - THICKEN, INTENSIFY, DREDGE, INCREASE
deeper shade - - - - - - DARKER
deepest within - - - - - INMOST
deer - - - STAG, DOE, HART (m.), HIND (f.), ELK, MOOSE
deer cry - - - - - - - - BELL
deer flesh - - - - - - - VENISON
deer horn - - - - - - - ANTLER
deer (pert. to) - - - - - CERVINE
deer (small) - - - - - - - - ROE
deer tail - - - - - - - - FLAG
deer trail - - - - - - - - SLOT
deface - - - - - - - - - MAR
defamatory statement - - - - LIBEL
defame - - - - - SLANDER, MALIGN
default - - - - FAILURE, NEGLECT
defeat - - - BEAT, BEST, FOIL, ROUT, OVERCOME, CONQUER, FRUSTRATE, FRUSTRATION, LOSS, VANQUISH, WORST
defeat at chess - - - - - - MATE
defeated - - - - - - - - BEATEN
defeated (be) - - - - - - - - LOSE
defect - - - - - - - FLAW, FAULT
defect in fabric - - - - - - SCOB
defective - - - - - - - - - BAD
defective explosive - - - - - - DUD
defective (prefix) - - - - - - MAL
defend - - - - - - - - PROTECT
defendant in libel suit - - - LIBELLEE
defender of liberty - - - - - PATRIOT
defense - - - PROTECTION, BULWARK
defense growth of cane - - CANEBRAKE
defensive armour - - - - - EGIS, MAIL
defensive barrier - - - - - STOCKADE
defensive bastions - - - - - - FORTS
defensive covering - - - - - - ARMOR
defensive ditch - - - - - - - MOAT
defensive enclosure - - - - - - BOMA
defensive head covering - - - HELMET
defensive plating on warship - ARMOR
defensive work of piles - - ESTACADE
defer - POSTPONE, PROLONG, ADJOURN
deference - - - - - HOMAGE, RESPECT
deficiency - - WANT, SHORTAGE, LACK, SCARCITY
deficient - - - - - - SCARCE, SHORT
deficit - - - - - - - - - SHORTAGE
defile - MOIL, POLLUTE, SOIL, PASS, UBRA, ABRA, TAINT, DEBASE
define - - - - - - - - - - EXPLAIN
definition - - - - - - - - MEANING
deflated - - - - - - - - - - FLAT
deflect - - - - - - - - - - DIVERT
defraud - - - - - TRICK, ROB, CHEAT
defray - - - - - - - - - - - PAY
defray in advance - - - - - - PREPAY
deft - - - - - - - - - - ADROIT
defy - - DARE, BEARD, BRAVE, HANDY
defy (colloq.) - - - - - - - STUMP
degenerate - - - ROT, DETERIORATE
degrade - CORRUPT, DEBASE, LOWER, ABASE, DEPOSE, DEMEAN
degrade oneself - - - - - - DEMEAN
degrading - - - - - - - - MENIAL
degree - EXTENT, STAGE, STEP, RANK, GRADE, RATE, STATION
degree of official standing - - - RANK
degree of progress - - - - - - STAGE
degree of value - - - - - - - RATE
dehydrate - - - - - - - - - DRY
deific - - - - - - - - - GODLIKE
deign - - - - - - - - VOUCHSAFE
deity - - - - - - - GOD, DIVINITY
deity of woods and flocks - - - FAUN
dejected - SAD, LOW, GLUM, SPIRITLESS, DISHEARTENED, DEPRESSED
Delaware capital - - - - - - DOVER
Delaware Indian - - - - - - LENAPE
Delaware town - - - - - - - LEWES
delay - STALL, RETARD, DEMUR, BELATE, WAIT, LINGER, LAG, REMORA, HINDER, LOITER, DEMURRAL, DETAIN
delay action - - - WAIT, FILIBUSTER
delay (law) - - - - - - - - MORA
delayed - - - - - - - - - LATE
dele - - - - - - - DELETE, REMOVE
delectate - - - - - - - - DELIGHT
delegate - - - - DEPUTE, DEPUTIZE, AUTHORIZE
delegation - - - - - - - MISSION
delete - - - - DELE, REMOVE, ERASE
deleterious - - - - - - - - - BAD
deletion - - - - - - - - ERASURE
deliberate - SLOW, CONSIDER, PONDER
deliberately ignore - - - - - - SNUB
Delibes ballet - - - - - - - NAILA
delicacy - - - CATE, TACT, CAVIAR
delicate - TENDER, FINE, FRAGILE, FRAIL
delicate fabric - - - - - - - - LACE
delicate food - - - - - - - - CATE
delicate gradations - - - - - NUANCES
delicate network - - - - - - - LACE
delicate ornamental openwork - FILIGREE
delicate perception - - - - - - TACT
delicate vine - - - - - - - SMILAX
delicious - - - - - - - AMBROSIAL
delight - - - REGALE, ELATE, PLEASE, ENTRANCE, REVEL, DELECTATE
delight in - - - - - - - - - REVEL

D

delighted - - - - - - - - - GLAD
delightfully - - - - - - ADORABLY
Delilah's lover - - - - - SAMSON
delineate - - LIMN, DRAW, PICTURE, DEPICT, PORTRAY, DESCRIBE
delineation - - - - - - - - - MAP
delirium - - - - - - - - - FRENZY
deliver - RID, SEND, RENDER, RESCUE, RELEASE, FREE, REDEEM
deliver a sermon - - - - - - PREACH
deliverer - - - LIBERATOR, REDEEMER
dell - - - - - DENE, RAVINE, GLEN
deltas - - - - - - - - TRIANGULAR
delude - - MISLEAD, BEGUILE, TRICK
deluge - - - - - FLOOD, INUNDATE
delusion - - - - - - - DECEPTION
delve - - - - - - - DIG, FATHOM
demand - - EXACT, INSIST, EXIGENCY, REQUIRE, CLAIM, NEED
demand as due - - - - - - - CLAIM
demand a repetition - - - - ENCORE
demean - DEGRADE, LOWER, CONDUCT, CONTROL, BEHAVE
demeanor - - MIEN, AIR, BEHAVIOUR
demented - - MAD, INSANE, CRAZY
demented person - - - - - MANIAC
demise - - - DEATH, DIE, DECEASE
demit - - ABDICATE, DISMISS, OUST, RESIGN
demobilize - - - - - - - DISBAND
demolish - RASE, RAZE, RUIN, DESTROY
demolisher - - - - - - - - RAZER
demon - IMP, OGRE, FIEND, DEVIL, RAHU
demonstrate - - - - - PROVE, EVINCE
demonstration - - - OVATION, PROOF
demoralize - - - - - - DISHEARTEN
demotic - - - - - - - - POPULAR
demulcent - - - - - - - - - SALEP
demur - - PROTEST, DELAY, OBJECT, HESITATE
demure - SERIOUS, SOBER, PRIM, COY, STAID, SEDATE, GRAVE, DECOROUS
demurral - - - - - - - - - DELAY
demurrer - - - - - - - - OBJECTOR
den - LAIR, DIVE, NEST, HUNT, CAVE, SANCTUM, CAVERN
denary - - - - - - - - - - TEN
dene - - - - - - - - DELL, DOWN
denial - NEGATIVE, NEGATION, REFUSAL, NAY, NO, REJECTION
denigrate - - - - - - - - BLACKEN
denizen - - - - - - - INHABITANT
Denmark - - - (See also Danish)
Denmark coin - - - - KRONE, ORE
Denmark measure - - - - RODE, ALEN
Denmark measure (pl.) - - - - ESER
Denmark native - - - - - - - DANE
Denmark weight - - - - - - - ESER
denominate - - - - - CALL, TITLE
denomination - - - - - - - - SECT
denote - - INDICATE, SIGNIFY, SHOW, MEAN, MARK
denoting central part - - - - - MID
denoting endeavor (gram.) - CONATIVE
denoting number - - - - NUMERICAL
denoting position in succession - ORDINAL
denoting a purpose - - - - - TELIC
denounce - - - CONDEMN, ARRAIGN
dense - CRASS, CLOSE, OBTUSE, THICK
dense growth of trees - FOREST, JUNGLE, CANEBRAKE
dense mist - - - - - - - - - FOG
dense smoke - - - - - - SMUDGE
dense throng - - - - - - - PRESS
dent - HOLLOW, DINT, NOTCH, INDENT, TOOTH
dentate - - - - - - - - TOOTHED
dentine - - - - - - - - - - IVORY
dentist's drill - - - - - - - BURR
dentist's plastic - - - - - - CEMENT
denude - - - - - BARE, STRIP, SCALP
denunciation - - - - - - THREAT, BAN
deny - - NEGATE, GAINSAY, DISOWN, REFUSE, DISAVOW, RENEGE, ABNEGATE, RENOUNCE, WITHHOLD, REJECT, CONTRADICT
depart - - - - - - - - - GO, LEAVE
depart quickly (slang) - - - - VAMOOSE
depart secretly - - DECAMP, ABSCOND
department - - - - DIVISION, PART
departure - - - - - EXIT, WITHDRAWAL
depend - - RELY, HINGE, LEAN, TRUST
dependable - - - - - - - - - TRUSTY
dependency of China - - - - - TIBET
dependent - - - - - - CONTINGENT
depended (be) - - - - - - - - HANG
despicable person - - - - - - - CAD
depict - PICTURE, DELINEATE, DRAW, PORTRAY
depiction of the beautiful - - - - ART
deplete - - DRAIN, LESSEN, EXHAUST, EMPTY
deplorably - - - - - - - - - SADLY
deploy - - - - - - - - - - UNFOLD
deportment - - - - - - - - CONDUCT
depone - - - - - - - - - - TESTIFY
deport - - BANISH, EXILE, CONDUCT
deportment (arch.) - - - - GESTE, GEST
depose - - - - - DEGRADE, DETHRONE
deposit - - - - LAY, LEAVE, PUT, SET
deposit of gold particles - - - - PLACER
deposit ice crystals - - - - - SNOWS
deposit of sediment - - - - - - SILT
depository - - - - - - - - - - BANK
depot - - - - - STATION, ENTREPOT, STOREHOUSE
depraved - BAD, CORRUPTED, BESTIAL
depravity - - - - - - WICKEDNESS
depreciate - - - - BELITTLE, LESSEN
depress - SADDEN, LOWER, DISCOURAGE, DISPIRIT, DAMPEN, DEJECT
depressed - - - - - - - - - - BLUE
depressing - - - - - - - - - TRISTE
depression - - - DENT, PIT, DIP, DINT
depression between mountain peaks - COL, DIP
depression in golf green - - - - - CUP
depression worn by running water RAVINE, GULLEY
deprivation - - - - - - - - - LOSS
deprive - BEREAVE, DIVEST, DISPOSSESS, AMERCE
deprive of - - - - - - - - - - LOSE
deprive of by deceit - - - - - MULCT
deprive of food - - - - - - - STARVE
deprive of moisture - - - - - - DRAIN
deprive of nature qualities - - DENATURE
deprive of reason - - - - - - DEMENT
deprive of sight - - - - - - - BLIND
deprive of weapons - - - - - - UNARM
depth - - - - - - - - - PROFUNDITY
depute - - - - - - - DELEGATE, SEND
deputize - - - - - - - - - DELEGATE
deputy - - - - - AGENT, SURROGATE
deranged - - - - CRAZED, DISORDERED
derby hat - - - - - - - - - BOWLER
derelict - - - - - - - - ABANDONED
deride - - TAUNT, SNEER, RIDICULE, MOCK, SCOFF, SCORN, GIBE, BELITTLE

deride (slang) - - - - - - - - - RAG
derision - - - - - - - - - - SCORN
derisive - - - - - - - - SCORNFUL
derisive cry - - - - - - HOOT, HISS
derivative of morphine - - - - HEROIN
derivative of phenol - - - - - - ANOL
derive - - DEDUCE, EVOLVE, OBTAIN, INFER, GET, TRACE
derived from fat - - ADIPIC, SEBACIC
derived by inference - - - - - ILLATIVE
derived from the maple - - - - ACERIC
derived from oil - - - - - - - OLEIC
derme - - - - - - - - - - - SKIN
derogate - - - - - - - - - DETRACT
derogatory remark - - - - - - SLUR
derrick pole - - - - - - - - - MAST
derry - - - - - - - - - - BALLAD
dervish's cap - - - - - - - - - TAJ
descend - - - - - - - - - - SINK
descend abruptly - - - - - - PLUNGE
descendant - - - - - - - SCION, SON
descendant of Dan - - - - - DANITE
descendant of Ham - - - - - HAMITE
descendant of Jacob - - - - - LEVITE
descendant (obs.) - - - - - - SIENT
descendant of Shem - - - - - SEMITE
descended to ground - - - - - - ALIT
descent - - - - - - STRAIN, SCARP
describe - - - - - RELATE, DELINEATE
describe as - - - - - - - - - LABEL
describe grammatically - - - - PARSE
descriptive adjective - - - - - EPITHET
descry - - - - - - - - - ESPY, SEE
desert - ABANDON, ABSCOND, FORSAKE, ICE, WASTELAND
desert dweller - - - - BEDOUIN, ARAB
desert plant - - - - - - - - CACTUS
desert train - - - - - - - - CARAVAN
desert wind - - - - SIMOOM, SIROCCO
deserter - - - TURNCOAT, RENEGADE, ABSCONDER, RAT
deserve - - - - - MERIT, METE, EARN
deserving blame - - - - - CULPABLE
desiccate - - - - - - - - - - - DRY
design - INTENTION, PLAN, PATTERN, PURPOSE, MODEL
design of scattered objects - - - - SEME
designate - SIGNATE, ASSIGN, LABEL, DUB, TERM, DISTINGUISH, NAME, APPOINT, ENTITLE, CONNOTE
designation - - - - - - - - - TITLE
designer - - - - - - - - - PLANNER
desirable part - - - - - - - - - FAT
desire - - CRAVE, LUST, WANT, YEN, WISH, CARE, LONGING, HOPE, THIRST, COVET, ASPIRE, ASPIRATION, YEARN
desire anxiously - - - - - - - YEARN
desire (colloq.) - - - - - - - - YEN
desire wrongfully - - - - - - - COVET
desired (be) - - - - - - - - - IDEAL
desiring food - - - - - - - - HUNGRY
desirous - - - - - - - - - - EAGER
desist - CEASE, FORBEAR, STOP, SPARE, REST, END
desolate - - - - - BARE, WOEBEGONE, ABANDONED
desolate region - - - - - - - DESERT
despair - - - - - - - - - ABANDON
despairing - - - - - - - - HOPELESS
desperado - - - - - - - - - RUFFIAN
desperate - - - - - - - - RECKLESS
despicable - - - - - - - VILE, SORDID
despicable character - - - - - - - CAD
despise - - HATE, DISDAIN, CONTEMN, DETEST
despoil - - SPOIL, PLUNDER, FLEECE
despoiled (arch.) - - - - - - - REFT
despondent - - - - - - - BLUE, SAD
despondent period - - - - - - BLUES
despot - - - - - - - TYRANT, SATRAP
despotic official - - - - - - - SATRAP
despotism - - - - - - - - TYRANNY
dessert - - - - - - - - ICE, MOUSSE
destine - - - - - - - - - - ALLOT
destiny - - - - - - FATE, LOT, DOOM
destitute - - - - - - - - - - DEVOID
destitute of (be) - - - - - - - LACK
destitute of hair - - - - - - - - BALD
destitute of teeth - - - - - EDENTATES
destitution - - - - - - - - POVERTY
destroyed - - - - - RASED, RUINED, EXTIRPATED, RAZED, DEMOLISHED, BROKEN, PERISHED
destroyed inside of - - - - - GUTTED
destroyer - - - - - - - - - - RASER
destruction - LOSS, DEMOLITION, RUIN, DEATH
destructive - - - - - - - - - DEADLY
destructive insect - - - - - - TERMITE
destructive sugar cane disease - - ILIAU
desultory - - - - - - - - - AIMLESS
detach - DISENGAGE, ISOLATE, DISUNITE
detached state - - - - - - ISOLATION
detachment - - - - PARTY, ISOLATION
detail - - - - - - - - ITEM, APPOINT
detailed information - - - - - - DATA
detain - - - - HALT, HINDER, RETARD, HARASS, DELAY, DETER, ARREST, WITHHOLD, INTERN
detect - - DISCOVER, ESPY, SPY, NOSE
detective - - - - - - - - - SLEUTH
detective (slang) - - - - - TEC, DICK
detent - - - - - - - - PAWL, CATCH
deter - RESTRAIN, HINDER, PREVENT, RETARD, DETAIN
deterge - - - - - - - - - CLEANSE
detergent - - - - - - - - - - SOAP
deteriorate - - - FAIL, DEGENERATE, DECLINE, WEAR
deteriorated - - - - - - - WORN, WORE
deteriorating - - - - - - - DECADENT
deterioration - - - - - - - DECADENCE
determinable - - - - - - - DEFINABLE
determinate - - - - - - - - SPECIFIC
determinate beneficial portion - DOSE
determination - - GRIT, RESOLUTION
determine - - - CONCLUDE, DESTINE, SETTLE, WILL, ASCERTAIN, DECIDE, RESOLVE
determine dimension of - - - MEASURE
determine position of - - - - LOCATE
determined - - - - - SET, RESOLUTE
determiners - - - - - - - - - GENES
detest - - - - - - DESPISE, LOATHE
dethrone - - - - - - - - - DEPOSE
detonate - - - - EXPLODE, FULMINATE
detract - - - - DEROGATE, WITHDRAW
devastate - - - - - - - - - - RASE
devastation - - - - - - - - - HAVOC
develop - - EVOLVE, GROW, GENERATE
develop in detail - - - - - ELABORATE
develop in enthusiasm - - - - - WARM
develop rapidly - - - - - - - - BOOM
developing a subject - - - - - TOPICAL
development - - EVOLUTION, PROGRESS
deviate - STRAY, LAPSE, ERR, DIGRESS, SWERVE
deviate from the vertical (mining) - HADE
device to charge with gas - - AERATOR
device to control draft - - - - DAMPER

D

device to deaden tone - - - - MUTE
device to fire a blast - - DETONATOR
device to grip - - - - - - - VISE
device to heat liquids - - - - ETNA
device to hoist large stones - - LEWIS
device that holds tight - - - CLAMP
device to keep wheel from turning - SPRAG
device to make cloth - - - - AGER
device for measuring - - - - RULE
device for measuring energy expended ERGOMETER
device to prevent backward motion DETENT
device for raising chicks - - BROODER
device to separate fine from coarse - SIEVE
device to spread lamp flame - - CRIC
device to stretch cloth - - - TENTER
device for unclosing - - - - OPENER
device for wedging things together CLAMP
devil - - SATAN, IMP, DEMON, FIEND
devil (of the) - - - - - - DIABOLIC
devilfish - - - - - - - - MANTA
devilish - - - - - - - - INFERNAL
devilkin - - - - - - - - - IMP
devilment - - - - - - - MISCHIEF
deviltry - - - - - - - - MISCHIEF
devise - - PLAN, CONTRIVE, INVENT, FRAME, CREATE
devoid - - - - - - - - DESTITUTE
devoid of moisture - - - - - - DRY
devoir - - - - - - - - - - DUTY
devolve - - - - - - - - - PASS
devote - - - - - APPLY, DEDICATE
devote to sacred use - - - DEDICATE
devoted - - APPLIED, LIEGE, FAITHFUL
devoted adherent - - - - - VOTARY
devoted to one's country - - PATRIOTIC
devotedly attached - - - - - FOND
devotee - - - - - - FAN, PARTISAN
devotes to - - - - - - - ADDICTS
devotion - - - - - - - - - PIETY
devour - - - - - - - - - - EAT
devoutly (musical) - - - - - DIVOTO
devoutness - - - - PIETY, DEVOTION
dewy - - - - RORIC, WET, MOIST
dewy (poet.) - - - - - - - ADEW
dexterity - - - - - - - ART, EASE
dexterous - - - - - CLEVER, DEFT
dexterous trick - - - - - - SLEIGHT
dextrorotary oil (chem.) - - - IRONE
diabolical - - - - - - - INFERNAL
diadem - - - - - - TIARA, CROWN
diagonal - - - - - - - - - BIAS
diagonally - - - - - - - - BIAS
diagram - - - - - - PLAN, CHART
diagrammatic chart - - - - GRAPH
dialect - - PATOIS, ARGOT, SPEECH, PATOIC, IDIOM
dialect used in sacred writings - - PALI
diameter measuring instrument - CALIPER
diametrally - - - - - - - UTTERLY
diamond cutting cup - - - - - DOP
diamond shaped figure - - LOZENGE
diatonic run (musical) - - - TIRADE
diatonic scale - - - - - - - GAMUT
dib - - - - - - - - - DAB, DAP
dibble - - - - - - - - DAP, DIB
dice - - - - - - - - - - CUBE
Dickens character - DORRIT, HEEP, DORA, WELLER, FAGIN, MICAWBER, PICKWICK
Dickens' pen name - - - - - - BOZ
dictate - - - - - - - - COMMAND
diction - - - - - - - - PARLANCE
dido - - - - ANTIC, CAPER, PRANK

die (a) - - - - - - - STAMP, PRINT
die - - - PERISH, DEMISE, DECLINE, EXPIRE, MOLD, STAMP, PRINT
die for making pipe - - - - - DOD
diet - - - - - - - - - FAST, FARE
diet (pert. to) - - - - - - DIETARY
differ - - - - - - - - - DISAGREE
different - DIVERSE, ANOTHER, OTHER, VARIANT, NOVEL
different ones - - - - - - - OTHERS
different persons - - - - - - OTHERS
differently - - - - - - - OTHERWISE
difficult - - - - HARD, KNOTTY, RUB
difficult accomplishment - - - FEAT
difficult (prefix) - - - - - - - DYS
difficult question - - - - - - POSER
difficulty - - - - SNAG, STRAIT, ADO
diffidence - - - - - - - SHYNESS
diffident - - - - - - - - COY, SHY
diffuse - RADIATE, STREW, DISPERSE, SPREAD
diffuse (arch.) - - - - - - - STROW
dig - - MINE, DELVE, BURROW, SPADE
dig up - - - - - - - - - UNEARTH
digest - - - TOLERATE, ASSIMILATE
digging implement - - - - SPADE, HOE
digit - TOE, FIGURE, NUMBER, FINGER
dignify - - - - - ENNOBLE, HONOUR
dignity - - - - - - - DISTINCTION
digress - - - - - - - - - DEVIATE
digressing - - - - - - - WANDERING
dike - - - - - - LEVEE, CAUSEWAY
dilapidated condition - - - DISREPAIR
dilate - - SWELL, ENLARGE, EXPAND, DISTEND
dilatory - - - REMISS, SLOW, LONG
dilettante - - - - - - - AMATEUR
diligence - - - - - - APPLICATION
diligent - - - - - - BUSY, SEDULOUS
dill - - - - - - - - - - - ANET
dillseed - - - - - - - ANET, ANISE
dilute - - - WATER, THIN, WEAKEN, ATTENUATE
diluted - - - - - - - - - - THIN
diluted alcoholic beverage - - - PUNCH
dim - OBSCURE, BLEAR, FAINT, FADED, PALE
dimension - MEASURE, MEASUREMENT
diminish - FADE, LESSEN, WAVE, BATE, ABATE, EBB, DECREASE, WANE, MODERATE, TAPER, LOWER
diminish by constant loss - - WASTE
diminish in depth - - - - NARROW
diminish gradually - - - - - TAPER
diminish strength of - - - - DILUTE
diminution - - - - - - ABATEMENT
diminutive - - SMALL, PETITE, DWARF
diminutive suffix - OLE, IE, ET, ULE, ETTE
din - - - - - - - NOISE, CLAMOR
dine - - - - - - - - - - EAT, SUP
diner - - - - - - - - - - EATER
dingy - - - - - - - - DULL, SOILED
dining alcove - - - - - - - DINETTE
dining room - - - - GRILL, CENACLE
dinner - - - - - - - - - REPAST
dinner course - - - - - - - ENTREE
dinner jacket - - - - - - TUXEDO
dint - - - FORCE, DENT, IMPRINT
diocesan center - - - - - - - SEE
dip - - - IMMERSE, DECLINE, SINK, INCLINE, LADE, PLUNGE, DAP
dip out - - - - - - - - - - BAIL
diphthong - - - - - - - - AE, EA
diplomacy - - - - - - - - TACT
diplomatic representative - MINISTER
dipper - - - - - - - - - - LADLE

dire - FATAL, DREADFUL
direct - LEAD, DRIVE, STEER, MANAGE, AIM, ADDRESS, WEND, IMMEDIATE, GUIDE, MANAGE, STRAIGHT, GOVERN, REFER
direct attention to - REFER
direct course - PILOT
direct one's way - WEND
direct opposition - CONTRADICTION
direct proceedings - PRESIDE
direct a weapon - AIM
direction - TREND, COURSE
direction (Scot.) - AIRT
directly opposite - DIAMETRICAL
director - STAGER, MANAGER, HEAD, LEADER
directory of church services - ORDO
dirge - LAMENT, EPICEDE
dirgelike - MONODIC
dirigible - BLIMP
dirigible balloon - AIRSHIP
dirk - SNEE, DAGGER, PONIARD
dirt - GRIME, SOD, TRASH, REFUSE, SOIL, LOAM
dirt and water - MUD
dirty - GRIMY, FOUL, SOILED
disable - MAIM
disaffect - ALIENATE
disagree - DISSENT, DIFFER
disagreeable - NASTY, MEAN, VILE
disappear - VANISH
disappoint - FAIL
disapprove of - CONDEMN
disarrange - MUSS
disassociate - SEPARATE
disaster - WOE, CALAMITY, MISFORTUNE
disavow - RETRACT, DENY, ABJURE
disavowal - DENIAL
disband - SCATTER, DEMOBILIZE
disbelief in God - ATHEISM
disbelieve - DOUBT
disburden - EASE, RID, UNLOAD
disburse - PAY, SPEND
disc - PATEN
discard - SHED, SCRAP
discarded material - SCRAP
discern - ESPY, SEE, LOOK, SPY
discern beforehand - FORESEE
discerning - ASTUTE, NICE, SAGACIOUS
discernment - FLAIR
discernment of feeling - TACT
discharge - SHOOT, EMIT, EXUDE, PAY, PAYMENT
discharged obligation - PAID, PAYMENT
disinclined - AVERSE
disciple - APOSTLE
disciple of Jesus - SIMON
disciple of Socrates - PLATO
disciples (pert. to) - APOSTOLIC
disciplinarian - MARTINET
discipline - TRAIN, CHASTEN, FERULE
disclaim - DISAVOW, DENY, REPUDIATE
disclose - REVEAL, BARE, OPEN, UNEARTH, UNVEIL, TELL
disclosed place - SPOT
disclosure - EXPOSE
discolour - STAIN, SPOT
discolouration - STAIN
discoloured - STAINED, FADED
discoloured by partial decay - DOTY
discomfort - PAIN
discompose - UPSET
disconcert - ABASH, RATTLE, UPSET, JAR, FAZE
disconcerting - PARLOUS
disconnect - SEVER, SEPARATE
discontinue - SUSPEND, DESIST, QUIT
discord - JAR
discordant - HARSH, SCRAPY
discount - REBATE, AGIO
discourage - APPAL, DEPRESS, DETER
discourage through fear - DETER
discouraging - DISHEARTENING
discourse publicly - PRELECT
discourteous - IMPOLITE, RUDE
discover - SPY, ESPY, DETECT, INVENT, FIND, LOCATE
discoverer of Cape of Good Hope - DIAZ
discoverer of North Pole - PEARY
discoverer of wine - NOAH
discoverer of x-ray - ROENTGEN
discovery - FIND, DETECTION
discredit - ABASE
discreet - CAREFUL, PRUDENT
discrete - SEPARATE
discretion - TACT
discretionary - ARBITRARY
discriminating - ASTUTE, NICE, JUDICIAL
discriminating cognition - SENSE
discrimination - ACUMEN
discus - QUOIT
discuss - DEBATE, ARGUE
discussion - ARGUMENT, DEBATE
disdain - POOH, SCORN, DESPISE, SPURN
disease - MALADY, GOUT, POX
disease of animals - MANGE
disease of cereals - SMUT, ERGOT
disease of fowl - PIP
disease of plants - SCAB
disease of rye - ERGOT
disease of sheep - GID
disease of tobacco - CALICO
disease of wheat - RUST
diseased - UNHEALTHY
disembark - LAND
disembodied spirit - SOUL
disenchant - DISILLUSION
disencumber - RID
disengage - RAVEL, FREE, DETACH
disengaged - OPEN
disentangle - RAVEL, EVOLVE
disentangle wool - CARD
disfigure - MAR, DEFACE
disgrace - SHAM, HUMBLE, SHAME, IGNOMINY
disgruntled person - SOREHEAD
disguise - VEIL, MASK, CLOAK, INCOGNITO
disgust (Scot.) - UG
dish - PLATE, PLATTER, TUREEN, BOWL
dish of crackers and water - PANADA
dish of eggs and milk - CUSTARD
dish of greens - SALAD
dish of maize and pepper - TAMALE
dishearten - DEMORALIZE, UNMAN, DEJECT
dishevel - TOUSLE
dishonour - STAIN, ABASE
disillusion - DISENCHANT
disincline - INDISPOSE, AVERSE
disintegrate - ERODE
disjoin - SEVER, SEPARATE
dislike - AVERSION, HATRED, ANTIPATHY, MIND
dislodged turf (piece) - DIVOT
dismal - BLEAK, DREAR, GRAY, TRISTE, DREARY, LURID, MOURNFUL
dismay - DREAD, APPALL, FEAR, APPAL, TERRIFY

D

dismiss - - - - - - OUST, DEMIT
dismiss (arch.) - - - - - - - DEMIT
dismiss from office (law) - - AMOVE
dismissal (slang) - - - - - - SACK
dismounted - - - - - - - - ALIT
disorder - - - - - - CHAOS, MESS
disorder in a state - - - SEDITION
disordered - - - MESSY, DERANGED, MUSSY
disorderly - LAWLESS, UNRULY, MESSY
disorderly behaviour - - - - RIOT
disorderly medley - - - - - - MESS
disown - - - - - REPUDIATE, DENY
disparage - - - - BELITTLE, SLUR
dispassionate - - IMPARTIAL, COOL
dispatch - - SEND, MESSAGE, HASTE
dispatch bearer - - - - - MESSENGER
dispatch boat - - - - - - - AVISO
dispatch by certain way - - - ROUTE
dispel - - - DISPERSE, DISSIPATE
dispense - - - - - - - DISTRIBUTE
dispense in small quantities - - DOLE
dispenser of alms - - - - - ALMONER
disperse - SCATTER, DISPEL, SPREAD, DIFFUSE
dispersion - - - - - - - STAMPEDE
dispirit - OVERDARE, DEPRESS, MOPE
displace - - - - SUPPLANT, JUMBLE
display - POMP, PARADE, SHOW, AIR, EVINCE, MANIFEST, EXPOSE, WEAR
display strong feeling (colloq.) - EMOTE
displease - - - OFFEND, AFFRONT
displeasure - - - - - - - ANGER
disport - - - - - - - PLAY, BATH
disposable - - - - - - - - SPARE
disposal - - - - - - ARRANGEMENT
dispose - - DIVEST, SETTLE, ARRANGE
dispose for price - - - - - - - SELL
disposed - INCLINED, PRONE, SOLD, APT
disposed to attack - - - AGGRESSIVE
disposed to laugh - - - - - RISIBLE
disposition - - MIEN, NATURE, MOOD
disposition to see things as they are REALISM
dispossess - - - DEPRIVE, DIVEST
disprove - - - - - REFUTE, REBUT
dispute - CONTEST, ARGUE, CHAFFER, WRANGLE
dispute (colloq.) - - - - - - SPAT
disquiet - - - - - UNEASE, PAIN
disquieted - - - - - - - UNEASY
disquietude - - - - - - - UNREST
disregard - OVERRIDE, WAIVE, IGNORE, NEGLECT
disregard temporarily - - - SHELVE
disregarded - - - - - - UNHEARD
disreputable - - - - SEAMY, SHADY
disrespectful - - - - - - INSOLENT
disrupt - - - - - - - - - SPLIT
dissemble - - - - - - - - MASK
disseminate - - - SOW, PROPAGATE, SCATTER, STREW, SPREAD
dissent - - - DISAGREE, PROTEST
dissenter - - - - - - - HERETIC
dissertation - - - - - - TREATISE
dissimilar - - DISPARATE, DIFFERENT
dissipate - WASTE, SQUANDER, DISPEL
dissociate - - - - - - - - PART
dissolve - - - - - - - - - MELT
distance - - - REMOTENESS, SPACE
distance (in the) - - - - - AFAR
distance from equator - - - LATITUDE
distance through - - - - DIAMETER
distant - FAR, REMOTE, YON, AFAR, FORMAL, ALOOF

distant (arch.) - - - - - - - YON
distance marker - - - MILESTONE, MILEPOST
distant but visible - - - - - - YON
distant (prefix) - - - - - TEL, TELE
distaste - - - AVERSION, DISLIKE
distasteful - - - - - - REPULSIVE
distend - INFLATE, DILATE, EXPAND, SWELL
distilled beverage - - - - ARRACK
distilling vessel - - - - - RETORT
distinct - - PLAIN, CLEAR, EVIDENT
distinct part - - - ARTICLE, SECTION
distinction - - - - - HONOUR, REPUTE
distinctive aspect - - - - - VISAGE
distinctive atmosphere - - - - AURA
distinctive mark - - - - - - BADGE
distinctive quality - - - SPECIALTY
distinctive system - - - - - - ISM
distinguish - - DISCERN, DESIGNATE
distinguished - - - - - - EMINENT
distinguished soldier - - - WARRIOR
distinguishing taste - - - - - SAVOR
distort - - - WARP, SCREW, GNARL
distorted - - - - - - - - - WRY
distract - CONFUSE, DIVERT, HARASS
distracted - - - - - - - FRANTIC
distraught - - - - - - - - MAD
distress - - - - - - - PAIN, GRIEF
distressed - - - - - - AGGRIEVED
distressing - - - - - - - - SORE
distressing (dial.) - - - - - SARE
distribute evently - - - - EQUALIZE
distributed - - DEALT, METED, DOLE, DELE, ALLOTTED, DISPENSED, ASSORT
distributor - - - - - - - DEALER
district - - - - - - - - REGION
distrustful - - - - - - - SHY, SLY
disturb - - - ROIL, RILE, UNSETTLE, AGITATE, AIL, MOLEST, ANNOY, RUFFLE, STIR, VIOLATE
disturb the peace - - - - - - RIOT
disturb a public speaker - - - HECKLE
disturbance - - RUMPUS, COMMOTION
disturber - - - - - - - - MESSER
disunite - - - - - DETACH, SEVER
disuse - - - - - - - - - LAPSE
ditch - TRENCH, MOAT, SEWER, RUT
dithery - - - SHIVERING, BOTHERED
ditto - - - - - - - - - - SAME
ditty - - - - - - SONG, REFRAIN
diurnal - - - - - - - - - DAILY
diva - - - - - - - - - SINGER
divan - - - - - - - SOFA, COUCH
dive - - - - - - - - - PLUNGE
divers - SEVERAL, SUNDRY, VARIOUS
diverse - - - UNLIKE, DIFFERENT, MULTIFORM
diversify - - - - - - - - - VARY
diversion - - PASTIME, SPORT, GAME
diversity - - - - - - - - VARIETY
divert - ENTERTAIN, AMUSE, DEFLECT, SPORT, RECREATE, DISTRACT
divest - - - DISPOSSESS, DISPOSE, DEPRIVE
divest of praise - - - - - - DEBUNK
divide - SHARE, SUNDER, APPORTION, BISECT, FORK, HALVE, SEPARATE, CLEFT
divide grammatically - - PUNCTUATE
divide proportionately - - - AVERAGE
divide in three parts - - - TRISECT
divided - - - - - CLEFT, SEPTATE
dividing edge - - - - - - - LINE
dividing line - - - - - - BISECTOR
dividing wall - - - - - - - SEPTUM

D

divination by the stars - - ASTROLOGY
divine - - - - MINISTER, GODLIKE
divine creative word (theol.) - LOGOS
diving bird - LOON, TERN, SMEW, AUK, GREBE
diving duck - - - - - - - - SMEW
divinity - - - - - - - - - - DEITY
divisible by two - - - - - - - EVEN
division - SHARE, CLASS, SQUADRON, PARTITION, SCHISM, GAME, SECTION, PART
division of Ancient Greece - - DEMES, DEME
division of army - - - - - - CORPS
division of book - - - - - CHAPTER
division of British Isles - - - WALES
division of building - - - - - ROOM
division of city - - WARD, PRECINCT
division of corolla - - - - - - PETAL
division of creed - - - - - - TENET
division of game - - - - - - - HALF
division of geological time - - - EON
division of Greece - - - - - NOMES
division of highway - - - - - - LANE
division of an Igorot town - - - ATO
division of India - - - - - - AGRA
division of Israelites - - - - - TRIBE
division of the Koran - - - - - SURA
division of mankind - - - - - - RACE
division of music - - - - - - - BAR
division of National Park - - - ESTES
division of opera - - - - - - SCENA
division of poem - - CANTO, VERSE, STANZA
division of polo grame - - CHUKKER
division of race - - - - - - - HEAT
division of Roman legion - - COHORT
division of society - - CASTE, CLAN
division of stained glass window - PANEL
division of stock - - - - - - SHARES
division of year - - - - - - SEASON
divorce allowance - - - - - ALIMONY
divulge - - - - - - - BARE, VOICE
dizzy (be) - - - - - - GIDDY, SILLY
dizzy attack - - - - - - - - SPELL
do - PERFORM, ACT, ACHIEVE, FARE
do again - - - - - - - - ITERATE
do alone - - - - - - - - - - SOLO
do away with - - - - - - ABOLISH
do the bidding of - - - - - - OBEY
do something in return - - - REPAY
do up - - - - - - - - - - WRAP
do without - - - - - - - - SPARE
docile - - TRACTABLE, GENTLE, TAME
docility - - - - - - - - TAMENESS
dock - - - - - - - - - - - PIER
dock worker - - - - - - STEVEDORE
docket - - - - - - - - - - LABEL
doctrine - DOGMA, TENET, CREED, ISM, BELIEF, GOSPEL, HEDONISM
doctrine of human welfare - - GOSPEL
doctrine that the universe is God - - PANTHEISM
document - - - - PAPER, SCRIPT
document (formal) - - - - INDENTURE
dodder - - - - - - - - - - SHAKE
Dodecanese Islands - LEROS, PISCOPI, LERO
dodge - - - - - - ELUDE, EVADE
doer - - - - - - - ACTOR, AGENT
doff - - - - - - - - - - REMOVE
dog - CANINE, PUG, HOUND, BEAGLE, TERRIER
dog (large) - - - - - - ALAN, DANE
dog of mixed breed - - - - MONGREL
dog's name - - - - - - - - - FIDO
dog star - - - - - - - - - SIRIUS
dogs (pert. to) - - - - - - CANINE
dogfish - - - - ROSSET, TOPE, SEPT
dogma - - - - - TENET, DOCTRINE
dogmatic principle - - - - - DICTUM, DICTA (pl.)
dogrose fruit - - - - - - - - - HIP
dogwood - - - - - - OSIER, CORNEL
doily - - - - - - - - - - - - MAT
doit - - - - - - - - - - - - WHIT
dole - ALMS, GRATUITY, METE, SHARE, GRIEF
dole out - - - - - - - - - RATION
doleful - - - - - - - - - - - - SAD
dolour - GRIEF, SORROW, MOURNING
dolourous - - - - - - - - GRIEVOUS
dolphin - - - - - - PORPOISE, INIA
dolphinlike fish - - - - - - - - INIA
dolt - - - - ASS, CLOD, DUNCE. OAF, SIMPLETON, FOOL
doltish - - - - - - - - - - STUPID
domain - REALM. DEMESNE, EMPIRE
domain of supernatural beings - FAERIE
dome - - - - - - EDIFICE, CUPOLA
domestic - - - - - - MAID, MENIAL
domestic cat - - - - - - - - MANX
domestic servant - MAID, HOUSEMAID
domestic spirit - - - - - - KOBOLD
domestic worker - - - - - - SERVANT
domesticate - - - - - - - - - TAME
domesticated birds - - - - - POULTRY
domesticated ox - - - - - - - - YAK
domicile - - - - - MENAGE, HOUSE
dominance - - - - - - SUPREMACY
dominant - - - - - - PREVAILING
dominant feature - - - - - - MOTIF
dominate - - - - - CONTROL, RULE
dominate (colloq.) - - - - - - BOSS
dominating - - - - - - - - - BOSSY
domineer - - - - - - - - - - LORD
domineering (colloq.) - - - - BOSSY
domineering woman - - - - - HUSSY
Dominican Republic measure - - ONA
dominion - - SWAY, EMPIRE, REIGN
domino - - - - - - - - - - - TILE
domino spot - - - - - - - - - PIP
don - - - - - - - - - - - - WEAR
Don Juan's mother - - - - - - INEZ
donate - - PRESENT, GIVE, BESTOW
donate (Scot.) - - - - - - - - - GIE
donation - - - - - - - - - - GIFT
done - - - - - - - - - - - OVER
done with the hands - - - - MANUAL
donkey - - - ONAGER, BURRO, ASS
donkey call - - - - - - - - - BRAY
donor - - - - - GIVER, BESTOWER
doom - - - FATE, CONDEMN, LOT, SENTENCE, DESTINY
door - - - PORTAL, STOA, ACCESS
door fastening - - - - - HASP, LATCH
door frame upright - - - - - STILE
door handle - - - - - - - - - KNOB
door knocker - - - - - - - RAPPER
door piece - - - - - - - - - - SILL
door post - - - - - - - - - ALETTE
doorkeeper - - PORTER, OSTIARIUS, TILER
doorsill - - - - - - - THRESHOLD
doorway - - - - - - - - ENTRANCE
dope - - - - - - - - - - - DRUG
dor - - - - - - - - - - - - BEETLE
dormant - - LATENT, TORPID, ASLEEP
dormouse - - - - - - LEROT, LOIR
dorp - - - - - - - - - - HAMLET

D

dorsal - - - - - - - - - - TERGAL
dose of medicine - - - - - PORTION
dot - - - DOWRY, PERIOD, SPECK, SCATTER, POINT, IOTA, STIPPLE
Douay Bible name - - - - - - AIA
double - DUAL, WIN, BINARY, DUPLEX, TWAIN
double curve - - - - - - - - ESS
double (prefix) - - - - - - DI, DIS
double moldboard plow - - - LISTER
double in narrow folds (var.) - - PLEAT
double quartet - - - - - - - OCTET
double tooth - - - - - - - - MOLAR
doubly - - - - - - - - - - TWICE
doubly (prefix) - - - - - - - - BI
doubt - - MISTRUST, UNCERTAINTY, QUERY
doubter - - - - - - - - - SKEPTIC
doubtful - - - - - - - - - DUBIOUS
doughy - - - - - - - - - - PASTY
dour - - - - - - - - - - SULLEN
douse - - - - - - DUCK, IMMERSE
dove - - - - - - PIGEON, CUSHAT
dove's home - - - - - - - - - COTE
dove (Scot.) - - - - - - - - DOO
dovelike - - - - - - - COLUMBINE
dower - - - - - - DOS, ENDOWMENT
down - - - - - - - - - - - DENE
down (to) - - - - - - - - - FLOOR
down (prefix) - - - - - - - - - DE
down cast - - - - - - - - - - SAD
downfall - - - - - - - - - - RUIN
downhearted - - - - - - - - - SAD
downpour - - - - RAINSTORM, SPILL
downright - - - - - - - - - STARK
downy surface - - - - - - - - NAP
dowry - - - - - - - - - DOS, DOT
dowry (pert. to) - - - - - - DOTAL
doze - - - - - - - - - NAP, SLEEP
doze (obs.) - - - - - - - - SLOOM
dozen - - - - - - - - - - TWELVE
drab - - - - - - - - - - - - DULL
draft - POTION, SKETCH, CONSCRIPT
draft animal - - - - MULE, OXEN, OX
draft harness part - - - - - - HAME
drafting of troops - - - - - - LEVY
drag - - - - - - LUG, HAUL, TRAIL
dragnet - - - - - - - - - - TRAWL
drain - SEWER, DEPLETE, MILK, SUMP
drain basin - - - - - - - - - SINK
drainage pit - - - - - - - - - SUMP
drama - - - - - - - - - - - PLAY
drama (pert. to) - - - - - THESPIAN
dramatic division - - - - - - SCENE
dramatic piece - - SKIT, MONODRAM
dramatic portrayal - - - - - ACTING
drape - - - - - - CURTAIN, ADORN
draped garland - - - - - - FESTOON
drapery - - - - - - - - - CURTAIN
draw - EXTRACT, ATTRACT, PORTRAY, HAUL, DRAG, DELINEATE, TIE, TOW, PULL, LURE, LIMN, DEPICT
draw after - - - - - - - TRAIL, TOW
draw along - - - - - - - - - - DRAG
draw back - - - - - - - - - RECEDE
draw as conclusion - - - - - DERIVE
draw forth - EDUCE, ELICIT, EXTRACT, EVOKE
draw game - - - - - - - - - - TIE
draw harshly over - - - - - SCRAPE
draw lots - - - - - - - - - BALLOT
draw by means of dots - - - - STIPPLE
draw off - - - - - - - - - - DRAIN
draw through a bent tube - - SIPHON
draw out - - - LENGTHEN, EXTRACT, EDUCE, LADE
draw out by suction - - - ASPIRATE
draw sap from tree - - - - - BLEED
draw through eyelets - - - - - LACE
draw tight - - - - - - - TAUT, FRAP
draw to - - - - - - - - - - ATTRACT
draw to a point - - - - - - - TAPER
draw together - - - - - - - - LACE
draw up shoulders - - - - - SHRUG
draw water - - - - - - - - - LADE
drawing - - - - - TRACTION, SKETCH
drawing room - - - - SALON, SALOON
drawn tight - - - - - - - - - TAUT
dread - FEAR, AWE, HORROR, TERROR
dreadful - DIRE, HORRID, TERRIBLE, FRIGHTFUL
dream - REVERIE, IMAGINE, VISION, ROMANCE, FANCY
dream (Fr.) - - - - - - - - - REVE
dreamt - - - - - - - - - FANCIED
dreamy - - - - - FANCIFUL, LANGUID
drear - - BLEAK, DISMAL, GLOOMY
dreary - - - - - - - - - - DISMAL
dredge - - - - - - - - - DEEPEN
dredge to collect starfish - - - - MOP
dreg - LEE, LEA, SETTLING, REMNANT
drench - SATURATE, SOUSE, DOUSE, SOAK, HOSE
dress - ATTIRE, GARB, FROCK, GOWN, ALIGN, RIG, CLOTHE, ARRAY, TOG
dress (colloq.) - - - - - - - - TOG
dress material - - - TRICOT, VOILE, MOHAIR
dress ornament - - - - - - - - SASH
dress ostentatiously - - - - - PRIMP
dress stone - - - - - - - - - - NIG
dress trimming - - RUCHE, RUCHING, PIPING, GIMP, INSERTION
dress with beak - - - - - - PREEN
dressed - - - - - - - - - - CLAD
dressed pelt - - - - - - - - - FUR
dresser - - - - - - - - - BUREAU
dresser in silk manufacturing - FRAMER
dressing for food - - - - - - SAUCE
dressing gown - - - - - - KIMONO
dressmaker - - - - - - - MODISTE
dressy - - - - - - - - - STYLISH
drew - - - - - - - - - - LIMNED
dried - - - - - - - - - - - SERE
dried brick - - - - - - - - ADOBE
dried bud used in seasoning - - CLOVE
dried cocoanut kernel - - - - COPRA
dried flower bud - - - - - - CLOVE
dried grape - - - - - - - RAISIN
dried grass - - - - - - - - - HAY
dried leaves of purple foxglove - - - DIGITALIS
dried orchid tubers - - - - - SALEP
dried plum - - - - - - - - - PRUNE
dries - - - - - - - - - - - SERES
drift - - - - - TENOR, TREND, SAG
drift to leeward, as a vessel - CRAB, SAG
driftage - - - - - - - - - FLOTSAM
drill - - - BORE, TRAIN, PRACTICE, PERFORATE
drill hall - - - - - - - - - ARMORY
drink - - BEVERAGE, GIN, POTATION, NECTAR, IMBIBE, SWIG
drink another's health - - - - PLEDGE, TOAST
drink of the gods - - - - - - NECTAR
drink heavily - - - - - - - - - TOPE
drink liquor - - - - - - - - TIPPLE
drink made from manna - - - - MEAD
drink made from molasses - - - - RUM

drink (small) - - - DRAM, SIP, NIP
drinker - - - - TOPER, TIPPLER
drinking bout - - - - - - WASSAIL
drinking cup - - TASS, AMA, MUG, TANKARD, BEAKER, STEIN
drinking glass - - TUMBLER, GOBLET
drinking mug - - - - - - - STEIN
drinking toast (Latin) - - - - PROSIT
drinking vessel - - GOURD, BEAKER, STEIN, MUG, CUP, GOBLET, TUMBLER, TANKARD
drip - - - - - - - DROP, TRICKLE
drive - IMPEL, RIDE, PROPEL, URGE, FORCE
drive away - REPEL, BANISH, DISPEL, SCAT, SHOO
drive back - - - - - - - REPULSE
drive ball into cup - - - - - - HOLE
drive forth - - - - - - - PROPEL
drive nail at angle - - - - - - TOE
drive off - - - - - - - - - - REPEL
drive out - - - - - - ROUT, ROUST
drive slantingly - - - - - - - TOE
drive with light blows - - - - - TAMP
drivel - - - - - - DOTE, SLAVER
driver - - - PROPELLER, COACHMAN
driver of vehicle - - HACKMAN, RIDER
driving back - - - - - - REPELLENT
driving line - - - - - - - - REIN
driving rain (colloq.) - - - - - PELTER
drizzle - - - - - - - - SPRINKLE
droll - - - - WHIMSICAL, COMIC
droll fellow - - - - - - - - - WAG
dromedary - - - - - - - - - CAMEL
drone - IDLER, HUM, SNAIL, BAGPIPE
drool - - - - - - - - - - SLAVER
droop - - - - SAG, WILT, DECLINE, LANGUISH, LOP, LOLL, FLAG, SLOUCH
drooping - NUTANT, SLOUCHING, LOP
drop - - - DRIP, FALL, PLUMMET, TRAPDOOR, SINK, BEAD
drop gently - - - - - - - - - - DAP
drop (pharm.) - - - - - - - GUTTA
drop suddenly (imitative) - - - PLOP
dropped - - - - - - - - - - FELL
dropsy - - - - - - - - - - EDEMA
dross - - - - - - - SCUM, WASTE
dross of a metal - - - - - - SLAG
drought - - - - - - - - DRYNESS
drove - - - - HERD, HORDE, FLOCK
drown - - - - - - - - SUBMERGE
drowse - - - - - - - - NOD, NAP
drowsy - - - - - - - - SLEEPY
drub - - BELABOR, CUDGEL, THRASH
drudge - - MOIL, SLAVE, PLOD, FAG
drudgery - - - - - - - - - - MOIL
drug - - - ALOES, HEROIN, DOPE, OPIUM, STUPEFY, URAL
drug plant - - - - - - - - ALOE
drum - - - BEAT, SNARE, TAMBOUR
drum (small) - - - - - - - TABOR
drumbeat - - - - FLAM, RATAPLAN
drunkard - - - - - - - - - - SOT
drupaceous fruit - - - - - - PLUM
dry - SEC, ARID, TED, SERE, THIRSTY, DULL, SEAR, PARCH
dry biscuit - - - - - - - - CRACKER
dry goods dealer - - - - - - DRAPER
dry lake basin - - - - - - - PLAYA
dry multiple fruits - - - - - CONES
dry by rubbing - - - - - - - WIPE
dry scale of fern stem - - - - PALEA
dry spell - - - - - - - DROUGHT
dry up - - - - - - - - - PARCH
dry as wine - - - - - - SEC, BRUT
drying cloth - - - - - - - TOWEL

dryness - - - - - - - - - DROUGHT
dual sound - - - - - - - - CHORD
dub - - - - CALL, ENTITLE, NAME
dubious - - PRECARIOUS, DOUBTFUL
dubious apostle - - - - - - THOMAS
duchy (pert. to) - - - - - - DUCAL
duck - - - - - - - - - - DOUSE
duck (European) - - - - - - SMEW
duck (kind) - PINTAIL, TERN, EIDER, TEAL, MALLARD, GOLDENEYE, SMEW
duck (male) - - - - - - - - DRAKE
duckbill - - - - - - - - PLATYPUS
duct - - - - VAS, PASSAGE, CANAL
ductile - - - - - - - - - TENSILE
dude - - - - - - - - DANDY, FOP
dudgeon - - - - - - - - - PIQUE
due - - - - PAYABLE, TOLL, OWING
duel - - - - - - - - - - COMBAT
duenna - - - - - - - - CHAPERON
dues - - - - - - - - - - - FEES
duet - - - - - - - - - - - DUO
dulcet - - - - - - - - MELODIOUS
dull - DIM, BLUNT, SLOW, SLUGGISH, MOPE, STOLID, STODGY, VAPID, DRAB, DRY, BLUR, TARNISH, DINGY, STUPID, LEADEN, LETHARGIC, GLASSY, UNINTERESTING
dull colour - - - - - - - DRAB, DUN
dull finish - - - - - - MATTE, MAT
dull gray - - - - - - - - LEADEN
dull gray brown - - - - - - - DUN
dull and heavy - - - - - - LEADEN
dull by inaction - - - - - - - RUST
dull monotony - - - - - - SAMENESS
dull and motionless - - - - - GLASSY
dull person - - - BORE, DUNCE, LOG
dull red - - - - - - - - - MAROON
dull (Scot.) - - - - - - - - DREE
dull sound - - - - - - - - - THUD
dull surface of metal - - - - - - MAT
dull and tedious - - - - - - PROSY
dull whitish tint - - - - - - GRAY
dullness - DRAB, HEBETUDE, VAPIDITY
Dumas character - - - - - - ATHOS
Dumas' novel - - - - - - CAMILLE
dumb - - - - MUTE, STILL, STUPID
dumb show - - - - - - PANTOMIME
dumpiness - - - - - - PUDGINESS
dun - - - - SWARTHY, IMPORTUNE
dunce - - - - DOLT, FOOL, NINNY, IGNORAMUS
dune area (pl.) - - - - - - - AREG
duo - - - - - - - - - - - PAIR
dupe - TOOL, VICTIM, DECEIVE, GULL, FOOL, VICTIMIZE
dupe (slang) - - - - - - - PIGEON
duplex - - - - - - - - - DOUBLE
duplicate - - - - - - BIS, REPLICA
duplicate (colloq.) - - - - - DITTO
duplicate copy - - - - - - ESTREAT
duplicity - - - - - - - - FRAUD
durable - - - PERMANENT, LASTING
durable wood - - - - - - - CEDAR
duration - - - TIME, SPACE, TERM, ETERNITY
duress - - - - - - - CONSTRAINT
during - - - - - - - - - - - AT
during the course of - - - - - - IN
during the time when - - - - - WHILE
dusk - - - - - - - - - - GLOOM
dusky - - - - - - - - - - - DARK
dust - - - - - - - - - - POWDER
dusting powder - - - - - EPIPASTIC
Dutch (abbr.) - - - - - - - - - DU
Dutch admiral - - - - - - - TRAMP
Dutch Antilles - - - - - - - ARUBA

Dutch cheese - - - - - - - EDAM
Dutch city - - - - - - - - - EDE
Dutch coin - - - - - - - - DOIT
Dutch commune - - - - - - - EDE
Dutch East Indies Island - - TIMOR, MOENA, JAVA
Dutch food - - - - - - - - EEL
Dutch geographer - - - - - - - AA
Dutch island - - - - - - - ARUBA
Dutch liquid measure - - KAN, AAM
Dutch measure - - - VAT, AAM, KOP
Dutch measure of length - - ROEDE
Dutch meter - - - - - - - - EL
Dutch painter - - DOW, HALS, CUYP, STEEN
Dutch republic founder - - WILLIAM
Dutch South African - - - - BOER
Dutch theologian - - - - ERASMUS
Dutch village - - - - - - DOORN
Dutch weight - - - - - - - - AAM
Dutch wine measure - - - - - AAM
dutiful - CONSCIENTIOUS, OBEDIENT
duty - TASK, CHORE, TARIFF, DEVOIR, IMPOST, TAX
dwarf - - - STUNT, TROLL, PYGMY
dwarf animal - - - - - - - - RUNT
dwarf cattle (S.A.) - - - - - NIATA
dwarf European shrub - - ELDERWORT
dwarf goblin - - - - - - - - GNOME
dwarf negrito of Mindaneo - - AETA
dwarfish - - - - - - - - NONOID
dwell - - - - LIVE, ABIDE, RESIDE
dwell on - - - - - - - - - - HARP
dwell upon moodily - - - - BROOD
dweller - - - - TENANT, RESIDENT
dwelling - - HOME, HOVEL, ABODE, TENEMENT, MANSION
dwelling alone - - - - - - EREMITIC
dwelling in caves - - - - - SPELAEAN
dwelling on a crag (var.) - - EYRIE
dwindle - - - - - - - - - PETER
dye - COLOUR, STAIN, HENNA, ANIL, EOSIN
dye base - - - - - - - - ANILINE
dye indigo - - - - - - - - - ANIL
dye plant - - - - - - - - - ANIL
dye process using wax - - - - BATIK
dye to shape pipe - - - - - DOD
dye substance - - ANILINE, SUMAC
dye yielding coal tar product - ANILINE
dyer - - - - - - - - -COLOURER
dying fire - - - - - - - - EMBERS
dynamic - - - - - - - ENERGETIC
dynamite (kind) - - - - - DUALIN
dynamite inventor - - - - - NOBEL
dynamo - - - - - - - GENERATOR
dynamo part - - - - - - ARMATURE
dynast - - - - - - - - - - RULER
dynasty - - - - - - - - - - REALM
dysprosium - - - - - - - - - DY

E

each (to) - - - - - - APIECE, EVERY
eager - - - ANXIOUS, AVID, KEEN, EARNEST, AGOG, INTENT, DESIROUS, AFIRE, ARDENT, ATHIRST, FERVENT
eager (slang) - - - - - - - ITCHY
eagerness for action - - - - - ELAN
eagle - - - - - - - - - ERN, ERNE
eagle's nest - - AERIE, EYRIE, AERY
eaglestone - - - - - - - - - ETITE
ear - AURICLE, HARKEN, PINNA, HEED, LUG, SPIKE
ear auricle - - - - - - - - PINNA
ear bone - - - - - AMBOS, STAPES
ear of corn part - - - - - - - COB
ear covering - - - - - - - EARLAP
ear doctor - - - - - - - OTOLOGIST
ear as of grain - - - - - - SPIKE
ear like part - - - - - - - - - LUG
ear lobe - - - - - - - - LUG, EARLOP
ear (pert. to) - - - - - OTIC, AURAL
ear ossicle - - - - - - - - STAPES
ear part - - - - - - - PINNA, LOBE
ear (Scot.) - - - - - - - - - LUG
ear shell - - - - - - - - ABALONE
earache - - - - - - - - - - OTALGIA
earlier - - - - - PREVIOUS, SOONER
earlike projection - - - - - - LUG
early - - - - - - BETIMES, SOON
early alphabetic character - - - RUNE
early alphabetic character (pert. to) - RUNIC
early American capitalist - - - ASTOR
early Archbishop of Canterbury - - - CRANMER
early Briton - - - - - - - - - PICT
early Chinese coin - - - - - - - PU
early Christian champion - - - - CID
early Christian pulpit - - - - AMBO
early colonist's greeting to Indian - NETOP
early counting device - - - - ABACUS
early in the day (poet.) - - - - RATHE
early English colonizers - - SAXONS
early English court - - - - - - LEET
early English money - - - - - - ORA
early European invader - - - - ALAN
early flowering perennial - PRIMROSE
early Greek Christian father - IRENAEUS
early Greek doctor - - - - - GALEN
early harpsichord - - - - - SPINET
early inhabitant of Great Britain - CELT
early Irish tenant - - - - - - SAER
early Irishman - - - - - - - AIRE
early Mexican Indian - - - - TOLTEC
early musical character - - - - NEUME
early musical instrument - REBEC, SPINET
early Norse gods - - - - - - - VANIR
early Peruvian chief - - - - - - INCA
early physician - - - - - - - - GALEN
early (poet.) - - - - - - - - - RATH
early prohibitionist - - - - - - DOW
early Scots - - - - - - - - - PICTS
early Syrian king - - - - ANTIOCHUS
early theologian - - - - - - - ARIUS
early theologian (pert. to) - - - ARIAN
early Venetian coin (var.) - - - BETSO
early version of Scriptures - - - ITALA
earn - GAIN, MERIT, DESERVE, ATTAIN, ACHIEVE
earn profit - - - - - - - - - - NET
earn with difficulty - - - - - - EKE
earnest - - SERIOUS, EAGER, PLEDGE, ZEALOUS
earnings - - - - - - - - - SALARY
earring - - - - - - - - - PENDANT
earth - TERRA, SOIL, GEAL, DIRT, LOAM, WORLD, SOD, GLOBE, CLAY, LAND
earth (comb. form) - - GEO, GE, GEA
earth (dial.) - - - - - - - - - ERD
earth (Latin) - - - - - - - - - TERRA
earth of lime and clay - - - - MARL
earth mound - - - - - - - RIDEAU
earth (poet.) - - - - - - - - - MARL
earthen container - - - - - - - POT
earthen cup - - - - - - - - - MUG
earthenware - - CROCKERY, FAIENCE, CROCK, POT, JUG
earthkin - - - - - - - - - TERELLA
earthly - - - - - - - - - MUNDANE

earthnut - - - - - - - - PEANUT
earthpea - - - - - - - - PEANUT
earthquake - - - - - - - - SEISM
earthy - TEMPORAL, TERRENE, COARSE
earthy deposit - - - - - - - MARL
earthy iron ore - - - - - - - OCHER
earthy material - - MOLD, CLAY, MARL
earthy pigment - - - - - - - SIENNA
earthy sediment - - - - - - - SILT
ease - - COMFORT, ALLAY, RELIEVE, REPOSE, REST, FACILITY, LIGHTEN, RELIEF, DECREASE
easily - - - - READILY, SMOOTHLY
easily affected - - - - - SENSITIVE
easily angered - - IRACUND, IRASCIBLE
easily bent - - - - - - - - - LIMP
easily broken - - - FRAIL, CRUMBLY
easily frightened - - - - - - TIMID
easily moved - - MOBILE, EMOTIONAL
easily tempted - - - - - FRAIL, WEAK
easily vaporized - - - - - - VOLATILE
East - - - - - - - ORIENT, LEVANT
East (pert. to) - - - - - - - EOAN
East African coin - - - - - - - PESA
East African hartebeest - - - - - TORA
East Asia fiber herb - - - - - RAMIE
East Asia weight - - - - - - - TAEL
East Indian antelope - - SASIN, SEROW
East Indian ascetic - - - - - - FAKIR
East Indian boiled butter - - - - - GHI
East Indian bridegroom's gold piece TALI
East Indian cart - - - - - - TONGA
East Indian caste - - - - - - - DOM
East Indian cavalryman - - - - SOWAR
East Indian cedar - - - - - - DEODAR
East Indian cereal grass - RAGEE, RAGI
East Indian chief of police - DAROGA, DAROGAH
East Indian coin - - - RUPEE, ANNA
East Indian country or region (var.) DES
East Indian cymbals - - - - - - TAL
East Indian fiber plant - - - - - - DA
East Indian food staple - - - - - RAGI
East Indian fruit - - - - - CARDAMON
East Indian gateway - - - - - - TORAN
East Indian granary - - - - - - GOLA
East Indian grass - KASA, GLAGAH, RICE
East Indian harvest - - - - - - RABI
East Indian hat plant - - - - - SOLA
East Indian helmet - - - - - - TOPEE
East Indian herb - PIA, SOLA, SESAME, REA
East Indian lady's maid - - - - AYAH
East Indian language - - - - - TAMIL
East Indian litter - - - - - - DOOLIE
East Indian millet - - - - - DHURRA
East Indian money - - - - - - ANNA
East Indian native - - BENGALI, TAMIL
East Indian agent - - - - - GOMASHTA
East Indian native sailor - - - - LASCAR
East Indian palm - - - - - - - NIPA
East Indian palm civet - - - - MUSANG
East Indian peasant - - - - - - RYOT
East Indian perennial - - - - - RAMIE
East Indian pheasant - - - - - MONAL
East Indian plant - SOLA, BENNE, RAMIE
East Indian poet - - - - - - TAGORE
East Indian police station - - - THANA
East Indian sacrificial rice dish PAYASAM
East Indian sailor - - - - - - LASCAR
East Indian shrubbery - - - - - HERB
East Indian singing bird - - - - SHAMA
East Indian soldier - - - - - - SEPOY
East Indian songbird - - - - - SHAMA
East Indian split pulse - - - - - DAL
East Indian spring crop - - - - - RABI
East Indian sword - - - - - - - PATA
East Indian temple - - - - - PAGODA
East Indian tent - - - - - - - - PAWL
East Indian timber tree - - DAR, SAL, SALAI, TEAK
East Indian title - - AYA, SAHIB, MIAN
East Indian tree - KHAIR, ACH, NIEPA, SAL, SALAI, PALAY, BANYAN, TEAK
East Indian vehicle - - - - - - TONGA
East Indian village cattle - - - - DHAN
East Indian vine - - - - - - - - ODAL
East Indian water vessel - - - - - LOTA
East Indian weight - SER, BAHAR, TOLA
East Indian wild honeybee - - DINGAR
East Indian wild sheep - - - - - URIAL
East Indian wood - - - - - ENG, ALOE
East Indian woody vine - - - - - ODAL
East Mediterranean region - - LEVANT
Eastern church part - - - - - - BEMA
Eastern inhabitant - - - - - - ASIAN
Eastern Mediterranean - - - - - LEVANT
Eastern potentate - - - - AMEER, EMIR
Eastern roving miracle man - - FAKIR
Eastern term of respect - - - - SAHIB
eastward - - - - - - - - EASTERLY
easy - - EFFORTLESS, COMFORTABLE, TRACTABLE, GENTLE, FACILE, SIMPLE
easy chair - - - - - - - - - ROCKER
easy to do - - - - - - - - - FACILE
easy gait - - - - - - - LOPE, AMBLE
easy gallop - - - - - - LOPE, CANTER
easy job - - - - - - - - SINECURE
easy to manage - - - - - - - DOCILE
easy talk (slang) - - - - - - - SNAP
easy task (slang) - - - - - - - SNAP
eat - DINE, CORRODE, DEVOUR, SUP, GNAW, RUST, FEED
eat away - - - ERODE, EROSE, GNAW
eat greedily - - - - - GORGE, GOBBLE
eat little by little - - - - - - GNAW
eat sparingly - - - - - - - - - DIET
eatable - - - - - - - COMESTIBLE
eaten away - - - - - EROSE, ERODED
eating (pert. to) - - - - - - DIETARY
eating place - - - - - - - - DINER
eating regimen - - - - - - - - DIET
ebb - - RECEDE, DECLINE, SUBSIDE, REFLUX, WANE, DECREASE, SINK
ebb tide - - - - - - - - - - NEAP
ebbing and flowing - - - - - - TIDAL
Eber's father - - - - - - - ELPAAL
Eber's son - - - - - - - - - PELEG
ebon - - - - - - - - - DARK, BLACK
ebullient - - - - - - - - AGITATED
eccentric - - - - - - ODD, ERRATIC
eccentric person (slang) - - - - NUT
eccentric wheel portion - - - - - CAM
eccentricity - - - - ODDITY, CROTCHET
Ecclesiast - - - - - - - - - - FRA
ecclesiastical - - - - - - - - SYNOD
ecclesiastical cape - - - - - - ORALE
ecclesiastical council - - - - - SYNOD
ecclesiastical court - - - - - - ROTA
ecclesiastical headdress - - - - MITER
ecclesiastical linen cloth - - - FANON
ecclesiastical plate - - - - - - PATEN
ecclesiastical residence - - - - MANSE
ecclesiastical salver - - - - - - PATEN
ecclesiastical scarf and vest - - ORALE
ecclesiastical service - - - - - MATIN
ecclesiastical unit - - - - - - PARISH
ecclesiastical vestment - - ALB, ORALE, AMICE, STOLE

E

echo - IMITATE. REPEAT. RESOUND
eclat - - - - GLORY, SPLENDOUR
eclogue - - - - - - - - - IDYL
economical - - - - FRUGAL, SPARING
economize - - - - - - - - SCRIMP
economy - - - - - - - FRUGALITY
ecru - - - - - - - - - - - BEIGE
ecstasy - - RAPTURE, BLISS, TRANCE
ecstatic utterance - - - - RHAPSODY
Ecuador province - - - - - - - ORO
Ecuador volcano - - - - - ANTISANA
eddy - - SWIRL, WHIRLPOOL, POOL, VORTEX
edematous - - - - - - - - - EDEMIC
edemic - - - - - - - EDEMATOUS
Eden's river - - - - - - - - PISON
edenic - - - - - - - - BLISSFUL
edge - - - LIP, BRIM, RIM, BRINK, SHARPEN, MARGIN, VERGE, BORDER, SHARPNESS, SIDLE, HEM
edge of crater - - - - - - - - - LIP
edge of garment - - - - - - - HEM
edge of hat - - - - - - - - - BRIM
edge of hill - - - - - - - - - BROW
edge of page (on) - - - - - MARGINAL
edge (poet.) - - - - - - - MARGE
edge of road - - - - - - - WAYSIDE
edge of roof - - - - - - - - EAVE
edged - - - - - - - - - - SHARP
edged implement - - - - - - RAZOR
edged tool - AXE, EDGER, AX, SWORD
edging - - - - - - - - - - - RIM
edgy - - - - - - - - - - - SHARP
edible - COMESTIBLE, ESCULENT, VIAND
edible bird - - - - - - - ORTOLAN
edible bulb - - - - - - - - ONION
edible clam - - - - - - - - GAPER
edible fish - - - - - - - - PORGY
edible fruit portion - - - - - - PULP
edible fungus - - - - - - - MOREL
edible grain - - - - - - - - CEREAL
edible mollusk - - - - - - ASI, CLAM
edible mudworm - - - - - - - IPO
edible part of anything - - - - MEAT
edible part of fruit - - - - - - PULP
edible plant - - - - - - VEGETABLE
edible plant (pert. to) - - - - VEGETAL
edible plant seed - - - - - - - BEAN
edible purple seaweed - - - - - LAVER
edible root - GARLIC, CARROT, BEET, PARSNIP, YAM, RADISH
edible root stock - - - - - - - TARO
edible seaweed - AGAR, DULSE, LAVER
edible seed - - - LENTIL, PEA, BEAN
edible tuber - - - OCA, POTATO, TARO
edict - - DECREE, ARRET, MANIFESTO, STATUTE
edification - - - - - - UPBUILDING
edifice - - - - - HOUSE, BUILDING
edify - - - - - - - - CONSTRUCT
Edison's middle name - - - - - ALVA
edit - REVISE, REDACT, PUBLISH, ISSUE, COMPILE
edition - - - - - - ISSUE, PRINTING
edition of paper (certain) - - - EXTRA
editor - - - - - - - - REDACTOR
educated - - - LITERATE, TRAINED, INSTRUCTED, LETTERED, TAUGHT
educated persons - - - - - LITERATI
education - - - - - - - TRAINING
educational institution - - ACADEMY, SEMINARY, SCHOOL
educational institution (abbr.) - - H.S.
educator - - - - - - - - TEACHER
educe - - - ELICIT, EVOLVE, EVOKE
educt - - - - - - - - - EXTRACT

eel - - - - - - - - - - - ELVER
eel (kind) - - MORAY, CONGER, SIREN
eel shaped amphibian - - - - - SIREN
eel trap - - - - - - - - - - EELPOT
eerie - - UNCANNY, WEIRD, MACABRE, SCARY
efface - - - - - - - ERASE, SPONGE
effacement - - - - - - - - ERASURE
effect - - - - - - - - RESULT, DO
effective - - - - - - - - OPERATIVE
effective as an agent - - - - - CAUSAL
effeminate - - - - EPICENE, WOMANISH
effeminate boy - - - - - - - - SISSY
effeminate fellow - - - - - - - - FOP
effete - - - - - - - - - - BARREN
efficacious - - - - - - - - - VALID
efficacy - - - - - - - - - - DINT
efficient - - - - - - ABLE, CAPABLE
efficient cause of action - MAINSPRING
effigy - - - - - - - - IMAGE, DOLL
effluence - - - - - - - EMANATION
effort - - ATTEMPT, EXERTION, ESSAY, NISUS, STRUGGLE
effort to gain support - - PROPAGANDA
effortless - - - - - - - - - - EASY
eft - - - - - - - - - - - - NEWT
egest - - - - - - - - - - EXCRETE
egg - OVUM, URGE, INCITE, OVA (pl.), ROE
egg cells - - - - - - - - - - OVA
egg (comb. form) - - - - - OVO, OO
egg dish - - - - - OMELET, OMELETTE
egg drink - - - - - - - - - - NOG
egg measure - - - - - - - - - PIK
egg on - - - - - - - - URGE, ABET
egg shaped - OVATE, OVOID, OVATED, OOIDAL, OVIFORM
egg shaped ornaments - - - - - OVA
egis - - - - - - - - - - - SHIELD
eglantine - - - - - - - SWEETBRIER
ego - - - - - - - - - - - - SELF
egoism - - - - - - - - - - VANITY
egotism - - - - - - - - - - PRIDE
egotistic - - - - - - - - CONCEITED
egregious - - - - - - - - - GROSS
egress - - - - - - - - - - - EXIT
egret - - - - - - - - HERON, PLUME
Egyptian - - - - - - - - - - COPT
Egyptian administrative official - MUDIR
Egyptian catheaded goddess - - BAST
Egyptian city - - - - - - - - CAIRO
Egyptian cotton - - - - - - - PIMA
Egyptian crown - - - - - - - ATEF
Egyptian dancing girl - - ALME, ALMA
Egyptian deity - BES, AMON, MIN, PTAH, ISIS, RA, DERA, OSIRIS, APET
Egyptian god of earth - - - - - - GEB
Egyptian god of procreation - - - MIN
Egyptian god of wisdom and magic THOTH
Egyptian goddess - ISIS, PTAH, SATI, MAAT, APET
Egyptian gold or silver alloy - - ASEM
Egyptian king - - - - - - RAMESES
Egyptian lizard - - - - - - - ADDA
Egyptian measure - - - - - DERA, KET
Egyptian monarch - - - RAMESES, TUT
Egyptian month - - - - - - - - APAP
Egyptian provincial governor - - MUDIR
Egyptian queen of the gods - - - SATI
Egyptian religious astral body - - KA
Egyptian religious heart - - - - - AB
Egyptian religious soul - - - - - - BA
Egyptian river - - - - - - - - NILE
Egyptian sacred bull - - - - - APIS

E

Egyptian skind - - - - - - - ADDA
Egyptian snake - - - - - - - - ASP
Egyptian solar deity (var.) - - - SU
Egyptian soul in religion - - - - BA
Egyptian structure - - - - PYRAMID
Egyptian sun disk - - - - - - ATEN
Egyptian sun god - RA, TEM, AMMON, AMON
Egyptian symbol of immortality - SCARAB
Egyptian symbolic eye - - - - UTA
Egyptian underground member - MUMMY
Egyptian unit of capacity - - - ARDEB
eidolon - - - PHANTOM, ICON, IMAGE
eight - - - - OCTET, OCTA, OCTAVE
eight (comb. form) - - - OCTI, OCTA
eight line stanza - - - - - - TRIOLET
eighth of a gallon - - - - - - PINT
eighth of a mark (Shetland) - - - URE
eighth part of a circle - - - - OCTANT
eight sided figure - - - - - OCTAGON
Eire - - - - - - - - - - - ERIN
either - - - - - - - - - - - OR
ejaculation - - - - - - - - - ALAS
eject - EMIT, OUT, OUST, ELIMINATE, EXPEL, EVICT
eject by force - - - - - OUSE, OUST
eject in a jet - - - - - - - SPOUT
eject violently - - - - - - - SPEW
ejection - - - - - - - - EVICTION
elaborate - - - - - - - - ORNATE
elaborate discourse - - - - - ORATION
elaborate melody - - - - - - - ARIA
elan - DASH, ZEAL, ARDOR, IMPULSE, SPIRIT
elapse - - - - - - - PASS, EXPIRE
elastic - - - - RESILIENT, SPRINGY
elastic bitumen - - - - - ELATERITE
elastic mineral resin - - - ELATERITE
elastic wood - - - - - - - - ASH
elate - - - EXALT, EXCITE, GLADDEN
elated - - - - JUBILANT, EXULTANT
elation - - - - - - - - - - JOY
elbow - - - - - - - - - - ANCON
elbow (to) - - - - - - - - JOSTLE
elder - - - - - - - SENIOR, PRIOR
elderly person - - - - - - - OLDSTER
eldest - - - - - - - - - - OLDEST
elect - - CHOOSE, CHOSEN, PREFER, DECIDE
election - - - - - - - - - POLL
election reports - - - - - - RETURNS
elector - - - - - - - - - - VOTER
electric atmosphere - - - - - - AURA
electric catfish - - - - - - - RAAD
electric circuit - - - - - - - LOOP
electric coil - - - - - - - SOLENOID
electric current - - - - - - A.C., D.C.
electric current strength - - - VOLTAGE
electric generator - - - - - DYNAMO
electric light (kind) - - - - - - ARC
electric od - - - - - - - - ELOD
electrical degree - - - - - - - EE
electrical current device - - RESISTOR
electrical device - - CODER, REVERSER, GENERATOR, CONDENSER
electrical generator - - - - - DYNAMO
electrical transmission - - - - RADIO
electrical unit - - FARAD, REL, VOLT, AMPERE, OHM, WATT
electrical unit (colloq.) - - - - AMP
electricity (kind) - - - - - - STATIC
electricity (pert. to) - - - - - VOLTAIC
electrified particle - - - - - IAN, ION
electromotive force - - - - PRESSURE
elegance - - GRACE, POLISH, REFINED
elegant - - - - - - - - - REFINED
element - - NEON, FACTOR, ARSENIC, SILVER, CONSTITUENT, BARIUM, COMPONENT
element of borax - - - - - - - BORON
element of the earth's crust - SILICON
element found in organic substances CARBON
elemental - PRIMAL, PRIMARY, SIMPLE
elementary - - SIMPLE, RUDIMENTAL
elementary substance - - - - - METAL
elephant's ear - - - - - - - - TARO
elephant carrying bird - - - - - ROC
elephant goad - - - - - - - ANKUS
elephant jockey - - - - - - MAHOUT
elephant pavilion - - - - - HOWDAH
elevate - HEIGHTEN, REAR, LIFT, RAISE, EXALT
elevated - - - - - - - - LOFTY, HIGH
elevated highway - - - - - OVERPASS
elevated line - - - - - - - - - EL
elevation - - - EXALTATION, HEIGHT
elevation to celestial things - ANAGOGE
elevation of land - - MOUNTAIN, HILL
elevator - - - - - - - - - - - LIFT
elevator carriage - - - - - - - CAR
elevator well - - - - - - - - SHAFT
elf - GNOME, SPRITE, FAY, PERI, FAIRY, PIXIE
elflike creature - - - - - - - PERI
elicit - - - - - - - EDUCE, EVOKE
elide - - - DELE, IGNORE, ANNUL, SUPPRESS, OMIT
eliminate - - - REMOVE, EXCLUDE, ERADICATE, EJECT
elision - - - - - - - - - OMISSION
elite - - - - - - - - - - - PICK
elixir - - - - - - - - - - PANACEA
elk - - ELAND, MOOSE, WAPITI, STAG
ellipse - - - - - - - - - - OVAL
elliptical - - - - - - - OVAL, OVATE
elocutionist - - - - - - - - READER
eloin - - - - - - - - - - ABSCOND
elongate - - - LENGTHEN, STRETCH
elope - - - - - - - - - - ABSCOND
eloquence - - - - - - - - ORATORY
eloquent - - - - - - - - EXPRESSIVE
eloquent discourse - - - - - ORATION
else - - - - - - - - OTHER, BESIDES
elucidate - - - - - - - - - SOLVE
elude - EVADE, AVOID, DODGE, ESCAPE, BAFFLE
elusive - - - - LUBRICOUS, EVASIVE
elver - - - - - - - - - - - - EEL
Elysium - - - - - - EDEN, PARADISE
emaciated - - - - - - - - - SKINNY
emanate - - - - - - - - ORIGINATE
emanation - - - AURA, EFFLUENCE, ECTOPLASM
emancipate - - - - - - - - DELIVER
emancipation - - - - - - - - AURA
emancipator - - - - - - - LIBERATOR
embalm - - - - - - - - - PRESERVE
embankment - - - - - - - - - LEVEE
embark - - - - - - - - - - - SHIP
embassy - - - - - - - - - LEGATION
embassy member - - - - - - ATTACHE
embellish - - - - - ADORN, DECORATE
ember - - - - - - - - COAL, CINDER
embezzle - - - - - - - - - - STEAL
embezzler - - - - - - - - PECULATOR
embitter - - - - - - - - - - - SOUR
emblem - - BADGE, IMAGE, SYMBOL TYPE, STANDARD
emblem of authority - - BATON, MACE
emblem of Neptune - - - - - TRIDENT
emblem on a shield - - - - - IMPRESA

E

emblem of subjection - - - - - YOKE
emblematic - - - - - - - - TYPICAL
embodiment - - - - - - - - AVATAR
embody - - - - - - - INCORPORATE
embolden - - - - - - - - - - ABET
emboss - - - - - - - - - - RAISE
embrace - - - - CLASP, ADOPT, HUG, COMPRISE, FOLD, CONTAIN
embrace (dial.) - - - - - - - - COLL
embrocation - - - - - - - LINIMENT
embroider - - - - ADORN, EMBELLISH
embroidery frame - - - - - TABORET
embroidery silk - - - - - - - FLOSS
embroidery thread - - - - - ARRASENE
embroidery yarn - - - - - - - CREWEL
embroil - - - - - - - - - ENTANGLE
embrown - - - - - - - - - - - TAN
emend - - REFORM, AMEND, RECTIFY, REVISE
emendation - - - - - - CORRECTION
emendator - - - - - - - - AMENDER
Emerald Isle - - - - - - - - - ERIN
emerge - - - - - - - - - - ISSUE
emergency - - - - - - - JUNCTURE
emery - - - - - - - - - CORUNDUM
emigrant settlement - - - - - COLONY
eminence - - - - FAME, HEIGHT, HILL
eminence commanding a plain - RIDEAU
eminent - NOTED, PROMINENT, GREAT
eminent person - - - - - - GRANDEE
eminently - - - - - - - - NOTABLY
emissary - - - - - - - - - AGENT
emit - - - - - EJECT, ERUPT, EXUDE, DISCHARGE, VOICE, ISSUE, SHED, RADIATE
emit a current of air - - - - - BLOW
emit light and heat - - - - - - GLOW
emit odour - - - - - - - - - SMELL
emit piercing sound - - - - - SCREAM
emit ray - - ERADIATE, RADIATE, BEAM
emit swiftly - - - - - - - - - DART
emit vapor - - - - - - - - - STEAM
emmet - - - - - - - - - - - - ANT
emolument - - - - - SALARY, PROFIT
emotion - - - - - - - - - FEELING
emotional cry - - - - - EXCLAMATION
emperor - - - - - RULER, IMPERATOR
emperor (former) - - - - - - - TSAR
emperor's wife - - - - - - EMPRESS
emphasis - SALIENCE, STRESS, ACCENT
emphasize - - - - - ACCENT, STRESS
emphatic - - - - - - - - FORCIBLE
empire - - - - - - NATION, REALM
Empire State - - - - - - - NEW YORK
employ - - - - - USE, HIRE, ENGAGE
employ with diligence - - - - - PLY
employees - - - - - - - - - - MEN
employment - - - - - - - - - WORK
emporium - - - - - - - - - - MART
emptiness - - - - - - - - - INANITY
empty - VOID, INANE, BARE, VACANT, VAIN, DEPLETE
empty form - - - - - - - - - BLANK
empty by lading - - - - - - - SCOOP
empty of liquids - - - - - - - DRAIN
empyrean - - - - - - - - - - ETHER
emu - - - - - - - - - - - - - RHEA
emulate - - - - - VIE, RIVAL, EQUAL
emulator - - - - - - - - - - RIVAL
enact - PLAY, DECREE, PERFORM, PASS
enact law - - - - - - - - LEGISLATE
enamel - - - - - - - - - - - GLAZE
enamored - - CAPTIVATED, SMIT, FOND
encamp - - - - - - - BIVOUAC, TENT
encampment - - - - - - - - - CAMP
encase - - - WRAP, CASE, ENSHEATH, SURROUND
enchanted - - - - - RAPT, CHARMED, BEWITCHED
enchantress - - MEDEA, SIREN, CIRCE
encircle - RING, ENCLASP, SURROUND, BELT, HOOP, ENVIRON
encircled - - - - - - - - - - - GIRT
encircling strip - - - - - - - - BELT
enclose - CASE, SURROUND, HEM, PEN, INSERT
enclose within walls - - - - - MURE
enclosed - - - - - - - - - INTERNAL
enclosed field - - - - - - - - AGER
enclosure - - PEN, YARD, CAGE, COOP
enclosure for cattle - - KRAAL, CORRAL
enclosure of close piling - - STARLING
enclosure for pasture - - - - PADDOCK
enclosure for sheep - - - - - - KRAAL
enclosure for storage - - - - - - BIN
encompass - - - - - - - - - - BELT
encore - - - - - - - - - BIS, AGAIN
encounter in battle - - - - - ENGAGE
encounter boldly - - - - - - - BEARD
encourage - - - ABET, HEARTEN, EGG, CHEER, IMPEL
encroach - TRESPASS, INVADE, INTRUDE
encroachment - - INROAD, INTRUSION
encumber - - - - - - LOAD, HAMPER
encurl - - - - - - - - - - - TWINE
encysted tumor - - - - - - - - WEN
end - TERMINATE, FINIS, OMEGA, CEASE, OUTCOME, TIP, CLOSE, PURPOSE, TERMINAL, FINALE, CLIMAX, LIMIT, DESIST, SURCEASE
end aimed at - - - - - - - - - GOAL
end car of freight train - - - CABOOSE
end (comb. form) - - - - - - - TELO
end man of minstrel show - - - BONES
end (musical) - - - - - - - - - FINE
end wall part - - - - - - - - GABLE
end of a yard (naut.) - - - - - ARM
endeavoured - STRIVEN, TRIED, AIMED, ESSAYED, ASSAYED, ATTEMPTED
endeavouring - - - - - - CONATIVE
ended - - - - - - - - - - - OVER
ending - - - - - - - FINALE, FINIS
endless - - - - ETERNAL, EVERLASTING CONTINUAL, INFINITE, PERPETUAL
endless monotony - - - - - TREADMILL
endless time - - - - - - - ETERNITY
endmost - - - - - - - - - FARTHEST
endorse - SANCTION, OK, RATIFY, BACK
endorsement - - - - - - - - BACKING
endow - - DOWER, INVEST, FURNISH, VEST, GIFT, BESTOW
endowed with authority - - - - VESTED
endowed with life - - - - - ANIMATE
endower - - - - - - - - - ENVESTOR
endowment - - - - FUND, DOS, DOWER
endue - - - - - - - - - - - INVEST
endure - LAST, BEAR, ABIDE, STAND, SUSTAIN, TOLERATE, WITHSTAND
endure (Scot.) - - - - - - - - DREE
endure sharp pain - - - - - - SMART
enduring - - PERSISTENT, PERMANENT
enemy - - - - - - - - - - - - - FOE
energetic - - - FORCEFUL, VIGOROUS, DYNAMICAL, ACTIVE, FORCIBLE
energy - - VIGOR, POWER, VIM, FORCE
energy (colloq.) - - - - - - - - - PEP
enervate - - - - - - - WEAKEN, SAP
enfold - - - - - - - - - WRAP, LAP
enforce - - - - - - - - - - COMPEL
engage - - - - HIRE, EMPLOY, RETAIN, BETROTH, OCCUPY
engage the attention - - - - INTEREST
engage in competition - - - - COMPETE
engage in - - - - - - - - - - - WAGE

engage in military service - - - ENLIST
engage in play - - - - - RECREATE
engage with each other - - - - MESH
engaged in trade - - - COMMERCIAL
engagement - - - - - - - - DATE
engaging - - - - - - - ATTRACTIVE
engender - - BREED, PRODUCE, EXITE, OCCASION, BEGET, GENDER
engine - - - - MOTOR, LOCOMOTIVE
engine part - - - - - - - TURBINE
engine of war - - - - - - - - RAM
engineer - - - - - - - - MANAGE
engineer's shelter - - - - - - - CAB
engineering degree - - - - E.E., C.E.
engineering unit - - - - - - - BEL
engineless aircraft - - - - - GLIDER
engirdle - - - - - - - - - - ZONE
English - - SAXON (See also British)
English actor and manager - - - TREE
English architect - - - - - - WREN
English Arctic explorer - - - - ROSS
English author - READE, MILNE, ROGET, OPIE, STERNE, CAINE, BRONTE, HARDY
English baby carriage - - - - - PRAM
English banker poet - - - - - ROGERS
English bishop - - - - - - - - KEN
English borough - - - - - - - LEEDS
English cathedral - - - - - - - ELY
English cathedral city - - - - TRURO
English cathedral passage - - - SLYPE
English cathedral town - - - - - ELY
English cheese - - - - - - STILTON
English chemist and physicist - FARADAY
English city - - - LEEDS, CHESTER, WALLSEND
English clergyman - - - - - - STERNE
English clown - - - - - - GRIMALDI
English coins - - PENCE, SHILLINGS, FARTHINGS, GUINEAS
English Colonel governor - - - - GAGE
English comedian - - - - - - TOOLE
English composer - - - - ARNE, ELGAR
English county - SHIRE, DORSET, KENT, ESSEX
English dance - - - - - - - MORRIS
English dean - - - - - - - - INGE
English diarist - - - - - - - PEPYS
English divine - - - - INGE, DONNE
English dramatist - PEELE, UDAL, KYD, LYLY, PINERO, MARLOWE
English dynasty - - - TUDOR, STUART
English Egyptologist - - - - - PETRIE
English essayist - - - - - - - LAMB
English field marshal - - - - - HAIG
English floral emblem - - - - - ROSE
English forest tract - - - - - ARDEN
English hedgerow - - - - - - - REW
English historian - - - GROTE, ACTON
English humorist - - - - - - STERNE
English hymn writer - - - - - - LYTE
English journalist - - - - - - HENTY
English law court - - - - - - - LEET
English malt liquor - - - - - PORTER
English manufacturing town - - LEEDS, DERBY
English measure of length - - - - ELL
English monk - - - - - BEDE, BEDA
English murderer - - - - - - - ARAM
English musician - - - - - - - ARNE
English name for letter Z - - - - ZED
English national emblem - - - - ROSE
English novelist - - BRONTE, DICKENS, RAMEE, READE, CAINE
English painter - - - - - - TURNER
English philologist - - - - - - ARAM
English philosopher - - - - - BACON
English physician - - - - - - - ROSS
English physicist - - - - - FARADAY
English poet - KEATS, SPENSER, DONNE, BLAKE, GRAY
English policeman (colloq.) - - BOBBY
English political party - - - - TORY
English port - - - - - - - PRESTON
English Quaker - - - - - - - - PENN
English race course - - - - - - ASCOT
English race horse - - - - - - ASCOT
English river - URE, AVON, EXE, DEE, THAMES, TEE, USK, AIRE, OUSE, TYNE, WYE, TEES, TRENT, MERSEY, SEVERN
English royal family - TUDOR, STUART
English royal stables - - - - - MEWS
English sandhill - - - - - - - DENE
English school - HARROW, ETON, RUGBY
English schoolmaster - - - - - ARAM
English seaport - - - - DOVER, DEAL
English spy - - - - - - - - ANDRE
English stage - - - - - - - PLATEAU
English statesman - - - - GREY, PITT
English streetcar - - TRAM, TRAMCAR
English suburb - - - - GORLESTON
English surgeon - - - - - - - LISTER
English title - - - - - - - BARONET
English town - - - ETON, LEEDS, ELY
English unit of measure - - - - STACK
English university official - - - BEADLE
English weight - - - - - - - STONE
English wood pigeon - - - - CULVER
engrave by means of dots - - - STIPPLE
engrave by a needle - - - - - - ETCH
engraving - - - - - - - - - - CUT
engrossed - - - - RAPT, ENGAGED
engrossment - - - PREOCCUPATION
engulf - - - - - - - - - - WHELM
enhance - - - - - - - - - HEIGHTEN
enigma - MYSTERY, RIDDLE, CHARADE, PUZZLE
enigmatic - - - PUZZLING, MYSTIC
enigmatical person - - - - - SPHINX
enjoin - COMMAND, BID, PRESS, FORBID
enjoy - - - - - - - - - - - LIKE
enjoyment - - FUN, PLEASURE, RELISH
enlarge - SPREAD, MAGNIFY, DILATE, INCREASE, EXPAND, AMPLIFY, GROW
enlarge an opening - - - - - - REAM
enlarged stem - - - - - - - - BULB
enlargement of thyroid gland - GOITER
enlarger - - - - - DILATOR, REAMER
enlighten - - - - - - - - ILLUMINE
enlist - - - - - - ENROLL, RECRUIT
enlist as seaman - - - - - - - SHIP
enlisted soldier - - - - - - PRIVATE
enlistment - - - - - - - - - ENTRY
enliven - - - ANIMATE, EXHILARATE, QUICKEN
enliven (slang) - - - - - - - - PEP
enlivener - - - - - - - - ANIMATOR
enmesh - TANGLE, ENTANGLE, ENLACE
enmity - - - HATE, HATRED, RANCOR
ennead - - - - - - - - - - - NINE
ennoble - - - - - ELEVATE, HONOUR
ennui - - - - - - - - - - BOREDOM
enormous - - - - - - - - HUGE, VAST
Enos's father - - - - - - - - SETH
enough (poet.) - - - - - - - - ENOW
enough (be) - - - - - - - - - - DO
enrage - - MADDEN, ANGER, INFLAME
enraged - ANGERED, MAD, INCENSED, MADDENED, ANGRY
enrapture - - ENTRANCE, TRANSPORT
enrich - - - - - - - - FATTEN, LARD
enroll - ENLIST, RECORD, POLL, ENTER, JOIN

E

enroll as voters - - - - - - - POLL
enrollment - - - - - LISTING, LIST
ensconce - - - - - - - - SETTLE
ensemble - - - - - - WHOLE, DECOR
ensheath - - - - - - - - ENCASE
ensign - - - - - - - - - - BANNER
ensnare - TANGLE, TRAP, ENTRAP, NET
ensnarl - - - - - - - - ENTANGLE
ensue - - RESULT, FOLLOW, SUCCEED
entail - - - - - - - - - INVOLVE
entangle - - MAT, EMBROIL, SNARE, RAVEL, MESH, ENSNARL, KNOT, WEB
enter - PIERCE, RECORD, PENETRATE, REGISTER, ENROLL, INSERT, JOIN
enter with hostile intent - - - INVADE
enterprise - - - - - - - - VENTURE
entertain - - AMUSE, TREAT, REGALE, BEGUILE, FETE, DIVERT, HARBOR
entertain royally - - - - REGALE, FETE
enthrall - - - - - - - - CAPTIVATE
enthrone - - - - - - - - - ENSEAT
enthusiasm - PEP, SPIRIT, ELAN, ARDOR, VERVE
enthusiast - - - - - - - - ZEALOT
enthusiastic - - - - - - EAGER, KEEN
enthusiastic acclaim - - - - OVATION
enthusiastic follower - - - - - - FAN
enthusiastic promoter (slang) - BOOSTER
enthusiastic reception - - - - OVATION
entice - LURE, ATTRACT, TEMPT, ALLURE, LEER, CHARM, INVITE, WIN, DECOY, INVEIGLE
entice by artifice - - - - - - DECOY
entice (dial.) - - - - - - - - TOLE
enticement - - - - - - LURE, BAIT
enticing woman - - - - - - - SIREN
entire - - TOTAL, COMPLETE, WHOLE, INTEGRAL, ALL
entire man - - - - - - - EGOS, EGO
entire range - - - - - - - - GAMUT
entirely - - - - - - TOTALLY, QUITE
entirety - - - - - - - - TOTALITY
entitle - - - NAME, DUB, DESIGNATE, QUALIFY
entitle anew - - - - - - - RENAME
entitle with authority - - - - - - VEST
entity - - - - - - - - - ENS, UNIT
entomb - - - - - - - - - - INTER
entomion - - - - - - - - MASTOID
entourage - - - - - - ENVIRONMENT
entrance - - - CHARM, ADIT, ENTRY, PORTAL, INLET, DOORWAY, INGRESS, GATEWAY, DELIGHT, GATE, DOOR, TRANSPORT
entrance hall - FOYER, LOBBY, ATRIUM
entranced - - - - - - - - - RAPT
entranceway - - - - - GATE, PORTAL
entrant - - - - - - - - - BEGINNER
entrap - - NOOSE, DECEIVE, DECOY, TREPAN, ENSNARE, BAG
entreat - PRAY, BESEECH, SUPPLICATE, CRAVE, IMPLORE, PLEAD, REQUEST, ADJURE, WOO, BEG
entreat earnestly - - - - - - - WOO
entreaty - - - PLEA, APPEAL, PRAYER
entrepot - - - - - - - - - - DEPOT
entrust - CONSIGN, CONFIDE, COMMIT
entry - ENTRANCE, ENGRESS, ACCESS, PASSAGE, ITEM
entry in an account - - - - ITEM, DEBIT
entry showing indebtedness - - - - DEBIT
entwined - - - - - - - WOVE, LACED
enumerate - - - - - - - - - NUMBER
enumeration - - - TALE, CATALOGUE
enunciate - - - - - - SPEAK, UTTER
enure - - - - - - - - - - HARDEN
envelop - - ENVEST, WRAP, SURROUND
envelope - - - - - COVER, WRAPPER
environ - - - SURROUND, ENCIRCLE
environment - - - SETTING, MEDIUM, ENTOURAGE
envoy - - - - - - - - - - - LEGATE
envy - - - - - - - COVET, JEALOUS
enwrap - - - - - - - - - - - ROLL
enzyme - - - - - - - - - - - ASE
eon - - - - - - - - - - - - AGE
eos - - - - - - - - - - - AURORA
ephemeral - - - - - - - MOMENTARY
epic - - HEROIC, POEM, NOBLE, GRAND
epic poem - - - - EPOS, EPO, EPOPEE
epical - - - - - - - HEROIC, NOBLE
epicure - - GOURMET, GASTRONOME
epicurean - - - - - - GASTRONOMIC
epidemic - - - - - - - WIDESPREAD
epidermic outgrowth (botanical) - - - RAMENTUM
epigrammatic saying - - - - - ADAGE
epinette - - - - - - - - - - LARCH
Episcopal jurisdiction - - - - - - SEE
Episcopal pastor - - - - - - RECTOR
episode - - INCIDENT, EVENT, SCENE
epistle - - - - - - LETTER, MISSIVE
epithesis (rhet.) - - - - - PARAGOGE
epithet - - - - - - - - - - - NAME
epitome - - - SYNOPSIS, SUMMARY
epoch - - - - - - AGE, ERA, EVENT
epoch of geological history - - EOCENE
epochal - - - - - - - - - - - ERAL
epode - - - - - - - - - AFTERSONG
epopee - - - - - - - - EPOS, POEM
equal - PEER, ISO, EVEN, EQUITABLE, COMPEER, COORDINATE, SAME, ADEQUATE, TIE, PAR
equal (comb. form) - - - - PARI, ISO
equal footing - - - - - - - - - PAR
equal of (was) - - - - - - RIVALED
equality - - - - - - - PAR, PARITY
equalize - - - - - - - - - - - EVEN
equally - - - - - - - - - ALIKE, AS
equally advanced - - - - - ABREAST
equals - - - - - - - - - - - TIES
equanimity - - - - - - - - - POISE
equestrian - - - - - - - - - RIDER
equiangular figure - - - - - ISAGON
equidistant lines - - - - PARALLELS
equilibrium - - - - - - - - - POISE
equine - HORSE, MARE, DONKEY, ASS
equip - - - - - - RIG, ATTIRE, GEAR
equip with crew - - - - - - - - MAN
equipment - - - GEAR, RIG, TACKLE
equipoise - - - - - - - - - - POISE
equipped with tires - - - - - - SHOD
equitable - - - - - EVEN, EQUAL, FAIR
equitable part - - - - - - - - SHARE
equitably - - - - - - - REASONABLY
equity - - - - - - - - - FAIRNESS
equivalence - - - - - - - - - - PAR
equivalent - - - - - - TANTAMOUNT
era - AGE, PERIOD, TIME, EPOCH, DATE
era (pert. to) - - - - - - - - - ERAL
eradicate - - - ELIMINATE, UPROOT, REMOVE, ERASE
eradicator - - - REMOVER, ERASER
eral - - - - - - - - - - - EPOCHAL
erase - - - DELETE, DELE, EFFACE, EXPUNGE, CANCEL
eraser - - - - - - - - - - - RUBBER
erasure - - - - - - - - - - DELETION
erbium - - - - - - - - - E.R., E.B.
ere - - - - - SOON, ANON, BEFORE

erect - - - REAR, UPRIGHT, RAISE, CONSTRUCT, BUILD
erect (be) - - - - - - - - STAND
ere long - - - - - - - ANON, SOON
eremite - - - - - - HERMIT, RECLUSE
erewhile - - - - - - - - FORMERLY
ergo - - - - - - - - - - - HENCE
eri - - - - - - - - - - SILKWORM
erica - - - - - - - HEATH, HEATHER
Erin - - - - - - - - - - - - ÉIRE
ermine - - - - - - - - - - STOAT
eroded - - - - - EATEN, CORRODED
erodent - - - - - - - - - CAUSTIC
erose - - - - - - UNEVEN, TOOTHED
err - - - STRAY, SIN, SLIP, BLUNDER
errand - - - COMMISSION, MISSION
errant - - - - - - ARRANT, ERRATIC
errantry - - - - - - - - - - ROVING
erratic - - - - - ERRANT, UNSTABLE
erroneous - - - - - MISTAKEN, FALSE
erroneous statement - - - - - FALLACY
error - - MISSTEP, MISTAKE, BLUNDER SLIP, FALLACY
error in printing - - - - - ERRATUM, ERRATA (PL.)
error (slang) - - - - - - - - MISCUE
Erse - - - - - - - - - - - - GAELIC
erudite - - - - - - LEARNED, WISE
erudite critic - - - - - - - - PUNDIT
erudition - LORE, WISDOM, LEARNING
erupt - - - - - - - - - - - - - EMIT
Peruvian llama - - - - - - - ALPACA
Esau's later name - - - - - - - EDOM
Esau's wife - - - - - - - - - ADAH
escapade - - - - - - - - - - PRANK
escape - EVADE, FLEE, LEAKAGE, ELUDE, AVOID
escape by artifice - - - - - - EVADE
escape notice of - - - - - - - ELUDE
escape (slang) - - - - - - - - - LAM
escape work in logging - - - - - SNIB
eschew - - - - - - - - AVOID, SHUN
escort - CONVOY, USHER, ACCOMPANY, SQUIRE, CONDUCT, ATTEND
escrow - - - - - - - - - - - - DEED
esculent - - - - - - - - - - EDIBLE
esker - - - - - - - - ASAR, OSAR, OS
Eskimo canoe - - - - - KAYAK, UMIAK
Eskimo house - - - - - - - - - TOPEK
Eskimo hut - - - - - - - IGLU, IGLOO
Eskimo outer garment - - - - - PARKA
Eskimo settlement - - - - - - - ETAH
esne - - - - - - - - - - - - - SERF
esoteric - - - MYSTERIOUS, INNER, CONFIDENTIAL, ABSTRUSE, PROFOUND
espionage agent - - - - - - - - - SPY
espouse - - - - - - - - WED, MARRY
esprit - - - - - - - - - - - - SOUL
espy - - - - - - - - DETECT, DESCRY
espy (colloq.) - - - - - - - - - SPOT
essays - - - THESES, TRIES, TESTS, EFFORTS, ATTEMPTS, PAPERS, THEMES
essence - - ATTAR, SUBSTANCE, PITH, PERFUME, YOLK, NATURE, SOUL
essence of a thing - - - - - - - SELF
essential - VITAL, VIRTUAL, NECESSARY, NEEDFUL
essential ingredients - - - - ESSENCE
essential to life - - - - - - - - VITAL
essential part - - ELEMENT, FACTOR, MARROW, VITAL, PITH
essential part of an individual - - SELF
essential quality - - - - - - - METAL
essentially - - - - - - - - - PER SE

establish - - - SETTLE, REAR, BASE, INSTATE, SET, INSTITUTE, PLANT
establish firmly - - - - - - - PLANT
establish one's place of abode - LOCATE
establish ownership - - - - - - CLAIM
established rule or model - - STANDARD
established value - - - - - - - - PAR
establishment - - - - - - - MENAGE
estate - MANOR, CONDITION, PROPERTY
estate going to widow - - - - - DOWER
esteem - REGARD, REVERE, ESTIMATE, VALUE, HONOUR, PRIZE, RESPECT, CONSIDER
ester of acetic acid - - - - - ACETATE
esthetics - - - - - - - - - - - ARTS
estimate - RATE, CALCULATE, MEASURE, GAGE, RANK, ESTEEM, ASSESS, JUDGE, APPRAISE
estimated reparation for injury - DAMAGES
estimation - - - - - REPUTE, REGARD
estop - PLUG, BAR, IMPEDE, HINDER, OBSTRUCT
estrange - - - - - - - - - ALIENATE
etagere - - - - - - - - - WHATNOT
etamine - - - - - - - - - BUNTINGS
etch - - - - - - - - - - - ENGRAVE
etch with dots - - - - - - - STIPPLE
eternal - - EVERLASTING, DEATHLESS, ENDLESS, CEASELESS, INFINITE, TIMELESS
Eternal City - - - - - - - - - ROME
eternity - - - EON, AEON, DURATION, IMMORTALITY
etesian - - - - - - - - - PERIODIC
ether - - - - - - - - - - - - ESTER
ethereal - - - - - - - - AIRY, AERIAL
ethereal salt - - - - - - - - - ESTER
ethical - - - - - - - - - - - MORAL
ethical talk - - - - - - - - SERMON
ethics - - - - - - - - - - - MORALS
Ethiopian title - - - - - RAS, NEGUS
ethnic - - - - - - - - - - - RACIAL
ethnological group - - - - - - TRIBE
etiolate - - - - - - - - - - BLEACH
enthusiasm - - - - - - - - - - ELAN
Etruscan gods - LARES, LARS, PENATES
Etruscan title - - - - - - - - - LARS
eucharistic plate - - - - - - - PATEN
eulalia - - - - - - - - - - - - NETI
eulogy - - - - - - - - PRAISE, ELOGE
euphemism - - - - - - - - DISGUISE
euphony - - - - - - - - - - - METER
Eurasian mountains - - - - - - - URAL
European - POLE, DANE, FINN, SWEDE, SLAV, LAPP, LETT, SERB, SLOVAK, CROAT
European apple tree - - - - - - SORB
European bass - - - - - - - - BRASSE
European bird - - - SERIN, MOTACIL, ORTOLAN, PIE
European bison - - - - - - - AUROCHS
European blackbird - - MERLE, OUSEL
European bunting - - - - - - ORTOLAN
European capital city - - - - - - RIGA
European cavalryman - - - - - - HUSSAR
European cavalryman (var.) - - ULAN
European countryman - - - PEASANT, PEASANTRY
European deer - - - - - - - - - ROE
European dormouse - - - - - - - LEROT
European dwarf elder - - - DANEWORT
European farmer - - - - - - - PEASANT
European finch - SERIN, TERIN, CITRIL, TARIN
European fish - - - - - - - - - - ID

European flounder - - - - - - - DAB
European government monopoly - REGIE
European gulf - - - - - - RIGA, ADEN
European gull - - - - - - - - - MEW
European herb - - - - - - - BENNET
European herring - - - - - - - SPRAT
European industrial valley - - - - RUHR
European juniper - - - - - - - CADE
European kite - - - - - - - - GLEDE
European larkspur - - - - STAVESACRE
European lavender - - - - - - - ASPIC
European lime - - - - - - - - - TEIL
European mint - - - - - - - - - IVA
European mountains - - ALPINE, URAL, ALPS
European mountain range - ALPS, ALTAI
European native - - - - SERB, CROAT
European night heron - - - - - - QUA
European oriole - - - - - - - LORIOT
European peninsula - - - - - CRIMEA
European perennial plant - TARRAGON
European principality - - - - MONACO
European rabbit - - - - - - - - CONY
European republic - - ESTONIA, EIRE
European river - - - - - - SAAR, BUG
European river basin - - - - - - SAAR
European rustic - - - - - - PEASANT
European sea - - - - - - - - AEGEAN
European shark - - - - - - - - TOPE
European ship canal - - - - - - - KEIL
European siskin - - - - - - - - TARIN
European song thrush - - - - - MAVIS
European strait - - - - - BOSPOROUS
European thrush - - - - MAVIS, OUSEL
European tree - - - - - SORB, LENTISK
European viper - - - - - - ASP, ADDER
European wild cherry - - - - - GEAN
European yew - - - - - - - - - - IF
evade - ELUDE, DODGE, SHUN, ESCAPE, GEE, SHIRK, AVOID, BAFFLE
evade meanly - - - - - - - - SHIRK
evade payment - - - - - - - - BILK
evaluate - - - - - - - - - APPRAISE
evanescent - - - - - - - - FLEETY
evangel - - - - - - - - - - GOSPEL
evaporable - - - - - - - - VOLATILE
Eva's friend - - - - - - - - - TOPSY
evasive - SHIFTY, DECEITFUL, BAFFLING, ELUSIVE
Eve's temptation - - - - - - - APPLE
even - - LEVEL, SMOOTH, EQUALIZE, FLUSH, EQUAL, BALANCE, UNVARIED
even chance - - - - - - - - TOSSUP
even now - - - - - - - - - ALREADY
even (poet.) - - - - - - - - - EEN
even score - - - - - - - - - - - TIE
evening - - - - - - - - - - - NIGHT
evening dance - - - - - - - - - BALL
evening love song - - - - - SERENADE
evening party - - - - - - - - SOIREE
evening (poet.) - - - - - - - EEN, EVE
evening song - - - - - - - SERENADE
evening star - - - - - - - - - VESPER
evenness of mind - - - - EQUANIMITY
evensong - - - - - - - - - VESPERS
event - FACT, INCIDENT, DEED, EPISODE, EPOCH
eventual - - - - - - - - - ULTIMATE
eventually - - - - - - - - - FINALLY
eventuate - - - - - - - - - - RESULT
ever - - - - - - - - - - ONCE, AYE
ever (poet.) - - - - - - - - - - EER
evergreen oak - - - - - - - - - HOLM
evergreen shrub - - - - BOX, MYRTLE, OLEANDER, HOLLY, FURZE
evergreen tree - PINE, CEDAR, CAROB, SPRUCE, OLIVE, YEW, HOLLY, BALSAM, FIR
everlasting - - - ETERNAL, ENDLESS, AGELONG, UNENDING
everlasting (poet.) - - ETERN, ETERNE
eversion - - - - - - - - OVERTHROW
every - - - - - - - - EACH, COMPLETE
every day - - - - - - - - - - - - DAILY
every other - - - - - - - - ALTERNATE
everyone - - - - - - - - - - EACH, ALL
evict - OUST, OBJECT, BANISH, EXPEL, EJECT
evidence - TESTIMONY, PROOF, SHOW
evident - PATENT, APPARENT, CLEAR, PLAIN, MANIFEST, OBVIOUS
evident (arch.) - - - - - - - - APERT
evil - - - - - BAD, BANC, SIN, ILL, INIQUITY, SINFUL, HARM, CORRUPT, VICE
evil act - - - - - - - - - - - CRIME
evil doer - - - - - - - - MISCREANT
evil intent - - - - - - - - - MALICE
evil (prefix) - - - - - - - - - - MAL
evil spirit - - DEMON, SATAN, FIEND, DEVIL
evince - SHOW, MANIFEST, DISPLAY, EXHIBIT
evoke - - - - - - - - EDUCE, ELICIT
evolve - - EDUCE, DEVELOP, DERIVE
ewer - - - - - - - - - - - - - - JUG
ex ruler - - - - - - - - - - - - TSAR
exact - DEMAND, ACCURATE, PRECISE, WREAK, LITERAL
exact copy - - - - - - - DUPLICATE
exact counterpart - - - - - - MATCH
exact likeness - - - - - - - IMAGE
exact reasoning - - - - - - - LOGIC
exact retaliation - - - - - REVENGE
exact satisfaction - AVENGE, REVENGE
exaction - - - - - - - - - - - - TAX
exactness - - - - - - - - PRECISION
exactly - - - - - - - - - PRECISELY
exaggerate - OVERTELL, OVERSTATE, OVERDO
exaggerate a stage role - - OVERACT
exalt - LAUD, RAISE, ELEVATE, HONOUR
exalt the spirits of - - - - - ELATE
exaltation - - - ELATION, ELEVATION
exalted - ELATED, SUBLIME, GLORIFIED
exalted in character - - - - - NOBLE
examination - - - - - - - - - TEST
examination of accounts - - - - AUDIT
examination for correction - REVISION
examination grade - - - - - - MARK
examine - TEST, SCRUTINIZE, INSPECT, SCAN, OVERHAUL
examine critically - - CENSOR, SIFT, PROBE
examine judicially - - - - - - - TRY
examine minutely - - - - - - - SIFT
examine secretly - - - - - - - - SPY
examine by touch - - - - - - - FEEL
example - - - - - - - NORM, CASE
exasperate - - - - ANGER, IRRITATE
exasperation - - IRE, HEAT, ANGER
exhausted - - - - - - - - - - TIRED
excavate - - - - - - - - - DIG, PIT
excavate mineral - - - - - - - STOPE
excavated passageway - - - - - CUT
excavation - - PIT, HOLE, CUT, MINE
excavation for digging ore - - MINE
excavation for extracting ore - STOPE
exceed - PASS, BETTER, TRANSCEND, OVERSTEP, SURPASS

E

exceedingly - - - VERY, GREATLY, EXTREMELY
exceedingly (musical direction) - TRES
exceedingly variable - - - PROTEAN
excel - - TOP, SURPASS, CAP, OUTDO
excel (poet.) - - - - - - - OVERDO
excellence - - - - - MERIT, VIRTUE
excellent - - FINE, CAPITAL, GOOD, RARE
excellent (slang) - - - - - - SUPER
excelling all others - - - - - - BEST
except - - - BUT, SAVE, EXCLUDE, UNLESS, OMIT, BAR
exercise control over - - DOMINATE
excess (in) - - - - - - - - OVER
excess of solar over lunar year - EPACT
excessive - - - - - - - - - RIOT
excessive degree (in) - - - - - TOO
excessively - - - - - - OVER, TOO
exchange - - TRADE, SWAP, BARTER, BANDY
exchange (colloq.) - - - - - - SWAP
exchange discount - - - - - - AGIO
exchange for money - - - - - - SELL
exchange premium or discount - AGIO
excise - - - - - - - - - - - TAX
excite - - - ELATE, AROUSE, STIR, STARTLE
excite attention - - - - - INTEREST
excite bitter feelings - - - EMBITTER
excite suddenly - - - - - - STARTLE
excited - - - - - - AGOG, NERVOUS
excitement - - FUROR, FRENZY, STIR, ELATION
exclamation - AHEM, AH, HO, ALAS, FIE, TUT, WOW, RATS, EXPLETIVE, OUCH
exclamation of abhorrence - - - FOH
exclamation to attract attention (var.) - HOLA
exclamation of contempt - PAH, FOH
exclamation of disgust - AW, BAH, FIE, TUSH, UGH
exclamation of displeasure - BAH, BOO
exclamation of pity - - - - - - AY
exclamation of regret - - - - - ALAS
exclamation of reproach - - - - FIE
exclamation of repugnance - - - UGH
exclamation of triumph - - - - AHA
exclude - - DEBAR, ELIMINATE, BAR, BAN, EXCEPT
exclusive - - - - - - - - SELECT
exclusive person - - - - - - SNOB
exclusively - - - SOLELY, ALL, ONLY
excommunicate - - - - - - - BAN
excoriate - - - - - - - - ABRADE
excrescence - - - - - - - - WART
excrete - - - - - - - - - EGEST
exculpate - - - - - - - VINDICATE
excursion - - TOUR, TRAMP, JAUNT
excursion party - - - - - - PICNIC
excursion for pleasure - - - JAUNT
excursionist - - - - - - TOURIST
excusable - - - - - - - - VENIAL
excuse - - - APOLOGY, PLEA, ALIBI, PARDON, PRETEXT, EXTENUATE
excuse (colloq.) - - - - - - ALIBI
excuse for not appearing in court - - ESSOIN
execrate - - - CURSE, ABOMINATE
execute - - - - - - - - - - DO
execute tastefully - - - - - ARTISTIC
execute unlawfully - - - - - LYNCH

exempt - - - - - - - RELEASED
exercise - - - - - - LESSON, USE
exercise control over - - DOMINATE, PRESIDE
exercise sovereign power - - - REIGN
exercise superior power - - OVERRIDE
exercising foresight - - - PROVIDENT
exert - - - - - - - - - - STRAIN
exert force - - - - - - - - - ACT
exert pressure upon - - - - - PRESS
exert return influence - - - - REACT
exertion - - - - - - EFFORT, ACT
exhalation - - - - STEAM, BREATHE
exhale - - - - - - - - - - EMIT
exhaust - DEPLETE, SPEND, SAP, FAG, WASTE
exhaust moisture - - - - - - - DRY
exhausted - FAGGED, SPENT, PETERED, DEPLETED, WORN, TIRED, FAINT
exhaustion - - - - - - DEPLETION
exhibit - - EVINCE, DISPLAY, SHOW, STAGE, WEAR
exhibit emotion - - - - - - EMOTE
exhibit malign satisfaction - - GLOAT
exhibit theatrically - - - - STAGE
exhibit to view - - - - - - PRESENT
exhibiting spontaneous movement - - MOBILE
exhibition - - - - - SHOW, PAGEANT
exhibition room - - - - - - GALLERY
exhilarate - - ENLIVEN, STIMULATE
exhortation to duty - - - - SERMON
exigency - - - - - - NEED, DEMAND
exile - - - - - - DEPORT, BANISH
exist - - - - - - - - - - - LIVE
existence - ESSE, ALIVE, ENS, LIFE, BEING, ENTITY
existent - - - - - - - - - ALIVE
existing in name only - - - TITULAR
exit - - - - - - - EGRESS, DOOR
exonerate - - - - - CLEAR, ACQUIT
exorbitant - - - - - - - - UNDUE
exorbitant interest - - - - - USURY
exoteric - - - - - PUBLIC, EXTERNAL
exotic - - - - - FOREIGN, STRANGE
expand - - GROW, DILATE, STRETCH, DISTEND, OPEN, ENLARGE
expand (poet.) - - - - - - - OPE
expanded - - - - - - - - - OPEN
expanse - - - ROOM, AREA, TRACT
expanse of heaven - - - - - - COPE
expanse of level land - - - - PLAIN
expansible - - - - - - DILATABLE
expansion - - - - - - - - SPAN
expansive - - - - - - - - WIDE
expatriate - - - - - - - BANISH
expect - - HOPE, AWAIT, ANTICIPATE
expectation - - - - - - - - HOPE
expected (be) - - - - - - NATURAL
expectorate - - - - - - - - SPIT
expedient - - - - - - - - POLITIC
expedition - - - - - TREK, SAFARI
expel - OUST, EJECT, EVICT, BANISH
expel air from lungs - - - - COUGH
expel forcibly - - - - - - - EVICT
expel from the bar - - - - - DISBAR
expel from the country - - - DEPORT
expel air - - - - - - - - - BLOW
expend - - - - - - - SPEND, PAY
expend lavishly - - - - - - POUR
expense - - - - - - COST, OUTLAY
expensive - - - - - - DEAR, COSTLY
experience - - FEEL, UNDERGO, LIVE

E

experienced - - - MET, UNDERWENT, LIVED, TASTED
experiences regret - - - - REPENT
experiencing sensation and feeling - - SENTIENT
experiment - - - - - - - - TEST
experimental workshop (colloq.) - LAB
expert - - - SKILLED, ADEPT, ACE
expert in precious stones - - LAPIDARY
expiate - - - - - - - - - ATONE
expiration - - - - - - - - - END
expire - - - DIE, PERISH, ELAPSE
explain - INTERPRET, DEFINE, SOLVE
explain clearly - - - - - ELUCIDATE
explainer - - - - - - - EXPONENT
explanation - - - - - - - - KEY
expletive - - - - - - EXCLAMATION
expletive (mild) - - EGAD, GOSH, GEE
explode - BLAST, DETONATE, BURST
exploding meteor - - BOLIS, BOLIDE
exploit - - FEAT, DEED, GEST, ACT, GESTE
explosion - - - - - - BLAST, POP
explosion device - - - CAP, PETARD, TORPEDO, GRENADE
explosive - - MELINITE, TNT, TONITE
explosive charge - - - - - - - CAP
explosive device - - - GRENADE, CAP
explosive powder (abbr.) - - - NITRO
explosive (powerful) - - - - - TONITE
explosive projectile - - - - - BOMB
explosive sound - - - - - POP, BOOM
expose - BARE, DETECT, DISCLOSURE, REVEAL, OPEN, DISPLAY
expose to moisture - - - - - - RET
expose oneself to - - - - - - INCUR
expose to ridicule - - - - - PILLORY
exposition - - - - - - - - - FAIR
expositors of Scripture - - EXEGETES
expostulate - - - - - - - PROTEST
express - - - - - - - - - - VOICE
express contempt - - - SNEER, HISS
express disapproval - DEPRECATE, HISS, REBUKE
express displeasure - - - - - RESENT
express dissatisfaction - - COMPLAIN
express emotion in tearful manner - - SNIVEL
express gratitude - - - - - - THANK
express official disapproval - - VETO
express in words - - - - - - PHRASE
expressed by numbers - - NUMERICAL
expressing denial - - - - - NEGATIVE
expressing homage - - - - REVERENT
expressing outcry - - EXCLAMATORY
expressing veneration - - REVERENT
expression - - - - - PHRASE, TERM
expression of approval - - - - SMILE
expression of inquiry - - - - - - EH
expression peculiar to a language - - - IDIOM
expression of pity - - - - - - - AY
expression of request (arch.) - PRITHEE
expression of sorrow - - - - - ALAS
expressive - - - - - - ELOQUENT
expressive action - - - - - GESTURE
expressive bodily movement - GESTURE
expressive of endeavor - - CONATIVE
expressive movements - - GESTURES
expunge - - DELETE, DELE, ERASE, SPONGE
expungent instrument - - - ERASER
exquisite - - FINE, ELEGANT, LOVELY
extend - SPREAD, LIE, STRETCH, RUN, REACH, PROLONG
extend the depth - - - - - DEEPEN
extend a financial obligation - RENEW
extend over - - - LAP, SPAN, COVER
extend to - - - - - - - - - REACH
extend toward - - - - - - - LEADS
extended - LONG, LENGTHY, SPREAD, RAN
extended journey - - - - - - TOUR
extended metaphors - - ALLEGORIES
extended view - - - - - PANORAMA
extended written exposition - TREATISE
extension - - - - - RENEWAL, ANNEX
extension of building - - - - - WING
extent - - - AREA, AMBIT, DEGREE, SCOPE, SPAN, LENGTH, SIZE, LIMIT, RANGE
extenuate - - - PALLIATE, MITIGATE, EXCUSE
exterior - - - SURFACE, OUT, OUTER
exterior of bark - - - - - - - ROSS
exterior (anat.) - - - - - - - ECTAL
external - - OUTER, CORTICAL, OUT, OUTSIDE
external angle - - - - - - - ARRIS
external appearance - - FACE, MIEN, GUISE
external bony scale - - - - - SCUTE
external (comb. form) - - - - - ECTO
external part - - - - - - OUTSIDE
external world - - - - - - NONEGO
extinct - - - - - - - - - - DEAD
extinct bird - - - - - - MOA, DODO
extinct elephant - - - - - MAMMOTH
extinct reptile - - - - - DINOSAUR
extinction - - ABOLISHMENT, DEATH
extinguish - - - - - - - - QUENCH
extinguishing - - - - - - STIFLING
extirpate - - - - - ROOT, DESTROY
extol - - - PRAISE, LAUD, BOAST
extort money from - - - - - BLEED, BLACKMAIL
extra - - - - - SPARE, MORE, OVER
extra pay for British soldiers in India BATTA
extra payment - - - - - - - BONUS
extra quantity - - - - - - - PLUS
extra supply - - RELAY, RESERVOIR
extra working hours - - - OVERTIME
extract - - DRAW, EXCERPT, WRING, EDUCT
extract fat - - - - - - - - RENDER
extract of soapbark - - - SAPONIN
extract with difficulty - - - - - PRY
extraordinary - - - PHENOMENAL, UNUSUAL
extraordinary in size - - - - GIANT
extraordinary thing (slang) - STUNNER
extravagant - - - OUTRE, PRODIGAL, WASTEFUL
extravagant person - - - - - WASTER
extreme - - LIMIT, DIRE, RADICAL, INTENSE, ULTRA, RANK
extreme emotions - - - - - - RAGES
extremely - - SO, EXCEEDING, END, VERY
extremity - - - - - - - - - END
extremity of an axis - - - - - POLE
exuberate - - - - - - - - ABOUND
exudation of trees - - - - - - GUM

exude - - EMIT, DISCHARGE, OOZE, SEEP
exult - - - REJOICE, CROW, ELATE
exultant - - - - - - - - ELATED
eye - OGLE, OBSERVE, WATCH, VIEW, ORB, VISION, REGARD, SIGHT, OPTIC
eye (of the) - - - - - - - OPTIC
eye of bean - - - - - - - HILUM
eye of bean (pert. to) - - - HILAR
eye coat - - - - - - - - RETINA
eye globe - - - - - - - EYEBALL
eye membrane - - - RETINA, IRIS
eye (part) - - RETINA, UVEA, IRIAN, PUPIL, LENS, CORNEA, IRIS
eye part (pert. to) - AREOLAR, UVEAL
eye (Scot.) - - - - - EE, EEN (pl.)
eye (slang) - - - - - - - - GLIM
eye socket (anat.) - - - - - - ORBIT
eyeball coat (part) - - - - - CORNEA
eyeglass - - - - - MONOCLE, LENS
eyeglass frame - - - - - - - RIM
eyelash cosmetic - - - - - MASCARA
eyelashes - - - - - - - - CILIA
eyelet - - - - - - - - LOOPHOLE
eyelid infection - - - - - - - STY
eyes - - - - - - - - - - PEEPERS

F

fable - - - - - - - STORY, MYTH
fable maker - - - - - - - AESOP
fabled demon - - - - - - - OGRE
fabled diminutive being - - GNOME
fabled giant - - - - - - - TITAN
fabled monster - - CENTAUR, OGRE, SPHINX
fabric - ETOILE, VOILE, WEB, MOIRE, TERRY, MATERIAL, RAYON, LENO
fabric edge - - - - - - - SELVAGE
fabric filling - - - - - WELT, WEFT
fabric (glossy) - - - - - - - SATIN
fabric (kind) - - - - - - - TULLE
fabric woven from metal threads - LAME
fabricate - - - - - - - - MAKE
fabrication - - - - - - - - - LIE
fabricator - - - - - COINER, FORGER
fabulous bird - - - - - - - - ROC
fabulous cannibal - - - - - - OGRE
fabulous horselike animal - UNICORN
fabulous monster - - - - - SPHINX
fabulous sea nymph - - - - - SIREN
fabulous tale - - - - - - LEGEND
face - FRONT, PRESTIGE, CONFRONT
face brazenly or impudently - OUTSTARE
face of a coin - - - - - - - HEAD
face downward - - - - - - PRONE
face of a gem - - - - - - - FACET
face hair - - - - - - - - BEARD
face on hewn stone - - - - - PANEL
face up a glacier - - - - - - STOSS
face value - - - - - - - - - PAR
face with a retaining wall - - - REVET
face with stone - - - - - - REVET
facetious - - - - - WITTY, JOCOSE
facetious person - - - - - HUMORIST
facial bone - - - - - - - - - JAW
facial expression - POUT, LEER, GRIN
facile - - - - - - - - - - EASY
facility - - - - - - - - EASE, ART
facing - - - - - - - - TOWARD
facsimile - - - - - - - REPLICA
fact - - - REALITY, DATUM, TRUTH
faction - SIDE, CLIQUE, SECT, PARTY
factional division - - - - - SCHISM
factor - AGENT, MANAGER, ELEMENT
factor in heredity - - - - - - GENE
factory - - - - - - - - MILL, PLANT
factory hand - - - - - - - OPERATOR
facts - - - - - - - - - - - - DATA
factual - - - - - - - - - - REAL
faculty of perception - - - - SENSE
fad - - WHIM, FANCY, HOBBY, CRAZE
fade - - WANE, VANISH, PALE, DIM
faded (Fr.) - - - - - - - - PASSE
Faerie Queen - - - - - - - - - UNA
Faerie Queen author - - - - SPENSER
Faerie Queen character - - AMORET, ALMA, ATE
fag - TIRE, FATIGUE, WEARY, EXHAUST
fag end - - - - - - - - - - - RUMP
fail - - PETER, MISS, DISAPPOINT, DEFAULT
fail to attain - - - - - - - - MISS
fail to catch - - - - - - - - MUFF
fail in duty - - - - - - - - - LAPSE
fail to follow suit - - - - - RENEGE
fail to move freely - - - - - - BIND
fail to remember - - - - - FORGET
fail (slang) - - - - - - - FLUNK
failing - - - - - - - - FALTERING
failure - - LOSER, LOSS, CESSATION, DEFAULT
failure to keep - - - - - - - LOSS
failure (slang) - - - - - DUD, FLOP
fain - - - - - - - - - - CONTENT
faint - - DIM, SWOON, PALE, WEAK
faint glow - - - - - - - - GLIMMER
fainting spell - - - - - - SYNCOPE
fair - BLOND, DECENT, JUST, BAZAAR, CLEAN, IMPARTIAL, GRACIOUS, EQUITABLE, COMELY
fair (arch.) - - - - - - - - - MART
fairness - - - - - JUSTICE, EQUITY
fairy - - - - - - ELF, SPRITE, FAY
fairy child - - - - - - - - - ELFIN
fairy creature - - - - - - - - PERI
fairy king - - - - - - - - OBERON
fairy queen - - TITANIA, UNA, MAB
fairy (Shakespeare) - - - - - PUCK
fairy world - - - - - - - - FAERIE
fairylike - - - - - - - - - ELFIN
faith - - - TROTH, BELIEF, CREDIT, CONFIDENCE, TRUST
faithful - LIEGE, TRUE, LEAL, LOYAL, DEVOTED
faithful (poet.) - - - - - - - LEAL
fake - - FRAUD, FALSIFY, SPURIOUS, FEIGN, COUNTERFEIT, SHAM
fake hair - - - - - - - - - - WIG
faker - - - - - - - - - - FRAUD
fakir - - - - - - - - - - - YOGI
falcon - - - LANNERET, PEREGRINE, EAGLE, HAWK
falconheaded deity - - - - - - RA
falconheaded sun god - - - - SOKARI
falderal - - - - - - - - NONSENSE
fall - - - DROP, TUMBLE, SUBSIDE, PLUMMET, SLIP
fall awkwardly - - - - - - TUMBLE
fall back - - - - - - - - RETREAT
fall back in former state - - RELAPSE
fall in drops - - - - - DRIP, PATTER
fall in drops (obs.) - - - - - DRIB
fall forward - - - - - - - TOPPLE
fall from power - - - - - - - WANE

F

fall headlong - - - - - - - PITCH
fall heavily, as rain - - - - - PELT
fall into disuse - - - - - - LAPSE
fall into partial ruin - - DILAPIDATE
fall profusely - - - - - - - POUR
fall short - - - - - - - LACK, FAIL
fall suddenly - - - - - - - PLOP
fall upon - - - - - - - - ASSAIL
fallacious - - - - - - MISLEADING
fallacy - - - - - - - - - ERROR
fallible - - - - - - - - ERRABLE
falling - - - - - - - - CADENT
falling back - - - - - - - RELAPSE
falling moisture - - - - - - - RAIN
falling star - - - - - - - METEOR
falling weight of pile driver - - TUP
fallow land - - - - - - - - LEA
false - - ERRONEOUS, LIE, UNTRUE, SHAM, SPURIOUS, ERRONEOUS, FAKE
false amnion - - - - - - - SEROSA
false belief - - - - - - - ERROR
false god - - - - - - - - BAAL
false gods - - - - - - - - IDOLS
false idea - - - - - - - FALLACY
false jewellery - - - - - - - PASTE
false move - - - - - - - MISSTEP
false (prefix) - - - - - - - PSEUDO
false pretenses - - - - - - SHAMS
false report - - - - - - - CANARD
falsehood - - - - TALE, LIE, FIB
falsify - - - - - - - FORGE, FAKE
falter - WAVER, FAIL, HESITATE, LAG
fame - EMINENCE, RENOWN, LAUREL
famed - - - - - - - - - NOTED
familiar - - - - - - - - - OLD
familiar friends - - - - - - - KITH
families of man (pert. to) - - RACIAL
family - GENUS, KINDRED, HOUSEHOLD
family name (obs.) - - - COGNOMEN
famine - - - - - - - - DEARTH
famish - - - - - - - - STARVE
famous - NOBLE, NOTED, RENOWNED, EMINENT
famous electrician - - - - - - TESLA
famous Florentine family - - - MEDICI
famous friend - - - - - - DAMON
famous murder and murderer - ARAM
famous naturalist - - - - - - SETON
famous soprano - PATTI, LIND, ALDA
famous uncle - - - - - - - - SAM
fan - - WINNOW, DEVOTEE, ROOTER, COOL
fan palm - - - - - - - PALMETTO
fanatic - - - - - - - - ZEALOT
fanatical - - - - - - - - RABID
fanatics (colloq.) - - - - - - FANS
fancied - - IMAGINARY, IMAGINED, DREAMT
fancied object of fright - - BUGABOO
fanciful - - - - UNREAL, DREAMY
fanciful story (colloq.) - - - - YARN
fancy - FAD, WHIM, DREAM, CAPRICE, IDEA, VAGARY, IDEATE
fancy (poet.) - - - - - - - WEEN
fancywork (kind) - - TATTING, LACE, EMBROIDERY
fane - - - - TEMPLE, SANCTUARY
fangs - - - - - - - - - TEETH
fanleaf palm - - - - - - - TALIPOT
fanon - - - - - - - - - ORALE
fantasy - - - DREAM, IMAGINATION
far - - REMOTE, AWAY, ADVANCED, WIDELY
far across - - - - - - - - WIDE
far apart - - - - - - - DISTANT
far below - - - - - - - - DEEP
far down - - - - - - - DEEP, LOW
far off - - - - - REMOTE, DISTANT
far off (comb. form) - - - - - TELE
far reaching - - - - - - - - LONG
far away regions - - - - - - THULES
farce - - - - - COMEDY, MOCKERY
fare - PASSENGER, DIET, DO, PROSPER
farewell - AVE, ADIEU, TATA, ADIOS
farewell (Latin) - - - - - - - VALE
farina - - - - - - - - - STARCH
farinaceous - - - - - - - - MEALY
farinaceous drink - - - - - PTISAN
farinaceous food - - - - - - SAGO
farm - - - - - TILL, PLOW, RANCH
farm building - - SILO, BARN, SHED
farm (kind) - - - - - - - - DAIRY
farm machine - - - - - - TRACTOR
farm yard - - - - - - - BARTON
farmer - - - PLANTER, CULTIVATOR, SOWER
farming - - - - - - AGRICULTURE
Faroe Island windstorm - - - - - OE
farther below - - - - - - - DEEPER
farther than - - - - - - - BEYOND
farthest - - - - - - - - ENDMOST
farthest back - - - - - - REARMOST
farthest in - - - - - - - INMOST
farthest within - - - - - INNERMOST
fascinating woman - SIREN, CHARMER
fascination - - - - - - - - SPELL
fashion - STYLE, MODE, SHAPE, MOLD, FAD, VOGUE, FRAME
fashion clothes - - - - - - TAILOR
fashion follower - - - - - - MODIST
fashionable - - - - - - - STYLISH
fashionable assemblage - - - SALON
fashioning - - - - - - - FINGENT
fast - - - RAPID, FLEET, SPEEDY, SECURELY, SECURE, DIET, APACE, FIRMLY, FIRM
fast driver - - - - - - - SPEEDER
fasten - NAIL, LACE, TIE, PIN, SEAL, GLUE, TETHER, BOLT, SECURE, RIVET, BIND, PASTE, MOOR, ATTACH, CLAMP, BRACE, LOCK
fasten boat - - - - - - - - MOOR
fasten firmly - - - - CLAMP, RIVET
fasten hermetically - - - - - - SEAL
fasten securely - RIVET, BRACE, LOCK, CLAMP, NAIL, SEAL
fastened shoe on horse - - - SHOD
fasten with wooden pin - - - - PEG
fastener - HASP, LOCK, STRAP, PIN, CLAMP, BOLT, CLASP, RIVET, DOWEL, SNAPPER, SNAP, CLEAT
fastening - - - - - - - - CLASP
fastening pin - - - - - - - DOWEL
fastening rod - - - - - - - BOLT
fastidious - - - FINICAL, ELEGANT, REFINED, NICE, DAINTY
fat - - - OBESE, OBESITY, PLANE, FLESHY, PLUMP, PORTLY, OILY, LARD, SUET
fat (hard) - - - - - - - - SUET
fat (medium) - - - - - - - LIPA
fat (pert. to) - - - - - - ADIPIC
fat of swine - - - - - - - - LARD
fatal - - - LETHAL, DIRE, MORTAL, DEADLY
fatal epidemic disease - - - - PEST
fate - DOOM, LOT, DESTINY, KISMET

fateful - - - - - - - - OMINOUS
father - - SIRE, PAPA, ABBE, ABBA, PARENT, DAD, PADRE, BEGET, PA
father of all - - - - - - - JUBAL
father (Arabic) - - - - - - - ABU
father (colloq.) - - - - - - - PA
father (Fr.) - - - - - - - - PERE
father of gods and men - - - ZEUS
father of modern engraving - - - PYE
fatherly - - - - - - - PATERNAL
fathom - - - - - - - - - DELVE
fatigue - IRK, OVERDO, TIRE, WEARY, HARASS, FAG
fatigued - - - - - - - - AWEARY
fatiguing - - - - - - - TEDIOUS
Fatima's husband - - - - - ALI
fatten - - - - - - - - - ENRICH
fatty - - - - - - - - - ADIPOSE
fatty animal tissues - - - - SUET
fatty fruit - - - - - - - - OLIVE
fatuity - - - - - - - - STUPIDITY
fatuous - - INANE, INSENSATE, SILLY
faucet - - - - - - - TAP, SPIGOT
fault - - - DEFECT, OFFENSE, SLIP, BLEMISH, FOIBLE
fault finding - - - - - - CAPTIOUS
faultily - - - - - - - - - AMISS
faultless - - - - - - - - IDEAL
faulty - - - - WRONG, BAD, AMISS
faun - - - - - - - - - - SATYR
favonian - - - - - - - PROMISING
favour - BOON, PREFER, INDULGENCE
favour (obs.) - - - - - - - - ESTE
favour of (in) - - - - - - - - PRO
favourable - - - - GOOD, PARTIAL
favourable argument - - - - - - PRO
favourable attention - - - - - - EAR
favourable (most) - - - - - OPTIMAL
favourable termination of malady - LYSIS
favourably - - - - - - APPROVINGLY
favourite - - - - - - - PET, DEAR
fawn - - - - - - - - - CRINGE
fawn upon - - - - TOADY, FLATTER
fawning - - - - - - - - SERVILE
fawning for favors - - - PARASITIC
fawnskin - - - - - - - - NEBRIS
fay - - - - - - - - ELF, SPRITE
fealty - - - - - - - - FIDELITY
fear - AWE, TERROR, DREAD, PANIC
fearful - - DIRE, NERVOUS, TIMID, AFRAID
fearless - - - - - - - - DARING
feast - - - REGALE, FETE, BANQUET, REPAST, FIESTA
feast (pert. to) - - - - - - FESTAL
feat - - DEED, ACT, EXPLOIT, STUNT
feather - PENNAS, PLUMAGE, PLUME, PINNA
feather neckpiece - - - - - - BOA
feather shaft - - - - - - - SCAPE
feathered vertebrate - - - - - BIRD
featherlike - - - - - - - PINNATE
feature - - - - LINEAMENT, STAR
federation - - - - - LEAGUE, UNION
fee - HIRE, CHARGE, PAYMENT, PRICE
fee paid to lawyer - - - - - RETAINER
feeble - ANILE, INEFFECTIVE, LAME, WEAK, INFIRM
feebleminded - - - - - - - ANILE
feebleminded person - - - - DOTARD
feed - - NOURISH, NURTURE, EAT, GRAZE, SUBSIST
feed to the full - - - - - - - SATE
feed upon - - - - - - - - BROWSE
feeding box - - - - - - - MANGER
feel - SENSE, TOUCH, EXPERIENCE, GROPE
feel absence of - - - - - - - MISS
feel concern - - - - - - - - CARE
feel discontent - - - - - - REPINE
feel disgust (Scot.) - - - - - - UG
feel indignant at - - - - - RESENT
feel one's way - - - - - - - GROPE
feel regret - - - - - - SUE, REPENT
feel remorse - - - - - - - REPENT
feel sorry for - PITY, REPENT, REGRET
feel sympathy or pity - - - - YEARN
feel a thrilling sensation - - TINGLE
feeler - - TENTACLE, ANTENNA, PALP
feeling - EMOTION, SENSATION, SENSE
feeling of hostility - - - - - ANIMUS
feeling of unrest - - - - - - ALARM
fees - - - - - - - - - - - DUES
feet (having) - - - - - - - PEDATE
feet (of the) - - - - - - - - PEDAL
feet (slang) - - - - - - - - - DOGS
feign - PRETEND, SHAM, SIMULATE, ACT, FAKE
feign sickness - - - - - MALINGER
feint - - - - - - PRETENSE, TRICK
feldspar - - - - - - - - - ALBITE
felicitate - - - - CONGRATULATE
felicity - - - - BLISS, HAPPINESS
felid - - - - - - - - - - - CAT
feline - - - - - - CATLIKE, KITTY
feline animal - - - - - - - - CAT
feline elixir - - - - - - - - CATNIP
fell - - - - - - - - - DROPPED
felled by cutting - - - - - - HEWN
felled trees - - - - - - - ABATTIS
fellow - - - - - - - - CHAP, GUY
fellowship - - - - - - - SODALITY
felon - - - - - - - - - CRIMINAL
felonious - - - - - - - MALICIOUS
felony - - - - - - - - - - CRIME
female - - - - - - - - GIRL, LADY
female bird - - - - - - - - - HEN
female chicken - - - - - - - - HEN
female demon - - - - - - - OGRESS
female elephant - - - - - - - COW
female pig - - - - - - - - - SOW
female praying figure - - - ORANT
female prophet - - - - - - SEERESS
female rabbit - - - - - - - - DOE
female red deer - - - - - - HIND
female ruff - - - - - - REE, REEVE
female saint - - - - - - - - STE
female sandpiper - - - - - - - REE
female sex - - - - - - - DISTAFF
female singer - - - - - - - DIVA
female warrior - - - - - - AMAZON
feminine suffix - - - - - - INA, ESS
fen - MARSH, BOG, SWAMP, MORASS, MOOR
fence - - - - - - RAIL, BULWARK
fence bar - - - - - - - - - RAIL
fence barrier - - - - - - - - BARS
fence in - - - - - - - - IMPALE
fence part - - - - - - - PALING
fence picket - - - - - PALE, PALING
fence of shrubs - - - - - - HEDGE
fence steps - - - - - - - STILES
fence of strong stakes - - PALISADE
fencer dummy - - - - - - - - PEL
fencer's leather shield - - PLASTRON
fencing implement - - - - - - FOIL
fencing leaping movement - - - VOLT
fencing position - - CARTE, TIERCE

F

fencing sword - - - EPEE, RAPIER
fencing sword (var.) - - - - SABRE
fencing term - - TOUCHE, TACAUTAC, RIPOSTE, SASA
fencing thrust - - - - - - - HAY
fencing weapon - RAPIER, EPEE, FOIL, SWORD
fend - - - - - - - GUARD, PARRY
feral - - - - - - - SAVAGE, WILD
feria - - - - - - - - HOLIDAYS
ferine - - - - - - - - - - WILD
ferity - - - - - - - - RUDENESS
ferment - - - - - - - - - YEAST
fermented drink - - - - MEAD, WINE
fermented liquor - - - - - ALE, BEER
fermented milk drink - - - - KUMISS
fern (kind) - - - - - - MULEWORT
fern leaf - - - - - - - - - FROND
fern rootstock - - - - - - - - ROI
ferocious - - - - GRIM, SAVAGE, WILD
ferret - - - - - - - - - - SEARCH
ferret out - - - - - - - - - - PRY
ferrum - - - - - - - - - - IRON
ferry (poet.) - - - - - - - - FORD
ferryman of the Styx - - - - CHARON
fertile spot - - - OASIS, OASES (pl.)
fertilizer - - - - - - - - - MARL
ferule - - PUNISHMENT, RULER, ROD
fervent - - - - - - WARM, EAGER
fervid - - - - - - ARDENT, INTENSE
fervor - - - - - - - ARDOR, ZEAL
festal - - - - - - - - - - JOYOUS
fester - - - - - - - - - - RANKLE
festival - FETE, GALA, FAIR, CARNIVAL, FIESTA
festival paper missiles - - CONFETTI
festive - - - - - - JOYOUS, GALA
festive array - - - - - - - - GALA
festive dance - - - - - - MASQUE
festivity - - - - - - - - - - GALA
festoon - - - - - - - DECORATE
fetch - - - - - - - - - - - BRING
fete - - - CELEBRATE, CELEBRATION
fetid - - - - - - - - - - - OLID
fetish - - - - - - - - - - - OBI
fetter - BIND, IRON, SHACKLE, CHAIN, BAND, MANACLE
fettle - - - - ARRANGE, CONDITION
feud - - - - - VENDETTA, STRIFE,
feudal estate - - - - - FEOD, FIEF
feudal labourer - - - - - - - SERF
few - - - - - - - - - - - - SOME
fewer - - - - - - - - - - - LESS
fewest - - - - - - - - - - LEAST
fiat - - - - - - - - - - - DECREE
fib - - - - - - - - - - - - - LIE
fibber - - - - - - - - - - - LIAR
fiber of American aloe - - - - - PITA
fiber - HEMP, THREAD, BAST, RAMIE
fiber (kind) - - - - - SISAL, ISTLE
fiber of peacock feathers - - MARL
fiber plant - - ALOE, RAMIE, SISAL, COTTON, FLAX, ISTLE, HEMP
fickle (be) - - - - - - - - - VEER
fictional kingdom - - - - - - - OZ
fictitious name - - - - - - - ALIAS
fictitious narrative - - - - - PARABLE
fidelity - - - - CONSTANCY, FEALTY
fidgety - - - - - - - - - RESTIVE
field - - - - - - - - - LEA, ARENA
field of activity - - - - - - TERRAIN
field (arch.) - - - - - - - - GLEBI
field of combat - - - - - - ARENA
field of glacial snow - - - - - FIRN
gield of granular snow - - - - - NEVE
field hospital - - - - - AMBULANCE
field (pert. to) - - - - - AGRARIAN
fiend - - - - - - - - SATAN, DEVIL
fierce - - - - - GRIM, SAVAGE, WILD
fiery - - - - - - - - HOT, INTENSE
fiesta - - - - - HOLIDAY, FESTIVAL
fifty-second asteroid - - - - EUROPA
fig (kind) - - - - - - ELEME, ELEMI
fig tree - - - - - - - - - - - UPAS
fight - SCRAP, BATTLE, MELEE, FRAY, STRIVE, COMBAT
fight against - - - - - - - - RESIST
fight (arch.) - - - - - - - MILITATE
fight (general) - - - - - - - MELEE
fighter - - - - - - - - - - WARRIOR
figurative - - - - ALLEGORIC, TROPE
figurative language - - - - IMAGERY
figuratively promising - - - - - ROSY
figure - - - - - DIGIT, CALCULATE
figure out (slang) - - - - - - - DOPE
figure of speech - - TROPE, SIMILE, METAPHOR, IRONY
figured linen - - - - - - - DAMASK
fiji chestnut - - - - - - - - - RATA
filament - - - - - - HAIR, THREAD
filbert - - - - - - - - - HAZELNUT
filch - - - - - - - - - - - - STEAL
file - - - - - - - - - - RASP, ROW
file (coarse) - - - - - - - - - RASP
filing card projection - - - - - - TAB
Filipino servant - - - - - - - - BATA
fill - - - - - - - - SATE, SATURATE
fill hole by sewing - - - - - - DARN
fill out - - - - - - - - - - - - PAD
fill with air - - - - - - - - AERATE
fill wth extreme fear - - - - TERRIFY
fill with mud - - - - - - - - - - SILT
fill with reverential fear - - - - AWE
filled - - - - - - - - - - - REPLETE
filled pastry shell - DARIOLE, ECLAIR
filled to repletion - SATURATED, SATED
filled space - - - - - - - - PLENUM
filled with crevices - - - - - AREOLAR
fillet for hair - - - - - - - - SNOOD
fillet at top of column - - - - - ORLE
filling of a fabric - - - - - - - WEFT
fillip - - - - - - - - - - - - - FLIP
filly - - - - - - - - - - - - - FOAL
film - - - - - - - - - - NEGATIVE
film on copper - - - - - - - PATINA
film on liquid - - - - - - - - - SCUM
filmy - - - - - - - - - - - - GAUZY
filmy clouds - - - - - - - - - CIRRI
filter - - - - PURIFY, STRAIN, SIEVE
filter through - - - - SEEP, STRAIN
filthy - - - - - - - - - - - - - VILE
final - - LAST, DECISIVE, ULTIMATE, CONCLUDING
final acquittance - - - - - QUIETUS
final cause (denoting) - - - - TELIC
final judgment - - - - - - - - DOOM
final Mohican - - - - - - - - UNCAS
final purpose - - - - - - - - - GOAL
final statement of account - - AUDIT
finale - END, CLOSE, TERMINATION, FINISH, CODA, ENDING
finale of sonata - - - - - - - CODA
financial - - - - - - - - MONETARY
financial institution - - - - - BANK
financial instrument - - - MORTGAGE
financial shortage - - - - - DEFICIT

F

finch - - - SERIN, LINNET, TERIN, BUNTING, TANAGER
find - - - - - - LOCATE, DISCOVER
find fault - - - - - - RAG, CARP
find out - - - DETECT, SEE, LEARN
find position of - - - - - - LOCATE
find sum of - - - - - - - - - ADD
fine - DAINTY, THIN, MULCT, AMERCE, KEEN, NICE
fine assessed for murder - - - - CRO
fine black powder - - - - - - SOOT
fine clothes - - - - - - TOGGERY
fine and delicate - - - - - - LACY
fine fabric - - - - - - SATIN, LAWN
fine fur - - - - - - - - - - SABLE
fine gravel - - - - - - - - - SAND
fine hair - - - - - - - - - - FUR
fine lime mortar - - - - - PUTTIES
fine line of a letter - - - - - SERIF
fine linen fabric - - CAMBRIC, LAWN
fine meal - - - - - - - - - FARINA
fine meshed material - - - - - TULLE
fine network - - - - - - - - - LACE
fine particles of stone - - - - SAND
fine porcelain - - - - - - LIMOGES
fine powder - - - - - - - - DUST
fine quartz particles - - - - - SAND
fine race horse - - - - - - ARABIAN
fine rain - - - - - - - - - - MIST
fine ravelings - - - - - - - - LINT
fine thread - - - - - - SILK, LISLE
finely discriminating - - - - - NICE
finely ground substance - - - - FLOUR
finely webbed - - - - - - SPIDERY
finely wrinkled - - - - - RUGULOSE
finer - - - - - - - - - THINNER
fingent - - - - - - - FASHIONING
finger game - - - - - - - - MORA
finger (pert. to) - - - - - - DIGITAL
finger or toe - - - - - - - - DIGIT
fingerless glove - - - - - - MITTEN
finial - - - - - - - EPI, CANOPY
finial on pagoda - - - - - - - TEE
finical - - - - - - - FUSSY, NICE
finis - - - - - - - - ENDING, END
finish - - - - - - - - - - FINALE
finished - - - OVER, DONE, CLOSED, COMPLETED
finished edge - - - - - - - - HEM
finished gentleman - - - ARISTOCRAT
finished (poet.) - - - - - - - - OER
Finnish city - - - - - - - - - ABO
Finnish poem - - - - - - - - RUNE
Finnish seaport - - - - - - - - ABO
fire - - - SHOOT, IGNITE, KINDLE, INFLAME
fire basket - - - - - - - CRESSET
fire (comb. form) - - - - PYR, IGNI
fire feeder - - - - - - - - STOKER
fire particle - - - - - - - - SPARK
fire whistle - - - - - - - - SIREN
fire worshipper - - - - - - - PARSEE
firearm - PISTOL, RIFLE, GUN, PIECE, WEAPON, REPEATER, SHOTGUN
firecracker - - - - - PETARD, RETARD
fired clay - - - - - - - - - - TILE
firedog - - - - - - - - - ANDIRON
fireman - - - - - - - - - - STOKER
fireplace - - - - - - - INGLE, GRATE
fireplace part - - - SPIT, GRATE, HOB
fireplace projection - - - - - - HOB
fireplace shelf - - - - - - - MANTEL
fireside - - - - - - - - - HEARTH

firm - - STABLE, SOLID, IMMUTABLE, STEADY, IRON, ADAMANT, SECURE, FAST
firm grasp - - - - - - - - - GRIP
firm to maintain high prices - CARTEL
firma (terra) - - - - - - DRY LAND
firmament - - - - - - SKY, HEAVEN
firmly - - - - - - - - - - - FAST
firmly united - - - - - - - - SOLID
firmness - - - - - - - - - - IRON
firmness of mind - - - - CONSTANCY
Firpo's first name - - - - - - - LUIS
first - - - ERST, PRIME, FOREMOST, ORIGINAL, INITIAL, PRIMARY, CHIEF, PRIMAL, PREEMINENT
first ages - - - - - - - PRIMEVAL
first appearance - - - - - - DEBUT
first appearance of new moon - PHASIS
first choice - - - - - - - REFUSAL
first class - - - - - - - EXCELLENT
first class man at West Point - - PLEBE
first five books of Bible - - - TORAH
first Jewish high priest - - - - AARON
first king of Israel - - - - - - SAUL
first known vegetable - - - - - - PEA
first letter - - - - - - - - INITIAL
first magnitude star - - ALTAIR, VEGA
first man (pert. to) - - - - ADAMIC, ADAMICAL
first name - - - - - - - FORENAME
first Polish premier - - PADEREWSKI
first pope - - - - - - - - - PETER
first principle - - - - - ARCHE, SEED
first rate (slang) - - - - - - SUPER
first team (colloq.) - - - - - VARSITY
first tone - - - - - - - - - - DO
firsthand work - - - - - - ORIGINAL
fish - PERCH, GAR, SHAD, PAR, SCROD, HAKE, RAY, ID, CARP, DACE, BASS, SPRAT, STURGEON, DARTER, OPAH, WRASSE, TARPON, LING, EELPOUT, CHUB, SENNET, ANGLE, SNAPPER, IDE
fish appendage - - - - - - - - - FIN
fish basket - - - - - - - - - CREEL
fish delicacy - - - - - - - - - ROE
fish eating animal - - - - - - OTTER
fish eating bird - - - - - - PELICAN
fish eggs - - - - - - - - - - - ROE
fish like mammal - - - - - PORPOISE
fish like vertebrate - - - - - - - RAY
fish hawk - - - - - - - - - OSPREY
fish hook (part) - - - - - - - BARB
fish from moving boat - - - - - TROLL
fish net - - - - - - - TRAWL, SEINE
fish part - - - - - - - FIN, SCALE
fish (pert. to) - ICHTHYIC, PISCATORY
fish pickle - - - - - - - - - - ALEC
fish propeller - - - - - - - - - FIN
fish relish - - - - - - - BOTARGO
fish sauce - - - - - - - - - - ALEC
fish (small) - SPARAT, SMELT, SHINER, MINNOW, IDE, ID, SARDINE, FRY, DARTER, DACE
fish spear - - - - - - - - GIG, GAFF
fish trap - - - - - - - - - EELPOT
fish which clings to another fish REMORA
fisher - - - - - - PRAWNER, ANGLER
fisherman - - - - - SEINER, ANGLER
fisherman's basket - - - - - - CREEL
fishes - - - - - - - - - - ANGLES
fishhook - - - - - - - - - - ANGLE
fishhook line - - - - - - - - - SNELL

F

fishhook (part) - - - - - - - BARB
fishing appurtenance and device - - NET
fishing boat - - TRAWLER, CORACLE, SMACK
fishing hook arrangement - - - - GIG
fishing line cork and linefloat - - BOB
fishing line part - - - - - - - SNELL
fishing net - - - - - - - - SEINE
fishing pole - - - - - - - - ROD
fishing spear - - - - - - - - GAFF
fishing tackle (dial.) - - - - - TEW
fishlike vertebrate - - - - - - RAY
fishing worm - - - - - - - TAGTAIL
fissile rock - - - - - - - - SHALE
fissure - - RIME, RENT, CLEFT, RIMA, CRACK, SEAM, RIFT, CRANNY
fissure through which liquid escapes - - LEAK
fit - APT, PROPER, PREPARED, CORRECT, ADAPTED, WELL, SUIT, READY, ADAPT
fit of anger - - - - - - - - RAGE
fit one inside another - - - - NEST
fit out - - - - - - - - - PREPARE
fit of passion - - - - - - TANTRUM
fit for plowing - - - - - - ARABLE
fit for stormy voyage - - - SEAWORTHY
fit of temper (colloq.) - - - TANTRUM
fit together - - - MESH, PIECE, NEST
fit together at an angle - - - MITER
fit with garments - - - - - - TAILOR
fit of wrath - - - - - - - - RAGE
fitting - - - APPROPRIATE, PAT, APT
fitting in behaviour - - - - - DECENT
fitting closely - - - - - - - SNUG
five dollar bill - - - - - VEE, CEE
five parts (having) - - - PENTALOGY
five sided figure - - - - - PENTAGON
five year period - - PENTAD, LUSTRUM
fix - - REPAIR, MEND, CORRECT, SET, ADJUST, SETTLE
fix by agreement - - - - - - SETTLE
fix attention on - - - - - - - PORE
fix conclusively - - - - - DETERMINE
fix firmly - - - BRACE, ROOT, ANCHOR
fix grade of - - - - - - - - RATE
fix in the ground - - - - - - - SET
fix income upon - - - - - - ENDOW
fix in stable condition - - - - ANCHOR
fixed - - STATIONARY, STABLE, STEADY
fixed allowance - - - - - - RATION
fixed charge - - - - - - - RATE, FEE
fixed course - - - - - - - - ROTE
fixed quantity - - - - - - - - UNIT
fixed ratio - - - - - - - - - RATE
fixed task - - - - - - - - - STINT
fixed time - - - - - - - - - TERM
fixed value on - - - - - - - ASSESS
fizzle (slang) - - - - - - - - FLOP
flabbergast - - - - - - - - AMAZE
flaccid - - - - - - - - - - LIMP
flag - - - SAG, STANDARD, BANNER, STREAMER, IRIS, PENNON, PENNANT, LANGUISH, DROOP, BANNERET
flag pole - - - - - - - - - STAFF
flagolet - - - - - - - - - - PIPE
flagrant - - - - - - - GROSS, RANK
flail - - - - - - - - - - BEAT
flair - - - - - - - - - - TALENT
flake - - - - - - - - - - SCALE
flake (comb. form) - - - - - - LEPIS
flaky - - - - - - - SCALY, LAMINAR
flaky mineral - - - - - - - - MICA
flambeau - - - - - - - - - TORCH
flamboyant - - - - - - - - ORNATE
flame - - - - - - - BLAZE, FLARE
flame up suddenly - - - - - - FLARE
flaming - - - - - - - AGLOW, AFIRE
flank - - - - - - - - - - - SIDE
flannel - - - - - - - - - - - LANA
flap - - - - - - - - - - TAB, FOLD
flapper - - - - - - - - - FLIPPER
flaring out - - - - - - - - - EVASE
flash - - - - SPARK, GLINT, SPARKLE
flash of lightning - - - - - - - BOLT
flashy - - - - - - - SPORTY, GAUDY
flat - - - LEVEL, TENEMENT, PLANE, INSIPID, TAME, VAPID, APARTMENT
flat bodied fish - - SKATE, DAB, SOLE, RAY, TURBOT
flat bodied ray - - - - - - - SKATE
flat bottle - - - - - - - - - FLASK
flat bottom boat - BATEAU, SCOW, PUNT, BARGE, KEEL, ARK
flat bottom freight boat - - - - BARGE
flat bottom lighter - - - - - PONTOON
flat bottom scow - - - - - - - ARK
flat cap - - - - - - - - - - BERET
flat circular piece - - - - DISK, DISC
flat disc - - - - - - - - - - PLATE
flat dish - - - - - - - - - PLATTER
flat fish - - DAB, SOLE, SKATE, RAY, TURBOT
flat headed nail - - - - - - - TACK
flat hat - - - - - - - - - - BERET
flat hill - - - - - - - MESA, MOOR
flat part of a stair - - - - - - TREAD
flat piece - - - - - - - - SLAB, FIN
flat piece in chair back - - - - SLAT
flat plate of metal - - - - - PLATEN
flat projecting layer of rock - - SHELF
flat projecting part - - - - - - LEDGE
flat round piece - - - - - - - DISC
flat stick - - - - - - - - - FERULE
flat stone - - - - - - - FLAG, SLAB
flat surface - - - - - - AREA, PLANE
flat top - - - - - - - - - - BERET
flattened at the poles - - - - OBLATE
flatter - - - - - BLANDISH, ADULATE
flattery - - - - - - - - - BLARNEY
flaunt - - - - - - - - - - PARADE
flavour - SALT, SAPOR, SAVOR, TASTE, AROMA, ANISE
flavour (has) - - - - - - - TASTES
flavoured with plant of mint family- SAGY
flavouring - - - - - ORGEAT, ANISE
flavoursome- - - - - - - - SAPOROUS
flaw - - - - - - - - - - - DEFECT
flawless - - - - - - - - PERFECT
flax (dial.) - - - - - - - - - - LIN
flax fiber - - - - - - - - - - - TOW
flaxen fabric - - - - - - - - - LINEN
flaxen hair - - - - - BLONDE, BLOND
flaxseed - - - - - - - - - LINSEED
flay - - BEAT, SKIN, CANE, REPROVE
fledgling - - - - - - - - - NESTLING
flee - VANISH, HASTEN, ESCAPE, SHUN
flee (slang) - - - - - - - - - - LAM
fleece - - - SHEAR, CHEAT, DESPOIL, SWINDLE
fleeced - - - - - - - - - - SHORN
fleer - - - - - - - - - MOCK, SCOFF
fleet - - - - RAPID, SWIFT, SPEEDY
fleet animal - - - - - - - - - HARE
fleet horse - - - - - - - - COURSER
fleet (small) - - - - - - - - FLOTILLA
fleet of vessels - - - - - - - ARGOSY
fleet of war vessels - - - - - ARMADA
fleeting - - - - - - - - TRANSITORY

F

fleeting (obs.) - - - - - - - EVANID
flesh - - - - - - - - - - - MEAT
flesh of calf - - - - - - - - VEAL
flesh eating - - - - CARNIVOROUS
flesh of swine - - - - - - - PORK
fleshes hides - - - - - - - - SLATES
fleshy - - - - - - - - - - - FAT
fleshy fruit - POME, PEAR, DATE, DRUPE
fleshy portion of soft palate - - UVULA
fleshy underground stem - - - TUBER
fleur-de-lis - - - - - - - LIS, IRIS
flew - - - - - - - - - - - WINGED
flexible - - LITHE, ELASTIC, LIMBER, PLIABLE, WILLOWY, PLIANT
flexible bond - - - - - - - - TIE
flexible branch - - - - - - - WITHE
flexible knifelike implement - SPATULA
flexible leather strip - - - - - STRAP
flexible palm stem - - - - - RATTAN
flexible pipe - - - - - - - - HOSE
flexible rod - - - - - - - - WATTLE
flexible shoot - - - - - - - - BINE
flexible and tough - - - - - - WITHY
flicker - - - - FLARE, WINK, WAVER
flier - - - - - - - - - - AVIATOR
flight - - - - - - - - - AVIATION
flight (pert. to) - - - - - - - VOLAR
flight of stairs - - - - - STAIRCASE
flightless bird - - - - - - - - MOA
flimflam - - - - - - - - - - FOB
flimsy - - - - - - - - - - SLIGHT
flinch - - - - - - - - - - WINCE
fling - - SLING, THROW, TOSS, HURL
flintlock - - - - - - - - MUSKET
flip - - - - - TOSS, SNAP, FILLIP
flippant - - - - - - - - - - GLIB
flipper - - - - - - - - - FLAPPER
flirt - - - - - - - - - COQUETTE
flirtatiousness - - - - - - COQUETRY
flit - - - - - - DART, SKIM, FLUTTER
float - RAFT, DRIFT, WAFT, SWIM, RIDE, BUOY, SAIL
float as a cloud - - - - - - - SAIL
float lightly along - - - - - - WAFT
float upward - - - - - - - - RISE
floating box for fish - - - - - - CAR
floating organic life of the sea PLANKTON
floating structure - - - - - - - RAFT
floating in water - - - - - - NATANT
floating on water - - - - - - AWASH
floating with the current - - DRIFTING
flock - - - - - - HERD, TROOP, BEVY
flock of quail - - - - - - - - BEVY
flock of seals - - - - - - - - POD
flog - - - LASH, TAN, BEAT, CANE, TROUNCE
flood - DELUGE, TORRENT, INUNDATE, OVERFLOW, SPATE
flood survivor - - - - - - - NOAH
floodgate - - - - - - - - - SLUICE
floor - - - - - - - - - STORY, DOWN
floor covering - - - RUG, MAT, CARPET
flora - - - - - - - - - - - PLANTS
floral leaf - - - - - - PETAL, SEPAL
floral organs - - - - - - - - STAMENS
Florentine iris - - - - - ORRIS, IREOS
florid - - - - - - - - RUDDY, ORNATE
Florida bay - - - - - - - - - TAMPA
Florida city - - - - ORLANDO, TAMPA
Florida fish - - - - - - - - SALEMA
Florida Indian - - - - - - SEMINOLE
Florida plain - - - - - - - SAVANA
floss silk - - - - - - - - - SLEAVE
flotsam - - - - - - - - - DRIFTAGE
flounce - - - - - - - - - FURBELOW
flounder - - - - - - - DAB, GROVEL
flour receptacle - - - - - - - - BIN
flourish - WIELD, PROSPER, BLOSSOM, BRANDISH
flourish defiantly - - - - - BRANDISH
flourish of trumpets - - - - - FANFARE
flout - DERIDE, SNEER, MOCK, GIBE, JEER
flow - - - - - RUN, STREAM, POUR, ABUNDANCE, RECOVER
flow against - - - - - - - - - LAP
flow back - - - - - - - - - - EBB
flow (comb. form) - - - - - - RHEO
flow forth - - - - - - - - - EMANATE
flow forth in a stream - - - - - POUR
flow off - - - - - - - - - - DRAIN
flow out - - - - - - - - - - EMIT
flow steadily - - - - - - - - STREAM
flow through - - - - - - - - - SEEP
flow of water - - - - - - - - FLOOD
flowed - - - - - - - - - - - RAN
flower - - - - - - BLOSSOM, BLOOM
flower (the) - - - - - - - - - ELITE
flower border - - - - - - - PLATBAND
flower bud used as a spice - - CLOVE
flower cluster - - CORYMB, RACEME, CYME
flower (of) - - - - - - - - - FLORAL
flower leaf - - - - - - - - - PETAL
flower part - - STAMEN, PETAL, SEPAL, COROLLA, SPADIX, ANTHER, PERICARP
flower plot - - - - - - - - - - BED
flower shaped ornament - - - ROSETTE
flowering herb - - - - - - HEPATICA
flowering plant - - ARUM, AGERATUM, LUPIN, CANNA, FERN, COLUMBINE, YUCCA, LUPINE, HYDRANGEA, SPIREA, GERANIUM, VALERIAN, AVENS, CYCLAMEN, LOBELIA
flowering shrub - - SPIREA, JAPONICA, OLEANDER, LILAC, AZALEA, SUMAC, WARATAH
flowering tree (thorny) - - - ACACIA
flowering vine - - - - - - - WISTERIA
flowering water plant - - - - - LOTUS
flowerless plant - FERN, LICHEN, MOSS
flowing and ebbing - - - - - - TIDAL
flowing forth - - EMANENT, EMANATION
fluctuate - WAVER, VEER, VARY, SWAY
flue - - - - - - - - CHIMNEY, PIPE
fluent - - - - - - - - - - - GLIB
fluffy substance - - - - - - - FLOSS
fluid - - - - - - - - - - - LIQUID
fluid rock - - - - - - - - - - LAVA
flurry - - - ADO, AGITATION, AGITATE
flush - - - - - - - - EVEN, REDDEN
flushed - - - - - - - - - - - RED
flushed with success - - - - - ELATED
fluster - - - - - - FUDDLE, CONFUSE
flute - - - - - - - - - NEI, PICCOLO
flutelike instrument - - - - FLAGEOLET
flutter - - - - - - - - - WAVE, FLIT
fly (a) - - - - - TSETSE, BOT, GNAT
fly - - - SOAR, FLIT, AVIATE, HASTEN
fly before the wind - - - - - - SCUD
flyer - - - - - - AERONAUT, AVIATOR
flying - - - - - - - - - - AVIATION
flying corps (British) - - - - - R.A.F.
flying device - - - - - - - - - KITE
flying Dutchman's heroine - - SENTA
flying expert - - - - - - - - - ACE
flying water - - - - - - - - - SPRAY

F

foal - - - - - - - - - FILLY
foam - FROTH, SUDS, LATHER, SPUME
fob - - - - - - - PENDANT, CHEAT
focus - - - - CENTER, CONCENTRATE
fodder - HAY, ENSILAGE, GRASS, SILAGE
fodder pit and tank - - - - - - SILO
fodder plant - - - - - - - - - VETCH
fodder stored in a silo - - - - SILAGE
fodder trough - - - - - - - MANGER
foe - - - - - - - - - - - ENEMY
fog - VAPOUR, MIST, OBSCURE, HAZE
fog (Scot.) - - - - - - - - - - HAR
foghorn - - - - - - - - - - SIREN
foible - - - - - FAULT, WEAKNESS
foil - - - - - - FRUSTRATE, OUTWIT
foil for comedian (slang) - - - STOOGE
fold - PLAIT, PLY, PLICATE, FLAP, RUGA, RUMPLE, CREASE, LOOP, EMBRACE, PLEAT, LAP, SEAM
fold on animal's throat - - - - DEWLAP
fold or circle - - - - - - - - LOOP
fold of cloth - - - - - - - - PLEAT
fold of coat - - - - - - - - LAPEL
fold (to) - CREASE, SEAM, PLEAT, PLY, LAP
fold over and stitch - - - - - - HEM
fold of sail - - - - - - - - - REEF
folded - - - - - - - - - - - PLIED
folded into 8 leaves - - - - OCTAVO
folding bed - - - - - - - - - - COT
folding supporting frame - - - - EASEL
foliage - - - - - - - - - - LEAVES
foliage plant - - - IRESINE, CROTON
folio - - - - - - - - - - - PAGE
folks - - - - - - - - - - - PEOPLE
follow - ENSUE, TRACE, TRAIL, RESULT, CHASE, TAIL
follow after - - - - - - TRAIL, TAIL
follow backward - - - - - - RETRACE
follow close behind - - - - - - TAIL
follow closely - - - DOG, HEEL, TAG
follow in place of - - - - - SUPERSEDE
follower - - - - - - ADHERENT, FAN
follower of fashion - - - - - MODIST
follower of French school - - ROMANTIC
follower of Greek philosophy - - ELEATIC
follower of realism - - - - - REALIST
follower (slang) - - - - - - - FAN
follower of (suffix) - - - - - - - ITE
following - - - - AFTER, SECT, NEXT
following the exact words - - LITERAL
following at once - - - - - - - NEXT
folly - - - - SENSELESS, RASHNESS
foment - - - INSTIGATE, INCITE, ABET
fond - - DOTING, LOVING, ATTACHED, DOTE
fond of (be) - - - - - - - - DOTES
fond of books - - - - - - LITERARY
fond manner - - - - - - - DEARLY
fondle - - CARESS, NESTLE, PET, COSSET
fondness - - - - - - - - - - LOVE
fondness for women - - - - PHILOGYNY
font - - - - - - - - - - - SOURCE
food - - - - - - - ALIMENT, MEAT
food of birds - - - - - - - - - SEED
food fish - - COD, TUNA, LING, CERO, SALEMA, POMPANE, TROUT, SHAD, SMELT, MULLET, ALEWIFE, SALMON, ROBALO, SPOT, MACKEREL
food in general - - - - - MEAT, BREAD
food of the gods - - - - - AMBROSIA
food of hawk - - - - - - - - - RAT
food from heaven - - - - - - MANNA
food material - - - - - - - TAPIOCA
food medium for bacteria - - - - AGAR
food merchant - - - - - - - GROCER
food of owls - - - - - - - - - MICE
food plants (pert. to) - - - - VEGETAL
food program - - - - - - - - - MENU
food (slang) - - - EATS, CHOW, GRUB
food staple - - - - - - - - - CORN
food starch - - - - - - - - - SAGO
food supplied to Israelites - - - MANNA
food of wild turkey - - - - - - PECAN
fool - - NINNY, DOLT, DECEIVE, DUPE, DUNCE, JESTER, ASS
foolhardy - - - - - - - - - - RASH
foolish - - DAFT, MAD, UNWISE, DAFFY
foolish person - - - - - SIMP, DOTARD
foolish (slang) - - - - - - - - BATTY
foolish talk - - - WISHWASH, DRIVEL
foolishness - - - - - - - - - FOLLY
foot - - - - - - - - - - - - IAMB
foot (comb. form) - - - - - - - PODO
foot coverings - - - - - SHOES, BOOTS
foot of four syllables - - - - - PAEON
foot lever - - - - - PEDAL, TREADLE
foot like part - - - - - - - - - PES
foot part - - - - - TOE, SOLE, INSTEP
foot pedal - - - - - TREADLE, LEVER
foot (pert. to) - - - - - - - - PEDAL
foot (poet.) - - - - - - - - SPONDEE
foot swelling - - - - - - - - BUNION
foot of three syllables - - - - ANAPEST
foot travel - - - - - - - - - - PAD
foot traveller - - TRAMP, PEDESTRIAN
foot of two syllables - - - - - IAMBIC
football play - - - - - - - SPINNER
football player - - - - - - - - END
football position - - - - - - TACKLE
football team - - - - - - - ELEVEN
football term - - - - - - - - - DOWN
footfall - - - - - - - - - - - STEP
footless - - - - - - APOD, APODAL
footless animal - - APOD, APODA (PL.)
footprint - - - - STEP, TRACE, TRACK
footway - - - - - - - - - - PATH
footway along canals - - - TOWPATH
fop - - - - - - - - - DUDE, DANDY
foppish - - - - - - - - - - APPISH
for - - - - - - PRO, SINCE, PER, TO
for each - - - - - - - - - - - PER
for example - - - - - - - - - - AS
for example (abbr.) - - - - - - EG, EC
for fear that - - - - - - - - LEST
for instance - - - - - - - - - -AS
for purpose of - - - - - - - - - TO
for shame - - - - - - - - - - FIE
for space of - - - - - - - - DURING
for this reason - - - - - - - -. SO
for that - - - - - - - - - THEREFORE
forage - - - - - - - - - - - RAID
forage plant - - - - - - - ALFALFA
foray - - - - - - - - RAID, PILLAGE
forbear - - PARENT, ANCESTOR, DESIST
forbearance - - - - - - - TOLERANCE
forbearing - - - - - - - - - PATIENT
forbid - BAN, TABU, PROHIBIT, VETO, VOTE, ENJOIN
forbidden - - TABOO, TABU, BANNED
forbidden (var.) - - - - - - - - TABU
forbidding - - - - - - - - - - GRIM
forboder - - - - - - PORTEND, OMEN
force - VIS, POWER, DINT, PRESSURE, COMPEL, IMPEL, CONSTRAIN, DRIVE, VIM, URGE, VIOLENCE, ENERGY
force air through nose - - - - - SNORT
force back - - - - - - - - - REPEL

force of a blow - - - - - - - BRUNT
force down - - - - - - - - - RAM
force in - - - - - - - - INTRUDE
force (Latin) - - - - - - - - - VIS
force of men - - - - - - - - POSSE
force of nature - - - - - - ELEMENT
force onward - - - - - - - - URGE
force in operation - - - - - - ENERGY
force to produce rotation - - TORQUE
force with legal authority - - - POSSE
forceful - - - DYNAMIC, ENERGETIC
forcible - COGENT, VIOLENT, EMPHATIC, ENERGETIC, VIGOROUS
forcibly - - - - - - - - - - AMAIN
ford - - - - - - - - - - - WADE
fore - - - - - - - - - - - FRONT
fore limbs - - - - - - WINGS, ARMS
fore part of ship - - - - - BOW, PROW
forearm (of the) - - - - - - CUBITAL
forebear - SPARE, PARENT, ANCESTOR
forebode - - - - - - - - - - AUGUR
foreboding - - - - - - OMEN, DIRE
foredoom - - - - - - PREDESTINATE
foredoomed to death (Scot.) - - - FEY
forefather - - - - ELDER, ANCESTOR
forefinger - - - - - - - - - INDEX
forego - - - - - - - WAIVE, REMIT
forehead - - - - - - - - - - BROW
foreign - - ALIEN, EXOTIC, PEREGRINE, STRANGE
foreign (cómb. form) - - - - - XENO
foreigner - - - - - STRANGER, ALIEN
foreknowing - - - - - - - PRESCIENT
forelorn - - - - - - - - - - LORN
foreman - - - - - - - - - - BOSS
foremost - FIRST, FRONT, PRIME, MAIN
forenoon - - - - - - MORNING, MORN
foreordain - - - - - - - - - DESTINE
forepart - - - - - - - - - - FRONT
forerun - - - - - - PRECEDE, USHER
forerunner - - - - - - - - - HERALD
forest - - - WOOD, TREES, WOODS, WOODLAND
forest divinity - - - - - - - NYMPH
forest patrol warden - - - - - RANGER
forest (pert. to) - - - - - - SYLVAN
forestall - - - - - - - - - PREVENT
forestless tract - - - - - - - STEPPE
foretell - - - - PREDICT, PRESAGE, PROPHESY
foretell (Scot.) - - - - - - - - SPAE
foreteller - - - - - - - - - - SEER
forethought - - - - - - - - - CARE
foretoken - - - - - - - - - OMEN
forever - - - - ETERNALLY, AY, AYE
forever (Austr.) - - - - - - - - AKE
forever (contr.) - - - - - - - - EER
foreword - - - - - - - - - PREFACE
forewarning - - - - - - - - PORTENT
forfeit - - - - - - - - - - - LOSE
forge - - - - - - - FALSIFY, FRAME
forge nozzle (Scot.) - - - - - - TEW
forger - - - - - - - - - FABRICATOR
forget - - - - - - - - - - NEGLECT
forgetfulness - - - - - - - - LETHE
forgive - - - - - - - PARDON, REMIT
forgiveness - - - - - - - - REMISSION
forego - - - - - - - - - - REFRAIN
fork - - - - - - - - - - - DIVIDE
forked - - - - - - - - - - - BIFID
forlorn - - BEREFT, LORN, WRETCHED
form - - - SHAPE, CEREMONY, MOLD, CREATE, FRAME, MAKE, VARIETY, STYLE
form after in model - - - - - IMITATE
form angle in dressmaking - - MITER
form of architecture - - - - - - IONIC
form a book is published in - EDITION
form of croquet - - - - - - - - ROQUE
form of diversion - - - - - - - CARDS
form of Esperanto - - - - - - - - IDO
form into fabric - - - - - - - - KNIT
form glossy surface on - - - ENAMEL
form of government - - - - - POLITY
form of greeting - - - - - - - - BOW
form into groove - - - - - - CHANNEL
form hollows in - - - - - - - - - PIT
form ideas - - - - - - - - - IDEATE
form into jelly - - - - - - - - - GEL
form in layers - - - - - - LAMINATE
form into league - - - - - FEDERATE
form of life annuity - - - - - TONTINE
form to a line - - - - - - - - ALINE
form (pert. to) - - - - - - - MODAL
form of polite address - - - - MADAM
form into ringlets - - - - - - - CURL
form in small grains - - - - - PEARL
form into a terrace - - - - - EMBANK
form a texture from - - - - - - WEAVE
form of type - - - - - - - - ITALIC
form words from letters - - - - SPELL
form of worship - - RITUAL, LITURGY
form of writing - - - - - - - - PROSE
formal - - - DISTANT, STIFF, PRECISE
formal address - - - - - - - LECTURE
formal agreement - - - - - CONTRACT
formal agreement between nations TREATY
formal assertion - - - - - ALLEGATION
formal choice - - - - - - - ELECTION
formal curse - - - - - - - ANATHEMA
formal dance - - - BALL, HOP, PROM
formal discourse - - - - - - LECTURE
formal discussion - - - - - - DEBATE
formal document - - - - - INDENTURE
formal farewell - - - - - - - - CONGE
formal objection - - - - - - - PROTEST
formal official agreement - - TREATY
formal permission - - - - - - LICENSE
formal procession - - - - - - PARADE
formal public assembly - - - - - DIET
formal reproof - - - - - - - LECTURE
formal social introduction - - - DEBUT
formal talk - - - - - - - - ADDRESS
formative - - - - - - - - - PLASTIC
formal base element - - - - - METAL
formed by agency of water - NEPTUNIAN
formed in a cluster - - - - GROUPED
former - ERST, QUONDAM, SOMETIME, OLD, EX, WHILOM, PREVIOUS
former Albanian king - - - - - - ZOG
former (arch.) - - - - - - - - ERST
former Archbishop of Canterbury ANSELM
former Austrian province - - DALMATIA
former Belgian king - - - - - LEOPOLD
former Chinese capital - - - - PEKING
former czar - - - - - - - - - IVAN
former days - - - PASTS, PAST, AGO
former emperor - - - - - - - - TSAR
former English coin - - - GROAT, RYAL
former English law court - - - - LEET
former English Prime Minister - - PITT
former European coin - - - - - - ECU
former fencing dummy - - - - - PEL
former fighter - - - - - - - - GREB
former French marshal - - - - - SAXE
former French president - - - BLUM

F

former German grand duchy - - HESSE, BADEN
former German monetary unit - - TALER
former German president - - - TALER
former Greek king - - - - - GEORGE
former Hungarian district - - - BANAT
former Hungarian kingdom - - SERBIA
former Japanese province - - SATSUMA
former Korean currency unit - - WON
former Mexican president - - - DIAZ
former military device - - - PETARD
former military signal - - GENERALE
former operatic star - - EAMES, ALDA
former Portuguese gold coin - - COROA
former Portuguese money of account REIS
former Prussian university town - HALLE
former public conveyance - - - STAGE
former Roman emperor - - OTTO, NERO
former Rumanian king - - - - CAROL
former Rumanian queen - - - MARIE
former Russian emperor - - - - PAUL
former Russian police - - - - BERIA
former Russian queen - - - - MARIE
former Russian ruler - - TSAR, LENIN, PAUL
former Russian state council - - DUMA
former Scottish king - - - - ROBERT
former Scottish musical instrument - GUE
former Spanish coin - - REAL, PESETA, PISTOLA
former Spanish kingdom - ARAGON, LEON
former spelling of eat - - - - - ETE
former spelling of eel - - - - - ELE
former spelling of rise - - - - - RIS
former spelling of three - - - - TRE
former Swedish king - - - - - ERIC
former tennis champ - - - - - LOTT
former times - - - - - - - - YORE
former times (poet.) - - - - - ELD
former trading vessel - - - - CRAY
former Turkish court - - - - PORTE
former Turkish sultan - AHMED, SELIM
former Turkish title - - - - - DEY
former U.S. senator - - - - -NYE
former Venetian coin - - - - DUCAT
former Venetian rulers - - - - DOGES
former Vichy leader - - - - PETAIN
formerly - - - ERST, ONCE, ONETIME, EREWHILE, AGO
formerly (prefix) - - - - - - - EX
forming a septum - - - - - SEPTAL
Formorian known for beauty - - - BRES
formula - - - - - - - - - - RULE
formula of religious faith - - - CREED
formula for solution - - - - - KEY
forsake - - - - - - - - - DESERT
forsaken - - - - - - - - - LORN
fort - - - - - - - - - - CASTLE
fort wall - - - - - - - - PARAPET
forth or away - - - - - - - OUT
forthwith - - - - - - - - - NOW
fortification - REDAN, RAVELIN, ABATIS, REDOUBT
fortification weapons - - ARMAMENTS
fortified place - - GARRISON, CASTLE, FORT
fortify - - - ARM, STRENGTHEN, MAN
fortress - CASTLE, CITADEL, RAMPART, STRONGHOLD
fortunate (India) - - - - - - SRI
fortunately - - - - - - - HAPPILY
fortune - - LOT, FATE, CHANCE, HAP
fortune teller - SEER, PALMIST, SIBYL
forward - - - AHEAD, ANTERIOR, TO, ALONG, SEND, FRONT, ON, TRANSMIT
forward part - - - - - - FRONT, FORE
forward part of boat - - - - - - BOW
forward payment - - - - - - REMIT
forward by stages - - - - - - RELAY
fosse - - - - - - - - - - - MOAT
fossil (kind) - - - - - - CALAMITE
fossil resin - - - - - - - RETINITE
fossil wood - - - - - - - - PINITE
fossilized coral - - - - - CORALITE
fossilized resin - - - - - - - AMBER
foster - NURSE, CULTIVATE, CHERISH, REAR, PROMOTE
fought - - - - - - - - - - STRIVEN
foul - DIRTY, UNFAIR, STORMY, RANK
foundation - - - BASE, BASIS, ROOT, BOTTOM, BED
foundation timber - - - SILLFOUNDED, BASED
founded on experiment - - EMPIRICAL
founder of elocution school - DELSARTE
founder of first city - - - - - CAIN
fountain - - - - - - - - - - WELL
fountain of Corinth - - - - - PIRENE
fountain drink - - - - - - - SODA
four (comb. form) - - - - - - TETRA
four footed animal - - - - - - BEAST
four legged reptile - - - - - LIZARD
four sided pillar - - - - - OBELISK
four winged insect - - - - - - MOTH
fourscore and ten - - - - - NINETY
fourth calif - - - - - - - ALI, ULI
fowl - - - - - - HEN, GOOSE, BIRD
fox (female) - - - - - - - - VIXEN
fox (Scot.) - - - - - - - - - - TOD
fox (var.) - - - - - - - - - RENARD
fox with large ears - - - - FENNEC
foxy - - - - - - - - - SLY, WILY
foyer - - - - - - - - - - - LOBBY
fra - - - - - - - - - - - - MONK
fracas - - - MELEE, QUARREL, BRAWL
fraction term - - - - - - NUMERATOR
fractional paper currency - - - SCRIP
fracture - - - - - - - - - - BREAK
fragile - - FRAIL, DELICATE, BRITTLE
fragment - - SCARP, ORT, BIT, SNIP, SHREAD, CRUMB, SHARD, CHIP, RELIC, RAG, SCRAP, PIECE, SHRED, TATTER
fragment of cloth - - - - - - - RAG
fragment left at a meal - - - - ORT
fragment of pottery - - - - - SHERD
fragrance - - - - - - - - - AROMA
fragrant - - - - REDOLENT, OLENT, AROMATIC, SWEET, ODOUROUS
fragrant flower - - - - LILAC, JASMINE
fragrant flowered shrub - - - - TIARA
fragrant oil - - - - - - - - ATTAR
fragrant ointment - - - - SPIKENARD
fragrant plant - - - - - - PINESAP
fragrant resin - - - - - - - NARD
fragrant rootstock - - - - - - ORRIS
fragrant seed - - - - - - - ANISE
fragrant shrub - - ROSEMARY, TIARA
frail - FRAGILE, SLENDER, PUNY, WEAK, DELICATE
frame - - FORGE, COMPOSE, ADJUST, FASHION, DEVISE, SHAPE, FORM
frame for beacon - - - - - CRESSET
frame of bed - - - - - - BEDSTEAD
frame of a car - - - - - - CHASSIS
frame of mind - - - - - - - MOOD
frame of vessel - - - - - - - HULL
frame work - - - - - - - - TRUSS

framework - - CADRE, RACK, TRESTLE
framework of bars - - - - - - GRATE
framework of crossing laths - - LATTICE
framework to hold fodder - - - RACK
framework of slats - - - - - - CRATE
framework supporting a bridge - TRESTLE
framework of a window - - - CASING
framing in which glass panes are set SASH
frank - - - CANDID, OPEN, HONEST
frankness - - - - - - - - CANDOR
Franks (pert. to) - - - - - - SALIC
frantic - DESPERATE, FRENZIED, MAD, FURIOUS
fraternal - - - - - - BROTHERLY
fraternize (colloq.) - - - - - COTTON
fraud - CHEAT, SWINDLE, DECEIT, FAKE, JAPE, FAKER, HUMBUG, TRICKERY
fraudulent - - - - - - - DECEITFUL
fray - - - - - MELEE, FIGHT, SET-TO
free - RID, CLEAR, RELEASE, GRATIS, DELIVER, INDEPENDENT, LIBERATE, LOOSE, RESCUE, ABSOLVE, LOOSEN, UNCHECKED
free card of admission - - - - PASS
free from anxiety - - - - REASSURE
free from danger - - - - - RESCUE
free from dirt - - - - - - CLEAN
free from disorder - - - STRAIGHTEN
free of germs - - - - - - ASEPTIC
free of impurities - REFINE, CLEANSE, CLEAN
free from moisture - - - - - DRIED
free by payment - - - - - RANSOM
free from restraint - - LOOSEN, UNBEND
free from risk - - - - - - - SAFE
free from spherical aberration APLANATIC
free from tension - - - - - LOOSEN
free from writing - - - - - BLANK
freedom - - - - - - - - LIBERTY
freedom of access - - - - - ENTREE
freedom from punishment - - IMPUNITY
freedom from risk - - - - - SAFETY
freehold right - - - - - - ODAL
freehold in Shetland Isles - - - UDAL
freeholder - - - - - - - - YEOMAN
freeze - ICE, REFRIGERATE, CONGEAL, GELATE
freeze together - - - - - - GELATE
freight - - - - - - LADE, CARGO
freight boat - - BARGE, ARK, FLATBOAT
freight car - - - GONDOLA, CABOOSE
freighted - - - - - - - - - LADEN
French - - - - - - - - - GALLIC
French abbe - - - - - - - ABBOT
French abbot - - - - - - - - ABBE
French African capital city - - - TUNIS
French African colony - - - ALGERIA, DAHOMEY
French annuity and security - - RENTE
French article - - - LE, UN, LA, UNE
French artist - - - - - - - - DORE
French astronomer - - - - - - PONS
French author - RENAN, DUMAS, VERNE, HUGO, LOTI, GIDE
French authoress - - - - - - - SAND
French bond - - - - - - - - RENTE
French brandy - - - - - - COGNAC
French cap - - - - - - - - BERET
French cardinal - - - - - RICHELIEU
French caricaturist - - - - - - NOE
French cathedral city - AIX, REIMS, SENS
French chamber of upper Parliament SENAT
French champagne - - - - - - - AY
French cheese - - - - - - - - BRIE
French city - NANTES, ARLES, NANCY, RENNES, SENS, CAEN, LYONS, ARIENS, AY, SEVRES, CANNES, AMIENS, LILLE, NICE, LIMOGES, AIX
French cleric - - - - - - - - ABBE
French coin - - - SOU, ECU, FRANC, CENTIME, OBOLE
French coin (minor) - - - - - DENIER
French commune - - - NESLE, VOIRON
French composer - LALO, WIDOR, RAVEL
French concrete - - - - - - - BETON
French dance - - - - - - - - BAL
French department - - - ORNE, NORD, SOMME, AIN, OISE, ISERE, EURE
French department officer - - PREFECT
French district - - - - - - ALSACE
French dramatist - - RACINE, MOLIERE
French dugout - - - - - - - ABRI
French emperor - - - - - NAPOLEON
French engraver - - - - - - - DORE
French essayist - - - - - - - GIDE
French friar - - - - - - - - FRERE
French historian - - - - - - TAINE
French illustrator - - - - - - - DORE
French income - - - - - - - RENTE
French Indo-China capital - - - HANOI
French law functionaries cap - MORTIER
French lawyer - - - - - - - AVOCAT
French lily - - - - - - - LIP, LYS
French marshall - - - - NEY, MURAT
French mathematician - - - - - BOREL
French native - - - - - - - BRETON
French naval station - - - - - BREST
French novelist - - SUE, PROUST, LOTI
French opera - - - - - - - FAUST
French operatic singer - - - - - CALVE
French painter - TISSOT, DORE, COROT, DEGAS, MANET, GELEE, MONET
French parliament - - - - - - SENAT
French philosopher - - - - ROUSSEAU
French phoneticist - - - - - - PASSY
French poet - - - VERLAINE, ARAGON
French policeman - - - - GENDARME
French porcelain - - - - - - LIMOGES
French possessive - - - - - - - MES
French preposition - - - - - - ENTRE
French priest - - - - - - - - ABBE
French pronoun - - - - - - - - TE
French Protestant insurgent - CAMISARD
French province - - - - - - ALSACE
French psychologist - - - - - BINET
French quisling - - - - - - - LAVAL
French railroad stations - - - - GARES
French region - - - - - - - BRESSE
French revolutionist - - - - - MARAT
French river - ISERE, OISE, MARNE, LYS, MEUSE, SAAR, SAONE, AIN, RHONE, LOIRE, SEINE, VESLE, SCARPE, YSER, SOMME, ORNE
French satirist - - - - - - RABELAIS
French scientist - - - - - - - CURIE
French sculptor - - - - - - - RODIN
French seaport - - - - CAEN, CALAIS
French security - - - - - - - RENTE
French shooting match - - - - - TIR
French soldier - - POILU, CHASSEUR
French suffix - - - - - - - - OT
French symbol - - - - - - - - LILY
French theologian - - - - - - CALVIN
French tobacco - - - - - - - TABAC

F

French town - - - VALENCE, NERAC, BAREGES, AY, LENS, LAON
French village - - - - - - - HAM
French wine - - - - - - - MEDOC
French winter resort - - - - - PAU
French writer - - VERNE, ROUSSEAU, PROUST, DUMAS, GAUTIER
Frenchman - - - - - - - - GAUL
frenetic - - - - - - - - FRENZIED
frenzied - FRANTIC, BERSERK, FRENETIC
frenzied manner - - - AMUCK, AMOK
frenzy - - - RAGE, FUROR, DELIRIUM, EXCITEMENT
frequent - - - - - - - - HAUNT
frequent use - - - - - - PRACTICE
frequented place - - - - - RESORT
frequently - - - - - - OFT, OFTEN
fresh - MODERN, NEW, BRISK, RECENT
fresh supply - - - - - - - - RELAY
fresh water annelid - - - - - NAID
fresh water catfish - - - - - POUT
fresh water fish - DACE, BASS, ID, IDE, ROACH, EELPOUT, BURBOT
fresh water porpoise - - - - - INIA
fresh water snail - - - - NERITINE
freshen appearance of masonry - REGRATE
freshet - - - - - - FLOOD, SPATE
fret - - STEW, NAG, WORRY, CHAFE, AGITATE, REPINE, IRRITATE, FUSS, VEX, ANNOY
fret away - - - - - - - - - GNAW
fretful - - PEEVISH, TESTY, PETTISH, PETULANT
friar - - - - - - - - MONK, FRA
friar's cowl - - - - - - - CAPUCHE
friar's title - - - - - - - - - FRA
fried meatball - - - - - - RISSOLE
fried quickly - - - - - - - - SAUTE
friend - - ALLY, CRONY, CHUM, AMI, COMPANION
friend (Fr.) - - - - - - - - - AMI
friend (greeting to Indian) - - NETOP
friend (law) - - - - - - - - - AMI
friendly - - - - - AMICABLE, KIND
friendly associate - - - - - - - ALLY
friendly dwarf of myths - - - - TROLL
friendly hint - - - - - - - - - TIP
friendly relations - - - - - AMITY
friendship - - - - - - - - AMITY
frigate bird - - - - - ATAFA, IWA
frigate mackerel - - - - TASSARD
fright - - - - TERROR, PANIC, AWE
frighten - - ALARM, STARTLE, SCARE
frighten away - - - - - - - SHOO
frightened (arch.) - - - - AFEARED
frightened (colloq.) - - - - - SCARY
frightful - - - - - - - - DREADFUL
frigid - - - COLD, ICY, ARCTIC, STIFF
frigidly - - - - - - - - - - ICILY
frill - - - - - - - - - - RUFFLE
fringed - - - - - - - - LACINIATE
frisk - GAMBOL, SPORT, CAPER, DANCE, FROLIC, ROMP
frisky - - - - - - - PEART, LIVELY
fritter - - - - - - - - - WASTE
frivolity - - - - - LEVITY, INANITY
frivolous - - - - - - - INANE, GAY
fro - - - - - - - - - - - BACK
frock - - - - - - - - - - - DRESS
frog - - RANA, RAMA, ANURAN, ANURA
froglike - - - - - - - - - - RANINE
frogs (pert. to) - - - - - - - RANINE
frolic - - LARK, CAPER, ROMP, PLAY, SPREE, FUN, PRANK, SPORT, FRISK, GAMBOL
frolicsome - - GAY, MERRY, SPORTIVE
from (Ger.) - - - - - - - - - VON
from here - - - - - - - - - HENCE
from the interior - - - - - - - OUT
from (prefix) - - - - - - - - - DE
from that place or there - - THENCE, SINCE
from this place - - - - - - HENCE
from this time - - - - - - - HENCE
from what place - - - - - WHENCE
from within - - - - - - - - - OUT
front - FORE, VAN, FACE, FOREMOST
front of an army - - - - - - - VAN
front of boat - - - - - - - - - BOW
front of building - - - - - - FACADE
front of hoof - - - - - - - - - TOE
front of mouth - - - - - - PREORAL
front of Muses - - - - HIPPOCRENE
front part of helmet - - - - - VISOR
front of ship - - - - - - BOW, PROW
front wheels of auto - - - - CAMBER
frontlet - - - - - - - - - - TIARA
frost - ICE, CHILL, COLD, RIME, FOAM
frosting - - - - - - - - - - - ICE
frosting device - - - - - - - - ICER
frosty - - - RIMY, AUSTERE, COLD
froth - - - - FOAM, YEAST, SPUME
froth from soapsuds - - - - - LATHER
froward - - - - - - - - - PERVERSE
frown - - - - - - - - - - GLOWER
frowning - - - - GLUM, SCOWLING
frowzy woman - - - - - - - - DOWD
frozen - - - - ICY, GELID, GLACE
frozen delicacy - - - - - - - ICE
frozen desserts - - - - - MOUSSES
frozen dew - - - - - - - - - RIME
frozen rain - - - - - - - - - SNOW
frugal - - - SPARING, ECONOMICAL PROVIDENT, THRIFTY, CHARY
frugality - - PARSIMONY, ECONOMY
fruit - - - - - - - - - - CITRON
fruit bearing part of cereal plant - EAR
fruit of beech tree - - - - - - MAST
fruit (comb. form) - - - - - - CARP
fruit dot - - - - - - - - - - SORUS
fruit drink - - - - ADE, LEMONADE
fruit (dry) - - - - - - - - - CONE
fruit of dwarf mallow - - - - CHEESE
fruit of fir - - - - - - - - - CONE
fruit of fungi (pert. to) - - - TELIAL
fruit of gourd family - - - - - PEPO
fruit of hawthorn - - - - - - HAW
fruit husk - - - - - - - - LEMMA
fruit kernel - - - - - - - - - PIT
fruit (kind) - - - - - - - - GRAPE
fruit of nut - - - - - - - KERNEL
fruit of palm - - - - - - - - DATE
fruit part - - - - - - CORE, RIND
fruit peel - - - - - - - - - RIND
fruit of pine - - - - - - - - CONE
fruit pit - - - - - - - - - PYRENE
fruit preserve - - - - - - - - - JAM
fruit pulp - - - - - - - - - - PAP
fruit refuse - - - - - - - - - MARC
fruit of rose - - - - - - - - - HIP
fruit seed - - - - - - - - - - PIP
fruit stone - - - - - - - - - - PIT
fruitless - - - USELESS, ABORTIVE
frustrate - - - FOIL, DEFEAT, BALK, THWART
frustrate (var.) - - - - - - BAULK
frustration - - - - - - - - DEFEAT
fry quickly - - - - - - - - SAUTE
frying pan - - - - SKILLET, SPIDER
fuddled - - - - TIPSY, FLUSTERED

fuel - PEAT, STOKE, CHARCOAL, GAS, COKE, OIL
fuel oil - KEROSENE
fuel transporting vessel - COALER
fugitive - RUNAGATE, RUNNER
fugitive of foreign country - EMIGRE
fulfill - COMPLETE, IMPLEMENT
full - PLENARY, AMPLE, REPLETE, LADEN
full of depressions - PITTED
full dress (colloq.) - TAILS
full of fears - TIMOROUS
full of fissures - RIMOSE
full of force - AMAIN
full grown - ADULT
full of roots - ROOTY
full of sharp points - PRICKLY
full of small spaces - AREOLAR
full of (suffix) - OSE
fullness - REPLETION
fully attended - PLENARY
fulminate - DETONATE
fulsom - REPULSIVE, COARSE
fumble - GROPE
fume - RAVE, SMOKE, REEK, INCENSE, RAGE
fun - SPORT, PLAY
functional animal part - ORGAN
fund - STORE, ENDOWMENT
funds - SUPPLIES
fundamental - ESSENTIAL, BASIC, BASAL, ORGANIC
fundamental mass of life tendencies - ID
fundamental quantity - UNIT
fundamental tone in music - KEY
fundamental truth - PRINCIPLE
funeral announcement - OBIT
funeral car - HEARSE
funeral of fire - PYRE
funeral oration - ELOGE, ELOGY
funeral pile - PYRE
funeral tune - DIRGE
funereal - MOURNFUL
fungi (kind) - RUST
fungi (pert. to) - AGARIC
fungus - AGARIC, YEAST
fungus disease - ERGOT
fungus disease of plants - SCAB
fungus growth - MILDEW, MOLD
fungus parts (pert. to) - TELIAL
funny COMICAL, HUMOUROUS, COMIC, ODD
fur - PELT
fur animal - OTTER, SABLE, SEAL, GENET, MINK, MARTEN, CALABAR
fur of coypu - NUTRIA
fur mat - RUG
fur for the neck - NECKLET
fur neckpiece - BOA
fur scarf - TIPPET
furbelow - FLOUNCE
furious - RABID, RAVING, FRANTIC
furl, as a sail - ROLL, FOLD
furnace - HEATER, OVEN, KILN
furnace tender - STOKER
furnish - PROVIDE, LEND, IMBUE, AFFORD, RIG, ENDOW, RENDER, CATER, EQUIP
furnish a crew - MAN
furnish a match for - PARALLEL
furnish for service - EQUIP
furnish with authority - VEST
furnish with band - BELT
furnish with feathers - FLEDGE
furnish with a guard - SHOE
furnish with money - ENDOW
furnished with critical notes - ANNOTATE
furnished with shoes - SHOD
furnished with towers - TURRETED
furniture wheel - CASTER
furor - RAGE, FRENZY, CRAZE
furrow - STRIA, RUT, GROOVE, LINE, PLOW
further - PROMOTE, ABET, YET, REMOTE
furthermore - ALSO
furtive - SLY, STEALTHY, SNEAKY
furtive look - PEEP
furtiveness - STEALTH
fury - RAGE, IRE, VIOLENCE, ANGER, WRATH
furze - GORSE
fuse - MELT, ANNEAL
fuse partly - FRIT
fused metal and refuse - SLAG
fusible alloy - SOLDER
fusible substance - METAL
fusion - COALITION
fusion worker - WELDER
fuss - ADO, BOTHER, TODO, FRET, BUSTLE
fussy - FINICAL
futile - USELESS, IDLE, INEFFECTUAL

G

G.I. bed - SACK
gab - PRATE
gabble - CHATTER
gad - RAMBLE
Gad's son - ERI
Gael - CELT, SCOT
Gaelic - ERSE
Gaelic sea god - LER
gag - JOKE, SILENCE
gage - ESTIMATE, PLUM
gaiety - MIRTH, GLEE
gaily - MERRILY
gain - NET, WIN, PROFIT, ATTAIN, ADVANCE, IMPROVE, ACQUIRE, OBTAIN, LUCRE, EARN, PROGRESS
gain advantage over - WORST
gain the attention - INTEREST
gain by compulsion - EXTORT
gain control over - MASTER
gain by effort - EARN
gain knowledge - LEARN
gain possession of - ACQUIRE
gain sight of - SPY
gain success - PROSPER
gain superiority - MASTER
gain by toil - EARN
gain in trade - MAKE
gainsay - DENY
gait - LOPE, STEP, PACE, STRIDE, TROT, AMBLE
gait (fast) - GALLOP
gaited horse - PACER
gaiter - SPAT
gala - FESTIVE, FESTIVITY
Galahad's mother - ELAINE
Galatea's sweetheart - ACIS
galaxy - BEVY
gale - WIND, GUST
Galilee town - CANA
gall - CHAFE, HARASS, IRRITATE
gall on an oak - OAKAPPLE
gallant - CAVALIER, SPARK, BRAVE, KNIGHT
gallery - ARCADE
galley (ancient) with 2 oar banks - BIREME
galley (ancient) with 3 oar banks - TRIREME
galley of Northmen - AESC

G

gallic - - - - - - - - - - FRENCH
gallop along - - PELT, LOPE, CANTER
gallop slowly - - - - - - - - LOPE
galore - - - - - - - - ABUNDANT
galosh - - - - - OVERSHOE, GALOE
galvanize - - - - - - - - - ZINC
gamble - - FROLIC, BET, DICE, GAME
gambler - - - - - - - DICER, PLAYER
gambler's capital - - - - - - - STAKE
gambling - - - - - - - - - GAMING
gambling game - - - - - - - STUSS
gambling house - - - - - - - CASINO
gambol - - - FRISK, CAPER, ROMP, FROLIC
game - - SPORT, CONTEST, PLUCKY, MOCKERY, DIVERSION, JEST, GAMBLE
game bird - - GROUSE, PTARMIGAN, SNIPE
game of chance - LOO, BINGO, KENO, LOTTO
game fish - - TARPON, BASS, CERO, TROUT, MARLIN
game of forfeits - - - - - PHILOPENA
game like Napoleon - - - - - - PAM
game like marbles - - - - - - TAW
game played with clubs - - - - GOLF
game of skill - - - - - - - CHESS
game for stakes - - - - - - - LOO
gamin - - - - - ARAB, TAD, URCHIN
gaming cube - - - - - - - DICE, DIE
gaming tile - - - - - - - - DOMINO
gamut - - - - - - - - - - SCALE
Gandhi's title - - - - - - - MAHATMA
gang - - - - - - - CREW, SQUAD
Ganges dolphin - - - - - - - SOOSOO
gangrenous stomatitis - - - - - NOMA
gangster - - - - - - - - - GUNMAN
gannet - - - - - - - - - - SOLAN
ganoid fish - - - - - - - - - AMIA
gap - - - BREACH, HIATUS, NOTCH, OPENING, CLEFT
gap in mountain ridge - - - - - COL
gar - - - - - - - - NEEDLEFISH
garb - - - ATTIRE, DRESS, CLOTHE, ARRAY, APPAREL
garbed - - - - - - - - - - CLAD
garden - - - - - - CULTIVATE, HOE
garden bed - - - - - - - - - PLOT
garden flower - - - - - - AGERATUM
garden fruit - - - - - - - - TOMATO
garden implement - - TROWEL, HOE, WEEDER, RAKE
garden loam (colloq.) - - - - - DIRT
garish - - - - - - GAUDY, SHOWY
garishly - - - - - - - - GAUDILY
garland - - - ANADEM, WREATH, LEI
garment - ROBE, ABA, STOLE, VESTURE
garment fastener - - - - - - PATTE
garner - - - REAP, GLEAN, GATHER, COLLECT
garnet - - - OLIVINE, GROSSULAR
garnish of toast - - - - - - - SIPPET
garret - - - ATTIC, MANSARD, LOFT
gas of the air - - - - - - - ARGON
gas (kind) - - - - - - - ACETYLENE
gaseous - - - - - - - - AERIFORM
gaseous (comb. form) - - - - - AERI
gaseous compound - - - - - ETHANE
gaseous element - - - NEON, OXYGEN
gaseous hydrocarbon - - - - ETHANE
gaseous mixture - - - - - - - - AIR
gash - - - - - - SLIT, CUT, SLASH
gasoline - - - - - - - - - PETROL
gasoline engine part - - - - - TIMER
gasp - - - - - - - - - - - PANT
gasping - - - - - - - - - - AGASP
gastronome - - - - - - - - EPICURE
gastropod - - - - - - SNAIL, SLUG
gastropod mollusk - ABALONE, SNAIL
gat - - - - - - - - - - CHANNEL
gata - - - - - - - - - - - SHARK
gate - - - - - ENTRANCE, PORTAL, PASSAGEWAY
gate keeper's cottage - - - - - LODGE
gateway - - - - - - - - - ENTRANCE
gateway to Shinto temple - - - - TORII
gather - - AMASS, ASSEMBLE, MASS, SHIRR, BREW, CONGREGATE, HARVEST, REAP, COLLECT, GARNER, GLEAN, MUSTER
gather after a reaper - - - - - GLEAN
gather by degrees - - - - - - GLEAN
gather gleanings - - - - - - - GLEAN
gather by inference - - - - - DERIVE
gather together - - - RAKE, AMASS, MUSTER, MASS
gathering - - BEE, CROWD, HARVEST, REUNION
gathering implement - - - - - RAKE
gaudily - - - - - - - - - GARISHLY
gaudy - - TAWDRY, GARISH, FLASHY
gaudy ornament - - - - - - - TINSEL
gaudy spectacle - - - - - - PARADE
gauge - - - - - - - - - APPRAISE
gauge to measure slate - - - - SCANTLE
gaunt - - - - RAWBONED, LEAN, LANK, THIN, GRIM, SPARE
gauntlet - - - - - - - - - GLOVE
gauze - - - - - - - - - - - LENO
gauzy fabric - TULLE, CHIFFON, TISSUE
gave birth to - - - - - - - BEGOT
gavel - - - - - MALLET, SILENCER
gay - - - - MERRY, BLITHE, RIANT, SPORTIVE
gaiety - - - - FESTIVITY, MERRIMENT
gaze - - STARE, LOOK, PEER, GLARE
gaze askance - - - - - - - - LEER
gaze fiercely - - - - - - - - GLARE
gaze narrowly - - - - - - - - PEER
gaze with close attention - - - - PORE
gaze with satisfaction - GLOAT, ADMIRE
gazelle - - - - - - - - - CORA, GOA
gazelle (kind) - - - - - - - ARIEL
gazelle of Sudan - - - - - - - DAMA
gazing - - - - - - - - - STARING
gear - HARNESS, OUTFIT, CLOTHING, RIG, TACKLE, TRAPPINGS
gear tooth - - - - - - - - - - COG
gel - - - - - - COAGULATE, JELLIFY
gelatine case - - - - - - - CAPSULE
gelatinous matter - - - - - - AGAR
gelatinous precipitate - - - - - GEL
gelid - - - - - FROZEN, ICY, COLD
gem - - - - MUFFIN, STONE, IOLITE
gem carved in relief - - - - - CAMEO
gem weight - - - - - - - - CARAT
gemel - - - - - - COUPLED, TWIN
gender - - - - - - SEX, ENGENDER
gene - - - - - - - - - - - FACTOR
genealogical record - - - - - - TREE
genealogy - - - - - - - - PEDIGREE
general aspect of landscape - SCENERY
general assembly - - - - - PLENUM
general character - - TENOR, NATURE
general course of action - - CAREER, TREND
general direction - - - - - - TREND
general fight - - - - - - - MELEE
general fitness - - - - - - APTITUDE
general ill health - - - - - CACHEXIA
general pardon - - - - - - AMNESTY
general purport - - - - - - TENOR

general type - - - - - - AVERAGE
general view - - - - - SYNOPSIS
generally disliked - - - - UNPOPULAR
generate - GENDER, PRODUCE, CREATE, DEVELOP
generation - - - - - - - - - AGE
generative cell - - - - - - GAMETE
generator - - - - - - - - DYNAMO
generous - - - - - - - - LIBERAL
genil - - - - - - - - - - GENIE
genius - - - - - - - - - TALENT
genius quality - - - - - - ARTISTRY
genre - - - - - - - - - KIND, TYPE
gens - - - - - - - - - - - CLAN
genteel - - - - - - - - NICE, POLITE
gentle - SOFT, DOCILE, TAME, KIND, MILD, TENDER, MEEK, EASY, BLAND
gentle (arch.) - - - - - MANSUETE
gentle blow - - - - - - DAB, PAT
gentle breeze - - - - ZEPHYR, AURA
gentle push - - - - - - - NUDGE
gentleman - - - - - - - - - - SIR
gentleman's country seat - - CHATEAU
gentlewoman - - - - - - - - LADY
genuflect - - - - - - - - - KNEEL
genuine - SINCERE, STERLING, REAL, TRUE
genuinely - - - - - - - - - TRULY
genus - - - - KIND, CLASS, VARIETY
genus of ambrosia - - - - RAGWEED
genus of annual herbs - - CALENDUAL
genus of auks - - - - - - ALLE, ALCA
genus of beet - - - - - - - - BETA
genus of birds (large) - - - - - OTIS
genus of the Blue Grass - - - - - POA
genus of bristly grasses - - SETARIA
genus of the burbots - - - - - LOTA
genus of cabbage - BRASSICA, COS, KALE
genus of candytuft - - - - - IBERIS
genus of cattle - - - - - - - - BOS
genus of cetaceans - - - - - - INIA
genus of chestnut tree - - CASTANEA
genus of chocolate trees - - - - COLA
genus of clearwing moth - - - - SESIA
genus of clothes moth - - - - - TINEA
genus of cow - - - - - - - - - BOS
genus of the currant - - - - - RIBES
genus of dogs - - - - - - - - CANIS
genus of ducks - - - - ANAS, ANSER
genus of ebony trees - - DIOSPYROS
genus of flowering shrubs - - ACACIA
genus of frog - - - - - RANA, ANURA
genus of garden spiders - - ARANEA
genus of garter snake - - - - ELAPS
genus of gastropods - - - - - TRITON
genus of geese - - - - ANSER, SOLAR
genus of goose barnacles - - - - LEPAS
genus of grass - - - - - - - - POA
genus of grasses - - - - AVENA, POA
genus of herbs - RUTA, ARUM, LIATRIS
genus of hog - - - - - - - - - SUS
genus of honey bee - - - - - - APIS
genus of hornbills - - - - - BUCEROS
genus of house mouse - - - - - MUS
genus of insect - - - - - - - NEPA
genus of kites - - - - - - - ELANUS
genus of lily - - - - - - - - - ALOE
genus of lindens - - - - - - - TILIA
genus of lizards - - - - IGUANA, UTA
genus of man - - - - - - - - HOMO
genus of maples - - - - - - - ACER
genus of medicinal herbs - - - SENNA
genus of medicinal plants - - - - ALOE
genus of mollusks - - - - - - - EOLIS
genus of monkeys - - - - - ALOUATTA
genus of moose - - - - - - - ALCES
genus of myrtle trees - - - - PIMENTA
genus of nuthatches - - - - - SITTA
genus of oak - - - - - - - QUERCUS
genus of oat - - - - - - - - AVENA
genus of Old World aquatic plants - - TRAPA
genus of olive trees - - - - - - OLEA
genus of orchids - - - - - - LAELIA
genus of palms - - - - - - - ARECA
genus of peacock - - - - - - - PAVO
genus of perchlike fish - - - - ANABAS
genus (pert. to) - - - - - - GENERIC
genus of pickerel - - - - - - - ESOX
genus of pig - - - - - - - - - SUS
genus of pineapples - - - - - ANANAS
genus of plants - - - - - - - - ALOE
genus of plants with conical trunks - - DIOON
genus of rails - - - - - - - - SORA
genus of rose - - - - - - - - ROSA
genus of rye - - - - - - - - SECALE
genus of sac fungi - - - - - - VERPA
genus of sandworts - - - - ARENARIA
genus of sea birds - - - - - - - SULA
genus of shad - - - - - - - - ALOSA
genus of sheep - - - - - - - - OVIS
genus of shrubs - ITEA, ROSA, OLEA, ERICA
genus of shrubs (large) - - - - ARALIA
genus of spider monkeys - - - ATELES
genus of sticklike insects - - - EMESA
genus of succulent plants - - - - ALOE
genus of sumac - - - - - - - - RHUS
genus of swan - - - - - - - - OLOR
genus of sweet flag - - - - - ACORUS
genus of swine - - - - - - - - - SUS
genus of toads - - - - - - - - ANURA
genus of tropical American plants - - BOMAREA
genus of tropical herbs - - - - URENA, LAPORTEA
genus of tropical trees - - - - MALOO
genus of turtle - - - - - - - - - EMY
genus of typical shrikes - - - - LANIUS
genus of vipers - - - - - - - - ECHIS
genus of Virginia willow - - ITES, ITEA
genus of wasp - - - - - - - - VESPA
genus of widgeons - - - - - - MARECA
geographical diagram - - - - - CHART
geographical dictionary - - GAZETTEER
geological age - - - - - - - - ERA
geological direction - - - - - STOSS
geological formation of layers of clay - LIAS
geological period - EOCENE, MIOCENE
geological rock formation - - - - IONE
geological term - - - - - - - STOSS
geometrical curve - PARABOLA, SPIRAL, POLAR
geometrical figure - - CONE, PRISM, ELLIPSE, CIRCLE, RHOMB, RHOMBUS, LUNE
geometrical proportion - - THEOREM
geometrical ratio - - - - - - - - PI
geometrical reference to locate point - ABSCISSA
geometrical solid - - CONE, CYLINDER
Georgian Caucasus - - - - - SVANE
Geraint's wife - - - - - - - - ENID
germ - - - - SEED, SPORE, MICROBE
germ cells - - - - - - - OVA, EGGS
German - - - - - - - TEUTON, HEGEL
German admiral - - - - - - - - SPEE
German affirmative - - - - - - - JA
German article - - - - - - - - DER

G

German author - - - - - - - - MANN
German beer - - - - - - - - MUM
German chancellor - - - - ADENAUER
German city - - ULM, ESSEN, EMDEN, EMS, TRIER, DRESDEN, TREVES, LEIPSIG
German coin - - - - - TALER, MARK
German composer - - - - ABT, BACH
German district - - - - SAAR, RUHR
German East African coin - - - - PESA
German emperor's title - - - - KAISER
German engraver - - - - - - - STOSS
German hall - - - - - - - - - SALA
German inventor - - - - - - - OTTO
German kobold - - - - - - - - NIS
German mathematician - - - - KLEIN
German militarism home - - PRUSSIA
German money - - - - - - - - MARK
German painter - - - - DURER, MARC
German (part) - - - - - - - PRUSSIA
German philosopher - - - HEGEL, KANT
German physicist - - - - - - - OHM
German poet - - - - - - - - HEINE
German port - - - - - - - - STETTIN
German religious reformer - - LUTHER
German river - - ESER, ODER, EDER, ELBE, WESER, EMS, RHINE, ISAR, RUHR, SAAR
German river basin - - - - - - SAAR
German ruler - - - - - - - - KAISER
German sculptor - - - - - - - STOSS
German socialist - - - - - - - MARX
German soldier - - - - - - - UHLAN
German state - - - - HESSE, SAXONY
German title - - - - - - HERR, VON
German tribe - - - - - - - ALAMANNI
German watering place - - - - - EMS
germane - - - - - - - - RELEVANT
germinate, as a seed - - - - - SPROUT
germinated grain - - - - - - - MALT
gest or geste - - EXPLOIT, GESTURE
gesticulate - - - - - - - - GESTURE
gesture - - - - - - MOTION, GEST
gesture of affection - - - - - CARESS
gesture of contempt - - - - - - FIG
gesture of helplessness - - - - SHRUG
get - - - - OBTAIN, RECEIVE, SECURE, PROCURE, WIN, BECOME, ACQUIRE, DERIVE
get along - - - - - - - - - - FARE
get away - - - - - - SCAT, ESCAPE
get away from - - - - ESCAPE, EVADE
get away (slang) - - - - LAM, SCRAM
get back - - - - - RECOVER, REGAIN
get and bring - - - - - - - FETCH
get on - - - - - - - - - - FARE
get out (colloq.) - - - - - - SCRAM
get ready - - - - - - - - PREPARE
get sight of - - - - - - - - ESPY
get to in time - - - - - - - CATCH
get up - - - - - - - - GEE, ARISE
getup - - - - - - - - - COSTUME
gewgaw - - - - - - - - - BAUBLE
ghastly - - - - - - - - LURID, WAN
ghost - - SPECTER, SHADE, SPOOK, APPARITION, PHANTOM, SPIRIT
ghostly being - - - - - - VAMPIRE
giant - TITAN, HUGE, OGRE, MONSTER
giant howitzer - - - - - - - SKODA
giant killer - - - - - - - - DAVID
giant (old word) - - - - - - - ETEN
gib - - - - - - - - - - - JIB
gibberish - - - - - - - - - JARGON
gibbet - - - - - - TREE, GALLOWS
gibbon - - - - - - - - - - - APE
gibbous - - CONVEX, FLOUT, TAUNT
gibe - SNEER, QUIP, DERIDE, AGREE, JAPE, TAUNT, FLOUT
gift - - - - PRESENT, GRANT, TALENT, DONATION, ENDOW
gift to bride - - - - - - - - DOWER
gift of charity - - - - - DOLE, ALMS
gift to employee - - - - - - - BONUS
gift to poor - - - - - - - - - - ALMS
gig - - - - - - - - - - - ROWBOAT
gigantic - MAMMOTH, TITAN, IMMENSE, HUGE, TITANIC
gigantic in power - - - - - - TITAN
giggle - - SNICKER, TEHEE, SNIGGER, TITTER
gilded bronze - - - - - - - ORMOLU
gill - - - - - - - - - - BRANCHIA
gin - - - - - - - - - SNARE, TRAP
gin (kind) - - - - - - - - - - SLOE
giraffe - - - - - - - - CAMELOPARD
giraffelike animal - - - - - - OKAPI
girdle - - SASH, BELT, CEST, BAND, CINCTURE, ZONE
girl - MAID, LASSIE, DAMSEL, LASS, MAIDEN, DAMOSEL
girl (dial.) - - - - - - - - - - GAL
girl student - - - - - - - - - COED
girl's toy - - - - - - - - - - DOLL
gist - - PITH, CORE, PITCH, POINT
give - DONATE, RENDER, CONTRIBUTE, PRESENT, PROFFER, HAND, BESTOW, IMPART
give an account of - - - - - REPORT
give authority to - - - - - EMPOWER
give away - - - - - - - - - BETRAY
give back - - - - RESTORE, RETURN
give bevel to - - - - - - - - - CANT
give in charge - - - - - - - CONSIGN
give confidence to - - - - - - ASSURE
give consecutive letters of - - - SPELL
give contrary order - - COUNTERMAND
give counsel - - - - - - - - ADVISE
give courge to - - - - - - - - NERVE
give ear to - - - - - - - - - HEED
give ease to - - - - - - - ALLEVIATE
give edge to - - - - - - - - - - SET
give expression to - - - - - - VOICE
give force to - - ENERGIZE, VALIDATE
give formally - - - - - - - PRESENT
give forth - - - - - - EMIT, UTTER
give a grant - - - - - - - CHARTER
give high value to - - - - - IDEALIZE
give indication of - - - - - PROMISE
give information - - - - - - - - TELL
give legal force to - - - - - VALIDATE
give the meaning - - - - - - DEFINE
give new colour to - - - - - - - DYE
give nourishment - - - - - - - FEED
give off - - - - - - - - - - - EMIT
give off fumes - - - - - - - - REEK
give one's word - - - - - - PROMISE
give out - - - - - METE, ISSUE, EMIT
give pain or sorrow to - - - - AGGRIEVE
give permission - - - - - - - CONSENT
give a place to - - - - - - - SITUATE
give pleasure - - - - - - - - DELIGHT
give reluctantly - BEGRUDGE, GRUDGE
give right to - - - - - - - - ENTITLE
give rise to - - - - - - - - GENDER
give (Scot.) - - - - - - - - - - GIE
give serrated edge - - - - - - TOOTH
give sloping edge to - - - - - - BEVEL
give strength to - - - - - - - NERVE
give substance to - - - - - - - FEED
give temporarily - - - - - - - LEND
give testimony under oath - - DEPONE
give up - - - RESIGN, CEDE, YIELD,

DESPAIR
give up all expectations - - DESPAIR
give utterance to - - - - - - - SAY
give variety to - - - - - DIVERSIFY
give vent to - - - - - - - - EMIT
give wavy appearance to - - - - CRIMP
give way - - - - - - - - - - YIELD
give wrong title to - - - - MISNAME
give zest to - - - - - - - SAUCE
given to jesting - - JOCULAR, JOCOSE
giver - - - - - - - - - - DONOR
giving milk - - - - - - - MILCH
glace - - - - - - - - - - FROZEN
glacial block formation - - - - SERAC
glacial deposits - ESKERS, MORAINES
glacial direction - - - - - - STOSS
glacial fissure - - - - - - CREVASS
glacial ice pinnacle - - - - - SERAC
glacial transition stage - - - - NEVE
glacial ridges - OSAR, ESKERS, ESKARS
glacial snowfields - - - - - - NEVES
glad - - - ELATED, HAPPY, JOYFUL, GRATIFIED, DELIGHTED, PLEASED
gladden - - - CHEER, ELATE, PLEASE
gladly - - - - - - - LIEVE, FAIN
glance - - - - - - - - - - LOOK
glance over - - - - - - - - SCAN
gland (comb. form) - - - - - - ADEN
glandiform - - - - - - - ADENOID
glandular organ - - - - - - LIVER
glare - - - - - - - - - - STARE
glaring light - - - - - - - FLARE
glass - - - - TUMBLER, MIRROR
glass for artificial gems - - - STRASS
glass container - PHIAL, JAR, CRUET, AMPULE
glass container (small) - - - - VIAL
glass tinged with cobalt - - - SMALT
glass tube for blowpipe - - MATRASS
glass vessel (var.) - - - - - AMPULE
glasses (colloq.) - - - - - - SPECS
glassy - - - - - SMOOTH, DULL
glassy volcanic rock - - - OBSIDIAN
glaze - - - - - - - - - ENAMEL
glaze on Chinese porcelain - EELSKIN
glazed sleazy cloth - - - - - SILESIA
glazier's tack - - - - - - - BRAD
gleam - - - SHINE, GLOW, RADIATE, LIGHT, GLINT, GLIMMER, SPARKLE
glean - - - - - - GARNER, GATHER
glee - - - - MIRTH, JOY, GAIETY
glen - - - - - - - - - - DELL
glib - - SMOOTH, FLUENT, FLIPPANT
glibness - - - - - - UNCTUOSITY
glide - - - - - SLIDE, SAIL, SLIP
glide airplane - - - - - - VOLPLANE
glide hurriedly - - - - - - SKITTER
glide over - - - - - - - - SKIM
glide over ice - - - - - - - SKATE
glide over snow - - - - - - - SKI
glide smoothly along - - - - - FLOW
glide as a snake - - - - - SLITHER
glide on strips of wood - - - - SKI
glide through - - - - - - - - SAIL
glimmer - - - - - - - - - GLEAM
glint - - - FLASH, GLITTER, GLEAM
glisten - - - - - - SPARKLE, SHINE
glistening brightness - - - - - SHEEN
glitter - - SHINE, GLINT, SPANGLE, SPARKLE
glittering - - - - - - - - SHEEN
globate - - - - - - - - SPHERICAL
globe - ORB, BALL, SPHERE, EARTH, STEER
globose fruit - - - - - - - ORANGE
globular - - - SPHERICAL, ROUND
globule - - - - - - - - - - BEAD
globule of liquid - - - - - - DROP
gloom - - MELANCHOLY, MURK, DUSK
gloomy - - DREARY, LURID, GLUM, DREAR, SAD, MOROSE, SATURNINE, STYGIAN, DARK, TENEBROUS
gloomy dean - - - - - - - - INGE
gloomy state of mind (colloq.) - DUMPS
glorify - - - - - BLESS, EXALT, LAUD
glorious - - - - - - SRI, MAJESTIC
glory - - SPLENDOUR, ECLAT, PRIDE, RENOWN, HALO
gloss - - LUSTER, PALLIATE, SHEEN, LUSTRE
glossy - - - SLEEK, SILKEN, NITID, LUSTROUS, SHINY
glossy fabric - SILK, SATEEN, SATIN, RAYON, SATINET
glossy paint - - - - - - - ENAMEL
glossy woolen cloth - - - - CALAMANCO
glove - - - - - MIT, GAUNTLET, MITT
glove leather - - - - - - - - NAPA
glow - - - - GLEAM, SHINE, BLOOM
glower - - - - - - - - - - SCOWL
glowing - - - - - - - - - RADIANT
glowing fragment of carbon - - COAL
glowing fragment of coal - - EMBER
glue - - - - - - - PASTE, FASTEN
glum - MOROSE, DEJECTED, SULLEN
glut - - - - - - - - SATE, SATIATE
glut oneself - - - - - - - BATTEN
glutinous - - - - - - - - VISCID
glutinous material - - - - - GELATIN
gluttonous animal - - - - - - HOG
gluttonize - - - - - - - - - GORGE
gluttony - - - - - - - - - GREED
gnar - - - - - - - - SNARL, GROWL
gnarl - - - - - - - TWIST, DISTORT
gnarled - - - - - - - - - KNOTTY
gnat - - - - - - - - - - MIDGE
gnaw - EAT, NIBBLE, PECK, CORRODE
gnaw away - - - - ERODE, CORRODE
gnawing animal - - - - - - RODENT
gnome - - - - - - - - ELF, GOBLIN
gnomon of a sun dial - - - - - STILE
go - - PROCEED, PRECEDE, DEPART, LEAVE, WENT, WEND, BETAKE
go abroad - - - - ENTRAIN, EMBARK
go after - - - - - - - - - FOLLOW
go against - - - - - - - - OPPOSE
go ahead - - - - - LEAD, PRECEDE
go aloft - - - - - - - - - ASCEND
go around - - - - - - - - - BYPASS
go astray - - - - - - - - - - ERR
go away - - SCAT, SHOO, DEPART, BEGONE, LEAVE
go back - - RETREAT, REVERT, EBB
go back over - - - - - - RETRACE
go before - - - - - PRECEDE, LEAD
go-between - - - - - - - - - AGENT
go by - - - - - - - - - - - PASS
go by auto - - - - - - - - - MOTOR
go by plane - - - - - - - AERO, FLY
go down - - - DESCEND, SINK, SET
go easily - - - - - - - AMBLE, LOPE
go at easy gallop - - - - - - CANTER
go fast - - - - - - - - - - SCOOT
go first - - - - - - - - - - LEAD
go forth - - - - - - - - - DEPART
go frequently - - - - - - - RESORT
go from one country to another - MIGRATE
go from place to place - - - - TRAVEL
go furtively - - - - - SNEAK, STEAL
go heavily - - - - - - - - LUMBER
go hunting - - - - - - - - - GUN
go into seclusion - - - - - - RETIRE

G

go on - - - - - - - GEE, PROCEED
go on board - - - - - - - EMBARK
go on with - - - - - - - RESUME
go out of sight - - - - - DISAPPEAR
go over - - - - - - - - - RETRACE
go (poet.) - - - - - - - - - WEND
go quickly (colloq.) - - SCOOT, DART
go rapidly - - - - - - RACE, TEAR
go the rounds - - - - - - PATROL
go (Scot.) - - - - - - - - - GAE
go silently - - - - - - - - STEAL
go slowly - - - - - - - - MOG
go to - - - - - - - - - - ATTEND
go to bed - - - - - - - - RETIRE
go to law - - - - - - - - - SUE
go to see - - - - - - - - - VISIT
go too far - - - OVERSTEP, OVERRUN
go up in rank - - - - - - - RISE
go without food - - - - - - - FAST
go wrong - - - - - - - - - - ERR
goad - SPUR, PROD, INCITE, STING
goal - END, AIM, TARGET, AMBITION, MECCA
goal of pilgrimage - - - - - MECCA
goat antelope - - - - - - - SEROW
goat cry - - - - - - - MAA, BLEAT
goat (kind) - - - - - ALPACA, IBEX
goat (wild) - - - - - - - - - IBEX
gob - - - - - - - - - - - MASS
goblet - - - - - - CHALICE, HANAP
goblin - - - - - - SPRITE, GNOME
gobloid river fish - - - - - - TETARD
god - - - - - - - - - IDOL, DEITY
god of altar fire - - - - - - - AGNI
god of ancient Memphis - - - - PTAH
god of fields and herds - - - - FAUN
god of flocks and pastures - - - - PAN
god of gates - - - - - - - - JANUS
god of love - - AMOR, EROS, CUPID
god of lower world - - - - - - - DIS
god of manly youth - - - - - APOLLO
god of metal working - - - - VULCAN
god of mirth - - - - - - - - COMUS
god of mischief - - - - - - - - LOKI
god of Polynesian pantheon - - TANE
god of revelry (classic myth) - - COMUS
god of sea - POSEIDON, NEPTUNE, LER
god of shepherds - - - - - - - PALES
god of thunder - - - - - DIS, THOR
god of underworld - - - - - - DIS
god for whom January is named - JANUS
god for whom Tuesday is named - TYR
god of war - ARES, MARS, IRA, ODIN, THOR, TYR
god wearing the solar disk - - - - RA
god of winds - - - - - - - AEOLUS
goddess - - - - - - - - - DEA, GE
goddess of agriculture - OPS, DEMETER, CERES
goddess of arts and sciences - ATHENA
goddess banished from Olympus - ATE
goddess of the chase - DIANA, ARTEMIS
goddess of dawn - - - - - - - - EOS
goddess of destiny - - - - - - - FATE
goddess of discord - - - - ERIS, ATE
goddess of earth - - - - - - GE, ERDA
goddess of fertility - - - - MA, OPS
goddess of grain - - - - - - - CERES
goddess of growing vegetation - CERES
goddess of harvest - - - - OPS, CERES
goddess of healing - - - - - - - EIR
goddess of hearth - - - - - - - VESTA
goddess of hope - - - - - - - SPES
goddess of horses - - - - - - EPONS
goddess of the hunt - - - - - DIANA
goddess of infatuation - - - - - ATE
goddess of justice - - - - - ASTRAEA
goddess (Latin) - - - - - - - - DEA
goddess of love - - - - EROS, VENUS
goddess of marriage - - - - - - HERA
goddess of mischief - - - - ERIS, ATE
goddess of moon - - LUNA, SELENE, SELENA
goddess of morning - - - - - AURORA
goddess of peace - - - - IRENE, IRINE
goddess of plenty - - - - - - - OPS
goddess of rainbow - - - - - - - IRIS
goddess of retribution - - - - - ARA
goddess of sea - - - - - - - - RAN
goddess of seasons - - - - - HORAE
goddess of sorrow - - - - - - - MARA
goddess of vegetation - - - - - CERES
goddess of vengeance - ARA, NEMESIS
goddess of victory - - - - - - - NIKE
goddess of war - - - - - - - - ALEA
goddess of wisdom - - - - - MINERVA
goddess of the wood - DIANA, NYMPH
goddess of youth - - - - - - - HEBE
godlike - - - - - - - DEIFIC, DIVINE
godly person - - - - - - - - SAINT
gods (the) - - - - - - - - - DI, DIE
gods (the) (var.) - - - - - - - - DII
gods of Teutonic pantheon - - - AESIR
goes at certain gait - - - - - LOPES
goggler - - - - - - - - - - - SCAD
going across land - - - - - OVERLAND
going on - - - - - - - - - - DOING
going the other way - - - - OPPOSITE
going up - - - - - - - - ANABASIS
gold - - - - - - - - - - - - AULIC
gold (alchem.) - - - - - - - - - SOL
gold bar - - - - - - - - - - INGOT
gold (her.) - - - - - - - - - - - OR
gold in Latin American countries - ORO
gold paint - - - - - - - - - - GILT
gold seeker in Alaska - - KLONDIKER
gold symbol - - - - - - - - - - AU
gold unit of Lithuania - - - - - LIT
golden - - - - PRECIOUS, AUREATE
golden oriole - - - - - - - - LORIOT
golf attendant - - - - - - - - CADDY
golf club - - CLEEK, SPOON, PUTTER, BRASSY, DRIVER, MIDIRON, IRON, BRASSIE, MASHIE
golf club nose - - - - - - - - - TOE
golf cone - - - - - - - - - - - TEE
golf course - - - - - - - - - LINKS
golf course depression - - - - CUP
golf course parts - GREENS, FAIRWAYS, TEES
golf hazard - - - - - - - - - TRAP
golf holes unplayed - - - - - - BYE
golf mound - - - - - - - - - - TEE
golf position - - - - - - - - STANCE
golf score - - BOGEY, STROKE, PAR
golf stroke - - - - PUTT, DRIVE, CHIP
golf term - - - - - PAR, TEE, DIVOT
golf turf - - - - - - - - - - DIVOT
golfer's target - - - - - - - - CUP
golfer's warning cry - - - - - - FORE
Goliath's home - - - - - - - - GATH
Goliath's slayer - - - - - - - DAVID
gone - - - - - - - - - PAST, LOST
gone by - - - - - - - - - AGO, PAST
gone by (poet.) - - - - - - - AGONE
goober - - - - - - - - - - PEANUT
good - - - ADMIRABLE, BENEFICIAL
goodbye - - - - - - - - ADIEU, TATA
good fortune - - - - - - - - - HAP
good health (colloq.) - - - - - - O.K.
good looking - - PRETTY, HANDSOME
good luck charm - - - - - - MASCOT

good manners - - - - - - BREEDING
good name - - - - - - - HONOUR
good order of management - - EUTAXY
good (prefix) - - - - - - - - - EU
good promise - - - - - - - HOPE
good spirit - - - - - - - - GENIE
good turn - - - - - - - - FAVOR
good will - - - - AMITY, KINDNESS
goods - - - - - - - - - - WARES
goods cast adrift - - - LIGAN, LAGAN
goods on hand - - - - - - - STOCK
goods for sale - - - - - - - WARES
goods as shipped - - - - - - INVOICE
goods shipped by public carrier FREIGHT
goods thrown overboard - - - JETSAM
goose (kind) - - - - SOLAN, BRANT
goose (male) - - - - - - - - GANDER
Gopher state - - - - - MINNESOTA
gordian - - - - - - - - INTRICATE
gore - - - - - - - - STAB, BLOOD
gorge - RAVINE, CHASM, GLUT, ABIDES, STUFF
gorgon - - - - - - - - - MEDUSA
gorilla - - - - - - - - - - - APE
gormandizer - - - - - - - GLUTTON
gorse - - - - - - - - - - FURZE
goslings - - - - - - - - - - GEESE
gospel - - - - EVANGEL, DOCTRINE
gossip - - - - - TATTLE, RUMOUR
gossip (dial.) - - - - - - - NORATE
got to - - - - - - - - - REACHED
Goth - - - - - - - - - BARBARIAN
Gounod opera - - - - - - - FAUST
gourd - - - - - - - - - CALABASH
gourd plant - - SQUASH, MELON, PEPO
gourmand - - - - - - - - EPICURE
gourmet - - - - - - - - - EPICURE
govern - - RULE, CONTROL, REGULATE, DIRECT, REIGN
governed by bishops - - - EPISCOPAL
governing principle - - - RULE, HINGE
government duty - - - - - - TARIFF
government grant - - - - - - PATENT
government levy - - - - - - - TAX
government representative - - CONSUL
government by women - - - GYNARCHY
governor - - - - - - - - - REGENT
gown - - - - - - - - - - DRESS
grab - SEIZE, COLLAR, SNATCH, CLUTCH, TRAP
grace - - - - - - - CHARM, ADORN
graceful - - - - - - - - - ELEGANT
graceful flowing melody - - CANTILENA
graceful woman - - - - - - - SYLPH
gracious - - - POLITE, BENIGN, FAIR
grade - - INCLINE, STANDING, RANK, DEGREE, SORT, RATE, RATING, CLASS
graded - - CLASSED, RANKED, RATED
gradient - - - - - - - - - SLOPE
gradual - - - - - - - - - SLOW
gradually enervate - - - - - - SAP
graduated glass tube - - - - BURETTE
graduates - - - - - - - - - ALUMNI
graduation certificate - - - DIPLOMA
grafted - - - - - - - - - - ENTE
grail - - - - - - - - - CHALICE
grail knight - - - - - - LOHENGRIN
grain - - GRANULATE, KERNEL, CEREAL
grain (artificial) - - - - - - - MALT
grain beating instrument - - - FLAIL
grain of a cereal - - - - - - - OAT
grain fungus - - - - - - - ERGOT
grain grinder - - - - - - - MILLER
grain for grinding - - - - - - GRIST
grain (pert. to) - - - - - - - OATEN
grain stalk - - - - - - - - STRAW
grain warehouse - - - - - ELEVATOR
graminaceous plant - - - - - GRASS
grammatical case - - - - - - DATIVE
grammatical construction - - - SYNTAX
grammatical error - - - - SOLECISM
grammatical form - - - - - - - CASE
grammatical tabulation - - PARADIGM
grampus - - - - - - - ORC, ORCA
grand - - - - AUGUST, GREAT, EPIC
grand slam at cards - - - - - VOLE
grandchild (Scot.) - - - - - - - OE
grandeur - - - - - - - - - ECLAT
grandiloquent - - - - - BOMBASTIC
grandiose - - - - - - - IMPRESSIVE
grandiose poem - - - - - - - - EPIC
grandparents (pert. to) - - - - AVAL
granitic - - - - - - - - AUSTERE
grant - - - CONCEDE, CEDE, BESTOW, ALLOW, CONFER, YIELD, GIFT, LEND
grant use of - - - - - - - - - LEND
granular material - - - - - - - SAND
granulate - - - - - - - - - GRAIN
grape - - UVA, RASP, ACINI, ACINUS
grape (dried) - - - - - - - RAISIN
grape drink - - - - - - - - WINE
grape (kind) - MALAGA, TOKAY, NIAGARA
grape plant - - - - - - - - - VINE
grape pomace - - - - - - - - RAPE
grape preserve - - - - - - - UVATE
grape refuse - - - - - - - - MARC
grapes (pert. to) - - - - - - ACINIC
graph - - - - - - - - - - CHART
graphic - - - - - - - - - - VIVID
graphic symbol - - - - - CHARACTER
graphite - - - - - - - - PLUMBAGO
grapple - - - - - - - - - CLINCH
grapple for oysters - - - - - - TONG
grapple with - - - - - - - - TACKLE
grasp - - APPREHEND, SEIZE, CLUTCH, TAKE, CLASP, GRIP
grasp firmly - - - - - - CLASP, GRIP
grasping - - - - - - - AVARICIOUS
grass - - - - - - - GRAZE, PASTURE
grass covered earth - - - - - - SOD
grass flower part - - - - - - PALEA
grass (kind) - - - RIE, REED, SEDGE, FODDER, POA, SWARD, GRAMA
grass-like herb - - - - - - - SEDGE
grass to make baskets - - - - OTATE
grass mowed and cured - - - - HAY
grass stem - - - - - - - - - REED
grass used for fodder - - - - - HAY
grasshopper - - - LOCUST, KATYDID
grassland - - - - - - LEA, MEADOW
grassy field - - - - - - MEADOW, LEA
grassy land surface - - - - - SWARD
grassy open place in forest - - GLADE
grassy plot - - - - - - - - - LAWN
grate - - RUB, RASP, GRILL, ABRADE, IRRITATE, GRIND, SCRAPE, GRIT
grated together - - - - - - GRITTED
gratified - - - - - - - - - - GLAD
gratify PLEASE, HUMOUR, SATE, WREAK
grating - GRID, GRILLE, RASPY, GRATE, GRILL
grating sound - - - CREPITUS, CREAK
grating utensil - - - - - - - GRATER
grating (var.) - - - - - - - - GRILL
gratis - - - - - - - - - - - FREE
gratitude - - - - - - - - - THANKS
gratuitous - - - - - - - - - - FREE
gratuitous benefit - - - - - - BOON
gratuity - - - - - - TIP, DOLE, FEE

G

grave - SATURNINE, SOLEMN, SOBER, DEMURE, SOMBER, PIT
grave robber - - - - - - - GHOUL
gravel - - - - - - - - GRIT, SAND
gravity - - - WEIGHT, SERIOUSNESS
gravy - - - - - - - - - - - SAUCE
gravy dish - - - - - - - - - - BOAT
gray - ASHEN, LEADEN, ASHY, HOARY, TAUPE, DISMAL
gray cloth - - - - - - - - - - DRAB
gray (dark) - - - - - - - - - TAUPE
gray rock - - - - - - - - - - SLATE
gray with age - - - - - - - - HOAR
grayish - - - - - - - - - - - SLATY
grayish green - - - - - - - RESEDA
grayish white - - - - - - - - ASHEN
graze - - PASTURE, GRASS, BROWSE, FEED
graze past - - - - - - - - - SHAVE
grazing tract - - - RANGE, PASTURE, PASTURAGE
grease - - LARD, OIL, FAT, LUBRICATE, LUBRICANT, BRIBE
greasy - - - - - - SMOOTH, LARDY
great - - VAST, IMMENSE, EMINENT, LARGE, GRAND
great age - - - - - - - - ANCIENT
great bear - - - - - - - - - - URSA
Great Britain - - - - - - - - ALBION
great deal - - - LOTS, LOT, MUCH
great desert - - - - - - - - SAHARA
great distance - - - - - - AFAR, FAR
great hurry - - - - - - - - - - RUSH
great intensity (of) - - - - - - DEEP
Great Lake - - ERIE, HURON, ONTARIO, SUPERIOR, MICHIGAN
Great Lake (pert. to) - - - - - ERIAN
great lavender - - - - - - - - ASPIC
great number - - - - - - MULTITUDE
great outpouring - - - - - - FLOOD
great personage - - - - - - - MOGUL
great (prefix) - - - - - - - - ARCH
great quantities - - - - - - WORLDS
great relish - - - - - - - - - GUSTO
greater - - - - - - - - - - - MORE
greater in length than breadth - OBLONG
greater merit - - - - - - - - - FINER
greater quantity - - - - - - - - MORE
greatest - - LARGEST, MOST, SUPREME
greatest age - - - - - - - - OLDEST
greatest amount - - - - - - - - MOST
greatly - - - - - - - - - - - MUCH
Grecian - - - - - - - - - HELLENIC
Greece - - - - - - - - - - - HELLAS
Greece (division of) - - - - - - DEME
Greece (pert. to) - - - - - - - GRECO
greed - - - - - AVARICE, CUPIDITY
greedy - - - - - - - - - - - - AVID
greedy person - - - - - MIDAS, PIG
Greek - - - - - - - - - - - ARGIVE
Greek assembly - - - - - - - - AGORA
Greek avenging spirit - - - - ERINYS
Greek capital - - - - - - - - ATHENS
Greek city - - - - - SALONIKA, ARTA
Greek coin - - OBOL, OBOLO, LEPTON
Greek coin (ancient) - - - - - STATER
Greek communes - - - - - - - DEMES
Greek country - - - - - - - - - ELIS
Greek counsellor in Trojan War - NESTOR
Greek deity - - - - - - - - - - EOS
Greek dialect - - - - - EOLIC, IONIC
Greek district - - - - - - - ARGOLIS
Greek enchantress - - MEDEA, CIRCE
Greek epic poem - - ILIAD, ODYSSEY
Greek fablist - - - - - - - - AESOP
Greek festival - - - - - - - - DELIA
Greek fury - - - - - ERINYS, ALECTO
Greek garment - - - - - - - - TUNIC
Greek ghost - - - - - - - - - - KER
Greek god - LETO, APOLLO, EROS, ARES
Greek god of sea (pert. to) POSEIDONIAN
Greek god of war - - - - - - - - ARES
Greek goddess - - - - - - - - ATHENA
Greek gravestone - - - - STELA, STELE
Greek hall - - - - - - - - - - - SAAL
Greek hero - - - - - - - - - - - AJAX
Greek historian - - - - - - XENOPHON
Greek island - - - MELOS, MILO, NIO, SAMOS, IOS, CRETE, RHODES, DELOS
Greek island (pert. to) - - - - CRETAN
Greek legendary hero - - - - - IDAS
Greek market place - - AGORE, AGORA
Greek mathematician - - ARCHIMEDES
Greek measure of distance - - STADIUM
Greek measure of length - - - - BEMA
Greek moon goddess - - - - - SELENA
Greek mountain - - - - - - - - OSSA
Greek mythological character - - LEDA
Greek mythological hero - - - - - IDAS
Greek mythological heroine - ATALANTA
Greek mythological monster - - HYDRA
Greek name - - - - - - - - - - ELIS
Greek patron of shepherds - - - - PAN
Greek peninsula - - - - - - - MOREA
Greek philosopher - - PLATO, GALEN, STOIC, ARISTOTLE, ZENO
Greek physician - - - - - - - - GALEN
Greek poem - - - - - - EPODE, EPIC
Greek poet - HOMER, PINDAR, ARION, HESIOD
Greek port - - - - - - - - - - ENOS
Greek portico - - - - - - - - - STOA
Greek priestess - - - - - - - - HERO
Greek province - - - - - - - - NOME
Greek resistance movement - - - - EDES
Greek room - - - - - - - - - - SAAL
Greek sea - - - - - - - - - IONIAN
Greek seaport - - - - - - ENOS, VOLO
Greek spirits - - - - - - - - ERINYES
Greek statesman - PERICLES, ARISTIDES
Greek sylvan deity - - - - - - - SATYR
Greek tense - - - - - - - - - AORIST
Greek theater - - - - - - - - - ODEON
Greek town - - - - - - - - - - SERES
Greek town (ancient) - - - - - SPARTA
green - - - - - - VERDANT, WREATH
green film on copper - - - - - PATINA
green herbage - - - - - - - - - GRASS
green leaved plants - - - - - GRASSES
green mineral - - - - - - - - ERINITE
Green Mountain Boys' leader - - ALLEN
green pigment - - - - - - - - - - BICE
green plum - - - - - - - - - - GAGE
green rust on bronze - - - - - PATINA
green tea - - - - - - - - - - HYSON
green with growing plants - - VERDANT
greenish yellow - - - - - - - - OLIVE
Greenland Eskimos - - - - - - - - ITA
Greenland settlement - - - - - - - ETAH
greet - - - SALUTE, HAIL, WELCOME, ADDRESS
greeting - SALUTATION, BOW, HELLO, HI, SALUTE
greeting (form) - - - - - - - - SALUTE
gregarious - - - - - - - - - - SOCIAL
gregarious cetacean - - - - PORPOISE
grenade - - - - - - - - - - - BOMB
grey - - - - - - - - - ASHEN, ASHY
grid - - - - - - - - - - - GRATING
griddle cake - - - - - - - - - SCONE
gridiron - - - - - - - - - - - GRILL

G

grief - DOLOUR, WOE, DISTRESS, DOLE, SORROW
grief (utterance for) - - - - - PLAINT
grief (var.) - - - - - - - - - - WO
grieve - SIGH, LAMENT, MOURN, PINE, SORROW
grievous - SORE, SORRY, DOLOUROUS, BURDENSOME
grill - - - GRIDIRON, GRATE, BROIL
grill with pepper - - - - - - - DEVIL
grille - - - - - - - - - - GRATING
grim - FIERCE, STERN, TERRIBLE, GAUNT
grimace - - - - - - GRIN, MOP, MOW
grime - - - - - - - - DIRT, SULLY
grimy - - - - - - - - - - - DIRTY
grin - - - - - - - - SMILE, SNEER
grin contemptuously - - - - - SNEER
grind - - - - GRATE, CRUSH, BRAY
grind to powder - - BRAY, TRITURATE
grind together - GNASH, CRUNCH, GRIT
grinding - - - - - MOLAR, GRITTING
grinding tooth - - - - - - - MOLAR
grip - - - VALISE, GRASP, HANDBAG, SEIZE, CLUTCH
gripe - - - - DISTRESS, COMPLAIN
gripping device - - - - - CLAMP, VISE
grist mill tenders - - - - - MILLERS
grit - SAND, GRAVEL, PLUCK, GRIND, COURAGE
gritty - - - - - - - - - - PLUCKY
groan - - - - - - - - - - - MOAN
groom - - - - - - - - - HOSTLER
groom hair - - - - - - - - - COMB
groove - - RUT, SLOT, SCORE, STRIA
groove part of joint - - - - - RABBET
groove wheel - - - SHEAVE, PULLEY
grooved - - - - - - - - - STRIATE
grope - - - - - - - - FUMBLE, FEEL
gross - - ANIMAL, CRASS, EGREGIOUS, BRUTISH
grotesque figure - - - - - - - GUY
grotesque imitation - - - - TRAVESTY
grotto - - - - - - - - - - - CAVE
ground - - - - SOIL, TERRAIN, LAND
ground for complaint - - - - GRIEVANCE
ground corn - - - - - - - - - MEAL
ground gained in football game YARDAGE
ground as a golf club - - - - - SOLE
ground grain - - - - - GRIST, MEAL
ground for grazing - - - - PASTURAGE
ground squirrel - - - - - - GOPHER
groundless - - - - - - - - BASELESS
groundwork - - - - - - BASE, BASIS
group - - BAND, SET, CLASS, BEVY, SQUAD, TEAM
group of animals or plants - - GENUS
group of bees - - - - - - - SWARM
group of graduate students - SEMINAR
group having similar views - - - SECT
group of houses - - - - - - - DORP
group of nine - - - - - - - ENNEAD
group of plants - - - - - - - GENUS
group taken at one time - - - BATCH
group of tents - - - - - - - - CAMP
group of three (in) - - - TERNATELY
group together - - - - - - ASSEMBLE
group of words - - - - - - SENTENCE
grove - - - - - - - - - - - WOOD
grovel - - WELTER, CRINGE, FLOUNDER
grow - - - WAX, INCREASE, BECOME, EXPAND, RAISE, ENLARGE, MATURE, DEVELOP, THRIVE
grow to be - - - - - - - - BECOME
grow in clusters - - - - - RACEMOSE
grow dim - - - - - - - FADE, BLEAR
grow exuberantly - LUXURIATE, VEGETATE
grow genial - - - - - - - - - THAW
grow larger - - - - - - - - - WAX
grow less - - - - - - - - - - WANE
grow less severe - - - - - - RELENT
grow out - - - - - - - - - - ENATE
grow profound - - - - - - - DEEPEN
grow rich - - - - - - - - - FATTEN
grow together - - - - - - COALESCE
grow uninteresting - - - - - - PALL
grow wan - - - - - - - - - - PALE
grower - - - - - - - - CULTIVATOR
growing in heaps - - - - - ACERVATE
growing in muddy places - - ULIGINOSE
growing in pairs - - - - - - BINATE
growing under water - - - SUBMERSE
growing vegetation - - - - - VERDURE
growl - SNARL, GNARL, GNARR, GNAR
grown - - - - - - - - - - - ADULT
growth - - - - - - TUMOR, STATURE
growth of scar tissue on skin - KELOID
grub - - - - - - - - - - - - LARVA
grudging covetousness - - - - - ENVY
gruel - - - - - - - - - - PORRIDGE
grumble - MUTTER, COMPLAIN, CROAK
grumble (colloq.) - - - - - - YAMMER
grunt - - - - - - - - - COMPLAIN
grunter - - - - - - - - - - - PIG
Guam capital - - - - - - - - AGANA
guarantee - - INSURE, AVOUCH, BAIL, ASSURE, PLEDGE, ENDORSE
guarantee payment - - - - ENDORSER
guaranty - - - - PLEDGE, WARRANTY, SECURITY
guard - PROTECT, KEEPER, FEND, TEND, SENTINEL
guard of sword hilt - - - - - - BOW
guard on tip of a foil - - - - BUTTON
guardian - - - - - PATRON, WARDEN
guardian deities - - - - - - - GENII
guardian of the peace - - - - POLICE
guardian spirit - - - - - - - ANGEL
guardianship - - - - - - - TUTELAGE
Guatemalan Indian - - - - - - MAYA
Gudrun's husband - - - - - - ATLI
guerdon - - - - - - - - - REWARD
guessing game - - - - CHARADE, MORA
guest - - VISITOR, CALLER, VISITANT, PATRON, LODGER
guest (comb. form) - - - - - - GENO
guffaw - - - - - - - - - - HEEHAW
Guiana tree - - - - - - - - - MORA
guidance - - - - - - - LEADERSHIP
guide - STEER, PILOT, DIRECT, LEAD, CLUE, LEADER
guide to navigation - - - - - - BUOY
guide thread through a maze - - CLUE
guider - - - - - PILOT, CONDUCTOR
guider of a course - - - - - RUDDER
guideway in a knitting machine - SLEY
guiding - - - - - - - - - - POLAR
guiding light - - - - - - - BEACON
guilder - - - - - - - - - - GULDEN
Guido's high note - - - - - - - ELA
Guido's low note - - - - - - - - UT
Guido's note - - - - - - - ALAMIRE
Guido's second note - - - - - - ARE
guile - - - - - - - - - - - DECEIT
guileful - - - - - - - - DECEITFUL
guileless - - - - - - - - - - NAIVE
guillemot - - - - - - - MURRE, LOOM
guiltlessness - - - - - - INNOCENCE
guilty party - - - - - - - - CULPRIT
guinea pig - - - - - - - - - - CAVY
Guinevere's husband - - - - - ARTHUR
guise - - - - - - - - - SEMBLANCE

guitar - - - - - - - - - - LUTE
gulch - - - - - - CANYON, RAVINE
gulden - - - - - - - - - GUILDER
gulf - - - - - - - CHASM, ABYSS
gulf of Arabian Sea - - - - - - ADEN
gulf in Baltic Sea - - - - - - RIGA
gulf of Caribbean Sea - - - - DARIEN
gulf at head of Adriatic Sea - TRIESTE
gulf of New Guinea - - - - - - HUON
gulf of Red Sea - - - - - - - SUEZ
gulf of Riga Island - - - - - OESEL
gulf of South China Sea - - - SIAM
gulf of St. Lawrence peninsula - GASPE
gull - - - - - - - - - DUPE, COB
gull-like bird - - - - - TERN, TERNES
gully - - - - - - - - - - RAVINE
gum - - - - MISCATORY, ADHESIVE
gum (kind) - - - - - - TRAGACANTH
gum resin - ELEMI, DAMAR, SANDARAC, COPAL, AVA
gum tree - - - - - - - - - BALATA
gum tree (sour) - - - - - - TUPELO
gumbo - - - - - - - - - - OKRA
gumbo (var.) - - - - - - - - OCRA
gummed piece of paper - - - STICKER
gun - - - - - - - RIFLE, CANNON
gun dog - - - - - - SETTER, POINTER
gun salute - - - - - - - - SALVO
gun sighter - - - - - - - - RADAR
gun (slang) - - - - - - - GAT, ROD
gunman - - - - - - - - - GANGSTER
gunner - - - - - - - - - SHOOTER
gunner's gang - - - - - - - CREW
gunpowder ingredient - - - - NITER
guns of a warship - - - - BATTERY
Guru Nanak follower - - - - - SIKH
gush - - - POUR, SPURT, SPOUT, JET
gush forth - - - - - - EMIT, SPURT
gust - - - - - GALE, WAFT, WIND
gust of wind - - - - - - - SQUALL
gusty - - - - - - - - - - WINDY
gut - - - - - - - - - - PLUNDER
guttural - - - - - - - - - VELAR
guttural sound - - - - - - - GRUNT
guy - - - - - - - - - CHAFF, JOSH
guy (colloq.) - - - - - GAG, FELLOW
gymnast - - - - - - - - - TURNER
gymnastic bar - - - - - - - TRAPEZE
gyp - - - - - - - - - - SWINDLE
gypsum (var.) - SELENITE, ALABASTER
gypsy - - - - - - - - ROM, ROMANY
gypsy book - - - - - - - - - LIL
gyre - - - - - - - - - - VORTEX
gyve - - - - - - - - - SHACKLE

H

habiliment - - - - - - - - ROBE
habit - - USAGE, CUSTOM, ROUTINE, ATTIRE, WONT
habitat plant form - - - - - - ECAD
habitation - - - - - - ABODE, LAIR
habitual - - - - - - - CUSTOMARY
habitual reserve in speech - RETICENCE
habitually complaining - - QUERULOUS
habitually silent - - - - TACITURN
habituate - - - - - - INURE, ENURE
habituate to a climate - - ACCLIMATE
hack - - - - - - - - - - - CAB
hackle - - - - - - - - - - COMB
hackneyed - - - - - - TRITE, BANAL
hackneyed expression - - - - CLICHE
had on - - - - - - - - - - WORE
Hades river - - - - - - LETHE, STYX
Hades stop - - - - - - - - EREBUS
haft - - - - - - - - HANDLE, HILT
hag - - - - BELDAM, CRONE, WITCH
haggard - - - - - - - - - - GAUNT
Haggard's book - - - - - - - SHE
hail - - - AVE, GREET, CALL, SALUTE, ACCOST
Haile Selassie title - - - NEGUS, RAS
hair - - - - - - - - - - FILAMENT
hair on animal's neck - - - - MANE
hair braid - - - - - - - - PIGTAIL
hair cloth - - - - - - - - - - ABA
hair (comb. form) - - - - - - - PIL
hair disease - - - - - XERASIA, MANGE
hair dressing implement - - - COMB
hair dye - - - - - - - - - - HENNA
hair on eyelid - - - - - - - EYELASH
hair fillet, covering and ribbon - SNOOD
hair line (var.) - - - - - - - SERIF
hair ointment - - - - - - - POMADE
hair ornament - - - - - - - COMB
hair of plants - - - - - - - VILLI
hair roll - - - - - - - - - - RAT
hairless - - - - - - - - - - BALD
hairy - - - PILARY, HIRSUTE, PILAR, COMATE
hale - - - STRONG, ROBUST, HEARTY, VIGOROUS, PULL
half - - - - - - - - - - PARTIAL
half boot - - - - - - - - - - PAC
half breed - - - - - METIS, MESTEE
half diameters - - - - - - - RADII
half an em - - - - - - - - - - EN
half a farthing - - - - - - - MITE
half man, half goat - - - - - FAUN
half man, half horse - - - CENTAUR
half mask - - - - - - - - DOMINO
half note - - - - - - - - - MINIM
half penny - - - - - - - - - MAG
half (prefix) - - - SEMI, DEMI, HEMI
half score - - - - - - - - - - TEN
half shrubby mint - - - - - - SAGE
half sole - - - - - - - - - - TAP
half suppressed laugh - - SNICKER
half tone - - - - - - - SEMITONE
half turn (manege) - - - - CARACOLE
half wild dog of India - - - - PARIAH
half woman, half bird - - - - SIREN
half year's stipend (Scot. law) - ANNAT
hall - - - - - - - AULA, CORRIDOR
hall (Ger.) - - - - - - - - - SAAL
hallow - - - - - - - HOLY, BLESS
hallowed - - - - - - HOLY, SACRED
hallowed place - - - - - - - SHRINE
halma (game like) - - - - - - SALTA
halo - - AREOLA, NIMBUS, AUREOLE, AUREOLA
halt - - STEM, PAUSE, LAME, ARREST, HESITATE
halting place - - - - - - - - ETAPE
halve - - - - - - DISSECT, DIVIDE
hamlet - - - - - - - - - - - DORP
Hamlet character - - - - - - OPHELIA
Hamlet's home - - - - - - ELSINORE
hammer - SLEDGE, MAUL, POUND, BEAT, MALLET, OLIVER
hammer to break stone - - - - KEVEL
hammer head (end) - - - PEEN, POLL
hammer in medicine - - - - PLESSOR
hammer out - - - - - - - - - ANVIL
hammer part - - - - - - - - - PEEN
hammer (small trip) - - - - OLIVER
hamper - - TRAMMEL, CRATE, CRAMP, BASKET, HINDER, HANAPER, ENCUMBER
hamper of slats - - - - - - - CRATE
hanaper - - - - - - - - - HAMPER
hand - - - GIVE, POINTER, PROFFER

hand (arch.) - - - - - - - - NIEVE
hand propeller - - - - - - - - - OAR
hand pump - - - - - - - SYRINGE
hand satchel - - - - - - - - GRIP
hand (slang) - - - - - - - - - FIN
handbag - GRIP, RETICULE, SATCHEL, VALISE
Handel's opera - - - - - - BERENICE
handful - - - - - - - - - - WISP
handful of hay - - - - - - - WISP
handle - - ANSA, HILT, HAFT, TREAT, MANAGE, HELVE, WIELD
handle of a hatchet - - - - - HELVE
handle to turn rudder - - - - - TILLER
handle of a pail - - - - - - - BAIL
handle roughly - - - - - PAW, MAUL
handle with skill - - - - - - WIELD
hands on hips - - - - - - - AKIMBO
handsome man - - - - - - - ADONIS
handsome (Scot.) - - - - - - BRAW
handwriting - - - - - - - - SCRIPT
handy - - - - - CONVENIENT, DEFT
handy person - - - - - - - DABSTER
hang - PEND, DRAPE, SUSPEND, HOVER, CLING
hang about - - - - - - - - HOVER
hang as if balanced - - - - - PEND
hang down - SAG, DROOP, LOP, SLOUCH
hang easily - - - - - - - - - LOLL
hang fluttering on the wing - - HOVER
hang loosely - - DRAPE, DANGLE, LOLL
hang over - - - - - - - - IMPEND
hanger-on - - - - - PARASITE, HEELER
hanging - - DRAPE, PENSILE, PENDENT
hanging for back of altar - - DOSSAL
hanging mass of ice - - - - - ICICLE
hanging ornament - TASSEL, PENDANT
hangings of a stage - - - - - SCENERY
hangman's loop - - - - - - - NOOSE
hangnail - - - - - - - - - AGNAIL
hanker - - - - - - - - - - - LONG
hanker after - - - - - - - - COVET
hansom - - - - - - - - - - - CAB
hap - LUCK, CHANCE, BEFALL, FORTUNE
haphazard - - - - RANDOM, CASUAL
happen - - OCCUR, BETIDE, BEFALL, CHANCE
happen again - - - - - - - - RECUR
happening too soon - - - - PREMATURE
happenings - EVENTS, NEWS, INCIDENTS
happiness - - - BLISS, JOY, FELICITY
happy - - - - GLAD, ELATE, BLEST
harangue - - - NAG, TIRADE, ORATE, SCREED, SPIEL
harass - NAG, BESET, FRET, BOTHER, PERPLEX, PLAGUE, VEX, ANNOY, GRIPE, PESTER, BAIT, IRK, TEASE, DISTRACT, FATIGUE, GALL
harness for oxen - - - - - - - YOKE
harass with clamour - - - - - - DIN
harbinger - - - - - - - - - HERALD
harbour COVE, PORT, ENTERTAIN, HOLD
harbour boat - - - - - - - - - TUG
hard - AUSTERE, RENITENT, CALLOUS, ADAMANT, ARDUOUS, SEVERE, SOLID, SET, IRON
hard ascent - - - - - - - - - PULL
hard brittle biscuit - - - - CRACKNEL
hard drawn - - - - - - TAUT, TENSE
hard fat - - - - - - - - - - SUET
hard finish - - - - - - - - ENAMEL
hard hearted - - - - - - - PITILESS
hard to manage - - - - - - ORNERY
hard metal - - - - - - - - - STEEL
hard mineral - - - - EMERY, SPINEL
hard outer covering - - SHELL, CRUST
hard porous structure - - - - - BONE
hard (prefix) - - - - - - - - - DYS
hard question - - - - - - - - POSER
hard resin - - - - - - - - - COPAL
hard rock - - - - - - - - - FLINT
hard rubber - - - - - - - - EBONITE
hard shelled fruit - - - - - CHESTNUT
hard substance - - - - - - - ADAMANT
hard tissue - - - - - - - - - BONE
hard twisted thread - - - - - - LISLE
hard water - - - - - - - - - - ICE
hard wood - - ASH, TEAK, OAK, LANA, EBONY, ELM
harden - - GEL, SET, ENURE, OSSIFY, STEEL, INURE, USE
harden fish nets - - - - - - - - TAN
harden sails - - - - - - - - - TAN
hardened clay - - - - - - - METAL
hardened mass - - - - - - - - CAKE
hardly - - - - - - - - - SCARCELY
hardship - - - - - - TRIAL, RIGOR
hardwood - - - - - - - - - EBONY
hardwood tree - - ASH, OAK, HICKORY
hardy - HALE, SPARTAN, ROBUST, WELL
hard covering - - - - - - - - SHELL
Hardy heroine - - - - - - - - - TESS
hardy shrub - - - - - - - - - ROSE
hare - - - - - - - LEPUS, RABBIT
harem - - - - - - - - - SERAGLIO
harem room - - - - - - - - - ODA
hark - - - - - - - - - - - LISTEN
harken - - - - - LISTEN, HEAR, EAR
harm - BANE, DAMAGE, INJURE, EVIL, HURT, INJURY
harm (obs.) - - - - - - - - - DERE
harmful - - - INJURIOUS, ILL, BAD
harmless - - - - - - - - INNOCENT
harmonious - - - - - - - - MUSICAL
harmonize - - ATTUNE, AGREE, TONE, BLEND, TUNE, CHIME
harmonize (colloq.) - - - - - - - GEE
harmony - - PEACE, UNION, UNISON
harness - - - - - - - - - - - GEAR
harness horse - - - - - - - - PACER
harness maker (arch.) - - - - LORIMER
harness part - HAME, REINS, TRACE, BRIDLE, REIN, HALTER
harness together - - - - - - - - TEAM
harp - - - - - - - - - - - - LYRE
harper - - - - - - - - - MINSTREL
harplike striking of a chord - ARPEGGIO
harpoon - - - - - - - - - - SPEAR
harrier - - - - - - - - - - - HAWK
harry - - - - - PESTER, PERSECUTE
harsh - - - STERN, SEVERE, ACERB, RASPING, RAUCOUS, RIGOROUS
harsh cry - - - - - - - - - - BRAY
harsh noise - - - - - - - - STRIDOR
harsh sounding - - - - - - STRIDENT
harsh tasting - - - - - BITTER, ACERB
harsh voiced person - - - - - STENTOR
harshness - - - - - RIGOR, STRIDENCE
hart - - - - - - - - - - - - - STAG
hartebeest - - - - - LECAMA, CAAMA
harvest - - - REAP, CROP, GATHERING
harvesting machine - MOWER, BINDER
has being - - - - - - - - - - - - IS
has courage - - - - - - - - - DARES
hasp - - - - - - - - - - - CATCH
haste - - - SPEED, HURRY, DISPATCH, QUICKNESS
hasten- HIE, RUN, HURRY, FLY, SCURRY, RACE
hasten away - - - - - - - SCAMPER
hasten off - - - - - - - - - - FLEE

H

hasty - - RASH, SUDDEN, IMPATIENT, BRASH, ABRUPT, IMPULSIVE
hasty (colloq.) - - - - - - - BRASH
hasty pudding - - - - - HASH, MUSH
hat - - BONNET, HEADGEAR, TOQUE, FEDORA, CAP, MILLINERY
hat crown - - - - - - - - - - POLL
hatch - - - - - - - - - CONCOCT
hate - - - DETEST, ABHOR, LOATHE, DESPISE, MALIGNITY
hateful - - - - - - CURSED, ODIOUS
hateful person - - - - - - - TOAD
hatred - - RANCOR, DISLIKE, ODIUM, AVERSION, ENMITY
hatter's mallet - - - - - - - - BEATER
haughtiness - - - - ARROGANCE, AIRS
haughty - - ARROGANT, PROUD, LOFTY
haul - TOW, LUG, PULL, CART, DRAW, DRAG, HALE, TUG
haul (naut.) - - - - - - - - - HEAVE
haulage - - - - - - - - - CARTAGE
haunt - - DEN, RESORT, VISIT, LAIR, FREQUENT, NEST, DIVE
hautboy - - - - - - - - - - - OBOE
have - - - - - - - - OWN, POSSESS
have ambition - - - - - - - - ASPIRE
have apex rounded and notched - RETUSE
have being - - - - - - - - - BE, ARE
have confidence - - - - - HOPE, TRUST
have courage - - - - - - - - - DARE
have dealings with - - - - - - TRADE
have effect - - - - - - - - - - TELL
have faith in - - - - - - - - - TRUST
have fondness for - - - - - - - - CARE
have harsh sound - - - - - - - GRATE
have impression of - - - - - - IDEATE
have life - - - - - - - - - - - - BE
have mercy on - - - - - - - - SPARE
have meter - - - - - - - - - - SCAN
have on - - - - - - - - - - - WEAR
have recourse to - - BETAKE, REFER, RESORT
have same opinion - - - - - - AGREE
have strong wish for - - - - - COVET
have title to - - - - - - - - - - OWN
have weight or effect - - - - MILITATE
haven - - - PORT, REFUGE, SHELTER
having ability - - - - - - - - - - ABLE
having arrived - - - - - - - - - - IN
having branches - RAMOSE, RAMULOSE
having a breathing sound - - ASPIRATE
having broad views - - - - - - ECLECTIC
having a clouded appearance - - MOIRE
having a comb - - - - - - - CRESTED
having equal angles - - - - ISOGONAL
having faculty of perception - SENTIENT
having feeling - - - - - - - SENTIENT
having feet - - - - - - - - - PEDATE
having a flat breastbone - - - RATITE
having flavor - - - - - - - - SAPID
having a good memory - - RETENTIVE
having a handle - - - - - - ANSATE
having hoofs - - - - - - - UNGULATE
having an intestine - - - - - ENTIRIC
having irregular margin - - - - EROSE
having a large nose - - - - - NASUTE
having limits - - - - - - - - FINITE
having lips - - - - - - - - LABIATE
having little depth - - - - - - SHOAL
having made and left a will - TESTATE
having narrow orifice - - - STENOPAIC
having no connection - - - - UNALLIED
having no curves - - - - - STRAIGHT
having no feet - - - - - - - - APODAL
having no interest or care - - SUPINE
having no lateral ranges of columns APTERAL
having no owner - - - - - UNOWNED
having no stem - - - - - - - SESSILE
having no tonal quality - - - - ATONAL
having no worries - - - - - CAREFREE
having obligation to - - - - - OWING
having offensive smell - - - - - OLID
having organs of hearing - - - - EARED
having painful feet - - - - - FOOTSORE
having purpose (gram.) - - - - TELIC
having quality of (suffix) - - - - - IVE
having raised strips - - - - - RIDGY
having recourse - - - - - RESORTING
having rectangular insets - - PANELED
having retired - - - - - - - - ABED
having rhythmical fall - - - - CADENT
having ribs - - - - - - - - COSTATE
having risen - - - - - - - - - - - UP
having rough edges - - - - - RAGGED
having rows - - - - - - - - - TIERED
having same relation to each other MUTUAL
having spikes - - - - - - - - TINED
having stamens - - - - - STAMINATE
having started - - - - - - - - - OFF
having strong impulse - - - - DRIVING
having supports - - - - - - - PIERED
having tendons - - - - - - SINEWED
having thin sharp tone - - - - - REEDY
having toothed margin - - - - - EROSE
having tufts - - - - - - - - BUNCHY
having two heads - - - - - BICIPITAL
having two horns - - - - - - BICORN
having two sides - - - - - BILATERAL
having two wings - - - - - DIPTERAL
having a veil - - - - - - - - VELATE
having a vibrant note - - TREMOLANT
having a wide application - - GENERIC
having wings - - - - - ALATED, ALATE
Hawaiian - - - - - - - - - KANAKAS
Hawaiian bird - - - - - OO, IO, OOAA
Hawaiian city - - - - - - - - - HILO
Hawaiian cloth - - - - - - - - TAPA
Hawaiian dance - - - - - - - - HULA
Hawaiian district - - - - - - - PUNA
Hawaiian farewell - - - - - - ALOHA
Hawaiian ferns - - - - - - - IWAIWA
Hawaiian fish - - - - - - LANIA, AHI
Hawaiian food - - - - - - - - - - POI
Hawaiian game of cat's cradle - - HEI
Hawaiian garland - - - - - - - - LEI
Hawaiian goose - - - - - - - - NENE
Hawaiian hawk - - - - - - - - - IO
Hawaiian herb - - - - - - - - NOLA
Hawaiian loincloth - - - MARO, MALO
Hawaiian salutation - - - - - ALOHA
Hawaiian taro paste - - - - - - POI
Hawaiian thrush - - - - - - - OMAO
Hawaiian timber tree - - - - - - KOA
Hawaiian town - - - - - - - - - HILO
Hawaiian tree - - - - - - KOA, AALII
Hawaiian valley - - - - - - - MANOA
Hawaiian wreath - - - - - - - - LEI
hawk headed deity - - - RA, HORUS
hawk (kind) - KESTREL, ELANET, FALCON, IO, HARRIER
hawk (large) - - - - - - - CARACARA
hawk-like bird - - - - - - - - - KITE
hawk nest - - - - - - - - - AERIE
hawk parrot - - - - - - - - - - HIA
hawk summons - - - - - - - - - WO
hawker - - - - - - - - - - PEDDLER
hawk's cage - - - - - - - - - MEW
hawk's leash - - - - - - - - - LUNE
hawser - - - - - - - - - - - ROPE
hawthorn blossom - - - - - - - MAY
hay - - - - - - - - - - - - FODDER
hay storage compartment - MOW, LOFT

haycock - - - - - - - - - RICK
haying machine - - - - - - TEDDER
haystack - - - - - - - - - - RICK
hazard - - RISK, PERIL, LOT, STAKE, DANGER, DARE
hazardous - - - DANGEROUS, UNSAFE
hazardous (slang) - - - - - - RUM
haze - - - - - - - - - FOG, MIST
hazelnut - - - - - - - - - FILBERT
haziness - - - - - - - MISTINESS
hazy - - - - - - - - - - VAGUE
he (Fr.) - - - - - - - - - - - IL
he flew too near the sun - - ICARUS
head - PATE, LEAD, POLL, DIRECTOR, LEADER, COP
head of convent - - - - - - ABBESS
head covering - - - - - HOOD, HAIR
head of ecclesiastical province - EPARCH
head (Fr.) - - - - - - - - - - TETE
head organ - - - - - - - - - - EYE
head part - - - - - - - - - SCALP
head and shoulders - - - - - - BUST
head (slang) - - - - - - - - - NOB
head of a thing - - - - - - - COP
headdress - - - - - - - TIARA, HAT
headdress (poet.) - - - - - - - TIAR
headgear - - - - - - - HOOD, HAT
headgear for a horse - - - - - BRIDLE
heading - - - - - - CAPTION, TITLE
headland - - CAPE, NESS, RAS, HOOK
headliner - - - - - - - - - - STAR
headman - - - - - - - - - - CHIEF
headpiece - - - - - - - - - - TAM
headstrong - - - - - - - - RASH
heal - - - - - - - - - - - CURE
healing art (dealing with) - - MEDICAL
healing ointment - - - BALM, BALSAM
healthy - - - - HALE, WELL, SANE
heap - - PILE, MASS, STACK, AMASS
heap adulation on - - - - - - PRAISE
heap of hay - - - - - - - - - MOW
heap of hay (obs.) - - - - - - - TAS
heap of stones - - - - SCREE, CAIRN
heap up - - - - - - - - - - AMASS
hear - HARKEN, REGARD, HEED, LISTEN
hear by accident - - - - - OVERHEAR
hear judicially - - - - - - - - TRY
hear ye - - - - - - - - - - OYEZ
hearer - - - - - - - - - - AUDITOR
hearing - - - - - - - - - AUDITION
hearing (pert. to) - - - - - - OTIC
hearsay - - - - - - - - - RUMOUR
heart - - - - - COR, CORE, SPIRIT
heart chamber - - - CAMERA, AURICLE
heart (pert. to) - - - - - - CARDIAC
heart shaped - - - - - - - CORDATE
hearten - - - - - ENCOURAGE, CHEER
hearth - - - - - - - - - FIRESIDE
hearty - - - - - - - HALE, SINCERE
heat - - - - - - - - - - WARMTH
heat excessively - - - - - - - TOAST
heat to extreme heat - - - - - ROAST
heat producer - - - - - - - - FUEL
heat (pert. to) - - THERMICAL, CALORIC
heat and spice - - - - - - - - MULL
heated - - - - - - - - - - - HOT
heated compartment - - - - - - OVEN
heated to liquid state - - - - MELTED
heated wine beverage - - - - - REGUS
heath - - - - - - - - ERICA, MOOR
heathen - - - - - - - - - - PAGAN
heathen diety - - - - - - - - IDOL
heather - - - - - - - - GORSE, ERICA
heather family - - - - - ERICACENE
heating implement - - - STOVE, ETNA, RADIATOR, BOILER
heating plant - - - - - - - - BOILER

heave - CAST, SURGE, RAISE, STRAIN, THROW, LIFT, HOIST
heave up - - - - - - - - - - HOIST
heaven - - - - - - FIRMAMENT, SKY
heaven's arch firmament - - - - - SKY
heaven personified - - - - - - ANU
heaven storming tower - - - - - BABEL
heavenly - - - - CELESTIAL, SUPERNAL
heavenly being - - - - - - - - ANGEL
heavenly body - - STAR, SUN, COMET, METEOR, LUMINARY, MOON, LAMP, PLANET
heavenly bread - - - - - - - - MANNA
heavenly food - - - - - - - - MANNA
heavenly spirit - - - - - - - ANGEL
heavens - - - - - - - - - SKIES, SKY
heaver - - - - - - - - - - - HOISTER
heavy - - - - - - - LEADEN, STOLID
heavy affliction - - - - - - - - WOE
heavy blow (slang) - - - - - - ONER
heavy boot - - - - - - - - - - STOGY
heavy gaseous element - XENON, RADON
heavy hair - - - - - - - - - - MANE
heavy hammer - - - - - - - - SLEDGE
heavy harrow - - - - - - - - - DRAG
heavy impact - - - - - - - - - SLAM
heavy metal - - - - - - - - - - LEAD
heavy mooring rope - - - - - - CABLE
heavy nail - - - - - - - - - - SPIKE
heavy shoes - - - - BROGANS, BOOTS
heavy spar - - - - - - - - - BARITE
heavy and sweet - - - - - - - SIRUPY
heavy swell - - - - - - - - - - SEA
heavy wood - - - - - - - - - EBONY
hebetate - - - - - - - - - - BLUNT
Hebrew - - - - - - (See also Jewish)
Hebrew deity - - - - - - - - BAAL, EL
Hebrew festival - - - - - - - - SEDER
Hebrew high priest - - - - - - - ELI
Hebrew judge - - - - - - - ELON, ELI
Hebrew king - - - - - - - SAUL, DAVID
Hebrew kingdom - - - - - - - ISRAEL
Hebrew lawgiver - - - - - - - MOSES
Hebrew letter - PE, TAV, DALETH, MEM, AYIN, RESH, AB, TETH
Hebrew lyre - - - - - - - - - - ASOR
Hebrew measure - OMER, CAB, HIN, KAB
Hebrew month - TISRI, SHEBAT, ELUL, ADAR, NISAN, AB
Hebrew musical instrument - - - - ASOR
Hebrew name for God - - - - - - EL
Hebrew plural ending - - - - - - IM
Hebrew prophet - - AMOS, JEREMIAH, HOSEA, DANIEL, ELIAS, ISAIAH, ELISHA
Hebrew proselyte - - - - - - - - GER
Hebrew synagogue pointer - - - - YAD
Hebrew vowel point - - - - - - TSERE
Hebrew weight - - - - - - - - OMER
Hebrides Island - - - - - - - - IONA
hector - - - - - - - - TEASE, BULLY
Hector's father - - - - - - - - PRIAM
heddles of a loom - - - - - - - CAAM
hedge - - - BUSH, THICKET, BARRIER, SKULK
hedge laurel - - - - - - - - TARATA
hedgehog-like animal - - - - - TENREC
hedgerow (Prov. Eng.) - - - - - REW
heed - - NOTICE, NOTE, ATTENTION, MIND, EAR, CARE, HEAR
heed (arch.) - - - - - - - - - RECK
heedful - - - - - ATTENT, ATTENTIVE
heedless - CARELESS, RASH, IMPRUDENT
heedlessness - - - - - - - TEMERITY
heehaw - - - - - - - - BRAY, GUFFAW
heel - - - - - - - - - - - - CANT
heel (comb. form) - - - - - - - TALO

H

heel over - - - - TIP, TILT, CAREEN
hegemony - - - - - - LEADERSHIP
height - - - - ALTITUDE, STATURE, ELEVATION, EMINENCE
heighten - - - - ELEVATE, ENHANCE
heinousness - - - - - FLAGRANCY
heir - - - - - - - LEGATEE, SCION
held in common - - - - - - JOINT
held in esteem - - - - - REPUTABLE
Helen's abductor - - - - - - PARIS
Helen of Troy's husband - - MENELAUS,
Helen of Troy's mother - - - - LEDA
heliacal - - - - - - - - - - SOLAR
helical - - - - - - - - - - SPIRAL
Helio's daughter - - - - - - CIRCE
helix - - - - - - - - - - - SPIRAL
hell - - - - - - - - - - INFERNO
Hellas - - - - - - - - - - GREECE
Hellenic - - - - - - - - - GRECIAN
hello (Latin) - - - - - - - - AVE
helm - - - - - - - STEER, TILLER
helmet faceguard - - - - - - VISOR
helmet front - - - - - - - AVENTAIL
helmet (light) - - - - - - - SALLET
helmet plume - - - - - - PANACHE
helmet shaped organ - - - - - GALEA
helmsman - - - PILOT, STEERSMAN
helot - - - - - - - - SLAVE, SERF
help - BENEFIT, STEAD, ATTEND, ABET, AID, ASSIST, SUCCOR, BEFRIEND
help over a difficulty - - - - - - TIDE
helper - - - - - - - - ALLY, AIDE
hem - - RESTRICT, MARGIN, BORDER
hem in - - - - - - - - - - BESET
hematite - - - - - - - - - ORE
hemp fiber - - - - - - TOW, SISAL
hemp (kind) - - - - - - SUNN, RINE
hempen cloth - - - - - - HESSIAN
hen's cry - - - - - - - - CACKLE
hence - - - ERGO, SO, THEREFORE
Hengist's brother - - - - - - HORSA
henna - - - - - - - - - - - DYE
henpeck - - - - - - - - - - NAG
Henry VIII's family - - - - - TUDOR
Henry VIII's nickname - - - - - HAL
Henry Clay's home - - - - - - ASHLAND
Hera's rival - - - - - - - - - - IO
herald - - - MESSENGER, PROCLAIM
heraldic - - - - - - - - - - BAY
heraldic bearing - - - - - - - ORLE
heraldic cross - - - - PATEE, PATTE
heraldic grafted - - - - - - - ENTE
heraldic sitting - - - - - - - SEJANT
heraldic star - - - - - - - ESTOILE
heraldic winged - - - - - - - AILE
heraldic wreath - - - - - - - ORLE
heraldry - - - - - - - - - - ENTE
heraldry gold - - - - - - - - - OR
heraldry green - - - - - - - - VERT
heraldry iris - - - - - - - - - LIS
heraldry wavy - - - - - - - - UNDE
herb - SAGE, SEDUM, CATNIP, ANISE, MOLY, DILL, RUE
herb of aster family - - - - - ARNICA
herb of bean family - - - PEA, LOTUS
herb of chicory family - - - - ENDIVE
herb (cloverlike) - - - - - - MEDIC
herb dill - - - - - - - - - - ANET
herb eve - - - - - - - - - - IVA
herb of goose foot family - - - BLITE
herb grace - - - - - - - - - RUE
herb of Himalayas - - - - - - ATIS
herb of mint family - - - - CATNIP
herb of mustard family - - - - CRESS
herb of nettle family - - - - HEMP
herb of nightshade family - - TOMATO
herb of parsley family - - - - DILL
herb of pink family - - - - CAMPION
herb pod - - - - - - - - - - OKRA
herb related to chicory - - - ENDIVE
herb for soup - - - - - - - - OKRA
herb (strong scented) - - - - CATNIP
herb used for seasoning - - - PARSLEY
herb with acid leaves - - - - SORREL
herb with aromatic root - - GINSENG
herb with aromatic seeds - - - ANISE
herb with stinging hairs - - - NETTLE
herbaceous perennial - - - - BANANA
herbage - - - - - - - - - - GRASS
herbivorous mammal - - - - TAPIR
herd - - - - - - - - DROVE, FLOCK
herdsman - - - - - - - - - HERDER
here - - - - - - - PRESENT, NOW
hereditary - - - - - - - - - LINEAL
hereditary character - - - - STRAIN
hereditary factor - - - - - - GENE
heretic - - - - - - - - DISSENTER
heretical doctrinal views - - HERESIES
heretofore - - - - - - - - ERENOW
heritage - INHERITANCE, BIRTHRIGHT
hermit - - - - - EREMITE, RECLUSE
hermit crab family (pert. to) - PAGURIAN
hermit saint - - - - - - - - GILES
hermitage - - - - - - - - CLOISTER
hero of an epic - - - - - - - IRA
hero of Marne - - - - - - JOFFRE
Herod's granddaughter - - - SALOME
Herodias' daughter - - - - SALOME
heroic - - - EPIC, BRAVE, EPICAL, VALIANT, ISSUSTRATE
heroic in scale - - - - - - - EPIC
heroic tale - - - SAGE, GEST, SAGA
heroically brave and enduring - SPARTAN
heroism - - - - - - - - - - VALOR
heron - - - EGRET, CRANE, AIGRET, BITTERN, RAIL
herring-like fish - SPRAT, LILE, SHAD, ALEWIVES, ALEWIFE
herring (pert. to) - - - - CLUPEOID
herring (small) - - SPRAT, ALEWIFE
hesitant - - - - - - - - - LOATH
hesitate - HAW, DEMUR, FALTER, HALT, PAUSE, WAVER
hesitate in speech - - - - STAMMER
hew - - - - CHOP, CUT, CLEAVE
hewing tool - - - - - - - - AXE, AX
hex - - - - - - - WITCH, BEWITCH
hiatus - - - - - - - GAP, OPENING
hibernating animal - - - - SLEEPER
Hibernian - - - - - - - - - - IRISH
hickory - - - - - - - - - - PECAN
hidden - - INNER, SECRET, LATENT, PERDU, INNATE, DEEP, COVERT
hidden obstacle - - - - - - - SNAG
hide - STOW, PELT, SECRETE, CONCEAL, SKIN, CACHE, COVER, VEIL, CONCEDE, ENSCONCE, CLOAK, SCREEN
hide by intervention - - - - ECLIPSE
hideous - - - - UGLY, HORRIBLE
hideous man - - - - - - - - OGRE
hiding place - - - - - CACHE, NICHE
hie - - - - - - - - HURRY, SPEED
high - - TALL, UP, LOFTY, COSTLY, ELEVATED
high (comb. form) - - - - - - ALTI
high estimation - - - - - - HONOR
high expectation - - - - - - HOPE
high fleecy cloud - - - - - CIRRUS
high hill - - - - - - - - - - TOR
high honour - - - - - - - HOMAGE
high mountains - - - - ANDES, ALPS
high note - - - - - - - - ELA, ALA

high pitched sound - - - - - - TING
high priest - - - - - - - - EL!
high rank - - - - - - - EMINENCE
high regard - - - - - - - HONOR
high in the scale - - - - - - - ALT
high silk hat (colloq.) - - - - - TILE
high steep cliff - - - - PRECIPICE
high temperature - - - - - - HEAT
high volley - - - - - - - - LOB
high waters - - - - - - - FLOODS
high wind - - - - - - - - GALE
higher - - - - - - - - UP, ABOVE
higher in place - - - - - - UPPER
higher point - - - - - - - - UP
higher in situation - - - - - UPLAND
highest - - - - - UPMOST, SUPREME
highest mountain - - EVEREST, PEAK
highest point - ACME, PEAK, PINNACLE, NOON, APEX, SUM
highest rank (of the) - - - - CURULE
highest ranking prelate - - - PRIMATE
highlander - - - - - - - - - SCOT
highlander costume - - - - - - KILT
highlander pouch - - - - - SPORRAN
highly decorated - - - - - - ORNATE
highly favoured - - - - - - BLESSED
highly respected - - - - - HONORED
highly seasoned - - - - - - DEVILED
highly seasoned dish - OLLA, RAGOUT
highly seasoned stew - - - - RAGOUT
highway - - - - - - PIKE, AVENUE
highway division - - - - - - - LANE
highway over railroads - - - OVERPASS
highly wrought - - - - - ELABORATE
highwayman - - - BANDIT, LADRONE, FOOTPAD
Highwayman author - - - - - NOYES
hike - - - - - - - - - - TRAMP
hilarity - - - - - - - - MERRIMENT
hill - - - - - - - - - EMINENCE
hill (flat) - - - - - - - - - MESA
hilltop - - - - - - - - - - KNAP
hilt - - - - - - - HANDLE, HAFT
Himalayan animal - - - - - - PANDA
Himalayan antelope - SEROW, GORAL
Himalayan monkshood - - - - - ATIS
Himalayan peak - - - - - - EVEREST
Himalayan wild sheep - - - - NAHOOR
hind bow of saddle - - - - - CANTLE
hinder - IMPEDE, OBSTRUCT, ARREST, LET, DELAY, HAMPER, ESTOP, DETER, BAR, RETARD, HARASS, DETAIN, CRAMP
hindered (arch.) - - - - - - - LET
hindmost - - - - - - - - - LAST
hindrance - - RESTRAINT, BALK, RUB, LET, BAR
Hindu acrobat - - - - - - - NAT
Hindu army man - - - - - - SEPOY
Hindu ascetic - - - - - - - YOGI
Hindu avatar - - - - - - - RAMA
Hindu charitable gift - - - - - ENAM
Hindu cymbals - - - - - - DAL, TAL
Hindu deity - SIVA, RAMA, UMA, DEVA, VARUNA
Hindu deity with seven arms - - AGNI
Hindu demon - - - - - ASURA, RAHU
Hindu garment - - - - - - - SARI
Hindu god (unknown) - - - - - - KA
Hindu goddess - - - - - - - DEVI
Hindu gods' abode - - - - - - MERU
Hindu guitar - - - - - - - SITAR
Hindu handkerchief - - - - MALABAR
Hindu hero - - - - - - - - RAMA
Hindu holy city - - - - - - BENARES
Hindu measure - - - - - - - RYOTS
Hindu merchant - - - - - - BANIAN
Hindu month - - - - - - PUS, ASIN
Hindu nature gods - - - - - - DEVA
Hindu peasant - - - - - - - RYOT
Hindu pillar - - - - - - - - - LAT
Hindu police station - - - - - THANA
Hindu policeman - - - - - - SEPOY
Hindu political leader - - - - GANDHI
Hindu prayer rug - - - - - - ASAN
Hindu prince - - RAJA, RAJAH, RANA
Hindu princess - - - - RANI, RANEE
Hindu progenitor - - - - - - MANU
Hindu proprietor - - - - - - MALIK
Hindu queen - - - - - RANEE, RANI
Hindu red dye - - - - - - - ALTA
Hindu religious philosophy - - YOGA
Hindu sacred literature - - - VEDA
Hindu school of philosophy - VEDANTA
Hindu social class - - - - - CASTE
Hindu supreme deity - - - - VARUNA
Hindu cymbals - - - - - - - TAL
Hindu title - - - - MIR, SAHIB, RAJAH
Hindu title of courtesy - - - - SAHIB
Hindu title of respect - - - - SWAMI
Hindu trinity - - - - - - - - SIVA
Hindu weight - - - - - - TOLA, SER
Hindu word (sacred) - - - - - - OM
Hindustan - - - - - - - - - INDIA
Hindustan hill dweller - - - - - TODA
Hindustan (poet.) - - - - - - - IND.
hinge - - - - JOINT, DEPEND, PIVOT
hinged plate in suit of armor - TUILLE
hint - - CLUE, CUE, TRACE, CLEW, SUGGEST, INTIMATE, TIP, IMPLY, ALLUSION, INTIMATION
hip - - - - - - - - - - - - COXA
hire - CHARTER, ENGAGE, RENT, FEE, EMPLOY, LET, CONTRACT, LEASE
hired assassin - - - - - - - BRAVO
hireling - - - - - - - - SLAVE, ESNE
hirsute - - - - - - - - - - HAIRY
hirsute adornment - - - BEARD, HAIR
hiss - - - - - - - - - SISS, BOO
hissing - - - - - - - SIBILANT, SIS
historian - - - - - - - CHRONICLER
historical goblet - - - - - - HANAP
historical period (pert. to) - EROL, ERAL
historical society (abbr.) - - - D.A.R., S.A.R.
history - - - - - - - - - ANNALS
history of person's life - BIOGRAPHY
hit - - SWAT, BATTED, STRIKE, BAT, SMITE, BUMP
hit aloft - - - - - - - - - - LOB
hit gently - - - - - - - - - - TAP
hit ground before ball in golf - SCLAFF
hit hard (slang) - - - - - - - LAM
hit (slang) - - - - - - SWAT, LAM
hitch - - - - - - - - - OBSTACLE
hither - - - - - - - - - - - HERE
Hitler's race - - - - - ARIAN, ARYAN
Hitler's hives - - - - - - - UREDO
hitter - - - - - - - - - - BATTER
ho there - - - - - - - - - HOLLA
hoar - - - - - - - - - - - WHITE
hoar frost - - - - - - - - - RIME
hoard - - - - - - - - - - - SAVE
hoarder - - - - - - - - - - MISER
hoarse - - - - - - - - - RAUCOUS
hoarseness - - - - - - - - - FROG
hoary - - - - - - - - - - - GRAY
hoax - - - - - - - - - - CANARD
hoax (slang) - - - - - - KID, SPOOF
hobby - - - - - - - FAD, AVOCATION
hobo - - - - - - - - - - - TRAMP
hocus - - - - - - - - - - - CHEAT

H

H

hod - - - - - - - - - - SCUTTLE
hodgepodge - - - - - - - - OLIO
hoe - - - CULTIVATE, GARDEN, TILL
hog fat - - - - - - - - - - LARD
hog (female) - - - - - - - - - SOW
hog (male) - - - - - - - - - BOAR
hog thighs - - - - - - - - - HAMS
hog (wild) - - - - - - - - - BOAR
hog (young) - - - - SHOAT, GRUNTER
hoist - - BOOST, CAT, RAISE, WINCH, HEAVE
hoisted - - - - - - - - - - HOVE
hoisting apparatus - DERRICK, CAGE, GIN, ELEVATOR, CAPSTAN, DAVIT, CRANE
hold - - - HAVE, RETAIN, CLUTCH, HARBOUR, KEEP, AVAST
hold in affection - - - - - - ENDEAR
hold attention - - - - - - - INTEREST
hold back - - DAM, RETARD, DETER, RESTRAIN, STEM, HINDER, DELAY, RESIST, DETAIN
hold balance - - - - - - - - POISE
hold in check - - - - - - RESTRAIN
hold in common - - - - - - - JOINT
hold in custody - - - - - - - DETAIN
hold dear - - - - - LOVE, CHERISH
hold in equilibrium - - - - - POISE
hold fast - - - CLING, ANCHOR, PIN
hold firmly - - - - - - - - - GRIP
hold in greater favour - - - - PREFER
hold inviolable - - - - - - RESPECT
hold one's ground - - - - - - STAND
hold oneself aloof - - - - - REFRAIN
hold out - - - - - - - - - - STAND
hold in respect - - - - - - - - AWE
hold by right - - - - - - - - - OWN
hold same opinion - - - - - - AGREE
hold a session - - - - - - - - - SIT
hold in suspense - - - - - - - HANG
hold together - - - - COHERE, CLAMP
hold under spell - - - - - - - CHARM
hold up - - - - - - - - - - - BEAR
holder - - - - CONTAINER, OWNER
holder of a lease - - - - - - LESSEE
holding - - - - - TENURE, PROPERTY
holding at bridge - - - - - - - TENACE
holding device - - - - - - - - VISE
hole - ORIFICE, APERTURE, OPENING, CAVITY, PERFORATION, EYELET
hole in the ground - - - - - BURROW
hole in one (slang) - - - - - - ACE
hole repairer - - - - - - - - DARNER
holidays - FIESTAS, VACATIONS, FERIA
Holland city - - - - - - - - - EDE
Holland seaport - - - - - - - EDAM
hollow - - DEPRESSION, CAVERNOUS, CONCAVE, DENT
hollow cylinder - - - - - - - - TUBE
hollow dish - - - - - BOWL, BASIN
hollow glass vessel - - - - - BOTTLE
hollow grass stem - - - - - - REED
hollow metallic vessel - - - - - BELL
hollow and round - - - - - CONCAVE
hollow vessel (suffix) - - - - - CYTE
holly - - - - - - - - - - - ILEX
holm - - - - - - - - - OAK, ILEX
holy - - SACRED, BLESSED, HALLOW
holy (French fem.) - - - - - SAINTE
holy person - - - - - - - - SAINT
holy picture - - - - - - - - - ICON
holy scriptures - - - - - - - BIBLE
Holy Thursday (name) - - - - - SKIRE
holy water font - - - - PILA, PATEN
homage - - - - - - - - - RESPECT
home - - - - - - - - - - ABODE
homecoming - - - - - - - - RETURN
home of Eri - - - - - - - - ASSAM
homeless child - - - - - - - - WAIF
homeless outcast - - - - - - - ARAB
homeless street wanderer - - - ARAB
Homer's epic - - - - ILIAD, ODYSSEY
homicide - - - - - - - - - MURDER
homicide satisfaction - - - - - CRO
homily - - - - - - - - - - SERMON
hominy - - - - - - - - - - - SAMP
homo sapiens - - - - - - - - - MAN
homologate - - - - - - - - - AGREE
homonym - - - - - - - - NAMESAKE
hone - - - - - - - - - - - - STROP
honest - SE, TRUE, UPRIGHT, FRANK
honey - - - - - - - - - - - - MEL
honey badger - - - - - - - - RATEL
honey buzzard - - - - - - - - PERN
honey container - - - - - - - COMB
honeycomb compartment - - - - CELL
honeyed - - - - - - - - - SUGARY
honour - VENERATE, REVERE, CREDIT, ESTEEM, REPUTATION, RENOWN, EXALT, ENNOBLE, RESPECT
honour with festivities - - - - - FETE
honourably retired - - - - - EMERITUS
honourary commission - - - - BREVET
Honshu bay - - - - - - - - TOYAMA
hooded cloak - - - - - - - CAPOTE
hoodlike cap - - - - - - - - - COIF
Hood's hero - - - - - - - - - ARAM
hoodwink - - - - - BLEAR, DECEIVE
hook - - - - GORE, CLASP, HEADLAND
hook money - - - - - - - - - LARI
hook part - - - - - - - - - - BARB
hooligan - - - - - - - - - RUFFIAN
hoop - - - - ENCIRCLE, RING, BAIL
Hoosier humorist - - - - - - - ADE
Hoosier poet - - - - - - - - RILEY
Hoosier state (abbr.) - - - - - IND.
hop - - - - - LEAP, SPRING, VINE
hop kiln - - - - - - - - - - - OAST
hop stem - - - - - - - - - - - BINE
hope - DESIRE, RELIANCE, ANTICIPATE, TRUST, WISH, EXPECTATION
hopelessness - - - - - - - DESPAIR
horal - - - - - - - - - - - HOURLY
horde - - - CROWD, DROVE, SWARM, THRONG, ARMY, HOST
horizontal - - - - - - - FLAT, LEVEL
horizontal bar in fireplace - ANDIRON
horizontal beam over door - - LINTEL
horizontal coping stone - - - TABLET
horizontal timber - - - - - - - SILL
horn - - - - - - - ANTLER, KLAXON
horn blast - - - - - - - - - TOOT
horn-like marine skeleton - - CORAL
horn of the moon - - - - - - CUSP
horned horse - - - - - - - UNICORN
horned quadruped - - - - - - - IBEX
hornet - - - - - - - - - - - WASP
hornless cow - - - - - - - - MULEY
horny - - - - - - - - - CERATOID
horny scales - - - - - - - - SCUTES
horrent - - - - - - - - BRISTLING
horrible - DIRE, HIDEOUS, DREADFUL
horrid - - - - - - - - - - DREADFUL
horrify - - - - - - - - - - - APPAL
horror - - - - - - - DREAD, TERROR
hors d'oeuvre - - - - - - - CANAPE
horse - NAG, STEED, HUNTER, MILER, ARAB, PACER, FENCER
horse blanket - - - - - - - MANTA
horse colour - - - - - ROAN, PINTO
horse disease - - - - GLANDER, SOOR
horse (female) - - - - - - - - MARE

horse fodder - - - - - - - - OATS
horse's foot part - - - - PASTERN
horse of a gait - - - GAITER, PACER, TROTTER
horse's gait - - - - - - - - RACK
horse harness part - - - HAME, REINS
horse headstall flap - - - BLINDER
horse (kind) - ROAN, PADNAG, PACER
horse leg (part of) - - - - - FETLOCK
horse mackerel - - - - - - - SCAD
horse in a race - - - - - - - ENTRY
horse that rises up - - - - - REARER
horse (small) - TIT, PONY, COB, BIDET
horse tender - - - - - - - GROOM
horse used for driving - - - - COB
horse with cut tail - - - - BANGTAIL
horse's working gear - - - HARNESS
horsehair line - - - - - - - SNELL
horseman - - - - - - - - - RIDER
horse's goads - - - - - - - SPURS
horse's seat - - - - - - - SADDLE
horsemanship's turns - - - CARACOLE
horticultural plot - - - - - GARDEN
hose - - - - - - - - - - DRENCH
hospital division - - - - - - WARD
host - - - ARMY, THRONG, HORDE
hostelry - - - - - - - - - - INN
hostile - - - - - - - - INIMICAL
hostile feeling - - - - - - ANIMUS
hostler - - - - - - - - - GROOM
hot - - - TORRID, PEPPERY, FIERY, HEATED
hot tempered - - - - - - IRASCIBLE
hot wind - - - - - - - - SIROCCO
hotel - - - - - - - - - - - INN
hound - - - BASSET, DOG, PURSUE
hour of the day - - - - - - - TIME
hourly - - - - - - - - - - HORAL
house - - - - - - LODGE, DOMICILE
house for bees - - - - - - - HIVE
house (pert. to) - - - - - - DOMAL
house plant - - - - - - - - CALLA
house of religious retirement - - - - MONASTERY
house (small) - CABIN, COTTAGE, COT
house of worship - - - - - - TEMPLE
houseboat - - - - - - - - BARGE
household - - - - MENAGE, FAMILY
household animal - - - - - - - PET
household gods - PENATES, DI, LARS
household linen - - - - - - NAPERY
household task - - - - - - CHORE
hover about - - - - - - - - FLIT
hove - - - MOVED, CAST, HOISTED
hovel - - - - - - - - - - - HUT
hover - - - - - - - POISE, LINGER
how nice! - - - - - - - - - - AH
however - - - - - - - - YET, BUT
howitzer - - - - - - - - - SKODA
howl - - - - ULULATE, WAIL, ROAR
howling - - - - - - - - - UBULANT
hoyden - - - - - - - - - TOMBOY
hub - - - - - - - - - - - NAVE
hubbub - CLAMOUR, TUMULT, NOISE, UPROAR
Hudson cliffs - - - - - - PALISADES
Hudson village - - - - - - - NYACK
hue - - COLOUR, TINT, CRY, SHADE, TINGE
hug - - - - - - - - - - EMBRACE
huge - GIANT, ENORMOUS, MASSIVE, GIGANTIC, VAST
huge being - - - - - - - - - GIANT
huge person or thing - - - - MONSTER
huge (poet.) - - - - - - - - ENORM
hulled corn - - - - - - - - SAMP
hulled oats - - - - - - - - GROATS

hum - CROON, DRONE, BOOM, BUZZ
human - - MAN, ADAMITE, MORTAL
human affairs - - - - - - - LIVES
human being - PERSON, MAN, MORTAL
human trunk - - - - - - - - TORSO
humane - - - - - - - - - - KIND
humanity - - - - - MAN, MORTALITY
humble - - ABASE, LOW, DISGRACE, LOWER
humbug - - - - FRAUD, IMPOSTURE
humdrum - - - - - - MONOTONOUS
humid - - - - - DAMP, WET, MOIST
humidity - - - - - - - - DAMPNESS
humiliate - SHAME, MORTIFY, ABASE, DEBASE, ABASH
humiliation - - - - - - - ABASEMENT
hummingbird - - - - - AVA, COLIBRI
humour - WIT, MOOD, INDULGE, BABY, WHIM, COMICALITY, GRATIFY
humourist - - - - - - - - - - WIT
humourist (colloq.) - - - - - - WAG
humourous - - - - - FUNNY, DROLL
humourous play - - FARCE, COMEDY
Hun - - - - - - ASIATIC, VANDAL
hundred weight (metric) - - QUINTAL
Hungarian composer - - LISZT, LEHAR
Hungarian dance - - - - - CZARDAS
hunger - - - - - - - - ESURIENCE
hungry - - - - RAVENOUS, STARVED
hunt - - - CHASE, TRAIL, SEARCH, PURSUE, SEEK
hunted animals - - - - - - - GAME
hunter - - - - - - - - - NIMROD
hunter's cap - - - - - - - MONTERO
hunter of rodents - - - - - RABBITER
hunter (var.) - - - - - - - - YAGER
hunting dog - SETTER, HOUND, ALAND, BEAGLE, BASSET
hunting dog (arch.) - - - - - - ALAN
hunting expedition - - - - - SAFARI
hunting game stealthily - - - ASTALK
huntsman horn - - - - - - - - BUGLE
hurdle - - - - SURMOUNT, BARRIER
hurl - - CAST, SLING, TOSS, THROW, FLING, PELT
hurl (poet.) - - - - - - - - EVANCE
hurricane - - - - - - - - - STORM
hurried - - - - - - - - - - HASTE
hurried (musical) - - - - - AGITATO
hurry - SPEED, RUSH, HASTE, HASTEN, HIE
hurt - PAIN, PAINED, DAMAGE, INJURY, HARM, INJURE
hurt (obs.) - - - - - - - - - DERE
hurtful - - - - - - MALEFIC, SORE
husband (pert. to) - - - - - MARITAL
husband or wife - - - - - - SPOUSE
hush - - - - - - - - TUT, SILENCE
husk - - - - - - - - SHELL, SHUCK
husks of fruit - - - - LEMMA, HULLS
husks of grain - CHAFF, STRAW, BRAN
hut - HOVEL, CABIN, SHANTY, SHACK
hybrid - - - - - - - CROSSBREED
hydrated aluminum silicate - SEVERITE
hydraulic pump - - - - - - - - RAM
hydrocarbon - - - - MELENE, BENZENE
hydrocarbon found in natural gas - - - ETHANE
hydrocarbon from pine tar - - RETENE
hydrocarbon radical - - - - - ETHYL
hydrocarbon (white) - MELENE, BENZENE
hydrophobia - - - - - - - - RABIES
hydrous magnes silicate - - - - TALC
hymn - - - - - - - - - - PSALM
hymn of praise - - - - - - - PAEAN
hymn tune - - - - - - - - CHORAL

H I

Hyperion's daughter - - - - - - EOS
hypnotic state - - - - - - TRANCE
hypnotism pioneer - - - - - MESMER
hypochet, alcohol rad. - - - - - AMYL
hypocrisy - - - - - - - - - - CANT
hypocrite - - - - - - - - TARTUFFE
hypocritical talk - - - - - - - CANT
hypothetical force - - - - - - - OD
hypothetical maiden - - - - - - IO
hypothetical structural unit - - - - ID
hysteria in males - - - - - TARASSIS

I

I (the) - - - - - - - - - - - - EGO
Ibsen character - ASE, NORA, ELLIDA, HEDDA
ice - SLEET, CHILL, DESSERT, FROST, FROSTING, SHERBET
ice cream container - - - - - - CONE
ice creeper - - - - - - - CRAMPON
ice crystals - - - - - - - - SNOW
ice (floating mass) - - FLOE, BERG, ICEBERG
ice runner - - - - - - - - SKATE
ice sheet - - - - - - - - GLACIER
Icelandic language - - - - - NORSE
Icelandic literary work - - - - EDDA
Icelandic measure - - - - KORNTUNNA
Icelandic measure of length - - LINA
Icelandic monetary unit - - - - KRONA
Icelandic mythical king - - - - ATLI
Icelandic prose narrative - - - - SAGA
Icelandic story - - - - - - - SAGA
ichthyic - - - - - - - - - PISCINE
icon - - IMAGE, PICTURE, PORTRAIT
icterine - - - - - - - YELLOWISH
icy - - - - - - - - FRIGID, GELID
Idaho capital - - - - - - - - BOISE
Idaho county - - - - - - - - - ADA
idea - - OPINION, CONCEPT, NOTION, THEORY, IMPRESSION, BELIEF, FANCY, THOUGHT, INTENTION
ideal - - AIM, PATTERN, STANDARD, FAULTLESS, PERFECT, MENTAL
ideally perfect place - - - - - UTOPIA
idealize - - - - - - - - - BEAUTIFY
ideate - - - - - - CONCEIVE, FANCY
identical - - - - - SAME, SELFSAME
identification - - - - - - - NOTCH
identification mark - - TAG, MARKER
idiocy - - - - - - - - - STUPIDITY
idiom - - - - - - - - - - DIALECT
idiot - - - MORON, OAF, SIMPLETON
idiotic - - - - - - - - - - DAFT
idle - - - INACTIVE, LOITER, LOAF, USELESS, LAZY, INDOLENT, VACANT, SLUGGISH, VAIN, FUTILE, OTIOSE, LAZE
idle (colloq.) - - - - - - - - - LAZE
idle talk - - PATTER, GAB, GOSSIP, PRATE, PALAVER
idle talk (colloq.) - - - - - - - GAS
idle tattler - - - - - - - - GOSSIP
idler - ROUNDER, DRONE, DAWDLER, LAZER, LOAFER
idly - - - - - - - - - INDOLENTLY
idol - - - - - - - - - - - - IMAGE
idolater - - - - - - - - - - PAGAN
idolatrous (arch.) - - - - IDOLOUS
idolatry - - - - - - - - - BAALISM
idolize - - - - - - - - - - - ADORE
idyl - - - - - ECLOGUE, PASTORAL
if - - - - - - - - - - - PROVIDED
if not - - - - - - - - - - - - ELSE
igneous rock - - BASALT, PORPHYRY
ignite - - - - - FIRE, KINDLE, LIGHT
ignoble - - - - - - - - MEAN, BASE
ignominy - - - - - - - - DISGRACE
ignoramus - - - - - - - - - DUNCE
ignorant - - - NESCIENT, UNAWARE, UNLEARNED
ignorant person - - - - - - - DUNCE
ignore - ELIDE, DISREGARD, SLIGHT
Igorot town division - - - - - - ATO
Igorot tribesman - - - - - - - - ATA
Iliad character - - - - - - - - AJAX
ilex - - - - - - - - - - - - HOLLY
Iliad author - - - - - - - - HOMER
Iliad hero - - - - - - - - - - AJAX
ilk - - - - - - - SORT, BREED, KIND
ill - BANEFUL, EVIL, BAD, HARMFUL, UNKIND, WOE, POORLY, AILING, UNWELL
ill boding - - - - - - - - - - DIRE
ill bred person - - BOOR, CAD, CHURL
ill gotten gain - - - - - - - - PELF
ill humour - - - - - - - - DUDGEON
ill humored - - - - - - - - MOROSE
ill made verse - - - - - DOGGEREL
ill mannered child - - - - - - - BRAT
ill natured - - - - - - - - - NASTY
ill natured state - - - - - NASTINESS
ill (prefix) - - - - - - - - - - MAL
ill tempered - - - - - - - - CRUSTY
ill tempered woman - VIRAGO, SHREW
ill treat - - - - - - - - - - - ABUSE
ill use - - - - - ABUSE, MALTREAT
ill will - - RANCOR, MALICE, ANIMUS
illegal act - - - - - - - - - CRIME
illeum (comb. form) - - - - - - ILEO
illimitable - - - - - - BOUNDLESS
Illinois city - - - - - - - - ALTON
Illinois village - - - - - - - - ODELL
illiterate - - - - - - - - IGNORANT
illiterate dialect - - - - - - PATOIS
illness - - - - - - - - - - MALADY
illuminant - - - - - - - - - - - GAS
illumine - - - - - - - - ENLIGHTEN
illusion - - - - - - - - - - MIRAGE
illusive - - - - - - - - DECEPTIVE
illustrate - - - - - ADORN, PICTURE
illustrate with action - - - - GESTURE
illustration (kind) - - - - - ETCHING
illustrious - - - - NOBLE, BRILLIANT
image - - IDOL, EMBLEM, LIKENESS, STATUE, ICON, COPY, PICTURE, EFFIGY, EIDOLON
image of a saint (var.) - - - - - IKON
imaginably true - - - - - POSSIBLE
imaginary - - - - - - - - MYTHICAL
imaginary belt in heavens - - ZODIAC
imaginary monster - - - - - CHIMERA
imaginary small beings - - - - FAIRIES
imaginary world beyond this - - LIMBO
imagination - - - - - IDEA, FANTASY
imaginative - - - - - - - - - POETIC
imaginative comparison - - - - SIMILE
imaginative and dreamy - - - - POETIC
imaginative verse - - - - - - POETRY
imagine - - IDEATE, DREAM, FANCY, CONJECTURE
imbecile - - - - - - CRETIN, ANILE
imbed - - - - - - - - - - - PLANT
imbedded dirt - - - - - - - - GRIME
imbibed - - - - - DRANK, ABSORBED
imbue - - INGRAIN, STEEP, INFUSE, TINCTURE, PERVADE, PERMEATE, SATURATE
imbue with vigor - - - - - - NERVE
inflammable material - - - - TINDER
imitate - - APE, EMULATE, SIMULATE, COPY, ECHO, MOCK, MIMIC

I

imitation - - - - - - PASTE, SHAM
imitation gold - - - - - - OROIDE
imitation pearl - - - - - - OLIVET
imitative - MIMETIC, COPYING, APISH
imitator - - APE, COPIER, PARODIST
immaculate - - - - - - - - SPOTLESS
immature - - - - - - - - - UNRIPE
immediate - - - - - - - - - DIRECT
immediate payment - - - - - CASH
immediately - - - - - PRESTO, NOW
immediately following - - - - NEXT
immediately previous - - PRECEDING
immense - - - - VAST, ENORMOUS, GIGANTIC, GREAT, VASTY
immerse - - DIP, SUBMERGE, DOUSE
immigration center - - - - - - ELLIS
imminent (be) - - - - - - IMPEND
immobile - - - - - - - - - STILL
immortality - - - - - - ETERNITY
immovable - - - - - ADAMANT, STILL
immunity - - - - - - - PRIVILEGE
immutable - - - - - - - - - FIRM
imp - - - - - - - SPRITE, DEMON
impair - - MAR, WEAR, DAMAGE, SAP, RUIN
impair by hard use - - - - - BATTER
impair by inaction - - - - - - RUST
impair by time - - - - - - - RUST
impairer - - - - - - - - SAPPER
impairment due to use - - - - - WEAR
impart knowledge to - - - - - INFORM
impart - - - INSTIL, TELL, CONVEY, INSPIRE, GIVE
impart new vigor - - - - - RECREATE
impartial - - - UNBIASED, FAIR, JUST
impassive - - - - - - - - - STOLID
impatient - RESTIVE, HASTY, TOLERANT
impecunious - - - - - - - - - POOR
impede - OBSTRUCT, HINDER, ESTOP, CLOG
impediment - - - - - - REMORA, BAR
impel - - - - - URGE, SEND, INDUCE, CONSTRAIN, FORCE, DRIVE, COMPEL, INCITE, SPUR, ACTUATE
impend - - - - - - - - - THREATEN
impenetrable - - - - - - - - HARD
imperative - - - - - - - - URGENT
imperator - - - - - - - - EMPEROR
imperceptible - - - - - - - MINUTE
imperfection - - - - - - - BLEMISH
imperfect - - - - - - - - DAMAGED
imperfect (prefix) - - - - - - - MAL
imperfect shell - - - - - - - - DUD
imperfectly crystallized diamonds - BORT
imperial - - - - - - REGAL, MAJESTIC
imperial domains - EMPERIES, EMPIRES
imperil - - - - - - - - - - MENACE
impertinence - - - - - - - - - SASS
impertinent - OFFICIOUS, SAUCY, SASSY
impertinent girl - - - - - - - MINX
impetuous - - RASH, EAGER, ABRUPT, FIERY
impetuosity - - - - - - - - DASH
impetus - - - - - - - MOMENTUM
implacable - - - - - - INEXORABLE
implanted - - ROOTED, INCULCATED, INFIXED, LODGED
implement - - TOOL, SPADE, UTENSIL, FULFILL
implement for bruising or mixing - - - PESTLE
implement to dig - - - - - - SPADE
implement to remove hair from hides - SLATER
implement to smooth loose material - - TROWEL
implement used with a mortar - PESTLE
implicate - - INVOLVE, INCRIMINATE
implicit - - - - - - - - - ABSOLUTE
implied - - - - - - - - - - TACIT
implore - BEG, ENTREAT, PLEAD, PRAY
implorer - - - - - - - - SUPPLICANT
imply - - - - - - - - - MEAN, HINT
impolite - - - - - - - - - - RUDE
import - - INTEREST, SENSE, MATTER
importance - - - - - - - - - STRESS
important - MOMENTOUS, PROMINENT
important (is) - - - - - - - MATTERS
important individual - - - PERSONAGE
important official - - - - - MAGNATE
important standing - - - - - PRESTIGE
importune - SOLICIT, PRAY, TEASE, DUN
impose - - - - - - - - OBTRUDE, LAY
impose by fraud - - - - - - - - PALM
impose as necessary result - - ENTAIL
impose as taxes - - - - - - - - LEVY
imposed labors - - - - - - - - TASKS
imposing elderly matron - - DOWAGER
impossible position (var.) - - - STIMEY
impost - - - - - - DUTY, TOLL, TAX
imposture - - - DECEPTION, SHAM, HUMBUG, DECEIT
impoverished - - - - - - BEGGARED
impractical - - - - - - - THEORETIC
imprecation - - - - - OATH, CURSE
imprecation of evil - - - - - - CURSE
impregnate with salt - - - - MARINATE
impregnation - - - - - - SATURATION
impress - - PRINT, STAMP, MARK, AWE
impress deeply - - - ENGRAVE, AFFECT
impress by repetition - - - - - DINS
impress upon indelibly - - - - INGRAIN
impressed - AWED, MARKED, STAMPED
impression - - - - - - - - DENT, IDEA
impression of type - - - - - - PRINT
impressionable - - - - - - PLASTIC
impressive - - GRANDIOSE, IMPOSING
imprimatur - - - - - - - - APPROVAL
imprint - - - - - - - - STAMP, DINT
imprison - - - CAGE, INTER, SCONCE, INCARCERATE, JAIL, CONFINE
imprisonment - - - - - - - DURANCE
improbable tale - - - - - - - YARN
improper - - - - - - - - - - AMISS
improve - - BETTER, AMEND, EMEND, GAIN, REVISE
imprudent - - - INDISCREET, RASH, HEEDLESS
impudent - SAUCY, RUDE, BRASH, PERT
impudent (colloq.) - - - - - - - SASSY
impulse - - - - - - - - - - ELAN
impulsively - - - - - - - - HASTILY
impure from ore - - - - - - - OCHER
impute - - - - - - - - - - ASCRIBE
in - - - - - - - - AT, AMONG, INTO
in abundance (colloq.) - - - - GALORE
in advance - - - - - - AHEAD, BEFORE
in another manner - - - - - - - ELSE
in any case - - - - - - - - - EVER
in bed - - - - - - - - - - - ABED
in behalf of - - - - - - - - PRO, FOR
in the capacity of - - - - - - AS, QUO
in the character of - - - - - - - QUA
in circulation - - - - - - - - AFLOAT
in circumference - - - - - - - AROUND
in company - - - - - - - ALONG, WITH
in a detached position - - - - ISOLATED
in a difficult position - - - CORNERED
in direction of - TO, AXIAL, TOWARD, ON
in disordered condition - - LITTERED, MESSY
in dotage - - - - - - - - - - ANILE
in equal degree - - - - - - - - - AS

I

in error - - - - - - - - - - WRONG
in excessive quantity - - - - - - TOO
in existence - - - - - - - - EXTANT
in fact - - - - - - - INDEED, TRULY
in favour of - - - - - - - PRO, FOR
in the fork - - - - - - - - - ALAR
in a frenzied manner - - - - - AMOK
in front - - - - - - - AHEAD, APACE
in front of - - - - - - - - - BEFORE
in good season and time - - BETIMES, EARLY
in harmony - - - - - - - - - AGREE
in high spirits - - - ELATED, EXULTED
in higher position - - - - - - ABOVE
in highest degree - - - - SUPREMELY
in honor of - - - - - - - - - AFTER
in the lead - - - - - - - - - AHEAD
in like manner - - - - - - - - - SO
in a line - - - - - - - - - - AROW
in the main - - - - - - - GENERALLY
in the major mode (mus.) - - - - DUR
in the midst of - - - - - - - AMONG
in the name of Allah - - - BISMILLAH
in name only - - - - - - - NOMINAL
in the near future - - - - - - SOON
in no place - - - - - - - - NOWHERE
in no way - - NOT, NOWISE, NOHOW
in one's dotage - - - - - - - SENILE
in operation - - - - - - - - GOING
in order that - - - - - - - - - LEST
in a party's platform - - - - - PLANK
in passing - - - - - - - - - OBITER
in the past - - - - - - - - - - AGO
in place of - FOR, ELSE, STEAD, INSTEAD
in position for motion (naut.) - - ATRIP
in position of a thrust - - - - - ATILT
in (prefix) - - - - - - - - - - - EN
in progress - - - - - - - - - AFOOT
in proper shape - - - - - - - - TAUT
in pursuit of - - - - - - - - - AFTER
in quick time - - - - - - - - PRESTO
in reality - - - - - - - - - INDEED
in respect to - - - - - - - - - - OF
in reverse direction - - - BACKWARDS
in a row - - - - - - - - ALIGNMENT
in a row (poet.) - - - - - - - - AROW
in same degree - - - - - - - - - SO
in same place - - - - IBIDEM, IBID
in same place (abbr.) - - - - - - IB.
in same state - - - - - - - - - SO
in a short time - - - - - - - SOON
in a silly way - - - - - - - INANELY
in a slanting direction - - - - ASKEW
insofar as - - - - - - - - - - QUA
in some measure - - - - - - PARTLY
in a sorry manner - - - - - SORRILY
in store for - - - - - - - - AWAIT
in such a manner - - - - - - - - SO
in sufficient time - - - - - - - DULY
in a tail-like manner - - - - CAUDALLY
in that case - - - - - - - SO, THEN
in this - - - - - - - - - - HEREIN
in this matter - - - - - - - - - SO
in this place - - - - - - - - - HERE
in this way - - - - - - - - - THUS
in time of - - - - - - - - - DURING
in time (mus.) - - - - - - - - TRAIN
in tired manner - - - - - - - WEARILY
in a trice - - - - - - - - - - ANON
in truth - - - - - - - - - - VERILY
in a vertical line (naut.) - - - - APEAK
in what place - - - - - - - - WHERE
in what way or manner - - - - - HOW
inability - - - - - - - - INCAPACITY
inability to speak - - - - - - ALALIA
Inachus' daughter - - - - - - - - IO
inactive - - INERT, INDOLENT, IDLE, INANIMATE, OTIOSE, PASSIVE, RESTING, RETIRED
inactivity - - - - - - - - - IDLENESS
inadequate to - - - - - - - - SHORT
inadequately - - - - - - - SLENDERLY
inane - - - EMPTY, SILLY, FATUOUS, STUPID, VACUITY
inanimate - - - - - - - - - INACTIVE
inanimate substance - - - - - THING
inanity - - - - - - - - - FRIVOLITY
inappropriate - - - - - - - - - INEPT
inattentive - - - - - HEEDLESS, NODS
inattentive because of anxiety - DISTRAIT
inaugurate - - - - - - - - - - OPEN
inborn - - INNATE, INBRED, NATURAL, NATIVE
inbred - - - - - - INBORN, INNATE
incandescent lamp - - - - - - - BULB
incandescent particle - - - - - SPARK
incantation - - - - - - - - - SPELL
incapacity - - - - - - - - INABILITY
incarcerate - - - - - - - IMPRISON
incarnation - - - - AVATOR, AVATAR
incarnation of Vishnu - - - - - RAMA
incase - - - - - - CASE, SURROUND
incendiarism - - - - - - - - - ARSON
incense - - - - - - - - - - - FUME
incense burner - - - - - - THURIBLE
incensed - - IRATE, ENRAGED, WROTH
incentive - - MOTIVE, SPUR, STIMULUS
incessant - - - - - - - - CONTINUAL
incident - EPISODE, EVENT, HAPPENING, ACT
incidental - - - - - - - - BYE, STRAY
incidental allusion - - - - REFERENCE
incidental narrative - - - - - EPISODE
incinerate - - - - - - - - CREMATE
incipient - - - - - - - - - - INITIAL
incipient laugh - - - - - - - - SMILE
incise - - - - - - - - - - - - CUT
incision - - - - - - - - - - - CUT
incisive - - - - - - - - - - SHARP
incite - - EGG, EXHORT, EDGE, URGE, ABET, GOAD, SPUR, FOMENT, STIMULATE, IMPEL
incite to activity - - - - - - - PROD
inclement - RAW, STORMY, RIGOROUS
inclination - TREND, BENT, PENCHANT, SLANT, RAKE, GRADE, TILT, WILL, BEVEL
inclination of the head - - - - - BOW
incline - - LEAN, GRADE, DIP, SLOPE, SLANT, TEND, TILT, TREND
incline downward - - - - - - - - DIP
incline from vertical (mining) - - HADE
inclined - - - - - - - - - - - PRONE
inclined (arch.) - - - - - - - - - FAIN
inclined channel - - - - - - - FLUME
inclined (poet.) - - - - - - - - LEANT
inclined railway - - - - - - - - RAMP
inclined trough - - - - - - - - CHUTE
inclose in a house - - - - - - - ROOF
inclosed field (civ. law) - - - - - AGER
inclosure - - - - - CAGE, PEN, YARD
include - - - - - - - - - - EMBRACE
including everything - - - - - OVERALL
incognito - - - - - - - - - DISGUISE
incoherent uproar - - - - - - BEDLAM
income - - - - - - - - - - REVENUE
income item - - - - - - - - REVENUE
incomparable - - - - - - - - - RARE
incompetence - - - - - - - INABILITY
incomplete - - - - - BROKEN, PARTIAL
incongruous - - - - - ALIEN, ABSURD
inconsiderable - - - - - - - NOMINAL

inconsistent - CONTRARY, INCONGRUOUS
incorporate - - BLEND, MIX, EMBODY
incorrect - - - - - - - ERRONEOUS
increase - GROW, ENHANCE, ENLARGE, DEEPEN, ADD, SPREAD, RISE, RAISE, WAX
increase by adhesion or inclusion - - - ACCRETION
increase intensity of - - - - DEEPEN
increase knowledge of - - - - ENRICH
increase in size - - - - - - - WAX
increase temporary exertion - - SPURT
increased power - - - - - - LEVERAGE
increasing to a climax - - - ANABATIC
increment - - - - - - - - - INCOME
incriminate - - - - - - - IMPLICATE
incrustation - - - - - - - - SCAR
incrustation on teeth - - - - TARTAR
inculcate - IMPLANT, INSTIL, INSTILL
incur - - - - - - - RUN, CONTRACT
incurable sufferer - - - - - - LEPER
incursion - - - - - - - - - - RAID
indecent - - - - - - - - - NASTY
indeed - - - - REALLY, YEA, TRULY
indefatigable - - - - - - - TIRELESS
indefinite - - - AMBIGUOUS, VAGUE
indefinite amount - - - - - - - ANY
indefinite article - - - - - - AN, A
indefinite nominative - - - - - - IT
indefinite number - - - - - - SOME
indefinite occasion - - - - SOMETIME
indefinite pronoun - - - ONE, ANYONE
indefinite quantity - SOME, MANY, ANY
indehiscent legume or fruit - - - UVA
indelible skin design - - - - TATTOO
indemnify - - - - - - - - - - PAY
indent - - - DEPRESS, NOTCH, DENT
independent - - - - - - - - FREE
independent laborers' association - ARTEL
independently - - - - - - - - APART
independently inheritable element - GENE
indeterminate - - - - - - - - VAGUE
indeterminate quantity - - - - SOME
India noble title - - - - - - - RAIA
India (poet.) - - - - - - - - - IND.
Indian - AMERIND, DELAWARE, ERIE, UTE, OTEE, KAW, MOHAVE, OTO, OTOE, OSAGE, KERES, EWERS, CREE, HOPI, MOHAWK, SEMINOLE, SAC, REDSKIN, APACHE, SERRANO, AHT, ONEIDA
Indian antelope - - - - - - - NILGAI
Indian arrow poison - - - - - CURARE
Indian boat - - - - - - - - CANOE
Indian building material - - LATERITE
Indian carpet - - - - - - - - AGRA
Indian caste - - - - - - - - - SHIR
Indian chick pea - - - - - - GRAM
Indian chief - - - - - - SAGAMORE
Indian city - AGRA, BENARES, LAHORE, MADIRA
Indian clan symbol - - - - - TOTEM
Indian class society - - - - - CASTE
Indian coin - - ANDA, RUPEE, ANNA, PAISA, SPARE, ANNAS
Indian (comb. form) - - - - - - INDO
Indian corn - - - - - - SAMP, MAIZE
Indian currency - - - - - - WAMPUM
Indian divisions - - TRIBAL, TRIBES, AGRAS
Indian, Ecuador - - - - - - - CARA
Indian, extinct Siouan tribe - SAPONI
Indian festival - - - - - - - MELA
Indian fetish - - - - - - - - TOTEM
Indian god - - - - - - - MANITOU
Indian groom - - - - - - SICE, SYCE
Indian handstone to grind grain - MANO
Indian harvest - - - - - - - - RABI
Indian hemp - - - - - - RAMIE, KEF
Indian hut - - - - - - - - - LODGE
Indian jungle - - - - - - - - SHOLA
Indian landing place - - - - - GHAT
Indian madder - - - - - - - - EL, AAL
Indian measure - - - - - - - - KOS
Indian measure (var.) - - - - - HAUT
Indian memorial post - - - - - - XAT
Indian mercenary soldier - - - SEPOY
Indian moccasin - - - - - - - - PAC
Indian monetary unit - - - - - ANNA
Indian mountain pass - - - - - GHAT
Indian mulberry - - AL, AAL, ASH, ACH
Indian native - - - - - - - - SEPOY
Indian noble title - - - - - - - RAIA
Indian nurse - - - - - - - - - AMAH
Indian Ocean Sea - - - - - ARABIAN
Indian Ocean vessel - - - - - DHOW
Indian peace pipe - - - - - CALUMET
Indian peasant - - - - - - - - RYOT
Indian policeman - - - - - - - SEPOY
Indian pole - - - - - - - - - TOTEM
Indian pony - - - - - - - - CAYUSE
Indian prince - - - - - - - - AMEER
Indian province - - - - - - - ASSAM
Indian race - - - - - - - JAT, TAMIL
Indian river - - - UL, GANGES, DEO
Indian robber - - - - - - - - DACOIT
Indian sacred city - - - - - BENARES
Indian sacred emblem - - - - - TOTEM
Indian seaport - - - - - - - - SURAT
Indian silk - - - - - - - - - - ERI
Indian snake - - - - - - - - KRAIT
Indian soldier - - - - - - - - SEPOY
Indian song bird - - - - - - SHAMA
Indian sovereign - - - - - - - - RAJ
Indian spirit - - - - - - - MANITOU
Indian spring crop - - - - - - RABI
Indian state - - - - - - - PAKISTAN
Indian symbol - - - - - - - - TOTEM
Indian tent - - - - TEPEE, TEEPEE
Indian thorny tree - - - - - - BEL
Indian title of address - - - - SAHIB
Indian town - - - - - PATAN, ARCOT
Indian tree - - - - - - - - - DAR
Indian tribe - - - - - - - - - - AO
Indian utterance - - - - - - - UGH
Indian village - - - - - - - PUEBLO
Indian war cry - - - - - - - WHOOP
Indian war trophy - - - - - - SCALP
Indian warrior - - - - - - - BRAVE
Indian weight - - - - - - TOLA, SER
Indian woman - - - - - - - - SQUAW
indicate - - - DESIGNATE, DENOTE, CONNOTE, BODE, BETOKEN, READ, SIGNIFY
indicating more than one - - - PLURAL
indicating succession - - - ORDINAL
indication - - SIGN, EVIDENCE, NOTE
indication of misfortune - - - THREAT
indicative - - - - - - - EXPRESSIVE
indicator - - - - - - POINTER, DIAL
indict - - - - - - - - - - ARRAIGN
indifference - - - - - - - - APATHY
indifferent - SUPINE, COOL, APATHETIC
indifferent to pain or pleasure - STOIC
indigence - - - - - - WANT, POVERTY
indigenous - - - - NATIVE, NATURAL
indigent - - - - - - - POOR, NEEDY
indigestion - - - - - - - - APEPSY
indignant at (be) - - - - - - RESENT
indignation - - - - - - - - - WRATH
indigo dye and plant - - - - - - ANIL
indirect suggestion - - - - - - HINT

I

indiscreet - - - - - - - IMPRUDENT
indistinct notion - - - - IMPRESSION
indisposed - - - - - AILS, AIL, ILL
indisposition - - - - - - - AILMENT
indisposition to motion - - - INERTIA
indistinct - - - DIM, BLUR, OBSCURE
indite - - - - - - - - - WRITE, PEN
individual - ONE, PERSON, SELF, EGO, SOLE
individual (comb. form) - - - - - IDIO
individual performance - - - - - SOLO
individuality - - - - - - SELF, EGO
individually distinct - - - - DISCRETE
Indo-Chinese city - - - - - - HANOI
Indo-Chinese kingdom - - - - - ANAM
Indo-Chinese language - - BAMA, TAI
Indo-Chinese native - - - - - - TAI
Indo-Chinese race - - - - NAGA, TAI
Indo-Chinese stock - - - - - - OAI
Indo Malayan chevrotain - - - - NAPU
indolence - - - - - - - - - SLOTH
indolent traveler - - - - - - LOITERER
indolent - INERT, OTIOSE, LAZY, IDLE
Indonesian - - - - - - - - - - ATA
indoor game - - - - - - - - - POOL
indoor swimming pool - - NATATORIUM
indorsement - - - - - - - - - O.K.
induce - URGE, PREVAIL, LEAD, MAKE, PERSUADE
induct into secret society - - INITIATE
inductive reasoning - - - - - EPAGOGE
indulge - - HUMOR, PAMPER, PLEASE
indulgence - - - - - - - - FAVOUR
indulgent - - - - - - - - - - EASY
industrial product - - - - - - OUTPUT
industrialist - - - - - - - MAGNATE
ineffective - - - - - - - - - FEEBLE
ineffectual - - - - - - WEAK, FUTILE
inefficient - - - - - - - - - LAME
inept - - - - - - ABSURD, CLUMSY
inequality - - - - - - - ODD, ODDS
inequity - - - - - - - - DISPARITY
inert - INACTIVE, LIFELESS, SLUGGISH, TORPID, INDOLENT
inert gaseous element - NEON, ARGON, KRYPTON
inexorable - IMPLACABLE, UNRELENTING
inexperienced - - - - - CALLOW, LAY
inexperienced person - - - FLEDGLING
infallibility - - - - - - - INERRANCY
infallible - - - - - - - - INERRANT
infamous - - - - - - - - NOTORIOUS
infant - - - - - - - - - BABE, BABY
infant's outfit - - - - - - - LAYETTE
infantile - - - - - - - - - CHILDLIKE
infantry unit (abbr.) - - - - - - REG.
infatuation - - - - - - - - - FOLLY
infect - - - - - - - - - - - - TAINT
infectious disease - - - - - TETANUS
infer - - DEDUCE, CONCLUDE, DERIVE
inferior - - - - - WORSE, LOW, BAD
inferior animal - - - - - - - BEAST
inferior cloth - - - - SURAT, SHODDY
inferior dwelling - - - - - TENEMENT
inferior horse - - - - - TIT, PLATER
inferior (prefix) - - - - - - - - SUB
inferior quality - - - - - - - - - ILL
inferior wares - - - - - - - SECONDS
infernal - - - - - - - - - DEVILISH
infernal regions - - - - - - AVERNUS
inferno - - - - - - - - - - - - HELL
Inferno author - - - - - - - - DANTE
infinite - - - ENDLESS, BOUNDLESS, ETERNAL
infinitive part - - - - - - - - - - TO
infirm - - - - ANILE, LAME, FEEBLE

infix - - - - - - - - - - - IMPLANT
inflame - - - RANKLE, FIRE, ENRAGE
inflame with passion - - - - - MADDEN
inflammable hydrocarbon - - OCTANE, BENZENE
inflammable liquid - - - - - - - GAS
inflammable substance - - - - TINDER
inflammation of shoulder - - - OMITIS
inflammatory disease - - - - - GOUT
inflated - BLOATED, BALLOONED, BLEW, DISTENDED
inflect a verb - - - - - - CONJUGATE
inflexible - - - - - - - - RIGID, IRON
inflexibility - - - - - - - - - - RIGOR
inflict - - - - - - - - WREAK, DEAL
influence - - - - INTEREST, AFFECT, PRESTIGE, BIAS, PERSUADE
influence corruptly - - - - - - BRIBE
influence by reward - - - - - - BRIBE
influx - - - - - - - - INFLOW, INSET
infold - - - - - - - - - - LAP, WRAP
inform - - - - - - - - APPRISE, TELL
informal conversation - - - - - CHAT
informal gathering - - - - - - SOCIAL
informant - - - - - - - - APPRISER
information - - - - - - - DATA, WORD
information seeker - - - - - - - SPY
informed - - - - - - - - - - - AWARE
informed (slang) - - - - - - HEP, HIP
informer - - - - - - - - - - - - SPY
infrequent - - - - - - RARE, SELDOM
infuriate - - - - - MADDEN, ENRAGE
infuse - - - - - - - IMBUE, INSTILL
ingenious - - - - - - - - - ARTFUL
ingenuity - - - - - - - - - ART, WIT
ingenuous - - - - - - - - - - NAIVE
ingle - - - - - - - - - - FIREPLACE
ingrained - - - - - - - - - - INNATE
ingredient - MATERIALS, COMPONENT, ELEMENT
ingredient in brewing - - - - - MALT
ingredient of certain soups - - - LALO
ingredient of horny tissue - - KERATIN
ingredient of salad dressing - - - OIL
ingredient of varnish - - RESIN, LAC
ingredients - - ESSENCE, ELEMENTS, COMPONENTS
ingress - - - - - - ENTRY, ENTRANCE
inhabit - - - - - - - - - - - PEOPLE
inhabitant - - - - - INMATE, DENIZEN
inhabitant of city - - - - - - - - CIT
inhabitants of (suffix) - - ITES, OTES
inhabited - - - - - - - - - PEOPLED
inhabited place - - - - - - - - CITY
inheritable element - - - - - - GENE
inherent - - - - - RESIDENT, INNATE
inheritance - - - - - - - - HERITAGE
inheritor - - - - - - - - - - - HEIR
inheritor of real property - - DEVISEE
inhibit - - - - - - - - - - - CHECK
inhume - - - - - - - - - - - - INTER
inimical - - - - - HOSTILE, AVERSE, UNFRIENDLY
inimitable - - - - - - - - MATCHLESS
iniquity - - - - CRIME, SIN, EVIL, VICE
initial - - - - - - FIRST, INCIPIENT
initiate - - INSTITUTE, START, BEGIN
initiative (slang) - - - - - - - - PEP
initiatory - - - - - - - - - - MAIDEN
injunction - ORDER, PRECEPT, MANDATE
injure - HARM, DAMAGE, MAIM, HURT, MAR, WRONG
injurious - - - - - - - - - - - - EVIL
injury - LESION, HARM, DAMAGE, HURT
ink - - - - - - - - - - - - BLACKEN
inky - - - - - - - - - - - - - BLACK

inland body of water - - RIVER, POND, BROOK
inland sea between Europe and Asia - - CASPIAN
inlay - - - - - - INSERT, INSET
inlet - - - - RIA, BAY, COVE, SLEW, ENTRANCE, ORIFICE
inlet (Scot.) - - - - - - - - GIO
inlet from sea - - - - - ARM, BAYOU
inmost part - - - - - - - - CORE
inn - - - HOTEL, TAVERN, HOSTEL, HOSTELRY
innate - HIDDEN, NATURAL, INHERENT, INGRAINED, INBORN
inner - - HIDDEN, INTERNAL, WITHIN, INSIDE, OBSCURE
inner bark - - - - - - - - - BAST
inner coat of the eye - - - - - RETINA
inner coat of the iris - - - - - UVEA
inner moon of Mars - - - - - PHOBUS
inner part - - - INSIDE, CORE, HEART
inner part of corn - - - - - - - COB
inner point - - - - - - - - - - INTO
inner scale of grass flower - - PALEA
inner wall of protective ditch - ESCARP
innermost part - - - - - - - - CORE
innervate - - - - - - - - STIMULATE
innocent - - - BLAMELESS, HARMLESS
innovation - - - - - - - - - NOVELTY
innuendo - - - - - SLUR, SUGGESTION
innumerable host - - - - - - MYRIAD
Ino's grandfather - - - - - - AGENOR
inopulent - - - - - - - - - - POOR
inorganic - - - - - - - - MINERAL
inquire - - - - - INVESTIGATE, PRY
inquire the cost - - - - - - - PRICE
inquired (Scot.) - - - - - - SPERED
inquiry - - - - - - - - - - SEARCH
inquiry for lost goods - - - - - TRACER
inquisitive - - - - - - NOSY, PRYING
inquisitive (colloq.) - - SNOOPY, NOSEY
insane - - - DEMENTED, MAD, LOONY
insane person - - - - - - - - LUNATIC
insanity - - - - - DEMENTIA, LUNACY
insatiable desire - - - - - CACOETHES
inscribe - - WRITE, DEDICATE, LETTER
inscription - - - - - - - - LETTERING
inscription on tombstone - - EPITAPH
inscrutable person - - - - - - SPHINX
insect - MANTIS, FLEA, TERMITE, GNAT, ANT, APHIS, APHID, BEE, BUG, MOTH, WASP, FLY, MITE, NIT, EARWIG, DOR, CRICKET, BEETLE, MIDGE
insect back (part.) - - - PRONOTUM
insect egg - - - - - - - - - - NIT
insect exudation - - - - - - - LAC
insect feeler - - - - ANTENNA, PALP
insect food - - - - - - - BEEBREAD
inseet larva - - - - - - - - - GRUB
insect leg's segment - - - - - COXA
insectivorous mammal - - - - TENREC
insectivorous bird - - - - - - VIREO
insecure - - RISKY, UNSAFE, PERILOUS
insensate - - UNFEELING, INFEELING
insert - - - - - ENTER, ENCLOSE, PUT
insert in something - - - - - - INLAY
insert surreptitiously - - - - - FOIST
insertion - - - INSET, INTRODUCTION
inset - - - - - - - - INLAY, INFLUX
inside - - - INTO, INTERIOR, WITHIN, INNER, INTERNAL
inside influence (slang) - - - - - PULL
inside of - - - - - - - - - - WITHIN
inside of hand - - - - - - - - - PALM
insight - - - - - - - - - - - KEN
insignia of office - - REGALIA, BADGE
insignificant - - TRIVIAL, NULL, TINY
insignificant part - - - - - - IOTA
insignificant person - - - - - - SNIP
insignificant thing - - - - - - SNIP
insipient - - - - - - - - - STUPID
insipid - - - - VAPID, FLAT, STALE
insist - - - PERSIST, DEMAND, URGE
insist upon - - - - - - - - - URGE
insistent - - - - - - - - - URGENT
insolent - - - - - - - - - - SAUCY
inspect - - - - - - - PRY, EXAMINE
inspector - - - - - - - - EXAMINER
inspector of electric lamps - - - AGER
inspector of weights and measures - - SEALER
inspire - - - UPLIFT, IMPART, STIR
inspire with dread - - - - - - - AWE
inspiring - - - - - - - - - STIRRING
inspirit - - - - - - - - CHEER, LIVEN
install - - - - - - - - SEAT, INVEST
instance - - - - - - - - - - - CASE
instant - - - - - - MOMENT, TRICE
instantaneous exposure - - SNAPSHOT
instauration - - - - - - - - RENEWAL
instate - - - - - - INSTALL, INVEST
instead - - - - - - - - - - - ELSE
instead of - - - - - - - - - - FOR
instigate - ABET, FOMENT, EGG, SUBORN
instill - - - - - - - - - - INFUSE
institute - - - ESTABLISH, INITIATE
institute suit - - - - - - - - - SUE
institution of learning (pert. to) COLLEGIAL
instruct - - TRAIN, TEACH, EDUCATE, SCHOOL, EDIFY
instruct privately - - - - - - TUTOR
instruct in rudiments - - - - INITIATE
instruction - - - LESSON, TEACHING
instructive discourse - - - - LECTURE
instructor - - - - - - - - - TEACHER
instrument - - - - - - TOOL, ORGAN
instrument board - - - - - - - PANEL
instrument to comb - - - - - - - CARD
instrument to decompose light - PRISM
instrument of discipline - - - - FERULE
instrument for grooving - - SCORERS
instrument or means - - - - - ORGAN
instrument to measure mountain heights AROMETER
instrument to measure strength of electrical current - - - - - - AMMETER
instrument to mow grass - - - SCYTHE
instrument to record time - - - DATER
instrument to remove skin - - PEELER
instrument for spreading yarn - EVENER
instrument to work gold leaf - - PALLET
instrumental composition - - SONATA, ARIOSO, RONDO
instrumental duet (mus.) - - - - - DUO
instrumentality - - - AGENCY, MEAN
insubordinate - - - - - - REBELLIOUS
insufficient - - - - - - - - - SCANTY
insular - - - - - - - - - - ISOLATED
insulate - - - - - - - - ISLE, ISOLATE
insult - - - AFFRONT, OFFEND, SLAP
insulting language - - - - REVILEMENT
insulting reproach - - - - - - - TAUNT
insurance certificate - - - - - POLICY
insurance protection - - - - COVERAGE
insure - - - - - - - - UNDERWRITE
insurgent - - - - - - - - - - REBEL
insurrection - - - - - - - - - REVOLT
integral - - - - - COMPOSITE, ENTIRE
inte~rity - - - - - - - - - - HONOR
intellect - - - - - - - - MIND, BRAIN
intellect (pert. to) - - - - - - NOETIC

intellectual - MENTAL
intellectual attitude - POSE
intellectually - IDEALLY, MENTALLY
intelligence - SENSE, MIND, REASON, WIT
intelligent - RATIONAL, SENSIBLE
intelligible - CLEAR
intend - MEAN, PURPOSE, PROPOSE, AIM
intended - MEANT, AIMED
intended for discussion - MOOT
intenerate - SOFTEN
intense - ARDENT, EXTREME, ACUTE, FIERCE, FERVID, DEEP
intensify - DEEPEN, AGGRAVATE
intensive - CONCENTRATED
intent - PURPOSE, EAGER, RAPT, CONNOTATION
intention - AIM, PURPOSE, IDEA
intentional - DELIBERATE
inter - INHUME, ENTOMB
intercede - MEDIATE
intercession - PRAYER
interdict - BAN, BAR
interdiction - VETO, BAN
interest - ZEAL
interest rate (excessive) - USURY
interested - CARED, CONCERNED, IMPORTED, BENEFITED, OCCUPIED, RAPT
interfere - MEDDLE
interfere with - MOLEST
interim - INTERMISSION, MEANTIME
interior - INSIDE, INNER
interior (comb. form) - ENTO
interior poet - RIMESTER
interjection - HA, HO, OH, AH
interjection to attract attention - AHEM
interjection enjoining silence - TST, PST
interlace - BRAID, WEAVE
interlacement - KNOT
interlock - KNIT
intermediate - BETWEEN
intermediate (law) - MESNE
intermediate number - SOME
interment - BURIAL
intermingle - BLEND
intermission - RECESS, INTERIM
intermix - MINGLE
intern - CONFINE
internal - INNER, ENCLOSED, INSIDE
internal fruit decay - BLET
internal organs - VISCERA
international agreement - TREATY, CARTEL
international combination - CARTEL
International language - RO
international understanding - ENTENTE
interpose - INTERRUPT
interprets - DECODES, RENDERS, CONSTRUES, REDE, READS
interprets (arch.) - REDES
interrogate - ASK, INQUIRE
interrogation - INQUIRY
interrogative - EH, WHAT
interrupt - INTERPOSE
interruption - HIATUS, GAP, BREAK
intersect - MEET, CROSS, JOIN
intersecting - SECANT
intersection - CROSSING
interstice - CREVICE, AREOLA
intertwine - LACE
interval - SPACE, TIME, RESPITE, SPAN, GAP
interval of rest - RESPITE
interval of time - LAPSE
intervening - BETWEEN
intervening (law) - MESNE
intervening stud - TRESTLE
interweave - BRAID, MAT, PLAIT, LACE, RADDLE
intimate - HINT, NEAR, SUGGEST
intimate associate - FRIEND
intimate (colloq.) - HOMY, HOMEY
intimation - CUE, HINT
intimidate - COW, AWE, DETER, DAUNT, OVERAWE
into - WITHIN, INSIDE, IN
into place - TO
into a ship - ABOARD
intolerant - BIGOTED
intolerant person - BIGOT
intone - CHANT, SING
intoxicated - EBRIOSE
intoxicating - HEADY
intoxicating drink - GROG
intransitive - NEUTER
intrench firmly - PLANT
intrepid - DREADLESS, BRAVE, BOLD, DAUNTLESS
intrepidity - NERVE
intricate - DEDAL, GORDIAN, COMPLICATED, COMPLEX
intricate organ of human body - EAR
intrigue - CABAL, PLOT
intrinsic nature - ESSENCE
introduce - HERALD, INSERT, PRESENT, USHER
introduce from abroad - IMPORT
introduction - ENTREE, PRELUDE, PREAMBLE, DEBUT, PROLOGUE, PREFACE, INSERTION
introductory - EXORDIAL, PROLOGUE
introductory explanatory statement PREAMBLE
intrude - TRESPASS
intrusive - MEDDLESOME
intrust - COMMIT
inundate - FLOOD, DELUGE
inundation - FLOOD
inure - HARDEN, SEASON, HABITUATE, ACCUSTOM, USE
inurn - ENTOMB
inutile - USELESS
invade - RAID, ENCROACH
invalid - NULL
invalidation - ANNULMENT
invaluable - PRICELESS
invariable - STEADY
invariant - CONSTANT
invasion craft - L.S.T.
invent - CREATE, FEIGN, COIN, ORIGINATE, DEVISE, CONTRIVE, DISCOVER
invention - FIGMENT
inventor - ORIGINATOR
inventor of modern locks - YALE
inventor of musical instruments - JUBAL
inventor of sewing machine - HOWE
inventor of telegraph - MORSE
inverse - OPPOSITE
invert - TRANSPOSE, REVERSE
invest - INSTATE, INSTALL, ENVELOP, ENDUE, VEST, ENDOW
investigate - PROBE, INQUIRE
investor - ENDOWER
invigorate - RENEW, STRENGTHEN
invisible - UNSEEABLE
invisible emanation - AURA
invitation - BID
invite - BID, ASK, ENTICE
invoke by prayer - IMPRECATE
involuntary wait - DELAY

involve - TANGLE, ENTAIL, IMPLICATE ENGAGE, EMBROIL
inward - - - - - - - - - SECRET
iota - - - - JOT, ATOM, WHIT, DOT
Iowa college - - - - - - - - COE
Iowa county - - - - - - - - ADAIR
Iowa town - - - - - - - - AMES
ipecac plant - - - - - - - - EVEA
Iranian - - - - - - - - PERSIAN
Iranian ambassador to U. S. - - - - ALA
Iranian premier - - - - - MOSSADEGH
Iranian title - - - - - - - - SHAH
Iraq capital - - - - - - - BAGDAD
Iraq district - - - - - - - AMARA
irascible - - - - - - TOUCHY, TESTY
irate - - WROTH, WRATH, ANGRY, MAD
ire - - RAGE, ANGER, WRATH, FURY, PASSION
Ireland - - - - - - - - EIRE, ERIN
irenic - - - - - - PEACEFUL, SERENE
iridescences - - - - - - IRISATIONS
iridescent - - - - - OPALINE, IRISED
iridescent gem - - - - - - - - OPAL
iridescent jewels - - - - - - - OPALS
iris of the eye (pert. to) - - - - IRIAN
iris (her.) - - - - - - - - - - LIS
iris (kind) - - - - - - - - - ORRIS
iris layer - - - - - - - - - - UVEA
iris layer (pert. to) - - - - - UVEAL
iris plant - - - - - IRID, IXIA, FLAG
Irish - - - - - - - - - - - CELTIC
Irish ancient capital - - - - - - TARA
Irish author - - - - - - - - - SHAW
Irish battle cry - - - - - - - - ABU
Irish bay - - - - - - - - - - SLIGO
Irish Chamber of Deputies - - - - DAIL
Irish city and county - - - - - - CORK
Irish coin - - - - - - - - - - RAP
Irish cudgel - - - - - - - - ALPEEN
Irish dramatist - - - - STEELE, SHAW
Irish epic tale - - - - - - - - TANA
Irish expletive - - - - - ARRA, ARRAH
Irish fish - - - - - - - - - POLLAN
Irish floral emblem - - - - SHAMROCK
Irish lassie - - - - - - - - COLLEEN
Irish love - - - - - - - - - - GRA
Irish Neptune - - - - - - - - - LER
Irish novelist - - - - - LEVER, MOORE
Irish peasant - - - - - - - - - KERN
Irish playwright - - - - MOORE, SHAW
Irish poet - - WILDE, MOORE, YEATS
Irish rank in society - - - - - - AIRE
Irish river - - - - - - NORE, LAGAN
Irish sea god - - - - - - - - - LER
Irish var. of John - - - - - - - SEAN
Irishman - - - - - - - - - - CELT
irk - - - - - - - - - ANNOY, CHAFE
irksome - - - - - - - - - TEDIOUS
iron - FE., FETTER, FERRUM, FIRMNESS, HARD, SMOOTH, MANACLE, FIRM, PRESS
iron alloy - - - - - - - - - - STEEL
iron block in stamp battery - - - - VOL
iron corrosion - - - - - - - - - RUST
iron hook - - - - - - - - - - GAFF
iron ore - - - - - - - - MAGNETITE
iron pyrites (lumps of) - - - - - PEAS
ironer - - - - - - - - - - MANGLE
ironic - SARCASTIC, SATIRICAL, SATIRIC
ironic discourse - - - - - - - SATIRE
ironwood - - - - - - - - - - - TITI
irony - - - - - - SATIRE, MOCKERY
Iroquois tribe - - - - - - - - ONEIDA
irrational numbers - - - - - - SURDS
irregular - - - - - ABNORMAL, EROSE
irregular moving part - - - - - - CAM
irregular verse - - - - - - DOGGEREL
irreverent - - - - - - - - AWELESS
irrigate - - - - - - - - - - WATER
irritability - - - - - - - - - CHOLER
irritable - - - - - - - - TESTY, EDGY
irritable person - - - - - - - TARTAR
irritate - GALL, FRET, PEEVE, GRATE, VEX, TEASE, RILE, NETTLE, ANGER, EXASPERATE, PROVOKE
irritate (colloq.) - - - - - - - - RILE
irritation - - - - - - - - ITCH, PIQUE
Isaac's son - - - - - - - - - ESAU
isinglass - - - - - - - - - - MICA
island - - - - - - - - - - AIT, ALT
island in Caroline group - - - - - YAP
island at earth's center - - - - - MERU
island (Fr.) - - - - - - - - - - ILE
island group - - - - - FAROE, SAMOA
island group near Guam - - - - - TRUK
island in Hebrides group - - - - IONA
island in North Sea - - - - - - TEXEL
island near China - - - - - - QUEMOY
island off France - - - - - - - - - IF
island off Ireland - - - - - - - - ARAN
island off Italy - - - - - ELBA, CAPRI
island off Tuscany coast - - - - ELBA
island (poet.) - - - - - - - - - ISLE
island of Saints - - - - - - - - ERIN
island (small) - - - - ISLE, ISLET, ILOT
islands in Atlantic - - - - - - FAROE
isle - - - - - - - - - - - ALT, AIT
isle off Ireland - - - - - - - - ARAN
islet - - - - - - CAY, BAY, AIT, ALT
Ismaelian title - - - - - - - - - AGA
Isolde's love - - - - - - - TRISTRAM
isolate - - - - - - ISLAND, INSULATE
isolated - SINGULAR, ALONE, DETACHED, INSULAR
isolated steepsided hills - BUTTES, KNOBS
isolation - - - - - - - - SOLITUDE
Israelite - - - - - - - JEW, HEBREW
Israelite judge - - - - ELON, SAMSON
Israelite king - - - - - - - - DAVID
Israelite tribe - GAD, DAN, ASHER, LEVI, ASER
issue - - PRINT, OUTCOME, EMERGE, EMIT, ARISE
issue copiously - - - - - - - - SPOUT
issue forth - - - - - - - - EMANATE
issue from confinement - - - - ESCAPE
issue in installments - - - - - SERIAL
issuing in rays - - - - - - - - RADIAL
isthmus - - - - - - - - - - - KRA
it is silent (musical) - - - - - TACET
Italian - - - - - - - ROMAN, LATIN
Italian actress - - - - - - - - DUSE
Italian Adriatic island - - - - - LIDO
Italian anatomist - - - - - - - ASELLI
Italian article - - - - - - - - - - IL
Italian artist - - - - - - - - CELLINI
Italian astronomer - - SECCHI, GALILEO
Italian building - - - - - - - - CASA
Italian cathedral city - - - - - MILAN
Italian chief magistrate - - - - - DOGE
Italian city - TARANTO, PISA, ASTI, MILAN, NOLA, VENICE, TRIESTE, ALBA, FERRARA, TEANO, ROME, TRENT, TURIN, ESTE, GENOA, SASSARI, BRA
Italian coins - - LIRE, LIRA, SOLDOS
Italian (comb. form) - - - - - - ITALO
Italian composer - - - - - - - VERDI
Italian condiment - - - - - - TAMARA
Italian custom house - - - - - DOGANA
Italian department - - - - - CALABRIA
Italian family - - - - - - - - - ESTE

I
J

Italian goddess of beauty - VENUS
Italian goddess of health - SALUS
Italian house - CASA
Italian island - COS, LIDO, ELBA, CAPRI
Italian lake - COMO
Italian legislative chamber - CAMERA
Italian measure - STERO
Italian millet - TENAI
Italian mountains - APENNINES
Italian music reformer - GUIDO
Italian name for Italy - ITALIA
Italian naval base - POLA
Italian novelist - SERAO
Italian opera - AIDA, NORMA, PAGLIACCI
Italian painter - RENI, TITIAN, RAPHAEL
Italian people (ancient) - SABINES
Italian physicist - VOLTA
Italian poet - DANTE, TASSO
Italian political organization (pl.) - FASCI
Italian princely house - ESTE
Italian province - PISA, PARMA, ESTE, COMO, MANTUA
Italian river - PO, ARNO, TIBER, PIAVE
Italian saint - NERI
Italian seaport - POLA, TRIESTE, GENOA
Italian seaport native - VENETIAN
Italian seaside resort - LIDO
Italian secret society - CAMORRA
Italian silver coin - LIRE
Italian soprano - PATTI
Italian statesman - SALANDRA
Italian tenor - CARUSO
Italian territory disputed - TRIESTE
Italian title - DONNA
Italian title (abbr.) - SRA
Italian town - CANNINO, PISA, ASTI, ESTI, BRA, TRENT
Italian university - PADUA
Italian violin - AMATI
Italian violin (old) - CREMONA
Italian wine - ASTI
Italian woodwork - TARSIA
Italian writer - CELLINI
Italian yes - SI
item - DETAIL, ENTRY, MAXIM
item of property - ASSET
item of value - ASSET
item which demands publication - MUST
itemize - LIST
iterate - REPEAT
itinerant merchant - PEDDLER
itineration - EYRE
Ivan the Terrible's title - TSAR
Ivanhoe character - ROWENA
ivory - DENTINE

J

jab - POKE
jabber - BABBLE, SPUTTER
jabber (colloq.) - YAP
jackal headed deity - ANUBIS
jackdaw - DAW
jackdaw (Scot.) - KA
jacket - REEFER, ETON
jacket (short) - ETON
Jacob's brother - ESAU
Jacob's father-in-law - LABAN
Jacob's son - DAN, LEVI, REUBEN, GAD
Jacob's twin brother - ESAU
Jacob's wife - LEAH
jade - HARASS
jaeger - SKUA
jaeger gull - TEASER
jagged parts - SNAGS
jam - CRUSH, CROWD
jail - PRISON, IMPRISON, LOCKUP
janizaries chief - DEY
Jap - NIP
Japanese aborigine - AINU, AINO, AETA
Japanese admiral - ITO, TOGO
Japanese boxes - INRO
Japanese Buddhist church - TERA
Japanese carriage - RICKSHAW
Japanese church - TERA
Japanese city - OSAKA, UJINA, NAGASAKI, KOBE
Japanese coin - SEN, YEN, RIL, RIN, BU
Japanese dancing girl - GEISHA
Japanese drink - SAKE, SAKI
Japanese emperor - MIKADO, HIROHITO
Japanese family badge - MON
Japanese festival - BON
Japanese fighter plane - ZERO
Japanese fortress - TRUK
Japanese (indigenous) - AINU
Japanese marine measure - RI
Japanese measure - RI, SE, RIN, CHO
Japanese medicine box - INRO
Japanese monetary unit - YEN
Japanese money - SEN
Japanese mountain - USU
Japanese native - AINUS
Japanese outcast - ETA
Japanese pagoda - TAA
Japanese peninsula - KOREA
Japanese plane - ZERO
Japanese plant - UDO
Japanese porgy - TAI
Japanese rice paste - AME
Japanese sash - OBI
Japanese seaport - KOBE, NAGASAKI
Japanese statesman - ITO
Japanese weight - MO, SHI
jape - GIBE, FRAUD, JEST, TRICK
jar - JOLT, SHOCK, DISCONCERT, SHAKE, CLASH, DISCORD
jar (wide mouth) - OLLA, URN
jargon - CANT, SLANG, PATTER, LINGO, ARGOT
Jason's follower - ARGONAUT
Jason's helper - MEDEA
Jason's ship - ARGO, ARGONAUT
jaundiced - YELLOW
jaunt - SALLY, TRIP
Java cotton - KAPOK
Java poisonous tree - UPAS
Java silk fabric - IKAT
javelin - DART, SPEAR
jay bird - PIE
jealousy - ENVY
jeer - SCOFF, FLOUT, BOO, TAUNT
jeer at - TAUNT
Jehovah's prophet - ELIAS
jejune - DRY, ARID
jellify - GEL
jellyfish - MEDUSA
jellylike material - GEL
jeopardies - DANGERS, PERILS
jerk - YANK, BOB
jerking motion - BOB
Jerusalem hill - ZION
Jerusalem hill (var.) - SION
Jerusalem mosque - OMAR
Jerusalem oak - AMBROSE
jest - JOKE, GAME, JAPE
jester - FOOL
Jesuits founder - LOYOLA
Jesus - SAVIOR, SAVIOUR
jet - SPOUT, GUSH, JUT, BLACK

jet black - - - - - - - RAVEN, EBON
jetting spring - - - - - - - GEYSER
jetty - - - - - - - - - - - - PIER
Jew (pious) - - - - - - - - - TOBIT
jewel - - - STONE, GEM, OPAL, BIJOU
jewel mounting - - - - - - SETTING
jeweller's weight - - - - - - CARAT
jewellry alloy - - - - - - - OROIDE
Jewish festival - - - - - - - SEDER
Jewish high priest - EZRA, ELI, AARON
Jewish - - - - - (See also Hebrew)
Jewish law - - - - - TORAH, TALMUD
Jewish leader - - - - - - - MOSES
Jewish month - NISAN, ADAR, TISRI, ELUL, AB, SEBAT, TEBET, SHEBAT
Jewish proselyte - - - - - - - GER
Jewish ram's horn - - - - - SHOFAR
Jewish teacher - - - - - - - RABBI
Jewish weight - - - - GERAH, OMER
Jezebel's husband - - - - - - AHAB
jib - - - - - - - - - - GIB, TALK
jibe - - - - - - - - - - - TAUNT
jiffy - - - - - - - - - - MOMENT
jiggle - - - - - - - - - - TEETER
jimson weed - - - - - - - DATURA
job - - - - - - - - - - - TASK
jockey - - - - - - - - - - RIDER
jocose - - - - - - - - FACETIOUS
jocular teasing - - - - - - BANTER
jocularity - - - - - - - - - - WIT
jog - - - - - - - - NUDGE, TROT
jog along - - - - - - TROT, PROD
Johann Sebastian - - - - - - BACH
John (Scot.) - - - - - - - - - IAN
johnnycake - - - - - - - - - PONE
join - UNITE, MEET, TEAM, CONNECT, MORTISE, ADD, MELD, MERGE, ENTER, INTERSECT, ANNEX, YOKE, ENGAGE, ALLY
join battle - - - - - - - - ENGAGE
join closely - - - - - WELD, ENLINK
join the colors - - - - - - ENLIST
joined - - - - - - - - - - - MET
joint - - - - HINGE, TENON, SEAM
joint of arm - - - - ELBOW, WRIST
joint of door - - - - - - - - HINGE
joint of leg - - - - - - - - - KNEE
joint legatee - - - - - - - COHEIR
joint of stem - - - - - - - - NODE
jointly - - - TOGETHER, MUTUALLY
joists - - - - - - - - - STUDDING
joke - - - - - - - - - JEST, GAG
joker - - - - - - - - - WIT, WAG
jollity - - - - - - - - - - MIRTH
jolly - - - - - - - JOVIAL, MERRY
jolt - - - - - - - - - JAR, BUMP
josh - - - - - - - - - - - - GUY
josh (slang) - - - - - - - - - RIB
Joshua's father - - - - - - - NUN
jostle rudely - - - - - - - ELBOW
jot - IOTA, MITE, SPECK, WHIT, ATOM, ACE, PARTICLE
journal - - - - - - - - - - PAPER
journey - FARE, TRAVEL, TRIP, TREK, TOUR
journey on foot - - - - - - TRAMP
joust - - - - - - - - - - - - TILT
jousting - - - - - - - - - - ATILT
Jove - - - - - - - - - - JUPITER
jovial - - - - - - - - - - - JOLLY
joy - - - BLISS, GLEE, GLADNESS, ELATION
joyful - - CHEERFUL, BLITHE, GLAD
joyful hymn - - - - - - - - CAROL
joyous - GLAD, HAPPY, RIANT, FESTAL, FESTIVE
jubilance - - - - - - - - - ELATION
jubilant - - - - - - - - - ELATED
Judah's son - - - - - - - - - - ER
Judea procurator - - - - - - PILATE
judge - CONSIDER, ARBITER, DECIDE, DEEM, OPINE, ARBITRATOR, REFEREE, ESTIMATE
judge's chamber - - - - - CAMERA
judge's circuit (arch.) - - - - - ITER
judge's court bench - - - - - BANC
judge's gavel - - - - - - - - MACE
judge in old England - - - - - EYRE
judge's robe - - - - - - - - GOWN
judgment - - DOOM, SENSE, AWARD, VERICT, OPINION, SENTENCE
judgment seat - - - - - - - - BAR
judicial command - - - - - MANDATE
judicial order - - - - - - - - WRIT
judicial writ - - - - - - - - ELEGIT
jug - - - - - - - - - EWER, CRUSE
Jugoslavian coin - - - - - - - DINAR
Jugoslavian town - - - - - - - STIP
juice of plant - - - - - - - - - SAP
juicy - - - - - - - - - SUCCULENT
juicy plant - - - - - - - - - - UVA
Jules Verne character - - - - - NEMO
Julius Caesar character - - CASSIUS
jumble - - - - - - DISPLACE, PIE
jumbled type - - - - - - - - - - PI
jump - - - - - - - - - LEAP, HOP
jump about - - - - PRANCE, CAPER
jumped - - - - - - - - - - - LEAPT
jumping amphibian - - - - - - TOAD
jumping stick - - - - - - - - POGO
junction - - - - - UNION, MEETING
junction lines - - - - SUTURE, SEAM
junction of two streams - CONFLUENCE
juncture - SEAM, UNION, EMERGENCY
juncture line - - - - - - - - SEAM
june bug - - - - - - - - - - - DOR
jungle carnivore - - - - - - - LION
junior - - - - - - - - - - YOUNGER
juniper (kind) - - - - - - - - CADE
juniper tree - - - - - - - - - EZEL
juniperlike desert shrub - - - RETEM
Jupiter - - - - - - - - ZEUS, JOVE
Jupiter's son - - - - - - - CASTER
Jupiter's temple - - - - - - CAPITOL
jurisdiction - - - - - - - - SPHERE
jurisdiction (law) - - - - - - - SOC
jurisprudence - - - - - - - - - LAW
jury - - - - - - - - - - - - PANEL
jury list - - - - - - - - - - PANEL
just - - - - - - FAIR, IMPARTIAL
just clear the ground (naut.) - ATRIP, AWEIGH
justice - - - - - - LAW, FAIRNESS
justify - - - - - - - - - VINDICATE
jut - - - - - - - - - - - - - - JET
jutting headland - - - - - - - RAG
jutting rock - - - - - - TOR, CRAG
juvenile - - - - YOUNG, YOUTHFUL

K

Kaffir warriors - - - - - - - - IMPI
kaka - - - - - - - - - - PARROT
Kansas city (a) - - - - IOLA, ABILENE
kava - - - - - - - - - - - - - AVA
kedge - - - - - - - - - - - ANCHOR
keel - - - - - - - - - - - CAPSIZE
keen - SHARP, NICE, ACUTE, SHREWD, PUNGENT, FINE
keen enjoyment - - - - GUSTO, ZEST
keen perseverance - - - - - FERRET

K

keenness of mind - - - - ACUMEN
keep - - - RETAIN, HOLD, MAINTAIN
keep afloat - - - - - - - - BUOY
keep apart - - - SEPARATE, SECLUDE
keep away from - - - - - - AVOID
keep back - DETAIN, HINDER, STIFLE, DETER, RETAIN
keep bow to the sea (naut.) - - ATRY
keep clear of (arch.) - - - - ESCHEW
keep close to - - - - - - - - HUG
keep company - - - - - - CONSORT
keep from action - - - - - - DETER
keep from happening - - - PREVENT
keep from proceeding - - - - DETER
keep intact - - - - - - - PRESERVE
keep on - - - - - - - CONTINUE
keep order - - - - - - - - POLICE
keep from progressing - - - - DELAY
keep in reserve - - - - - - - HOLD
keep in safety - - - - - - PRESERVE
keep from shaking - - - - STEADY
keep in store for special use - RESERVE
keeo tally - - - - - - - - SCORE
keeper - - - CUSTODIAN, WARDEN
keeper of sheep (Bib.) - - - - ABEL
keeve - - - - - - - - TUB, VAT
keg - - - - - - CASK, BARREL
ken - - - - - - - - - INSIGHT
Kentucky bluegrass - - - - - POA
Kentucky city - - - - - - - PARIS
Kentucky college - - - - - - BEREA
Keresan Indian - - - - - - - SIA
kern - - - - - - - - - - - BOOR
kernel - - - - NUT, GRAIN, BARREL
kettle - - - - - - - - - - - POT
kettle mender - - - - - - - TINKER
kettledrum - - - ATABAL, TYMPANI, TIMBAL
key - CAY, WHARF, PITCH, SOLUTION
key fruit - - - - - - - - SAMARA
key of harp pitch - - - - - DITAL
keyed up with interest - - - - AGOG
keyhole guard - - - - - - - TAPPET
keynote - - - - - - - - - TONIC
Keystone State - - - - - - - - PA.
Khayyam - - - - - - - - - OMAR
kick a football - - - - - - - PUNT
kidnap - - - - - - - - - ABDUCT
kidney bean - - - - - - - - BON
kidneys - - - - - - - - - RENAL
kill - - - - - - - - - - - SLAY
kill game illegally - - - - - POACH
killed - - - SLAIN, SLEW, SLEWED
killed Achilles - - - - - - - PARIS
killer - - - - - - - - ASSASSIN
killer whale - - - - - - ORC, ORCA
killing cold - - - - - - - - FROST
killing of one's mother - - MATRICIDE
kiln - - - OST, OVEN, OAST, OSIER, FURNACE, STOVE
Kim's author - - - - - - - KIPLING
kin - - OSIER, RELATIVE, RELATED, AFFINITY
kind - SORT, ILK, GENUS, HUMANE, GENTLE, GENRE, FRIENDLY, TYPE
kind of - - - - - - - - - - SORT
kindle - FIRE, FUME, LUME, IGNITE, LIGHT
kindled - - - - - - - - - - - LIT
kindling - - - - - - - - AKINDLE
kindly - - - - - - - - - - BENIGN
kindness - - - FAVOR, TENDERNESS
kindred - GENS, KINSHIP, FAMILY, SIB
kindred collectively - - - - - - SIB
kinds - - - - - - - - - - GENERA

kine - - - - - - - - CATTLE, COWS
king - - - - - - - - - - - - RULER
King Arthur's abode - - - CAMELOT, AVALON
King Arthur's father - - - - UTHER
King Arthur's lance - - - RON, RONE
King Arthur's mother - - - - IGRAINE
King Arthur's nephew - - MORDRED or MODRED
King Arthur's resting place - - AVALON
king of Ancient Persia - - - - XERXES
king of Boshan - - - - - - - - - OG
king of Cologne - - - - - - GASPAR
king of Crete - - - - - - - - MINOS
King David's ruler - - - - - - - IRA
king of England and Denmark - CANUTE, CNUT
king of fairies - - - - - - OBERON
king fish - - - - - - - - - - BARB
king (French) - - - - - - - - - ROI
king of golden touch - - - - - MIDAS
king of Huns - - - - - - - - ATTILA
king of Israel - - SAUL, OMRI, AHAB, DAVID, ASA
king of Judah - - ASA, AHAZ, HEROD
king of Judea - - - - - HEROD, ASA
king of jungle - - - - - - - - LION
king (Latin) - - - - - - - - - REX
king of light - - - - - - - - - ARC
king of Phrygia - - - - - - - MIDAS
king of Pylos - - - - - - - NESTOR
king of Siam - - - - - - - ANANDA
king (Slavonic title) - - - - - KRAL
king of Troy - - - - - - - - PRIAM
king of Tyre - - - - - - - - HIRAM
king of underground - - - - - SATAN
king of Visigoths - - - - - - ALARIC
king of W. Saxons - - - INE, ALFRED
kingdom - - - - - REALM, EMPIRE
kingdom of Alexander the Great - - - MACEDONIA
kingdom in Arabia - - - - - - IRAQ
kingdom in East Asia - - - - - KOREA
kingdom in India - - ANAM, NEPAL
kingdom south of Assyria - - - ELAM
kingdom of southeast Asia - - - SIAM
kingly - - - - - - - - - - REGAL
Kingsley's river - - - - - - - DEE
kink - - - - - - - - - CROCHET
kinsfolk - - - - - - - RELATIVES
kinship - - - KINDRED, RELATION
kinsman - - RELATION, SIB, RELATIVE
Kipling's novel - - - - - - - KIM
Kish's son - - - - - - - - - SAUL
kismet - - - - - - - - - - FATE
kiss - - - - - - BUSS, OSCULATE
kit - - - - - - - - - - - OUTFIT
kitchen implement - - STONER, CORER
kitchen stove - - - - - - - RANGE
kitchen of a vessel - - - - - GALLEY
kite - - - - - - - - - - ELANET
kite part - - - - - - - - - - TAIL
kittenish - - - - - - - - PLAYFUL
kiwi - - - - - - - - - - - - ROA
Kizi Kumuk - - - - - - - - - LAK
klaxon - - - - - - - - - - HORN
knack - - - - - - ART, SKILL, HANG
knaggy - - - - - - - - - - ROUGH
knap - - - HILLTOP, KNOB, MOUND
knave - - - RASCAL, ROGUE, VARLET
knave of clubs - - - - - - - PAM
knave in cribbage - - - - - - NOB
knead - - - - - - MASSAGE, MOLD
knead (dial.) - - - - - - - - ELT
knee length garment - - - - TUNIC
kneecap - - - - - - - - PATELLA

kneel - GENUFLECT, TOLL, PROCLAIM
kneepan (of the) - - - - PATELLAR
knell - - - - - - - - RING, TOLL
knick knack - - - PRETTY, TRINKET, TRIFLE
knife case - - - - - - - SHEATH
knife to cut loops - - - - TREVET
knife (kind) - - - - - BOWIE, BOLO
knife (large) - MACHETE, SNEE, BOLO
knife sharpener - - - - - - STEEL
knife to shear velvet - - - - TREVET
knifelike instrument - - - SPATULA
knight - - - - - CAVALIER, GALLANT
knight errant - - - - - - PALADIN
knight of Round Table - - LANCELOT
knightly wandering - - - ERRANTRY
knight's cloak - - - - - - TABARD
knight's wife - - - - - - - - LADY
knit - CONTRACT, UNITE, INTERLOCK
knitted blanket - - - - - AFGHAN
knob - - - - - - NODE, NUB, LUMP
knob for fastening - - - - BUTTON
knobby - - - - - - - - - NODOSE
knock lightly - - - - - - - - TAP
knockout (slang) - - - - KAYO, KO
knot - - NODE, NOOSE, TIE, GNARL, ENTANGLE, NODULE, MAT
knot of hair - - - - - - - CHIGNON
knot (pert. to) - - - - - - NODAL
knot of short hair - - - - - NOIL
knot in wood - - GNARL, BURL, KNAR, GNAR
knot of wool - - - - - - - - NOIL
knot of yarn - - - - - - - SKEIN
knotted lace - - - - - - - TATTING
knotty - - GNARLY, GNARLED, NODAL, NODOSE
know - - - - - - - - - - - KEN
know (arch.) - - - - - - WOT, WIS
know (Scot.) - - - - - - - - - KEN
knowing - - AWARE, SHREWD, WISE
knowledge - LORE, KEN, COGNITION, WISDOM
knowledge gained - - - - - LESSON
knowledge (pert. to) - - - GNOSTIC, GNOSTICAL
knowledge (Scot.) - - - - - - KEN
known facts - - - - - - - - DATA
kobold - - - - NISSE, NIS, GOBLIN
Koran chapter - - - - - - - SURA
Korea - - - - - - - - - - CHOSEN
Kruman tribal group - - - - - KRA
Krupp steel works - - - - - ESSEN

L

La Boheme heroine - - - - - - MIMI
Laban's daughter - - - - - - LEAH
label - - - - TAG, STAMP, BRAND, DESIGNATE, DOCKET, CLASSIFY, MARK, TAB
labium - - - - - - - - - - - LIP
labour - - - - - - - - - - - TOIL
labour hard - - - - - - - - STRIVE
labour organization - - - - - UNION
labour to weariness - - - - - FAG
laboured breath - - - - GASP, PANT
labourer - - - - - - - PEON, SERF
laborious - - - - - - - TOILSOME
Labrador tea - - - - - - - LEDUM
labyrinth - - - - - - - - - MAZE
lace - - THREAD, EMBROIDER, TIE, CLUNY
lace collar - - - - - - - BERTHA
lace edging - - - - - - - - FRILL
lace pattern - - - - - - - - TOILE
lacerate - - - REND, TEAR, MANGLE
lacet - - - - - - - - - - - BRAID
lachrymal drop - - - - - - - TEAR
lachrymosely - - - - - - - TEARILY
laciniate - - - - - - - - FRINGED
lack - - - - - - - NEED, DEARTH
lack of harmony - - - - - DISCORD
lack of knowledge - - - - NESCIENCE
lack of moisture - - - - - DRYNESS
lack of vigour - - - - - - - ATONY
lackadaisical (slang) - - - - - BLAH
lacking - - - - - - DESTITUTE, SHY
lacking brilliance - - - - - - GREY
lacking depth - - - - - - SHALLOW
lacking elevation - - - - - - - LOW
lacking good taste - - - - INELEGANT
lacking height - - - - - - - - LOW
lacking interest - - - - - - - DRY
lacking melody - - - - - TUNELESS
lacking moisture - - - - - - - DRY
lacking spirit - - - - - - - POKY
lacking stiffness - - - - - - LIMP
lacking strength - - - - - - WEAK
lacking in vision - - - - - PURBLIND
lacking vital energy - - - - ATONIC
Laconia capital - - - - - - SPARTA
laconic - - - - - - - - - - TERSE
lacquer - - - - - - - - - - - LAC
lacteal fluid - - - - - - - - MILK
lad - - - - - - - - STRIPLING, BOY
ladderlike - - - - - - - - SCALAR
lade - LOAD, BAIL, BURDEN, FREIGHT, DIP
laden - - - - - - - - FREIGHTED
lading - - - - - - - - - CARGOES
ladle - - - - - - - SCOOP, DIPPER
lady - - - - - - - - - - FEMALE
lady's reception room - - - - BOUDOIR
lady of Troy - - - - - - - - HELEN
lady's waiting maid - - - - - ABIGAIL
lag - TRAIL, LINGER, FALTER, LOITER, DAWDLE, DELAY, TARRY
lag behind - - - - - LOITER, TRAIL
laggard - - - - - LOITERER, REMISS
lair - - - DEN, TIER, ROW, HAUNT, AMASS, CAVE
laity - - - - - - - - - - PEOPLE
laity (pert. to) - - - - - - - LAIC
lake (small) - - - - - - - - MERE
lake tributary - - - - - - - INLET
lamb - - - - - - - - - - - - TAG
lamb's mother - - - - - - - - EWE
Lamb's pen name - - - - - - ELIA
lame - - - HALT, INFIRM, FEEBLE
lament - - DEPLORE, BEMOAN, SIGH, GRIEVE, BEWAIT, REGRET, WAIL, BEWEEP, PINE, MOAN, CRY
lamentably - - - - - - - PITIFULLY
lamentation - - - - - - - - MOAN
lamia - - - - - - - - - - - WITCH
lamina - - - - - - - - - - - LEAF
laminar - - - - - - - SCALY, FLAKY
laminated - - - - - - - - - SLATY
laminated rock - - - - - - - SHALE
lamp - - - TORCH, LIGHT, LANTERN
lamp cord - - - - - - - - - WICK
lamp fuel - - - - - - - KEROSENE
lamp iron frame - - - - - - CRESSET
lamp part - - - - - - - - BURNER
lamp (slang) - - - - - - - - GLIM
lampoon - SATIRE, RIDICULE, SQUIB, SKIT
lamprey - - - - - - - - - - EEL
lanate - - - - - - - - - - WOOLY
lance - SPEAR, OPEN, PIERCE, DART

L

lance support - - - - - - - REST
land - TERRA, SOIL, GROUND, SHORE, EARTH, COUNTRY, DEBARK, ALIGHT
land (to) - - - - DEBARK, ALIGHT
land area - - - - - - - - - AR
land belonging to parish church - GLEBE
land conveyance - - - - - - - DEED
land held absolutely - - - - ALOD
land measure - ARE, ROD, ACRE, AR, METER, ROOD, DECARE
land or naval force - - - ARMAMENT
land point - - - - - - - - SPIT
land tenure (pert. to) - - AGRARIAN
land turtle - - - - - - - TORTOISE
landed - - - - - - - - - - ALIT
landed estate - - - - - - - MANOR
landed property - - - - - - ESTATE
landing - - - - - - - - WHARF
landing place - - - - QUAY, WHARF
landing place of the Ark - - ARARAT
landscape - - - - SCENE, SCENERY
landscape gardener - - - TOPIARIST
lane - - - - - - - - - - PATH
language - - - - - TONGUE, RO
language based on tones - - CHINESE
language of Buddhist scriptures - PALI
language of Mindanao - - - - ATA
language peculiar to a people - IDIOM
language of Savage Island - - - NIUE
languid - - WAN, LISTLESS, FEEBLE, INDIFFERENT, DREAMY, SLACK
languish - - - PINE, DROOP, FLAG
languor - - - - - - - LASSITUDE
lank - - - LEAN, GAUNT, SLENDER
lanky - - - - - - - - - LEAN
lanneret - - - - - - - - FALCON
lap - CIRCUIT, FOLD, UNFOLD, ENFOLD, TRUNCATE
lapidated - - - - - - - - STONED
lapped joint - - - - - - - SCARF
lapse - - - - - - - - - - SLIP
lapwing - - - - - - - - - PEWIT
larch - - - - - - - - TAMARACK
lard - - - - - - - - ADEPS, FAT
larded - - - - - - - - ENRICHED
larder - - - - - - - - - PANTRY
large - - HUGE, GREAT, BUG, BULKY
large (comb. form) - - - - MACRO
large amount - - - - - - - PLENTY
large animal - - - - - - BEHEMOTH
large artery - - - - - - - AORTA
large bag net - - - - - - TRAWL
large barrel - - - - - - - - TUN
large basin - - - - - - - - LAVER
large basket - - - - - - HAMPER
large bell - - - - - - - - GONG
large bird - - - - - EMU, PELICAN
large boat - - - - - SCOW, BARGE
large body of land - - - CONTINENT
large book - - - - - - - - TOME
large bottle for liquids - - - CARBOY
large bundle - - - - - - - - BALE
large butterfly - - - - - - URSULA
large collection (colloq.) - - - RAFT
large container - - - - - TUB, VAT
large convex moulding - - - - TORUS
large deer - - - - - - - - - ELK
large dish - - - - PLATTER, TUREEN
large dog - - - - - - DANE, ALAN
large drinking vessel - - - TANKARD
large farm - - - - - - - - RANCH
large field tent - - - - MARQUEE
large fish - - SHARK, TUNA, SKATE, SNAPPER
large hall - - - - - - - - AULA
large handkerchief - - - - MADRAS
large hawk - - - - - - - CARACARA
large house - - - - - - - MANSION
large investor - - - - CAPITALIST
large knife - - - - - - - - SNEE
large lake - - - - - - - - - ERIE
large lizard - MONITOR, IGUANA, SEPS
large number - SCORE, HOST, BILLION, MYRIAD
large number (colloq.) - - - - RAFT
large number (slang) - - - - SLEW
large oil can - - - - - - - OILER
large oven - - - - - - - - KILN
large ox - - - - - - - - - YAK
large parrot - - - - - MACAW, KEA
large pill - - - - - - - - BOLUS
large quantity - - - - MASS, SEA
large receptacle for liquids - - TANK
large reptile - - - - - ALLIGATOR
large roofing slate - - - - - RAG
large room - - - - - - - - AULA
large rowboat - - - - - - - BARGE
large sea bird - - - - - - GANNET
large serpent - PYTHON, ABOMA, BOA
large shark - - - - - - MANEATER
large ship - - - - - - - ARGOSY
large snake - - - - - - - - BOA
large stork - - - - - - - - AYAYA
large stout cord - - - - - - ROPE
large stove - - - - - - - - KILN
large stream - - - - - - - RIVER
large vessel - - - - VAT, TANKARD
large violin - - - - - - - - VIOLA
large water pipe - - - - - - MAIN
large waterfowl - - - - - - EGRET
large whale - - - - - - - SPERM
lariat - - - - - - - RIATA, LASSO
lark - - - - - - - - - - FROLIC
lark's home - - - - - - - - LEA
larva - - - - - - - - GRUB, LOA
larva of fly - - - - - - - MAGGOT
larval stage of crustaceans - NAUPLIUS
lash - - FLOG, TIE, WHIP, SATIRIZE, BERATE
lash with tongue - - - - - - BASTE
lass - - - - - MAID, MAIDEN, GIRL
lassitude - - - - INERTIA, LANGUOR, DEBILITY
lasso - RIATA, REATA, ROPE, LARIAT
last - - FINAL, ENDURE, CONTINUE, OMEGA, ULTIMATE
last act - - - - - - - - - FINALE
last (arch.) - - - - - - - - DURE
last month - - - - - - - ULTIMO
last month (abbr.) - - - - - - ULT.
last movement of sonata - - RONDO
last part of ancient odes - - - EPODE
last state of insect - - - - IMAGO
Last Supper represent. - - - - CENA
last syllable but one - - - - PENULT
last traces - - - - - - - - ASHES
last under use - - - - - - - WEAR
lasted (arch.) - - - - - - - DURED
lasting - - - - - - - - DURABLE
lasting seven years - - SEPTENNIAL
Latvia's capital - - - - - - - RIGA
late - - - RECENT, TARDY, DELAYED
late afternoon service - - - VESPERS
late (comb. form) - - - - - - NEO
late information - - - - - - NEWS
late intelligence - - - - - - NEWS
lately - - - - - - - PRESENTLY
latent - HIDDEN, DORMANT, POTENTIAL, QUIESCENT
later - - - AFTER, TARDIER, NEWER
later in life - - - - - - - ELDER
later origin - - - - - - - NEWER

lateral boundary - - - SIDE
laterally - - - SIDEWISE
lath - - - SLAT
lather - - - SUDS, SOAP, FOAM
Latin - - - ROMAN, ITALIAN
Latin epic - - - AENEID
Latin greetings - - - AVE
Latin poet - - - OVID
Latin pronoun - - - IPSE
Latinia's mother - - - AMATA
latite - - - LAVA
latitude - - - SCOPE
latterly - - - RECENTLY
lattice structure - - - TRELLIS
lattice-work bowers - - - ARBORS
Latvian - - - LETT, LETTIC
Latvian capital - - - RIGA
Latvian coin - - - LAT
Latvian river - - - AA
laud - PRAISE, EXTOL, EXALT, GLORIFY
laugh - - - CHORTLE
laugh loudly - - - SNORT
laugh to scorn - - - DERIDE, FLEER
laughable - - - RISIBLE
laughing - - - RIANT
laughing (rare) - - - RIDENT
launder - - - WASH
laundry machine - - - IRONER
laurel - - - FAME
laurel tree - - - BAY
lava - - - LATITE
laval (cooled) - - - AA
lava (rough-Hawaiian) - - - AA
lave - - - BATHE, WASH
lavender - - - ASPIC
Lavinia's mother - - - AMATA
lavish - - - PROFUSE
lavish fondness on - - - DOTE
law - - - CANON, CODE, JUSTICE, STATUTE, RULE, ACT
law breaker - - - CRIMINAL
law to deed - - - REMISE
law (delay) - - - MORA
law (intervening) - - - MESNE
law (Latin) - - - IUS, LEX
law note - - - UT
law officer - - - SOLICITOR
law (pert. to) - - - CANONIC
lawful - - - LEGAL, LICIT
lawless - - - UNRULY, DISORDERLY
lawmaker - - - SOLON
lawn (fine) - - - BATISTE
lawyer - - - LEGALIST, BARRISTER
lawyer fee - - - RETAINER
lawyer profession - - - BAR
lax - - - SLACK, LOOSE, REMISS
lay - - - PUT, SONG, BALLAD
lay aside - - - TABLE
lay away - - - STORE, REPOSIT
lay bare - - - EXPOSE, DENUDE
lay burden upon - - - SADDLE
lay by - - - STORE
lay hidden - - - LURKED
lay officers of religious sect - ELDERS
lay siege to - - - INVEST
lay stretched out - - - SPRAWLED
lay in surrounding matter - - - EMBED
lay up a store of - - - HIVE
lay waste - - - RAVAGE, DESOLATE, DEVASTATE
layer - - - STRATUM, STRATA
layers - COATS, STRATA, BEDS, ROWS, TIERS, THICKNESS, PLIES
layers of iris - - - UVEA
layers of iris (pert. to) - - - UVEAL, STRATAL
layers of metal - - - SEAM
layers of mineral - - - VEIN
laymen - - - LAICS, SECULARS
leaf - - - TENDRIL, SPATHE, PETAL, LAMINA, PAGE
leaf of book - - - PAGE
leaf of herb - - - BLADE
leaf of palmyra palm - - - OLE
leaf part - - - BLADE
leaf vein - - - RIB
leaf of water lily - - - PAD
leafless flower organ - - - TENDRIL
leaflike appendage of flower - - BRACT
leafstalk - - - PETIOLE
leafy shelter - - - BOWER
league - - - FEDERATION, UNION
leak - - - DRIP, SEEP
leakage - - - ESCAPE
leal - - - LOYAL
lean - - LANK, GAUNT, TIP, INCLINE, TILT, REST, SPARE, SLANT, DEPEND, TANK, TRUST
lean over on one side - - HEEL, LIST
lean-to - - - SHED
Leander's love - - - HERO
leap - SPRING, HOP, BOUND, VAULT, JUMP
leap (dial.) - - - LEP
leap over - - - SKIP
leap playfully - - - GAMBOL
leaping animal - - - KANGAROO
learn - - - ACQUIRE, MEMORIZE, ASCERTAIN, CON
learned - ERUDITE, WISE, ERUDITION, SCHOLARLY
learned Brahmin - - - PUNDIT
learned man - - - PUNDIT
learning - - - LORE
lease - - CHARTER, LET, HIRE, RENT, TENURE, CONTRACT
least - MINIMUM, SLIGHTEST, FEWEST
least audible - - - FAINTEST
least number - - - FEWEST
least possible - - - MINIMAL
least whole number - - - UNIT
leather factory - - - TANNERY
leather on football shoe - - - CLEAT
leather (kind) - NAPA, OXHIDE, LEVANT, KID, CALF, ROAN, COWHIDE
leather (long, narrow piece of) - STRAP
leather (sheepskin) - - - ROAN
leather (soft) - - SUEDE, NAPA, ROAN
leather working tool - - - POMMEL
leave - - DEPART, VACATE, RETIRE, PERMISSION, GO, QUIT
leave country - - - EMIGRATE
leave empty - - - VACATE
leave helpless - - STRAND, MAROON
leave out - - - OMIT, ELIDE, MISS
leave a public carrier - - - DETRAIN
leave (slang) - - - SCRAM
leaven - - - YEAST
leaves - - - FOLIAGE
leaving - - - ORT
leaving a will - - - TESTATE
ledge - - - SHELF
ledger bait (var.) - - - LEGER
ledger entry - - - ITEM
lee - - - SHELTER
leer - - - OGLE, MOCK, ENTICE
leery - - - SUSPICIOUS
left - - - GONE, DEPARTED
left after expenses - - - NET
left complete - - - INTACT
left entire - - - INTACT
left hand page (abbr.) - - - V.O.

L

left hand side of an account - DEBTOR, DEBIT
left hander - - - - - - SOUTHPAW
left side (on) - - - - - - - APORT
leftover - - - - - - - - REMNANT
leg - - - - - - - CRUS, SUPPORT
leg (colloq.) - - - - - - - - PIN
leg covering - - - - - PUTTEE, HOSE
leg joint - - - - - - ANKLE, KNEE
leg mutton - - - - - - - - AVINE
leg part - - - - - - SHIN, SHANK
legacy recipient - - - - - - LEGATEE
legal - LAWFUL, DOMINATE, VALID, LICIT
legal action - - - - - RES, REPLEVIN
legal attachment - - - - - - LIEN
legal charge - - - - - - DUE, FEE
legal claim - - - - - - - - LIEN
legal conveyance - - - - - - DEED
legal defense (form) - - - - - ALIBI
legal dispossession - - - - EVICTION
legal document - - - - - - - WRIT
legal fees - - - - - - - - DUES
legal hearing - - - - - - - TRIAL
legal instrument - - - - - - WRIT
legal instrument under seal - ESCROW
legal offense - - - - - - - CRIME
legal official - - - - - - - NOTARY
legal order - - - - - - - - WRIT
legal order for writs - - - PRECIPES
legal paper - - - - - - - - DEED
legal profession - - - - - - - BAR
legal records - - - - - - - ACTA
legal strength - - - - - - VALIDITY
legal suffix - - - - - - - - - EE
legal tender notes - - - - - DOLLARS
legal tribute - - - - - - - - DUES
legal wrong - - - - - - - - TORT
legalist - - - - - - - - LAWYER
legate - - - - - - - - - ENVOY
legatee - - HEIR, HEIRESS, RECIPIENT
legend - - - - - - - - SAGA, MYTH
legendary - - - - - - - - STORIED
legendary bird - - - - - - - - ROC
legendary founder of Rome - - REMUS
legendary hero - - - - - - - PALADIN
legendary singing siren - - - - LORELEI
leger - - - - - - - - - - LIGHT
legerdemain - - - - - - - - MAGIC
legible - - - - - - - - READABLE
legion - - - - - - - - - MULTITUDE
legislate - - - - - - - - - ENACT
legislative body division - - HOUSE, SENATE
legislator - - - - - SOLON, SENATOR
legume - - POD, BEAN, LENTIL, PEA, LOMENT, UVA
leguminous plant - - LENTIL, PEAS, PULSE, PEA
lei - - - - - - - - - - WREATH
leisure - - - - - - - - - - TIME
leisurely - - - - - - - - - GRADUAL
lemon yellow - - - - - - - ORPIMENT
lemur - - - - - - - - LORIS, LORI
lemurine animal - - - - - - TARSIER
lemuroid animal - - - - - - - POTTO
lend - - - LOAN, AFFORD, FURNISH
lene - - - - - - - - - - - SMOOTH
length - - - - - - - - - - EXTENT
length of life - - - - - - - - YEARS
length measure (var.) - - - - METRE
lengthen - - - EXTEND, ELONGATE, PROLONG
lengthen out - - - - - - - DISTEND
lengthwise of - - - - - - - - ALONG
lengthy - - - - - - LONG, EXTENDED
lenient - - - - CLEMENT, MERCIFUL
lenitive - - - - - - - - ASSUASIVE
lens (type of) - - - - - - - - TORIC
lens shaped seed - - - - - - - LENTIL
lent - - - - - - - - - - AFFORDED
lenten - - - - - - - - - - - SOMBER
lentil - - - - - - - - - - - LEGUME
Leo - - - - - - - - - - - - - LION
leonine - - - - - - - - - - LIONLIKE
leopard - - - - - - - - - PANTHER
leopard-like animal (var.) - - CHETAH
leper - - - - - - LAZAR, OUTCAST
leprosy sufferer - - - - - - - LEPER
lerot - - - - - - - - - - DORMOUSE
Les Miserables author - - - - - HUGO
less - MINUS, MINOR, FEWER, SMALLER
less adulteration - - - - - - - PURER
less common - - - - - RARE, RARER
less dangerous - - - - - - - - SAFER
less intricate - - - - - - - SIMPLER
less (musical) - - - - - - - - MENO
less pleasant - - - - - - - - SEAMY
less (prefix) - - - - - - - - - MIS
less ripe - - - - - - - - GREENER
less severe - - - - - - - - RELENT
less than sufficient - - - - - SCANT
less than twice - - - - - - - ONCE
lessee - - - - - - TENANT, RENTER
lessen - LOWER, BATE, ABATE, REDUCE, WANE, EASE, TAPER, DIMINISH, SHRINK, DEPLETE
lessen gradually - - - - - - - TAPER
lesser - - - - - - SMALLER, MINOR
lesson - - - - - - - - - EXERCISE
lesson taught by fable - - - - MORAL
let - - - - - - - LEASE, RENT, HIRE
let air out of - - - - - - - DEFLATE
let the bait bob (angling) - - - - DIB
let down - - - - - - - - - - LOWER
let down tension - - - - - - - RELAX
let fall - - - - - - - - SLIP, DROP
let fall in drops - - - - - - - DISTILL
let go - - - - - - - - - - RELEASE
let in - - - - - - - - - - - ADMIT
let liquid in or out - - - - - - LEAK
let slip by - - - - - - - - - LAPSE
let stand - - - - - - - - - - STET
let stand (musical) - - - - - - STA
lethal - - - - - - - FATAL, DEADLY
lethargic - - - - - - - DULL, SLEEPY
lethargic sleep - - - - - - - SOPOR
lethargic state - - - - - - - - COMA
lethargy - STUPOR, TORPOR, APATHY, COMA
letter - EPISTLE, MISSIVE, INSCRIBE
letter container - - - - - ENVELOPE
letter of challenge - - - - - CARTEL
lettered - - - - LITERATE, EDUCATED
lettering - - - - - - - INSCRIPTION
letters received through Post Office MAIL
lettuce - - - - - - - COS, ROMAINE
Levantine - - - - - - - - ORIENTAL
Levantine ketch - - - - - SAIC, PROA
levee - - - - - - - - - DIKE, QUAY
level - - - - EVEN, FLAT, PLANE, AIM
level forestless tract - - - - - STEPPE
level piece of ground - - - - - - BED
level to the ground (to) - - - - - RASE
levelled - - - - - - - - FLATTENED
lever - - - - - - - - PRY, CROWBAR
lever in a loom - - - - - - - - LAM
lever moved by a cam - - - - TAPPET
levers (var.) - - - - - - - - PRISES
levity - - - - - - - - - FRIVOLITY
levy - TAX, ASSESS, COLLECT, WAGE
lexicon - - - - - - - - WORDBOOK

liability to err - ERRANCY
liable - APT
liable to punishment - GUILTY
liar - FIBBER
libel - SLANDER, CALUMNY, MALIGN
liberal - GENEROUS, BROAD
liberal gift - LARGESS
liberate - REDEEM, RELEASE, FREE
liberator - DELIVERER
Liberia capital - MONROVIA
libertine - ROUE
liberty - FREEDOM, PRIVILEGE
Libyan seaport - DERNA
license - PERMIT, AUTHORITY
lichen - MOSS
licit - LAWFUL, PERMITTED, LEGAL
lick up - LAP
lid - COVER, TOP
lidless - UNCOVERED
lie - FIB, FALSEHOOD
lie about - LOLL
lie in ambush - LURK
lie at anchor - MOOR
lie dormant - SLEEP
lie at ease - BASK, LOLL
lie hidden - LURK
lie stretched out - SPRAWL
lie in wait - LURK
lie in warmth - BASK
liege - DEVOTED, LOYAL, FAITHFUL, VASSAL, OVERLORD
lien - CLAIM, MORTGAGE
lieu - PLACE, STEAD
lieve - WILLING
life - VITALITY, EXISTENCE, BIOGRAPHY
life annuity (kind) - TONTINE
life of business - SALES
life fluid - BLOOD
life insurance (kind) - TONTINE
lifeboat (kind) - CATAMARAN
lifeless - INERT, AMORT, DEAD
lifelessness - INERTIA
lifelike - NATURAL
lifetime - AGE
lift - HOIST, RAISE, ELEVATE, HEAVE, ELEVATOR, PRY, EXALT
lift of boat crane - DAVIT
lift high - EXALT
lift price - UP
lift in spirits - ELATE
lift up - EXALT, HEAVE
lift with lever - PRY
lifting implement - TONGS
ligament - BOND
ligate - BANDAGE
light - LAMP, GLEAM, PALE, IGNITE, AIRY, LEGER, BRIGHTEN
light armed European cavalryman - HUSSAR
light boat - CANOE, SKIFF
light brushing sound - SWISH
light carriage - GIG, SHAY, PHAETON, SURREY, CALASH
light cloak or cape - MANTILLA
light collation - TEA
light coloured and mild - CLARO
light crimson - ROSE
light of day - SUN
light of evening - STAR
light and fine - LEGER
light hasty lunch - SNACK
light hearted - GAY
light helmet - SALLET
Light Horse Harry - LEE
light javelin (var.) - ASSEGAI
light (kind) - ARC
light maul - MALLET
light openwork material - GAUZE
light outer garment - DUSTER
light overcoat - TOPCOAT
light racing boat - SHELL
light rain - SHOWER
light repast - TEA, COLLATION
light sailing vessel - YAWL
light shirt - CAMISE
light sketch - PASTEL
light substance - CORK
light tan - ALMOND
light touch - DAB, PAT
light up - ILLUME
light vapour in the air - HAZE
light volatile liquid - ETHER
light wood - BALSA, POPLAR
lighted coal - EMBER
lighten - EASE
lighter - SPARKLER
lightheaded - GAY
lighthouse - PHAROS
lighting (arch.) - LEVIN
lighting implement - LAMP
lightly - AIRILY
like - ADMIRE, AS, SIMILAR, ENJOY, RELISH
like a bear - URSINE
like better - PREFER
like dust - POWDERY
like grown boy - MANLY
like a hare - LEPORINE
like a ladder - SCALAR
like a tail - CAUDAL
like a wing - PTERIC
likelihood - CHANCE
likely - PROBABLE, VERISIMILAR, CREDIBLE
likened - COMPARED
likeness - IMAGE, SIMULACRE
likeness produced by art - PORTRAIT
likewise - TOO, ALSO, EKE
lilac color - MAUVE
liliaceous herb - PARIS
lily (the) - LIS
lily (day) - NIOBE
lily (kind) - CALLA, SEGO, ALOE, ONION, YUCCA, TULIP, ARUM
lily maid - ELAINE
limb - BOUGH, BRANCH
limb appendage - ENDITE
limber - LIMP, PLIANT
lime - CEMENT
lime tree - TEIL, LINDEN
limit - TERM, SOLSTICE, END, RESTRICT, BOUNDARY, CONFINE, EXTENT, STINT
limited - FINITE
limited amount - ALLOWANCE
limited in number - FEW
limited to small area - LOCAL
limited by time - TEMPORAL
limitless - UNBOUNDED
limn - PAINT, SKETCH, DRAW
limned - DREW
limner - PAINTER
limp - LIMBER
limp (dial.) - CLOP
Lincoln's assassin - BOOTH
Lincoln's secretary of state - SEWARD
linden - TEIL, BASSWOOD
linden tree - LIN, TEIL
line - ROW, STREAK, REIN, CORD, BOUNDARY, COURSE, STRING, RULE, MARK

L

line to attach fishhook - - - - SNELL
line of descent - - - - - - STRAIN
line of juncture - - - - - - SEAM
line made by folding - - - - CREASE
line of mowed grain - - - - - SWATH
line of persons - - - - - - - CUE
line of poetry - - - - - - - VERSE
line of revolution - - - - - - AXIS
line the roof of - - - - - - - CEIL
line walls of - - - - - - - - CEIL
line where the compass points to north AGONE
line with ridges - - - - - - - RIB
line with soft material - - - - - PAD
lineage - - - - - - RACE, PEDIGREE
lineament - - - - - FEATURE, LINE
lined - - - - - - - - - - RULED
linen cloths - - - - - - - NAPERY
linen fabric - - - - - - - CRASH
linen (fine) - - - - DAMASK, LAWN, CAMBRIC
linen fluff - - - - - - - - LINT
linen plant - - - - - - - - FLAX
linen (sheer) - - - - - - - TOILE
linen vestment - - - - - - - - ALB
liner - - - - - STEAMSHIP, STEAMER
lines - - - - - - - - ROWS, TIERS
lines (consisting of) - - - - LINEAR
lines of different colours - - - STRIPES
linger - HOVER, LAG, LOITER, TARRY, WAIT, STAY, DELAY, DAWDLE
lingering - - - - - - - - - SLOW
lingo - - - - - - - - - - JARGON
lining of iris - - - - - - - - UVEA
lining of a well - - - - - - - STEEN
link - YOKE, NEXUS, COUPLE, UNITE, TIE, ATTACH
link together - - CATENATE, COUPLE
linseed - - - - - - - - - FLAXSEED
lion headed dog - - - - - - - CHOW
lionlike - - - - - - - - - LEONINE
lip - - - - - LABIUM, EDGE, BRIM
lips (pert. to) - - - - - - - LABIAL
liqueur - - - - - - - - - - CREME
liquid - - - - - - - - - - FLUID
liquid compound - - - - - - OLEIN
liquid container - - PAIL, TANK, CAN
liquid dose - - - - - - - - POTION
liquid fat (var.) - - ELAINE, ELAIN, OLEIN
liquid flying in small particles - SPRAY
liquid food - - - - - - - - - SOUP
liquid measure - - - GALLON, MINIM, PINT
liquid medicinal preparation - LOTION
liquid particle - - - - - - - - DROP
liquid pitch - - - - - - - - - TAR
liquify by heat - - - - - - - - MELT
liquor - RUM, NOYAU, ANISETTE, ALE, GROG, TIPPLE, HYDROMEL
liquor used as mild tonic - - BITTERS
lira (abbr.) - - - - - - - - - - LR
lissome - - LITHE, SUPPLE, NIMBLE
list - ROTA, ROLL, ROSTER, ITEMIZE, AGENDUM, CAREEN, REGISTER, CATALOG, CATALOGUE
list of actors - - - - - - - - CAST
list of electors - - - - - - - POLL
list of errors - - - - - - - ERRATA
list of names - ROSTER, ONAMASTICON, ROLL, ROTA
list of things to be done - - AGENDA
listen - HARKEN, HARK, ATTEND, HEAR
listen secretly - - - - - - EAVESDROP
listener - - - - - - - - - AUDITOR
listless - - - - - - - - - LANGUID

literal - - - - - - - - - - EXACT
literary - - - - - - - - - LITERATE
literary burlesque - - - - - - PARODY
literary composition - PAPER, TRAGEDY, ESSAY, THESIS
literary fragments - - - - - - - ANA
literary supervisor - - - - EDITOR, ED.
literate - - - EDUCATED, LITERARY, LETTERED
lithe - - - SUPPLE, PLIANT, LISSOME, AGILE, FLEXIBLE
litigation - - - - - - - - - - LAW
litter - - - - - - - - BIER, CLUTTER
little - - - - - - BIT, SMALL, PETTY
little ball - - - - - - - - - PELLET
little eye - - - - - - - - - - OCELLI
little face - - - - - - - - - FACET
little heart (obs.) - - - - - HEARTLET
little island - - - - - - - - - ISLET
little lie - - - - - - - - - - - FIB
little parcel - - - - - - - - PACKET
little piece - - - - - - - - - MORSEL
little (Scot.) - - - - - - - - - SMA
liturgical pause - - - - - - - SELAH
live - RESIDE, ARE, BE, BRISK, SUBSIST, QUICK, SURVIVED
live coal - - - - - - - - - - EMBER
live in the country - - - - RUSTICATE
live in a tent - - - - - - - - CAMP
lived - - - - - - - - - - - - WAS
lived 905 years - - - - - - - ENOS
liveliness - - - - - - - BRISKNESS
lively - - BRISK, NIMBLE, ANIMATED, PERT, AGILE, SPIRITED
lively dance - - - - - - - - - REEL
lively song - - - - - - - - - - LILT
liven - - ANIMATE, ACTIVATE, INSPIRIT
liver secretion - - - - - - BILE, GALL
livid - - - - - - ASHEN, DISCOLORED
living - - - - - - - - - - - ALIVE
living at - - - - - - - - - - - OF
living being - - - - - - - ORGANISM
living human - - - - - - - - PERSON
living on land or in water - AMPHIBIAN
lixivium - - - - - - - - - - - LYE
lizard - AGAMA, GILA, IGUANA, LACERTA, EFT, ADDA, SKINK, SEPS, MONITOR
lizard-like amphibian - SALAMANDER, NEWT
llama (kind) - - - - - - - - ALPACA
lo - - - - - - - - - - - - - SEE
loa - - - - - - - - - - - - LARVA
load - LADE, BURDEN, CARGO, SADDLE
load, as with a burden - - - SADDLE
loaded - - - - - - - - - - LADEN
loadstone - - - - - - - - - MAGNET
loaf - - - - - IDLE, LOITER, LOUNGE
loafer - - - - - - - - - - - IDLER
loam - SOIL, EARTH, MARL, DIRT, CLAY
loam deposit - - - - - - - - LOESS
loamy - - - - - - - - - - CLAYEY
loan - - - - - - - - - - - - LEND
loath - ABHOR, HATE, AVERSE, DETEST, RELUCTANT, ABOMINATE, HESITANT
loathsome - - - - - - - - - - FOUL
lobby - - - - - FOYER, VESTIBULE
lobe of ear - - - - - - - - EARLOP
lobe (having) - - - - - - - LOBATE
lobed - - - - - - - - - - - LOBATE
lobster chela - - - - - - - PINCER
lobster claw - - - - - - - - CHELA
lobster row - - - - - - - - CORAL
local - - - - SECTIONAL, REGIONAL
local ordinance - - - - - - - BYLAW
local position - - - - - - - - SITE
locale - - - - - - POSITION, PLACE

localities - - - LOCI, SITES, SPOTS, REGIONS, PLACES
localized vector - - - - - ROTOR
locate - - - - - - - - SPOT, FIND
located - - - - - SITUATE, STANDS
location - - SITE, SEAT, SPOT, PLACE
lock - - - - - BOLT, HASP, FASTEN
lock of hair - - - - TRESS, RINGLET
lock opener - - - - - - - - - KEY
lockup - - - - - - - - - - JAIL
locomotive - - - - - - - ENGINE
locomotive driver - - - - ENGINEER
locomotive part - - - - - - - CAB
locomotive service car - - - TENDER
locus - - - - - - - - - - PLACE
locust - - - - - - CICADA, ACACIA
locust tree - - - - - - - - ACACIA
lode - - - - - - - - - - - REEF
lodge - ROOM, CABIN, HOUSE, IMPLANT, LAY, LIE
lodge doorkeeper - - - - - - TILER
lodge for the night - - - - - BED
lodger - - - - - - - - - GUEST
lodging - - - - - - - - - ABODE
loft - - - - - - - - - - ATTIC
lofty - - - ELEVATED, AERIAL, TALL, EMINENT, HAUGHTY, AERY, HIGH
lofty mountain - - - - - - - - ALP
lofty peak - - - - - - - PINNACLE
lofty place - - - - - - - EMINENCE
lofty in style - - - - - - - EPIC
lofty tree - - - - - - - - DATE
log - - - - - - - - - - - RECORD
log float - - - - - - - - - - RAFT
log from which shingles are cut - SPALT
loge - - - - - - - - BOOTH, BOX
logger's boot - - - - - - - - PAC
loggia - - - - - - - - - ARCADE
logical - - - - - - - REASONABLE
logical basis of a fact - - - RATIONALE
logograph - - - - - - - - ANAGRAM
Lohengrin's father - - - - PARSIFAL
Lohengrin's wife - - - - - - - ELSA
loiter - - LINGER, LAG, IDLE, TARRY, SAUNTER, DELAY
loiterer - - - - - - - - LAGGARD
loitering - - - - - - - DALLIANCE
loll - - - RECLINE, DROOP, SPRAWL, LAZE
loment - - - - - - - - - LEGUME
London district - - - - - - - SOHO
London hawker (short form) - - COSTER
London statue - - - - - - - MAGOG
lone - - - - SOLE, SOLO, SOLITARY
lonely - - - - - - - - SECLUDED
long - TALL, HANKER, LENGTHY, CRAVE, YEARN
long arched gallery - - - - ARCADE
long cut - - - TRENCH, GASH, SLASH
long distance race - - - - MARATHON
long distance runner - - - - - MILER
long drink - - - - - - - - - SWIG
long fish - - - - - - - - - - EEL
long for - PINE, CRAVE, DESIRE, YEARN, HANKER
long groove - - - - - - - - SLOT
long handled implement - HOE, POLEAX
long handled spoon - - - - - LADLE
long hill - - - - - - - - - RIDGE
long intently - - - - - - - - PANT
Long Island summer resort - - ISLIP
long journey - - - - - - - - TREK
long knife - - - - - - - YATAGAN
long legged bird - STEVE, STILT, WADER, EGRET, STORK, AVOCET, CURLEW, CRANE, RAIL, HERON
long low seat - - - - - - - SETTEE
long napped fabric - - - - - PLUSH
long narrow board - - - - SLAT, LATH
long narrow piece - - - - - - STRIP
long necked bird - - - - - - SWAN
long piece - - - - - - - - - BAR
long pointed tooth - - - - - FANG
long rectangle - - - - - - OBLONG
long seat - - - - - BENCH, SETTEE
long since - - - - - - - - YORE
long and slender - - SPINDLE, REEDY
long slender spear - - - - - LANCE
long space of time - - - - - - EON
long standing - - - - - - - - OLD
long step - - - - - - - - STRIDE
long stick - - - - - - - - - POLE
long thin piece - - - - - - SLIVER
long time - - - - - - - - - YEARS
long tooth - - - - - - TUSK, FANG
long trying time - - - - - - SIEGE
long used - - - - - - - - - OLD
long view - - - - - - - - - VISTA
long winged bird - - - - - PETREL
long standing (of) - - - - - - ELDER
longer than broad - - - - - OBLONG
longest lived insect - - - - - CICADA
longest standing - - - - - - OLDEST
longing - - - YEN, APPETITE, DESIRE
longitude marker - - - - - MERIDIAN
longitudinally - - - - - - ENDWISE
longwinded - - - - - - - - PROLIX
look - GAZE, SEARCH, SEE, DISCERN, PEER, EYE, SEEM, APPEARANCE, APPEAR, GLANCE, LO, LEER
look after - - - - - TEND, ATTEND
look aimlessly - - - - - - - GROPE
look angrily - - - - - - - - GLARE
look approvingly - - - - - - - SMILE
look askance - - - - - - LEER, OGLE
look at - - - - - - - - - - VIEW
look attentively - - - - - - - PORE
look briefly - - - - - - - - GLANCE
look of contempt - - - - - - SNEER
look despondent - - - - - - GLOOM
look fixedly - - - - - - GLARE, STARE
look for - - - - - - - CRAVE, SEEK
look forward to - - - - - ANTICIPATE
look at hastily - - - - - - - GLANCE
look into - - - - - - - - - - PRY
look joyous - - - - - - - - - SMILE
look at malignly - - - - - - - LEER
look obliquely - - - - - - - - LEER
look on with contempt - - - DESPISE
look out - - - - - - - - BEWARE
look pryingly (colloq.) - - - - - PEEK
look searchingly - - - - - - - PEER
look slyly - - - - PEEK, PEEP, OGLE
look steadily - - - - - - - - GAZE
look sulky - - - - - - - - - POUT
look sullen - - - - - POUT, GLOWER
look upon - - - - - - - - REGARD
look upon approvingly or with favour - - SMILE
look well on - - - - - - - BECOME
looking glass - - - - - - - MIRROR
loom part - - - - - - - - - REED
loop - NOOSE, CURVE, CIRCLE, FOLD, TAB, PICOT
loop on edge of lace or ribbon - PICOT
loop for lifting - - - - - - - - TAB
loop pile dress fabric - - - - - AGARIC
loophole - - - - - - - - - EYELET
loose - - - FREE, SLACK, RELEASE, UNBOUND
loose earth - - - - - - - - DIRT
loose end - - - - - - - - TAG, DAG

L

loose fragments of rock - - - GRAVEL
loose hanging shred - - - - - - DAG
loose outer garment - - CAPE, MANTLE, ROBE
loose overcoat - - - - - - PALETOT
loose particles of rock (pert. to) DETRITAL
loose with lever - - - - - - - PRY
loosely woven fabric - - - - - ETAMINE
loosen - - - RELAX, SLACKEN, UNTIE, RELEASE, FREE
loot - SACK, ROB, PLUNDER, BOOTY, PILLAGE, SPOIL
lop - - PENDENT, CHOP, TRIM, DROOP
lop off - - - - - - - - - - PRUNE
lop off roughly - - - - - - - SNAG
lope - - - - - - - - - - - CANTER
lopsided - - - - - - - - - - ALOP
loquacity (colloq.) - - - - - - GAB
lord's chief manor place - - DEMESNE
lord's demesne - - - - - - - MANOR
lore - - - - - - - - - - LEARNING
lorica - - - - - - - - - - CUIRASS
lorn - - - - - - - - - - FORLORN
lose - WASTE, STRAY, MISPLACE, MISS
lose blood - - - - - - - - - BLEED
lose colour - - - - - - PALE, FADE
lose from container - - - - - - SPILL
lose footing - - - - - - - - - SLIP
lose freshness - - WILT, STALE, FADE
lose heat - - - - - - - - - - COOL
lose hope - - - - DESPAIR, DESPOND
lose luster - - - - - FADE, TARNISH
lose one's footing - - - - - - - SLIP
lose vigor - - - - - - - - - - FLAG
lose vital fluid - - - - - - - BLEED
loss - - - DEFEAT, FAILURE, DAMAGE
loss of hope - - - - - - - - DESPAIR
loss of a sound in pronouncing - ELISION
lost - - - MISSING, GONE, RUINED
lost animal - - - - - - - - ESTRAY
lot - FATE, DESTINY, PORTION, HAZARD, SHARE, FORTUNE
lottery (form of) - - - - - - RAFFLE
lotto (form of) - - - - - - - KENO
lotus (arch.) - - - - - - - - - LOTE
loud - - - - - - NOISY, CLAMOROUS
loud call - - - - - - - - - - CRY
loud cry - - - - - - - - - - HOWL
loud cry (dial.) - - - - - - - YAWP
loud hollow sound - - - - - - BOOM
loud lamentation - - - - - - - WAIL
loud noise - - - - - BANG, DIN, ROAR
loud ringing sound - - - - - - CLANG
loud shout - - - - - - - - HALLOO
loud sound - - - - - - - - - NOISE
loud voiced person - - - - - STENTOR
Louis XIV's title - - - - - - - ROI
Louisiana county - - - - - - PARISH
Louisiana court decree - - - - ARRET
lounge - - - - - - LOLL, SOFA, LOAF
louse egg - - - - - - - - - - NIT
lout - BOOR, YAHOO, OAF, BUMPKIN, BLOCKHEAD
love - FONDNESS, CHARITY, AFFECTION, GRA
love (Anglo-Ir.) - - - - - - - GRA
love apple - - - - - - - - TOMATO
love greatly - - - - - - - - - DOTE
love missive - - - - - - - VALENTINE
love (pert. to) - - EROTIC, AMATORY
love potion - - - - - - - - PHILTER
love story - - - - - - - - ROMANCE
loved - - - - - - - - - - - DEAR
lover - - - - - - - - - SWAIN, AMI
lover of one's country - - - - PATRIOT
loving - - - - - - - AMATIVE, FOND
loving too much - - - - - - DOTING
low - - - MOO, BASE, SOFT, HUMBLE, INFERIOR, SOFTLY, BELLOW
low bow - - - - - - - - - - SALAAM
low bred dog (var.) - - - - - TYKE
low cloud - - - - - - - - - NEBULA
low couch - - - - - - - - - DIVAN
low deck of ship - - - - - - - ORLOP
low flat bottomed boat - - - - KEEL
low form of animal life - - - AMOEBA
low gaiter - - - - - - - - - - SPAT
low growing plant - - - - - - VIOLET
low haunt - - - - - - - - DEN, DIVE
low island - - - - - - - - - - KEY
low monotonous sound - - - - - DRONE
low necked - - - - - - - - DECOLLETE
low noise - - - - - - - - - - HUM
low note - - - - - - - - - - - UT
low place between hills - - - - DALE
low plant - - - - - - - - - SHRUB
low section of a city - - - - - SLUM
low shoe - - - - - - - - - - PUMP
low slipper - - - - - - - - - MULE
low sound - - HUM, MURMUR, DRONE, RUMBLE
low spirits - - - - - - DUMPS, BLUES
low tree - - - - - - SCRUB, SHRUB
low tufted plant - - - - - - - MOSS
low voice - - - - - - - - - - ALTO
low wagon - - - - - - - - - - DRAY
lower - - - REDUCE, LESSEN, ABASE, NETHER, FROWN, DIMINISH, SINK, DEBASE, HUMBLE, DEMEAN, DEPRESS, DEGRADE, BATE
lower the bottom - - - - - - DEEPEN
lower corner of a sail - - - - CLEW
lower end of mast - - - - - - HEEL
lower part of jaw - - - - - - - CHIN
lower part of leg - - - SHIN, SHANK
lower point (to) - - - - - - - DOWN
lower in rank - - - DEGRADE, JUNIOR
lower region - - - - - - - - HADES
lower Silurian division - - - - - BALA
lower in value - - - - - - - DEBASE
lowest - - - BASEST (See also Low)
lowest deck of vessel - ORLOPS, ORLOP
lowest ebb - - - - - - - - - NEAP
lowest form of wit - - - - - - - PUN
lowest limit - - - - - - - MINIMUM
lowest part - - - - - - - BOTTOM
lowest part in music - - - - - BASS
lowest point - - - - - - - - NADIR
lowest quarter on ship - - - STEERAGE
lowest timber of a ship - - - - KEEL
lowing sound - - - - - - - - - MOO
loyal - - LEAL, TRUE, LIEGE, FAITHFUL
loyalist - - - - - - - - - - TORY
lozenge - - - - - - - - - - PASTIL
lubricant - - - - - - - - - GREASE
lubricate - - OIL, GREASE, GRAPHITE
lubricator - - - - - - - - - OILCAN
lubricous - - - - - ELUSIVE, SLIPPERY
lucent - - - - - - - - - - SHINING
lucerne - - - - - - - - - - ALFALFA
lucid - - - - - - - - CLEAR, SANE
lucidity - - - - - - - - - CLARITY
Lucifer - - - - - - - - - - - SATAN
luck - - - - - - - - HAP, CHANCE
lucre - - - - - - - - - GAIN, MONEY
ludicrous - - - - - COMICAL, COMIC
lug - - - - - - - - DRAG, HAUL, EAR
lugubrious - - - - - - - - DOLEFUL
lukewarm - - - - - - - - - - TEPID
lull - - - - - - - - QUIET, RESPITE
lumber - - - - - - - - - - TIMBER

lumber saw - - - - - - - - - RIP
lumberman - - - - - - - - - HEWER
lumberman's boots - - - - - OVERS
lumberman's tool - - - - - - - ADZE
luminary - - - - - - - - - CANDLE
luminous body - - - - - - - - STAR
luminous bow between two electrodes - ARC
luminous envelope around the sun - - CORONA
luminous phenomenon - - - - METEOR
lump - - MASS, NODULE, NUB, PIECE, KNOB
lump of clay (ceramics) - - - - - BAT
lump of earth - - - - - - - - CLOD
lump (slang) - - - - - - - - - GOB
lump (small) - - - - - - - - NODULE
lumpy - - - - - - - - - - KNOBBY
lunacy - - - - - - - - - INSANITY
lunar creator - - - - - - - - LINNE
lunar months - - - - - - - - MOONS
lunary - - - - - - - - MOONWORT
lunatic - - - - - - - - BEDLAMITE
lunge - - - - - - - - - - THRUST
lurch - - - - - - - - - - CAREEN
lure - - BAIT, ENTICE, TEMPT, DRAW, ATTRACT, DECOY
lurid - - - - - - - - - - DISMAL
lurk - - - - - - - - - - - PROWL
luster - - - - SHEEN, GLOSS, SHINE
lustrate - - - - - - - - - - PURIFY
lustrous - - - - - - - - - GLOSSY
lustrous mineral - - - - - - - SPAR
lusty - - - - - - - - - - ROBUST
lute - - - - - - - - - - - CEMENT
luxuriant - - - - - - - - - - LUSH
luxuriate - - - - - - - - - - BASK
Luzon capital - - - - - - - MANILA
Luzon Indonesian - - - - - - IGOROT
Luzon native and savage - - ATTA, ATA, AETA, IGOROT
Luzon tribe - - - - - - - - - ATAS
Luzon tribesman - - - - - - - AETA
lye - - - - - - - - - - - CAUSTIC
lying down - - - - - - - - - - ABED
lying under - - - - - - - SUBJACENT
lymphs - - - - - - - - - - - SERA
lyra - - - - - - - - - - - - HARP
Lyra star - - - - - - - - - - VEGA
lyrelike instrument - - - - - - ASOR
lyric - - - - - - - POEM, MUSICAL
lyric ode (last part) - - - - - EPODE
lyric poem (pert. to) - - - - - ODIC
lyric poem (kind) - ODE, EPODE, RONDEL

M

macabre - - - - - - - - - - EERIE
macaw - - ARA, ARARA, ARAR, PARROT
Macbeth character - - - - - BANQUO
macebearer - - - - - - - - BEADLE
macerate - - - - - - - - - - STEEP
machetes - - - - - - - - - - BOLOS
machination - - - - - - - ARTIFICE
machine - - - - - - ENGINE, MOTOR
machine bar - - - - - - - - - ROD
machine for binding papers - - STAPLER
machine to compress hay - - - - BALER
machine to cut hay - - - - - MOWER
machine to grind grain - - - - MILL
machine to notch girders - - - COPER
machine part (slang) - - - - - GADGET
machine to raise pile on cloth - NAPPER
machine to raise weights - - - - GIN
machine to separate cotton and seeds - GIN
machine to spread hay - - - - TEDDER
machine tool - - - - - - - - - LATHE
machine to turn wood - - - - - LATHE
mackerel-like fish - TUNNY, PLAINTAIL
maculate - - - - - - - SPOT, STAIN
mad - - - INSANE, FRANTIC, IRATE
Madagascar animals - AYEAYES, TENRECS
madam (contr.) - - - - - - - - MAAM
madden - - - - - - ENRAGE, CRAZE
made of certain cereal - - - - OATEN
made of grain - - - - - - - CEREAL
made of flowers - - - - - - - FLORAL
made of tile - - - - - - - TEGULAR
made up of distinct parts - COMPOSITE
made of wood - - - - - - - - TREEN
madman - - - - - - - - - MANIAC
madness - - - - - - - - - - MANIA
Madras weight - - - - - - - POLLAM
maestro - - - - - - - CONDUCTOR
magazine - - - - - ARSENAL, STORE
mage - - - - - - - - - - WIZARD
maggot - - - - - - - - - - LARVA
magi - - - - - - - - - SORCERER
magic - - - - - - - RUNE, SORCERY
magical ornament - - - - - - AMULET
magician - - - - - - - - HOUDINI
magician's stick - - - - - - - WAND
magician's word - - - - - - PRESTO
magnate - - - - - - - - - OFFICIAL
magnesium - - - - - - - - TALC, MG
magnet - - - - - - - - LODESTONE
magnet end - - - - - - - - - POLE
magnificence - - - POMP, SPLENDOR, GRANDEUR
magnificent - - - SPLENDID, GRAND, PALATIAL, SUPERB
magnify - - - - - GREATEN, ENLARGE
magnitude - - - - - - - - - - SIZE
mahogany pine - - - - - - TOTARA
maid - LASS, NYMPH, GIRL, DOMESTIC
maiden - - - - - LASS, DAMSEL, GIRL
mail - - - - - - - - POST, ARMOR
mail service (pert. to) - - - - POSTAL
maim - - - CRIPPLE, LAME, INJURE, DISABLE
main - - OCEAN, PRINCIPAL, CHIEF, FOREMOST
main blood stream - - - - - - AORTA
main body - - - - - - TRUNK, MASS
main course - - - - - - - - ENTREE
main highway - - - - - - - - - PIKE
main idea - - - - - - - - - - GIST
main shock - - - - - - - - BRUNT
Maine capital - - - - - - AUGUSTA
Maine city - - - - - - - - - - BATH
Maine lake - - - - - - - - SEBAGO
Maine town - ORONO, MILO, BANGOR, HIRAM
maintain - - KEEP, PRESERVE, CLAIM, ASSERT, VINDICATE, ALLEGE, CONTEND
maintain order - - - - - - - POLICE
maintenance - - RETENTION, UPKEEP
maize - - - - - - - - - - - CORN
majestic - LEONINE, STATELY, IMPERIAL, SUPERB, GLORIOUS
make - CREATE, CONSTRUCT, FABRICATE, MANUFACTURE, INDUCE, RENDER, FORM
make active - - - - - - - ENERGIZE
make additions to - - - - - - - EKE
make allegations against - - - ACCUSE
make allusion to - - - - - - MENTION
make amends - - - ATONE, REDRESS, REDEEM

M

make angry - - - - - - - - RILE
make arrangements - - - - - - PLAN
make ashamed - - - - - - - ABASH
make believe - SHAM, PRETEND, FEIGN
make beloved - - - - - - - ENDEAR
make better - - - - - AMELIORATE
make a botch of - - - - - - - FLUB
make certain - - - ASSURE, INSURE
make changes - - - - - - INNOVATE
make cheerful - - - - - - - CHIRK
make chess move - - - - - - CASTLE
make choice - - - - - - - - OPT
make clean and put in order (mil.) POLICE
make clear - - - - EXPLAIN, FOCUS
make cloth - - - - - - - - WEAVE
make common interest of - - - POOL
make compact - - - - - - CONDENSE
make complicated - - - - - - SNARL
make corrections in literary work - EMEND
make crackling sound - - - - CRINK
make damp - - - - - - - MOISTEN
make dejected - - - - - - - MOPE
make designs by lines - - - - ETCH
make destitute - - - BEREFT, BEREAVE
make dizzy - - - - - - - - STUN
make docile - - - - - - - - TAME
make easy - - - - - - - - GENTLE
make an edging - - - - - - - TAT
make empty - - - - - - - - VACATE
make an end of - - - - - - DESTROY
make enduring - - - - - - - ANNEAL
make entreaty - - - - - - - PRAY
make equal - - - - - - - - EQUATE
make ethereal - - - - - - - AERATE
make evenly proportioned - - EQUATE
make evident - - - - - - - EVINCE
make excuses (slang) - - - - STALL
make expiation for - - - - - ATONE
make eyes - - - - - - - - - OGLE
make faint - - - - - - - - BEDIM
make famous - - - - - - - RENOWN
make fast - - - SECURE, GIRD, BELAY
make fast (naut.) - - - - - - BELAY
make feeble - - - - - DEBILITATE
make financial amends - - - REDRESS
make finer - - - - - - - - STRAIN
make firm - - - - - - - - - FIX
make first move - - - - - - - LEAD
make flat and even - - - - - LEVEL
make fleshy - - - - - - - FATTEN
make fool of - - - - - - STULTIFY
make a foray - - - - - - - - RAID
make fun - - - - - - - - - PLAY
make fun of - - - - - - - GUY, RIB
make glad - - - - - - - - PLEASE
make glass into a sheet - - PLATTEN
make glossy - - - - - - - - SLEEK
make of goods - - - - - - - BRAND
make grating sound - - - - - RASP
make grooves - - - - - - - SCORE
make harmonious - - - TUNE, ATONE
make harsh sound - - - - - - BRAY
make haste - - - - - - - - SPEED
make a hedge - - - - - - - PLASH
make a hole - - - - - - - - BORE
make ill - - - - - - - - - - AIL
make an imitation of - - - - PATTERN
make infirm - - - - - - - - LAME
make into fabric - - - - WEAVE, KNIT
make into law - - - - - - - ENACT
make into leather - - - - - TAN, TAW
make into parcels - - - - - PACKAGE
make into a steep slope - - - ESCARP
make into texture - - - - - - WEAVE
make into thread - - - - - - - SPIN

make irate - - - - - - - - ANGER
make Irish - - - - - - - - ERINIZE
make irrevocable - - - - - - - BIND
make joyful - - - - ELATE, GLADDEN
make knotted lace - - - - - - - TAT
make known - - - - NOTIFY, IMPART
make laborious research - - - DELVE
make late - - - - - - - - BELATE
make laws - - - - - - - LEGISLATE
make lean - - - - - - - - EMACIATE
make less bright - - - - - - - DIM
make less compact - - - - - LOOSEN
make less dense - - - - - - RAREFY
make less flexible - - - - - STIFFEN
make less loose - - - - - TIGHTEN
make long deep incision - - - - GASH
make lustrous - - - - - - - - GILD
make merry - - - - - - - - REVEL
make misstep - - - - - - - - TRIP
make mistakes - - - - - - BLUNDER
make motion - - - - - - - GESTURE
make muddy - - - - - - - - - ROIL
make necessary - - - - - - - ENTAIL
make needlework - - - - - - - SEW
make note of - - - - - - - - JOT
make obeisance - - - - - - - KNEEL
make objection - - - - - - PROTEST
make oneself useful - - - - - AVAIL
make out - - - - - - - - DISCERN
make over - - - REMODEL, REFORM, REMAKE, RENOVATE
make parallels - - - - - COLLIMATE
make petulant - - - - - - - PEEVE
make plump - - - - - - - FATTEN
make possible - - - - - - - ENABLE
make precious - - - - - - - ENDEAR
make pretext of - - - - - - PRETEND
make proud - - - - - - - - ELATE
make public - - - - - - DELATE, AIR
make quiet - - - - - - - - - HUSH
make quilt - - - - - - - - - PIECE
make a rattling noise - - - - CLATTER
make ready - - - PREPARE, FOREARM
make reparation - - - ATONE, EXPIATE
make request - - - - - - - APPEAL
make requittal for - REPAY, RETALIATE
make resolute - - - - - - - STEEL
make rigid - - - - - - - - TENSE
make safe - - - - - - - - SECURE
make safe (Scot.) - - - - - - - GAR
make secure - - - - - - - FASTEN
make serious - - - - - - - SOBER
make a showy display - - - SPLURGE
make a shrill sound - - - - - HOOT
make sleek - - - - - - - - PREEN
make a slight quick sound - - - TICK
make slower - - - - - - - RETARD
make soapsuds - - - - - - LATHER
make sorrowful - - - - - - SADDEN
make speech - - - ORATE, PERORATE
make spiritless - - - - - MOPE, PALL
make succession of small sounds - PATTER
make suitable - - - - - - ADAPT, FIT
make tight - - - - - - - - TAUTEN
make too small - - - - - - SCRIMP
make trial of again - - - - - RETEST
make turbid - - - - - - ROIL, MUD
make unfit - - - - - - - - - SPOIL
make unhappy - - - - - - - SADDEN
make uniform - - - - - - - - EVEN
make untidy - - - - - - - - LITTER
make unyielding - - - - - - - STEEL
make up - - - - - - - - COMPRISE
make up for - - - - - - - - ATONE
make use of - - - - - - - EXERCISE
make vapid - - - - - - - - - PALL

make vigorous - - ENERGIZE, LIVEN
make void - - - - - - - - ANNUL
make well - - - - - - - CURE, HEAL
make white - - - - - - - BLEACH
make wine - - - - - - - - - VINT
make words from letters - - - - SPELL
make worse - - - - - - AGGRAVATE
make wrathful - - - - - - - ANGER
make wrinkles - - - - - - - CREASE
make young again - - - REJUVENATE
maker of roofing material - - - TILER
maker of wills - - - - - - TESTATOR
makeup of a publication - - - FORMAT
making excuses - - - - - APOLOGETIC
mala - - - - - - - WRONGS, EVILS
malady - - - - - - - - - DISEASE
Malaga raisin (kind) - - - - - LEXIA
malapert - - - - - - - - - - SAUCY
malaria and malarial fever - - - AGUE
Malay animal - - - - - - - - NAPU
Malay ape - - - - - - - - - - LAR
Malay canoe - - - - - - - - - PROA
Malay coin - - - - - - - TRA, ORA
Malay condiment - - - - - - SEMBALL
Malay dagger - - - - - - - - KRIS
Malay disease - - - - - - - - AMOK
Malay fan palm - - - - - - GEBANG
Malay garment - - - - - - - SARONG
Malay gibbon - - - - - - - - - LAR
Malay island - - - SUMATRA, TIMOR, BORNEO, OMA, JAVA
Malay isthmus - - - - - - - - KRA
Malay rattan - - - - - - - - SEGA
male - - - - - - - - - - MAS, MAN
male ancestry - - - - - - PATERNITY
male antelope - - - - - - - - BUCK
male attendant - - - - - - - - PAGE
male bee - - - - - - - - - - DRONE
male bovine animal - - - - - - STEER
male ferret - - - - - - - - - - HOB
male figure for supporting column - - TELAMON
male forebears - - - - - - - SIRES
male chicken - - - - - - - ROOSTER
male hog - - - - - - - - - - BOAR
male of the lanner - - - - LANNERET
male red deer - - - - - - HART, STAG
male servant - - - - - - - - - BOY
male server - - - - - - - - WAITER
male sheep - - - - - - - - - - RAM
male swan - - - - - - - - - - COB
male swine - - - - - - - - - BOAR
malediction - - - - - - - - CURSE
malefic - - - - - - - - - HURTFUL
malevolent - - - - - - - EVIL, ILL
malevolent water sprite (var.) - - NIS
malice - - - - - - - - - - SPITE
malicious - - SPITEFUL, LEER, CATTY, FELONIOUS, EVIL
malicious burning of property - - ARSON
malicious damage - - - - - SABOTAGE
malign - EVIL, DEFAME, LIBEL, REVILE
malignant spirit - - - - - - - - KER
maligner - - - - - - - - - REVILER
malignity - - - - - - RANCOR, HATE
mall - - - - - - - - AVENUE, POST
malleable - - - - - - - - - - SOFT
malleable metal - - - - - - - - TIN
mallet - GRAVEL, MAUL, GAVEL, HAMMER
malodorous - - - - - - - - - FETID
malt liquor - ALT, ALE, STOUT, PORTER, BEER
malt liquor factory - - - - - BREWERY
Malta capital - - - - - - - - VALETTA
Malta village - - - - - - - - - LIA
maltreat - - - - - - - - - - ABUSE

mammon - - - - - RICHES, WEALT
man - - - - - - - - - - - - - MALE
man of all work - - - - - FACTOTUM
man in charge of horses - - - GROOM
man of courage - - - - - - - - LION
man dressed as woman - - - - - BESSY
man of great strength - - - - SAMSON
man of great wealth - - - - - NABOB
man (slang) - - - - - - - - - GENT
man of learning - - - - SAVANT, PUNDIT
man-like monkey - - - - - - - - APE
man's arch-enemy - - - - - - SATAN
man's best friend - - - - - - - DOG
man's hat - - - - - - - - - FEDORA
man with deep singing voice - - BASSO
manacle - - IRON, SHACKLE, FETTER
manage - - - CONTRIVE, REGULATE, HANDLE, WIELD, DIRECT, MANIPULATE, ADMINISTER, CONTROL, OPERATE, ENGINEER
manageable - - - - - - - - WIELDY
management - - - - - - - - REGIME
management of money - - - - FINANCE
manager - - - STEWARD, DIRECTOR, FACTOR, BOSS
menagerie - - - - - - - - - - ZOO
Manchurian port - - - - - - - HARBIN
Manchurian province - - - - - JEHOH
mandate - - - - - ORDER, COMMAND, INJUNCTION
mandatory precept - - - - - - - WRIT
manducate - - - - - - - - - - CHEW
manger - - - - - - - - - - - STALL
mangle - LACERATE, MUTILATE, IRONER
mania - - - - - - CRAZE, MADNESS
maniac - - - - - - - - - - MADMAN
manifest - - PATENT, SIGNIFY, PLAIN, DISPLAY, EVINCE, PALPABLE, OVERT, CLEAR, EVIDENT
manifest derision - - - - - - SNEER
manifestation of affection - - CARESS
manifesting exhilaration - - EBULLIENT
manifesto - - - - - - - - - - EDICT
manifold - - - - - - - - - MULTIPLE
Manila hemp - - - - - - - - ABACA
Manila hemp braid - - - - - - TAGAL
manipulate - HANDLE, TREAT, MANAGE, USE, WIELD
mankind - - - - - - - - - - WORLD
manly - - - - - - - VIRILE, RESOLUTE
mannequin - - - - - - - - - MODEL
manner - MIEN, AIR, CUSTOM, STYLE, SORT, MODE, MEANS, WAY
manner of building - - - - STRUCTURE
manner of pitching a baseball - DELIVERY
manner of running - - - - - - - GAIT
manner of utterance - - - - ELOCUTION
manner of walking - - - - - - - GAIT
mannerly - - - - - - - - - - POLITE
manor - - - - - - - ESTATE, MANSION
manor court (kind) - - - - - - - LEET
manse - - - - - - - - - PARSONAGE
mansion - - - - - - - PALACE, MANOR
mantle - - - - - - - - CLOAK, ROBE
mantle worn over armour - - - TABARD
manual - - - - - - - - - TEXTBOOK
manual art - - - - - - - - - CRAFT
manual digit - - - - FINGER, THUMB
manual of instruction - - - - TEXTBOOK
manual vocation - - - - - - - TRADE
manufacture - - - - - - - - - MAKE
manufacturer of fermented liquor - - - BREWER
manuscript (abbr.) - - - - - - - MS
many - SEVERAL, MULTIPLE, NUMEROUS, VARIOUS

M

map - - - - PLAT, CHART, SKETCH
map (kind) - - - - - - - - RELIEF
map out - - - - - - - - PLAN
map of solar system - - - - - ORRERY
maple (pert. to) - - - - - - ACERIC
maples - - - - - - - - - - - ACER
mar - DEFACE, DAMAGE, SPOIL, IMPAIR, TARNISH, INJURE
maraud - - - - - - - - - PLUNDER
marble - AGATE, TAW, ALLEY, MIG, MIB
marble game - - - - - - - - - TAW
march - - - - - - - - - - PARADE
march back and forth - - - - - PACE
march king - - - - - - - - - SOUSA
march on - - - - - - - - - TROOP
marching cry - - - - - - - - - HEP
margin - - LIP, BORDER, EDGE, HEM, VERGE, SCOPE, BRIM
marginal note - - - - - - - - APOSTIL
margosa - - - - - - - - - - NEEM
Mariana Island canoe - - - - - PROA
marinate - - - - - - - - - PICKLE
marine - MARITIME, OCEANIC, NAUTICAL
marine animal - - - - - - - - CORAL
marine carnivore - - - - - - - OTTER
marine crustacean - - - - - LOBSTER
marine fish - - OPAH, SCAROID, LING, EELPOUT
marine gastropod - - - TRITION, YET, LIMPET, NERITE
marine mammal - - - - - - - - SEAL
marine mollusk - - MUSSEL, SCALLOP
marine plant - MOSS, SEAWEED, ENALID
mariner - SAILOR, SEAMAN, NAVIGATOR
marionette - - - - - - - - - PUPPET
maritime - MARINE, NAVAL, NAUTICAL
mark - - TRACK, TRACE, LANE, TAB, TARGET, LABEL, NOTE, BRAND, CHARACTERIZE
mark aimed at in curling - - - - TEE
mark of a blow - - - - - DENT, DINT
mark by cutting - - - - - - ENGRAVE
mark of infamy - - - - - - - STIGMA
mark of injury - - - - - - - - SCAR
mark the limits - - - - - - - DEFINE
mark of omission - - - CARET, DELE, APOSTROPHE
mark out - - - - - - - - - DEFINE
mark paid - - - - - - - - - RECEIPT
mark of pronunciation - - - - - TILDE
mark to retain - - - - - - - - - STET
mark to shoot at - - - - - - - TARGET
mark the skin - - - - - - - - TATTOO
mark used in checking - - - - - TICK
mark with asterisk - - - - - - - STAR
mark with cuts - - - - - - - - SCORE
mark with different colours - VARIEGATE
mark with ridges - - - - - - - - RIB
mark with spots - - DAPPLE, NOTATE, MOTTLE
mark with squares - - - - - CHECKER
mark of wrinkle - - - - - - - CREASE
marked by duplicity - - - - - - - SLY
marked melodic phrase - - LEITMOTIF
marked off in small spaces - AREOLATE
marked with lines - - - - - - LINEATE
marker - - - - - - - - - - - - PEG
market - - - - STORE, SELL, MART
market place - - - - - MART, AGORA
market town - - - - - - - - - BOURG
marketable - - - - - - - - SALABLE
marksman - - - - - - - - - - - SHOT
marl - - - - - - - - - - - - - LOAM
marmoset - - - - - - - - - TAMARIN
marriage - - - MARITAL, CONNUBIAL, WEDLOCK, UNION, MATRIMONY

marriage (comb. form) - - - - - GAMO
marriage dot - - - - - - - - DOWER
marriage (pert. to) - - - - - MARITAL
married woman - - - - - - - MATRON
marry - - - - - MATE, WED, ESPOUSE
Mars (comb. form) - - - - - - - AREO
Mars (pert. to) - - - - AREAN, MARTIAN
marsh - FEN, SWAMP, SWALE, MORASS, BOG
marsh (soft) - - - - - - - - SALINA
marsh bird - - - - SNIPE, RAIL, SORA
marsh crocodile - - - - - - - - - GOA
marsh elder - - - - - - - - - - - IVA
marsh grass (tall) - - - - REED, SEDGE
marsh marigold - - - - - - - COWSLIP
marsh plant - - - - - - - - CATTAIL
marshy - - - - - PALUDINAL, PALUDIC
marshy land - - - - - - - FEW, SWALE
marshy place - - - - - - - - - SLEW
mart - - - - - - - - STORE, MARKET
martial - - - - - - - - - - WARLIKE
Martin Eden author - - - - - LONDON
Martinique volcano - - - - - - PELEE
marvel - WONDER, PRODIGY, MIRACLE
marvellous - PRODIGIOUS, WONDERFUL
masculine - - - - - - - - MALE, LUIS
masculine or feminine name - CELESTINE
mash - - - - - - - - - - - - CRUSH
mash down - - - - - - - STOMP, RICE
mask - - - - VISOR, DISGUISE, VEIL, CONCEAL
mason's hammer point - - - - - PEEN
mason's maul - - - - - - - - - GAVEL
Masonic doorkeeper - - - - - - TILER
masonry support - - - - - - - - - PIER
masquerade costume - - - - - DOMINO
mass - - WAD, BULK, LUMP, THRONG, ASSEMBLE, GOB, HEAP, PAT
mass book - - - - - - - - - MISSAL
mass meeting - - - - - - - - RALLY
mass (comb. form) - - - - - - - MAS
mass of floating logs - - - - - DRIVE
mass of floating vapor - - - - CLOUD
mass of ice - - - - BERG, SERAC, FLOE
Massachusetts cape - - - - - ANN, COD
Massachusetts city - - - - - - SALEM
Massachusetts mountain - - - - - TOM
Massachusetts town - - - - - - - LEE
massacre - - - - CARNAGE, SLAUGHTER
massage - - - - - - - - KNEAD, RUB
Massenet opera - - - - - - - THAIS
massive - - - - - - - - - - - HUGE
mast - - - - - - - - - - - - - SPAR
master - - - - - CONQUER, SUBDUE
master stroke - - - - - - - - - COUP
masticate - - - - - - - - - - - CHEW
mastiff - - - - - - - - - - - - ALAN
mastoid of bone - - - - - - ENTOMION
mat - CARPET, KNOT, CUSHION, DOILY, ENTANGLE
matador - - - - - - - - BULLFIGHTER
match - MATE, PAIR, TEAM, SUIT, TWIN, COPE, PEER, TALLY
matchless - - INIMITABLE, PEERLESS
mate - - - - - - - - - - - - MATCH
material - - REAL, DATA, CORPOREAL, FABRIC, SUBSTANCE, INGREDIENT, STUFF
material to make mantles - - - CERIA
material for violin strings - - - - GUT
maternal - - - - - - - - MOTHERLY
maternity - - - - - - - MOTHERHOOD
matgrass - - - - - - - - - - - - NARD
mathematical arc - - - - - - RADIAN
mathematical instrument - - - - SECTOR
mathematical line in space - - VECTOR

mathematical quantity - - - - SURD
mathematical ratio - - - - - - SINE
mathematical term - - COSINE, SINE, PI
matrimonial - - - - - - - NUPTIAL
matrimony - - - WEDLOCK, MARRIAGE
matrix - - - - - - - - - MOLD, BED
matron - - - - - - - - - - DAME
matronly - - - - - - - - - SEDATE
matter - SUBSTANCE, AFFAIR, CONCERN, SIGNIFY, IMPORT
matter (arch.) - - - - - - - RECK
matter of fact - - - - - - - LITERAL
matter formed on iron - - - - RUST
mattress - - - - - - - - - - BED
mattress covering - - - - - - TICK
mature - AGE, RIPEN, MELLOW, RIPE, SEASON, GROW
mature feather - - - - TELEOPTILE
matured - - - - - - - GROWN, RIPE
matutinal beverage - - - - COFFEE
maul - - - - - - - ABUSE, GAVEL
maul (small) - - - - - - - MALLET
mauser - - - - - - - - - - RIFLE
maw - - - - - - - - - - - CRAW
maxilla - - - - - - - - - - JAW
maxim - SAW, ADAGE, MOTTO, TENET, ITEM, PRECEPT, PRINCIPLE, PROVERB, AXIOM, MORAL
maximum - - - - - - - - - MOST
May apple - - - - - - - MANDRAKE
Mayan month - - - - - - - UINAL
meadow - - - - - - LEA, GRASSLAND
meadow mouse - - - - - - - VOLE
meadow (poet.) - - - - - - - MEAD
meadow prairie - - - - - SAVANNA
meadow saxifrage - - - - - - SESELI
meager - - - SCANT, SCANTY, BARE
meal - - - - - - - - - - REPAST
meal (fine) - - - - - - - - FARINA
meal to be ground - - - - - - GRIST
meal of parched corn - - - - NOCAKE
mean - - INTEND, BRUTAL, AVERAGE, SIGNIFY, CRUEL, STINGY, SHABBY, BASE, SNIDE, IMPLY, PURPOSE, DENOTE
meander - - - TWINE, MAZE, WANDER
meaning - - - SENSE, INTENDING, DEFINITION
means - - - RESOURCES, PURPOSES, WEALTH
means of access - - - - - - DOOR
means of conveyance - - - - VEHICLE
means of crossing a fence - - - STILE
means of defense - MUNIMENT, ABATIS
means of education - - - - TRAVEL
means of entrance - - - DOOR, GATE
means of escape - - - - LOOPHOLE
means of ingress - - - - - - GATE
means of livelihood - - - - - TRADE
means of restraint - - - - - REINS
means of transmitting force - - LEVER
means of transmitting power - - BELT
meant - - - - - - - - PURPOSED
meantime - - - - - - - - INTERIM
measure - METE, GAGE, ESTIMATE, ARE, ACRE, METER, DIMENSION
measure of ancient Egypt - - - - KET
measure of capacity - - PINT, LITER, BUSHEL, PECK, GILL, LITRE, STERE, QUART, TON
measure of cloth - - - - - - - ELL
measure of cut wood - - - - CORD
measure of distance - MILE, ROD, METRE
measure of Eritrea - - - - - DERAH
measure of Hungary - - - - MAROK
measure of length - ELL, METER, MILE, METRE, CUBIT, PIK, DRA, FOOT, YARD, ROD
measure of paper - - - REAM, QUIRE
measure thickness of - - - - CALIPER
measure of wire - - - - - - - MIL
measure of weight - - CARAT, OUNCE, GRAIN
measure of wood - - - - - - CORD
measure of yarn - - - - - - - LEA
measured in electronic units - - OHMIC
measured medication - DOSE, DOSAGE
measured pace - - - - - - - TROT
measured by the sun - - - - SOLAR
measurement - - METRIC, DIMENSION
measurement downward - - - DEPTH
measurement (kind) - - - - LINEAR
measurement (pert. to) - - METRICAL, DIMENSIONAL
measuring instrument - - ALTIMETER, METER, CALIPER, TAPELINE
measuring stick - - - ELLWAND, POLE, YARDWAND, ROD
meat - - - - - - - - - - - FLESH
meat ball - - - - - - - - RISSOLE
meat in dough shells - - - RAVIOLI
meat dish - - - - - - - - - HASH
meat jelly - - - - - - - - - ASPIC
meat (kind) - - - - - - - - TRIPE
meat paste - - - - - - - - - PATE
meat pie - - - - - - - - - PASTY
meat pin - - - - - - - - SKEWER
meat and vegetable dish - - - RAGOUT
meaty - - - - - - - - - - PITHY
Mecca - - - - - - - - - - GOAL
Mecca shrine - - - - - - - CAABA
mechanical advantage - - - LEVERAGE
mechanical arrangement - - DEVICE
mechanical bar - - - - - - - LEVER
mechanical contrivance - - - ENGINE
mechanical device - - LEVER, WHEEL, MACHINE, PUMP, ROBOT
mechanical man - ROBOT, AUTOMATON
mechanical repetition - - - - ROTE
mechanism - - - - - - - ACTION
medal - - - - - - - - REWARD
meddle - - - - - - TAMPER, MESS
meddlesome - - - - - - INTRUSIVE
medial - - - - - - - - - AVERAGE
mediate - - - ARBITRATE, SETTLE, INTERCEDE
medical fluids - - - - SERA, SERUM
medical root - - - - - - - JALAP
medical term - - - - - - - - ANA
medical tincture - - - - - ARNICA
medicated compress - - - - STUPE
medicated pellet - - - - - - PILL
medicinal - - - - - - - CURATIVE
medicinal cigarette - - - - CUBEB
medicinal herb - - BONESET, SENNA, ALOE, ARNICA
medicinal nut - - - - - - - COLA
medicinal pellet - - - - - - - PILL
medicinal plant - - HERB, ACONITE, EPHEDRA, ALOE, IPECAC, CAMOMILE, SENNA, TANSY
medicinal root - - - - - - - JALAP
medicinal seaweed - - - - - - AGAR
medicinal shrub - - - - - - SENNA
medicinal tablet - - - - - - TROCHE
medicine - - - - - - DRUG, TONIC
medicine to allay pain - - ANODYNE
medicine distributor - - - DISPENSER
medicine dropper - - - - - PIPETTE
medieval - (See also Ancient, Old, etc.)
medieval cap - - - - - - - ABACOT
medieval chemical science - ALCHEMY

M

medieval dagger - - - - - - ANLACE
medieval European kingdom - - ARLES
medieval fabric - - - - - - - SAMITE
medieval fortified building - - CASTLE
medieval French coin - - - - - OBOLE
medieval French kingdom - - - - ARLES
medieval hat - - - - - - - - ABACOT
medieval knight - - - - - - PENNON
medieval military catapult - - ONAGER
medieval military engine - - - BOAR
medieval playing card - - - - TAROT
medieval poem - - - - - - - - LAI
medieval romantic island - - AVALON
medieval scarfs - - - - - LIRIPIPES
medieval shield - - - - - - - ECU
medieval ship - - - - - - - - - NEF
medieval silk fabric - - - - - SAMITE
medieval sport - - - - - - - - TILT
medieval story - - - - - - - - SAGA
medieval stringed instrument - REBAB
medieval sword - - - - - - - ESTOC
medieval tale - - - - - - - - - LAI
medieval weapon - SPEAR, PIKE, MACE, LANCE
mediocre - - - - - LALA, ORDINARY
meditate - - - - - MUSE, PONDER, CONTEMPLATE, MULL, RUMINATE, STUDY
meditate moodily - - - - - - BROOD
meditative - - - - - - - - RUMINANT
Mediterranean fish - - - - - OMBER
Mediterranean island - MALTA, CRETE, CAPRI, ELBA, SARDINIA, SICILY
Mediterranean sailing vessel - - SAIC, SETEE, MISTIC, TARTAN, XEBEC, POLACRE, FELUCCA
medium - - - - - - - - - AVERAGE
medium of communication - - ORGAN
medium of discussion - - - - FORUM
medium's emanation - - ECTOPLASM
medley - - - - - - OLIO, MELANGE
meed - - - - - - - - - - REWARD
meek - - SUBMISSIVE, TAME, GENTLE
meet - - - - CONFER, ASSEMBLE, ENCOUNTER, JOIN, CONVENE, INTERSECT, PROPER, CONFRONT
meet by appointment - - - - - TRYST
meeting - - - - - TRYSTING, TRYST, ASSEMBLAGE, PARLEY, JUNCTION, CONCLAVE
meeting room for students - SEMINAR
meeting of spiritualists - - - SEANCE
mel - - - - - - - - - - - HONEY
melancholy - SAD, GLOOM, RUEFUL, BLUE
melange - - - - - - - - - MIXTURE
meld - - - - - - - - - - - - JOIN
melee - - SKIRMISH, BATTLE, FEUD, AFFRAY, FRAY, BRAWL
mellow - AGE, MATURE, RIPE, RIPEN, SOFTEN, SOFT
melodic - - - - - - - - - TUNEFUL
melodious - ARIOSE, TUNEFUL, DULCET, MUSICAL
melody - TUNE, ARIA, AIR, STRAIN, LAY, SONG, MUSIC
melt - - - FUSE, THAW, DISSOLVE, LIQUEFY
melt down - - - - - - - - RENDER
member of ambassador's staff - ATTACHE
member of Australian army - - ANZAC
member of electorate - - - - - VOTER
member of gang - - - - - MOBSTER
member of governing board - REGENT
member of laity - - - LAYMAN, LAIC
member of religious community - - - CENOBITES
member of religious order - - - MONK
member of tribe - - - - - TRIBESMAN
membership - - - - - - - - - - SEAT
membership charges - - - - - DUES
membrane - - - - - - - - - - TELA
memento - - - - - - - - - RELIC
memoir - - - - - - - - - - - ELOGE
memorandum - - NOTES, NOTE, MEMO
memorial post - - - - - - - - XAT
memorial stone - - - - - - - CAIRN
memorize - - - - - - LEARN, ROTE
memorizing through repetition - ROTE
Memphis divinity - - - - - - - PTAH
men of letters - - - - - - LITERATI
men who handle a boat - - - - CREW
menace - THREAT, THREATEN, IMPERIL
menage - - HOUSEHOLD, DOMICILE
menagerie - - - - - - - - - - - ZOO
mend - REPAIR, DARN, HEAL, PATCH, FIX, SEW
mend coarsely - - - - - - - COBBLE
mend with weaving stitch - - - DARN
mendicant - - - - - - - - BEGGAR
menial - SERVILE, VARLET, SERVANT, DOMESTIC
menial worker - - - - - - DRUDGE
mending tool - - - DARNER, NEEDLE
Menelaus' brother - - - - AGAMEMNON
Menelaus' wife - - - - - - - - HELEN
mental - - - - IDEAL, INTELLECTUAL
mental acceptance - - - - RECEPTION
mental alertness and agility - - - WIT
mental bent - - - - - - - - - SLANT
mental concept - - - - - - - - IDEA
mental condition - - - - - MORALE
mental confusion - - - - - - - - FOG
mental derangement on one subject - - MONOMANIA
mental function - - - - - - - POWER
mental perception - - - - - - - TACT
mental state - - - - MOOD, MORALE
mental strain - - - - - - - TENSION
mental training - - - - - EDUCATION
mentality - - - - - - - - - - MIND
mentally - IDEALLY, INTELLECTUALLY
mentally agile and alive - - - - ALERT
mentally arrested person - - - - MORON
mentally deranged person MONOMANIAC
mentally dull - - - - - - - - - SLOW
mentally feeble (colloq.) - - - DOTTY
mentally sound - - - - - - - - SANE
mention - - - NAME, CITE, SPECIFY
mention officially - - - - - - - CITE
mentor - - - - - - - - - - ORACLE
menu card - - - - - - - - - CARTE
Mephistopheles - - - SATAN, DEVIL
mercantile establishment - - - STORE
mercenary - - - VENAL, HIRELING
merchandise - - - - - WARE, GOODS
merchant - DEALER, TRADER, SELLER, VENDER
merchant of Bagdad - - - - SINBAD
merchant marine - - - - - SEAMAN
merchant ship - - - - - - ARGOSY
Merchant of Venice character - PORTIA
merchant vessel's cubic capacity - - - TONNAGE
merciful - - - - LENIENT, CLEMENT
mercurial - - - - - - - - - - SWIFT
mercurous chloride - - - - - CALOMEL
Mercury's wand - - - - - CADUCEUS
Mercury's winged shoes - - TALARIA
mere - - - - - BARE, SIMPLE, ONLY, ABSOLUTE, POOL, POND
mere taste - - - - - - - - - - - SIP
mere youth - - - - - - - STRIPLING

merely - - - - - - - - ONLY, BUT
merganser - - - - - - - - SMEW
merge - FUSE, SINK, JOIN, COMBINE, UNITE, ABSORB, BLEND
merger - - UNION, COMBINE, TRUST
meridian - - - - - - - - NOONDAY
merit - - EARN, WARRANT, WORTH, DESERVE, RATE
merl - - - - - - - - - BLACKBIRD
mermaid - - - - - - - - - SIREN
merrily - - - - - - - - - GAILY
merriment - - GLEE, FUN, HILARITY, GAIETY
merry - GAY, SUNNY, HILARIOUS, JOLLY
merry-go-round - - - - - CAROUSEL
merry makings - - - - - - - REVEL
merry monarch - - - - - - - COLE
merry song - - - - - - - - LILT
Merry Widow composer - - - - LEHAR
merrymaker - - - - - - - REVELER
merrymaking - - - - - - - REVELRY
mesa - - - - - - - - - - PLATEAU
mesh - - NET, NETTING, ENTANGLE
mesh apparatus - - - - - - SIEVE
mesh-like cap for hair - - - SNOOD
meshed fabric - LACE, NET, NETTING, WEB, TULLE
meshed instrument - - - - STRAINER
Mesopotamia - - - - - - - IRAQ
Mesopotamians - - - IRAQIS, IRAQI
mess - - BOTCH, MEDDLE, DABBLE
message - - - - - - WORD, NOTE
messenger - CARRIER, PAGE, HERALD
messenger of the gods - - - HERMES
messenger from heaven - - - ANGEL
Messiah composer - - - - - HANDEL
messy - - - UNTIDY, DISORDERLY
met - - - - - - - - - SATISFIED
metal - STEEL, LEAD, ORE, SILVER, TIN
metal bar - - - RIVET, ROD, RAIL
metal bearing compound - - - ORE
metal bearing vein - - - - - LODE
metal bolt - - - - - - - - RIVET
metal case - - - - - - - CANISTER
metal circlet - - - - - - - RING
metal container - - - - - PAIL, CAN
metal cymbals - - - - - - - - TAL
metal disk - - PATEN, SEQUIN, MEDAL, GONG
metal dross - - - - - - - - SLAG
metal fastener - - RIVET, NUT, NAIL
metal flask - - - - - - - CANTEEN
metal lattice work - - - - - GRATE
metal lined eyelet - - - - GROMMET
metal machine bar - - - - - ROD
metal mass - - - - - - PIG, INGOT
metal merchandise - - - - HARDWARE
metal money - COIN, SPECIE, COINAGE
metal piece - - - - - - - - INGOT
metal plate - - DISC, PATEN, PLATEN
metal related to nickel - - - COBALT
metal rock - - - - - - - - - ORE
metal shell - - - - - - - - BOMB
metal spicule - - - - - - - NAIL
metal strand - - - - - - - WIRE
metal tag of a lace - - - - AGLET
metal thread - - - - - - - WIRE
metal worker - - - SMITH, RIVETER
metal working tool - - - - - SWAGE
metallic - - - - - - - - - TINNY
metallic alloy - - - - - - BRASS
metallic bracelet - - - - - BANGLE
metallic cement - - - - - - SOLDER
metallic chemical element - ARSENIC
metallic cloth - - - - - - - TINSEL
metallic container - - - - - - POT
metallic element - - ZINC, IRIDIUM, SILVER, IRON, LEAD
metallic element articles - - IRONWARE
metallic mixture - - - - - - ALLOY
metallic plate - - - - - - - - PATEN
metallic seal - - - - - - CAPSULE
metallic sound - - - - - - - CLANK
metallic zinc - - - - - - SPELTER
metalliferous rock - - - - - - ORE
metamere - - - - - - - - SOMITE
mete - - ALLOT, DOLE, DISTRIBUTE
meteor - - - - - LUMINOUS, ANTLID
meteor from Orion - - - - ORIONID
meteorological instrument - BAROMETER
meter - - - - - RHYTHM, MEASURE
method - SYSTEM, PLAN, WAY, ORDER, TECHNIQUE, PROCESS, RULE
method of action - - - - PLAN, RULE
method of cooking - - - - - BRAISE
method of mounting horizontal bar - KIP
method of operations - - - PROCESS
method (pert. to) - - - - - - MODAL
methodical - - - - - - - FORMAL
methodize - - - - - - - REGULATE
methyl ketol - - - - - - - ACETOL
metier - - - - - - - OCCUPATION
metric measure - - - LITER, STERE, DECARE, ARE, GRAM
metric unit - - - - - - DECIMETER
metric unit of weight - - - - - GRAM
metrical beat - - - - - - - ICTUS
metrical composition - VERSE, POEM
metrical foot - - - ANAPEST, IAMB, ANAPAEST
metrical foot part - - - - - - ARSIS
metrical land measure - AR, ARE, METER
metrical tale - - - - - - - ROMAN
metrical units of verse - - - - FEET
mettle - - - - - - - - COURAGE
mettlesome - - - - - - - SPUNKY
mewl - - - - - - - - WHIMPER
Mexican amphibian - - - - - AXOLOTL
Mexican blanket - - - - - - SERAPE
Mexican cake - - - - - - TORTILLA
Mexican city - - - - - - TAMPICO
Mexican coin and dollar - - - - PESO
Mexican coin and dollar (var.) - - REI
Mexican conqueror - CORTEZ, CORTES
Mexican corn mush - - ATOLE, AMOLE
Mexican cotton cloth - - - - - MANTA
Mexican cottonwood - - - - - ALAMO
Mexican dish - - - - - - - TAMALE
Mexican drink - - PULQUE, MESCAL
Mexican fiber - - - - - - - ISTLE
Mexican garment - - - - - SERAPE
Mexican guardian spirit - - - NAGUAL
Mexican hero - - - - - - - JUAREZ
Mexican hut - - - - - - - JACAL
Mexican Indian - - CORA, TLASCALAN, ALAIS, AZTEC, MAYA, XOVA
Mexican labourer - - - - - - PEON
Mexican mammal - - - - - OCELOT
Mexican peasant - - - - - - PEON
Mexican peninsula - - - - YUCATAN
Mexican president - - - - - ALEMAN
Mexican race (early) - - - - - TOLTEC
Mexican ranch - - - - - - HACIENDA
Mexican stirrup hood - - - TAPADERO
Mexican tea - - - - - - - APASOTE
Mexican town - - - - - - - - TULA
Mexican weight - - - - - - ARROBA
mezzanine - - - - - - - ENTRESOL
miasma - - - - - - - POLLUTION
miasmic - - - - - - - NOXIOUS
mica - - - - - - - - ISINGLASS

M

mica of muscovite - - - - - - TALC
Michigan city - - - - FLINT, IONIA
Michigan county - - - - - - KENT
microbe - - - - - - - - - - GERM
Micronesian Island group - - PELEW
microscopic - - - - - - - LITTLE
microscopic animal - - - - AMOEBA, ANIMALCULE
microscopic fungi - - - - - - YEAST
microsporophyll - - - - - - STAMEN
mid - - - - - - - - - CENTRAL
midday - - - - - - - - NOONDAY
middle - - - MESNE, CENTER, MID, MEDIAN
middle (in the) - - - - CENTRALLY
middle ages (pert. to) - - MEDIAEVAL, MEDIEVAL
middle distance runner - - - MILER
middle (law) - - - - - - - MESNE
middle part - - - - - - - WAIST
middle point - - - - - - - MESNE
midge - - - - - - - - - - GNAT
midshipman - - - - - PLEBE, REEFER
midst of - - - - - - - - AMONG
mien - - - BEARING, AIR, ASPECT
might - - - - - - - POWER, ARM
mighty - - - - - - STRONG, POTENT
mignonette colour - - - - - RESEDA
migrant - - - - - - - - - ROVING
migration - - - - - - - - - TREK
migratory worker - - - - - - HOBO
mild - TAME, GENTLE, SOFT, BLAND
mild and easy - - - - - - - FACILE
mild expletive - - GOSH, EGAD, GEE
mild oath - - - - - - - - EGAD
military artifice (use of) - - STRATEGY
military assistant - - - - - - AIDE
military barrier - - - - - - ABATTIS
military boat - - - - - - - - LST
military cap - - - - - KEPI, SHAKO
military chaplain (slang) - - - PADRE
military commission - - - - - BREVET
military decoration - - - - - MEDAL
military ditch - - - - - - - TRENCH
military force - - - - - ARMY, TROOP
military front - - - - - - - - SECTOR
military greeting - - - - - - SALUTE
military group - - - - CORPS, TROOP
military hat - - - - - SHAKO, KEPI
military inspection - - - - - REVIEW
military installation - - - - - CAMP
military officer - - - - - - - AIDE
military organization - - - - - ARMY
military post - - - STATION, BASE
military prisoners (abbr.) - - P.O.W.
military signal - - - - - - - TAPS
military spectacles - - - - PARADES
military storehouse - - - - ARSENAL
military truck - - - - - - CAMION
military unit - - - - - - BATTALION
military vehicle - - - - - - CAISSON
military warehouse - - - - - - ETAPE
militate - - - - - - - - - CONTEND
milk (comb. form) - - - - LACTO, LACT
milk curdler - - - - - - - RENNET
milk farm - - - - - - - - - DAIRY
milk (pert. to) - - - - - - LACTIC
milk (pharm.) - - - - - - - - LAC
milk protein - - - - - - - CASEIN
milkfish - - - - - - - - - - AWA
Milky Way - - - - - - - - GALAXY
Milky Way (pert. to) - - - - GALACTIC
mill - - - - - - - - - - FACTORY
mill (pert. to) - - - - - - MOLINE
mill wheat float - - - - - - LADLE
milled - - - - - - - - - KNURLED
milligram (abbr.) - - - - - - - MG
millinery - - - - - - - - - - HATS
millpond - - - - - - - - - - DAM
millstone fitting - - - - - - RYND
millstone support - - - - - - RYND
milt - - - - - - - - - - SPLEEN
mime - - - CLOWN, BUFFOON, APE
mimic - - APE, APER, IMITATE, MIME
mince - - - - - - - - - - - CHOP
mince and mix - - - - - - - HASH
minced oath - - - - - ECOD, EGAD
mind - - CARE, OBEY, TEND, HEED, MENTALITY, DISLIKE, BRAIN, SENTIENT
mind function - - - - - - IDEATION
mind (of the) - - - - - - - MENTAL
Mindanao Indonesian - - - - - ATA
Mindanao inhabitant - - - - - - ATA
Mindanao lake - - - - - - - LANAO
Mindanao language - - - - - - ATA
mindful of - - - - - - - - CARES
mine - - - - - - - - - - BURROW
mine approach - - - - - - - SLOPE
mine division - - - - - - - PANEL
mine entrance - - - - - - - ADIT
mine owner - - - - - - OPERATOR
mine sweeping vessel - - - TRAWLER
mine vein - - - - - - - - - LODE
mineral - - - METAL, IOLITE, ORE, ERINITE, SPINEL
mineral bed - - - - - - - - SEAM
mineral (brown) - - - - - - EGERAN
mineral deposit - - - - LODE, PLACER
mineral (hard) - - - - - - - EMERY
mineral (kind) - - EDENITE, EGERAN, EPIDOTE, IRITE, URALITE, GALACTITE, CAL, RUTILE, ARAGONITE, EMERY
mineral matter - - - - - - - STONE
mineral pitch for paving - - ASPHALT
mineral salt - - - - ALKALI, ALUM
mineral (soft) - - - - - - - - TALC
mineral spring - - - - - - - - SPA
mineral substance - - - - - - ORE
mineral vein - - - - - - - - LODE
mineral of zeolite family - NATROLITE
mineralized rock - - - - - - - ORE
mingle - - MIX, BLEND, INTERMIX
mingle harmoniously - - - - - BLEND
mingle with - - - - - - - - AMID
miniature - - - - - - - - SMALL
miniature representation - - - MODEL
minimize - - - - - - - - REDUCE
minimum - - - - - - - - - LEAST
mining blast - - - - - - - - SHOT
mining car - - - - - - - - TRAM
mining chisel - - - - - - - - GAD
mining excavation - - - - - - STOPE
mining refuse - - - - - - - ATTLE
minion - - - - - - - - - - SLAVE
minister - PASTOR, CLERIC, PRIEST, DIVINE, PREACHER, PARSON, ATTEND, SERVE, TEND
minister of Jehovah - - - - - SERAPH
minister to - - SERVE, TEND, ATTEND
minister's home - PARSONAGE, MANSE
minister's title (abbr.) - - - - REV.
ministerial - - - - - - - CLERICAL
ministering - - - - - - ATTENDANT
ministration - - - - - SERVICE, RITE
mink - - - - - - - - - - - VISON
Minnesota city - - - - ELY, DULUTH
Minnesota inhabitant - - - - GOPHER
minor - - - - - LESSER, SMALLER, SUBORDINATE
minor demon - - - - - - - - - IMP
minor details - - - - - - MINUTIAE

minor planet - - - - - - ASTEROID
minor prophet - - - AMOS, HOSEA
minority - - - - - - - - NONAGE
minstrel - - - - - - BARD, HARPER
minstrel show (part) - - - - - OLIO
minstrel song - - - - - - - - - LAY
mint - - - - - - - - - - - COIN
mint drink - - - - - - - - - JULEP
mint plant - - - BASIL, CATNIP
minus - - - - - - - - - - - LESS
minute - - - - WEE, SMALL, MITE
minute arachnid - - - - - - - MITE
minute difference - - - - - - SHADE
minute distinction - - - - - NICETY
minute groove or channel - - - STRIA
minute ice crystals - - - HOARFROST
minute interstice - - - - - - PORE
minute invertebrate animal - - INSECT
minute mark - - - - - - - - - DOT
minute object - - - - - - - - MITE
minute opening - - - - - - - PORE
minute organism - - - - - - SPORE
minute orifice - - - - STOMA, PORE
minute orifice (pl.) - - - - STOMATA
minute particle - - MOTE, MOLECULE, ATOM
minute unicellular fungus - - YEAST
miracle - - - - - MARVEL, WONDER
miracle man - - - - - - - - FAKIR
mirage - - - - - ILLUSION, SERAB
mire - - MUD, MUCK, STALL, BOG, MUDDY, OOZE
mirror - - - - - - GLASS, REFLECT
mirth - - - - GLEE, GAIETY, JOLLITY
miry - - - - - - - MUDDY, BOGGY
miscalculate - - - - - - OVERSHOOT
miscellany - - - - - - - - - ANA
mischief - - - ELFISH, DEVILMENT, DEVILTRY, BANE
mischievous - - EVIL, ELFISH, ELFIN, SLY, ARCH, DEVILISH
mischievous child - - - - - - IMP
mischievous doings - - - GOBLINRY, MALEFIC, PRANK
mischievous spirit - IMP, PIXIE, ELF
mischievous trick - - PRANK, CANTRIP
misconduct mark - - - - - DEMERIT
miscreant - - - - - - - - - VILLAIN
misdemeanor - - - - - - - - - SIN
misdeed - - - - - - - - CRIME, SIN
misdirect - - - - - - - - MISLEAD
miser - - - - - NIGGARD, HOARDER
miserable - - - - - - - - WRETCHED
miserly - - STINGY, PAIN, PENURIOUS
miserly (was) - - - - - - SCRIMPED
misery - - - - - - - - - - - WOE
misfortune - - - - ILL, EVIL, BLOW, DISASTER, WOE
misgiving - - - - - - - FEAR, QUALM
mishap - - - - - - - - - ACCIDENT
misjudge - - - - - - - - - - ERR
mislaid - - - - - - - - - - LOST
mislead - - - MISDIRECT, DELUDE, DECEIVE
misleading - - - - - - - FALLACIOUS
misleading argument - - - - FALLACY
misplace - - - - - - - - - - LOSE
misrepresent - - - - - - - - BELIE
miss - OMIT, FAIL, LOSE, OVERLOOK, SKIP, ERR
missel thrush - - - - - - - SHRIKE
missile - - DART, BULLET, BRICKBAT, ARROW, BOLAS, SPEAR, SHAFT
missile which returns to thrower - - - BOOMERANG
missing - - - - - - - - - - LOST

mission - - - ERRAND, PURPOSE, DELEGATION
missive - - - - - - - LETTER, EPISTLE
Missouri river - - - - - - - - OSAGE
misspend - - - - - - - - SQUANDER
misstep - - - - - - - - - - - TRIP
mist - - - - - - FOG, HAZE, BEDIM
mister (Sp.) - - - - - - - - - SENOR
mistake - - ERROR, BONER, BLUNDER
mistake (colloq.) - - - - - - - BONER
mistaken - - - - - ERRONEOUS, OFF
mistakes in published work - ERRATO, ERRATA
mistreat - - - - - - - - - - ABUSE
mistrust - - - - - - - - - - DOUBT
misty - - - - NEBULOUS, VAPOROUS
misunderstanding - - - - IMBROGLIO
misuse - - - - - - - - - - - ABUSE
mite - - - - - TICK, ACARID, ACARUS
mite or tick - - - - - - - - ACARUS
mitigate - - RELAX, ASSUAGE, ALLAY, TEMPER, EXTENUATE, SOFTEN, RELIEVE, ALLEVIATE, PALLIATE
mitt - - - - - - - - - - - - - GLOVE
mix - - - - - STIR, BLEND, MINGLE
mix together - - - - - COMMINGLE
mix up - - - - - - - MELEE, ADDLE
mix when wet - - - - - - - - - PUG
mix with hands - - - - - - - KNEAD
mixed dish - - - - - - - - - - SALAD
mixed drink - - - - - - - - - - NOG
mixed type - - - - - - - - - - - PI
mixture - - OLIO, MELANGE, HASH, BLEND
mixture of pork bits and meal - SCRAPPLE
mixture of spirits and water - - GROG, TODDY
mo (suffix) - - - - - - - - - BOOK
moa - - - - - - - - - - - PEACOCK
Moab mountain - - - - - - - - NEBO
moan - - COMPLAIN, WAIL, LAMENT
moaning sound - - - - - - - GROAN
moat - - - - - DITCH, FOSSE, FOSS
mob - - RABBLE, POPULACE, CROWD
moccasin - - - - - - PAC, LARRIGAN
mock - TAUNT, DERIDE, SNEER, GIBE, MOW, LEER, FLEER, IMITATE, FLOUT, SCORN
mock attack - - - - - - - - FEINT
mock orange - - - - - - - SYRINGA
mockery - - - FARCE, GAME, CRONY
mode - - FASHION, MANNER, STYLE
mode of action - - PLAN, OPERATION
mode of expression - - - - - STYLE
mode of government - - - - - REGIME
mode of procedure - - - - - METHOD
mode of standing - - - - - STANCE
model - NORM, TYPE, PATTERN, SHAPE, PARAGON, PARADIGM, DESIGN
model of perfection - - - - PARAGON, STANDARD
models to follow (arch.) - ENSAMPLES
moderate - - BATE, ABATE, RESTRAIN, COOL, SOME, TEMPERATE, DIMINISH, SEASON, MITIGATE
moderate amount - - - - - - - SOME
moderately good - - - - - - - FAIR
moderately slow and flowing (musical) ANDANTE
moderating - - - - - - - REMISSIVE
moderation - - - - - - - TEMPERANCE
modern - - - - - - - NEW, RECENT
modern circus - - - - - HIPPODROME
modern detecting device - - - - RADAR
modest - RETIRING, DEMURE, DECENT, PRIM, CHASTE

M

modest person - - - - - - - PRUDE
modesty - - - - - - - - DECENCY
modicum - - - - - - - TINCTURE
modified leaf - - - - - - - BRACT
modify - - - - - - - - - - ALTER
modish - - - - - - - - - CHIC
mogul - - - - - - - - - AUTOCRAT
Mohammedan - ISLAM (See also Moslem)
Mohammedan adopted son - - - - ALI
Mohammedan Ali's son - - - - AHMED
Mohammedan ascetic - - - - - FAKIR
Mohammedan call to prayer - MUEZZIN
Mohammedan caravansary - - - IMARET
Mohammedan chieftain - - - - EMIR
Mohammedan cleric - - IMAM, IMAN
Mohammedan daughter - - - - FATIMA
Mohammedan decree - - - - - IRADE
Mohammedan descendant - - - - EMIR
Mohammedan festival - - - - BAIRAM
Mohammedan Filipino - - - - - MORO
Mohammedan god - - - - - - ALLAH
Mohammedan judge - - CADI, MOLLAH
Mohammedan leader - - - - AGA, ATA
Mohammedan magistrate - - - - KADI
Mohammedan month - SAFAR, RAMADAN
Mohammedan name - - - - - - - ALI
Mohammedan nature spirit - - - GENIE
Mohammedan noble - - AMIR, AMEER
Mohammedan nymph - - - - - HOURI
Mohammedan prayer - - - - - SALAT
Mohammedan prayer call - - - - AZAN
Mohammedan priest - - - - - IMAM
Mohammedan priests (body of) - ULEMA
Mohammedan prince - AMIR, AMEER, AMEE, EMEER, EMIR, SULTAN
Mohammedan princess - - - - - EMIR
Mohammedan religion - - - - ISLAM
Mohammedan religious devotee - DERVISH
Mohammedan religious teacher - ALIM
Mohammedan ruler - - - - AGA, CALIF
Mohammedan ruler's decree - - - IRADE
Mohammedan saint - - - - - - - PIR
Mohammedan saint's tomb - - - - PIR
Mohammedan scholars - - - - ULEMA
Mohammedan scriptures - - - - KORAN
Mohammedan state head - - - - KALIF
Mohammedan Supreme Being - ALLAH
Mohammedan title - - - - - ALI, AGA
Mohammedan title of successors - CALIF
Mohammedan tomb - - - - - - - PIR
Mohammedan tribe - - - - - ARAIN
Mohammedan uncle - - - - - ABBAS
Mohammed's son - - - - - - - ALI
Mohammed's son-in-law - - - - - ALI
Mohawk chief - - - - - - - BRANT
moil - - - - - TOIL, SOIL, DRUDGE, DRUDGERY
moist - DAMP, HUMID, WET, DEWY, DANK
moisten - - - - - DAMPEN, BEDEW
moisten in a liquid - - - - - - SOP
moisture - - - - - - - - - - DEW
molar - TOOTH, GRINDING, CRUSHING
molar tooth - - - - - - - GRINDER
molasses - - - - - - - - - TREACLE
mould - - - MATRIX, SHAPE, FORM, FASHION, DIE, MUST
moulded mass of bread - - - - - LOAF
moulding - OGEE, OVOLO, FASHIONING, LISTEL
molding (large convex) - TORUS, TORI (pl.)
mole - - - - - - - - - - - PIER
moleskin colour - - - - - - - TAUPE
molest - - DISTURB, TEASE, ANNOY, TROUBLE
mollify - - SLEEK, ALLAY, SMOOTH, CONCILIATE
mollusk - - SNAIL, CLAM, ABALONE, MUSSEL, SHELLFISH, SCALLOP
mollusk shell - - - - - - - ABALONE
molt - - - - - - - - - - - - SHED
molten glass - - - - - - - - METAL
molten lava - - - - - - - - - - AA
molten rock - - - - - - - - - LAVA
moment - - - - INSTANT, TRICE, JIFF
momentary - - - - - - EPHEMERAL
momentary cessation - - - - - PAUSE
momentous - - WEIGHTY, IMPORTANT
momentum - - - - - - - - IMPETUS
monarch - - KING, EMPEROR, RULER, SOVEREIGN
monarch's son - - - - - - - PRINCE
monastery - - - - - - - - - ABBEY
monastery room - - - - - - - - CELL
monastic house - - - - - - - PRIORY
monastic office - - - - - - - - PRIOR
monetary - - - - - - - - FINANCIAL
monetary penalty - - - - - - - FINE
monetary unit - - - - - - - DOLLAR
money - - - - COIN, CASH, COINAGE, SPECIE
money on account - - - - - PAYMENT
money on account in Afghanistan - PAISA
money box - - - - - - - - - - TILL
money drawer - - - - - - - - - TILL
money due but not paid - - ARREARS
money (hard) - - - - - - - - SPECIE
money hoarder - - - - - - - - MISER
money made of silver wire - - - - LARI
money market - - - - - - - BOURSE
money matters - - - - - ECONOMIC
money owed - - - - - - - - - DEBT
money paid - - - - - - - - - - SCOT
money placed in bank - - - - DEPOSIT
money (slang) - - - - - - MOSS, TIN
money (Sp.) - - - - - - - - DINERO
Mongolian - - - - - - - - - - TATAR
Mongolian desert region - - - - GOBI
Mongolian province - - - - - CHAHAR
Mongolian tribesman - TARTAR, TATAR
mongoose - - - - - - - URVA, LEMUR
mongrel - - - - - CUR, MUT, MUTT
monitor - - - - REMINDER, MENTOR
monk - - - - - - - - - FRIAR, FRA
monk's hood - COWL, ACONITE, ATIS
monk's title - - - - - - - - - - FRA
monkey - STENTOR, TAMARIN, MONO, APE, TITI
monkey (kind) - SAI, MONO, MARMOSET
monkey-like animals - - - - LEMURS, AYEAYES
monocle - - - - - - - - EYEGLASS
monologue - - - - - - SOLILOQUY
monopoly - - - - - - - - - TRUST
monotonous - - DREARY, HUMDRUM
monotony - - - - - - - - SAMENESS
monster - - OGRE, GIANT, CENTAUR, SPHINX
monster (medieval) - - TARATA, TERAS
monstrosity - - - - - - - - - FREAK
monstrous - - - - - - - - OGRISH
Montana city - - - - HELENA, BUTTE
month preceding the present - ULTIMO
monument of one stone - - MONOLITH
moo - - - - - - - - - - - - - LOW
mood - - - - - - - TUNE, HUMOUR
moodily silent - - - - - - - SULKS
moody - - - - - MOROSE, PEEVISH
moon - LUNA, LUNAR, DIANA, LUNE
moon in her first quarter - CRESCENT
moon valley - - - - - - - - - RILLE

moon's age at beginning of year - EPACT
moon's crescent point - CUSP, HORN
moonwort - - - - - - - - LUNARY
moor - ANCHOR, FASTEN, FEN, HEATH
mooring buoy - - - - - - DOLPHIN
Moorish drum - - - - - - - TABOR
Moorish tabor - - - - - - - ATABAL
moose - - - - - - - - - - ELK
moot - - - - - - - - - - DEBATE
mop - - - - - - SWAP, SWAB, WIPE
mope - - - - - - - - SULK, PINE
moral - ETHICAL, TEACHING, MAXIM
moral excellences - - - - - VIRTUES
moral offense - - - - - - - - EVIL
moral science - - - - - - - ETHICS
moral teachings - - - - - PRECEPTS
morally healthy - - - - - - CLEAN
morals - - - - - - - - - - ETHICS
morass - BOG, SWAMP, MARSH, FEN
moray - - - - - - - - - - - EEL
mordant - - - - - - - - SARCASTIC
more - - - - - - EXTRA, GREATER
more distant - - - - - - - FARTHER
more evil - - - - - - - - - WORSE
more (musical) - - - - - - - - PIU
more remote - - - - - - - ULTIMATE
more than - - - - - - - - - OVER
more than enough - - - - - - TOO
more than one - - - - - - - PLURAL
more than sufficiently - - - - - TOO
moreover - - - - - - - - - BESIDES
morindin dye - - - - - - - - - AL
morn - - - - - - - - - FORENOON
morning - - - - - MORN, FORENOON
morning (abbr.) - - - - - - - - A.M.
morning (of the) - - - - - - - MATIN
morning (poet.) - - - - - - - MORN
morning prayer and song - - - - MATIN
morning (pert. to) - - - - - - MATINAL
morning song (poet.) - - - - - MATIN
morning star - - - - DAYSTAR, VENUS
Moro chief - - - - - - - - - DATO
Moro high priest - - - - - - - SARIP
Moro people in Philippines - - LANAO
Morocco cape - - - - - - - - - NUN
Morocco coin - - - - - - OKIA, RIAL
Morocco native - - - - - - - - MOOR
Morocco seaport - - - - - - - RABAT
Morocco tree - - - - - - - SANDARAC
morose - - GLOOMY, GLUM, SULLEN, MOODY, SOUR
morsel - - BITE, BUT, ORT, TIDBIT, PIECE, CRUMB
morsel of food - - - - CRUMB, BITE
mortal - - - - - - - FATAL, HUMAN
mortal remains - - - - - - - BONES
mortality - - - - - - - - HUMANITY
mortar - - - - - - CEMENT, PETARD
mortar tray - - - - - - - - - HOD
mortification - - - - - - - CHAGRIN
mortification of tissue - - GANGRENE
mortify - - - ABASH, SPITE, SHAME, HUMILIATE
mortise (part of) - - - - - - TENON
Moscow's citadel - - - - - - KREMLIN
Moses' brother - - - - - - - AARON
Moses' sister - - - - - - - - MIRIAM
Moslem - - (See also Mohammedan)
Moslem ascetic - - - - - - - FAKIR
Moslem deity - - - - - - - - ALLAH
Moslem enemy of Crusaders - SARACEN
Moslem flute - - - - - - - - - NEI
Moslem gold coin - - - - - - DINAR
Moslem javelin - - - - JEREED, JERID
Moselm judge - - - - - CADI, IMAM
Moslem name - - - - - - - - - ALI
Moslem noble - - - - - - - AMEER
Moslem official - - - - - - - AGA
Moslem priests - - - - IMAM, ULEMA
Moslem purist - - - - - - - WAHABI
Moslem religion - - - - - - - ISLAM
Moslem ruler - - - - - - - - NAWAB
Moslem saint - - - - - - - SANTON
Moslem scholars - - - - - - - ULEMA
Moslem Supreme Being - - - - ALLAH
Moslem woman's garment - - - - IZAR
mosque tower - - - - - - - MINARET
moss - - - - - - - - RAG, LICHEN
moss leaves - - - - - - - - - ALA
mosslike herb - - - - - STONECROP
most - - - - - MAXIMUM, GREATEST
most unimportant - - - - - - LEAST
motet - - - - - - - - - - ANTHEM
moth (kind) - REGAL, LAPPET, EGGER, TINEA
moth (large family of) - - - - ARCTIID
mother - - - - - - MATRON, MAMA
mother of Castor and Pollux - - LEDA
mother of Ishmael - - - - - - HAGAR
mother (Latin) - - - - - - - - MATER
mother of mankind - - - - - - - EVE
mother of pearl - - - - - - NACRE
mother (Phil. Isl.) - - - - - - - INA
mother (Tagalog) - - - - - - - INA
mother of the Titans - - - - - - GE
motherhood - - - - - - - MATERNITY
motherless calf (var.) - - - - - DOGY
motherly - - - PARENTAL, MATERNAL
motif - - - - - - - - - - - THEME
motion - - - GESTURE, MOVEMENT
motion of horse rearing - - - - PESADE
motion picture - - - - - - - - FILM
motion of sea - - - - - TIDAL, TIDE
motionless - - - - STILL, STAGNANT
motivating - - - - - - - - CAUSAL
motive - REASON, CAUSE, INCENTIVE
motor - - - - - - ENGINE, MACHINE
motor car (colloq.) - - - - - - AUTO
motor coach - - - - - - - - - BUS
motor part - - - - - - - - - CAM
motor truck - - - - - - - - LORRY
motorless plane - - - GLIDER, AVIETTE
mottle - - - - - - - - - - BLOTCH
mottled - - - - - - - - PINTO, PIED
mottled appearance in mahagony - ROES
motto - SAW, MAXIM, ADAGE, SLOGAN
mound - - HILL, KNOLL, DHER, TEE, DUNE
mound of sand - - - - - - - - DUNE
mount - RISE, ASCEND, SET, ARISE, CLIMB
mount of Cascade Range - - RAINIER
Mount Etna river - - - - - - - ACIS
Mount Everest site - - - - - - NEPAL
mount on which Noah landed - ARARAT
mountain - - - - ALP, BARROW, BERG
mountain aborigines - - - - - ATIS
mountain ash - - - - - - - ROWAN
mountain chain - - - - RANGE, SIERRA
mountain in Colorado - - - - - OWEN
mountain (comb. form) - - - - - ORO
mountain crest - - - - - - - ARETE
mountain defile - - - - - - - PASS
mountain gap - - - - - - - - - COL
mountain goat - - - - - - - - IBEX
mountain gorge - - - - - - - RAVINE
mountain irregular ridge - - - SIERRA
mountain lake - - - - - - - - TARN
mountain mint - - - - - - - - BASIL
mountain nymph - - - OREAD, DRYAD
mountain pass - - - - - GHAT, COL
mountain passage - - - - TUNNEL, COL

M

mountain pasture land - - - - ALP
mountain pool - - - - - - - TARN
mountain range - - RIDGE, SIERRA, ANDES, ALPS, URAL
mountain ridge - - - RANGE, ARETE, SIERRA
mountain ridge (flat top) - - - LOMA
mountain (Scot.) - - - - - - - BEN
mountain spinach - - - - - ORACH
mountain spur - - - - - - - ARETE
mountain, Thessaly - - - - - OSSA
mountain top - - - - - - - PEAK
mountain near Troy - - - - - IDA
mounted sentinel - - - - VEDETTE
mounting device - - - - - LADDER
mourn - - - - - SORROW, GRIEVE
mournful - - - - - PLAINTIVE, SAD, SORROWFUL, FUNEREAL, DISMAL
mournful cry - - - - - - - WAIL
mournful song - - - - - - - DIRGE
mourning - - - DOLOR, REGRETTING, SORROW
mourning hymn - - - - - - DIRGE
mourning poem - - - - - - ELEGY
mourning symbol - - - - - CREPE
mouselike mammal - - - - - SHREW
mouth - - - - - - - - - - OS
mouth (comb. form) - - - - - ORO
mouth (of the) - - - - - - - ORAL
mouth organ - - - HARMONICA, LIP, TONGUE
mouth of river - - - - - - DELTA
mouth of volcano - - - - - CRATER
mouthlike opening - - - - - STOMA
mouthpiece of bagpipe - - - - MUSE
movable - - - - - - PORTABLE
movable barrier - - - - GATE, DOOR
movable frame in a loom - - - SLEY
movable part - - - - - - - ROTOR
move - - - STIR, BUDGE, AGITATE
move about furtively - SLINK, PROWL, LURK
move about noisily - - - - CLATTER
move across - - - - - - TRAVERSE
move ahead steadily - - - - FORGE
move to another place - - TRANSFER
move away - - - - - - - - MOG
move away from - - - - - - SHY
move back - - - RECEDE, RETREAT, RETIRE
move back and forth - - WAG, SAW, WAVE, WAVER
move briskly - - - - - - - STIR
move in a circle - - - - - EDDY
move clumsily - - - - - LUMBER
move at easy pace - - - - AMBLE
move forward - - - - - PROGRESS
move with difficulty - - - - WADE
move from one place to another - - - TRANSFER
move at full speed (colloq.) - - - RIP
move furtively - - - STEAL, SNEAK
move heavily - - - - - - - LUG
move helically - - - - - - SPIRAL
move indolently - - - - - - LOLL
move lazily - - - - - - - SNAIL
move lightly and quickly - - - - FLIT
move merrily - - - - - - - DANCE
move on - - - - - - ONRUSH, GO
move on wheels - - - - - - ROLL
move over surface - - - - - - SLIDE
move rapidly - HURTLE, CAREER, FLY, FLIT, DART
move in reverse - - - - - - BACK
move rhythmically - - - - - DANCE
move round and round - - - - EDDY
move in short jerky manner - - - BOB
move sideways - - - - SIDLE, SLUE
move slowly - - - - - - - LAG, INCH
move smoothly - - GLIDE, SLIDE, SAIL
move stealthily - - - SLINK, SNEAK
move suddenly - - DART, START, FLIT
move swiftly - - - - DART, CAREER
move through water - - - - - - SWIM
move to and fro - - WAG, WAVE, FLAP
move in undulations - - - - - WAVE
move upward - - - - - - - RISE
move vigorously - - - - - BESTIR
move on wheels - - - - - - - ROLL
move with beating motion - - - FLAP
move with quick steps - - - - PATTER
move with rotation - - - - - - ROLL
move with vigor - - - - - - BESTIR
moved - - - - - - - - - - HOVE
movement - - - - TREND, MOTION
movement of the feet - - - - GAIT
movement of the sea - - - - - TIDE
movement of tumultuous crowd - - - STAMPEDE
moving - - - - - ASTIR, TRANSIENT
moving company - - - - - CARAVAN
moving compassion - - - - PITEOUS
moving force - - - - - - - AGENT
moving part - - - - - - - ROTOR
moving picture - - - - - - - FILM
moving power - - - - - - - MOTOR
mow - - - - - - - - MOCK, CLIP
much - - - - - - - - - GREATLY
muck - - - - MIRE, SLIME, SLOSH
mud - - MIRE, SLIME, SLOSH, SLUDGE
mud eel - - - - - - - - - SIREN
mud volcano - - - - - - - - SALSE
muddle - - - ADDLE, MESS, CONFUSE
muddled - - - - - - - - - ASEA
muddy - - - BESPATTER, MIRE, MIRY, ROILY, ROIL, SLUDGY
muddy ground - - - - - - - - SOG
mudworm - - - - - - - - - IPO
muffin - - - - - - - - - - GEM
muffle - - - - - - - DEADEN, MUTE
muffler - - - - - - SCARF, SILENCER
mug - - - - - - - STEIN, NOGGIN
mulberry - - - - - - AL, ACH, AAL
mulberry (pl.) - - - - - - - - AAL
mulct - - BILK, AMERCE, CHEAT, FINE
mule - - - - - - - - - - - ASS
mule cry - - - - - - - - - BRAY
mule driver - - - - - - MULETEER
mull - - - - - - - - MEDITATE
multiform - - - - - - - DIVERSE
multiple - - - - - - - - - MANY
multiplication result - - - - PRODUCT
multiplied by - - - - - - - TIMES
multiply - - - - - - - INCREASE
multitude - - - - - - HOST, LEGION
mummery - - - - - - - PUPPETRY
mummy - - - - - - - - EMBALM
municipality - - - - - - - - CITY
municipality (pert. to) - - - - CIVIC
murder - - - - - - HOMICIDE, SLAY
murk - - - - - - GLOOM, DARKNESS
murky - - - - - - - - - - DARK
murky condition - - - - - - - FOG
murmur - - - - - - REPINE, MUTTER
murmur softly - PURL, COO, HUM, PURR
murre - - - - - - - - - - - AUK
muscle - - - - - - - SINEW, THEW
muscle in arm - - - BICEPS, TRICEPS
muscle band - - - - - - - TENDON
muscle of mouth - - - - - - - LIP
muscle for stretching - - - - TENSOR

muscles - - THEWS, LEVATORS, SINEWS
muscovite - - - - - - - - - RUSS
muscular - - - - TOROSE, SINEWED
muse - - MEDITATE, REVE, COGITATE, PONDER, GAZE, RUMINATE
muse of astronomy - - - - - URANIA
muse of elegance - - - - - CALLIOPE
muse of history - - - - - - - CLIO
muse of love - - - - - - - - EROS
muse of music - - - - - - EUTERPE
muse of poetry - - - - - - - ERATO
mushroom - - - - - AGARIC, MOREL
music - - - - - - - - - - MELODY
music - - - - - - (See also Musical)
music (accented) - - - - - SFORZATO
music (as it stands) - - - - - - STA
music (as it is written) - - - - - STA
music (concluding passage) - - - CODA
music (high) - - - - - - - - - ALT
music (increase in volume) - CRESCENDO
music (it is silent) - - - - - - TACET
music (melodious) - - - - - - ARIOSO
music (moderately slow) - - ANDANTE
music (slow) - LENTO, ADAGIO, LARGO, RITARDO
music (smooth and connected) - LEGATO
music (soft) - - - - - - - - PIANO
music (stately) - - - - - - - LARGO
musical - - - - - - (See also Music)
musical - MELIC, LYRIC, HARMONIOUS, MELODIOUS, LYRICAL
musical air - - TUNE, SONG, MELODY
musical aria - - - - - - - - SOLO
musical bells - - - - CHIMES, CHIME
musical character - REST, CLEF, SHARP, NOTE
musical close - - - CADENCE, CODA
musical comedy - - - - - - - REVUE
musical composer - - - - - - ELGAR
musical composition - OPERA, ORATORIO, RONDO, SONG, SERENADE, NOCTURNE, CANTATA, SONATA, BALLADE, OPUS, TRIO, GLEE, SEXTET, SERENATA, ARIOSO
musical direction - - - - - - TACET
musical direction (abbr.) - - RIT, RALL
musical direction for silence - - TACET
musical drama - - - CANTATA, OPERA
musical drama (pert. to) - - OPERATIC
musical and emotional - - - - LYRICAL
musical ending - - - - - - - CODA
musical exercise - - - - - - ETUDE
musical (fast) - - - - PRESTISSIMO
musical group - - - - - - - BAND
musical half step - - - - SEMITONE
musical instrument - - REBEC, GORA, OBOE, SAXHORN, TUBA, BUGLE, SPINET, CORNET, OCARINA, MARIMBA, CONCERTINA, GUITAR, CELLO, LYRE, VIOL, UKE, FIFE, LUTE, REED
musical instrument part - - - - REED
musical interval - - - REST, OCTAVE, TRITONE, SECOND
musical key - - - - - - - - MINOR
musical line - - - - - - - - - TIE
musical measure (closing) - - - CODA
musical movement (slow) - - - LARGO
musical note - - - - - - - - SPA
musical organization - - - - - BAND
musical passage - - CODE, RECITATIVE
musical performance - CONCERT, RECITAL
musical pipe - - - - - - - - REED
musical pitch - - - - - - - - TONE
musical reed - - - - - - - - PIPE
musical salute - - - - - SERENADE
musical shake - - - TRILL, TREMOLO
musical show - - - - - - - - REVUE
musical sound - - TONE, TONAL, NOTE
musical sound (pert. to) - - - TONAL
musical stringed instrument - - HARP
musical study - - - - - - - ETUDE
musical syllable - DO, RE, MI, FA, SO, LA, TI
musical term - - - - - - - LARGO
musical timbre - - - - - - - TONE
musical tone - - - - - - - CHORD
musical triplet - - - - - - - TERCET
musical up beat - - - - - - ARSIS
musical waver - - - - - - TREMOLO
musical work - - - - - - - - OPUS
musical work (abbr.) - - - - - - OP.
musician - - - - - PIANIST, BUGLER
musician's baton - - - - - - WAND
musing - - - - - - - - - - REVERIE
musket - - - - - FUSIL, FLINTLOCK
musketeer - - - - - - - - - ARAMIS
muskmelon - - ATIMON, CANTALOUPE
muslin - - - - - - - - - TARLATAN
muss - - - - - - RUMPLE, CRUMPLE
mustang - - - - - - - - - BRONCO
mustard - - - - - - - - - SINAPIS
mustard plant - - - - CRESS, RADISH
muster - - - - ASSEMBLE, GATHER
musty - - - - - - - - - - MOLDY
mutate - - - - - - - - - - ALTER
mutation - - - - - - - - CHANGE
mute - - - DUMB, MUFFLE, SILENT, DEADEN, SPEECHLESS
mute consonant - - - - - - - LENE
muted - - - - - - - - - - SILENT
mutilate - - - - - - - - - MANGLE
mutiny - - - - - - - - - - REVOLT
mutter - - - - MURMUR, GRUMBLE
mutual - - - - - - - - RECIPROCAL
mutual discourse - - - - - COLLOQUY
mutual relations - - - - - CORRELATE
mutually planned - - - - - CONCERTED
muzzle - - - - - - - - - - SNOUT
my lady - - - - - MADAME, MADAM
mysterious - SPHINXINE, OCCULT, RUNIC
mysterious word in the Psalms - SELAH
mystery - - SECRET, ENIGMA, CABALA
mystic - - - - - - - - - - EPOPTIC
mystic ejaculation - - - - - - - OM
myth - - - - LEGEND, SAGA, FABLE
mythical - - - - - - - - IMAGINARY
mythical being - - - - - - - GIANT
mythical bird - - - - - - - RO, ROC
mythical character - - - - - PANDORA
mythical drink of the gods - - NECTAR
mythical ferryman - - - - - CHARON
mythical Greek mother - - - - - NIOBE
mythical hero - - - - - - - LEANDER
mythical Hindu deity - - - - - RAMA
mythical Hindu saga - - - - DHRAMA
mythical hunter - - - - - - - ORION
mythical king - - - - - ATLI, MIDAS
mythical king of Britain - LEAR, BRAN, LUD
mythical king of Crete - - - - MINOS
mythical king of Thebes - - - CREON
mythical kingdom - - - - - - - OZ
mythical lover - - - - - - - - HERO
mythical maiden - - - - - IO, DANAE
mythical monster - - - OGRE, GIANT, DRAGON
mythical mountain - - - - - - OSSA
mythical ocean island - - - - AVALON
mythical swimmer - - - - - LEANDER

mythical Titan - - - - - - - ATLAS
mythical world - - - - - - - LIMBO
mythological character - - - - YMIR
mythological horse - - - - PEGASUS
mythological hunter - - - - - ORION
mythological Norse giant - - - YMIR

N

nab - - CATCH, SEIZE, SNATCH, TRAP
nacre - - - - - - - - - - - PEARL
nag - TEASE, HORSE, SCOLD, PESTER, HENPECK
Naga Hills tribe in India - - - - AO
nahoor sheep - - - - - - - - SNA
naif - - - - - - - - - - ARTLESS
nail - BRAD, HOB, STUD, SPIKE, SPAD, FASTEN, SECURE, TACK, CLINCH
nail driven obliquely - - - - - TOED
nail marker - - - - - - - - SPAD
nail to survey - - - - - - - - SPAD
nail weight - - - - - - - - - KEG
naive - - - - ARTLESS, GUILELESS, INGENUOUS
naked - - - - - - - - NUDE, BARE
name - TERM, MENTION, ENTITLE, CALL, TILE, DUB
name claimed by Naomi - - - - MARA
name (Fr.) - - - - - - - - - NOM
name (Latin) - - - - - - - NOMEN
name for office - - - - - - NOMINATE
name of person, place or thing - NOUN
namelessness - - - - - ANONYMITY
namesake - - - - - - - HOMONYM
nana - - - - - - - - - - - NURSE
nap - - - PILE, SIESTA, DOZE, SLEEP, SLUMBER
nape - - - - - - SCRUFF, NUCHA
nape of neck (pert. to) - - - NUCHAL
napkin - - - SERVIETTE, BIB, DOILY
Naples (pert. to) - - - - NEAPOLITAN
Napoleonic marshall - - - - - - NEY
Napoleon's exile - - - - - - - ELBA
nappy - - - - - - - - - - SHAGGY
narcotic - - - OPIATE, DOPE, OPIUM
narcotic drug - - - - - - - HEMP
narcotic shrub - - - - - - - - KAT
narine - - - - - - - - - - NASAL
narrate - - - RELATE, TELL, RECITE
narration - - - - - - - - RECITAL
narrative - - - - - - STORY, RECITAL
narrative poem - - - - EPIC, LAY, EPOS
narrator - RELATER, RELATOR, RECITER
narrow - - - - STRAIT, CONTRACT
narrow (comb. form) - - - - - STEN
narrow aperture - - - - - - - SLOT
narrow arm of sea - - - FIRTH, FRITH
narrow bar - - - - - - - - - STRIPE
narrow board - - - - - - LATH, SLAT
narrow body of water - - - - STRAIT
narrow channel - - - - - - - STRAIT
narrow division - - - - - - - STRIP
narrow fabric - - - - - - BRAID, TAPE
narrow fillet (arch.) - - ORLE, LISTLE
narrow gash - - - - - - - - - SLIT
narrow glass vessel - - - - - - VIAL
narrow inlet - - - - - - - - - RIA
narrow minded - - - - - - BIGOTED
narrow opening - - RIMA, SLIT, SLOT
narrow pass - - - - - - - - ABRA
narrow passage - GUT, STRAIT, GORGE, LANE, ALLEY
narrow piece - - - - - - - - STRIP
narrow streak - - - - - - - - LINE
narrow strip - - - - RIBBON, STRAP
narrow strip of wood - SLAT, BATTEN, LATH
narrow strip of woven cloth - - TAPE
narrow track - - - - - - - - - LANE
narrow trimming - - - - - - EDGING
narrow waterway - - - - - INLET, RIA
narrow way - - - - - - - - - LANE
narrow wooded valley - - - - - DINGLE
nasal - - - - - - RHINAL, NARINE
nasal disturbance - - - - - - SNEEZE
nasal noise - - - - - SNORT, WHINE
nasal tone - - - - - - - - - TWANG
natal - - - - - - - - - - NATIVE
nation - - EMPIRE, COUNTRY, PEOPLE, REALM
national - - - - - PATRIOTIC, PUBLIC
national emblem - - - - - - - EAGLE
national guard - - - - - - - MILITIA
national hymn - - - - - - - ANTHEM
national park - - - - - - - - ESTES
national systems of rules - - - LAWS
native - - - - NATAL, SON, INBORN, INDIGENOUS, ABORIGINE
native American race - - - - AMERIND
native of Biblical country - - EDOMITE
native borax - - - - - - - - TINCAL
native of Burma - - - - - - - - VU
native carbonate of soda - - - NATRON
native chloride and bromide of silver EMBOLITE
native of Denmark - - - - - - DANE
native garment - - - - - - - SARONG
native Indian soldier - - - - - SEPOY
native of Ireland - - - - - - - CELT
native of Latvia - - - - - - - - LETT
native metal - - - - - - - - - ORE
native of Mindanao - - - - - - ATA
native (poet.) - - - - - - - - NATAL
natty - DAPPER, NEAT, SPRUCE, DANDY
natural - NORMAL, INBORN, INNATE, LIFELIKE, BORN
natural ability - - - - - - APTITUDE
natural abode - - - - - - - HABITAT
natural abomination - - - - - PLAGUE
natural capacity - - - - - - - TALENT
natural depression - - - - - - VALLEY
natural drift of events - - - - - TIDES
natural elevation - - - - - - - HILL
natural gas constituent - - - - ETHANE
natural gift - - - - - TALENT, DOWER
natural habitat (zool.) - - - - PATRIA
natural height - - - - - - - STATURE
natural power - - - - - - - - - OD
natural quality - - - - - - - - GIFT
natural sweet - - - - - - - - HONEY
naturalness - - - - - - - - - EASE
nature - - - - CREATION, ESSENCE, CHARACTER, TYPE, SORT
nature of bristles - - - - - - - SETAL
nature of wood - - - - - - LIGNEOUS
naught - - - ZERO, NOTHING, CIPHER
nautical - MARINE, NAVAL, MARITIME
nautical cask - - - - - - - - BARECA
nautical command - - - - - - AVAST
nautical fiy - - - - - - - - - BURGEE
nautical hailing call - - - - - AHOY
nautical hazard - - - - - - - - FOG
nautical instrument - - - - - SEXTANT
nautical map - - - - - - - - CHART
nautical mile - - - - - - - - KNOT
nautical pennant - - - - - - - FLAG
nautical rope - - - HAWSER, NETTLE
nautical term - - - - - APORT, ALEE
nautical term to cease - - - - AVAST
nautical term in raising - - - TRICE

N

Navajo Indian hut - - - - - - HOGAN
naval - MARINE, NAUTICAL, MARITIME
naval landing craft - - - - - L.S.T.
naval officer - - - - - - - - YEOMAN
naval officer (var.) - - - - - BOSUN
naval petty officer - - - - - YEOMAN
naval protective device - - PARAVANE
naval rig (kind) - - - - - - LATEEN
naval vessel flag - - - - - - PENNANT
naval weapon - - - - - - - TORPEDO
nave - - - - - - - - - - - - HUB
navigable part of a stream - CHANNEL
navigate - - - - - - - - - - SAIL
navigate the air - - - - FLY, AVIATE
navigator - - - - - - - - MARINER
near - AT, CLOSE, NIGH, INTIMATE, BY
near the back - - - - - - - DORSAL
near by - - - - - - - - - BESIDE
near the center - - - - - - - INNER
near the cheek - - - - - - - MALAR
near the chin - - - - - - - MENTAL
near the ear - - - - - - - - OTIC
near (poet.) - - - - - - - - ANEAR
near (prefix) - - - - - - - - - BE
near (Scot.) - - - - - - - - - NAR
near the stern - - - - - - - - AFT
near to - - - - - - - - - - - AT
nearby - - - - - - - - - - - - AT
nearer (the) - - - - - - - - THIS
nearer (dial.) - - - - - - - - NAR
nearest - - - - - - - - - - NEXT
nearest maturity - - - - - - RIPEST
nearest star - - - - - - - - SUN
nearly - - - - - - - - - ALMOST
nearly corresponding - - - - - SIMILAR
nearsighted person - - - - - MYOPE
neat - - TIDY, TRIM, TRIG, ORDERLY, ADROIT, PRIM, NATTY, SPRUCE, PRECISE
neb - - - - - - - - - - - - BEAK
Nebraska city - - - - - ORD, OMAHA
Nebraska county - - - - - - - OTOE
nebris - - - - - - - - - FAWNSKIN
nebular - - - - - - - - - CLOUDY
nebulous - - - - - - - - - - MISTY
necessary - - ESSENTIAL, REQUISITE
necessary to life - - - - - - - VITAL
necessitate - - - - - - - - - NEED
necessity - - - - - - - WANT, NEED
neck artery - - - - - - - CAROTID
neck chain - - - - - - - - TORQUE
neck circlet - - - - - - - COLLAR
neck covering - - - - - - - - MANE
neck ornament - - - - - - GORGET
neck part - - - - - - - - - NAPE
neck scarf - - - - - - - - ASCOT
neckband - - - - - - COLLAR, SCARF
neckpiece - BOA, BOAS, STOLE, COLLAR
necktie - - - CRAVAT, ASCOT, SCARF
necromancy - - - MAGIC, SORCERY, CONJURATION
need - - - - LACK, REQUIRE, WANT, NECESSITATE, POVERTY, DEMAND
need (urgent) - - - - - - EXIGENCY
needful - - - - - - - - ESSENTIAL
needing outside support - - DEPENDENT
needle shaped - - ACEROSE, ACERATE
needlefish - - - - - - - - - - GAR
needless - - - - - - - - - USELESS
needlework - - - - - - - - - SEWING
needy - - - - - - POOR, INDIGENT
negate - DENY, NULLIFY, CONTRADICT
negation - - - - NOT, NO, DENIAL, BLANKNESS
negative - - - - - - NAY, NOT, FILM
negative charged particle - - ANION
negative ion - - - - - - - - - ANION
negative prefix - - NON, IR, UN, DIS
negative vote - - - - - - - - - NAY
neglect - - - - - OMIT, DISREGARD
neglected - - - UNTENDED, UNDONE, FORGOT, DEFAULTED
neglectful - - - REMISS, CARELESS
negligent - - REMISS, LAX, CARELESS
negotiable - - - - - - - - - TREATY
negotiable instrument - - - - - NOTE
negotiate - - - - - TREAT, TRANSACT
Negrito - - - - - - - - - - - - ITA
Negro of Africa - - - - - - - - KREPI
Negro of Cameroons - - - - - - ABO
Negro of French West Africa - - HABE
Negro of Niger Delta - - - - - - IBO
Negro of Nigeria - ARO, EDO, VAI, IBO
neigh - - - - - - - - - - WHINNY
neighbouring - - - - - - - - VICINAL
neighbourly gathering - - - - - - BEE
neophyte - - - - - - - - BEGINNER
nephew (pert. to) - - - - - NEPOTAL
Neptune's spear - - - - - - TRIDENT
nerve - - - - - - - - - - - PLUCK
nerve cell framework - - - - - STROMA
nerve center - - - - - - - GANGLION
nerve (comb. form) - - NEUR, NEURO
nerve of leaf - - - - - - - - - VEIN
nerve network (sg.) - - RETE, ARETE, PLEXUS
nerve network (pl.) - - - - - - RETIA
nerve substance - - - - - - - ALBA
nervous - - - - - - - - - - UNEASY
nervous affliction - - - - TARANTISM
nervous disorder - - - - CHOREA, TIC
nervous excitability - - - - - NERVES
nervous system (pert. to) - - NEURAL
nervous twitching - - - - - - - TIC
nescient - - - - - - - - - IGNORANT
ness - - - - - - - - - - - - CAPE
nest - DEN, AERIE, RETREAT, HAUNT, NIDE
nest on a crag - - - - - - - AERIE
nestle - - - - - - CUDDLE, SNUGGLE
nestling - - - BIRD, BIRDLING, EYAS
net - - CLEAR, SEINE, MESH, GAIN, YIELD, SNARE, TRAP
net (kind of) - - - - - - - DRAGNET
nether - - - - - - - LOWER, UNDER
Netherlands measure - - - - - ROEDE
Netherlands seaport - - - ROTTERDAM
netlike - - - - - - - - - RETICULAR
nettle - - PROVOKE, IRRITATE, ANNOY
nettle rash - - - - - - - - - UREDO
network - - MESH, WEB, RETE, PLEXUS
network of thin strips - - - - LATTICE
network of threads - - - - - - LACE
neuter verbal noun - - - - - GERUND
neutral equilibrium - - - - - ASTATIC
neutral tint - - - - - - - - - GRAY
Nevada city - - - - - - RENO, ELKO
Nevada lake - - - - - - - - TAHOE
Nevada river - - - - - - - - RAESE
never a (dial.) - - - - - - - - NARY
never (contr.) - - - - - - - - - NEER
never ending - - - - - - PERENNIAL
nevertheless - - - - - YET, HOWBEIT
new - RECENT, NEOTERIC, FRESH, LATE, UNUSED, MODERN, UNTRIED
New Caledonia capital - - - - - NUMEA
new (comb. form) - - - - - - - NEO
New England river - MERRIMACK, SOCO
new expression - - - - - NEOLOGISM
New Guinea mission - - - - - - GONA

N

New Guinea city - - - - - - - LAE
New Guinea seaport - - - - - - LAE
New Guinea tribesman - - - KARON
New Hampshire city - - - - - KEENE
New Hampshire county - - - - COOS
New Hampshire lake - - - SUNAPEE
New Hampshire river - - - SACO, SOCO
New Haven university - - - - YALE
new member - - - - - - - ENTRANT
New Mexico county - - - - - OTERO
New Mexico dollar - - - - - - SIA
New Mexican Indian - - - SIA, TAOS
New Mexican river - - - - - GILA
New Mexican state flower - - YUCCA
new (prefix) - - - - - - - NEO, NEA
new star - - - - - - - - - NOVA
new start - - - - - - - - REDEAL
New Testament part - - - - GOSPEL
new wine - - - - - - - - - MUST
New World republic - - - - - HAITI
New York canal - - - - - - - ERIE
New York capital - - - - - ALBANY
New York Indian tribe - - - ONEIDA, ONONDAGA
New York island - - - - - - ELLIS
New York river - - MOHAWK, NIAGARA
New York State city - - UTICA, OLEAN, ELMIRA, TROY
New York State county - - YATES, TIOGA
New York State flower - - - - ROSE
New York State lake - SENECA, ONEIDA
New York State village - - - - AVON
New York town - - - OLAN, OSSINING
New Zealand aborigine - - - MAORI
New Zealand bird - - MOREPORK, KEA
New Zealand bird (extinct) - - - MOA
New Zealand clan - - - - - - - ATI
New Zealand demon - - - - TAIPO
New Zealand district - - - - OTAGO
New Zealand food fish - - - - - IHI
New Zealand hedge laurel - - TARATA
New Zealand mahogany pine - TOTARA, TATARA
New Zealand native - - - - - MAORI
New Zealand fort - - - - - PAH, PA
New Zealand parrot - - - - - - KEA
New Zealand parson bird - KOKO, POE
New Zealand plant - - - - - - KARO
New Zealand Polynesian - - - MAORI
New Zealand soldier - - - - ANZAC
New Zealand tree - AKE, TARO, RATE, TAWA, TARATA, TORU
New Zealand wood robin - - - MIRO
New Zealand woody vine - - - - AKA
New Zealander - - - - - - - MAORI
newcomer - - - - - - - - ENTRANT
newer - - - - - - - - - - LATER
newest - - - - - - - - - - - NEO
Newfoundland cape - - - - - - RACE
Newfoundland jurisdictional territory - - LABRADOR
newly gathered - - - - - - - FRESH
newly married man (var.) - - BENEDICT
newness - - - - - - - - RECENCY
news - - - - - - - - - - TIDINGS
news gatherer - - - - - - REPORTER
news monger - - - - - - - GOSSIP
news sheet - - - - - - - - PAPER
news stand - - - - - - - - KIOSK
newspaper issue - - - - - - EDITION
newspaper paragraph - - - - ITEM
newspapers - - - - PRESS, SHEETS
newt - - - - - - - - TRITON, EFT
next - - - - - - - - - - NEAREST
next to the last syllable - - - PENULT
nexus - - - - - - - - - - - LINK

nib - - - - - POINT, BEAK, PRONG
nibble - - - - - - - - PECK, GNAW
nice - FINICAL, PLEASANT, GENTEEL, AGREEABLE, SOCIABLE, FINE
nice discernment of purpose - - TACT
niche - - - - - - - CORNER, RECESS
nick - - - - - - - - - - - - NOTCH
nickel - - - - - - - - - - - - NI
nickel sulfide - - - - - - MILLERITE
nickname - - - - - - - - - AGNAME
nictitate - - - - - - - - - - WINK
nide - - - - - - - - - - - - NEST
Nigerian Negro - - - - - - IBO, ARO
Nigerian river - - - - - - - - - OLI
Nigerian town - - - - - - - - - ISA
Niger river - - - - - - - - - - NUN
niggard - - - - - - - - - - MISER
nigh - - - - - - - - - NEAR, CLOSE
night - - - - - - - - - - EVENING
night (Fr.) - - - - - - - - - NUIT
nightfall (poet.) - EVE, EEN, EVENTIDE
Nile charmer - - - - - - - - - CLEO
nimble - AGILE, ACTIVE, SPRY, LISSOME, ALERT
nimbus - - - - - - - - - - - HALO
nimrod - - - - - - - - - - HUNTER
nine - - - - - - - NONET, ENNEAD
nine (comb. form) - - - - - - ENNEA
nine days devotion - - - - - NOVENA
nine (group of) - - - - - - ENNEAD
nine-headed monster - - - - - HYDRA
nine inches - - - - - - - - - SPAN
nine part composition - - - - - NONET
nine sided figure - - - - - NONAGON
ninefold - - - - - - - - - NENARY
ninny - - - - - - - - FOOL, DUNCE
nip - - BITE, PINCER, PINCH, BLIGHT, PECK, CLAMP, CLIP
nipa palm - - - - - - - - - - ATAP
nipple - - - - - - - - - - - TEAT
nippy - - - - - - - - - - - SHARP
nisus - - - - - - - - - - EFFORT
niter (of) - - - - - - - - - NITRIC
nitid - - - - - - - GLOSSY, BRIGHT
nitrogenous compound - - - KENATIN, PROTEIN
no - - - - - - - - - - - - - NAY
no extent - - - - - - - - - - NOT
no (Germ.) - - - - - - - - - NEIN
no longer active - - - - - - RETIRED
no longer burning - - - - - - - OUT
no longer in existence - - - EXTINCT
no longer in use - - - - - OBSOLETE
no matter what one - - - - - - ANY
no more than - - - - - - BUT, MERE
no objection (colloq.) - - - - - O.K.
no score in tennis - - - - - - - LOVE
no (Scot.) - - - - - - - - - - NAE
no (slang) - - - - - - - - - - NIX
no value (of) - - - - - - - - NULL
Noah (New Testament spelling) - - NOE
Noah's son - - - SHEM, HAM, JAPHETH
Nobel's invention - - - - - DYNAMITE
nobility - - - - - - - - - PEERAGE
noble - EPIC, PEER, SUBLIME, EPICAL, BARON
nobleman - BARON, PEER, EARL, PRINCE, LORD, GRANDEE, MARQUIS
noblewoman - - - - - - - - PEERESS
nobody - - - - - - - - NONENTITY
nocturnal animal - - - - - - - COON
nocturnal bird - - - - - - OWL, BAT
nocturnal carnivore - - - - - - RATEL
nocturnal lemur - - - - - - - LORIS
nocturnal mammal - - WEASEL, LEMUR
nocturne - - - - - - - - SERENADE

nod - - BOW, DROWSE, BEND, SWAY
nodal - - - - - - - - - KNOTTY
nodding - - - - - - - - NUTANT
node - - - - - - - - - KNOB
nodose - - - - - KNOTTY, KNOBBY
nodule - - - - - - - - - - KNOT
nodule of stone - - - - - - - GEODE
nog - - - - - - - - - - PIN
noise - DIN, SOUND, ROAR, HUBBUB, CLAMOR, RACKET, RATTLE
noise abroad - - - - - - - BRUIT
noise of surf - - - - - - - - ROTE
noiseless - - - - - - - - SILENT
noisy - - LOUD, BLATANT, CLAMOROUS
noisy bird - - - - - - - - - PIE
noisy condemnation - - - - DECRIAL
noisy disturbance - - - BROIL, BABEL
noisy laugh - - - - - - - GUFFAW
noisy quarrel - - - FRACAS, AFFRAY
noisy speaker - - - - - - - RANTER
noisy throng - - - - - - - - ROUT
noisy violent woman - - - - VIRAGO
nom de plume - - - ALIAS, PEN NAME
nomad - BEDOUIN, ROVER, WANDERER
nomadic Arab - - - - - - BEDOUIN
nominal stock value - - - - - PAR
nominate - - - - - NAME, APPOINT
nominee - - - - - - - CANDIDATE
non-Brahmanical Hindu - - - - JAIN
non-conductor of electricity - - RESIN
non-conformist - - - - - - HERETIC
non-metrical language - - - - PROSE
non-Moslem subject - - - - - RAIA
nonplussed - - - - - - - TRUMPED
non-professional - LAY, LAIC, AMATEUR
non-Semitic - - - - - - - - ARYAN
non-venomous snake - - - - - BOA
nonactionable agreement - - - PACT
nonage - - - - - - - - MINORITY
noncircular rotating piece - - - CAM
none (dial.) - - - - - - - - NIN
nonentity - - - - - - - - NOBODY
nonmetallic element - BORON, SILICON, IODINE
nonmineral - - - - - - - - SPAR
nonmigratory of birds - - - RESIDENT
nonsense - - - BAH, BOSH, FUDGE, FALDERAL
nonsense poem - - - - - - LIMERICK
nonsensical - - - - - - - - INANE
nonsensical speech - - - - GABBLE
nook - - CORNER, IN, ANGLE, RECESS
noonday - - - - - - - - MERIDIAN
noose - - - - LOOP, ENTRAP, SNARE
Norfolk river - - - - - - - - TAS
norm - - - - PATTERN, STANDARD
normal - - - SANE, NATURAL, SAME, STANDARD, REGULAR
normal contour feather - - - PENNA
normal state - - - - - - - - ORDER
normal value - - - - - - - - PAR
Normandy horses (breed of) - PERCHERON
Norse capital - - - - - - - - OSLO
Norse deities home - - - - ASGARD
Norse deity - - VE, ODIN, EIR, THOR
Norse demi-goddess - - - - - NORM
Norse fate - - - - - - NORN, NORM
Norse fire demon - - - - - - SURTR
Norse galley - - - - - - - - AESC
Norse god - ODIN, TYR, THOR, AESIR, VE, EIR
Norse god of dead - - - - - - - HEL
Norse god of evil and discord - - LOKI
Norse god of poetry - - - - - BRAGI
Norse goddess - - - - - - EIR, NORN
Norse goddess of lower world - - HEL
Norse gods - - - - - - - - AESIR
Norse mythological deity - - - - VAN
Norse mythological giant - - - - ATLI
Norse saga - - - - - - - - EDDA
Norse saint - - - - - - - - OLAF
Norse sea deity - - - - - - - VAN
Norse tale - - - - - - - - - SAGA
Norse territorial division - - - - AMT
Norsemen (pert. to) - - - - - - RUNIC
Norway river - - - - - - - - KLAR
Norway saint - - - - - - - - OLAF
North Africa - - - (See also African)
North African gazelle - - - - - CORA
North African native - ERITREAN, HAMITE
North African plant - - - - - - ANISE
North African region - - SUDAN, LIBYA
North African seaport - - DERNA, ORAN
North African weight - - - - - ROTL
North American mountain - - LOGAN
North American weight - - - - ARTAL
North Atlantic fish - - - - - SALMON
North Atlantic island - - - - ICELAND
North Carolina county - - - - - ASHE
North Carolina river - - - - - - TAR
North Caucasian language - - - - AVAR
Northeastern Burma native - - - - VU
North Pole discoverer - - - - - PEARY
north Scandinavian - - - - - - LAPP
north star - - POLESTAR, LODESTAR, POLARIS
north Syrian deity - - - - - - - EL
north wind - - - - - - - - BOREAS
northern - - - - - - - - - BOREAL
north Adriatic wind - - - - - - BORA
north Albanian - - - - - - - GHEG
north bird - - - - - - - LOON, AUK
north constellation - - LEO, SERPENT
north European - - FINN, SLAV, LAPP, LETT
north part of Isle of Man - - - AYRE
north part of North America and Greenland - - - - - - - - NEARTICA
Northumbria part - - - - - - DEIRA
Norwegian - - - NORSE, NORSEMAN
Norwegian capital - - - - - - OSLO
Norwegian city - - NARVIK, ALESUND
Norwegian county - - - - - - - AMT
Norwegian dramatist - - - - - IBSEN
Norwegian land division - - - - AMT
Norwegian measure - - - - - - ALEN
Norwegian name - - - - OLAF, OLAV
Norwegian painter - - - - - - DAHL
Norwegian river - OI, NEA, ENA, KLAR
Norwegian snowshoe - - - - - - SKI
nose - - - - - SNIFF, SCENT, DETECT
nose (comb. form) - - - - - - RHIN
nose (pert. to) - - - RHINAL, NASAL
nose (slang) - - - - - - - - SNOOT
nostalgic - - - - - - - HOMESICK
nostril - - - - - - - - - - NARE
nostril (pert. to) - - - - - NARINE
not a (dial.) - - - - - - - - NARY
not abstract - - - - - - - CONCRETE
not accurate - - - - - - - - INEXACT
not acquired - - - - - - - - INNATE
not active - - - - - RETIRED, STATIC
not agreeing - - - - - - DISSIDENT
not all - - - - - - - - - - SOME
not any - - - - - - - - - - - NO
not any (law) - - - - - - - - NUL
not apparent to eye - - - - INVISIBLE
not apprehended by the mind - UNKNOWN
not artificial - - - - - - - NATURAL
not astir - - - - - - - - - - ABED
not at all - - - - - - - - - - - NO
not at home - - - - - - - - ABROAD

N

not beyond - - - - - - - - - WITHIN
not bound - - - - - - - - - - FREE
not bright - - - - - - - - GREY, DIM
not cautious - - - - - - - - UNWARY
not certain - - - - - - - - - UNSURE
not comely - - - - - - - - - UGLY
not complex - - - - - - - - SIMPLE
not concerted - - - - - - - - SOLO
not conscious - - - - - - - UNAWARE
not copied - - - - - - - - ORIGINAL
not covered - - - - - - - - - BALD
not crying - - - - - - - - TEARLESS
not difficult - - - - - - - - - EASY
not in direct light - - - - - - SHADY
not entirely - - - - - - - - - PARTLY
not even - - - - - - - - - - - ODD
not exciting - - - - - - - - - TAME
not extreme - - - - - CONSERVATIVE
not firmly - - - - - - - UNSTEADILY
not forming an angle - - - - - AGONIC
not general - - - - LOCAL, PERSONAL, ESPECIAL
not handsome - - - - - - - - HOMELY
not hard - - - - - - - - SOFT, EASY
not hollow - - - - - - - - - SOLID
not imitative - - - - - - - - ORIGINAL
not indigenous - - - - - - - - EXOTIC
not inhabited - - - - - UNPOPULATED
not involving morality - - - - AMORAL
not italic - - - - - - - - - ROMAN
not legal - - - - - - - - - - UNDUE
not legally disposed of by will - - - INTESTATE
not many - - - - - - - - - - FEW
not matched (Scot.) - - - - - - ORRA
not multifold - - - - - - - - - ONE
not obtuse - - - - - - - - - SHARP
not occupied - - - - - - - - - - IDLE
not one (dial.) - - - - - - - - NARY
not one or the other - - - - NEITHER
not out - - - - - - - - - - - SAFE
not paired - - - - - - - - - - ODD
not plentiful - - - - - - - - SCARCE
not positively - - - - - - NEGATIVELY
not precise - - - - - - - - INDEFINITE
not (prefix) - - IR, IL, IM, UN, NON, MIS, DIS
not present - - - - - - - - - ABSENT
not public - - - - - - - - PERSONAL
not real - IMAGINARY, FALSE, NOMINAL
not resilient - - - - - - - INELASTIC
not restricted - - - - - - - - LIBERAL
not rigid - - - - - - - - - - - LAX
not ripe - - - - - - - - - - GREEN
not sacred - - - - - - - - SECULAR
not the same - - - - ANOTHER, OTHER
not (Scot.) - - - - - - - - - - - NA
not settled - - - - - - - - ITINERANT
not severe - - - - - - - - - LENIENT
not sharp - - - - - - - - - - - DULL
not shut - - - - - - - - - - - AJAR
not slack - - - - - - - - - - - TAUT
not so - - - - - - - - - - - - NO
not so much - - - - - - - - - LESS
not sound and healthful - - - - MORBID
not specific - - - - GENERIC. GENERAL
not spontaneous - - - - - - LABOURED
not steady - - - - - - - - UNSTABLE
not stiff - - - - - - - - - - - LIMP
not stirring - - - - - - - - - ABED
not straightforward - - - - - EVASIVE
not strict - - - - - - - - - - - LAX
not suitable - - - - - - - INAPT, INEPT
not sweet - - - - - - - - - - - SEC
not tanned - - - - - - - - - - - RAW
not this - - - - - - - - - - - THAT
not uniform - - - - - - - IRREGULAR
not in use - - - - - - - - - - - IDLE
not watertight - - - - - - - - LEAKY
not widespread - - - - - - - - LOCAL
not yet settled - - - - MOOT, PENDING
notable act - - - - - - - - - - FEAT
notable personage - - - - - - - LION
notably - - - - - - - - - - EMINENTLY
notch - - NICK, GAP, DENT, SERRATE, INDENT
notch edge of - - - - - - - - INDENT
notched - CRENATE, SERRATED, SERRATE
notched bar - - - - - - - - - - RATCH
notched like a saw - - - - - - SERRATE
notched wheel - - - - - - - RATCHET
notching - - - - - - - - - INDENTING
note - - - - OBSERVE, HEED, REMARK
note of chromatic scale - DO, RE, MI, FA, SO, LA, TI
note the duration of - - - - - - TIME
note the speed - - - - - - - - - TIME
noted - EMINENT, MARKED, FAMOUS, FAMED
notes - - - - - - MEMORANDA, MEMO
noteworthy - - - - - - - - - SPECIAL
nothing - NIL, ZERO, NIHIL, NOUGHT
nothing (colloq.) - - - - - - - - NIX
nothing more than or nothing but - MERE
nothing to spare - - - - - - - BARELY
notice - - HEED, OBSERVE, SEE, SIGN, SPOT
noticeable - - - - - POINTED, SIGNAL
notion - - - - - - - IDEA, FAD, WHIM
notion (dial.) - - - - - - - - - IDEE
notoriety - - - - - - - - - - ECLAT
notorious - - - - - - INFAMOUS, ARRANT
notwithstanding - DESPITE, HOWEVER, BUT, YET
nought - - - - - - - NOTHING, ZERO
noun - - - - - - - - - SUBSTANTIVE
noun suffix - - - - - IER, AC, IST, ITE
noun with three cases only - TRIPTOTE
noun without case endings - - APTOTE
nourish - - - - - - - - - - - - FEED
nourishing - MEATY, ALIBLE, ALIMENTAL
nourishing substance - - - - - FOOD
Nova Scotia - - - - - - - - - ACADIA
Nova Scotia (pert. to) - - - - ACADIAN
Nova Scotia seaport - - - - - - TRURO
novel - - - - NEW, UNUSUAL, STRANGE, ROMANCE, DIFFERENT
novelty - - - - - - - - - INNOVATION
novice - - TYRO, BEGINNER, ACOLYTE
novice (var.) - - - - - - - - - - TIRO
now - - - - - - - - HERE, FORTHWITH
noxious - - - - - - - - ILL, MIASMIC
noxious influence - - - - - - MIASMA
noxious substance - - - - - - POISON
nuance - - - - - - - - - - - - SHADE
nub - - - - - - - PITH, LUMP, KNOT
nucha - - - - - - - - - - - - - NAPE
nuclear - - - - - - - - - - - - FOCAL
nucleus of atom - - - - - - - PROTON
nude - - - - - - - - - NAKED, BARE
nudge - - - - - - - - - - - - - JOG
null - - - - - VOID, CIPHER, INVALID
nullify - - - - - - - - - - - NEGATE
number - COUNT, ENUMERATE, DIGIT
number to be added to another - ADDEND
number of hills on which Rome was built SEVEN
number of members necessary to do business - - - - - - - QUORUM
number of Muses - - - - - - - - NINE
number of related events - - - SERIES
number from which another is subtracted

MINUEND
numbered (Bib.) - - - - - - - MENE
numbered disc - - - - - - - - DIAL
numbers at one's command - REPERTOIRE
numbers we use - - - - - - - ARABIC
numbness - - - - - - - - TORPOR
numeral style - - - - - - - - ARABIC
numerical - - - - - - - - - TEN
numerical (prefix) - - - - - - - UNI
numerous - - - - - MANY, PLENTIFUL
nun - - SISTER, PIGEON, RELIGIEUSE
nuptial - - - - - - - - MATRIMONIAL
nurl - - - - - - - - - - ROUGHEN
nurse - FOSTER, NANA, NURTURE, TEND
nurse shark - - - - - - - - - GAT
nursemaid (Fr.) - - - - - - BONNE
nurture - - BREED, CHERISH, NURSE, FEED
nut - - - - - - - - - - PROBLEM
nut confection - - PRALINE, NOUGATS
nut (kind) - - - KOLA, COLA, ALMOND
nutant - - - - - NODDING, DROOPING
nutriment - - - - - - - - FOOD, MEAT
nutritious - ALIMENTARY, ALIMENTAL, NOURISHING
nutritive - - - - - - - - - - ALIBLE
nuts collectively - - - - - - - MAST
nymph changed into a rock - - ECHO
nymph of hills - - - - - - - OREAD
nymph of Moslem paradise - - HOURI
Nyx's daughter - - - - - - - ERIS

O

oaf - - - - - - DOLT, LOUT, IDIOT
oak (kind) - - - BLACKJACK, ALDER
oar - - - - - PADDLE, ROW, ROWER
oar blade - - - - - - - PALM, PEEL
oar fulcrum - - - - - - - - - THOLE
oar part - - - - - - - - - - LOOM
oar pin and rester - - - - - - THOLE
oarsman - - - - - - - - - - ROWER
oath - - - - - - - - VOW, CURSE
oath (mild) - - - - - - DRAT, EGAD
oath (old) - - - - - - - ECOD, EGAD
obdurate - - - - - - - - - DOGGED
obedient - - - - - - - - - DUTIFUL
obedient (was) - - - - - CONFORMED
obeisance - - - - - - - - - HOMAGE
obese - - - - - - - - - - - FAT
obey - MIND, COMPLY, SUBMIT, YIELD
obfuscate - - - - - - - - - CONFUSE
object - - INTENTION, DEMUR, THING, AIM, EVICT, PROTEST, TARGET
object of affection - - - - - - IDOL
object of aim - - - - - - - - BUTT
object of bowlike curvature - - - ARC
object of bric-a-brac - - - - - CURIO
object of devotion - - - - - - - IDOL
objection - - - - - - - - PROTEST
objective - - - - GOAL, TARGET, AIM
objective case of pronoun - - - THEM
objector - - - - - DEMURRER, CAVILER
objurgate - - - - - - - - - SCOLD
obligate - - - - - - - - - - BIND
obligation - - DEBT, TIE, DUTY, DUE, BOND
obligatory - - - - - - - - BOUNDEN
obliged - CONSTRAINED, COMPELLED, ACCOMMODATE
obliged (be) - - - - - - - - - MUST
obliged to - - - - - - - - - - OWE
oblique - - LATERAL, SLANT, BEVEL, AWRY, SKEW, SIDELONG
oblique position - - - - - - - SLANT

obliterate - ERASE, EFFACE, RAZE, RASE, BLOT
obliteration - - - - - ERASURE, BLOT
oblivion - - - - - - AMNESTY, LETHE
oblong metal mass - - - - - - - PIG
obnoxious - - - - - - - OFFENSIVE
obscure - - DIM, SHADE, FOG, DEEP, INDISTINCT, SEE, DARKEN, INNER, BLUR
obsequious person - - - - - SATELLITE
observance - - - - - RITE, ATTENTION
observant - - - - - - - - ATTENTIVE
observation - - - - - - - - REMARK
observe - - - NOTICE, NOTE, REGARD, REMARK, EYE, LO
observe duty - - - - - - CELEBRATE
observer - - - - - - - - SPECTATOR
obsolete - - - - - - - - OLD, PASSE
obstacle - - BAR, SNAG, DAM, HITCH
obstinate - - - - - - STUBBORN, SET
obstruct - DAM, BAR, DETER, IMPEDE, CLOG, HINDER, OCCLUDE, ESTOP
obstruction - - - - BARRIER, SNAG, BAR
obtain - - - DERIVE, GAIN, PROCURE, SECURE, WIN, GET
obtain control of - - - - - - - TAKE
obtain laboriously - - - - - - - EKE
obtain loan - - - - - - - - BORROW
obtain with difficulty - - - - - - EKE
obtrude - - - - - - - - - - IMPOSE
obtuse - - - - CRASS, DENSE, BLUNT
obvious - - OVERT, PATENT, EVIDENT
obvious facts - - - - - - - - TRUISMS
occasion - ONCE, NONCE, TIME, BREED, ENGENDER
occasion (Scot.) - - - - - - - - SELE
occasional (Scot.) - - - - - - ORRA
occident - - - - - - - - - - - WEST
occlude - - - - - - OBSTRUCT, CLOSE
occult - - - - - - - - - - CRYPTIC
occultism - - - - - - - - - CABALA
occupant - - - - - TENANT, RESIDENT
occupation - - - - - CAREER, TENURE, BUSINESS, METIER, WORK, TRADE
occupied - - - - - - - - RAPT, BUSY
occupy - - - - - - - INTEREST, USE, ENGAGE
occupy completely - - - - - - FILL
occupy a seat - - - - SIT, PRESIDE
occupying the whole of - - - - - FILL
occur - - - - - HAPPEN, PASS, BETIDE
occur every year - - - - - - ANNUAL
occur at irregular intervals - SPORADIC
occur at stated intervals - - - REGULAR
occurred - - - - - - - - - BETIDED
occurrence - - EVENT, HAP, INCIDENT
occurring every third day - - TERTIAN
occurring regularly - - - - - PERIODIC
occurring in the spring - - - VERNAL
ocean - - - - - - - - - MAIN, SEA
ocean (pert. to) - - - - - - PELAGIC
ocean route - - - - - - - - - - LANE
ocean vessel - - - - - - - - - LINER
oceanic - - - - - - MARINE, PELAGIC
octave (musical) - - - - - - - EIGHTH
Octavia's husband - - - - - - - NERO
octopus's arms - - - - - - TENTACLES
ocular - - - - - - - - - - - VISUAL
odd - - - STRANGE, RARE, QUEER, ECCENTRIC, QUAINT, SINGULAR, UNEVEN, UNIQUE
odd (Scot.) - - - - - - - - - ORRA
odds - - - - - - - - - - CHANCES
Odin's brother - - - - - - - - - VE
Odin's son - - - - - - - - - - TYR
odious - - - - - - - - - - HATEFUL

O

odium - HATRED
odour - AROMA, SCENT, SMELL
odour (offensive) - OLID
odorous - FRAGRANT, REDOLENT
odylic force - OD
Odysseus' dog - ARGOS
Odysseus' wife - PENELOPE
of - ABOUT
of (Dutch) - VAN
of each (med.) - ANA
of (Fr.) - DE
of the matter - RE
of the past - YORE
of (prefix) - DE
of the side - LATERAL
of that kind - SUCH
of that thing - ITS
of us - OUR
off - AWAY, BEGONE, MISTAKEN
off hand - IMPROMPTU
offend - PIQUE, DISPLEASE, INSULT
offend morally - SIN
offense - CRIME, FAULT
offense against the law - DELICT
offensive - OBNOXIOUS
offensively bright - GARISH
offensiveness - ODIUM
offer - BID, TENDER, PROFFER, PROPOSE, PROPOSAL
offer for consideration - PROPOSE
offer objections - DEMUR
offer to pay - BID
offer for sale - VEND
offer solemnly - PLEDGE
offer of terms - PROPOSITION
offer to verify - AVER
offering - TRIBUTE
offering of goods - SALE
offering opposition - RESISTANT
office head - MANAGER
office holders - INS
officer in charge of horse provender - AVENER
officer of military police - PROVOST
officer's assistant - AIDE
official - MAGNATE
official candidate list - SLATE
official command - MANDATE, EDICT
official declaration - PROMULGATION
official decree - UKASE
official document - INDENTURE
official endorsement - VISA
official examiner - CENSOR
official message - BREVET
official negation - VETO
official note - MEMOIR
official paper - DOCUMENT
official proof of a will - PROBATE
official record - PROTOCOL, ROLL, ACTUM
official record of inhabitants - CENSUS
official seal - SIGNET
official sitting - SESSION
official stamp - SEAL
official transactions - ACTA
officiate - ACT
offset - UNDO
offshoot - SLIP
offspring - DESCENDANT, SON
often (poet.) - OFT
ogle - LEER, EYE, GAZE
ogrish - CRUEL, MONSTROUS
Ohio city - XENIA, LIMA, LORAIN
Ohio county - ROSS, ERIE
Ohio town - ADA
Ohio village - MEDINA
oil - OLEIC, OLEO, GREASE, LUBRICATE, ANOINT, PETROLEUM
oil of animal fats - OLEO
oil based ointment - CERATE
oil of bitter orange - NEROLI
oil bottle - CRUET
oil can - OILER
oil color vehicle - MEGILP
oil (comb. form) - OLEO
oil derivative - OLEIC
oil (kind) - KEROSENE
oil of orange - NEROLI
oil of orris root - IRONE
oil (pert. to) - OLEIC
oil of roses (var.) - ATAR, OTTO, ATTAR, OTTAR
oil ship - TANKER
oil (suffix) - OL
oil tree - EBOE
oil well - GUSHER
oil yielding herb - PEANUT
oilstone - HONE
oily - FAT, SEBACEOUS
oily ketone - IRONE
oily substance - FAT
ointment - CERATE, SALVE, POMADE, UNGUENT, BALSAM, BALM, NARD
ointment of the ancients - NARD
ointment (fragrant) - NARD
Okinawa capital - NAHA
Oklahoma city - ENID, TULSA, ADA
Oklahoma nickname of natives - SOONERS
okra - GUMBO
old - STALE, AGED, ANCIENT, FORMER
old age - SENILITY
old age (pert. to) - SENILE
old book of song - JASHAR
old Briton chariot - ESSED
old card game - PAM, LOO, LU
old ceremonial dance - PAVANE, PAVAN, PRIMERO
old coin - RAP
old dance of sailors - MATELOTE
old dice game - NOVUM
old dog - ROVER
old Dominion State (abbr.) - VA.
old Dutch measure - AAM
old English coin - GROAT, ORA
old English court - LEET
old English rent - TAC
old English tax - TALLAGE, PRISAGE
old fashioned - PASSE, ARCHAIC
old fashioned fellow - FOGY
old fashioned piece of needlework - SAMPLER
old fashioned rifle part - TIGE
old form of like - BELIKE
old form of three - TRE
old French coin - SOU, ECU, OBOLE
old French poem - DIT
old French verse form - VIRELAY, ALBA
old horse - PADNAG
old joke - GAG
old joke (colloq.) - CHESTNUT
old liquid measure - RUNLET
old love song - AMORET
old maid - SPINSTER
old man famed for wisdom - NESTOR
old maxim - SAW, ADAGE
old military device - PETARD
old money unit - TALENT
old moneyer's weight - PERIT
old Moslem coin - DINAR
old musical instrument - REBEC, LYRE, CITOLE, ROTA, ASOR. CITHERN, SPINET
old musical note - ELA, FE, UT, ARE

old Norse work - - - - - - - EDDA
old oath - - - - - - - - - - EGAD
old order of scratching birds - RASORES
old Persian - - - - - - PARTHIAN
old piano - - - - - - - - SPINET
old piece of satrap - - - - - OTANES
old playing card - - - - - - TAROT
old pronoun - - - - - - - - THEE
old proverb - - - - - - - - SAW
old rifle part - - - - - - - - TIGE
old Roman chest - - - - - - - CYST
old salt - - - - - - - - - TAR
old saying - - - - - - - - SAW
old Scot. coin - - - - DEMY, BAUBEE
old Scot. weight - - - - - - TRONE
old Spanish peninsula - - - - IBERIA
old stage call on trumpet - - SENNET
old stringed instrument - - PANDORA, REBEC
old style war vessel - - - - - FRIGATE
Old Testament book - - - - - ESTHER
Old Testament cony - - - - - DAMAN
Old Testament object - - - - - URIM
Old Testament word - - - - - TOPHET
old Teutonic alphabetical symbol - RUNE
old Teutonic alphabetical symbol (pert. to) RUNIC
old time beverage - - - - - POSSET
old time dagger - - - - - - SNEE
old time dance - - - - - - CAROLE
old time pistol - - - - - - - DAG
old time playing card - - - - - TAROT
old time spear - - - - - - JAVELIN
old times - - - - - - - - - YORE
old vessel - - - - GALLEON, FRIGATE
old violin (colloq.) - - - - - STRAD
old woman - - - - - - CRONE, HAG
old womanish - - - - ANILE, SENILE
Old World bird - - - STARLING, TEREK
Old World carnivore - - - - - GENET
Old World crow - - - - - - - ROOK
Old World finch - - - - - - SERIN
Old World fish - - - - - - - LOACH
Old World genus of herbs - - - PARIS
Old World lizard - - - - - - - SEPS
Old World plant - - - - - - - ALOE
Old World sandpiper - - - - - TEREK
Old World shrub - - - - - OLEANDER
Old World wading bird - - - - STORK
olden - - - - - - - - - - ANCIENT
olden times (poet.) - - - - ELD, YORE
older - - - - ELDER, SENIOR, STALER
older (abbr.) - - - - - - - - - SR.
oldest - - - - - - - - - - ELDEST
oldest Kashmir alphabet - - - SERADA
oldest member - - - - - - - - DEAN
oldest of the Pleiades - - - - - MAIA
oldtimer - - - - - - - - - VETERAN
oleaginous - - - - - - - - - OILY
olent - - - - - - - - - FRAGRANT
oleoresin - - - - - - ELEMI, AMIME
olfactory organ - - - - - - - - NOSE
olive - - - - - OLEA, RELISH, TAWNY
olive tree - - - - - - - - - - ASH
olive tree substance - - - - - OLIVIL
Oliver Twist character - - - - - FAGIN
olla - - - - - - - - - - POT, JUG
Olympian goddess - - - - ARTEMIS
omen - - SIGN, PRESAGE, PORTENT, FORBODE
ominous - - - - SINISTER, FATEFUL
ominous Biblical word - - - - - MENE
omission - - - - - - - - - ELISION
omission of end of a word - APOCOPE
omission of letter from word - SYNCOPE
omission mark - - - - - - - CARET
omit - - DELETE, SKIP, CUT, MISS, SPARE, EXCEPT, NEGLECT, ELIDE
omit from consideration - - - - ELIDE
omit from pronouncing - - - - ELIDE
on - - ABOVE, ALONG, ABOUT, UPON, FORWARD
on account of - - - - - - - - - FOR
on all sides - - - - AROUND, ABOUT
on board ship - - - - - - - - ASEA
on condition that - - - - - - SO, IF
on fire - - - - - - - - - - ABLAZE
on the left side - - - - - - APORT
on the line of - - - - - - - ALONG
on the mouth - - - - - - - - ORAL
on occasion of - - - - - - - - - AT
on right hand - - - - - - - DEXTER
on strike - - - - - - - - - - OUT
on that account - - - - - - THEREAT
on this - - - - - - - - HEREUPON
on this side (prefix) - - - - - - CIS
on top of - - - - - - - ATOP, UPON
on a wall - - - - - - - - - MURAL
on the way - - - - - - - - ENROUTE
on what account - - - - - - - - WHY
onager - - - - - DONKEY, CATAPULT
once - FORMERLY, OCCASION, EVER, SINGLY
once again - - - - - - - - - OVER
once again (poet.) - - - - - - OER
once more - - - - - ANEW, ENCORE
one - UNIT, UNITY, SAME, ANYBODY, UNITED, PERSON, SINGLE, AN
one before another - - - - - TANDEM
one in charge of collected funds - - - TREASURER
one in charge of horses - - - - GROOM
one (comb. form) - - - - UNI, MONO
one concerned with external actions - - EXTROVERT
one confined to institution - - INMATE
one continually on the go - GADABOUT
one dependent on charity - - PAUPER
one deprived of something - - LOSER
one devoted to monastic life - OBLATE
one engaged in gainful occupation - - EARNER
one of fine arts - - - - - - - MUSIC
one first in rank - - - - - PRIMATE
one gainfully employed - - - - EARNER
one of the genii - - - - - - - GENIE
one of gigantic size - - - - - TITAN
one of Gilbert Islands - - - - TARAWA
one given to a habit - - - - - ADDICT
one of the gorgons - - - - - MEDUSA
one habitually untidy - - - - SLOVEN
one having gigantic strength - - TITAN
one horse carriage - - - - - - SHAY
one impervious to pain or pleasure - - STOIC
one indefinitely - - - - - - - - AN
one (It.) - - - - - - - - - - UNA
one of King David's rulers - - IRA
one of laity - - - - - - - - - LAIC
one lately arrived - - - - NEWCOMER
one in the lead - - - - - PACEMAKER
one less than par - - - - - - BIRDIE
one living in a place - - - - RESIDENT
one masted vessel - - - - - - SLOOP
one of mixed breed - - - - - METIS
one more - - - - - - - - ANOTHER
one named after another - NAMESAKE
one named for office - - - - NOMINEE
one of Norse Fates - - - - - - NORN
one not in the army (slang) - - - - CIT
one omitted - - - - - - - - - OUT
one's own share - - - - - - - RATA

O

one of pleasant countenance - **SMILER**
one (prefix) - - - - - - **UNI, MONO**
one of the proteoses - - - **CASEOSE**
one of a ruling class - - - **ARISTOS**
one (Scot.) - - - - - - - **ANE, AE**
one in second childhood - - **DOTARD**
one of seven hills of Rome - **AVENTINE**
one of Shylock's coins - - - **DUCAT**
one skilled in colours - - - **COLOURIST**
one skilled in languages - - **LINGUIST**
one skilled in science - - **SCIENTIST**
one skilled in science (suffix) - - **IST**
one of Society Islands - - - **TAHITI**
one spot - - - - - - - - **ACE, PIP**
one storied house - - - **BUNGALOW**
one of three equal parts - - - **THIRD**
one of The Three Musketeers - **ARAMIS**
one of two - - - - - - - - **EITHER**
one of two equal parts - **HALF, MOIETY**
one unclean (Bib.) - - - - **LEPER**
one under care of another - - **PROTEGE**
one with indigestion - - - **DYSPEPTIC**
one with information - - - **INSIDER**
one with loud voice - - - **STENTOR**
one who is abandoned - - **DERELICT**
one who acts for another - - - **AGENT**
one who acts for a sheriff - - **ELISOR**
one who administers wills - **EXECUTOR**
one who advocates changes - **TURNABOUT**
one who blows horn - - - - **TOOTER**
one who breaks or transgresses - - - **VIOLATOR**
one who brings bad luck - - **JONAH**
one who brings good luck - - **MASCOT**
one who cannot be believed - - **LIAR**
one who colours fabrics- - - - **DYER**
one who conceals - - - - **SECRETOR**
one who considers himself superior - **SNOB**
one who constructs - - - - **FRAMER**
one who courts - - - - - - **SPOONER**
one who cowers - - - - - - **CRINGER**
one who damages - - - - **VANDAL**
one who dies for a cause - - **MARTYR**
one who displays his learning - **PEDANT**
one who dispossesses - - - **DEPRIVER**
one who does (suffix) - - - - - **IST**
one who drives a team - - **TEAMSTER**
one who entertains - - - - - **HOST**
one who evades duty - - - **SLACKER**
one who excels - - - - - - **ACE**
one who faces facts - - - - **REALIST**
one who fights - - - - - **COMBATANT**
one who follows backwards - **RETRACER**
one who forsakes a faith - - **APOSTATE**
one who frees - - - - - **LIBERATOR**
one who furnishes tips - - - - **TOUT**
one who gives a title - - - - **NAMER**
one who grinds grain - - - **MILLER**
one who has on - - - - - **WEARER**
one who hastens - - - - **EXPEDITER**
one who helps others - - - **ALTRUIST**
one who inflicts retribution - **NEMESIS**
one who inserts public announcements - **ADVERTISER**
one who invests for high profits - - - **SPECULATOR**
one who leases vessel - - **CHARTERER**
one who lessens by cutting - **TRUNCATOR**
one who levies imposts - - - **TAXER**
one who lives on another - **PARASITE, SPONGE**
one who looks on dark side - **PESSIMIST**
one who looks steadily - - - **GAZER**
one who makes affidavit - - **DEPONENT**
one who makes chair seats - - **CANER**
one who makes corrections - **EMENDATOR**
one who makes and leaves a will - - - **TESTATOR**
one who moves out of the country - - - **EMIGRANT**
one who offers - - - - - **TENDERER**
one who owes - - - - - - **DEBTOR**
one who pledges real estate - **MORTGAGER**
one who praises formally - **ENCOMIAST**
one who prepares athletes for contest - **TRAINER**
one who preserves for use - - **CURER**
one who presides - - - - **PRESIDER**
one who procrastinates - - **POSTPONER**
one who punishes - - - - **SADIST**
one who puns - - - - - - **PUNSTER**
one who reads the lessons in church - - **LECTOR**
one who receives - - - - **RECIPIENT**
one who receives stolen property - **FENCE**
one who rents - - - - - - **LESSEE**
one who repeats - - - - - **PARROT**
one who represents the newest - - **NEO**
one who requests - - - **POSTULATOR**
one who resembles another (slang) - - **RINGER**
one who ridicules - - - - **DERIDER**
one who rules for another - - **REGENT**
one who rules by fear - - **TERRORIST**
one who rules for sovereign - **VICEROY**
one who sacrifices his life to a cause - **MARTYR**
one who scares up game - - **BEATER**
one who seeks resemblances - - - - **ANALOGIST**
one who seizes a prisoner - - **CAPTOR**
one who sells small wares - - **MERCER**
one who sets a goal - - - - **AIMER**
one who shirks duty - - - - **TRUANT**
one who shows endurance - - **TROJAN**
one who sounds a bell - - - **TOLLER**
one who spreads needless fear - **ALARMIST**
one who stares openmouthed - - **GAPER**
one who suffers for a cause - **MARTYR**
one who takes another's money - - - **EMBEZZLER**
one who takes another unawares - - - **SURPRISER**
one who takes captive - - - **CAPTOR**
one who takes the initiative - **LEADER**
one who takes interest - - - **USURER**
one who testifies - - - **EYEWITNESS**
one who testifies by affidavit - - - - **DEPONENT**
one who throws football - - - **PASSER**
one who transfers property - **ALIENOR**
one who evaluates for tax purposes - - **ASSESSOR**
one who is versed in languages - - - **POLYGLOT**
one who is with another - **COMPANION**
one who works for wages - **EMPLOYEE**
one to whom bequest is made - **LEGATEE**
one to whom money is due - **CREDITOR**
one to whom money is to be paid - **PAYEE**
one on whom order is drawn - **DRAWEE**
one to whom property is leased - **LESSEE**
one to whom secrets are told - - - - **CONFIDANT**
one for whom a suit is brought - **USEE**
one to whom thing is sold - - **VENDEE**
one to whom trust is committed - - - **COMMITTEE**
one whose chief interest is in the past - **PRETERIST**
one for whose use a thing is done - **USEE**
one of Windward Islands - - **GRENADA**

oneness - - - UNITY
one's attendants - - - ENTOURAGE
one's own - - - PERSONAL
one's own share - - - RATA
one's strong point - - - FORTE
onion (variety) - - RARERIPE, LEEK, CIBOL
only - - - - SOLE, MERE, SOLELY, ALONE
onrush - - - ONSET
onset - ATTACK, START, OUTSET, DASH
onslaught - ONSET, ATTACK, ASSAULT
onus - - - BURDEN, WEIGHT
onward - - - ALONG
ooze - - EXUDE, SEEP, SLIME, SPEW, MIRE
open - OVERT, UNFOLD, LANCE, BARE, UNCLOSE, ACCESSIBLE, EXPOSED, DISCLOSE, UNLOCK, AGAPE, FRANK, UNSTOPPED, EXPAND, BLAND, UNFURL, EXPANDED, START
open auto - - - PHAETON
open court - - AREA, HIATUS, PATIO
open to debate - - - MOOT
open gallery - - - TERRACE
open to general use - - - PUBLIC
open hand (resembling) - - PALMATED
open inner court of building - - PATIO
open land - - - FIELD, HEATH, MOOR
open sea - - - MAIN
open shelved cabinet - - - ETAGERE
open space - - - AREA
open space in forest - - - GLADE
open tract in a forest - - - SLASH
open vessel - PAN, BASIN, BOAT, TUB
open to view - - - BARE, OVERT
open vocal sounds - - - VOWELS
open wide - - - GAPE, YAWN
open woodland space - - - GLADE
opened widely - - - AGAPE
opening - GAP, FISSURE, APERTURE, VENT, EYELET, HOLE, PORE, RIMA, HIATUS, RIFT
opening above door - - - TRANSOM
opening in cask - - - BUNGHOLE
opening in front of helmet - - - VUE, VISOR
opening the mouth wide - - - AGAPE
opening in net - - - MESH
opening in nose - - - NARE
opening in underground - - - CAVE
opening wide - - - AGAPE
open wound - - - SORE
openwork fabric - - - LACE
opera - - - AIDA
opera house - - - MET
opera singer - - - PATTI, ALDA
operate - - - WORK, RUN, MANAGE
operate on skull - - - TREPAN
operatic heroine - NEDDA, SENTA, ELSA
operatic solo - - - ARIA
operatic soprano - - - EAMES, MELBA
operation - - - PROCEDURE
operations (pert. to) - - - SURGICAL
operative - - - ARTISAN
operator - - - RUNNER
opercula (botanical) - - - LIDS
Ophelia's father - - - POLONIUS
ophidian - - - SNAKE
ophidian sibilation - - - HISS
opiate (colloq.) - - - DOPE
opiates - - - NARCOTICS
opine - - THINK, JUDGE, SUPPOSE, CONSIDER, ADJUDGE
opinion - - VIEW, CONCEPT, CREDO, THOUGHT, IDEA, JUDGMENT, REPUTE
opium - - - NARCOTIC, DRUG
opponent - - - FOE, RIVAL
opportune - - APROPOS, TIMELY, PAT
opportunity - - - OPENING
oppose - FACE, RESIST, WITHSTAND, REPEL
oppose manfully - - - BREAST
opposed - - - AVERSE
opposed to adnate - - - SOLUTE
opposed to endogen - - - EXOGEN
opposed to hook (golf) - - - SLICE
opposed (prefix) - - - ANTI
opposed to - - - AGAINST
opposed to right - - - LEFT
opposed to sec - - - BRUT
opposed to stoss - - - LEE
opposed to van - - - REAR
opposing - - - RESISTANT
opposing faction - - - SIDE
opposite - - - INVERSE, REVERSE
opposite to - - - AGAINST, REVERSE, SUBTEND
opposite of aweather - - - ALEE
opposite of liabilities - - - ASSETS
opposite middle of ship's side - ABEAM
opposite ones - - - OTHERS
opposition - - - AVERSION
opposition to war - - - PACIFISM
oppress - AGGRIEVE, LADE, PERSECUTE
Op's daughter - - - CERES
opt - - - CHOOSE, DECIDE
optic - - - EYE
optic (comb. form) - - - OPTO
optical glass - - - LENS
optical illusion and phenomenon - - - MIRAGE
optical instrument - PRISM, PERISCOPE, TELESCOPE
optical instrument part - - ALIDADE
optimistic - ROSEATE, ROSY, SANGUINE
option - - - CHOICE
optional - - - ELECTIVE
opulence - - - WEALTH
opulent - - RICH, PROFUSE, WEALTHY
opus - - - WORK, BURDEN
ora - - - MOUTHS
oracle - - - MENTOR
oracular - - - PROPHETIC, VATIC
orage - - - TEMPEST, STORM
oral - - - SPOKEN, PAROL, VERBAL, ALOUD, VOCAL
oral utterance - - - PAROL
orale - - - FANON
orange dye - MANDARIN, HENNA, CHICA
orange grove - - - ORANGERY
orange red stone - - - SARD
orange segment (Scot.) - - - LITH
orange (variety of) - - - OSAGE
orangutan - - - MIAS, APE
orate - - - DECLAIM, SPEAK, TALK, HARANGUE, SAY
oration - ADDRESS, SPEECH, PRAYER
oratorical - - - RHETORICAL
orb - - CIRCLE, SPHERE, EYE, GLOBE
orb of day - - - SUN
orbed - - - ROUND, LUNAR
orbit - - - PATH
orc - - - GRAMPUS, WHALE
orchestra conductor - - - DIRECTOR
orchestra section - - - BRASSES
orchestrate - - - SCORE
orchid with fragrant leaves - - FAHAM
orchid (kind) - ARETHUSA, POGONIA, FAHAM

O

orchid meal or root - - - - SALEP
ordain - - - - - - - - - DECREE
ordeal - - - - - - - - - TRIAL
order - COMMAND, MANDATE, METHOD, BADE, REGULATE, BID, SYSTEM
order of aquatic mammals - - CETE, CETACEA
order of architecture - - DORIC, IONIC
order back - - - - - - - REMAND
order of business - - - - AGENDA
order of mammals - - CETE, PRIMATE
order of march - - - - - - ROUTE
order of reptiles - - - - - - SAURIA
order of whales - - - - - - - CETA
orderly - - NEAT, SHIPSHAPE, TRIM
orderly arrangement - SYSTEM, SERIES
ordinal number - - - - - - SEVENTH
ordinal numeral suffix - - - - - ETH
ordinary - USUAL, AVERAGE, MEDIOCRE
ordinary language - - - - - - PROSE
ordnance device - - - - - - TRACER
ordnance (piece) - - - - - CANNON
ore - - - - - - - - - - - - METAL
ore deposit - - LODE, BONANZA, BED
ore digger - - - - - - - - MINER
ore excavation - - - - - - - MINE
ore of lead - - - - - - - GALENA
ore refiner - - - - - - - SMELTER
ore of silver - - - - - - ARGENTITE
ore vein - - - - - - - - - - LODE
Oregon capital - - - - - - - SALEM
Oregon Indian tribe - - - - KUSAN
organ bass note - - - - - - PEDAL
organ desk - - - - - - - CONSOLE
organ of insect - - - - - - STINGER
organ of motion - - - - - - MUSCLE
organ pipe - - - - - - REED, FLUE
organ shrub - - - - - - - - SALAL
organ of speech - LIP, VOICE, THROAT, TONGUE
organ stop - - - CELESTE, GAMBA, TREMOLO
organ stop (string toned) - - - VIOLA
organic - - FUNDAMENTAL, RADICAL
organic base of mustard - - SINAPINR
organic nitrogenous compound - - - PROTEIN
organic unit - - - - - - - MONAD
organism living on another - PARASITE
organism (minute) - - - - - SPORE
organism (simple) - - - - - MONAD
organization - - - - - - - SETUP
organized massacre - - - - POGROM
organized official body - - - BOARD
orgy - - - FROLIC, CAROUSAL, LARK
oriental - ASIAN, EASTERN, ASIATIC, LEVANTINE
oriental animal - - - - - - RASSE
oriental bird - - - - - MINO, MINA
oriental bovine animal - - - - ZEBU
oriental bow - - - - - - - - SALAAM
oriental building - - - - - PAGODA
oriental captain - - - - - - - RAS
oriental caravansary - - - - - SERAI
oriental cart - - - - - - - ARABA
oriental case - - - - - - - - INRO
oriental coin - - - - RIN, YEN, SEN
oriental commander - - - - - - RAS
oriental country - - - - - - INDIA
oriental country (poet.) - - - - IND
oriental dish - - - - - PILAW, PILAU
oriental drums - - - - - TOMTOMS
oriental dwelling - - - - - - - DAR
oriental obeisance (var.) - - SALAM
oriental flat housetop - - - TERRACE
oriental food fish - - - - - - - TAI
oriental garment - - - - - - - ABA
oriental gateway - - - - - - TORII
oriental governor - - - - - - - DEY
oriental greeting - - - - - - SALAM
oriental guitar - - SITAR, SAMISEN
oriental inn - - - - - - - - - SERAI
oriental interpreter - - - DRAGOMAN
oriental labourer - - - - - - COOLIE
oriental measure - - - - - - - PARAH
oriental measure of capacity - ARDEB
oriental musical instrument - SAMISEN
oriental native - - - KOREAN, ASIAN
oriental nature spirits - - - - GENII
oriental nurse - - - - - AMAH, AYAH
oriental plant - - - - - - - SESAME
oriental prince - - - - - - - - AMIR
oriental receptacle - - - - - - INRO
oriental ruler - - - - - - - - AMEER
oriental sacred tower - - - PAGODA
oriental sail - - - - - - - - LATEEN
oriental ship captain - - - - - - RAS
oriental shrub - TEA, HENNA, OLEANDER
oriental tea - - - - - - - - - - CHA
oriental wagon - - - - - - - ARABA
oriental weight - CANTAR, TAEL, CATTY, MO, ROTL
osier - - - - - - - - - - - - KILN
orifice - - - - HOLE, PORE, INLET
origin - ROOT, SOURCE, PARENTAGE, GENESIS, BEGINNING
origin (pert. to) - - - - - GENETIC
original - - - PRISTINE, FIRST, PRIMIGENIAL
original inhabitant - - - ABORIGINE
originate - - ARISE, INVENT, CREATE, BREED, COIN, EMANATE
originator - - - AUTHOR, COINER, INVENTOR
originator of atomic theory - - DALTON
Orion meteor - - - - - - ORIONID
Orion star - - - - - - - - - RIGEL
orison - - - - - - - - - - - PRAYER
orle - - - - - - - - - - - BEARING
ornament - TRINKET, AMULET, ADORN, PIN, ROSETTE
ornamental - - - DECORATIVE, BOW, BEAD, FANCY
ornamental ball - - BEAD, POMPON
ornamental belt - - - - - - - SASH
ornamental braid - - - - - - LACE
ornamental button - - - - - - STUD
ornamental device - - - - - - - PIN
ornamental disposition - - - DECOR
ornamental dress trimming - - GIMP
ornamental ensemble - - - - DECOR
ornamental fabric - - - - TAPESTRY
ornamental grass - - - - - - NETI
ornamental jet of water - - FOUNTAIN
ornamental loop - - - - - - PICOT
ornamental part of wall - DODO, DADO
ornamental plant - - - - VALERIAN
ornamental shrub - - - - - - LILAC
ornamental slipknot - - - - - - BOW
ornamental tree - - ALMOND, PALM
ornamental vessel - - - - VASE, URN
ornamental wrist band - - BRACELET
ornamentation - - - - - - - DECOR
ornamented leather - - - - - TOOLED
ornate - FLORID, DECORATED, SHOWY, ADORN, ELABORATE
ort - - - - - MORSEL, SCRAP, BIT
orthodox Mohammedan - - MOSLEM
orthographer - - - - - - - SPELLER
os - - - - - - - - - BONE, MOUTH
osar - - - - - - - - - - - ESKERS
oscillate - - - WAG, SWING, ROCK,

VIBRATE, SWAY
oscine bird - CROW, TANAGER
osculate - KISS
osier - WILLOW, DOGWOOD, WAND, ROD
Osiris' brother - SET
Osiris' crown - ATEF
Osiris' wife - ISIS
osmium (pert. to) - OSMIC
ossicle of middle ear - BONE
ossified tissue - BONE
ost - KILN
osteal - BONY
ostentation - PARADE, POMP, FLARE, GAUDY
ostentatious - ARTY, PRETENTIOUS, SHOWY, GAUDY
ostiarius - DOORKEEPER
ostiole - STOMA, PORE
ostrich - RHEA
ostrich-like bird - EMU
otalgia - EARACHE
Othello's false friend - IAGO
other - ELSE, DIFFERENT, ALTERNATIVE
otherwise - ELSE, OR, ALIAS
otherwise called - ALIAS
otherwise (law) - ALITER
otic - AURAL
otiose - INDOLENT, INACTIVE, IDLE
otiosity - IDLENESS
Ottoman - TURKISH, TURK
Ottoman court - PORTE
Ottoman standard - ALEM
Our Lord (abbr.) - D.N.
oust - REMOVE, EVICT, EXPEL, EJECT
out - EX, FORTH, EJECT, OUTSIDE, EXTERNAL
out of - FROM
out of bed - ASTIR
out of breath - WINDED, AGASP
out of date - PASSE, OLD
out of the ordinary - UNUSUAL
out and out - ARRANT
out of position - OFF
out of (prefix) - EC, DE, EX
out of the right way - ASTRAY
out of style - PASSE
out of the way - REMOTE, AFIELD, ASIDE
outbreak - RIOT, ERUPTION
outbreak of enthusiasm - HYSTERIA
outbuilding - SHED, BARN
outburst - ERUPTION
outcast - LEPER, PARIAH
outclass - SURPASS, EXCEL
outcome - ISSUE, RESULT, END, SEQUEL
outcropping (geol.) - BASSET
outcry - CLAMOR
outdo - CAP, EXCEL, TRUMP, EXCEED
outdoor bench - EXEDRA
outdoor game - POLO
outdoor lamp - LANTERN
outdoor party - FETE, PICNIC
outdoor staircase - PERRON
outer - EXTERNAL, EXTERIOR
outer boundary of plane figure - PERIMETER
outer covering - RIND, SKIN, WRAP, COAT, HUSK, CRUST, HULL, SHELL
outer covering of tire - SHOE
outer covering of tooth - ENAMEL
outer garment - PARKA
outer grain husk - BRAN
outer layer - RIND
outer seed integument - TESTA
outfit - RIG, EQUIPMENT, GEAR, KIT, TOG
outing - AIRING
outlandish - OUTRE
outlay - PRICE, EXPENSE, COST
outlet - VENT
outline - CONTOUR, SYNOPSIS, SKETCH, PLAN
outline of moving picture - SCENARIO
outline of play - SCENARIO
outlive - SURVIVE
outlook - ASPECT, PROSPECT, VISTA
outlying settlement - OUTPOST
outmatch - BEST
outmoded - PASSE, DATED
outpouring - TIRADE, TORRENTIAL, EMITTING, FLOOD
outrage - ABUSE
outset - ONSET
outside - OUT
outside (comb. form) - ECTO
outside covering - WRAPPER
outside piece of log - SLAB
outside (prefix) - ECT
outspoken - BLUNT, FRANK, CANDID
outstanding - NOTABLE, SALIENT
outstanding bill - DEBT
outstanding endowment - TALENT
outstanding event - FEAT
outstrips - BESTS
outward - ECTAD, OUTER
outwit - FOIL
ova - EGGS
oval - OVATE
oval-shaped figure - ELLIPSE
ovate - OVAL
oven - KILN, BAKER
over - ABOVE, AGAIN, ACROSS, FINISHED, EXTRA, COMPLETED, BEYOND, ENDED, PAST, DONE
over again - ANEW
over (contr.) - OER
over (poet.) - OER
over (prefix) - SUPER
overawed - COWED
overbearing - PROUD
overbearing (colloq.) - BOSSY
overbusy (is) - FUSSES
overcast and threatening - LOWERING
overcoat - ULSTER, TOPCOAT, PALETOT
overcome - ROUT, BEST, SURMOUNT, CONQUER, APPAL, DEFEAT
overcome with horror - APPAL
overdue part - ARREAR
overflow - FLOOD, TEEM
overflow of an estuary - EAGRE
overfond - DOTE
overgrown - WEEDY
overhang - BEETLE, JUT
overhanging roof edge - EAVE
overhasty - RASH, DARING
overhead - ABOVE, ALOFT
overjoyed - ELATED
overlay - ENCRUST
overlook - MISS, SKIP
overlord - LIEGE
overly - TOO, CARELESS
overpass - TRANSCEND
overpower - MASTER, AWE, REPRESS, SUBDUE
overpower with light - DAZZLE
overpower with sudden emotion - STUN
overseas - ABROAD
overseer - BOSS, CENSOR, CURATOR, TASKMASTER
overseer (Eng. hist.) - REEVE

O

P

overseer of morals and conduct - - - CENSOR
overshoe - - - - - - - - GALOSH
overspread - - - - - - - - COVER
overstrain - - - - - - - - SPRAIN
overstrained - - - - - - EPITONIC
overt - - OPEN, PUBLIC, MANIFEST, OBVIOUS
overthrow - - - - UPSET, EVERSION
overthrowing (law) - - - REVERSAL
overtop - - - SURPASS, TRANSCEND
overtrained - - - - - - - - STALE
overture - - - - - - - - PRELUDE
overturn - - - - - - - UPSET, TIP
overwhelm - - - - - - - SWAMP
overwhelming number - - - - ARMY
ovule - - - - - - - - SEED, EGG
ovum - - - - - EGG, SEED, SPORE
owed - - - - - - - - - - - DUE
owing - - - - - - - - - - - DUE
own - POSSESS, CONFESS, AVOW, HAVE
own (Scot.) - - - - - - - - AIN
owner - - - - HOLDER, POSSESSOR
ownership - - - - - - - - TITLE
ox - - - - - - - BOS, STEER, YAK
ox of Celebes - - - ANOA, GOA, NOA
ox of Tibet - - - - - - - - YAK
oxen stall - - - - - - - - CRIB
oxidize - - - - - - - - - RUST
oxlike antelope - - - - ELAND, GNU
oxlike quadruped - - - BISON, YAK
oxygen compound - - - - - OXIDE
oxygen (form of) - - - - - OZONE
oxygenate - - - - - - - - AERATE
oyster - - - - - BIVALVE, REEFER
oyster bed - - - - - - - - LAYER
oyster (young) - - - - - - - SPAT

P

pace - GAIT, STRIDE, RATE, AMBLE, STEP, TROT
Pacific - - - - - - - - - IRENIC
Pacific coast shrub - - SALAD, SALAL
Pacific discoverer - - - - BALBOA
Pacific Island aroid - - - - TARO
Pacific Island group - SAMOA, SAIPAN, HAWAII
Pacific Island pine - - - - EI, IE
Pacific Island tree - - - IPIO, IPIL
pacifist - - - - - - APPEASER, SOP
pacify - PLACATE, SOOTHE, APPEASE
pack - - - - - - - - STOW, CRAM
pack of cards - - - - - - - DECK
pack down - - - - - - - - TAMP
pack tightly - - - - - - - - CRAM
package - CARTON, PARCEL, BUNDLE
packing box - - - - - - - CRATE
packing disk for joints - - - GASKET
packing ring - - - - - - - GASKET
pact - - - - - TREATY, AGREEMENT
pad - - - - - - CUSHION, TABLET
padding for a coat - - - - - WAD
paddle - - - - - - - - OAR, ROW
pagan - HEATHEN, ETHNIC, IDOLATOR
page - - - - - - - - FOLIO, LEAF
pageant - - - - - - - - - POMP
pagoda ornament and finial - - - TEE
pagoda top - - - - - - - FINIAL
paid office with few duties - SINECURE
pail - - - - - - - - - - BUCKET
pail (Scot.) - - - - - - - COGGIE
pain - ACHE, PANG, STING, THROE, DISQUIET, MISERY, HURT, DISTRESS
painful - - - - - - - BITTER, SORE
paint - - COLOUR, PIGMENT, ROUGE, DECORATE, LIMN
paint brush - - - - - - - - PENCIL
paint coarsely - - - - - - - DAUB
paint pigment - - - - - - - - OCHER
paint with cosmetics - - - - ROUGE
paint with short strokes - - STIPPLE
painstaking - - - - - - - DILIGENT
painter - - - - - - ARTIST, LIMNER
painter and paperer - - DECORATOR
painter's stand - - - - - - EASEL
painter's tablet - - - - - - PALETTE
painting (kind) - - - - - - MURAL
painting of Madonna - - - SISTINE
painting medium - OILS, WATERCOLOR
painting method - - - - - ENCAUSTIC
painting in one color - - MONOTINT
painting of plaster - FRESCO, SECCO, FRESCOING
painting style - - - - - - - GENRE
pair - TEAM, BRACE, TWAIN, MATCH, TWO, DUO, DYAD
pair (var.) - - - - - - - - - DIAD
paired (her.) - - - - - - - GEMEL
paisley - - - - - - - - - SHAWL
pal - - - - - - - - - - - CHUM
palace - - - - - - - - - CASTLE
paladin - - - - - - - - CHAMPION
palanquin (form of) - - - - KAGO
palatable - - - - - SAVORY, SAPID
palate - - - - - - - - - - TASTE
palate (soft) - - - - - - - - UVULA
palatial - - - - - PALATINE, VELAR
palatine - - - - - - - - - PALATIAL
palatine bone - - - - - - PALATAL
palaver - - - - - - - - - DEBATE
pale - WAN, STAKE, PALLID, BLANCH, ASHY, DIM, WHITE, PICKET, ASHEN, FAINT, FADE
pale brown - - - - - - - - ECRU
pale green - - - - - - - - - NILE
pale or light - - - - - - - PASTEL
paleness - - - - - - - - - PALLOR
Palestine animal - - - - - - DAMAN
Palestine city - - - SAMARIA, HAIFA
Palestine coin - - - - - - - - MIL
Palestine mountain - CARMEL, GILEAD
Palestine mountain district - - GILEAD
Palestine plain - - - - - - SHARON
Palestine province - - - - - GALILEE
Palestine town - - - - - - - CANA
paletot - - - - - - - - OVERCOAT
pall - - - - - - - - - - - CLOY
palliate - - - EXTENUATE, MITIGATE, CONCEAL, GLOSS, SALVE
pallor - - - - - - - - - PALENESS
palm - - - - - - - - - - - ARECA
palm cockatoo - - - - - - - ARACA
palm of hand - - - - VOLAR, THENAR
palm (kind) - - - - - COCO, ASSAI
palm leaf - - - - - OLA, OLE, FROND
palm lily - - - - - - - - TI, TITREE
palm off - - - - - - - - - FOIST
palm stem (flexible) - - - - RATTAN
palm wine - - - - - - - - - TAREE
palmer - - - - - - - - - PILGRIM
Palmyra palm - - - - TAL, OLE, OLA
palp - - - - - - - - - - FEELER
palpable - - - TANGIBLE, MANIFEST
palpitate - - - - - - - - - THROB
paltry - - - - - - - - - - SMALL
pamper - - - CODDLE, SPOIL, PET, COSSET
pamphlet - - - - - - - - - TRACT
pan to burn incense - - - - CENSER

panacea - - - ELIXIR, CURE
Panama Canal dam - - - GATUN
Panama Canal lake - - - GATUN
Panama seaport - - - COLON
Panama town - - - GATUN
Panay Island native - - - ATI
pandiculate - - - STRETCH
panegyric - - - ELOGE, ENCOMIUM
panel - - - JURY
pang - - - AGONY, PAIN, ACHE, THROE
pant - - - GASP, THROB, BEAT, PUFF, YEARN
panther - - - PUMA, PARD, LEOPARD
pantry - - - LARDER
pants - - - TROUSERS, SLACKS
papal - - - APOSTOLIC
papal veil - - - ORALE
paper - - - ESSAY
paper fastener - - - CLIP
paper measure - - - REAM, QUIRE
paper-nautilus (zool.) - - - ARGONAUT
paper pulpvat stirrer - - - HOG
paper spoiled in the making - - - SALLE
par - - - PARITY, BALANCE
parachutist's cry - - - GERONIMO
parade - SPECTACLE, FLAUNT, DISPLAY, MARCH, REVIEW
paradigm - - - MODEL, PATTERN
Paradise - - - EDEN
paragon - - - MODEL, PATTERN, TYPE
paragraph - - - ITEM
Paraguay city - - - ITA
parallel - - - EVEN
parallel of latitude - - - TROPICS
parallelogram (kind) - - - RHOMB
paralytic - - - PARETIC
paramount - - - CHIEF, SUPREME
paramour - - - LOVER
parapet - - - RAMPART
paraphrase - - - REWORD
parasite (colloq.) - - - SPONGE
parasitic insect - - - FLEA, LOUSE, LICE
parasitic larva - - - BOT
parasitic shrub - - - MISTLETOE
parasol - - - SUNSHADE
parcel - - - PACKAGE, PACKET
parcel of land - - - LOT, LET
parcel out - - - ALLOT, METE
parch - - - SEAR
parch with heat - - - SCORCH
parched - - - THIRSTY, ARID, SEARED
parchment roll - - - SCROLL
parchment written on often - - - PALIMPSEST
pard - - - PANTHER
pardon - - - CONDONE, FORGIVE, REPRIEVE, REMIT, REMISSION, EXCUSE, ABSOLVE, AMNESTY
pardonable - - - VENIAL
pare - PEEL, REMOVE, REDUCE, CUT, SHAVE
parent - - - FOREBEAR
parentage - - - ORIGIN
parenthetical remark - - - ASIDE
paretic - - - PARALYTIC
parget - WHITEWASH, PLASTER, COAT
pari-colored - - - PIED
Paris' father - - - PRIAM
Paris' wife - - - OENONE
parish assistant - - - CURATE
parish (pert. to) - - - PAROCHIAL
parity - - - EQUALITY, PAR
park in Rockies - - - ESTES
parlance - - - DICTION
parlay - - - WAGER
parley - - - CONFERENCE, CONFER, DISCUSS
parliament - - - DIET
parlour - - - SALON
parodist - - - IMITATOR
parody - - - SKIT, TRAVESTY, SATIRE
parol - - - UNWRITTEN, ORAL
paronomasia - - - PUN
paroxysm - - - SPASM, FIT
parrot fish - - - LANIA, COTORO
parrot (kind) - - - LORY, ARA, MACAW, KAKA, PARAKEET, KEA
parry - - - FEND, AVOID
parsimonious - - - STINGY
parsley plant - - - DILL
parson - - - PASTOR, MINISTER
parson bird - - - TUI, TIRE, POE
parsonage - - - MANSE, RECTORY
part - - - SECTION, SEVER, PORTION, PIECE, SIDE, SUNDER, ROLE, BIT
part (small) - - - SNIPPET, BIT, IOTA
part above ground - - - TOP
part of flower - - - SEPAL, PETAL
part of head - - - SCALP
part of infinitive - - - TO
part of joint - - - TENON
part of meal - - - COURSE
part in play - - - ROLE
part of shoe - - - RAND
part song - - - MADRIGAL
part of speech - - - NOUN
part of whole - - - HALF
part with - - - LOSE
partake - - - SHARE, USE
parti-coloured - - - PIED
partial - HALF, BIASED, FAVOURABLE
partial darkness - - - SHADE, SHADOW
partial to - - - FAVOUR
partially - - - HALF
partially burned carbon - - - SOOT
partially fused composition - - - FRIT
partially paralyzed - - - PARETIC
participant - - - PLAYER
participate - - - SHARE
participator - - - PARTY
participial ending - - - ED, ING
particle - IOTA, MITE, SHRED, ATOM, GRAIN, SPECK, MOTE, ACE, JOT
particle of falling water - RAINDROP, DROP
particle of fire - - - SPARK, ARC
particular - SPECIAL, ESPECIAL, FUSSY
particular instance - - - CASE
particularly - - - NOTABLY
partisan - - - DEVOTEE
partition - - - SEVERANCE, DIVISION, CELL, WALL, SECTION, SEPTUM
partly open - - - AJAR
partly (prefix) - - - SEMI
partner - - - MATE, ALLY, SHARER
partner (colloq.) - - - PARD
partnership - - - ALLIANCE
partnership (colloq.) - - - CAHOOTS
party - - - SECT, FACTION
party member - - - DEMOCRAT
parvenu - - - UPSTART
pasquinade - - - LAMPOON
pass - - - ELAPSE, FARE, APPROVE, CIRCULATE, OCCUR, DEFILE, ADOPT, DEVOLVE, ENACT
pass around - - - SKIRT
pass away - - - ELAPSE, PERISH, DIE
pass between hills - - - DEFILE
pass between peaks - - - COL
pass by - - - ELAPSE
pass from one stage to another - - - BECOME

P

pass imperceptibly - - - - - - SLIDE
pass into use - - - - - - - ENURE
pass lightly over - - - - - SKIM
pass off as genuine - - - - - FOIST
pass in vapour - - - - EVAPORATE
pass on - - - - - - - - - - RELAY
pass over - - - - ELIDE, CROSS, OMIT
pass over lightly - - - - - - SKIM
pass a rope through - - - - - REEVE
pass slowly - - - - - DRAG, LAPSE
pass swiftly - - - - - - - - SWEEP
pass through - - PENETRATE, CROSS
pass through cautiously - - - - REEVE
pass through pores - - - - TRANSUDE
pass through a sieve - - - - - SIFT
pass as time - - - - - - - - SPEND
pass without touching - - - - - CLEAR
passable - - - - - - - - TOLERABLE
passage - TRANSIT, AISLE, APERTURE, ALLEY, WAY, ENTRY, ALEE, CANAL, CHANNEL, VOYAGE
passage (anat.) - - - - - - - - ITER
passage between cliffs - - - - - GAT
passage in a cathedral - - - - SLYPE
passage for fluid - - - - - - DUCT
passage from shore inland - - - - GAT
passage into - - - - - ENTRY, INLET
passage out - - - - - EXIT, EGRESS
passage of Scriptures - - - - - TEXT
passage with pomp - - - - - SWEEP
passageway - ARCADE, RAMP, AISLE, GATE
passe - - - - - - - - - OBSOLETE
passenger - FARE, RIDER, TRAVELLER, PASSER
passerby - - - - - - - - - PASSER
passerine bird - - STARLING, FINCH
passing whim - - - - - - - - - FAD
passion - - - - IRE, FEELING, LUST
passion in Buddhism - - - - - RAGA
passive - - - - - INERT, INACTIVE
Passover festival - - - - - - SEDER
passport indorsement - - - - - VISA
past - BY, AGONE, AGO, GONE, OVER
past (poet.) - - - - - - - - AGONE
past tense - - - - - - - PRETERIT
past tense suffix - - - - - - - - ED
paste - - CREAM, GLUE, ARTIFICIAL, IMITATION, CEMENT, FASTEN, ADHESIVE, DOUGH, STICK
pasteboard (piece of) - - - - - CARD
pasteboard container - - - - CARTON
pastime - - - - - DIVERSION, SPORT
pastor - RECTOR, PARSON, MINISTER, CLERGYMAN, KEEPER
pastoral - - - - RUSTIC, RURAL, IDYL, DRAMA, POEM
pastoral poem - IDYLL, IDYL, ECLOGUE
pastry - - - - - - - - - PIE, TART
pasturage - - GRASS, EATAGE, RANGE
pasture - - - - - LEA, GRASS, GRAZE
pasture grass - - - - - - - GRAMA
pasture for hire - - - - - - - AGIST
pasture plant - - - - - - - CLOVER
pasty - - - - - - - - - - DOUGHY
pasty cement - - - - - - - - MASTIC
pat - APT, TIMELY, TRAP, TAP, STROKE
Patagonian deity - - - - - SETEBOS
patch - - - - - PIECE, MEND, VAMP
patchwork composition - - - - CENTO
paten - - - - - - - - - - - - DISC
patent - - - - MANIFEST, COPYRIGHT, OBVIOUS
paternal - - - - - - - - FATHERLY
paternal inheritance - - - PATRIMONY
path - - TRAIL, LANE, ROUTE, WAY, FOOTWAY, TRACK, COURSE, ORBIT
pathetic - - - - - - - - - - - SAD
pathfinder - - - - - - - - PIONEER
patient - - - - - - - FORBEARING
patient fortitude - - - - ENDURANCE
patient man - - - - - - - - - JOB
patio - - - - - - - - - - - COURT
patrimonial - - - - - - - ANCESTRAL
patriotic - - - - - - - - NATIONAL
patriotic society - - - - - DAR, SAR
patrol - - - - - - - - SCOUT, WATCH
patrolman's assignment - - - - BEAT
patron - - PROTECTOR, BENEFACTOR, GUEST
patron saint of Christmas - - - SANTA
patron saint of cripples - - - - GILES
patron saint of France (var.) - - DENYS
patron saint of Ireland - - - - PATRICK
patron saint of lawyers - - - - - IVES
patron saint of Norway - - - - - OLAF
patron saint of sailors - - - - - ELMO
patron saint of sea - - - - - - ELMO
patron saint of Wales - - - - DAVID
patter - - - - - - - - - - JARGON
pattern - - - NORM, MODEL, IDEAL, DESIGN, PARADIGM
paucity - - - - - - - - SCARCITY
Paul's associate - - - - - - - SILAS
pause - - - - REST, SELAH, RESPITE, HESITATE, STOP
paver's mallet - - - - - - - - TUP
pavilion on elephant's back - HOWDAH
paving block - - - - - - - - PAVER
pawl - - - - - - - - - DETENT, COG
pawl (mach.) - - - - - - - - CLICK
pawn - - - - - - - - - - - - TOOL
pay - - - - - REMUNERATE, DEFRAY, DISBURSE, DISCHARGE, WAGES, STIPEND, COMPENSATE, EXPEND, WAGE
pay in advance - - - - - - PREPAY
pay attention - - - - - - - - HEED
pay back - RETALIATE, REMIT, RENDER, REIMBURSE
pay homage to - - - - - - - HONOR
pay one's part - - - - - ANTES, ANTE
pay out - - - - - - - - - - SPEND
payable - - - - - - - - - - - DUE
paying guest - - - - - - - BOARDER
paying social attention to (var.) - - - LIONIZING
payment - - - - FEE, COMPENSATION
payment back - - - - - - - REBATE
payment for instruction - - - - TUITION
pea - - - - - - - - - - - LEGUME
pea tree - - - - - - - - - - AGATI
peace - SERENITY, REPOSE, CONCORD, CALM, QUIETUDE
peace (Latin) - - - - - - - - - PAX
peace officer - - - - - - CONSTABLE
peace pipe - - - - - - - - CALUMET
peach state - - - - - - - - GEORGIA
peaceful - - - SERENE, IRENIC, CALM
peacock - - - - - MOA, STRUT, PAWN
peacock blue - - - - - - - - PAON
peacock butterfly - - - - - - - - IO
peak - ACME, CREST, SUMMIT, CUSP
peak (Fr.) - - - - - - - - - - - PIC
peal - - - - - RING, RESPOND, TOLL
peanut - EARTHPEA, EARTHNUT, MANI, GOOBER
pear - - - - - - - - - - - - NOME
pear orange - - - - - - - BERGAMOT
pear shaped fruit - - - - FIG, GUAVA
pear shaped glass vessel - - - ALUDEL
pearl - - - - - - - - - RING, NACRE
pearl blue colour - - - - - - - METAL

pearl mussel - - - - - - - UNIO
peart - - - - - - - - - - FRISKY
peas collectively - - - - - PEASE
peas (dial.) - - - - - - - PEASES
peasant - - - RYOT, RUSTIC, SERF
peat bog - - - - - - MOSS, CESS
peat cutter (Scot.) - - - - - PINER
pebble - - - - - - - - - - STONE
pebbles (sand) - - - - - - GRAVEL
pecan - - - - - - - - - HICKORY
peck - - - - - - - DOT, DAB, NIP
peculiar - STRANGE, SINGULAR, QUEER, ODD
peculiar to a language - - IDIOMATIC
peculiar leaf form (bot.) - - PITCHER
peculiar nature - - - - - - GENUS
peculiar saying - - - - - - IDIOM
peculiarity - - - - TRAIT, ODDITY
pecuniary penalty - - - - - - FINE
pedagogue - SCHOOLMASTER, TUTOR
pedal digit - - - - - - - - TOE
pedal extremity - - - - - - FOOT
pedant - - - - - - - - SCHOLAR
pedantic - - - - - - - - STILTED
peddler - - - - - - - - HAWKER
pedestal - - SUPPORT, BASE, ANTA
pedestal face - - - - - - - DADO
pedestal part - - - - - - - DADO
pedicel of an umbel - - - - RAY
pedigree - - - - - RACE, LINEAGE
peduncle - - PEDICEL, STEM, SCAPE
peek - - - - - - - - PEEP, PEER
peel - - BARK, PARE, REMOVE, SKIN, STRIP, RIND
peep - - - - - - - CHIRP, PEEK
peep show - - - - - - - - RAREE
peepers (colloq.) - - - - - - EYES
peer - - - GAZE, NOBLEMAN, LOOK, MATCH, NOBLE, PEEP, PEEK
peer of Charlemagne - - - OLIVER
Peer Gynt's author - - - - - IBSEN
Peer Gynt's mother - - - - - - ASE
peerage - - - - - - - - NOBILITY
peerless - - - - - - - MATCHLESS
peeve - VEX, ANNOYANCE, IRRITATE, ANNOY
peeve (colloq.) - - - - - - NETTLE
peevish - PETTISH, FRETFUL, CROSS, TESTY, MOODY, TECHY
peg - - DOWEL, PIN, MARKER, NOB
pegu ironwood - - - - - - - ACLE
pelagic - - - - - - - - OCEANIC
pelite - - - - - - - - - SHALE
pellet - - - - - - - - - - PILL
pellucid - - - - - - - - SHEER
pelt - FUR, SKIN, HIDE, HURL, THROW, PEPPER
pelt of Siberian squirrel - - CALABAR
pelted with rocks - - - - - - STONED
pen - - STY, QUILL, COOP, INDITE, WRITE, CAGE, CONFINE, ENCLOSE, RECORD
pen point - - - - - - - NIB, NEB
pen up - - - - - - - - - - MEW
penal - - - - - - - - - PUNITIVE
penalize - - - - - - - - PUNISH
penalty - - - - - - - FINE, LOSS
pencil - - - - - - - - - CRAYON
pend - - - - - - - - - - - HANG
pendant - - - - - TASSEL, EARRING
pendant ornament - LAVALIERE, TASSEL
pendent - - LOP, FOB, BOB, HANGING
pendulous - - - - - - - - - LOP
penetrate - - ENTER, PIERCE, BORE
penetrating - - - - - - ACUTE, RAW
penetrating flavor - - - - - - TANG
penitent - - - CONTRITE, REPENTANT
penitential period - - - - - - LENT
penitential psalm - - - - - MISERERE
penmanship - - - - - - - - WRITING
pennant - - - - - STREAMER, FLAG
pennies (abbr.) - - - - - - - CTS.
pennon - - - - - - FLAG, BANNER
Pennsylvania borough - SAYRE, ETAN
Pennsylvania city and lake port - ERIE, EASTON, ALTOONA
Pennsylvania coal mining town - JERMYN
Pennsylvania river - - - - - LEHIGH
Pennsylvania town - - - ONO, AVOCA
penny - - - - - - - - - - COPPER
pensile - - - - - - - - - HANGING
pentateuch - - - - - - - - - TORAH
penurious - POOR, STINGY, MISERLY, MEAN
people - DEMOS, NATION, POPULATE, LAITY, FOLKS, RACE, INHABIT, ONES
people conquered by Rome - - SABINE
people (pert. to) - - - - - NATIONAL
people of present day - - - MODERNS
pep - - - - - - - - - - - VERVE
pep (slang) - - - - - - - - GINGER
pep up - - - - - - - - - ENLIVEN
pepper - - - - - - - - - - PELT
pepper (kind) - - BETEL, AVA, KAVA
peppery - - - - - - - - - - HOT
per - - - - - - - - - - BY, FOR
perceive - - SEE, SENSE, REALIZE, APPREHEND
perceive by senses - - - - SENSATE
percent - - - - - - - - - - RATE
perceptible by touch - - - TACTILE
perception - - - SENSE, SENSATION
perch - - - - - ROOST, SEAT, SIT
perch-like fish - - - - - - - BASS
percolate - - - - - - SEEP, FILTER
percussion - - - - - - COLLISION
percussion drill - - - - - - - GAD
percussion instrument - DRUM, GONG, TRAP, TRIANGLE
peregrine - - - - FALCON, FOREIGN
peremptory order - - - - MANDATE
perennial - - - - - - COLUMBINE
perennial garden plant - - RHUBARB
perennial herb - PIA, MADDER, SEDUM
perfect - - - - - IDEAL, FLAWLESS, CONSUMMATE, COMPLETE
perfect (comb. form) - - - - TELEO
perfectionist - - - - - - IDEALIST
perfidious person - - - - TRAITOR
perforate - PUNCH, TEREBRATE, DRILL, BORE
perforated cask to drain sugar - - POT
perforated design - - - - - STENCIL
perforated disk - - - - - - WASHER
perforated implement - - - STRAINER
perforated metal disk in oil lamps - - DIFFUSER
perforated ornament - - - - - BEAD
perforation - - - - - - - - HOLE
perform - - - - - - DO, ACT, PLAY, ENACT
perform diligently - - - - - - PLY
perform offhand - - - - IMPROVISE
perform with ceremony (var.) - - - - SOLEMNIZE
performance - - - RENDITION, ACT
performer - - - - - - - - - DOER
performing service - - - MINISTRANT
perfume - - ESSENCE, ATTAR, SCENT, CENSE
perfume bag - - - - - - - SACHET
perfume compound - - - - PIPERONAL

P

perfume of flowers - - - - - - ATTAR
perfume (kind) - - - - - - - CIVET
perfume (var.) - - - - - - - ATAR
perfume with odors - - - - - CENSE
perfumed pad - - - - - - - SACHET
pergola - - - - - - - - - - ARBOR
perhaps (arch.) - - MAYHAP, BELIKE
peril - - MENACE, DANGER, HAZARD, RISK, JEOPARDY
perilous - - INSECURE, DANGEROUS
period - - - AGE, DOT, ERA, TIME
period of day - - - - - - - TIME
period of denial - - - - - - - LENT
period just before - - - - - - EVE
period of light - - - - - - - DAY
period of reduced prices - - - SALE
period of a thousand years - CHILIAD
period of time - - ERAL, TERM, EON, DECADE, EPOCH
period of year - - - - - - SEASON
periodic - - - - - - - REGULAR
perish - - - - EXPIRE, DIE, RUIN
perissodactyl ungulate - - - - TAPIR
permanent - - DURABLE, ENDURING
permeable by liquids - - - - POROUS
permeate - - - - PERVADE, IMBUE
permeating - - - - - - PERVASIVE
permission - LEAVE, CONSENT, LICENSE
permission to travel - - - PASSPORT
permission to use - - - - - - LOAN
permit - - - LET, ALLOW, LICENSE
permitted - - - - - - - - LICIT
pernicious - - - - BANE, EVIL, BAD
perpendicular - - - - SHEER, SINE
perpetrate - - - - - - - - - DO
perpetual - - PERENNIAL, CONSTANT, UNCEASING, ENDLESS
perpetually - - - - - - - - EVER
perplex - - - - HARASS, BOTHER
perplexing questions - - CONUNDRUM
perse - - - - - - - - - - BLUE
persecute - HARRY, BADGER, OPPRESS
perseverance - - - - - - - - GRIT
persevere - - - - - - - PERSIST
persevering person - - - - PLODDER
Persia - - - - - - - - - IRAN
Persian - - - IRANIAN, MEDE, PERSE
Persian angel - - - - - - - MAH
Persian coin - - - - - - RIAL, KRAN
Persian coin (ancient) - - - DARIC
Persian fairy and elf - - - - - PERI
Persian gazelle - - - - - - - CORA
Persian governor - - - - - - SATRAP
Persian judge - - - - - - - CADI
Persian king - - - - - - - XERXES
Persian measure of distance - - - - PARASANG
Persian money - - - - - - - DINAR
Persian poet - - - - - - - OMAR
Persian race - - - - - - - - LUR
Persian ruler - - - - - - - - SHAH
Persian title - - - - - - SHAR, MIR
Persian town - - - - - - - - - FAO
Persian water wheel - - - - - NORIA
Persian weight - - - ABBAS, SANG
persiflage - - - - - - - - - BANTER
persist - LAST, PERSEVERE, REMAIN, INSIST, ENDURE, CONTINUE
persistent - PERSEVERING, ENDURING
persistent aggressor - - - - - SINNER
person - - - - ONE, SOUL, BEING
person addressed - - - - - YOU, YE
person appointed to act as sheriff - - - ELISOR
person bearing the blame (slang) - GOAT
person of consequence - - SOMEONE
person doing servile work - - MENIAL
person of foresight - - - - - - SAGE
person from 60 to 69 - SEXAGENARIAN
person of long experience - - STAGER
person named for office - - NOMINEE
person not in office - - - - - - OUT
person, place or thing - - - - - NOUN
person of rank - - - - - - MAGNATE
person of servile nature - - - MENIAL
person of social distinction - - - NOB
person of superior air - - - - - PRIG
person on whom bill of exchange is drawn DRAWEE
person with loud voice - - - STENTOR
personal beliefs - - - - - OPINIONS
personal belongings - - TRAPS, GEAR
personal consideration and interest - SELF
personal pronoun (poet.) - - - - - YE
personality - EGO, SELF, CHARACTER
personality (slang) - - - - - - - IT
personification of rumor - - - - FAMA
personification of truth - - - - - UNA
persons collectively - - - PERSONNEL
perspicacious - - - - - - - ASTUTE
perspicacity - - - - - - - ACUMEN
perspiration - - - - - - - - SUDOR
perspire - - - - - - - - - SWEAT
persuade - URGE, INFLUENCE, INDUCE, COAX
persuade by argument - - - REASON, CONVINCE
persuasive - - - - - - - COGENT
pert - - - LIVELY, BOLD, IMPUDENT, SHORT
pert girl - - - - - - - - - - MINX
pertain - RELATE, CONCERN, BELONG
pertaining to - - - - - - - - ANENT
pertaining to (suffix) - AR, AC, ILE, IC
pertaining to that which is taught - - - DOCTRINAL
pertinent - RELATIVE, APT, RELEVANT
pertness - - - - - - - - - SAUCE
perturb - - - - - - - - AGITATE
peruke - - - - - - - - - - - WIG
perusal - - - - - - - - - READING
peruse - - - - READ, CON, SCAN
Peruvian capital - - - - - - LIMA
Peruvian chieftain - - - - - - INCA
Peruvian coin - - - DINER, DINERO
Peruvian dance - - - - - - CUECA
Peruvian Indian - - - - CANA, INCA
Peruvian plant - - - - - - - OCA
Peruvian race - - - - - - - INCA
Peruvian seaport - - - - - CALLOA
Peruvian tinamou - - - - - - YUTU
Peruvian tuber - - - - - - - OCA
Peruvian volcano - - - - - - MISTI
pervade - - PERMEATE, IMBUE, FILL
pervasive - - - - - - PERMEATING
perverse - - - - - - - FROWARD
pervert - - - - - - - - CORRUPT
pest - - - - - - BORE, EPIDEMIC
pester - - HARRY, HARASS, TEASE, ANNOY, NAG
pesterer - - - - - - - - NAGGER
pet - - - - - - - FONDLE, COSSET
pet lamb - - - - - - - - - COSSET
petal - - - - - - - - - - - LEAF
Peter the Great - - - - - - - TSAR
petiole - - - - - LEAFSTALK, STEM
petit - - - - - - - - - - SMALL
petition - - - SUE, BEG, PLEA, ASK, SOLICIT, SUIT
petitioner - - - - - - - APPLICANT

Petrarch's lady - - - - - - LAURA
petrified vegetation - - - - - COAL
petroleum - - - - OIL, GASOLINE
petticoat - - - - - - - - - - SLIP
pettifogger - - - - - - - SHYSTER
pettiness - - - - - - - SMALLNESS
petty - - - SMALL, TRIFLE, LITTLE
petty devil - - - - - - - - - IMP
petty malice - - - - - - - SPITE
petty officer - - - YEOMAN, SATRAP
petty officer (colloq.) - - - BOSUN
petty plunder - - - - - - - PILFER
petulant - - SHORT, CROSS, FRETFUL
phantom - IDOLON, GHOST, EIDOLON
pharmaceutical name for honey - - MEL
pharmacist - - - - - - DRUGGIST
phase - ASPECT, SIDE, APPEARANCE, STAGE
Phen goddess of love - - - ASTARTE
phial - - - - - - - VIAL, BOTTLE
philippic - - - - SCREED, TIRADE
Philippine aborigine - AETA, ATA, ITA
Philippine archipelago - - - - SULU
Philippine barge - - - - - - CASCO
Philippine dagger - - - - - - ITAC
Philippine dwarf race - - - - AETA
Philippine garment - - - - - SAYA
Philippine group - - - - - IGOROT
Philippine Island - - PANAY, LEYTE, MINDANAO, CEBU, SAMAR
Philippine Island province - - CAVITE
Philippine Island town division - - ATO
Philippine knife - - - - - - - BOLO
Philippine lizard - - - - - - - IBID
Philippine measure - - - - - - CABA
Philippine Mohammedan - - - MORO
Philippine mountain - - - APO, IBA
Philippine native - ATI, ATA, TAGALOG, AETA, MORO
Philippine Negrito - - - ITI, ITA, ATI
Philippine peasant - - - - - TAO
Philippine rice - - - - - - MACAN
Philippine rice polishings - - DARAC
Philippine termite - - - ANAY, ANAI
Philippine timber - - - - - - CAHUY
Philippine timber tree - - - AMAGA
Philippine tree - TUA, IPIL, DITA, DAO
Philippine tree (poisonous) - - LIGAS
Philippine tribe - - - ATAS, MOROS
Philippine weapon - - - - - - BOLO
Philippine woody pine - - - - IYO
Philistine foe - - - - - - SAMSON
Philistine giant - - - - - GOLIATH
Philistine god - - - - - - - BAAL
philosopher - - - - - - - - KANT
philosophical disciples - - - - SECT
philosophical doctrine - - PANTHEISM
Phoenician capital - - - - - TYRE
Phoenician goddess of fertility - ASTARTE
phonetic sign - - - - - - - LETTER
phosphorous compound source - APATITE
photo - - - - - - - - - - PICTURE
photograph - - - PRINT, SNAP, MUG
photograph bath - REDUCER, TONER, DEVELOPER, FIXER
photograph book - - - - - - ALBUM
photographed criminals - - MUGGED
phraseology - - - - - - - DIALECT
Phrygian cap - - - - - - - TIARA
Phrygian god of life - - - - ATYS
physical - - - - - - - MATERIAL
physician (arch.) - - - - - - LEECH
physician (colloq.) - MEDIC, MEDICO
physician (pert. to) - - - - IATRIC
physiognomy - - - - - - - - - FACE
pianist - - - - - - - - MUSICIAN
piano keyboard - - - - - - CLAVIER
piano keys (slang) - - - - - IVORIES
pianolike instrument - - - CELESTE
piazza - - - - - - - - - VERANDA
picaroon - - - - - - - - - ROGUE
pick - - - - PLUCK, SELECT, ELITE
pick bamboo shoots - - - - ACHAR
pick flaws - - - - - - CAVIL, CARP
pick out - - - - - - - - GLEAN
pick up by degrees - - - - GLEAN
pick up with beak - - - - - - PECK
picket - - - - - - - PALE, STAKE
pickle - - MARINATE, CORN, SOUSE
pickpocket (slang) - - - - - - DIP
picnic - - - - - - - - - - OUTING
pictorial sketch - - - - - - CARTOON
picture - DEPICT, PORTRAYAL, PHOTO, IMAGE, ICON, PASTEL
picture cast by a lens - - - - IMAGE
picture drawn with coloured crayons - - PASTEL
picture frame - - - - - - - EASEL
picture puzzle - - - - - - - REBUS
picture supporting framework - EASEL
picturesque - - - SCENIC, IDYLLIC
pie - - - - - - - - - - PASTRY
piebald horse - - - - - - - PINTO
piece - PATCH, PORTION, FRAGMENT, SEGMENT, CHIP, MISSILE, SECTION, PART, BIT, LUMP, STAB, MORSEL, SCRAP
piece of armor for thigh - - - TASLET
piece broken off - - - - - - - CHIP
piece of cloth - - - - - - - INSET
piece of connecting pipe - - - - TEE
piece of ground - - - - - - - LOT
piece of iron adjoining poles of magnet - ARMATURE
piece of meadow - - - - - - SWALE
piece of metal to hold another in place - GIB
piece of money - - - - - - - COIN
piece of news - - - - - - TIDINGS
piece of paper - - - - - SHEET, SLIP
piece to prevent slipping - - - CLEAT
piece of property - - - LOT, ASSET
piece put in - - - - INSET, GUSSET
piece of soap - - - - - - - CAKE
piece of timber - - - - - - PLANK
piece of turf - - - DIVOT, PEAT, SOD
piece of waste silk - - - - - - NOIL
piece of work - - - - - - - - JOB
piece out - - - - - - - - - - EKE
pied, as an animal - - - - - PINTO
pie plant - - - - - - - RHUBARB
pier - ANTA, DOCK, MOLE, WHARF, JETTY
pier treated as a pilaster - - - ANTA
pierce - - TAB, PENETRATE, ENTER, GORE, LANCE, PUNCTURE
pierce with horn - - - - - - GORE
pierce with many holes - - - RIDDLE
pierce with a stake - IMPALE, EMPALE
pigeon - DOVE, POUTER, BARB, NUN
pigeon food - - - - SALTCAT, PEA
pigeon hawk - - - - - - - MERLIN
pigeon house - - - - - - DOVECOT
pigeon nestling - - - - - - SQUAB
pigeon pea - - - - - - - TUR, DAL
pigment - - - - - - - - - PAINT
pigment from plants - - - - ETIOLIN
pigment used in water color - - BISTRE
pigs - - - - - - SWINE, GRUNTERS
pigtail - - - - - - - - - - QUEUE

pike - HIGHWAY, LUCE
pike-like fish - GARA, GAR, ROBALO
piker - TIGHTWAD
pillage - RANSACK
pilaster - ANTA, COLUMN
pile - HEAP, MASS, STACK, LOAD, NAP, SPILE
pile to be burnt - PYRE
pile of earth - HILL
pile of hay or straw - RICK, MOW
pile up - AMASS, STACK
pilfer - ROB, STEAL, PLUNDER
pilgrim - PALMER
pilgrim father - ALDEN
pilgrim from Holy Land - PALMER
pilgrim leader - STANDISH
pilgrim's protector - TEMPLAR
pilgrimage to Mecca - HADJ
pill - PELLET, BOLUS
pill bug - SLATER
pillage - LOOT, RAVAGE, RAPINE, PLUNDER, SACK, RANSACK, RIFLE, FORAY
pillager - MARAUDER
pillar - OBELISK, LAT, POST, SHAFT
pillar (resembling) - STELAR
pillow cover - SHAM
pilot - STEER, STEERSMAN, GUIDE, GUIDER, STEERER, AVIATOR
pilot fish - ROMERO
pin - FASTEN, BOLT, PEG, NOG, BADGE, SKITTLE
pin to fasten meat - SKEWER
pin used in certain game - SKITTLE
pinaceous tree - FIR
pinch - NIP
pinch and pull - TWEAK
pine - LANGUISH, MOPE, SULK, YEARN, LAMENT, GRIEVE
pine cone - STROBILE
pine extract - RESIN
pine for - GRIEVE
pineapple - PINA, ANANA, NANA, ANANAS
pineapple leaf - PINA
pinion - SHACKLE, WING
pink - ROSE, ROSY
pinna - EAR
pinnacle - TOP, APEX
pinnacle of ice in a glacier - SERAC
pinnacle ornament - FINIAL
pinnacle of rock - NEEDLE
pinochle score and term - MELD
pins, needles and thread - NOTIONS
pintado - SIERRA
pintail duck - SMEE
pious - SAINTLY
pipe - TUBE, FLAGOLET, HOSE, FLUE, CINCH, BRIER
pipe die - DOD
pipe to discharge liquid - SPOUT
pipe joint ring - GASKET
piper - TRILLER
piper's son - TOM
piquancy (colloq.) - GINGER
piquant - RACY, SALTY, ZESTY
pique - OFFEND, SPITE, RESENT, DUDGEON, STIR, VEXATION
piquet term - CAPOT
pirate - CORSAIR, ROVER, BUCCANEER, PRIVATEER
pirate flag - ROGER
piscine - ICHTHYIC
pistol (old) - DAG
piston - VALVE
pit - HOLE, GRAVE, EXCAVATE, ABYSS, CAVITY, GRAVITY
pitch - TAR, TONE, KEY, TOSS, THROW, GIST
pitcher - EWER, TOBY, TOSSER
pitcher-catcher combination - BATTERY
pitcher's mound - BOX
pitcher's plate - SLAB
pitfall - SNARE, TRAP
pith - CORE, GIST, NUB, ESSENCE
pith helmet - TOPEE, TOPI
pith of a matter - GIST
pithy - MEATY, TERSE
pithy saying - MOT
pitiable - FORLORN, SORRY
pitiless - CRUEL
pity - RUTH
piu (mus.) - MORE
pivot - TURN, HINGE, SLUE
pivot pin of a hinge - PINTLE
pivoted catch for wheel teeth - RATCHET
placard - SIGN, POSTER
placate - APPEASE
place - (See also Put)
place (a) - ESTRE
place - STEAD, STATION, PUT, SET, LOCALITY, LAY, SPOT, SEAT, LOCALE, DEPOSIT, SITUATE, LOCUS, RANK, LIEU, LOCALE, POSITION, ARRANGE
place of activity - HIVE
place alone - ISOLATE
place of amusement - RESORT
place to anchor - MOORAGE
place at an angle - SKEW
place in artificial basin - DRYDOCK
place away - STORE
place of barter - MART
place of bliss - PARADISE, EDEN
place burden on - LADE
place for canoes - PORTAGE
place in charge - ENTRUST
place (comb. form) - GEA
place in common fund - POOL
place of concealment - HIDEOUT
place of confinement - PRISON
place of contrasting colour - SPOT
place of darkness - EREBUS
place in different order - TRANSPOSE, REARRANGE
place down - LAY
place of education - SEMINARY
place elsewhere - RELOCATE
place end for end - REVERSE
place of endless perdition - TOPHET
place of entry - PORT
place favoring rapid growth - HOTBED
place firmly - POSIT
place forward in opposition against - PITTED
place of great delight - ELYSIUM
place in ground - PLANT
place for hiding things - RACK
place of ideal perfection - UTOPIA
place in an impossible position - STYMIE
place at intervals - SPACE
place of justice - BAR
place levy on - TAX
place in mass of matter - IMBED
place on a mound - TEE
place of nether darkness - EREBUS
place of occurrence - SCENE
place in office - SEAT
place one inside another - NESTLE, NEST
place opposite - APPOSE

place in order - - - - - - ARRANGE
place of pilgrimage - - - - - MECCA
place (pl.) - - - - - - - - - LOCI
place in position again - - READJUST
place of preparation - - PARATORIUM
place in proximity - - - - - APPOSE
place of rearing - - - - - - - - LAP
place of refuge - - - ARK, HARBOUR
place of retirement - - - - - RECESS
place in rows (var.) - - - - - ALINE
place for safe keeping - - REPOSITORY
place in safe keeping - - - - - STORE
place of safety - - - - - - - HAVEN
place of the seal (abbr.) - - - - L.S.
place for storing corn - - - - - CRIB
place for storing fodder - - - - - SILO
place for storing hay - - - - - MOW
place of trade - - - - - - - - MART
place trust in - - - - - - - REPOSE
place of worship - - CHAPEL, ALTAR
place under a ban - - - - - OUTLAW
place under legal constraint - OBLIGATE
place under a promise - - OBLIGATE
place under restraint - - - - - INTERN
place under water - - - SUBMERGE
place of uproar - - - - - - BEDLAM
place where charitable gifts are given out
ALMONRY, ALMONRIES
place where current is fast - - RAPIDS
place where everything is perfect - UTOPIA
place where food is kept - - LARDER
place where gold is obtained - PLACERS
place where instruments of war are kept -
ARMORY
place where metal is refined - FORGE
place where pineapples grow - PINERY
place where tools are ground - GRINDERY
place where trial is held in action - - -
VENUE
place where wealth exists - - INDIES
place to worship - - CHAPEL, ALTAR
place with only one outlet - CUL-DE-SAC
placid - - - - - - - CALM, SERENE
plague - - TEASE, TAUNT, TORMENT,
HARASS
plaid - - - - - - - - - - TARTAN
plain - - BARE, CLEAR, APPARENT,
SIMPLE, EVIDENT
plain clothes - - - - - - - - MUFTI
plaintive - - - - MOURNFUL, SAD
plaintive cry - - - - - - - - - WAIL
plait - - - - - - - - - - - BRAID
plaited trimming - - - - - - RUCHE
plan - - - PLOT, INTEND, DESIGN,
ARRANGE, DEVISE, CONTRIVE,
DIAGRAM, PLAT, SCHEME, METHOD,
PROJECT, OUTLINE
plan of action - - - - - - - IDEA
plan of future procedure - - PROGRAM
plan of a town site - - - - - - PLAT
plane figure with equal angles - ISAGONS
plane handle - - - - - - - - TOTE
plane (kind) - - ROUTER, GIRO, JET
plane - - - - - - - - - - - LEVEL
plane manoeuvre - - - - - - LOOP
plane surface - - FLAT, LEVEL, AREA
plane surface (of a) - - - - - AREAL
planet - - MARS, SATURN, ASTEROID,
NEPTUNE, URANUS, VENUS, PLUTO
planet's path (pert. to) - - - ORBITAL
planet's shadow - - - - - - UMBRA
planetarium - - - - - - - ORRERY
plank - - - - - - - - - - BOARD
plant - - SEED, ENDOGEN, EMBED,
FACTORY, SOW, SAPLING,
INTRENCH, TEASEL, SHRUB
plant of abnormal development - ECAD
plant axis - - - - - - - - - STALK
plant of bean family - - - PEANUT
plant bearing aromatic seeds - CUMIN,
ANISE
plant bud - - - - - - - - - CION
plant disease - - - - - - - SCAB, ROT
plant embryo - - - - - - - - SEED
plant of extraordinary size - - GIANT
plant exudation - - - - - - RESIN
plant exudation (var.) - - - - ROSIN
plant of gourd family - - - - MELON
plant that grows on sea bottom - ENALID
plant known as live forever - - ORPINE
plant life - - - - - - - - - FLORA
plant like wheat - - - - - - - RYE
plant of lily family - - - - - - ALOE
plant that lives two years - BIENNIAL
plant modified by environment - ECAD
plant of mustard family - - - - CRESS
plant not having woody stem - - HERB
plant organ - LEAF, TENDRIL, SOMA
plant part - - - - - - - - - STALK
plant of poaceae family - - - GRASS
plant protuberance - - - - - - WART
plant root - - - - - - - - - BULB
plant root used for soap - - AMOLE
plant seed - - - - - - - - - SOW
plant stem - - - - - - - - - BINE
plant substance - - - - - - RESIN
plant tissues - - - - - - - - SOMA
plant twig - - - - - - - - - - ROD
plant with aromatic seeds - - ANISE
plant with sensitive leaves - - MIMOSA
plant with sour juice - - - - - SORREL
planter - - - - - - - - - FARMER
plantigrade carnivore - - BEAR, PANDA
planting device - - - - - - SEEDER
planting machine - - - - - - SOWER
plants of a region - - - - - - FLORA
plash - - - - - - - PUDDLE, POOL
plaster - - STUCCO, SMEAR, DAUB,
PARGET
plaster cement - - - - - - - PUTTY
plaster support - - - - - - - LATH
plastic - - - FORMATIVE, PLIABLE
plastic kind of earth - - - - - CLAY
plat - - - PLOT, PLAN, MAP, CHART,
BRAID
plate - - - - - - - DISH, SAUCER
plate of glass - - - - - - - - PANE
plateau - - - - TABLELAND, MESA
platform - - STAGE, DAIS, ESTRADE
platinum loop - - - - - - - OESE
platypus - - - - - - - DUCKBILL
plausible - - - - - - - SPECIOUS
play - - - SPORT, ENACT, PERFORM,
DRAMA, TOY, DISPORT, CAVORT,
FROLIC, ROMP
play boisterously - - ROMP, ROLLICK
play at bridge - - - - - - FINESSE
play first card - - - - - - - - LEAD
play idly - - - - - - - - - STRUM
play the lead - - - - - - - - STAR
play lightly with - - - - - - - BABY
play at love - - - - - - - - FLIRT
play for money - - - - - - GAMBLE
play monotonously - - - - - STRUM
play a part - - - ACT, PERSONATE,
IMPERSONATE
play a part on stage - - - - - - ACT
play tenpins - - - - - - - - BOWL
play on words - - - - - - - - PUN
play wrongly - - - - - - - RENEGE

P

player - - - - - - ACTOR, GAMBLER
player at duck on a rock - - - - TENTER
player of Hamelin - - - - - - - PYSIR
player of shrill instrument - - - PIPER
player who cuts the cards - - - - PONE
playful - SPORTIVE, KITTENISH, FRISKY
playhouse - - - - - - - - - THEATER
playing card spot - - - - - - - - PIP
playing field - - - - - - - - ARENA
playlet - - - - - - - - - - - SKIT
plaza - - - - - - - - - - SQUARE
plea - - - - - - PETITION, PRAYER
plead - ENTREAT, APPEAL, IMPLORE, SOLICIT, BEG, ADVOCATE, ARGUE
plead for - - - - - - - - INTERCEDE
pleasant - SWEET, AGREEABLE, NICE, AMIABLE
pleasant (arch.) - - - - - - - LEPID
pleasant aspect - - - - - - - SMILE
pleasant odor - - - - - - - - AROMA
pleasant (slang) - - - - - - - PEACHY
pleasantry - - - - - - - - BANTER
please - - SUIT, GRATIFY, DELIGHT, INDULGE, ACCOMMODATE
please (arch.) - - - - - - - ARRIDE
pleased - - - - - - - - - - - GLAD
pleasing - - - - - NICE, WELCOME
pleasing to the taste - - - - - SWEET
pleasing tones - - - - - - - - MUSIC
pleasure - - - - - - - - ENJOYMENT
pleasure boat - - - - YACHT, CANOE
pleasure jaunt - - - - - - SAIL, RIDE
pleasure (obs.) - - - - - - - - ESTE
pleat or fold in cloth - - - - GATHER, PLICATE, FOLD
pledge - - - - VOW, TRUCE, COMMIT, EARNEST, SEAL, PROMISE, TOKEN, GUARANTY, GUARANTEE
pledge (civil law) - - - - - - - - VAS
pledge of honour - - - - - - - PAROLE
plenteous - - - - - - - - - - AMPLE
plentiful - - - - ABOUND, NUMEROUS, ABUNDANT
plexus - - - - RETE, RETIA, NETWORK
pliable - - SOFT, SUPPLE, FLEXIBLE, PLASTIC
pliable composition - - - - - - - WAX
pliant - - - LITHE, LIMBER, SUPPLE, FLEXIBLE
plicate - - - - - - FOLDED, PLEATED
pliers - - - - - - - - - - - PINCERS
plight - - - - - PREDICAMENT, CASE
plighted forth - - - - - - - - TROTH
plodder - - - - - - - - - - - PLUG
plods - - - - - - - SLOG, TRUDGES
plot - - - - - PLAN, PLAT, SCHEME, CONSPIRE, CHART, INTRIGUE, CABAL, CONSPIRACY, BED
plot of land - - - - - - LOT, PARCEL
plotted map - - - - - - - - - - PLAT
plotter - - - - ENGINEER, SCHEMER
plover - - - - - - - - - DOTTEREL
plover-like bird - - - - - - - - SURF
plow - - - - - - - - - TILL, FURROW
plow (part) - - - - - - - - - - SHETH
plow sole - - - - - - - - - - SLADE
pluck - - SPUNK, GRIT, NERVE, PICK
pluck or pull off - - - - - - - AVULSE
pluck (slang) - - - - - - - - - SAND
plucked on stringed instrument - - - - TWANGED
plucky - - - - - - - - GAME, GRITTY
plug - - - ESTOP, STOPPER, PLODDER
plum - - - - - - - - - - GAGE, SLOE
plum kernel - - - - - - - - - - - PIT
plumb bob and rule - - - - PLUMMET
plumage - - - - - - - - FEATHERS
plumbago - - - - - - - - GRAPHITE
plume - - PREEN, CREST, FEATHER, EGRET
plumlike fruit - - - - - - - - SLOE
plummet - - - - - - - - FALL, DROP
plump - - - - - - - - - - - - - FAT
plunder - DESPOIL, LOOT, ROB, RAID, PREY, GUT, SPOIL, SACK, STEAL, PILLAGE, PILFER, RAPINE, SPOLIATE, MARAUD
plunder (arch.) - - - - - - - - REAVE
plunder (slang) - - - - - - - - SWAG
plundered (arch.) - - - - - - - REFT
plundering - - - - - - - PREDATIVE
plundering (act of) - - - - - RAPINE
plunge - - - - - - - - - - DIVE, DIP
plunger - - - - - - - - - - - - RAM
Pluto's kingdom - - - - - - - HADES
ply - THICKNESS, FOLD, BIAS, LAYER, WIELD
plywood - - - - - - - - - - VENEER
pneuma - - - - - - - - - - - - SOUL
pneumatic tire tread - - - - - - SHOE
poach - - - - - - - - - - TRESPASS
pocket case - - - - - - - - - - ETUI
pocket in trousers - - - - - - - FOB
pocketbook - - - PURSE, RETICULE, BAG
pocosin - - - - - - - - - - - SWAMP
pod bearing vine - - - - - - - - PEA
pod of a plant - - - - - - - - BOLL
Poe's heroine - - - - - - - LENORE
Poe's poem - - - - - - - - LENORE
poem - EPIC, SONNET, EPODE, VERSE, EPOS, LAY, LYRIC, ELEGY, EPEPEE, BALLAD, BALLADE
poem (short narrative) - - - - BALLAD
poet - - BARD, LYRIST, RHYMSTER, RIMER
poetic canto - - - - - - - - PASSUS
poetic inspiration - - - - - - - MUSE
poetical measure and rhythm - METER
poetry (arch.) - - - - - - - - POESY
poetry (pert. to form) - - - - - ODIC
poetry (poet.) - - - - - - - - POESY
poignant - - - - - - - - - - ACUTE
point - - - - PEAK, NEB, TIP, APEX, INDICATE, AIM, SHARPEN, CUSP, APICE, GIST, NIB, DOT
point at - - - - - - - - - - - - AIM
point between extremes - - - - MESNE
point of compass - RHUMB, AIRT, AIRTH
point of concentration - - - - FOCUS
point of crescent moon - - - - CUSP
point of crisis - - - - - - - - APEX
point of culmination - - - - - - APEX
point of deer's antler - - - - - SNAG
point of departure for polar expedition - ETAH
point of difference - - - - - LIMEN
point directly overhead - - - - ZENITH
point of earth's axis - - - - - POLE
point of egress - - - - - - - - EXIT
point of intersection - - - - CROSSING
point of land - - - - - - - - - SPIT
point of magnet - - - - - - - - POLE
point in moon's orbit - - - - APOGEE, SYZYGY
point opposite the zenith - - - - NADIR
point set for journey's end - - - - - DESTINATION
point of a spear - - - - - - - - GAD
point of support of lever - - - FULCRUM
point of traffic congestion - BOTTLENECK
point under discussion - - - - - ISSUE

point a weapon - - - - - - - AIM
point where leaf springs from branch - - AXIL
point on which something turns - PIVOT
point at which bean sprouts - - EYE
pointed - - - - - CULTRATE, ACUTE
pointed arch - - - - - - - - OGIVE
pointed end - - - - - - - - - CUSP
pointed instrument - - AWL, NEEDLE, PROD
pointed mass of ice - - - - - SERAC
pointed metal spike - - - - - NAIL
pointed part - - - - - - - - - NIB
pointed piece of metal - - - - - NAIL
pointed piece of wood - - - - - STAKE
pointed process - - - - - - - AWN
pointed shaft - - - - - - - ARROW
pointed steel implement - - - NEEDLE
pointed stick - - - - - - - - STAKE
pointed tool - - - - - - - - - AWL
pointed weapon - - - SPEAR, ARROW
pointed wheel - - - - - - TRACER
pointer - - - - - - - - - HAND, TIP
pointer on a sun dial - - - GNOMON, GNAMON
pointless - - - - - - - - - INANE
poise - BALANCE, HOVER, CARRIAGE, EQUIPOISE, COMPOSURE
poison - - VENOM, BANE, CORRUPT, VIRUS, TAINT
poisonous - - - VENOMOUS, TOXIC
poisonous crystalline compound - - - AMARINE
poisonous element - - - - - ARSENIC
poisonous matter - - - - - - VIRUS
poisonous plant of bean family - LOCO
poisonous spider - - - - - TARANTULA
poisonous tree - - - - - - - UPAS
poisonous weed - - - - - - - LOCO
poke - - - - - PROD, JAB, DAWDLE
poke around - - - - - ROOT, PROBE
poke fun at - - - - - - - - - JOSH
poker chip - - - - - - - - - - DIB
poker hand (kind) - - - - - - - PAT
poker stake - - - - - - - - - ANTE
poky - - - - - - - - - - - SLOW
polar - - - - - - ARCTIC, GUIDING
pole - - - ROD, STAFF, STICK, PIKE, STAKE, MASH
pole to hold flax - - - - - DISTAFF
pole (pert. to) - - - - - - NODAL
pole (pointed) - - - - - - - STAKE
pole propelled barge - - - - - PUNT
pole (Scot.) - - - - - - - - CABER
pole sustaining rigging - - - - MAST
pole of a team drawn vehicle - NEAP
pole of a vehicle - - - - - - - NEAP
polecat - - - - - - - - - - SKUNK
police station record books - BLOTTERS
policeman's club - - - - - - MACE
polish - - GLOSS, SCOUR, ELEGANCE, RUB, SHINE, SHEEN, REFINEMENT
Polish cake - - - - - - - - - BABA
Polish chemist - - - - - - - CURIE
Polish county - - - - - - - POSEN
Polish river - - SAN, NAREW, BUG, SERET
polished - - - - - - - - - ELEGANT
polished manner - - - - - ELEGANTLY
polishing material - - RABAT, EMERY
polite - - - COURTEOUS, GRACIOUS, MANNERLY, URBANE, GENTEEL, CIVIL
politic - - - - - - - - - SHREWD
political combination - - - - - BLOC
political faction - - - - - - - BLOC
political group - - - BLOC, POLITY, PARTY
political party of 1870 - - GREENBACK
political party (abbr.) - - - - - GOP
politican - - - - - - - - STATESMAN
poll - ELECTION, VOTE, ENROLL, HEAD
polling place - - - - - - - - BOOTH
polliwog - - - - - - - - - TADPOLE
pollute - - - - - - TAINT, DEFILE
Pollux's twin - - - - - - - - CASTOR
polo mount - - - - - - - - - PONY
polo team - - - - - - - - - FOUR
poltroon - - - - - - - - - COWARD
polygon of 12 sides - - DODECAGON
Polynesian aborigine - - - - - MAORI
Polynesian apple - - - - - - - HEVI
Polynesian baking pit - - - - - UMU
Polynesian chestnut - - - - - RATA
Polynesian cloth - - - - - - - TAPA
Polynesian herb - - - - - - - - PIA
Polynesian island group - - - - SAMOA
Polynesian tree - - - - - - - - ARA
Polynesian yam - - - - UVE, UBE, UBI
pome - - - - - - - - APPLE, PEAR
pomegranate sirup - - - - GRENADINE
pomp - - - - - PAGEANT, CEREMONY
pompous - - - - - - - - - STILTED
pompous show - - - - - - - PARADE
pond - - - - - - - - - - - - MERE
ponder - PORE, COGITATE, MEDITATE, CONSIDER, BROOD, CONTEMPLATE, RUMINATE, MUSE, REFLECT, DELIBERATE
ponderous - - - - - - - - MASSIVE
poniard - - - - - - - - - - DIRK
pony - - - - - - - - - NAG, PINTO
pool - - - - - - - - PUDDLE, MERE
pool, as in card playing - - - - - POT
pool (Scot.) - - - - - - - - - DIB
poor - - - INDIGENT, NEEDY, BAD, PENURIOUS, SCANTY, INOPULENT
poor golf shot - - - - - - DUB, SLICE
poor player (slang) - - - - - - - DUB
poorer - - - - - - - - - - - WORSE
poorest - - - - - - - - - - WORST
poorest part of fleece - - - - - ABB
poorhouse - - - - - - - ALMSHOUSE
poorly - - - - - - ILL, ILLY, BADLY
poorly provided - - - - - - - - BARE
pop - - - - - - - - - - - - SODA
pop the question - - - - - - PROPOSE
Pope (pert. to) - - - - - - - - PAPAL
Pope's scarf, collar or veil - - ORALE
Pope's triple crown - - - - - TIARA
poplar - - - - - - - ALAMO, ASPEN
poplar (white) - - - - - - - - ABELE
Poppaea's husband - - - - - - NERO
populace - - - - - - - MOB, DEMOS
popular - - - - - - - - - DEMOTIC
popular ascription - - - - - REPUTE
popular sort - - - - - - - - - ILK
popular success - - - - - - - - HIT
populate - - - - - - - - - PEOPLE
porcelain (fine) - - - - - - LIMOGES
porcelain insulator - - - - - - CLEAT
porcelain (kind) - - - - - - - SPODE
porcelain worker - - - - - - POTTER
porch - - PLAZA, VERANDA, STOOP, PORTICO
porcine animal - - - - - - - PIG, HOG
pore - - - PONDER, STUDY, STOMA, OPENING
pore in stem of plant - - - - LENTICEL
porgy - - - - - - - - - - - - SCUP
porgy (red) - - - - - - - - - - TAI
porous - - - - - - - - - - SPONGY
porous clay - - - - - - - - LATERITE

P

porous rock - - - - - - - - TUFA
porridge - - - - GRUEL, STIRABOUT
porridge made from maize - - ATOLE
port - - - - - - HAVEN, HARBOUR
portmanteaux - - - - - - VALISES
portable bathtub - - - - - - TOSH
portable bed - - - - - - - - COT
portable bulwark - - - - - - MANTA
portable canopy - - - - - UMBRELLA
portable chair - - - - - - - SEDAN
portable hoisting machine - - - GIN
portable lamp - - - - - - LANTERN
portable lamp (arch.) - - LANTHORN
portable lodge - - - - - - - TENT
portable stove - - - - - - - ETNA
portal - - - - - - - - - - GATE
portend - - BODE, AUGUR, PRESAGE, FORBODE
portent - - - - - - - OMEN, SIGN
portentous - - - - - - - - - DIRE
porter - - CARRIER, SUISSE, REDCAP
portico - - - - - - - STOA, PORCH
Portia's maid - - - - - - NERISSA
portion - PIECE, SOME, SHARE, PART, DOLE, BIT, WHIT, DAB, LOT, HALF, SAMPLE, TASTE
portion allotted - - - - - ALLOWANCE
portion of duration - - - - - - TIME
portly - - - - - - - - - - - FAT
portrait - - - - - - - - - - ICON
portray - - PAINT, DRAW, PICTURE, LIMN, DEPICT, DELINEATE
portray dramatically - - - - - ENACT
portray by dumb show - - PANTOMIME
Portuguese capital - - - - - LISBON
Portuguese city - - - - - - - OVAR
Portuguese coin - - - - - - - REI
Portuguese money of account - - REI, ESCUDO
Portuguese poet and historian - MELO
Portuguese province - - - - - AZORES
Portuguese river - - - - SOA, SADO
Portuguese territory in India - - GOA
Portuguese title - - - - - - - DOM
pose - - - SIT, ATTITUDE, POSTURE, PROPOUND
Poseidon's son - - - - - - TRITON
position - - LOCALE, JOB, STATION, STAND, POST, STANCE, PLACE
position in ballet - - - - ARABESQUE
position in chess - - - - STALEMATE
position of trust - - - - - - OFFICE
position with no escape - - IMPASSE
position with pay and no work - - - - SINECURE
position with no responsibilities - - - SINECURE
positions - - - - - - - - - - LOCI
positive - - - - - - SURE, CERTAIN
positive command - - - - - - FIAT
positive declarations - - ASSERTIONS
positive electrode - - - - - - ANODE
positive pole - - - - - - - - ANODE
positive statement - - AFFIRMATION
positive terminal - - - - - - ANODE
positiveness - - - - - - DOGMATISM
possess - - - - - - - - OWN, HAVE
possess ability - - - - - - TALENTED
possess flavor - - - - - - - SAPID
possession (law) - - - - - - SEISIN
possessions - - - - - ESTATE, ASSETS
possessor - - - - - OWNER, HOLDER
post - MAIL, STATION, OFFICE, STAKE, MALL, PILLAR
post to secure hawsers - - - - - BITT
postage stamp border - - - TRESSURE
postal certificate - - - - - - STAMP
postal service - - - - - MAILS, MAIL
poster - - - - - BILL, PLACARD, AD
poster (colloq.) - - - - - - - - AD
posterior - - - - - - - - REAR, HIND
postpone - - - - - - DEFER, DELAY
postulate - - - - - - - - PREMISE
posture - - STANCE, ATTITUDE, POSE
posture on horseback - - - - - SEAT
pot - - - - - - - - - KETTLE, OLLA
potato - - - - - - - - TUBER, SPUD
potato masher - - - - - - - RICER
potato (slang) - - - - - - - - SPUD
potency - - - - - - - - - - - VIS
potent - POWERFUL, MIGHTY, STRONG
potential - - - - - - - - - LATENT
potential energy - - - - - - ERGAL
pother - - - - - - - - BUSTLE, ADO
potion taken to relieve sorrow - - - - NEPENTHE
potpourri - - - - - - - - - - OLIO
potter's wheel - - - - LATHE, PALLET
pottery fragment - - - - - - SHARD
pottery kiln - - - - - - - - STOVE
pottery (kind) - - - - - - - DELFT
pottery (pert. to) - - - - - CERAMIC
pouch - - - - - - - - - SAC, BAG
pound - BEAT, HAMMER, THUMP, RAM
pound down - - - - - - - - - TAMP
pour - - - STREAM, FLOW, DECANT
pour forth - - - - - - - EMIT, GUSH
pour off liquid - - - - - - - DRAIN
pour oil upon - - - - - - - ANOINT
pour out - - - - - - - - - STREAM
pouring holes in molds - - - - GATES
pout - - - - - - - - - SULK, MOPE
pouter - - - - - - - - - - PIGEON
poverty - - - PENURY, NEED, WANT, INDIGENCE
poverty-stricken - - - - - - NEEDY
powder - - TALC, DUST, PULVERIZE
powder for cookery - - - - - - SODA
powder dose paper - - - - CHARTULA
powdery - - - - - - - - - - DUSTY
powdery residue - - - - - - - - ASH
powdered rock - - - - - - - - SAND
power - ENERGY, FORCE, STRENGTH, ABILITY, MIGHT, STEAM, VIS, VIGOR
power (Fr.) (poet.) - - - - PUISSANCE
power of striving (psychol.) - CONATION
powerful - - - - - STRONG, POTENT
powerful deity - - - - - - - - - EL
powerful particle - - - - - - - ATOM
powerless - - - - - - - - IMPOTENT
pow-wow - - - - - - - CONFERENCE
practicability - - - - - - - - UTILITY
practicable - - - - - - - - POSSIBLE
practical - - - - - - - - - - UTILE
practical astronomy (obs.) - ASTROLOGY
practical jokes - - - PRANKS, HOAXES
practice - DRILL, REHEARSE, USE
practice magic - - - - - - CONJURE
practice swordplay - - - - - - FENCE
prairie wolf - - - - - - - - COYOTE
prairie - - - - - - - - - - - PLAIN
praise - - LAUD, BLESS, COMMEND, FLATTER, EXTOL, ACCLAIM, ADULATION, TRIBUTE
praise highly (slang) - - - - - TOUT
praiseworthy - - - - - - LAUDABLE
prance - - - - - - - CAPER, CAVORT
prank - - ANTIC, FROLIC, ESCAPADE, TRICK, DIDO

P

prate - - - GAB, BABBLE, PRATTLE
prattle - - - - - - PRATE, BABBLE
pray - - - ENTREAT, IMPORTUNE, IMPLORE, BESEECH
prayer - ORISON, AVE, LITANY, PLEA, ENTREATY
prayer (arch.) - - - ORISON, BENE
prayer ending - - - - - - - AMEN
prayer sung at mass - - - - - CREDO
preach - - - - - - - SERMONIZE
preacher - - - - - - - MINISTER
prearrange - - - - - - - - PLAN
prearranged list - - - - - - SLATE
precarious - - - - - - - DUBIOUS
precede - - - - - - LEAD, FORERUN
precede in time - PREDATE, ANTEDATE
preceded - - - - - - - FORERAN
precedence - - - - - - - PRIORITY
precept - - - - - - - - MAXIM
precious - - - DEAR, GOLDEN, RARE
precious stone - GARNET, SARD, OPAL, ZIRCON, GEM, LAZULI, BERYL, ASTERIA
precipice - - - - - - - - CLIFF
precipitate - - - - - - STEEP, RASH
precipitation - RAINFALL, RAIN, MIST
precipitous - - - - - - - - STEEP
precis - - - - - - - - SUMMARY
precise - NEAT, NICE, EXACT, PRIM, FORMAL
precise point - - - - - - - - TEE
precisely - - - - NICELY, EXACTLY
precisely contracted - - - - - - EEN
precision - - ACCURACY, EXACTNESS
preclude - - - - - - - DEBAR, BAR
precocious - - - - - - - BRIGHT
precursor - - - - - - - - HERALD
predative - - - - - - PLUNDERING
predatory bird - - - - - - - OWL
predatory insect - - - - - - MANTIS
predestinate - - - - - - FOREDOOM
predestine - - ORDAIN, PREORDAIN
predetermine - - - - - - DESTINE
predicament - FIX, SCRAPE, DILEMMA, PLIGHT, PICKLE
predicate - - CONNOTE, ASSERT, BASE
predict - FORETELL, BODE, PROPHESY
predictive - - - - - - - PROPHETIC
predominant - - - - - - - CHIEF
preeminent - - CAPITAL, FIRST, STAR
preeminehtly - - - - - SUPREMELY
preen - - - - - PERK, PLUME, TRIM
preface - - - - PROEM, FOREWORD
prefecture in West Central Formosa - - TAICHU
prefer - - - FAVOUR, CHOOSE, ELECT
preferable - - - - - - - RATHER
preference - - PREDILECTION, TASTE
preferred position - - - - - STANDING
prefix - - - - - - - - TRE, DI, ANTI
prehistoric implement - - - - - CELT
prehistoric reptile - - - - DINOSAUR
prejudice - - - - - - BIAS, POISON
prejudiced - - - - - PARTIAL, BIASED
prelate - - - - - - - - - - PRIEST
preliminary meeting - - - - CAUCUS
preliminary plan - - - - - - IDEA
prelude - - - - - OVERTURE, PROEM
premature development - - PRECOCITY
premier - - - - - - - - PRINCIPAL
premier of Israel - - - - - - DAVID
premise - - PROPOUND, STIPULATE, POSTULATE
premium - - - - - - BONUS, AGIO
premium paid for insuring - INSURANCE
premonition - - - - - - - - OMEN
premonition (colloq.) - - - - - HUNCH
preordain - - - - - - PREDESTINE
prepare - - ARRANGE, SET, READY, PRIME
prepare for action - - - - - ALERT
prepare for college (colloq.) - - PREP
prepare flax - - - - - - - - - RET
prepare for publication - - - - - EDIT
prepare for resistance - - FOREARM
prepare for roasting - - - - - TRUSS
prepare for tearing - - - - PERFORATE
prepared - - - - READY, FIT, ALERT
presage - - OMEN, BODE, PORTEND
prescribe - - - - - - - DEFINE, SET
prescribe punishment - - - - SENTENCE
prescribed rule - - - - - - - RITUAL
prescribed task - - - - - - - STINT
presence - - - - - - - - PROXIMITY
present (a) - - - - - - BOON, GIFT
present (be) - - - - - ATTEND, HERE
present (to) - - - - - GIVE, DONATE, INTRODUCE, PROFFER
present in brief - - - - - - - - SUM
present day - - - - - - - - MODERN
present oneself for duty - - REPORT
present time or occasion - - NONCE, NOW, TODAY
presently - - - - - - - - - ANON
preserve - - CAN, SAVE, MAINTAIN, PROTECT, CURE, SPARE
preserve by drying - - - - DESICCATE
preserve in metal container - - TIN
preserve from oblivion - - - EMBALM
preserved in vinegar - - - - PICKLED
preserving can - - - - - - - - TIN
preserver - - - - SAVER, PROTECTOR
preside - - - - - - - - - CONDUCT
press - IRON, URGE, IMPEL, SQUEEZE, CROWD, ENJOIN
press against - - - - - - - - PUSH
press closely - - - - - - - - - JAM
press down - - - - TAMP, DEPRESS
press for payment - - - - - - - DUN
press forward - - - - - - - - DRIVE
press hard - - - - - - - CORRAL
press into dough - - - - - - KNEAD
press into thin sheets, as metal - - - LAMINATE
press out moisture - - - - - WRING
presage - - - - - - - - - - OMEN
pressed milk curd - - - - - CHEESE
pressing - - - - - URGING, URGENT
pressing implement - - - - SADIRON
pressing machine - - - - - - BALER
pressing necessity - - - - EMERGENCY
pressure - STRESS, WEIGHT, FORCE, URGENCY
prestige - - - - - FACE, INFLUENCE, REPUTATION
presto - - - - - QUICKLY, SPEEDILY
presume - - - - VENTURE, SUPPOSE, IMPOSE
presume obnoxiously - - - - IMPOSE
presumptuous - - - - - - - ICARIAN
pretend - - FEIGN, SHAM, SIMULATE
pretender - - - - PEDANT, CLAIMANT
pretender to gentility - - - - - SNOB
pretense - - SHAM, PLEA, PRETEXT, FEINT, SUBTERFUGE
pretension - - - - - - - AFFECTATION
pretensions to knowledge - SCIOLISM
pretentious - - ARTY, ELABORATE, SHOWY
pretentious building - - - - EDIFICE
pretentious language - - - BOMBAST

P

pretentious scholar - - - - - PEDANT
pretext - PRETENSE, COVER, EXCUSE, PEG
pretty - - - - - - - - - COMELY
prevail - - - TRIUMPH, REIGN, WIN
prevail upon - - - LEAD, INDUCE
prevailed without restraint - RAGED
prevailing - - - - - - DOMINANT
prevailing character - - - - TONE
prevalent - - - WIDESPREAD, RIFE, DOMINANT
prevarication - - - - - FALSEHOOD
prevaricator - - - - - - - - - LIAR
prevent - STOP, PRECLUDE, AVERT, DETER, BLOCK, FORESTALL
prevent from free speech - - - - GAG
preventive - DETERRENT, RESTRAINING
perverse - - - - - - - - FROWARD
previous - ANTERIOR, PRIOR, FORMER, PRECEDING
previously - - ERST, BEFORE, SUPRA
previously (arch.) - - - - - - ERST
previously mentioned - - FORESAID
prey - - - VICTIM, BOOTY, QUARRY
prey upon - - - - - - - - - RAVEN
Priam's father - - - - - LAOMEDON
Priam's kingdom - - - - - - TROY
Priam's son - - - - - - - - PARIS
price - - - - RATE, COST, VALUE, CONSIDERATION, CHARGE, OUTLAY, FEE
price of transportation - - - - FARE
prick painfully - - - - - - STING
prickly - - - STINGING, BRAMBLY
prickly bush - - - - - - - - BRIER
prickly envelope of fruit - BUR, BURR
prickly herb - - - - - - - TEASEL
prickly pear - - - - - NOPAL, TUNA
prickly plant - THISTLE, ACANTHUS, NETTLE
prickly seed covering - - - - - BUR
prickly sensation - - - - - TINGLE
prickly shrub - ROSE, GORSE, BRIAR
pride - - - - - VANITY, CONCEIT, ARROGANCE, GLORY, VAINGLORY
priest - - - - - MINISTER, PRELATE
priest's cloth - - - - - - - AMICE
priest's vestment - - - - - - ALB
prim - - - NEAT, MODEST, DEMURE
prima donna - - - - - - - - DIVA
primal - - ELEMENTAL, CHIEF, FIRST
primary - - - FIRST, ELEMENTAL
primary importance - - - - - VITAL
prime - - FIRST, CHIEF, FOREMOST, PREPARE, CHOICE
prime minister - - - - - PREMIER
primer - - - - READER, TEXTBOOK
primeval - - - - - - - - PRISTINE
primeval deity - - - - - - - TITAN
primigenial - - - - - - - ORIGINAL
primitive - EARLY, PRISCAN, PRISTINE
primitive drum - - - - - - TOMTOM
primitive implement - - - - - CELT
primitive interdiction - - - - TABOO
primitive Japanese - - - - - - AINU
primitive migratory peoples - ARYANS
primitive social group - - - - TRIBE
primrose - - - - - - - - AURICULA
primrose (Scot.) - - - - - - SPINK
prince of Afghanistan - - - - - AMIR
prince of apostate angels - - EBLIS
prince of beasts - - - - - - LIONET
prince of darkness and evil - SATAN
princess of Colchis - - - - - MEDEA
princess of Crete - - - - - ARIADNE
principal - MAIN, PREMIER, CHIEF, CARDINAL
principal of elaterium - - - ELARERIN
principal element - - - - - STAPLE
principal ore of lead - - - - GALENA
principal personage - - - - - HERO
principally - - - - - - - - MOSTLY
principle - REASON, IDEAL, TENET, CREDO, MAXIM
prink - - - - - - - - - - - PRIMP
prinked (colloq.) - - - - - PRIMPED
print - - PUBLISH, IMPRESS, DIE, STAMP
printed compilation - - - - - ALBUM
printed defamation - - - - - - LIBEL
printed journal - - - - - - - PAPER
printer - - - - - - - - COMPOSITOR
printer's apprentice - - - - - DEVIL
printer (colloq.) - - - - - - - TYPO
printer's error - - ERRATO, ERRATUM
printer's mark - - - - - - - - STET
printer's measure - EM, EN, ENS, PICA
printer's spacing block - - - - QUAD
printer's tray - - - - - - - - CASE
printing - - - - - - - - - EDITION
printing form - - - - - MAT, TYPE
printing mark - - - - - - ASTERISK
printing need - - - - - - - - INK
printing pattern - - - - - STENCIL
printing plate - - - - - STEREOTYPE
printing preparation - - - - - INK
printing press part - - - - - PLATEN
prior - ANTERIOR, BEFORE, ELDER, PREVIOUS, ANTECEDENT
priority - - - - - - - - PRECEDENCE
priority in time (prefix) - - - - PRE
priory - - - - - ABBEY, CLOISTER
priscan - - - - - - - - - PRIMITIVE
prism - - - - - - - - - - - SOLID
prison - - - - - - - - GAOL, JAIL
prison compartment - - - - - CELL
prisoner - - - - - - - - - CAPTIVE
prisoner's place in court - - - - DOCK
prisoner's security - - - - - - BAIL
pristine - - PRIMITIVE, PRIMEVAL, UNTOUCHED, ORIGINAL
privacy - - - - - - - - SECLUSION
private - - - - - - - - SECLUDED
private detective - - - - - SPOTTER
private room - - - - - - - - - DEN
private wrong (law) - - - - - TORT
privateer - - - - - CORSAIR, PIRATE
privately - - - - - - - - - ASIDE
privation - - - - - - - - - LOSS
privilege - - - LIBERTY, IMMUNITY
prize - TREASURE, ESTEEM, VALUE, AWARD
prize in lottery - - - - - - TERN
pro - - - - - - - - - - - - - FOR
proa - - - - - - - - - - - CANOE
probabilities - - - - - - - - ODDS
probably (arch.) - - - - - BELIKE
probe - - - - - - - - - - - SEARCH
problem - - - - POSER, TASK, NUT
problem in arithmetic - - - - - SUM
problem (colloq.) - - - - - - - NUT
proboscis - - - - - - - NOSE, SNOUT
procedure - - - - - - OPERATION
proceed - - - - - - GO, CONTINUE
proceed laboriously - - - - - WADE
proceeding from side - - - LATERAL
proceeding (her.) - - - - - ISSUANT
proceeds - - STARTS, INCOME, GOES
process of decision - - - - - PEND
process of doing something - ACTION

procession - - - - - - - PARADE
proclaim - - - - KNELL, DECLARE
proclaim loudly - - - - - - BLARE
proclaim publicly - - - - - HERALD
proclamation - - - - - - - EDICT
proclivity - - - - - - - - TALENT
procrastination - - - - - - - DELAY
procurator of Judea - - - - - PILATE
procure - - GET, PROVIDE, OBTAIN
prod - GOAD, PUNCH, SLOG, POKE, THRUST
prod with the elbow - - - - - NUDGE
prodigal - - - - - LAVISH, WASTEFUL, EXTRAVAGANT
prodigal expenditure - - LAVISHMENT
prodigious - - - - - - MARVELLOUS
prodigy - - - - - - - - MARVEL
produce - - - - - CAUSE, GENERATE, ENGENDER, STAGE, YIELD, CREATE, CROP
produce designs on metal - - - ETCH
produce dull surface - - - - - MAT
produced by a river - - - - FLUVIAL
produced by the wind - - - - EOLIAN
produced in this country - DOMESTIC
producing heat - - - - - CALORIFIC
producing inflammation - - IRRITANT
producing motion - - - - - MOTILE
product - - - - - - - - - FRUIT
product of natural distillation - - DEW
production - - - - - - - OUTPUT
productive - RICH, FERTILE, CREATIVE
productive source of supply - - MINE
proem - - - - - PREFACE, PRELUDE
profane - - - - - - - DESECRATE
profess - - - - - - - - - AVOW
professed intention - - - - PRETENSE
profession - METIER, VOCATION, TRADE
professional mourner - WEEPER, WAILER
professional tramp - - - - - - HOBO
professionally befitting - - - ETHICAL
proffer - BID, TENDER, OFFER, GIVE, PRESENT, HAND
proficiency - - - - - - - - SKILL
proficient - ADEPT, VERSED, SKILLED
profit - - - AVAIL, GAIN, BENEFIT, ADVANTAGE
profitable (be) - - - - - - - PAY
profound - - DEEP, RECONDITE, SAGE
profound dread - - - - - - - AWE
profound sleep - - - - - - - SOPOR
profundity - - - - - - - - DEPTH
profuse - - - LAVISH, BOUNTIFUL, OPULENT
profuse talk - - - - - - - PALAVER
progenitor - - - - - - PARENT, SIRE
progeny - - - SEED, BREED, STRAIN, ISSUE
prognosticator - - - - - - PROPHET
program of things to be done - AGENDA
progress - - - - - - GAIN, ADVANCE
progress with difficulty - - - - WADE
progressive action - - - - - PROCESS
progressively through - - - - - ALONG
prohibit - BAR, BAN, DEBAR, ESTOP, VETO, FORBID
prohibition - - - - - - - BAN, EDICT
prohibitionist - - - - - - - - - DRY
project - - - SCHEME, ABUT, PLAN
project stiffly, as hair - - - - - STARE
projectile - - - - - - - - GRENADE
projecting bone of ankle - MALLEOLAR
projecting crane arm - - - - - GIB
projecting member of a board - TENON
projecting nose - - - - - - - SNOUT
projecting part - - - - - - - NOB
projecting part of a building - - APSE
projecting piece - - - - - - - - FIN
projecting piece of a cap - - - VISOR
projecting piece (flat) - - - - SHELF
projecting point - - - - - PEAK, JAG
projecting rim - - - - - - - FLANGE
projecting rock - - - - - - - - CRAG
projecting roof edge - - - - - EAVE
projecting tooth - - - - - - SNAG
projecting window - - - - - DORMER
projection - - - - - - - - - SNAG
projection from a card - - - - - TAB
projection of cog wheel - - - - TEETH
projection on gear wheel - - - - COG
prolong - LENGTHEN, EXTEND, DEFER, PROTRACT
prolonged declamation - - - - TIRADE
prolonged metaphor - - - - ALLEGORY
prolonged sound of s - - - - - HISS
promenade - - - - - - - - PARADE
prominence - - - - - - - SALIENCE
prominent - - - - EMINENT, STAR, IMPORTANT
prominent person - - - - - - - LION
promise - - PLEDGE, VOW, SWEAR, COVENANT, WORD
promising - - - - - - - FAVONIAN
promontory - - - - - - CAPE, NESS
promontory (var.) - - - - - - NASE
promote - - ABET, FOSTER, SERVE, FURTHER, ADVANCE
promote interest of - - - - - SERVE
promoter - - - - - - - - - AGENT
prompt - - - - - - - - - - - CUE
promptly - - - - - - - - - - SOON
prone - APT, PROSTRATE, ADDICTED, INCLINED
prone to fight - - - - - PUGNACIOUS
prong - - - - - - TINE, NIB, FORK
pronged tool - - - - - - - - - FORK
pronounce - ASSERT, UTTER, DECLARE
pronounce as a sentence - - - - PASS
pronounce holy - - - - - - - BLESS
pronouncements - - - - - - - DICTA
pronto - - - - - - - - - QUICKLY
pronunciation mark - DIACRITIC, TILDE
proof - - - - - - - - - EVIDENCE
proofreader - - - - - - - - REVISER
proofreader's mark - - CARET, STET
prop - STAY, BRACE, SHORE, BUTTRESS, STRENGTHEN
prop beam - - - - - - - - - SHORE
propagated - - - - - - - - - BRED
propagator - BREEDER, DISSEMINATOR
propel - - DRIVE, IMPEL, ROW, URGE
propel a boat - - - - - - - - ROW
propeller - - - - - DRIVER, FAN, OAR
propeller (type) - - - - - - - SCREW
proper - - DECENT, MEET, PRIM, FIT, RIGHT
property - - ESTATE, REALTY, ASSET, HOLDINGS
property charge - - - - - - - - LIEN
property of a matter - INERTIA, MASS
property of a person - - - - - ASSET
prophesy - - - - PREDICT, FORETELL
prophet - SEER, AMOS, ORACLE, SAGE, SEERESS
prophetic - - ORACULAR, PREDICTIVE
prophetical - - - - - VATICAL, VATIC
propitiate - - - - - ATONE, APPEASE, CONCILIATE
proponent - - - - - - - - ADVOCATE
proportion - - - - - - - RATIO, RATE

P

proposal - - SUGGEST, INTEND, OFFER
proposed act - - - - - - - - BILL
proposed international language - RO, IDO, OD
proposition previously proved - PREMISE
propound - - - - PREMISE, POSE
propped up - - - - - - - SHORED
proprietor - - - - - - - - OWNER
propulsion in planes - - - - - - JET
prorogue - - - - - - - - ADJOURN
prosaic - UNIMAGINATIVE, WORKADAY, COMMONPLACE
proscribe - - - - - - - - - BAN
prose - - - - - - - - - TEDIOUS
prosecuting office - - - - - - D.A.
prosecutor - - - - - - - - SUER
proselyte - - - - - - - CONVERT
prosit - - - - - - - - - TOAST
prosodic foot - - - - - - - IAMB
prospect - - - - OUTLOOK, VISTA
prosper - - THRIVE, FLOURISH, FARE
prosperity - - - - WELFARE, WEAL
Prospero's servant - - - - - ARIEL
prosperous times - - - UPS, BOOM
prostrate - - - - - - - - PRONE
prostrate (be) - - - - - - - - LIE
prosy - - - - - - DULL, TEDIOUS
protect - SHELTER, SHIELD, DEFEND, ARMOR, PRESERVE, BLESS
protect against infringement - PATENT
protect against loss - - - - - INSURE
protecting - - - - - - - TUTELAR
protecting power - - - EGIS, AEGIS
protection - ARMOR, EGIS, DEFENSE, AEGIS, LEE
protection for invention - - PATENT
protective - - - - - - DEFENSIVE
protective covering - ARMOR, RAINCOAT, PAINT
protective ditch - - - - - MOAT, FOSS
protective garment - APRON, DUSTER, COVERALL
protective head covering - - HELMET
protective influence - - - - - AEGIS
protective railing - PARAPET, BALCONY
protective secretion - - - - - - INK
protector - - - DEFENDER, PATRON
protein in milk - - - - - - CASEIN
protein in seeds - - - - - EDESTIN
pretentious dwelling - - - - - PALACE
protest - DEMUR, COMPLAINT, DISSENT
proton - - - - - - - - - - ATOM
protract - - - - - - EKE, PROLONG
protuberance - SNAG, WEN, NODE, NUB, BULGE, LOBE, WART
protuberance on horse's leg - SWIMMER
protuberance part of a cask - - BILGE
protuberance (pert. to) - - - LOBAR
protuberance of skull - - - - INION
protrude the lips - - - - - POUT
protruding - - - - - - - - LOBAR
protruding tooth - - - - - - TUSK
proud - - - - - - - - ARROGANT
prove - - - - - - - - - - - TEST
prove false - - - BETRAY, CONFUTE
prove foolish - - - - - - STULTIFY
proved statement - - - - THEOREM
proved wrong - - - - - - CONFUTED
proverb - - - ADAGE, SAW, MAXIM
proverbial friend - - - - - - DAMON
provide - STORE, PURVEY, FURNISH, AFFORD
provide food - - - - CATER, PURVEY
provide quarters for - - - - LODGE
provide scantily - - - - - - STINT
provide with flap - - - - - - - TAB
provide with hoops - - - - - - BAIL
provide with power - - - - ENDUE
provided - - - - - - - - - - - IF
provided that - - - - - - - - SO
provided a way of escape - - HEDGED
provided with shoes - - - - SHOD
provident - CAREFUL, THRIFTY, FRUGAL
provincial speech - - - - - PATOIS
provision - - GRIST, STORE, RATION
provision closet - - - - - - PANTRY
provisos - - - - - - - - - - IFS
provoke - - - NETTLE, IRE, CAUSE, IRRITATE
prow - - - - - - - - - STEM, BOW
prowl about - - - - - - - - LURK
proximity - - NEARNESS, PRESENCE
prudent - - WISE, SAGE, DISCREET, CHARY
prune - - - - - - - - - - - TRIM
prune or abridge (var.) - - - - RASEE
pruning shears - - - - - SECATEUR
Prussian city - - - ESSEN, ANKLAM
Prussian district - - - - - - STADE
Prussian mining valley - - - - RUHR
Prussian river - - - - RUHR, LENA
Prussian seaport - - EMDEN, STETTIN, KIEL
Prussian town - - - - - - EMA, EMS
Prussian watering town - - - - - EMS
pry - - - - LEVER, INSPECT, SNOOP, EXTRACT, PEEP
pry into - - - - - - - - - SNOOP
prying person - - - - - - - PEEPER
psalm - - - - - - - - - - HYMN
pseudonym - - - - - - - - - ALIAS
ptarmigan - - - - - - - - - RIPA
public - UNIVERSAL, OVERT, EXOTERIC, NATIONAL
public announcement - - - - - - AD
public announcer - - - - - - CRIER
public carrier - - - - - - RAILROAD
public declaration - - - MANIFESTO
public display - - - - - - - SCENE
public document - - - - - ARCHIVE
public estimation - - - - - REPUTE
public guardian - - - - - - POLICE
public house - - TAVERN, INN, HOTEL
public life - - - - - - - - CAREER
public lodging house - - - - - HOTEL
public meeting - - - - - - - FORUM
public notice - - - - - - - - EDICT
public officer - - - - - - - NOTARY
public opposed to local - - NATIONAL
public passage - - - - - - - - ROAD
public performer - - - - - ARTISTE
public prayer (pert. to) - - LITURGIC
public proclaimer - - - - - - CRIER
public promenade - - - - - ALAMEDA
public recreation ground - - - - PARK
public regard - - - - - - - - REPUTE
public room - - - - - - - - - HALL
public sale by auction - - - VENDUE
public sales announcer - - - - CRIER
public speaker - - ORATOR, RHETOR
public storehouse - - - - - - ETAPE
public vehicle - - CAB, BUS, TAXICAB
public walk - - - MALL, PROMENADE
public writer - - - - - - SCRIVENER
publicity - - - - AIR, ADVERTISING
publish - - - - EDIT, ISSUE, PRINT
published mistakes - - - - - ERRATA
published price - - - - - - - LIST
published without authority - PIRATIC,

PIRATE, PIRATED
Puccini opera - - - - - - - TOSCA
pucker - - - - - - - - - PURSE
puddle - - - - - - - POOL, PLASH
pudginess - - - - - - DUMPINESS
Pueblo Indian - - - - - - - HOPI
puerile - - - - - - - - - CHILDISH
Puerto Rican city - - LARES, PONCE
Puerto Rican municipality - - PONCE
puff - - - - - - - - - PANT, WAFT
puff up - - - BLOAT, SWELL, ELATE
pugilist - - - - - - - - PUG, BOXER
pugilist's assistant - - - - HANDLER
pule - - - - - - - - - - WHIMPER
pull - TUG, TOW, DRAW, LUG, YANK, HALE, HAUL
pull apart - - - - - - TEAR, REND
pull off - - - - - - - - - AVULSE
pull out - - - - - - - - - - BLOW
pull to pieces - - - - - - DEMOLISH
pull sharply - - - - - - - - YANK
pull up by roots - - - DERACINATE
pull with force - - - - - - - HAUL
pulley wheel - - - - - - - SHEAVE
pulp - - - - - - - - - - CHYME
pulpit - - - - - - - - - ROSTRUM
pulpy fruit - - UVA, GRAPE, DRUPE
pulsate - - - - - - - BEAT, THROB
pulsation - - - - - - - - - - BEAT
pulse - - - - - - - - - - THROB
pulverize - GRIND, STAMP, POWDER, PESTLE, FINE
pulverized earth - - - - - - - DUST
pulverized mixture - - - - LOAM
pulverized ore - - - - - - - PULP
pulverized rock - - - - - - - SAND
pulverizing implement - - - - PESTLE
puma - - - - - - - - - PANTHER
pummel - - - - - - - - - - BEAT
pump handle - - - - - - - SWIPE
punch - - - - PROD, PERFORATE
punch (colloq.) - - - - - - - PEP
punctilious person - PRECISIAN, PRIG
punctuation point - - HYPHEN, DASH
puncture - - - - - - PIERCE, STAB
puncture in ornamental pattern - PINK
pungency - - - - - - - RACINESS
pungent - - - BITTER, ACRID, KEEN, SHARP, RACY
pungent bulb - - - - - - - GARLIC
pungent odour - - - - - - - TANG
pungent plant - - - - - - - ONION
pungent seasoning - - - CONDIMENT, SPICE
punish - - - - CHASTISE, AVENGE, CASTIGATE, PENALIZE
punish by fine - - - - - - AMERCE
punishing (law) - - - - - - PEINE
punishing (pert. to) - PUNITIVE, PENAL
punishing rod - - - - - - FERULE
punitive - - - - - - - - - - PENAL
puny - - - - - - - - WEAK, FRAIL
pupil - - - - - STUDENT, SCHOLAR
puppet - - - - - DOLL, MARIONETTE
puppy - - - - - - - - - - WHELP
purchasable - - - - - - - - VENAL
purchase - - - - - - - - - - BUY
purchase (old word for) - - - ACATE
purchase to hoist anchor - - - - CAT
pure - - - CHASTE, CLEAN, CLEAR, ABSOLUTE, VESTAL
pure air (colloq.) - - - - - - OZONE
pure number - - - - - - - SCALAR
purge - - - - - - - - - - PURIFY
purification - - - - - - - LUSTRAL
purified potash - - - - - PEARLASH
purify - - REFINE, CLEANSE, AERATE, CLEAN, FILTER, LUSTRATE, PURGE
purl - - - - - - - - - RIB, EDDY
purloin - - - - - - - - - - STEAL
purple - - - - - - TYRIAN, MAUVE
purple colour - - - - - - MULBERRY
purple flowered evergreen shrub - - - BARETTA
purple seaweed - - - - - - - LAVER
purplish brown - - - - - - - - PUCE
purport - - - - - - - - - - TENOR
purporting to show taste - - - ARTY
purpose - END, AIM, DESIGN, INTEND, MISSION, MEAN, INTENTION, INTENT, GOAL
purpose in view - - - - - - - END
purposed - - - - - - MEAN, MEANT
purposes - - - - - - - - - MEANS
purposive - - - - - - - - - TELIC
purse - - - - - - WALLET, PUCKER
pursue - BOUND, PLY, TRACE, CHASE, STEER, CON, HUNT
pursue diligently - - - - - - - PLY
pursue stealthily - - - - - - STALK
pursuit - - - - - - - - - - CHASE
pursuit of (in) - - - - - - - AFTER
purvey - - SUPPLY, PROVIDE, CATER
purveyor of food - - - - - CATERER
purveyor to troops - - - - - SUTLER
push - - - - - JOSTLE, SHOVE, URGE
push down - - - - - - - - DEPRESS
push gently - - - - - - - - NUDGE
push in - - - - - - - - - - DENT
put - - - - - - - (See also Place)
put - DEPOSIT, PLACE, LAY, INSERT, LAID, SET
put in action - - - - - EXERT, BESTIR
put aside - - - - - - - - - - FOB
put aside temporarily - - - - TABLED
put away - - - - - RELEGATE, STORE
put back - - - - - REPLACE, RESTORE
put before - - - - - - - - - PREFIX
put burden on - - - - STRAIN, LADE
put in circulation - - - - - PUBLISH
put in container - - - - - - ENCASE
put on desert island - - - - MAROON
put in disordered condition - - LITTER
put down - - - DEPOSIT, LAY, LAID, DEPOSITED, DEPRESS
put on file - - - - - - - - FILED
put to flight - - - - - ROUT, ROUTED
put in forgotten place - - - - MISLAID
put forth - - - - - - - EXERT, ISSUE
put forth effort - - - - - - STRIVE
put forth shoot - - - - - - - SPROUT
put forward as an excuse - - PROPONE
put fuel on fire - - - - - - - STOKE
put on guard - - - - - - - WARN
put to hazard - - - - - - ENDANGER
put in - - - - - - INSERT, INSERTED
put into force - - - - - - - ACTIVATE
put into poetry - - - - - POETICIZE
put into practice - - - - - - - - USE
put load on - - - - - - - - - LADE
put new end pieces on - - - - RETIP
put off - - - - - POSTPONE, DEFER, PROCRASTINATE
put on - - - - - - - - - - - INDUE
put to one side - - - - - - - SHELVE
put in order - REGULATE, STRAIGHTEN, ARRANGE, FILE
put in order (mil.) - - - - - POLICE
put out - - - - - EXPEL, OUST, EVICT

P Q R

put out of existence - - - DESTROY
put out of place - - - - DISPLACE
put out with hope of return - - INVEST
put in possession (law) - - - SEIZE
put in reciprocal relation - CORRELATE
put to shame - - - - - - - ABASH
put to a strain - - - - - - - - TAX
put tennis ball into play - - - SERVE
put together - - - - - ADD, FRAME
put in type - - - - - - PRINT, SET
put up - - - - CAN, POST, ERECT
put to use - - - - APPLIED, APPLY
put in vessel - - - - - - - - POT
put with - - ADD, TOLERATE, ADDED
putative - - - - - - - SUPPOSED
puzzle (kind) - - ACROSTIC, RIDDLE, ENIGMA, REBUS, CHARADE
puzzlemaker's pet - - - - - - - AI
puzzling - - - - - - - ENIGMATIC
pygmy - - - - - - - - - - DWARF
pylon - - - - - - - - - - TOWER
pyramid builder - - - - - - CHEOPS
Pyrenees republic - - - - - ANDORRA
Pythias' friend - - - - - - DAMON

Q

quack - - - - - - - - CHARLATAN
quack medicine - - - - - NOSTRUM
quadruped - - HORSE, DEER, SHEEP, GOAT, BEAST
quadruped of ox - - - - - - - YAK
quagmire - - - - - BOG, FEN, LAIR
quagmire death (symbol) - - - ASP
quail - - - - - - - COWER, COLIN
quaint - - - - - - ODD, WHIMSICAL
quake - - - - - TREMBLE, TREMOR
Quaker - - - - - - - - - FRIEND
quaker - - - - - - - - - TREMBLER
quaking - - - - - - - - - ASPEN
qualification - - - - - - - ABILITY
qualified - - - - - FIT, ABLE, APT
qualify - - - - - TEMPER, ENTITLE
quality of sound - - - - - - - TONE
quantity - - - - - - - - - AMOUNT
quantity having magnitude - - SCALAR
quantity (large) - - - - - MASS, SEA
quantity of matter - - - - - - MASS
quantity of medicine - - - - DOSAGE
quantity of paper - - - - - - REAM
quantity (small) - - - - - - - IOTA
quantity of yarn - - - SKEIN, HANK
quarrel - ALTERCATION, FEUD, SPAT, FRACAS, AFFRAY, TIFF, ROW
quarry - - - - - - - - GAME, PREY
quarter of a circle - - - QUADRANT
quarter round molding - - - OVOLO
quartet of players - - - FOURSOME
quartz (kind of) - - PRASE, AGATE, FLINT, ONYX, SARD
quaver - - - - - - - TRILL, SHAKE
quay - - - - - - - LEVEE, WHARF
Quebec peninsula - - - - - - GASPE
queen of beasts - - - - - - LIONESS
queen of Carthage - - - - - - DIDO
queen of fairies - MAB, TITANIA, UNA
queen of gods - - - - - - - - HERA
queen of heaven - - - - - - HERA
queen of Navarre - - - - - MARGARET
queer - - ERRATIC, ODD, SINGULAR, PECULIAR
quell - - REPRESS, ALLAY, SUPPRESS
quench - - - - SLAKE, EXTINGUISH
querulous - - - - - - - - QUIZZICAL
query - - - - - - - - - - DOUBT
quest - - - - - - - - - - SEARCH
question before the house - - MOTION
questionable - - - - - - - - SHADY
questioner - - - - - INTERLOCUTOR
queue - - - - - - - - - - PIGTAIL
quick - FAST, RAPID, SPEEDY, SUDDEN, ACTIVE, LIVE, APACE
quick blast - - - - - - - TOOT, JIG
quick blow - - - - - - - - - - RAP
quick jerk - - - - - - - - - YANK
quick to learn - - - - - - - - - APT
quick look - - - - - - - - GLANCE
quick movement - - - - - - - DART
quick punch (colloq.) - - - - - CLIP
quick stroke - - - - - - - - - DAB
quick witty reply - - - - - REPARTEE
quicken - - ANIMATE, URGE, ENLIVEN
quickened gallop - - - - - - - RUN
quickly - - APACE, PRESTO, PRONTO
quickness - - - - - - - - - HASTE
quid of tobacco - - - - - - - CUD
quiescence - - - - - - - - LATENCY
quiescent - DORMANT, LATENT, STATIC
quiet - STILL, SERENE, SILENCE, STATIC, ALLAY, INERT, SILENT, LULL, STILLY, SOOTHE, REPOSEFUL, PEACE
quieting pain - - - - - ANALGESIC
quietness - - - - - - - - - PEACE
quietude - - - - - - - PEACE, REST
quill - - - - - - - - - - - - PEN
quill to wind silk - - - - - - COP
quintessence - - - - - - - CREAM
quip - - - - - - - - - - - GIBE
quirk - - - - - - - - - - - TWIST
quit - RETIRE, CEASE, LEAVE, VACATE, STOP
quite - ENTIRELY, ALL, COMPLETELY
quiver - - - - - TREMBLE, TREMOR
quivering - - - - - ASPEN, TREMOR
quizzical - - - - - - - QUERULOUS
quoit - - - - - - - - - - DISCUS
quoit throw (good) - - - - - RINGER
quota - - - - - - - - - - - SHARE
quotation - - - - EXTRACT, SNIPPET
quote - - - - - - - - CITE, ALLEGE
quoter - - - - - - - - - - ALLEGER

R

Ra's wife - - - - - - - - - - MUT
rabbit - - - - HARE, CONY, RODENT
rabbit (female) - - - - - - - - DOE
rabbit fur - - - - - - - - - LAPIN
rabbit home - - - - - - - - HUTCH
rabbit hutch - - - - - - - WARREN
rabbit (kind) - - - - - - - - - CONY
rabbit run - - - - - - - - WARREN
rabbit tail - - - - - - - - - SCUT
rabble - - - - - - - - RAFF, MOB
rabble rouser - - - - - - AGITATOR
rabid - - - - - - - MAD, FURIOUS
raccoon - - - - - - - COON, COATI
raccoon-like carnivore - - - - PANDA
race - - SPEED, CONTEST, LINEAGE, HASTEN, SUBSPECIES, PEOPLE, RUN
race of animals - - - - - - BREED
race course (part) - - - - - STRETCH
race horse - - - TROTTER, ARABIAN, MANTIS, PLATER
race (kind) - - - - - - - - - RELAY
race (short) - - - - - DASH, SPRINT
race track tipster - - - - - - TOUT
racer - - - - - - - - - - RUNNER

Rachel's father - - - - - - LABAN
raciness - - - - - - - PUNGENCY
racing boat - - - - - - - - SHELL
rack - TORMENT, TREE, FRAMEWORK
racket - - - - - - - - - - NOISE
radiant - - - - - BEAMING, GLOWING
radiate - - - - - SHINE, EMIT, GLOW
radiating part - - - - - - - RADIAL
radiation refracting device - - - LENS
radiation of short length wave - X-RAY
radical - - - RED, ORGANIC, SURD, EXTREME
radicate - - - - - - - - - ROOTED
radicel - - - - - - - - - ROOTLET
radio - - - - - - - - - WIRELESS
radio antenna - - - - - - - AERIAL
radio chain - - - - - - - NETWORK
radio wire - - - - - - - - AERIAL
radium emanation - - NITON, RADON
radix - - - - - - - - - - - ROOT
radon - - - - - - - - - - - RN
raff - - - - - - - - - - RABBLE
raft - - - - - - - - - - - FLOAT
raft breasted (ornith.) - - - RATITE
rafter - - - - - - - - - - BEAM
rag - - - TATTER, SHRED, REMNANT
rage - - STORM, RANT, FUROR, IRE, FURY, WRATH, FUME, VIOLENCE, FRENZY, TANTRUM
rage (be in a) - - - - - - - FUME
ragged - - - - - - - - - TATTERED
ragout of mutton or lamb - - HARICOT
raid - - - FORAGE, MARAUD, FORAY, INVADE, INVASION, INCURSION, ATTACK, ASSAULT
raiding vessel - - - - - - - RAIDER
rail - - FENCE, HERON, BAR, SORA
rail (to) - - REVILE, SCOFF, BERATE, FENCE, RANT
railbird - - - - COOT, SORA, CRAKE
railing on a bridge - - - - - PARAPET
raillery - - - - - - - - BANTER
railroad car - - - - - - - - TRAM
railroad signal - - - - - SEMAPHORE
railroad tie - - - - - - - SLEEPER
railroad (type) - - - - - MONORAIL
raiment - - - - - - DRESS, ATTIRE
rain - - - - - - - - - SHOWER
rain cloud - - - - - - - - NIMBUS
rain in fine drops - - - - - - MIST
rain forest of Amazon - - - - SELVA
rain hard - - - - - - - - - POUR
rain (pert. to) - - - - - - HYETAL
rainbow - - - - - - - IRIS, ARCH
raincoat - - - - - - - - PONCHO
rainspout (Scot.) - - - - - - RONE
rainstorm - - - - - - - DOWNPOUR
rainy - - - - - - - - - - - WET
raise - ELEVATE, LIFT, EXALT, REAR, BREED, HOIST, EMBOSS, BOOST, ERECT, GROW, UPLIFT, INCREASE
raise aloft - - - - - - - - HEFT
raise and fasten as an anchor - - CAT
raise a nap - - - - - TEASEL, TEASLE
raise objections - - - - - - CAVIL
raise (Scot.) - - - - - - - - EAN
raise spirits of - - - - - - - ELATE
raise temperature - - - - - - HEAT
raise to third power - - - - - CUBE
raise with a rope (naut.) - - - TRICE
raised flooring - - - - - - - STAGE
raised lawns - - - - - - TERRACE
raised platform - - - - - DAIS, STAGE
raised sacrificial structure - - ALTAR
raised strip - - - - - - - - RIDGE
raised stripe - - - - - - WELT, RIB
rajah's wife - - - - - RANEE, RANI
rake - - - - - - - RANSACK, ROUE
rally - - - - - - - REVIVE, RECOVER
ram - - BUFF, STUFF, ARIES, TUP, STRIKE, TAMP, BATTER, POUND
ram (the) - - - - - - - - - ARIES
ramble - MEANDER, GAD, ROVE, RANGE, STROLL, ROAM
rambling excursion - - - - - - TOUR
ramie - - - - - - - - - - FIBER
ramp - - - - - - - - SPRING, SLOPE
rampant - - - - - - - UNCHECKED
rampart - - WALL, REDAN, FORTRESS, BULWARK, PARAPET
rana - - - - - - - - - - - FROG
rancid - - - - - - - - - - RANK
rancor - - - - - - ENMITY, SPITE
rang - - - - - - - - - - CHIMED
range - - - - SCOPE, STOVE, SWEEP, RAMBLE, RANK, ADJUST, ROAM, AREA, PASTURAGE, GAMUT, EXTENT
range in rows - - - - - - - ALINE
range of columns - - - - COLONNADE
range of experience - - - - HORIZON
range of hills - - - - RIDGES, RIDGE
range of knowledge - - - - - - KEN
range of occurrence - - - INCIDENCE
range of perception - - - - - - KEN
range of Rocky Mountains - - - TETON
range of sight - - - - - - - - KEN
range of view - - - - - - - - SCOPE
ranger - - - - - - - - - - ROVER
Rangoon weight - - - - - - - - PAI
rangy - - - - - - - - - - ROOMY
ranine - - - - - - - - - FROGLIKE
rank - DEGREE, CASTE, GRADE, RATE, TIER, ROW, FOUL, ESTIMATE, CLASS, EXTREME, RANGE, RANCID, STATUS, FLAGRANT
rank of nobleman - - - - - BARONY
rank taste - - - - - - - - RANCID
rankle - - - - - - INFLAME, FESTER
ransack - - - - RAKE, PILLAGE, RIFLE
ransom - - - - - - - - - REDEEM
rant - - - - - RAGE, RAIL, BOMBAST
rap - - - - - - - - - - - BLOW
rapacious bird - - - - - - SHRIKE
rapier - - - - - - - - - - SWORD
rapid - FLEET, QUICK, FAST, SWIFT, SPEEDY
rapid speech - - - - - - - PATTER
rapidity - - - - - - - - - SPEED
rapidly - - - - - - SWIFTLY, APACE
rapine - - - - - PILLAGE, PLUNDER
rapt - ABSORBED, INTENT, ENTRANCED, TRANSPORTED
rapture - - - - - - BLISS, ECSTASY
rapturous state - - - - - - TRANCE
rapturous utterance - - - - RHAPSODY
rare - - - UNIQUE, ODD, SCARCE, INFREQUENT, UNUSUAL, TENUOUS
rare metal - - - - - - - - IRIDIUM
rarefy - - - - - - - - ATTENUATE
rarely - - - - - - - - - SELDOM
rascal - - - SCAMP, KNAVE, ROGUE, SCOUNDREL
rase - - - - - - - RUIN, DEMOLISH
rash - - - - HASTY, HEADSTRONG, OVERHASTY, HEEDLESS
rashness - - - - - TEMERITY, FOLLY
rasp - GRATE, SCRAPE, FILE, AFFECT, ABRADE
rasping - - - - - - - - - - HARSH
raspy - - - - - - - - - - GRATING

R

rasse - - - - - - - - - - - CIVET
rat - - - - - - - - - - - RODENT
rat-catching animal - - RATTER, CAT
rate - - - - - PACE, VALUE, GRADE, CALCULATE, SCOLD, DEGREE, RECKON, PRICE, CHARGE, MERIT, COST, REGARD, PERCENT
rate highly - - - - - - - - PRIDE
rate of movement - - - - PACE, TEMPO
rate of progress and motion - - SPEED, PACE
rather - - - - - - - - - SOMEWHAT
rather (Scot.) - - - - - - - - GEY
rather than - - - - - - - - - ERE
ratify - - SEAL, CONFIRM, ENDORSE
rating - - - - - - - - - - - GRADE
ration - ALLOWANCE, SHARE, ALLOT, APPORTION
ratio of mass to volume - - DENSITY
ration for needy - - - - - - - DOLE
rational - - - - - - SANE, SENSIBLE
rattan - - - - - REED, SEGA, CANE
rattle - - - - CLATTER, NOISE, SHAKE
rattlesnake - - - - - - - - RATTLER
raucous - - - - - - HOARSE, HARSH
ravage - - - - - - - - - - - RUIN
rave - - - - RANT, FUME, BOMBAST
ravel - - UNKNIT, ENTANGLE, TANGLE
raven - - - - - - - - - - - CROW
Raven character - - - - - - LENORE
raven's cry - - - - - - - - - CAW
ravenous - LUPINE, TOOTHY, HUNGRY
ravenous bird - - - - - - - - KITE
ravine - DELL, GULCH, DALE, GORGE, CANYON
raving - - - - - - - - - DELIRIOUS
raw - - - - CRUDE, BLEAK, CHILLY, PENETRATING
raw cotton - - - - - - - - - LINT
raw hide - - - - - - - - - - PELT
raw material - - - - - - - STAPLE
raw silk weight - - - - - - - PARI
rawboned animal - - - - - - SCRAG
ray - - - - - - - - - SHINE, BEAM
raze - - OBLITERATE, DESTROY, CUT, DEMOLISH
razer - - - - - - - - DEMOLISHER
razor-billed auk - - - - - - MURRE
razor sharpener - - - - - - STROP
reach - - ATTAIN, ARRIVE, EXTEND, ASPIRE, SPAN, COME
reach across - - - - - - - - - SPAN
reach for - - - - - - - - - ASPIRE
reach highest point - - - CULMINATE
reach toward and upward - - - - ASPIRE
react - - - - - - RESPOND, BEHAVE
reaction - - - - - - - - RESPONSE
read - - PERUSE, PORE, INTERPRET
read metrically - - - - - - - - SCAN
reader - - - - - - - - - - PRIMER
reader of lessons - - - - - - LECTOR
readily - - - - - - - - - - EASILY
readiness - - - - - - - - - - EASE
reading - - - - - - - - - PERUSAL
reading desk - - - - - - - LECTERN
reading matter - - - - - - - - COPY
readjust - - - - -- - - - - REFIT
reads same forward or backward - - - PALINDROME
ready - ALERT, PREPARED, WILLING, FIT, RIPE, APT, FOREARMED
ready (arch.) - - - - - - - - YARE
ready money - - - - - - - - - CASH
ready tied four-in-hand - - - - TECK
ready for trimming sails - - - - ATRIP
reaffirm - - - - - - - REASSERT
reagency - - - - - - - - REACTION
real - - TRUE, CONCRETE, ACTUAL, FACTUAL, GENUINE
real estate - - - - PROPERTY, REALTY
real estate absolutely owned - - ALOD
real estate contract - - - - - LEASE
real estate holding - - - - - - ALOD
real estate in law - - - - - - REALTY
real estate map - - - - - - - - PLAT
reality - - - - - FACT, DEED, TRUTH
realize - - - - SENSE, COMPREHEND, ACCOMPLISH, CONCEIVE, PERCEIVE, SEE
really - - - - - - - - - ACTUALLY
realm - - - DOMAIN, NATION, EMPIRE
reanimate - - - - - - - - - - REVIVE
reap - - - - - - - GATHER, GARNER
rear - - - HIND, POSTERIOR, ELEVATE, BEHIND, RAISE, ERECT, CONSTRUCT, BACK
rear (in the; to the) - - - - - ASTERN
rear of vessel - - - - - - - - - AFT
rearranged - - - - - - - REALIGNED
reason - - - CAUSE, MOTIVE, DEBATE
reasonable - - - - - - - - LOGICAL
reasoning - - - - - - - - - - LOGIC
reasoning faculty - - - - - - - - WIT
reassertion - - - - - REAFFIRMATION
rebate - - - - - DISCOUNT, REFUND
Rebecca's son - - - - - - - - ESAU
rebel - - - - - - RISE, INSURGENT
rebellion - - - - - - - - - REVOLT
rebellious - - - - - INSUBORDINATE
rebirth of a soul in a new form - - - REINCARNATION
rebound - - - - - - - DAP, CAROM
rebuff - SLAP, REPEL, SNUB, SCORN, REPULSE
rebuke - - SNUB, REPRIMAND, CHIDE
rebus - - - - - - - PUZZLE, RIDDLE
rebut - - CONTRADICT, DISPROVE, REFUTE
rebuttal - - - - - - - - DISPROVE
recalcitrant - - - - - - - - RENITENT
recall - REMEMBER, RETRACT, REMIND
recall in form of ideas - - - - IDEATE
recant - - RETRACT, ABJURE, REVOKE
recapitulation - - - SUMMARY, RESUME
recede - - - - - - - - - - - - EBB
receipt - - - - - - - - RECIPE, STUB
receive - - - - - GET, ACCEPT, TAKE
receive cargoes - - - - - - - - LADE
receive and register votes - - - - POLL
receive word - - - - - - - - - HEAR
receiver - - - - - - - - RECIPIENT
recent - NEW, LATE, MODERN, FRESH
recently - - - - - - - - - LATTERLY
recently commenced - - - - INCHOATE
recently hatched - - - - - - SQUAB
receptacle - - BIN, RECEIVER, TRAY, BOX, TANK
receptacle for fluid - - - - - - TANK
reception - - - - - - - - - - - TEA
reception room - - - PARLOUR, SALON
recess - - - - - - - - - NICHE, NOOK
recess in sea shore - - - - BAY, INLET
recess in wall - - - - - - - - NICHE
recess of a door - - - - - EMBRASURE
recessed portion of room - - - ALCOVE
recipe - - - - - - - - - - RECEIPT
recipient - - - - RECEIVER, LEGATEE
recipient of gift - PRESENTEE, DONEE
reciprocal - - - - - - - - - MUTUAL
reciprocal influence - - - - - REACT

reciprocate - - - - - - - RETURN
recital - - - ACCOUNT, NARRATION, NARRATIVE
recite - - RELATE, NARRATE, REPORT
recite metrically - - - - - - SCAN
recite in musical monotone - INTONE, CHANT
recite pompously - - - - - - SPOUT
reckless - - - RASH, BOLD, MAD, DESPERATE
reckon - - - - RATE, DATE, TALLY, COMPUTE, CALCULATE
reckoning (colloq.) - - - - - - TAB
reckoning table - - - - - - ABACUS
reckoning time - - - - - - DATING
reclaim - RECOVER, REDEEM, RESCUE
recline - - REPOSE, LIE, LOLL, REST
recluse - - - - - HERMIT, EREMITE
recognize - - - - - - - - - KNOW
recoil - - - - - - - - SHRINK, SHY
recollect - - - - - RECALL, BETHINK
recollection - - - - - - - - - MIND
recommence - - - - - - - - RESUME
recommit - - - - - - - - REMAND
recompense - - PAY, REWARD, MEED, RENEW, FEE
reconcile - - - - ATONE, RESIGN
recondite - - ABSTRACT, ABSTRUSE
reconnoiter - - - - - SCOUT, PICKET
reconstruct - - - - - - - - REMAKE
record - ANNAL, LOG, ENTER, ENROLL, PEN
record of acts - - - - - - - ACTA
record book - - - - - - - LEDGER
record of criminal investigation - - - DOSSIER
record of descent - - - GENEALOGY
record of performance - - - - - LOG
record of proceedings - ACTA, ACTUM
record of single event - - - - ANNAL
record (to) - - ENTER, ENROLL, LOG, PEN
recorded proceedings - - - - - ACTA
recount - - - - - - - - TELL, RELATE
recourse - - - - - - - - - RESORT
recover - RESTORE, REGAIN, RECLAIM, RALLY, RETRIEVE, FLOW
recreate - - - - - - - - - DIVERT
recreation - - - - - - PLAY, SPORT
recreation area - - - - - - - PARK
recreational contest - - - - - GAME
recruited - - - - - - - ENLISTED
rectangular - - - - - - - OBLONG
rectangular inserts - - - - PANELS
rectify - - CORRECT, AMEND, EMEND
rectitude - - - - - - - - - PROBITY
rector's dwelling - - - - - RECTORY
rectory - - - - - - - PARSONAGE
recuperate - - - - - - - - - RALLY
recur - - - - - - REVERT, RETURN
recurring part of decimal - REPETEND
red - - RUDDY, FLUSHED, CARMEN, CRIMSON, ROSY, ROSET, VERMILION, SCARLET, CERISE, ROSEATE, ANARCHIST
red-bellied terrapin - - - - - SLIDER
red and blue - - - - - - - - PURPLE
red cedar - - - - - - - - - SAVIN
red clay (kind) - - - - - - LATERITE
red dye - - - - - - - - - - ALTA
red flannel (former name) - - TAMINE
red-legged sandpiper - - - REDSHANK
red pepper - - - - - - - CAYENNE
red planet - - - - - - - - - MARS
red purple - - - - - - - - CLARET
red-yellow in hue - - TITIAN, AMBER
redact - - - - - - - - - - EDIT
redactor - - - - - - - - - EDITOR
redan - - RAMPART, FORTIFICATION
redbreast - - - - - - - - - ROBIN
redcap - - - - - - - - - PORTER
redden - - BLUSH, RUDDLE, FLUSH
reddish - - - - - - - - - ROSEATE
reddish brown - AUBURN, BAY, HENNA, SEPIA, SORREL, CHESTNUT, UMBER
reddish brown mineral - - - - RUTILE
reddish clay - - - - - - - LATERITE
reddish colour - - - - PEONY, CORAL
reddish orange dye - - - - - HENNA
reddish yellow - - ORANGE, AMBER, TOTEM, TITIAN
redeem - - - - - RECLAIM, RANSOM
redeemer - - - - SAVIOR, DELIVERER
redolent - - - FRAGRANT, ODOROUS
redress - - - - - - - - - REPAIR
redskin - - - - - - - - - INDIAN
reduce - LESSEN, ABATE, BATE, LOWER, DEBASE, PARE
reduce to ashes - - - - - CREMATE
reduce to bondage - - - - - ENSLAVE
reduce by cutting - - - - - - PARE
reduce in density - - - - - - THIN
reduce to fine state - - - - - REFINE
reduce to fluid state - - - - LIQUEFY
reduce from blown up stage - DEFLATE
reduce to lower grade - - - - DEMOTE
reduce to a means - - - - AVERAGE
reduce to a pulp - - - MASH, CRUSH
reduce in rank - - - - - - DEMOTE
reduce in richness - - - - - - THIN
reduce in size - - - - - - SHRINK
reduce to smallest part - - MINIMIZE
reduce to soft mass - - - MACERATE
reduce to a spray - - - - - ATOMIZE
reducing medium - - - - - - DIET
reduction - - - - - - - - - - CUT
reduction in sail area - - - - - REEF
ree - - - - - - - - - - - - RUFF
reed - - - - - - - - - - RATTAN
reed instrument - CLARINET, BASSON
reef - - - - - - - - SHOAL, LODE
reef oyster - - - - - - - REEFER
reefer - - - - - - - - - - JACKET
reek - - - - - - - - SMOKE, FUME
reel - SPIN, STAGGER, SPOOL, WAVER, SWAY, FALTER, BOBBIN, TROLL, WHIRL
reem - - - - - - - - - UNICORN
reeve - - - - - - - - - - THREAD
reexamine - - - - - - - - - REVISE
refer - - APPEAL, ALLUDE, ASCRIBE, RELEGATE, DIRECT, CITE, MENTION
referee - - - - - - - UMPIRE, JUDGE
reference - - - - - - - - ALLUSION
reference mark - - - - - - ASTERISK
reference table - - - - - - - INDEX
refill - - - - - REPACK, REPLENISH
refined - - - - - PURE, NICE, NEAT
refined gracefulness - - - - ELEGANCE
refined in manner - - - - - POLITE
refinement - - - POLISH, CULTURE, ELEGANCE
refit - - - - - - - - - READJUST
reflect - MIRROR, PONDER, RUMINATE
reflect deeply - - - - - - - PORE
reflect upon - - - - - - RUMINATE
reflux of the tide - - - - - - EBB
reform - - - - AMEND, REGENERATE, CORRECT
reform movement - - - - - CRUSADE
Reformation leader - - - - - LUTHER
R

refractory - - - - - - - - - UNRULY
refrain - CHORUS, ABSTAIN, FOREGO, DITTY
refreshed - - - - - - - - - RESTED
refreshing - - - - - - - - - TONIC
refreshing air - - - - - - - OZONE
refrigerant - - - - - - - - - - ICE
refrigerant dealer - - - - ICEMAN
refrigerate - - - - - - ICE, FREEZE
refuge - - - - - - HAVEN, RETREAT
refulgent - - - - - - - BRILLIANT
refund - - - - - - REPAY, REBATE
refusal - DENIAL, WASTE, NAY, VETO
refusal of assent - - - - - NEGATIVE
refuse - DENY, TRASH, VETO, WASTE, DIRT, SCUM, REJECT, DECLINE, MARC
refuse approval - - - - - - - VETO
refuse to have dealings with - BOYCOTT
refuse from down or fur fiber - KEMP
refuse from melting metal - - - SLAG
refuse in wine making - - - - - MARC
refute - - DENY, DISPROVE, REBUT
regain - - - - RECOVER, RESTORE
regain possession - - - - REPOSSESS
regal - - IMPERIAL, ROYAL, KINGLY, STATELY
regale - - - - - TREAT, ENTERTAIN
regard - - - OBSERVE, CONSIDER, ESTIMATION, HEAR, CARE, RATE, ESTEEM, EYE
regard favourably - - - - - APPROVE
regard highly - - - RATED, ESTEEM, HONOUR, DEEM, ADMIRE
regard reverently - - - - - - ADORE
regard studiously - - - - - - - CON
regard too favorably - - - OVERRATE
regard with honour - - - VENERATE, RESPECT
regard with indifference - - DISDAIN
regenerate - - - - - RENEW, REFORM
regent - - - - - - - - - - RULER
regime - - - - - - - - - - - RULE
region - CLIME, ZONE, TRACT, AREA, DISTRICT, REALM, TERRITORY, LOCALITY, TERRAIN
region beyond Jordan - - PEREA, ENON
region of darkness - - - - - EREBUS
region of ear - - - - - - - - - OTIC
region in general - - - - DEMESNE
region of influence - - - - - ORBIT
region of sunset - - - - - - - WEST
region of surpassing delight - PARADISE
regional - - - LOCAL, ZONAL, AREAL
regional weather conditions - CLIMATE
register - ENLIST, SLATE, TALLY, ROLL, LIST, ENTER
register of days of year - - CALENDAR
regret - - - RUE, REPENT, RESENT, MOURN, LAMENT, DEPLORE, SPURN
regretful - - - - - - - - - SORRY
regular - STATED, NORMAL, CANONIC, PERIODIC
regular customer - - - - - PATRON
regulate - SETTLE, MANAGE, ORDER, ADJUST, GOVERN, DIRECT
regulate action of - - - - - - PACE
regulate by moderating - - TEMPER
regulation - - - - - - - RULE, LAW
regulative - - - - - - - DIRECTIVE
rehearse - - - - - - - - PRACTICE
Reich division - - - - - - - - SAAR
reign - - - RULE, PREVAIL, GOVERN
reigning beauty - - - - - - BELLE
reimbue with courage - - - - REMAN
reimburse - - - - - - PAY, REPAY
reimpose - - - - - - - - - RELAY
rein - RESTRAIN, LINE, CURB, CHECK
reindeer - - - - - - - - - CARIBOU
reinstate - - - - - - - - RESTORE
reject - REPEL, DENY, SPURN, REFUSE
rejection - - - - - REPULSE, DENIAL
rejoice - - - - - - - - - - - EXULT
rejoinder - - - ANSWER, REPARTEE, RETORT, RESPONSE
rekindle - - - - - - - - - RELUME
relate - - - RECITE, TELL, PERTAIN, APPERTAIN, NARRATE, RECOUNT, DETAIL
relate in particulars - - - - DETAIL
related - - - - - - - - - KIN, AKIN
related by blood - - - - - AKIN, SIB
related on father's side - - AGNATE
related on mother's side - - - ENATE, ENATIC, ENATION
related succession - - - - - SERIES
relating to - - PERTAIN, PERTAINING
relating to right hand - - - DEXTER
relation - - - - - KINSHIP, KINSMAN
relation to harmony - - - - RAPPORT
relation through mother - - ENATION
relation to (in) - - PROPORTIONATE
relations - KINDRED, KITH, RELATIVES
relative - - - PERTINENT, KINSMAN, RELATION, KIN
relative condition - - - - - STATUS
relative of the emu - - - - - - RHEA
relative by marriage - - - - - IN-LAW
relatives - - - - - - KIN, KINSFOLK
relatively harmless - - - - - WHITE
relax - - - EASE, LOOSEN, SLACKEN, REMIT, UNBEND
relaxation - - - - - - - - - REST
release - - - LOOSE, FREE, DELIVER, RELET, UNDO, UNBIND, LOOSEN, LIBERATE, EXEMPT
release on honour - - - - - PAROLE
release from obligation - - ABSOLVE
released - - - - - - - - - EXEMPT
relegate - - - - - - - - - REFERS
relent - - - - - - - YIELD, SOFTEN
relentless - - - - - - - - - - GRIM
relet - - - - - - - - - - RELEASE
relevant - - - PERTINENT, GERMANE
reliable - - - - - - - - - - TRUSTY
reliance - TRUST, HOPE, CONFIDENCE
reliant - - - - - - - - CONFIDENT
relic - - - - - FRAGMENT, VESTIGE, REMAINDER, TOKEN, MEMENTO
relict - - - - - - - - - - - WIDOW
relief - - - - - AID, SUCCOR, EASE
relieve - - - LESSEN, EASE, ALLAY, MITIGATE, AID, SPELL, VENT
religieuse - - - - - - - - - - - NUN
religious assemblage - CONGREGATION
religious awakening - - - - - REVIVAL
religious band (abbr.) - - - - - - SA
religious belief - - - - - - - CREED
religious ceremony - - - - - - MASS
religious class - - - - - - - - SECT
religious community - - AGAPEMONE
religious composition - MOTET, ANTHEM
religious congregation - - - PARISH
religious discipline - - - - PENANCE
religious discourse - - - - - SERMON
religious dogma - - - - - - - TENET
religious faith - - - - - - RELIGION
religious festival - - EASTER, PURIM
religious group - - - - - - - - SECT
religious head - - - - - - - - POPE
religious hermit - - - - - - - MONK
religious holiday - - - - - - FIESTA
religious image - - - - - ICON, IKON

religious musical composition - - - CANTATA
religious denomination and order - SECT
religious observance - - - - - RITE
religious pamphlet - - - - - TRACT
religious poem - - - - - - - PSALM
religious recluse - - - - - - - NUN
religious song - - - CHANT, PSALM
religious songs collectively - HYMNODY
religious talk - - - - - - - CANT
religious woman - - - - - - - NUN
religious zealot - - - - - - FANATIC
relinquish - CEDE, GO, WAIVE, RESIGN, ABDICATE, LEAVE
relinquished - - - - - - - - LEFT
relinquishment - - - - - - WAIVER
reliquary - - - - - - ARCA, APSIS
relish - - FLAVOUR, ZEST, CANAPE, SAVOR, TASTE, ENJOYMENT, LIKE, OLIVE, GUSTO
reluctant - - - - - - AVERSE, LOATH
relume - - - - - - - - REKINDLE
rely - - - - DEPEND, TRUST, REST
rely on - - - - - - - LEAN, TRUST
remain - - - STAY, ABIDE, TARRY, CONTINUE
remain erect - - - - - - - STAND
remain near - - - - - - - HOVER
remainder - BALANCE, RECALL, RELIC, MONITOR, REST
remaining - - - REMNANT, OTHER, RESIDUAL, LEFT
remaining after deductions - - - NET
remaining fragment - - - - - RELIC
remains of a city - - - - - RUINS
remake - - - - - RECONSTRUCT
remanent - - - - - REMAINING
remark - - - SAY, NOTE, COMMENT, OBSERVE, WORD
remarkable - - - - - - - NOTABLE
remedial herb - - - - - - ARNICA
remedy - - - - - - CURE, REPAIR
remember - - - - - - REST, RECALL
remember when absent - - - IDEATE
remember with sorrow - - - REGRET
remind oneself - - BETHINK, RECALL
remise - - - - - - - - - DEED
remiss - NEGLIGENT, LAGGARD, LAX
remission - - FORGIVENESS, PARDON
remit - - SEND, FORGIVE, ABSOLVE, FOREGO, RELAX
remnant - - - - - - RAG, ORT, DREG
remnant of fire - - - - - - - ASH
remonstrate - - - - - - - PROTEST
remorse - - COMPUNCTION, ANGUISH
remote - FAR, DISTANT, OLD, SECLUDED
remotely - - - - - - - - - AFAR
remount a jewel - - - - - - RESET
removal of obstruction - - CLEARANCE
remove - - ELIDE, ELIMINATE, DELE, DELETE, OUST, PEEL, CONVEY, RID, DOFF, PARE, ERADICATE
remove afar off - - - ELOIN, ELOIGN
remove air - - - - - - - DEFLATE
remove beyond jurisdiction (law) - - - ELOIN
remove bone from - - - - - - BONE
remove a cargo - - - - - - UNLOAD
remove central portion - - - - CORE
remove cream - - - - - - - SKIM
remove error - - - - - - CORRECT
remove from active service - - RETIRE
remove from fixed position - UNSEAT
remove from high position - - DEPOSE
remove from position (naut.) - UNSHIP
remove hair - - - - - - - EPILATE
remove impurities - - - - - REFINE
remove moisture - - EVAPORATE, DRY
remove pits from - - - - - - STONE
remove in printing - - - - - - DELE
remove sprouts from - - - - - CHIT
remove utterly - - - - - - - RAZE
removed - - - - - - - - - - AWAY
remover - ELIMINATOR, ERADICATOR
remunerate - - - COMPENSATE, PAY
remuneration - - - PAY, EMOLUMENT
rend - - SPLIT, RIVE, TEAR, CLEAVE, RUPTURE, BREAK, RIP, LACERATE
render - - TRANSLATE, CONTRIBUTE, TRANSMIT, DELIVER, GIVE, BESTOW, SUNDER, MAKE, FURNISH
render accessible - - - - - - OPEN
render active - - - - - - ACTIVATE
rend asunder - - - - - SPLIT, RIVE
render desolate - - - - - - DESTROY
render easy - - - - - - - - PAVE
render enduring - - - - - - ANNEAL
render fat - - - - - - - - LARD
render ineffective - NEGATE, ENERVATE
render insane - - - - - - DERANGE
render muddy - - - - - - - ROIL
render senseless - - - - - - STUN
render suitable - - - - - - ADAPT
render turbid - - - - - - - - ROIL
render unconscious - - - - - - STUN
render useless - - - - - - - NULL
render vocal music - - - - - - SING
rendezvous - - - - - - - - TRYST
renegade - - DESERTER, APOSTATE, TRAITOR
renege - - REVOKE, DENY, RENOUNCE
renew - RESTORE, RESALE, RESUME, REGENERATE, RENOVATE, REVIVE
renew wine - - - - - - - - STUM
renewal - - - - - - - - REVIVAL
renewed attention - - - - - REVIVAL
renaissance (pert. to) - - - - REBORN
rennet (dial.) - - - - - - - KESLOP
renounce - REPUDIATE, DISOWN, DENY, ABJURE, RENEGE, WAIVE
renovate - REPAIR, RESTORE, ALTER, CLEANSE, RENEW, CLEAN, FURNISH
renovation - - - - - - - RENEWAL
renown - - FAME, GLORY, HONOUR
renown (slang) - - - - - - - REP
rent - - LEASE, HIRE, RIVEN, LET, BREACH, BREAK, SCHISM
rent for a booth - - - - - STALLAGE
rent (Scot. law) - - - - - - - PAIN
rent asunder - - - - - - - RIVEN
renter - - - - - - LESSEE, TENANT
renting contract - - - - - - LEASE
repair - - - MEND, RENOVATE, FIX, REDRESS, RESORT, REMEDY
repair shoes - - - - - - RETAP, TAP
reparation - - - AMENDS, REDRESS, AMEND, ATONE, ATONEMENT
reparation for injury - - - - DAMAGES
repartee - REJOINDER, RIPOSTE, REPLY, RETORT
repast - MEAL, FEAST, REFLECTION, DINNER, LUNCH
repast (pert. to) - - - - - PRANDIAL
repatriation - - - - - - - - AMENDS
repay - REFUND, REQUITE, RETALIATE
repeal - ABROGATE, ANNUL, RESCIND, REVOKE, ABOLISH
repeat - - ITERATE, PARROT, ECHO
repeat again - - - - - - REITERATE
repeat mechanically - - - - - PARROT
repeat sound - - - - - - - ECHO
repeatable - - - - - - - ITERANT

R

repeated knocking - - - - RATATAT
repeating - - - - - - - ITERANT
repel - - REPULSE, WARD, REJECT, OPPOSE
repent - - - - - - - ATONE, RUE
repentance - - - - - - - PENANCE
repentant - - PENITENT, CONTRITE
repercussion - - - - - - - RECOIL
repetition - - ENCORE, ECHO, ROTE, REITERATE, ITERATION, ITERANCE
repetitious - - - - - - - ITERANT
repine - - COMPLAIN, MURMUR, FRET
replaced - - - - RESET, RESTORED
replenish - - - - - - REFILL, FILL
replete - - ABOUNDING, RIFE, FULL
repletion - - - - - - - FULLNESS
replevin - - - - - - - - - - BAIL
replica - COPY, DUPLICATE, FACSIMILE
reply - - RETORT, RESPOND, ANSWER
report - -RUMOUR, RECITE, ACCOUNT
repose - REST, EASE, PEACE, COMPOSE
reposed - - - - - - LAIN, TRANQUIL
reposeful - - - - - - - - QUIET
reposition - - - - - - - - RESET
repository for valuables - SAFE, VAULT
reprehend - - - - - - - REPRISE
reprehensible - - - - CENSURABLE
representation - - - - - - - IMAGE
representative - - AGENT, DELEGATE, CONSUL, LEGATE
representative example - - - - - TYPE
representative of sacred beetle - SCARAB
representative specimen - - SWATCH
representing speech sounds - PHONETIC
repress - - - - RESTRAIN, BRIDLE
reprieve - - - - - - - - RESPITE
reprimand - - ADMONISH, REBUKE, SLATE, LESSON
reprimand (Scot.) - - - - - - STON
reprise - - - - - - - REPREHEND
reproach - - BLAME, SLUR, UPBRAID, TAUNT
reproach abusively - - - - REVILE
reprove - - REBUKE, CENSURE, FLAY
reptile - - - SNAKE, TURTLE, ASP
Republican party (abbr.) - - G.O.P.
repudiate - - - RENOUNCE, DISOWN, DISCLAIM, DENY, RECANT
repudiate formally - - - - - RECANT
repulse - REPEL, REJECTION, REBUFF
repulsive - - FULSOME, DISTASTEFUL
repulsive woman - - - - - - GORGON
repurchase - - - - - - - REDEEM
reputation - REPUTE, CREDIT, STAMP, HONOUR, PRESTIGE
repute - - - REPUTATION, OPINION
request - - ASK, ENTREATY, SOLICIT, ENTREAT, APPEAL
request formally - - - - PETITION
request for payment - - - - - - DUN
requiem mass - - - - - - - DIRGE
require - - - NEED, DEMAND, CLAIM
require little effort - - - - - - EASY
required conduct - - - - - - DUTY
requisite - - - NEEDFUL, NECESSARY
requisition for goods - - - - - ORDER
requite - REPAY, REVENGE, AVENGE, RETALIATE, REWARD
reround - - - - - - - - ACCRUE
rescind - REPEAL, RETRACT, REVOKE, ABROGATE, CANCEL
rescript - - - - - - - - DECREE
rescue - - SAVE, DELIVER, SUCCOR, FREE, RECLAIM
resemblance in sound - - ASSONANCE
resembling oats - - - - - - OATEN
resembling tiles - - - - - TEGULAR
resentful - - - BEGRUDGING, ENVY
reserve - SPARE, RETICENCE, RETAIN, SAVE
reserved - - TAKEN, ALOOF, OFFISH, COY, SHY, COLD
reserved in speech - - - RETICENT
reservoir for water - - - - - - POOL
resew - - - - - - - - RESTRICT
reside - ABIDE, DWELL, CINDER, LIVE
residence - - - - - - - - - HOME
residence of gentleman farmer - GRANGE
resident - - - CITIZEN, INHERENT, DWELLER, OCCUPANT
resident of convent - - - - - - NUN
resident of (suffix) - - - - - - - ER
residing at - - - - - - - - - OF
residing in - - - - - - - - - OF
residual - - REMANENT, REMAINING
residue - - - - - - - ASH, REST
resign - - - DEMIT, RELINQUISH, RECONCILE, RETIRE
resiliency - - - - - - - - - TONE
resilient - - - - - - - - ELASTIC
resin - LAC, ANIME, CONIMA, COPAL, ELEMIN
resin (fragrant) - ALOE, ELEMI, NARD
resin (gum) - - - - - - - ELEMI
resinous insect secretion - - - - LAC
resist - - - REBEL, OPPOSE, REPEL, WITHSTAND
resistance - - - - - - - - - - AID
resistance to attack - - - - DEFENSE
resistance to pressure - - RENITENCE
resistant - - - - - - - OPPOSING
resisting pressure - - - - RENITENT
resolute - - - DETERMINED, MANLY
resolution - - - - DETERMINATION
resolve - DECIDE, DETERMINE, ROTATE
resonant - - - - - - - - RINGING
resort - - SPA, HAUNT, RECOURSE, REPAIR
resound - - - - RING, PEAL, ECHO, REVERBERATE, CLANG, TOLL
resounding - - - - - - RESONANT
resources - - - - ASSETS, MEANS
respect - ESTEEM. AWE. REVERENCE. HOMAGE, DEFERENCE, HONOUR
respectable - - - - - - - DECENT
respectful - - - - - - - REVERENT
respiratory organ - - - - - - LUNG
respiratory sound - - - - - - RALE
respire - - - - - - - - BREATHE
respite - - REST, REPRIEVE, PAUSE, TRUCE, INTERVAL, LULL
resplendent - - - AUREATE, GOLDEN
respond - - REACT, ANSWER, PEAL, REPLY
respond to a stimulus - - - REACT
respond to a trick (slang) - - - BITE
responding instantly - - - PROMPT
response - - - ANSWER, REACTION, REJOINDER
rest (at) - - - - - - - - STATIC
rest - PAUSE, REPOSE, LEAN, SIT, RESPITE, EASE, LAIR, DESIST, RECLINE, RELY, SUPPORT
rest to support music - - - - LEAN
restate briefly (slang) - - - RECAP
restate in other words - PARAPHRASE
restaurant - - - - - - - - CAFE
restaurant car - - - - - - - DINER
resting - - - - - - - - INACTIVE
resting place - - - - ROOST, BED

resting place for a column - - PLINTH
restive - UNEASY, FIDGETY, RESTLESS
restless - UNEASY, TOSSING, RESTIVE
restless (be) - - - - - - - - TOSS
restless desire - - - - - - - ITCH
restless hankering - - - - - - ITCH
restlessness - - - - - - - UNREST
restoration - - - - - - - REVIVAL
restore - RENEW, REPLACE, RENOVATE, REINSTATE, RETURN
restore to citizenship - - REPATRIATE
restore confidence - - - REASSURE
restore to normal position - - RIGHT
restrain - - DAM, STINT, MODERATE, CURB, BATE, CHAIN, CHECK, REPRESS, TETHER, BRIDLE, CRAMP, BIND, DETER, CONFINE, ARREST, RULE, REIN
restrain through fear - - - DETER, OVERAWE
restraining - - - - - - PREVENTIVE
restraining instrument - - - - REIN
restraint - - - - DETENTION, STINT
restrict - LIMIT, HEM, RESEW, DAM, STINT
restricted - - - - - - - - STRAIT
result - EVENTUATE, OUTCOME, ENSUE, FOLLOW, UPSHOT, EFFECT
result of an inquiry - - - FINDINGS
result of a vote - - - - - - - POLL
resume - RENEW, REOPEN, CONTINUE
resumption - - - - - - - RENEWAL
resurrection - - - - - - - RENEWAL
resuscitate - - - - REVIVE, WAKE
ret - - - - - - - - - SOAK, STEEP
retail shop - - - - - - - - STORE
retain - SAVE, HOLD, KEEP, ENGAGE, RESERVE
retaining band - - - - - - - HOOP
retake - - - - - - - REPOSSESS
retaliate - AVENGE, REQUITE, REPAY
retaliate vindictively - - - REVENGE
retaliation - - - REPRISAL, REVENGE
retard - - - DELAY, SLOW, HINDER
retardation - - - - - - - - LAG
reticence - - - - - - - - RESERVE
reticent - - - SECRETIVE, TACITURN
reticular - - - - - - - - NETLIKE
reticule - - - - - - - - HANDBAG
retinue - - - - - - - SUITE, TRAIN
retinue of wives - - - - - - HAREM
retire - - - RETREAT, QUIT, LEAVE, RESIGN, WITHDRAW
retired - - - - - INACTIVE, ABED
retired from the world - - - RECLUSE
retired with honour - - - EMERITUS
retiring - - - - - - - - - SHY
retort - - - - - - - - REJOINDER
retract - - RECANT, DISAVOW, RECALL
retread a tire - - - - - - - RECAP
retreat - RECESS, RETIRE, WITHDRAW, NEST, REFUGE
retribution - - - REVENGE, AVENGE, NEMESIS, PAY
retrieve - - - - - - - - RECOVER
retrogression - - - - - - RETREAT
return - - - - - RESTORE, RECUR, RECIPROCATE, REVERT
return to - - - - - - - - REVISIT
return to custody - - - - - REMAND
return evil for evil - - - RETALIATE
return to former state - - REVERSION
return like for like - - - RETALIATE
return to mind - - - - - - - RECUR
return to office - - - - - - REELECT
return procession - - - - RECESSION
return to stockholder - - - DIVIDEND
return thrust - - - - - - - RIPOSTE
returning - - - - - - RECURRENT
reunion with Brahma - - - NIRVANA
reveal - - BARE, DISCLOSE, SHOW, UNVEIL, EXPOSE
reveal secret without discretion - BLAB
revel - FEAST, SPREE, DELIGHT, RIOT
reveler - - - - - - - ROISTERER
reveling cry - - - - - - - - EVOE
revelry - - - - - - - - RIOT, JOY
revenge - - REQUITE, RETRIBUTION, AVENGE, RETALIATE, RETALIATION
revenue - - - - - - - - - INCOME
revenue department - - - TREASURY
reverberate - RESOUND, ECHO, ROLL, RING
reverberation - - - - - - - ECHO
revere highly - - ADORE, VENERATE, ADMIRE
reverence - AWE, REVERE, VENERATION, HONOUR
reverent - - - - - - - WORSHIPFUL
reverentially - - - - - - AWESOMELY
reverie - DREAM, DAYDREAM, MUSING
reverse - TURN, OPPOSITE, VENERATE, REVERT, REVOKE, INVERT, SETBACK
reverse curves - - - - - - - ESSES
revert - - REVERSE, RECUR, RETURN
review - SURVEY, CONSIDER, REVISE, PARADE, CRITIQUE
review and amend - - - - REVISE
revile - MALIGN, ABUSE, SCOFF, VILIFY
reviler - - - MALIGNER, TRADUCER
revise - - AMEND, PROOFREAD, EDIT, REVIEW, CHANGE, EMEND
revision - - - - - - - - CHANGE
revival - - - - - - - - RENEWAL
revive - - - FRESHEN, RESUSCITATE, RALLY, REANIMATE, RENEW
reviver - - - - - - - - - RALLIER
revoke - - REPEAL, CANCEL, RENEGE, ADEEM, REVERSE, RECANT, RESCIND
revoke a legacy - - - - - - ADEEM
revolt - - - REBEL, MUTINY, RISE, REBELLION, UPRISING
revolution - - - - - - - ROTATION
Revolution hero - HALE, REVERE, ALLEN
Revolution leader - - - - - ALLEN
Revolution traitor - - - - ARNOLD
Revolution war general - - - ALLEN
revolutionary - - - - - - - WARS
revolve - ROTATE, GYRATE, SPIN, ROLT, TURN, WHIRL, ROLL
revolving arrow - - - - - - VIRE
revolving body - - - - - SATELLITE
revolving cylinder - - - - ROLLER
reward - MEND, PRIZE, MEED, MEDAL, REQUITE, GUERDON
reward for services - - - - - FEE
reword - - - - - - - PARAPHRASE
rhea - - - - - - - - - - - EMU
rhetorical - - - - - - ORATORICAL
rhetorical device - - - - - APORIA
rhetorical questions - - EPEROTESIS
rhinal - - - - - - - - - - NASAL
Rhine affluent - - - - - - - RUHR
rhinoceros beetle - - - - - - UANG
Rhone river town - - - - - ARLES
rhubarb - - - - - - - - PIEPLANT
rhymester - - - - POET, VERSIFIER
rhyming game - - - - - - CRAMBO
rhythm - - CADENCE, METER, TEMPO
rhythm in verse - - - - - - METER

R

rhythmic - - - CADENT, METRICAL
rhythmic beat - - - - - - - PULSE
rhythmic silence - - - - - - REST
rhythmic succession of sound - MUSIC
rhythmic swing - - - - - - - - LILT
ria - - - - - - - - - - - - INLET
riant - BLITHE, GAY, BRIGHT, SMILING
riata - - - - - - - - - - - - - ROPE
rib - - - - VEIN, VERTEBRA, PURL
ribald - - - - - - - - - - COARSE
ribbed fabric - - REP, TWILL, DIMITY
ribbon decoration - - - - - ROSETTE
ricochet - - - - - CAROM, GLANCE
rice in the husk - - - - - - PADDY
rice liquor - - - - - - - - - SAKE
rice paste - - - - - - - - - - - AME
rich - - - - - AFFLUENT, OPULENT, PRODUCTIVE, WEALTHY, SUMPTUOUS
rich brown - - - - - - - - - SEPIA
rich hangings behind a throne - DORSE
rich man - - - - - - - - - NABOB
rich in oil - - - - - - - - - - FAT
rich source - - - - - - - - - MINE
riches - - - - - - - - - MAMMON
riches (ill sense) - - - - - - LUCRE
richest part - - - - - - - - - FAT
richly laden ships - - - - - ARGOSIES
rick - - - - - HAYSTACK, HAYCOCK
rid - - - - - - - - - CLEAR, FREE
riddle - - - ENIGMA, SIFT, REBUS
ride - - - - - - - - - - - - DRIVE
ride in airplane - - - - - - - - FLY
rider - - - - - HORSEMAN, JOCKEY, PASSENGER
rides in a car (colloq.) - - - AUTOES
ridge - - - - - - - - - - - SPINE
ridge between channels - - - - ARRIS
ridge in cloth - - - - - - - - - RIB
ridge (colloq.) - - - - - - - - WELT
ridges of drift - OSAR, ESKAR, ESKER
ridge of earth - - - - - - - RIDEAU
ridge (narrow) - - - - - - - - OSAR
ridge of plant - - - - - - - - - RIB
ridge of rock - - - - - - REED, REEF
ridge of sand - - - - - DUNE, REEF
ridicule - DERIDE, SATIRE, SATIRIZE, LAMPOON, SNORT, BANTER, ROAST, SCOUT, TWIT
ridicule (colloq.) - - - - ROAST, PAN
ridiculous failure - - - - - - FIASCO
riding academy - - - - - - MANEGE
riding whip - - - - - - QUIRT, CROP
rife - REPLETE, CURRENT, ABOUNDING, WIDESPREAD
rifle - - - GARAND, GUN, PILLAGE, RANSACK, MAUSER
rifle bullet sound - - - - - - PING
rift - - - - FISSURE, CLEFT, BREAK
rig - - - - - - - - - - ATTIRE, GEAR
Riga Island gulf - - - - - - OESEL
right (to the) - - - - - - - - - GEE
right - - - PROPER, JUST, CORRECT
right angled - - - - - RECTANGULAR
right away - - - - - - - - PRONTO
right feeling - - - - - - EMPATHY
right hand page - - - - - - RECTO
right hand (pert. to) - - - - DEXTER
right handed - - - - - - - DEXTER
right to hold office - - - - - TENURE
right of suffrage - - - - - - - VOTE
right of using another's property - - - EASEMENT
righteous - - - - - - - - - MORAL
rigid - SET, TENSE, STARK, SEVERE, STIFF, STRICT, SOLID

rigor - - - HARDSHIP, STRICTNESS, ASPERITY, STIFFNESS
rigorous - SEVERE, DRASTIC, SPARTAN, STRAIT, INCLEMENT, STERN
rile - - - - VEX, ANNOY, IRRITATE
riler (colloq.) - - - - - - - ROILER
rill - - - - - - - STREAMLET, RILLET
rim - BORDER, EDGE, BRINK, EDGING
rim of cask - - - - - - - - - CHIME
rima - - - - - - - - - - - FISSURE
rimple - - - - - - FOLD, WRINKLE
rind - - - - - - - - - - PEEL, SKIN
ring - - PEAL, CIRCLE, TOLL, KNELL, ARENA, HOOP, ENCIRCLE, RINGLET
ring around moon - - - - - CORONA
ring of chain - - - - - - - - LINK
ring to hold reins - - - - - - TERRET
ring official - - - - - - - - TIMER
ring of rope - - - - - - GROMMET
ring shaped - - - - - - - - ANNULAR
ring shaped coral island - - - ATOLL
ring softly - - - - - - - - - TINGLE
ring-tailed tree dwelling mammal - - - LEMUR
rings through which reins pass - TERRET
ring to tighten a joint - - - - WASHER
ringed boa - - - - - - - - - ABOMA
ringing - - - - - - - - - RESONANT
ringing sound - - - - - - - - CLANG
ringlet - - - - - - - - TRESS, CURL
ringshaped - - - - - - - - ANNULAR
ringworm - - - - - - - - - TINEA
riot - - UPROAR, BRAWL, REVELRY, ORGY, REVEL
riotous - - - - - - - - - - AROAR
riotous behaviour - - - - - RAMPAGE
riotous celebrant - - - - - REVELER
riotous party - - - - - - - - - ORGY
rip - - - - - - - - - TEAR, REND
ripe - - MELLOW, MATURE, READY
ripen - - - - - - - - - - - MELLOW
ripened part of flower - - - PERICARP
riposte - - - - - - - - - REPARTEE
ripple - - - - - - - - - - WAVELET
ripple against - - - - - - - - - - LAP
rise - - ELEVATE, LEVITATE, MOUNT, SOAR, LIFT, ASCENT, REBEL, REVOLT, CLIMB, INCREASE, SOURCE
rise against authority - - - - MUTINY
rise and fall of sea - - - - - - TIDE
rise from a liquid - - - - - EMERGE
rise of ground - - - HILL, HUMMOCK
rise high - - - - - - - - - - TOWER
rise threateningly - - - - - - LOOM
risible - - - - - LAUGHABLE, FUNNY
rising - - - - - ASCENDANT, ASCENT
rising step - - - - - - - - - - STAIR
risk - DARE, VENTURE, HAZARD, STAKE, DANGER, CHANCE, PERIL
risky - - - - INSECURE, DANGEROUS
rite - - - - - - - - - - CEREMONY
ritual - - - - - - - - - CEREMONIAL
rival - - FOE, EMULATE, COMPETITOR, EMULATOR, COMPETING
rivalry - - - - - - - - - EMULATION
rive - - REND, CLEAVE, SPLIT, RENT
riven - - - - - - - - - - CLEFT, RENT
river - - - - - - - - STREAM, RUN
river bank - - - - - - - - - - RIPA
river bank (pert. to) - - - - RIPARIAN, RIVERAIN
river bed - - - - - - - WADY, WADI
river between France and Belgium - LYS
river between New York and Canada - - NIAGARA

river boat - - - BARGE, BARK, ARK
river bottom - - - - - - - - BED
river channel - - - - - - - - BED
river (comb. form) - - - - - POTAMO
river dam - - - - - - - - - WEIR
river deposit - - - - - - - - - SILT
river descent - - - - - - - - RAPIDS
river duck - - - - - - - - - TEAL
river embankment - - - - - - DAM
river famed in song - - - - WABASH
river flatboat - - - - - - - - ARK
river god's daughter - - - - - - IO
river isle - - - - - - - - - - AIT
river lowland - - - - - - - - FLAT
river mouth - - - - - - - - DELTA
river mud - - - - - - - - - - SILT
river mussel - - - - - - - - UNIO
river nymph - - - - - NAIAD, NAIS
river of forgetfulness - - - - - LETHE
river sediment - - - - - - - - SILT
river shore - - - - - - - - - BANK
river, small - - - - - - - - - TCHAI
river source - - - - - - FOUNTAIN
river tract - - - - - - - - - FLAT
river of underworld - - - - - - STYX
rivet - - - - - - - - BOLT, FASTEN
rivulet - - RILL, STREAMLET, CREEK
roa - - - - - - - - - - - - KIWI
road - - - - - - - - COURSE, WAY
road building substance - - - - TAR
road surface - - - - - - MACADAM
roam - - - - - - - - - - - RANGE
roam about idly - - - - - - - GAD
roar - BELLOW, SCREAM, YELL, BOOM, DIN, HOWL
roar of surf - - - - - - - - ROTE
roast - - - - - - - - - - - BAKE
roast meat - - - - - - - - CABOBS
roasted (Sp.) - - - - - - - ASADO
roasting iron and stick - - - - - SPIT
rob - - - STEAL, LOOT, PLUNDER, DEFRAUD, PILFER, BURGLE
robbed - - - - - - - - - - - REFT
robbery on high seas - - - PIRACY
robe - MANTLE, ATTIRE, ARRAY, TALAR
robe of office - - - - - - VESTMENT
Robin Hood's companion - LITTLE JOHN
Robin's last name - - - - - ADAIR
Robinson Crusoe's author - - DEFOE
robust - - STRONG, HALE, VIGOROUS, HARDY, RUGGED
robust (colloq.) - - - - - STRAPPING
rock - VIBRATE, TOTTER, STONE, ORE, SHAKE
rock boring tool - - - - - - TREPAN
rock debris - - - - - - - DETRITUS
rock of fine mud - - - - - - PELITE
rock (kind) - - SLATE, SPAR, AGATE, STONE, TRAP, BESALT, PRASE, SHALE, GNEISS, BASALT
rock material - - - - - - - - SAND
rock (sharp) - - - - - - - - CRAG
rock (to) - - - - - - - - - TEETER
rocked - - - - - - - - - SHAKEN
rockfish - - - - - - - - RENA, REINA
rockier - - - - - - - - - STONIER
rocky - - - - - - - - - - STONY
rocky debris - - - - - - DETRITUS
Rocky Mountain Park - - - - - ESTES
Rocky Mountain range - - - - TETON
rocky pinnacle - - - - - - - - TOR
rod - - STAFF, POLE, WAND, TWIG, FERULE, BATON, SPINDLE
rod for beating time - - - - BATON
rod for hand spinning - - - - DISTAFF
rod for punishing - - - - - - FERULE
rod on which wheel revolves - - AXLE
rod used in basketry - - - - - OSIER
rodent - - - PACA, HARE, MARMOT, MOUSE, RABBIT, GNAWER
rodent catching dog - - - - - RATTER
rodeo - - - - - - - - - ROUNDUP
roe - - - - - - - - - - - - EGGS
roe of lobster - - - - - - - - CORAL
rogue - - BEGGAR, KNAVE, RASCAL, SCAMP, PICAROON, SCOUNDREL
roguish - - - - - - - - SLY, ARCH
roguish youngster - - - - - URCHIN
roil - - - - - - - - - - - MUDDY
roily - - - - - - - TURBID, MUDDY
roister - - - - - SWAGGER, BLUSTER
Roland's companion - - - - - OLIVER
role - - - - - - - - - - - - - PART
roll - - ROTA, LIST, BUN, REGISTER, ROSTER, REVOLVE
roll (to) - - - - - - TRILL, REVOLVE
roll along - - - - - - - - TRUNDLE
roll of cloth - - - - - - - - - BOLT
roll (dial.) - - - - - - - - WHELVE
roll into thin sheets, as metal - - - - LAMINATE
roll of paper money (slang) - - WAD
roll of parchment - - - - - - - PELL
roll of thread - - - - - - - - - COP
roll of tobacco - - - - - - - - CIGAR
roll of tobacco (var.) - - - - - SEGAR
roll up - - - - - - - - - - - FURL
rolled tea - - - - - - - - - - - CHA
rolling stock - - - - - - - - - CARS
rolypoly - - - - - - - - ROUNDISH
Romaine lettuce - - - - - - - - COS
Roman - - - - - - - - - - - LATIN
Roman amphitheater - - COLOSSEUM
Roman army captain - - CENTURION
Roman basilica - - - - - - LATERAN
Roman boxing glove - - - - - CESTUS
Roman breastplate - - - - - LORICA
Roman bronze - - - - - - - - - AES
Roman chariot - - - - - - - - ESSED
Roman church cathedral - - LATERAN
Roman citadel - - - - - - - - - ARX
Roman clan - - - - - - - - - GENS
Roman coin - AS, AE, (anc.) SESTERCE
Roman cuirass - - - - - - - LORICA
Roman date - - - - - NONES, IDES
Roman day - - - - - - - CALENDS
Roman deity - - - - - - - - - - DIS
Roman dialect - - - - - - - - LADIN
Roman domestic bowl - - - - PATINA
Roman emperor (old) - CAESAR, OTHO, NERO, OTTO
Roman emperor (pert. to) - - NEROIC
Roman family - - - - - - - - GENS
Roman fate - - - - - - - - - NONA
Roman garment - - - STOLA, TUNIC, STOLAE, TOGA, PLANETAE
Roman general - - - - - AGRICOLA
Roman gladiator - - - MIRMILLION
Roman god - - - - - - - - DI, LARE
Roman god of metal working - VULCAN
Roman god of underworld - - - - DIS
Roman god of woods and herds - FAUN
Roman goddess - - - - - LUA, LUNA
Roman goddess of horses - - EPONA
Roman goddess of vegetation - CERES
Roman greeting - - - - - - - - AVE
Roman highway - - - - - - - - ITER
Roman hill - - - VIMINAL, PALATINE
Roman historian - - - NEPOS, LIVY

R

Roman house god - LAR, LARE, PENATE
Roman magistrate - - PRETOR, EDILE, TRIBUNE
Roman mantle - - - - - - - TOGA
Roman mark of authority - - FASCES
Roman marsh district (pert. to) - - - PONTINE
Roman meal - - - - - - - - CENA
Roman monetary unit - - - - - LEY
Roman money - - - - - - - - AES
Roman name - - - - - - - LUCIUS
Roman naturalist - - - - - - PLINY
Roman official - - PREFECT, EDILE, TRIBUNE
Roman orator - - - - - - - PLINY
Roman palace - - - - - - LATERAN
Roman patriot - - - - - - - CATO
Roman philosopher - - - - - SENECA
Roman poet - - - - OVID, HORACE
Roman priest - - - - - - - FLAMEN
Roman procurator of Judea - - PILATE
Roman room - - - - - ATRIA (pl.)
Roman sock (ancient) - - - - UDO
Roman statesman - - CATO, AGRIPPA
Roman temple - - - - PANTHEON
Roman tribune - - - - - - RIENZI
Roman tyrant - - - - - - - NERO
Roman weight - - - - - - - - AS
Roman writer - - - - - - TERENCE
romance - - - - - - NOVEL, DREAM
romance language - SPANISH, ITALIAN
Romanian city - - - - - - - SIBIU
Romanian coin - - - - - - LEU, LEY
romantic - - - - - SENTIMENTAL
romantic music - - - - - SERENADE
romantic person - - - - - IDEALIST
romantic song - - - - - - BALLAD
romantic tale - - - - - - - SAGA
romany - - - - - - - - - - GYPSY
romp - FROLIC, GAMBOL, FRISK, PLAY
romping girl - - - - - - - TOMBOY
rood - - - - - - CROSS, CRUCIFIX
roof - - - SLATE, SUMMIT, SHELTER
roof edge - - - - - - - - - EAVE
roof-like canvas cover - - - AWNING
roof material - - - - - TILE, PANTILE
roof of mouth - - - - - - - PALATE
roof of mouth (pert. to) - - PALATAL
roofing tile - - - - - - - PANTILE
roofing tin - - - - - - - - TERNE
rook - - - - - - - - CHESSMAN
rook cry - - - - - - - - - CAW
room - SPACE, LODGE, CHAMBER, AULA
room for pitchers and linens - - EWERY
room (small) - - - - - - - - CELL
room under a house - - - - CELLAR
roomy - - - - CAPACIOUS, RANGY
roost - - - - - - SET, SIT, PERCH
root - - - RADIX, BOTTOM, ORIGIN, BASIS, SOURCE, CHEER
root of certain plant - - - - BULB
root out - - ERADICATE, DERACINATE, EXTIRPATE, STUB
root (pert. to) - - - - - RADICULAR
root vegetable - - - - - - CARROT
root word - - - - - - - - ETYMON
rooted - - - - - - - - RADICATE
rooted grass - - - - - - - - SOD
rooter - - - - - - FAN, SUPPORTER
rootlet - - - - - - - - - RADICEL
roots to sew Indian canoes - - WATAP
rope - HAWSER, RIATA, NETTLE, CABLE
rope fiber - - - - - - - - SISAL
rope for hoisting a ship's yard - - TYE
rope to lead horse - - - - HALTER
rope to moor a boat - PAINTER
rose - - - - - - - - - PINK, TEA
rose (dial.) - - - - - - - - - RIS
rose essence - - - - - - - ATTAR
rose fruit - - - - - - - - - - HIP
rose red dye - - - - EOSIN, EOSINE
rose red gem - - - - - - - BALAS
rose shaped ornament - - - ROSETTE
roseate - - - - - - ROSY, REDDISH
rosette - - - - - - - - ORNAMENT
rosset - - - - - - - - DOGFISH
roster - - - - - - LIST, ROTA, ROLL
rostrum - - - - - - STAGE, PULPIT
rosy - - RED, ROSEATE, BLUSHING, BRIGHT, BLOOMING, PINK
rot - - - - - - - - DECAY, RUBBISH
rota - - - - - - - - - ROLL, LIST
rotary motor - - - - - - - TURBINE
rotate - - - TURN, SPIN, REVOLVE, RESOLVE, ALTERNATE, SWIRL
rotating coupler - - - - - - SWIVEL
rotating machine tool - - - - LATHE
rotating part - - - - - CAM, ROTOR
rotating pin - - - - - - - SPINDLE
rote - - - - - - - - - MEMORIZE
roue - - - - - - - - - - - RAKE
rouge - - - - - - CARMINE, PAINT
rough - - - - - - RAGGY, KNAGGY
rough breathing - - ASPER, ASPIRATE
rough cliff - - - - - - - - - CRAG
rough house - - - - - - - - SHACK
rough shelter - - - - - - - - SHED
rough stone - - - - - - - - RUBBLE
rough with bristles - - - - - HISPID
roughen - - - - - - - SHAG, NURL
roulade - - - - - - - - - - - RUN
roulette bet - - - - - - - - - BAS
round - CIRCULAR, ORBED, SPHERICAL
round about way - - - - - - DETOUR
round ball - - - - - - - - - PELLET
round body - - - - - - - - - BALL
round hill (Sp.) - - - - - - MORRO
round and hollow - - - - - CONCAVE
round muscle - - - - - - - - TERES
round projection - - - - - LOBE, NOB
round room - - - - - - - - ROTUNDA
round and tapering - - - - - CONIC
round up - - - - - - - - - RODEO
roundabout way - - - - - - DETOUR
rounded appendage - - - - - - LOBE
rounded appendage (pert. to) - LOBAR
rounded division (pert. to) - LOBAR, LOBATE
rounded hill - - - - - KNOLL, KNOB
rounded moulding - - - - - - OVOLO
rounded projection or protuberance - - LOBE, NOB
rounded roof - - - - - - - - DOME
rounded surface - - - - - CONVEXITY
roundish - - - - - - - - ROLYPOLY
roundup - - - - - - - - - - RODEO
rouse - STIR, BESTIR, WAKEN, SPUR, AWAKEN
rouse to vigilance - - - - - - ALARM
rout - - - - - - - - - - - DEFEAT
route - - WAY, COURSE, TRAIL, LINE, PATH
route to avoid traffic - - - BYPASS
routine - - - - - - - - HABIT, RUT
rove - - - PROWL, WANDER, STROLL
rove about - - - - - - GAD, RANGE
rover - - - RANGER, PIRATE, NOMAD
roving - ERRANT, ERRANTRY, MIGRANT
roving mircle man - - - - - - FAKIR
row - TIER, LINE, OAR, LAYER, SPAT,

QUARREL, BRAWL, RANK, ARGUMENT
row (bring into a) - - - - - - ALIGN
row gently - - - - - - - PADDLE
row of grain (cut) - - - - - - SWATH
rowan tree - - - - - - - - - SORB
rowboat - - GIG, CAIQUE, WHERRY, BARGE
rowboat (obs.) - - - - - - - SCULL
rowdyish fellow - - - - - LARRIKIN
rower - - - - - - - OARSMAN, OAR
royal - - - - - - - - - - REGAL
royal antelope - - - - - - - IPETE
royal fur - - - - - - - - - ERMINE
royal heir - - - - - - - - - PRINCE
royal jewel - - - - - - - - - REGAL
royal palace (pert. to) - - - PALATINE
rub - - - ABRADE, SCRAPE, POLISH, CHAFE, SCOUR
rub gently - - - - - - - STROKE
rub hard - - - - - - - - - SCRUB
rub lightly - - - - - - - - WIPE
rub off - - - - - - - - - ABRADE
rub out - - - - - - ERASE, EXPUNGE
rub with rough file - - - - - RASP
rubber - - - - - PARA, ERASER, GUM
rubber jar ring - - - - - - - LUTE
rubber-like substance - - - - - GUTTA
rubber soled shoe - - - - - SNEAKER
rubber tree - - - - - - - - - ULE
rubber watering tube - - - - - HOSE
rubbish - - TRASH, REFUSE, DEBRIS, ROT
rubbish (mining) - - - - - - ATTLE
rubbish pile - - - - - - - - DUMP
Rubinstein's first name - - - - ARTUR
ruby (kind) - - - - - - - - BALAS
ruby-like gem - - - - - - - GARNET
rudder - - - - - - - - - - GUIDER
rudder lever - - - - - - - - TILLER
rudder part - - - - - - - - YOKE
ruddle - - - - - - - - - - REDDEN
ruddy - - - - - - - - - - - FLORID
rude - BOORISH, UNCIVIL, UNCOUTH, IMPOLITE, IMPUDENT
rude dwelling - - - - - - - - HUT
rude fellow - - - - - - - - - CAD
rude girl - - - - - - - - - HOYDEN
rude house - - SHACK, CABIN, HUT, SHED
rude person - - - - - - - - BOOR
rude shelter - - - - - SHED, LEANTO
rudely concise - - - - - - - - CURT
rudeness - - - FERITY, CONTUMELY
rudimental - - - - - - ELEMENTARY
rudimentary - - - - - - ELEMENTAL
rue - - - - REGRET, REPENT, HERB
ruff - - - - - - - - - REE, TRUMP
ruffian - DESPERADO, THUG, HOOLIGAN
ruffle - - - ROIL, FRILL, DISTURB
ruffled strip on cuff - - - - - RUCHE
rug (small) - - - - - MAT, RUNNER
ruga - - - - - - WRINKLE, CREASE
rugate - - - - - - - - - WRINKLED
rugged - - - - - - - - - - ROBUST
rugged crest - - - - - - - - - TOR
rugged rock - - - - - - - - - CRAG
Ruhr city - - - - - - - - - ESSEN
ruin - - WRECK, UNDOING, IMPAIR, BANKRUPT, DOOM, DESTROY, DEVASTATE, RAVAGE, RASE, DEMOLISH, UNDO, BANE
ruined - - - - - - - - - - LOST
ruins - - - - - - - - - - DEBRIS
rule - - PRESIDE, REIGN, RESTRAIN, DOMINATE, FORMULA, LAW, GOVERN, REGIME, LINE
rule by unprincipled politicians - - - DEMAGOGY
ruler - - DYNAST, GERENT, REGENT, MONARCH, FERULE, OLIGARCH, EMPEROR, SOVEREIGN, KING
ruler in place of a king - - VICEROY
ruling authority - - - - - - REGENT
ruling few (the) - - - - - OLIGARCHS
ruling spirit of evil - - - - - - MARA
Rumanian coin - - - - - - LEU, LEY
rumen - - - - - - - - - - - CUD
ruminant - - SHEEP, CAMEL, GOAT, MEDITATIVE, LLAMA
ruminant stomach - - RUMEN, TRIPE
ruminant stomach used as food - TRIPE
ruminate - PONDER, MUSE, MEDITATE, REFLECT
ruminated (something) - - - - CUD
rumour - - REPORT, GOSSIP, HEARSAY
rumour personified - - - - - - FAMA
rumple - - - - - - TOUSLE, MUSS
rumple (colloq.) - - - - - - - MUSS
run - FLOW, RACE, OPERATE, EXTEND, SPEED, SPRINT, CONDUCT, BROOK
run after - - - - - - - - - CHASE
run aground - - - - - STRAND, SAND
run along a similar pattern - PARALLEL
run away - - - - - - - - - DECAMP
run away or from - - - - - - FLEE
run away (colloq.) - - - - - SCRAM
run away (slang) - - - - - - - - LAM
run between ports - - - - - - - PLY
run (dial.) - - - - - - - - - - RIN
run down - - - - - - - - DECRY
run easily - - - - - - LOPE, TROT
run fast - - - - - - - - - SPRINT
run off - - - - - - - ELOPE, BOLT
run out - - - - - - - - - - SPILL
run out (colloq.) - - - - - - PETER
run over - - - - - - - - - - SPILL
run rapidly before the wind - - SCUD
run (Scot.) - - - - - - - - - - RIN
run slowly - - - - - - - - TRICKLE
run in wavy line - - - - - ENGRAIL
run on wheels - - - - - - - - ROLL
run wild - - - - - - - - - - GAD
run without a load - - - - - - IDLE
runagate - - - - - - - - FUGITIVE
rune - - - - - - - - - - MAGIC
rung of ladder - - - - RATLINE, SPOKE
runner - MILER, SPEEDER, OPERATOR, RACER, SKI, FUGITIVE
runner for foot - - - - - - - - SKI
runner for office - - - - - CANDIDATE
runner of rootstock - - - - - STOLON
running contest - - - - - MARATHON
running knot - - - - - - - - NOOSE
running talk - - - - - - - - PATTER
rupees (abbr.) - - - - - - - - - RS
rupture - - - - - - - - - - - REND
rural - PASTORAL, ARCADIAN, RUSTIC, COUNTRIFIED, BUCOLIC
rural deity - - - - - - - - - FAUN
rural poem - - - - - - - - GEORGIC
rural residence - - - - - - - - VILLA
ruse - - - - - - - TRICK, ARTIFICE
rush - - HURRY, CATTAIL, CHARGE, SPEED, SURGE, STAMPEDE
rush forward - - - - - - SURGE, TEAR
rush headlong - - - - - - - - BOLT
rush suddenly - HURTLE, SALLY, TEAR
rush violently - - - - HURTLE, TEAR
rusk - - - - - - - - - BUN, BISCUIT

Russian - - - - SLAV, SOVIET, RED
Russian antelope - - - - - - SAIGA
Russian bay - - - - - - - - LUGA
Russian cavalryman - - - - COSSACK
Russian city - - TULA, GROSNY, OREL, DNO, MINSK, OSA, SAMARA, UFA
Russian coin - KOPECK, KOPEK, ALTIN, RUPEE
Russian coin (old) - - - - - - ALTIN
Russian composer - - - - - - CUI
Russian council - - - DUMA, SOVIET
Russian craft society - - - - - ARTEL
Russian czar - - - - - - - - IVAN
Russian emperor - - - - - NICHOLAS
Russian empress' title - - - - TSARINA
Russian gulf - - - - - - - - OB
Russian hemp - - - - - RIVE, RINE
Russian independent union - - ARTEL
Russian isthmus - - - - - PERSKOP
Russian labor union - - - - - ARTEL
Russian leader - - - - - - - LENIN
Russian local community - - - MIR
Russian measure of length - - VERST
Russian monarch - - - - - - TSAR
Russian money - - - - - - RUBLE
Russian mountain - - - - - - URAL
Russian musical composer - - - CUI
Russian name - - - - - IGOR, IVAN
Russian news agency - - - - - TASS
Russian novelist - - - - - - GORKI
Russian peninsula - - - - - - KOLA
Russian plain - - - - - - STEPPE
Russian revolutionary - - - - - LENIN
Russian river - - URAL, NEVA, DON, LENA, ROS, OB, NER, AMUR, DUNA, KARA, IRTISH, VOLGA, IK, ILET, AI
Russian ruler - - - - - IVAN, TSAR
Russian rustic dance - - - - ZIGANKA
Russian sea and lake - - ARAL, AZOF, AZOV
Russian stockade - - - ETAH, ETAPE
Russian storehouse - - - - - ETAPE
Russian sturgeon - - - - - STERLET
Russian tea urn - - - - - SAMOVAR
Russian town - - - - - - - ELISTA
Russian trade commune - - - - ARTEL
Russian union - - - - - - - ARTEL
Russian village - - - - - - - MIR
Russian wagon - - - - - - TELEGA
rust - - - CORRODE, TURMOIL, EAT
rusted - - - - - - - - - - - ATE
rustic - - RURAL, YOKEL, PEASANT, PASTORAL, BUCOLIC, SYLVAN, BOOR
rustic (colloq.) - - - - - - HODGE
rustic dance - - - - - - - - HAY
rustic gallant - - - - - - - SWAIN
rustic poem - - - - - - - ECLOGUE
rustic workman - - - - - - PEASANT
rut - - - GROOVE, DITCH, ROUTINE
Ruth's husband - - - - - - - BOAZ
Ruth's mother-in-law - - - - - NAOMI
rye disease - - - - - - - - ERGOT
rye drink - - - - - - - - - - GIN
Ryukyus island - - - - - - OKINAWA

S

S shaped curve - - - - - - - ESS
S shaped moulding - - - - - - OGEE
S shaped worm - - - - - - - ESS
S shaped wind - - - - - - - AFER
sabbath - - - - - - - - SUNDAY
saber - - - - - - - - - SWORD
sable - - - - - - - - - BLACK
sac shaped - - - - - - - SACCATE
saccharine - - - - - SWEET, SUGARY
sack - - LOOT, POUCH, BAG, PILLAGE
sack on ball field - - - - - - BASE
sacrament - - - - - - - RETE, RITE
sacrament of the Lord's Supper - - - EUCHARIST
sacred - - - - - - HOLY, HALLOWED
sacred animal - - - - - - - - TOTEM
sacred beetle - - - - - - - - SCARAB
sacred Buddhist language - - - - PALI
sacred bull - - - - - - - - - APIS
sacred city of Islam - - - - MEDINA
sacred hymn - - - - - - - - PSALM
sacred image - - - - - - ICON, IDOL
sacred image (var.) - - - - - - - IKON
sacred musical composition - - MOTET
sacred picture - - - - - - ICON, IKON
sacred poem - - - - - HYMN, PSALM
sacred song - - - - - - - - PSALM
sacred tune - - - - CHORALE, CHORAL
sacred vessel - - - - - - - - - ARK
sacred work - - - - - - - - - - OM
sacred writing - - - - - - SCRIPTURE
sacrificial table - - - - - - - ALTAR
sad - PLAINTIVE, MOURNFUL, DOLEFUL, GLOOMY, DOWNCAST, DEJECTED, DESPONDENT, WOEFUL, DEPRESSED
sadden - - - - - - - - - - DEPRESS
saddle animal - - - - - - - - LOPER
saddle cloth (Sp.) - - - - - - MANTA
saddle horse - - - - - - - - PALFREY
saddle loop - - - - - - - - STIRRUP
saddle pad - - - - - - - - - - PANEL
sadness - - - - - - - - - - SORROW
safe - - - - - - - - - - - - SECURE
safe keeping - - - - - - - STORAGE
sag - - - - - - - - - - DROOP, SINK
saga - - - - - TALE, MYTH, LEGEND
sagacious - - - - WISE, DISCERNING
sagacity - - - - - - - - - - ACUMEN
sage - WISE, SEER, SAPIENT, PROPHET, PRUDENT, SOLON
said to be - - - - - - - - REPUTED
sail - - NAVIGATE, VOYAGE, CRUISE, JIB, LATEEN
sail close to the wind - - - - - POINT
sail extended by spar - - - - SPRITSAIL
sail (kind) - - - - - - - JIB, LATEEN
sail nearer the wind - - - - - - LUFF
sail on a square rigged vessel - TOPSAIL
sail upward - - - - - - - - - - SOAR
sail yard (Scot.) - - - - - - RA, RAE
sailing race - - - - - - - - REGATTA
sailing vessel - SLOOP, SAIC, KETCH, YAWL
sailor - TAR, SALT, MARINER, GOB, SEAMAN
sailor's outfit - - - - - - - - - KIT
saint - - - - - - - - - - CANONIZE
Saint Andrew's crosses - SALTIRES
Saint Claire river port - - - - SARNIA
Saint of Avila - - - - - - - TERESA
Saint Paul's friend - - - - LUKE, SILAS
saintliness - - - - - - - - SANCTITY
saintly - - PIOUS, ANGELICAL, HOLY
saints collectively - - - - SAINTHOOD
sake - - - - - - - - - - - BEHALF
salable - - - - - - - - MARKETABLE
salad herb - - - - - - - - - ENDIVE
salad plant - - - - - - CRESS, ENDIVE
salamander - - - - NEWT, EFT, TRITON
salary - WAGES, STIPEND, EARNINGS, EMOLUMENT
sale - - - - - - AUCTION, BARGAIN

Salian Franks (pert. to) - - - SALIC
salience - - - PROMINENCE
salient - - - OUTSTANDING
saline - - - SALTY
saline solution - - - BRINE
salix - - - WILLOW
sally - - - SORTIE, START
sally forth - - - ISSUE
sally of the troops - - - SORTIE
salmon colour - - - ROUCOU
salmon (young) - - - PARR
salmonoid fish - - - TROUT
Salome's grandfather - - - HEROD
Salome's mother - - - HERODIAS
salon - - - PARLOUR
saloon - - - CAFE
salt - SAL, SEASON, MARINATE, ALUM
salt of acetic acid - - - ACETATE
salt of adipic acid - - - ADIPATE
salt of anisic acid - - - ANISATE
salt of arsenic acid - - - ARSENATE
salt of boric acid - - - BORATE
salt of citric acid - - - CITRATE
salt marsh - - - SALINA
salt marsh (var.) - - - SALIN
salt meat - - - SALAMI
salt of nitric acid - NITRATE, NITRITE
salt of oleic acid - - - OLEATE
salt (pert. to) - - - SALINE
salt of sea - - - BRINE
salt of silicic acid - - - SILICATE
salt solution - - - BRINE
salt of stearic acid - - - STEARATE
salt water - - - BRINE
salt water fish - - - COD
saltcellar (old word) - - - SALER
salted (Phil. Isl.) - - - ALAT
saltpeter - - - NITER, NITRE
salty - - - SALINE, BRINY
salutary - - BENEFICIAL, WHOLESOME
salutation - - AVE, BOW, GREETING, HELLO
salute - - - GREET, HAIL
salute musically - - - SERENADE
salve - - - OINTMENT, PALLIATE
salver - - - TRAY
sambar deer - - - MAHA
same - - ONE, SIMILAR, IDENTICAL, EQUAL, DITTO, ALIKE
same age (of the) - - - COEVAL
same as before - - - DITTO
same degree - - - SO
same kind (of) - - - AKIN
same (Latin abbr.) - - - ID
same opinion (of) - - - AGREE
same rank - - - PEER
same as schizont (med.) - - MONONT
sameness - - - MONOTONY
Samoan bird - - - IAO
Samoan city - - - APIA
Samoan mollusk - - - ASI
Samoan mudworm - - - IPO
Samoan seaport - - - APIA
Samoan warrior - - - TOA
samp - - - HOMINY
sample - - - TASTE, SPECIMEN
sample of fabric - - - SWATCH
sampler - - - TASTER
Samuel's mentor - - - ELI
sanctified - - - SAINT
sanctified person - - - SAINT
sanctify - - - BLESS
sanction - APPROVE, APPROVAL, FIAT, ABET, RATIFY, ENDORSE, ASSENT
sanctioned person - - - SAINT
sanctuary - - - FANE, BEMA
sanctum - - - DEN
sand - - - GRIT, BEACH, GRAVEL
sand bank - - - SHOAL
sand bird - - - SNIPE
sand clay mixture - - - LOAM
sand hill - - - DUNE, SUNE, DENE
sand ridge - - - DUNE, REEF
sand on sea bottom - - - PAAR
sandal - - - SLIPPER
sandal fastener - - - LATCHET
sandarac tree - - - ARAR, ADAR
sandarac wood - - - ALERCE
sandiness - - - ARENOSITY
sandpaper - - - STIB
sandpiper - REE, STINT, REEVE, RUFF
sandstone deposit - - - PAAR
sandy - - - ARENOSE
sandy soil - - - LOAM
sandy waste - - - DESERT, SAND
sane - - LUCID, RATIONAL, SOUND, WISE
sanguine - - - OPTIMISTIC
sanitary - - - HEALTHFUL
sap - VITALITY, ENERVATE, WEAKEN, EXHAUST, IMPAIR
sap of certain plants - - - MILK
sap spout - - - SPILE
sapid - - - SAVORY, TASTY
sapidity - - - SAVOR, TASTE
sapient - - - SAGE
sapling - - - PLANT
sapor - - - TASTE
sapper - - - IMPAIRER
sarcasm - - - IRONY
sarcastic - - - SATIRIC, IRONIC, SARDONIC, BITING, MORDANT
sardonic - - - SARCASTIC
sardonyx - - - SARD
sarlak - - - YAK
sartor - - - TAILOR
sash - - - SCARF, BELT, GIRDLE
Satan - - DEVIL, TEMPTER, LUCIFER
satchel - - - HANDBAG, BAG, VALISE
sate - GLUT, SATIATE, GRATIFY, FILL, SURFEIT
sated with pleasure - - - BLASE
satellite - - - MOON
satellite of the sun - - - PLANET
satellite of Uranus - - - ARIEL
satiate - SATE, FILL, PALL, SURFEIT, GLUT
satin dress fabric - - - ETOILE
satire - LAMPOON, IRONY, RIDICULE
satiric - - - IRONIC, SARCASTIC
satirist - - - CYNIC
satirize - - - BLAST
satisfaction - - - DELIGHT
satisfaction (old word) - - - GRE
satisfactory (is) - - - SUITS
satisfied - CONTENT, CONTENTED, MET
satisfy - - - SATE, SUIT, SATIATE, CONTENT, SERVE, PLEASE
satisfy demands - - - CATER
saturate - - - SOAK, IMBUE, STEEP, DRENCH, SOUSE, WET
saturated - - - SODDEN, WET
saturnine - - - GLOOMY
satyr - - - FAUN
sauce - - - GRAVY, PERTNESS
saucepan - - - POSNET
saucerlike ornaments - - - PATERAE
saucy - MALAPERT, PERT, INSOLENT, BRASH, SASS
saucy girl - - - MINX

S

saucy person - - - - - - - - PIET
saucy speech (slang) - - - - - LIP
saunter - - - - - - STROLL, LOITER
saurel - - - - - - - - - - - SCAD
savage - - - - - - - FERAL, FIERCE
savage island - - - - - - - - NIUE
savant - - - - - - SCIENTIST, SAGE
save - RESCUE, BUT, SPARE, EXCEPT, PRESERVE, HOARD, CONSERVE
save from wreck - - - - - SALVAGE
savior - - - - - - - - - REDEEMER
savor - - - TASTE, RELISH, SMACK, SAPIDITY
savory - - SAPID, PALATABLE, TASTY
savory meat jelly - - - - - - ASPIC
saw (a) - - - - - - - - - - MOTTO
sawfish - - - - - - - - - - - RAY
sawlike edge - - - - - - - SERRATE
saw part - - - - - - - - - SERRA
saxifrage - - - - - - - - - SESELI
Saxon - - - - - - - - - - ENGLISH
say - - UTTER, AVER, STATE, VOICE
say again or differently - - RESTATE
say further - - - - - - - - - ADD
saying - - - - - - - - - - ADAGE
scabbard - - - - - - - - - SHEATH
scad - - - - - - GOGGLER, SAUREL
scaffold - - - - - - - - - TRESTLE
scalawag - - - - - - - - - SCAMP
scale - - - CLIMB, FLAKE, GAMUT
scale (comb. form) - - - - - LEPIS
scale of hot iron - - - - - - - NILL
scale inspector - - - - - - SEALER
scale-like - - - - - - - - LAMELLAR
scale-like particle - - - - - - FLAKE
scale note - - - - - - - - ELA, SOL
scaleless amphibian - - SALAMANDER
scaling device - - - - - - - LADDER
scalloped on the margin - - CRENATED
scalp - - - - - - - - - - DENUDE
scaly - - - - - - - - - - LAMINAR
scamp - RASCAL, SCALAWAG, ROGUE
scamper - - - - - SCURRY, SKITTER
scan - - - - - - - - - - - STUDY
Scandinavian - - DANE, NORSE, FINN, SWEDE, LAPP
Scandinavian country - - - - SWEDEN
Scandinavian division - - - - - AMT
Scandinavian giant - - - - - TROLL
Scandinavian goddess - - - - - HEL
Scandinavian language - - - NORSE, ICELANDIC
Scandinavian legislative body - THING
Scandinavian literary work - - - - EDDA
Scandinavian measure - - - - - ALEN
Scandinavian Mongoloid - - - - LAPP
Scandinavian myth - - - - - - SAGA
Scandinavian mythical monarch - ATLI
Scandinavian name - - - - - - ERIC
Scandinavian navigator - - - - ERIC
Scandinavian (pert. to) - - - NORSE, NORDIC
Scandinavian poet - - - - - - SCALD
scandent - - - - - - - - CLIMBING
scant - - MEAGER, SLIGHT, SKIMPY, SPARSE
scantily - - - - - - - - - SPARSELY
scanty - - MEAGER, SPARSE, SCARCE, BARE, POOR, SPARE
scanty provider - - - - - - STINTER
scape - - - - - - - - - PEDUNCLE
scar - - - - - - - - - - BLEMISH
scar (dial.) - - - - - - - - - ARR
scarab - - - - - - - - - - BEETLE
scarce - - - SPARSE, RARE, SCANTY, DEFICIENT
scarcely - - - - - - - - - HARDLY
scarceness - - - - - - - - PAUCITY
scarcity - - DEARTH, FAMINE, WANT
scare - - FRIGHTEN, STARTLE, ALARM
scarecrow - - - - - - - - BUGABOO
scaremonger - - - - - - - ALARMIST
scarf - ASCOT, NECKTIE, SASH, TIPPET, TIE
scarf of feathers - - - - - - - - BOA
scarflike vestment - - - - - - ORALE
scarlet - - - - - - - - - - - - RED
scarlet bird - - - - - - - TANAGER
scarp - - - - - - - - - - FRAGMENT
scathe - - - - - - - - - - DAMAGE
scatter - - DISPEL, RADIATE, SOW, DISPERSE, STREW, SPREAD, DISSEMINATE, DISBAND, BESTREW, DOT
scatter (arch.) - - - - - - - STRAW
scatter carelessly - - - - - - LITTER
scatter grass for drying - - - - TED
scatter loosely - - - - STREW, STEW
scatter over - - - - - - - BESTREW
scattered rubbish - - - - - - LITTER
scene - - - VIEW, VISTA, OUTLOOK, EPISODE, LANDSCAPE
scene of action - - - ARENA, STAGE
scene of Biblical action - - - - GOB
scene of judgment of Paris - - - IDA
scenery (pert. to) - - - - - SCENIC, LANDSCAPE
scenic view - - - - - - - - SCAPE
scenic word enigma - - - - CHARADE
scent - - - PERFUME, NOSE, AROMA, SMELL
scent bag - - - - - - - - SACHET
scent of cooking - - - - - - NIDOR
scepter - - - - - - - - WAND, MACE
schedule - - - SLATE, TIME, TABLE
scheme - - PLOT, PLAN, CONSPIRE, PROJECT
schism - - - - - - RENT, DIVISION
scholar - - STUDENT, PUPIL, PEDANT, SAVANT
scholarly - - - - - - - LEARNED
scholastic rating - - - - - - GRADE
school - - - - - - - - TRAIN, TUTOR
school assignment - - - - - LESSON
school (Fr.) - - - - - - - - ECOLE
school master - PEDANT, PEDAGOGUE
school mistress - - - - - - - DAME
school of seals - - - - - - - - POD
school session - - - TERM, SEMINAR
school shark - - - - - - - - - TOPE
school of whales - - - - - - - GAM
science - - - - - - - - - - - ART
science of analysis - - - - ANALYTICS
science of being or reality - ONTOLOGY
science of bodies at rest - - STATICS
science of causes - - - - - ETIOLOGY
science of exact reasoning - - LOGIC
science of government - - POLITICS
science of life - - - - - - BIOLOGY
science of mountains - - - - OROLOGY
science of plants - - - - - - BOTANY
science of plants (pert. to) - BOTANIC
science of reality - - - - ONTOLOGY
science of reasoning - - - - - LOGIC
science of weights and measures - - - METROLOGY
scientific study of language - PHILOLOGY
scientist - - - - - - - - - SAVANT
scintillate - TWINKLE, SPARK, SPARKLE
scion - - - - BUD, SPROUT, HEIR, DESCENDANT, SON
scoff - SNEER, SCORN, RAIL, DERIDE, MOCK, FLEER, REVILE, JEER

S

scold - - BERATE, RATE, NAG, RANT, CHIDE, RAIL, OBJURGATE
scolded - - - - - - - - CHIDDEN
scolding woman - - - - - VIRAGO
sconce - - - - - - - - SHELTER
scoop - - - - - - - - - SHOVEL
scope - - RANGE, EXTENT, LATITUDE, AREA, MARGIN
scorch - BLISTER, CHAR, SINGE, SEAR, TOAST, USTULATE, PARCH
score - - - TALLY, GROOVE, TWENTY, SCRATCH
score in certain games - - - - GOAL
score at cribbage - - - - - - PEG
scoria - - - - - - - - - - SLAG
scorn - - SCOFF, SPURN, DISDAIN, REBUFF, MOCK, DERIDE, DERISION, CONTEMN
scornful - - - - - - - - DERISIVE
Scot - - - GAEL, TAX, CALEDONIAN
Scotch assessment - - - - - STENT
Scotch author - - - - - - - MILNE
Scotch biscuit - - - - - - - SCONE
Scotch cake - - - - - - - SCONE
Scotch celebration - - - - - KIRN
Scotch chemist - - - - - - DEWAR
Scotch child - - - - - - - BAIRN
Scotch city and town - - AYR, PERTH
Scotch county - - - - - - - ANGUS
Scotch dairymaid - - - - - - - DEY
Scotch dance - - - - - - - REEL
Scotch drapery - - - - - - - PAND
Scotch explorer - - - - - - - RAE
Scotch family of rulers - - - STUART
Scotch girl - - - - - - - - LASSIE
Scotch highlander - - - - - - GAEL
Scotch highlander language - - ERSE
Scotch hillside - - - - - - - BRAE
Scotch inlet - - - - - - - - GEO
Scotch island - - - - - - - IONA
Scotch Jacobite - - - - - - - MAR
Scotch jurist - - - - - - ERSKINE
Scotch king - - - - - - - ROBERT
Scotch landed proprietor - - - LAIRD
Scotch landowner - - - - - - LAIRD
Scotch mortgage - - - - - - WADSET
Scotch mountain - - - - - - NEVIS
Scotch musical instrument - - BAGPIPE
Scotch musician - - - - - - - PIPER
Scotch negative - - - - - - - NAE
Scotch petticoat - - - - - - - KILT
Scotch pirate - - - - - - - - KIDD
Scotch plaid - - - - - - - TARTAN
Scotch poet - - - - BURNS, HOGG
Scotch preposition - - - - - - TAE
Scotch river - - DEE, TAY, AFTON, CLYDE, DEVON
Scotch shepherd's staff - - - KENT
Scotch skirt - - - - - - - - KILT
Scotch sword - - - - - - CLAYMORE
Scotch weighing machine - - - TRONE
Scotchman - - - - BLUECAP, SCOT
Scotland (poet.) - - - - - - SCOTIA
Scott heroine - - - - - - - ELLEN
Scottish Gaelic - - - - - - - ERSE
scoundrel - - KNAVE, CAD, VARLET, ROGUE, RASCAL
scour - - - SCRUB, RUB, CLEANSE
scourge - - - - - - - - - BANE
scout - - - - - - - SPY, RIDICULE
scow - - - - - - - - - - BARGE
scowl - - - - - FROWN, GLOWER
scrap - - - BIT, SHRED, FRAGMENT, FIGHT, ORT
scrape - - - - - - - - GRATE, RASP
scrape off - - - - - - - - ABRADE
scrape together - - - - - - - RAKE
scrape with something sharp - SCRATCH, PAW
scraped linen - - - - - - - - LINT
scraping implement - - - - - - HOE
scrappy - - - - - - - DISCORDANT
scratch - RIST, SCRAPE, CLAW, SCORE
scratching ground for food - RASORIAL
scream - - - - - - - - - - YELL
screed - - - - - - - - - TIRADE
screen - - SIFT, SHADE, COVER, HIDE
screw - - - - - - - DISTORT, TWIST
screwball - - - - - - - - - - NUT
scribe - - - - - - WRITE, WRITER
scrimp - - - - - - - - - - STINT
scripture reading - - - - - - LESSON
scrub - - - - - - - - MOP, SCOUR
scruff - - - - - - - - - - - NAPE
scrutinize - - - SCAN, EXAMINE, EYE, PERUSE, PRY
scuffle - - - - - - - - - TUSSLE
scull - - - - - - - - OAR, SHOAL
sculptor's instrument - - - SPATULA
sculptured likeness - - - - - STATUE
sculptured male figure - - - TEAMON
sculptured stone tablet - - - - STELE
scum - - - - DROSS, SILT, REFUSE
scum of society - - - - - - - RAFF
scurrilous - - - - ABUSIVE, RIBALD
scurry - - - - - - - RUN, SCAMPER
scuttle - - - - - - - - - - - HOD
scye - - - - - - - - - - ARMHOLE
scythe handle - - - SNEAD, SNATH, SNATHE
scythe (Scot.) - - - - - - - - SY
sea - - - - - - BILLOWY, ZEE, WAVE, OCEAN, MAIN
sea (a) - - - - - - - - - - AEGEAN
sea anemones - - - - - - - POLYPS
sea animal - - - - - - CORAL, ORC
sea bird - PETREL, ERNE, TERN, GULL, SOLAN, AUK, ERN, GANNET
sea boat - - - - - - - - - LERRET
sea brigand - - - - - - - - PIRATE
sea coast - - - - - - - - - SHORE
sea cow - - - - - - - - - MANATEE
sea cucumber - - - - - - - TREPANG
sea demigod - - - - - - - - TRITON
sea duck - - - - - - EIDER, COOT
sea Dyak - - - - - - - - - - IBAN
sea eagle - - - - - - - - ERNE, TERN
sea ear - - - - - - - - - ABALONE
sea fighting force (pert. to) - - NAVAL
sea (Fr.) - - - - - - - - - - MER
sea god - - - - - - LER, NEPTUNE
sea gods' attendant - - - - - TRITON
sea going vessel - - - - - - - SHIP
sea green colour - - - - - - CELADON
sea gull - - - - - - - - COB, MEW
sea kale beet - - - - - - - - CHARD
sea mile - - - - - - - NAUT, KNOT
sea near Crimea - - - - - - - - AZOV
sea nymph - - NEREID, NAIAD, SIREN
sea (pert. to) - - - - MARINE, NAVAL
sea robbery - - - - - - - - PIRACY
sea shell - - - - - - - - - - CONCH
sea swallow - - - - - TERN, TRITON
sea undulation - - - - - - - - WAVE
seal - STAMP, CERE, SIGNET, RATIFY, CONFIRM, SIGIL, PLEDGE, CACHET
sealing wax ingredient - - - - - LAC
seam - SUTURE, STRATUM, JUNCTURE
seam of ore - - - - - - - - - VEIN
seaman - - - - - SAILOR, MARINER
seance - - - - - - - - - - SESSION

S

sear - BURN, BLAST, SCORCH, PARCH
search - RANSACK, HUNT, SEEK, GROPE, FERRET, INQUIRY, QUEST, PROBE
search for food - - - - - - FORAGE
search with hands - - - - - - GROPE
seashore - - - - - - - - COAST
seashore recreation - - - - - BATHING
season - - TIDE, WEATHER, WINTER, INURE, MATURE, AUTUMN, MODERATE
season of joy - - - - - - - JUBILEE
season for use - - - - - - - - AGE
seasoned - - - - - - - - - RIPE
seasoned wood - - - - - - - TIMBER
seasoning - - - - SPICE, ALLSPICE
seasoning herb - SAGE, THYME, BASIL, PARSLEY
seat - - - INSTALL, PERCH, CHAIR, BENCH, SETTEE
seat of Dartmouth College - - HANOVER
seat of government - - - - - CAPITAL
seat near altar - - - - - - - SEDILE
seat in office - - - - - - - INSTALL
seated - - - - - - - - - SITTING
seaweed - - ALGA, ALGAE (pl.), ORE, LAVER, KELP
seaweed ashes - - - - - VAREC, KELP
seaweed derivative - - - - - - AGAR
seaweed (pl.) - - - - - - - - ALGAE
sebaceous - - - - - - - - - OILY
sebaceous cyst - - - - - - - WEN
sec - - - - - - - - - - - DRY
secede - - - - - - - - WITHDRAW
secluded - PRIVATE, LONELY, REMOTE
secluded valley - - - - - - - GLEN
seclusion - - - - - - - - PRIVACY
second - - - - - - - - - - ABET
second childhood - - - - - DOTAGE
second copy - - - - - - - - DRAFT
second father of human race - NOAH
second growth crop - - - - - ROWEN
second growth of grass - - - - - FOG
second hand - - - - - - - - - USED
second largest bird - - - - - - EMU
second of two things mentioned - LATTER
secondary - - - - - - - - - - BYE
secondary consideration (of) - - MINOR
secondary school - - - - - - - PREP
secondhand - - - - - - - - - USED
secrecy - - - - - - - - VELATION
secret - - PRIVATE, HIDDEN, COVERT, CONCEALED, INNER
secret agent - - - - - - - - SPY
secret council - - - - - - CONCLAVE
secret military agent - - - - - - SPY
secret procedure - - - - - - STEALTH
secret writing - - - - - - - CODE
secretary - - - - - - - - - DESK
secrete - - - - - - HIDE, CONCEAL
secreting organ - - - - - - GLAND
secretion of cuttlefish - - - - - INK
secretive - - - - - - - - RETICENT
secretly - - - - - - - - INWARDLY
sect - - - - CULT, FACTION, PARTY
section - - DIVISION, PART, PIECE, PARTITION, AREA
sectional - - - - - - - - - LOCAL
secular - - - - - - - LAIC, LAYMAN
secure - SAFE, OBTAIN, GET, ACQUIRE, FAST, NAIL, FIRM, FASTEN
secure against intrusion - - - - TILE
secure in place - - - - - - FASTEN
secure temporarily - - - - - BORROW
secure with leather strips - - - STRAP
securely - - - - - - - - - - FAST
security - - PAWN, GUARANTY, BOND, TIE, BAIL, WARRANTY
security for appearance - - - - - BAIL
security for payment - - - - - - LIEN
sedate - - STAID, SOBER, SETTLED, TRANQUIL, MATRONLY
sedentary - - - - SETTLED, SESSILE
sediment - - - - - SILT, DREG, LEES
sedition - - - - - - - - - TREASON
seductive woman - - SIREN, VAMPIRE
sedulous - - - - - - - - DILIGENT
see - LO, BEHOLD, WITNESS, NOTICE, DESCRY
seed - GERM, OVULE, PLANT, PROGENY, SPORE, SOURCE, SOW, SEEDLET, CORN, PIP
seed of cereal - - - - - - - KERNEL
seed coat (hard) - - - - - - - TESTA
seed container - POD, BUR, LOMENT
seed covering - ARIL, TESTA, TESTAE, POD
seed of flowerless plant - - - - SPORE
seed integument - - - - - - - TESTA
seed of leguminous plants - - - PULSE
seed of opium poppy - - - - - - MAW
seed plant - - - - - - - - - HERB
seed pod - - - - - - - - - LOMENT
seed used as spice - - - - - NUTMEG
seed vessel - - - - - POD, LEGUME
seedlike fruit - - - - - - - - BEAN
seedy - - - - - - - - - - SHABBY
seek - CRAVE, SEARCH, ASPIRE, HUNT
seek after - - - - - - - - - - SUE
seek favor of - - - - - - - COURT
seek influence - - - - - - - CRAWL
seek laboriously - - - - - - DELVE
seek with hands - - - - - - GROPE
seel - - - - - - - - - - - BLIND
seem - - - - - - - APPEAR, LOOK
seen (be) - - - - - - - - - VISUAL
seep - PERCOLATE, TRANSUDE, OOZE, LEAK, EXUDE
seep through slowly - - - - - - DRIP
seer - - - - - - - PROPHET, SAGE
seesaw - - - - TEETER, VACILLATION
seethe - - - - - - - - BOIL, STEW
segment cf crustacean - - - - TELSON
segment of curve - - - - - - - - ARC
segment of vertebrate animal - SOMITE
segregate - - - - - - - - - SORT
seine - - - - - - - - - NET, TRAP
seize - - GRASP, GRAB, NAB, CATCH, TAKE, ARREST, CLASP, CLUTCH, GRIP
seizure - - - - - - - - - ARREST
seldom - - - - - - - - - RARELY
select - - - - - - - - CHOOSE, PICK
select body - - - - - - - QUORUM
select group - - - - - - - - ELITE
selected - - - - - - - - - CHOSEN
self - - - - - - - - - - - - EGO
self assurance - - - - - - - APLOMB
self centered person - EGOIST, EGOTIST
self (comb. form) - - - - - - AUTO
self command under strain - - NERVE
self conceit - - - - - - - - EGOTISM
self defense without weapons - - JUDO
self esteem - - - - - - - - - PRIDE
self evident truth - - AXIOM, TRUISM
self exaltation - - - - - - - - PRIDE
self interested - - - - - - - EGOIST
self luminous body - - - - - - - SUN
self moving machine - - AUTOMATON
self originated existence - - - ASEITY
self possessed - - - - - - - - COOL
self possession - - - - - - - APLOMB
self respect - - - - - - - - PRIDE
self reproach - - - - - - REMORSE

S

self righteous person - - - PHARISEE
self satisfied - - - - - - - SMUG
self (Scot.) - - - - - - - - SEL
self sufficient person - - - - PRIG
selfish rivalry and strife - EMULATION
selfsame - - - - - - - - IDENTICAL
sell - - - VEND, TRADE, DISPOSE
sell to customer - - - - - RETAIL
sell for - - - - - - - - - BRING
sell from door to door - - - PEDDLE
sell in small quantities - - - RETAIL
seller of provisions to troops - SUTLER
seller of small quantities - - RETAILER
semblance - - - - - - - - GUISE
semi-circular recess - - - - APSE
semi-diameter - - - RADII, RADIUS
semi-diameter of circle - - - RADIUS
semi-pellucid mineral - - - AGATE
semi-transparent material - - - VOILE
Seminole chief - - - - - - OSCEOLA
semiprecious stone - AGATE, OLIVIN, ONYX, GARNET, SARDS
semite - - - - - - - - - ARAB
semitic deity - - - - - - MOLOCH
semitic goddess - - - - - - ALLAT
semitic language - ARABIC, ARAMAIC
send - DISPATCH, DELIVER, TRANSMIT, FORWARD, DEPUTE
send along - - - - - - - - RELAY
send back - - - - REMIT, REMAND
send back to custody - - - REMAND
send down - - - - - - - - DEMIT
send forth - - - - - - - - EMIT
send off - - - - - - - - - EMIT
send out - - - - - EMIT, RADIATE
send out of country - - - - DEPORT
send out, as rays - - - - ERADIATE
send payment - - - - - - - REMIT
sending forth - - - - - - EMISSIVE
senile - - - - - - - - - - AGED
senile person - - - DOTARD, DOTER
senior - - - ELDEST, ELDER, OLDER
seniority - - - - - - - - - AGE
senna (former spelling) - - - SENE
sensation - - FEELING, PERCEPTION
sensational - - - - - - - - LURID
sensational feat - - - - - STUNT
sense - FEEL, MEANING, COMPREHEND, WIT, IMPORT, FEELING
sense datum - - - - - SENSATION
sense of dignity - - - - - PRIDE
sense of guilt - - - - - - SHAME
sense of smell - - OLFACTORY, NOSE
sense of taste - - - - - PALATE
senseless - - - INANE, FOLLY, MAD
sensible - - - - - - - RATIONAL
sensitive - - - - - - SORE, TENDER
sensitive mental perception - - TACT
sensitive to nonphysical forces - PSYCHIC
sensitive plant - - - - - - MIMOSA
sentence - - - DOOM, JUDGMENT, CONDEMN
sentient - - - - - - - - - MIND
sentient thing - - - - - - - BEING
sentimental - - - - - ROMANTIC
sentinel - - - - WARDEN, GUARD
sentry's greeting - - - - - - HALT
separate - - DIVORCE, PART, APART, PARTITIVE, ALIENATE, SEVER, DIVIDE, ASIDE, DISJOIN, SORT
separate and classify - - ASSORT, SIFT
separate and divide - - - - SLEAVE
separate entry - - - - - - - ITEM
separate from others - - - - SINGLE
separate particle - - - - - - ITEM
separate portion - - - - - - - LOT
separated - - - - - APART, SPACED
separately - - - - - - - - - APART
separation - - - - - - - DIVISION
separator - - - - - - - - - SORTER
separator in weaving - - - EVENER
sepulcher - - - - - - - - - TOMB
sepulchral - - - - - - - CHARNEL
sequel - - - - - OUTCOME, UPSHOT
seraglio - - - - - - - - - - HAREM
seraph - - - - - - - - - - ANGEL
seraphic - - - - - - - - - ANGELIC
Serbian - - - - - - - SERB, SLAV
sere - - - - - - - - - DRY, WITHER
serenade - - - - - - - NOCTURNE
serene - - CALM, PLACID, TRANQUIL, IRENIC
serenity - - - - - - - - - - PEACE
serf - ESNE, SLAVE, VASSAL, BONDMAN, THRALL, HELOT, VILLEIN, PEASANT
serfage - - - - - - - - - BONDAGE
serial - - - - - - - - SUCCESSIVE
series - - - - - - - - - - - SETS
series of ancestors - - - - - - LINE
series of columns - - - - COLONNADE
series of dropped stitches - - - RUN
series of links - - - - - - - CHAIN
series of meetings - - - - - SESSION
series of names - - - - - - - LIST
series of operations in warfare - - - CAMPAIGN
series of plant changes - - - - SERE
series of rings - - - - - - - COIL
series of stairs - - - - - - FLIGHT
series of tennis games - - - - SET
serious - SOBER, SOLEMN, SEVERE, EARNEST, GRAVE, GRIM, RAPT, DEMURE
serious attention - - - - - - CARE
serious discourse - - - - - SERMON
sermon - ADDRESS, ORATION, HOMILY
sermon subject - - - - - - - TEXT
sermonize - - - - - - - - PREACH
serous - - - - - - - - - WATERY
serous fluid - - - - - SERA, SERUM
serpent - ABOMA, ASP, SNAKE, ADDER, COBRA, BOA, PYTHON
serpentine - - - - - - - - - SNAKY
serpentine fish - - - - - - - EEL
serrate - - - - - - - - - NOTCH
serry - - - - - - - - - - CROWD
servant - - - - - SERVITOR, MENIAL
servant's garb - - - - - - LIVERY
serve - BESTEAD, SATISFY, MINISTER, ATTEND
serve food - - - - - - - - CATER
serve the purpose - - - - - - - DO
serve scantily - - - - - - - STINT
serve with legal writ - - - SUBPOENA
server - - - - - TRAY, ATTENDANT
service - - - - - - - - - - - USE
service tree - - - - - - - - SORB
service utensil - - - - - - - TRAY
serviceable - - - - - - - USEFUL
serviette - - - - - - - - NAPKIN
servile - MENIAL, SLAVISH, ABJECT, SUBMISSIVE, FAWNING
servile dependent - - - - - MINION
serving to protect - - - DEFENSIVE
serving to refute - - - - - ELENTIC
serving to restrain - - - DETERRENT
serving as a warning of danger - SEMATIC
servitude - - - - - - - - - - YOKE
sesame - - - - - - - TIL, SEMSEM
session - - - - - - - - - SEANCE
set - - - COTERIE, SERIES, CLIQUE, GROUP, HARD, ADJUST, RIGID,

APPOINT, MOUNT, CONGEAL, PUT, FIX
set apart - - - ISOLATE, ALLOCATE, DEVOTE
set back - - - RECESS, RECESSED
set body of a surface - - - - INLAY
set of boxes - - - - - - - - NEST
set fire to - - - BURN, IGNITE, LIT
set forth - - - - - - - - - SAIL
set forth (obs.) - - - - - - EXPONE
set forth by particulars - - ITEMIZE
set of four - - - - - - - TETRAD
set free - RELEASE, LIBERATE, DELIVER
set in from margin - - - - - INDENT
set of hives - - - - - - - APIARY
set of instruments - - - - - - KIT
set at intervals - - - - - - SPACE
set into body of a surface - - INLAY
set and leave in certain place - - PARK
set at liberty - - - - - - DELIVER
set in motion - - - - - - - STIR
set at naught - - - - - - OVERRIDE
set of nested boxes - - - - - - INRO
set in order - - - - FILE, ARRANGE
set of organ pipes - - - - - - STOP
set of ornaments - - - - - PARURE
set off nicely - - - - - - BECOME
set out - - - EMBARK, START, SAIL
set, as a plant - - - - - - - BED
set of players - - - - - - - TEAM
set right - - - - - - - CORRECT
set to rights - - - - - - - SETTLED
set of signals - - - - - - - CODE
set solidly - - - - - - - EMBED
set the speed - - - - - - - PACE
set of three - - - - - - - TIERCE
set to - - - - - - - - - - BOUT
set of type - - - - - - - - FONT
set up - - - - - - - - - REAR
set upright - - - - - ERECT, REAR
set value on - - - APPRAISE, RATE
setal - - - - - - - - - BRISTLY
setback - - - - - - - - REVERSE
Seth's brother - - - - - - - ABEL
Seth's mother - - - - - - - - EVE
Seth's son - - - - - - - - - ENOS
setose - - - - - - - - - BRISTLY
sets - - - - - - - - - - SERIES
settee - - - - - - - - - - SOFA
setter (kind) - - - - - - - GORDON
setting aside - - - - - - REVERSAL
settle money on - - - - - - ENDOW
settled - - - SEDATE, SEDENTARY, DETERMINED, AGREED, DECIDED, ADJUSTED, REGULATED, COLONIZED, LIT, DISPOSED
settled by common consent - - AGREE
settled course - - - - - - POLICY
settled habit - - - - - - - - RUT
settlement of claims - - CLEARANCE
settler - - - - - - - - - COLONIST
settling - - - - - - - - DREG, LEE
set-to - - - - - - - BOUT, FRAY
seven (comb. form) - - - - - HEPTA
seven part composition - - - SEPTET
seventh planet - - - - - - - URANUS
sever - CUT, DISUNITE, PART, DISJOIN, REND, SEPARATE, BREAK
sever violently - - - - - - - TEAR
several - - - - - - DIVERS, MANY
severance - - - - - - - PARTITION
severe - - STERN, STRICT, SPARTAN, DRASTIC, AUSTERE, CRUCIAL, RIGID, HARD, RIGOROUS, DISJOIN, HARSH
severe cold - - - - - - - FROST
severity - - - - RIGOR, STERNNESS
sew - - - - PLANT, STITCH, MEND
sew loosely - - - - - - - - BASTE
sewed joint - - - - - - - - - SEAM
sewer - - - - - - - DITCH, DRAIN
sewing aid - - - - - - - THIMBLE
sewing case - - - - - - - - - ETUI
sewing machine - - - - - STITCHER
sewing style - - - - - - - - SHIRR
sex - - - - - - - - - - GENDER
shabby - - - - - - SEEDY, MEAN
shack - - - - - - - - - - - HUT
shackle - FETTER, PINION, MANACLE, GYVE
shad - - - - - - - - ALOSE, ALOSA
shad-like fish - - - - - MENHADEN
shade - TONE, SHADOW, HUE, TINT, SCREEN, CAST, GHOST, NUANCE, TINGE
shade of the dead - - - - - - MANE
shade of difference - - - - - NUANCE
shade tree - - - - - ELM, LIN, ASH
shade with fine lines - - - - HATCH
shaded walk - - - - - MALL, ARBOR
shadow - - - - - - SHADE, DARKEN
shadowless men - - - - - - ASCIANS
shady - - - - - - - - SHELTERED
shady retreat - - - - - - - ARBOR
shady thicket - - - - - - - COVERT
shaft - - - - POLE, MISSILE, PILLAR
shaft of a column - - - - - - VERGE
shaft of a column (arch.) - - - - FUST
shaft of a vehicle - - - - - - THILL
shaggy - - - - - - BUSHY, NAPPY
shake - TREMOR, WAG, JAR, TREMBLE, SHIVER, BOB, DODDER, CONVULSE, RATTLE
shake continuously - - - - - CHURN
shake up fire - - - - - - - - STOKE
shake with cold - - - - - - SHIVER
Shakespearian actor - - - - - - TREE
Shakespearian character - - - - IRAS, SALERIO, OTHELLO, IAGO, OBERON, FALSTAFF
Shakespearian conspirator - - CASSIUS
Shakespearian forest - - - - - ARDEN
Shakespearian heroine - - - - PORTIA
Shakespearian king - - - - - - LEAR
Shakespearian lord - - - - - BIGOT
Shakespearian play - - - - OTHELLO
Shakespearian river - - - - - AVON
Shakespearian spirit in "Tempest" - - ARIEL
Shakespearian villain - - - - - IAGO
shaking - - - - - - - TREMOR, ASPEN
shaking apparatus - - - - - AGITATOR
shale - - - - - - - - - - - PELITE
shallow - - - - SHOAL, SUPERFICIAL
shallow box - - - - - - - - - TRAY
shallow dish - - - - - PLATE, SAUCER
shallow and impertinent - - - FLIPPANT
shallow receptacle - - - - - - - TRAY
shallow sound (var.) - - - - - LAGUNE
shallow trunk box - - - - - - - TRAY
shallow vessel - - - - - - - - BASIN
sham - - PRETEND, FEIGN, FALSE, IMPOSTURE, ARTIFICIAL, FAKE
sham (colloq.) - - - - - - - - FAKE
shame - HUMILIATE, ABASH, MORTIFY, DISGRACE, CHAGRIN, ABASEMENT
shameless - - - - - - - - ARRANT
shank - - - - - - - - SHIN, CRUS
shanty - - - - - - - - - - - HUT
shape - FORM, MODEL, MOLD, FRAME, CONTOUR, MOULD
shape conically - - - - - - - CONE
shape ideas - - - - - - - - IDEATE
shape with knife - - - - - WHITTLE

shaped like an arrowhead - SAGITTATE
shaped like pine cone - - - PINEAL
shaped with an ax - - HEWED, HEWN
shapeliness - - - - - - SYMMETRY
shard - - - - - - - - FRAGMENT
share - IMPART, PORTION, PARTAKE, QUOTA, DIVIDE, BIT, LOT, DOLE
share in - - - - - - PARTICIPATE
share in common - - - - - JOINT
sharer - - - - - - - - PARTNER
shark - - - GATA, MANEATER, TOPE
sharp - TART, ACUTE, KEEN, RATION, PUNGENT, EDGED, STERN, EDGY, BITING, NIPPY, INCISIVE, ACERB
sharp answer - - - - - - - RETORT
sharp bend - - - - - - - - KINK
sharp and biting - - - - - ACID
sharp blade - - - - - - - RAZOR
sharp blow - - - - - - - - RAP
sharp continuous knocking - - RATTAT
sharp cornered - - - - - - ANGULAR
sharp cry - - - - - - YELP, YELL
sharp edged - - - - - - CULTRATE
sharp end - - - - - - - - POINT
sharp and harsh - - - - - - ACERB
sharp pain - - PANG, STING, TWINGE
sharp piercing sound - - - - SHRILL
sharp point - - - - - - BARB, CUSP
sharp pointed - - ACUTE, ACULEATE
sharp process on plant - - - THORN
sharp projection - - - - - - BARB
sharp reply - - - - - - - RETORT
sharp shooter - - - - - - - SNIPER
sharp taste - - - TANG, TART, ACID
sharp tempered - - - - EDGY, ACID
sharp tip - - - - - - - - SPIRE
sharpen - - - STROP, WHET, HONE, POINT, EDGE
sharpened - - - - - - - - EDGED
sharpening machine - - - GRINDER
sharpening stone - - - - - - HONE
sharpness - - - - EDGE, ACUMEN
shatter - - - SMASH, BREAK, DASH
shave - - - - - - - SHEAR, PARE
shave head of - - - - - - TONSURE
shaved osier - - - - - - - SKEIN
shaven head - - - - - - - TONSURE
shaver - - - - - - - YOUNGSTER
shawl - - - - - - PAISLEY, WRAP
Shawnee's chief - - - - - TECUMSEH
shear - POLL, CLIP, SHAVE, FLEECE, STRIP
sheath - - CASE, ENCASE, SCABBARD
sheath internally - - - - - - CEIL
sheathed - - - - - - - - OCREATE
shed - LEANTO, SPILL, COTE, MOLT, EMIT
shed copiously - - - - - - - RAIN
shed feathers - - - - MOULT, MOLT
shed to house aircraft - - - HANGAR
sheen - - LUSTER, POLISH, GLOSS, BRIGHTNESS
sheep - - - - - - EWE, RAM, SNA
sheep (breed) - - - - - - MERINO
sheep coat - - - - FLEECE, WOOL
sheep cry - - - - - - - - BLEAT
sheep disease - - - - - - - - COE
sheep dog - - - - - - - - COLLIE
sheep (female) - - - - - - - EWE
sheep killing parrots - - - - KEAS
sheep (male) - - - - - - - - - RAM
sheep in its second year - - - - TEG
sheep shelter - - - - COTE, FOLD
sheep tender - - - - - SHEPHERD
sheepfold - - - - - - - - - COTE
sheepskin - - - - - - - - - OVINE
sheepskin leather - - - - - - ROAN
sheer - - - - ABSOLUTE, PELLUCID
sheer fabric - - - - - - - - - LAWN
sheet - - - - - - - - NEWSPAPER
sheet of floating ice - - - - - FLOE
sheet folded once - - - - - - FOLIO
sheet of glass - - - - PANE, PLATE
shelf - - - - - - - - - - LEDGE
shell - - - - - - - - SHOT, BOMB
shell fiercely - - - - - - - STRAFE
shell hole - - - - - - - - CRATER
shell hurling device - - - - MORTAR
shell that fails to explode - - - DUD
shellac - - - - - - VARNISH, LAC
shellfish - - - CLAM, DECAPODAL, ABALONES, CRAB, MOLLUSK
shellfish spawn - - - - - - - SPAT
shelter - - LEE, HAVEN, SHED, ABRI, TENT, PROTECT, ROOF, SCONCE, COVER, ASYLUM
shelter for animals - - - - - - COTE
sheltered - - - SHADY, LEE, COVERT
sheltered corner - - - - - - NOOK
sheltered inlet - - - - - - - COVE
sheltered side - - - - - - - - LEE
Shem descendant - - - - - SEMITE
Shem's father - - - - - - - NOAH
sheol - - - - - - - - - - HADES
shepherd's staff (Scot.) - - - KENT
sherbet - - - - - - - - - - ICE
sheriff's deputy - - - - - - BAILIFF
sheriff's group - - - - - - - POSSE
Sherlock Holmes author - - - DOYLE
Shetland Islands measure - - - URE
Shetland Islands tax - - - - SCAT
shield - - EGIS, PROTECT, BUCKLER, TARGE, ECU, ECUS
shield (arch.) - - - - - - - TARGE
shield division (her.) - - - - ENTE
shield shaped - - - - - - PELTATE
shift - - - - VEER, TOUR, CHANGE
shifting - - - - - - - AMBULANT
shifty - - - - - - - - - EVASIVE
shin - - - - - - - SHANK, CLIMB
shine - - - GLEAM, RADIATE, BEAM, GLITTER, RAY, POLISH, GLISTEN, GLOW, LUSTER, GLOSS
shingle - - - - - - - - - - SIGN
shining - - RADIANT, LUCENT, AGLOW
shins up (colloq.) - - - - SHINNIES
Shinto temple - - - - - - - - SHA
Shinto temple gateway - - - TORII
shiny - - - - - - - - - GLOSSY
ship - - - BOAT, VESSEL, EMBARK
ship biscuit - - - - - - HARDTACK
ship's boats - - - - - - - - GIGS
ship's body - - - - - - - - HULL
ship's bow - - - - - - STEM, PROW
ship's cabin - - - - - - - SALOON
ship's captain - - - - - - MASTER
ship's channel - - - - - - - - GAT
ship's company - - - - - - - CREW
ship's crane - - - - - - - DAVIT
ship's cubical content - - - TONNAGE
ship's deck - - - - - - - - POOP
ship's deck opening - - - - - HATCH
ship's defensive plating - - - ARMOR
ship's employee - - - - - STEWARD
ship's guide - - - - - - - RUDDER
ship's guns - - - - - - - - TEETH
ship's kitchen - - - - - - - GALLEY
ship's line - - - - - - - LANYARD
ship's load - - - - - - - - CARGO
ship's log (part) - - - - - ROTATOR
ship's officer - - - MATE, PURSER, NAVIGATOR

ship part - - - KEEL, MAST, RUDDER
ship personnel - - - - - - - CREW
ship (pert. to) - - - - - - - NAVAL
ship's petty officer (colloq.) - - BOSUN
ship (poet.) - - - - - - KEEL, PROW
ship prison - - - - - - - - BRIG
ship rear - - - - - - - - - - AFT
ship ropes (number) - - - - - SEVEN
ship's small boat - - - - - - YAWL
ship's storage room - - - - LASTAGE
ship's strengthening part - - KEELSON
ship's timber - KEEL, SNY, BITT, SPAR
ship's timber (vertical) - - - - - BITT
ship's timberpiece - - - - - - SNY
ship's windlass - - - - - CAPSTAN
shipboard - - - - - - - - ASEA
shipbuilding to bend upward - - SNY
shipping container - - - - - - CRATE
ships of war (pert. to) - - - - NAVAL, NAUTICAL
shipshape - - - - - - - ORDERLY
shipworm - - - - TEREDO, BORER
shipwrecked sailor - - - - CRUSOE
shire - - - - - - - - - COUNTY
shirk - - - - EVADE, AVOID, SHUN
shirker - EVADER, DESERTER, TRUANT
shirt (arch.) - - - - - - - SARK
shirt button - - - - - - - - STUD
shiver - SHUDDER, SHAKE, SPLINTER, TREMOR
shivering - - - - - - - - DITHERY
shoal - - - FLAT, SHALLOW, REEF
shoal as of fish - - - - - - SCULL
shock - APPAL, STRIKE, JAR, STARTLE, BRUNT
shoe - - - - - - - BOOT, BROGAN
shoe fastener - - - - - - LATCHET
shoe form - - - - - - - LAST, TREE
shoe (kind) - - - SANDAL, SLIPPER
shoe leather strip - - - - - - WELT
shoe part - - RAND, TOECAP, INSOLE, UPPER, VAMP
shoe store - - - - - - - BOOTERY
shoemaker thread (dial.) - - LINGEL
shoemaker tool - - - - - - - AWL
shoes (arch.) - - - - - - - SHOON
shoestring - - - - - - LACE, LACET
shoot - - - - CION, FIRE, SPROUT, DISCHARGE, DART, SPRIG
shoot forth - - - - - - - BURGEON
shoot for grafting - - - CION, SCION
shoot at from hiding - - - - SNIPE
shoot out - - - - - - - - DART
shoot of plant - - - SPROUT, SCION
shoot of woody plant - - - - - ROD
shooting star - - - METEOR, LEONID
shop - - - - - - - - - STORE
shop keeper - - - - - - TRADESMAN
shore - COAST, STRAND, LAND, BEACH, PROP, SUPPORT
shore bird - - - SNIPE, RAIL, STILT, AVOCET, PLOVER, REE
shore (poet.) - - - - - - STRAND
shore of the sea (pert. to) - LITTORAL
shorn of holdings - - - - - STRIPPED
short - - CURT, BRIEF, SUCCINCT, PERT, ABRUPT, DEFICIENT
short aria - - - - - - - ARIETTA
short article - - - - - - - - ITEM
short billed rails - - - - - - SORAS
short blunt piece - - - - - - STUB
short branch - - - - - - - SNAG
short and concise - - - - - TERSE
short contest - - - - - - - SETTO
short distance - - - - - STEP, PACE
short distance race - - - - - SPRINT
short dramatic piece - - - - - SKIT
short for explosive powder - - NITRO
short jerking motion - - - - - BOB
short lance - - - - - - - - DART
short letter - BILLET, LINE, NOTELET
short look - - - - - - - - GLANCE
short for matrix - - - - - - STEREO
short missive - - - - - - - BILLET
short napped fabric - - - - - - RAS
short note - - - - - - - - - LINE
short outdoor trip - - - - - AIRING
short piece of pipe - - - - - - TEE
short and to the point - - - TERSE
short race - - - - - DASH, SPRINT
short rest - - - - - - SIESTA, NAP
short rib in Gothic vaulting - - LIERNE
short run - - - - - - - - - SPRINT
short sentence - - - - - - CLAUSE
short sharp branch - - - - - - SNAG
short sharp sound - - - - - - POP
short skirt - - - - - - - - - KILT
short sled - - - - - - - - - - BOB
short sport - - - - - - - - PIKER
short stalk - - - - - - - - - STIPE
short stop - - - - - - - - PAUSE
short story - - - - - - - ANECDOTE
short surplice - - - - - - - COTTA
short talk - - - - - - STIPE, CHAT
short and thick - - STOCKY, DUMPY
short time - - - - - - - - - SPELL
short visit - - - - - - - - - CALL
shortage - - - - - - - - - DEFICIT
shorten - - CONTRACT, CUT, CURTAIL
shorten a mast - - - - - - - REEF
shortening - - - - - - - - - LARD
shortly - - - - - - - - - - SOON
Shoshone Indian - UTE, PAIUTE, PIUTE
shot - - - - - - - - - - - SHELL
shoulder (comb. form) - - - - - OMO
shoulder ornament - - - - - EPAULET
shoulder pack - - - - - - KNAPSACK
shoulder of road - - - - - - BERM
shout - - YELL, HOOT, CRY, HOOY, BAWL, ROOT
shout applause - - - - - - CHEER
shout of encouragement - - - - CHEER
shout for (slang) - - - - - - ROOT
shouting - - - - - - - - - HUE
shove - - - - - - - PUSH, THRUST
shovel - - - - - - SPADE, SCOOP
show - - - ARRAY, PARADE, EVINCE, DISPLAY, EXHIBIT, DENOTE, REVEAL, EVIDENCE
show approval - - - - - - - SMILE
show contempt - - SNEER, HISS, BOO
show difference - - - - - CONTRAST
show to be false - - BELIE, DISPROVE
show fondness - - - - - - - DOTE
show mercy - - - - - - - - SPARE
show off - - - - - - - - - PARADE
show pique - - - - - - - - RESENT
show play of colours - - - OPALESCE
show pleasant surprise - - - - SMILE
show to a seat - - - - - - - USHER
show sorrow for - - - - - - - PITY
show to be true - - - - - - PROVE
shower - - - - - - - - - - RAIN
shower icy particles - - - - - SLEET
showery - - - - - - - - - - RAINY
showy - ORNATE, GARISH, PRETENTIOUS
showy clothes - - - - REGALIA, FINERY
showy (colloq.) - - - - LOUD, DRESSY
showy display - - - - - - SPLURGE
showy fern - - - - - - - OSMUND
showy ornament - - - - - - TINSEL
shred - - - - RAG, PARTICLE, SCRAP,

S

TATTER, WISP, SNIP, FRAGMENT
shred of waste silk - - - - - - NOIL
shrew - VIRAGO, VIXEN, TERMAGANT
shrewd - - - CANNY, KEEN, ASTUTE, POLITIC, SMART, KNOWING, ACUTE, CLEVER, SLY
shrewd (slang) - - - - - - - - CAGEY
shrewd woman - - - - - - - VIRAGO
shrewdness - - - - - - - - ACUMEN
shrill - - - - - - PIPE, STRIDENT
shrill bark - - - - - YAP, YELP, YIP
shrill cry - - - - - SHRIEK, SCREAM
shrill note - - - - - - - - - SKIRL
shrimplike crustacean - - - - PRAWN
shrink - CONTRACT, COWER, RECOIL, LESSEN, WANE, CRINGE, SHRIVEL
shrink in fear - - - - - - - CRINGE
shrivel - - WITHER, WIZEN, BLAST, SHRINK
shrivel with heat - - - - - - PARCH
shroud - - - - - - - - - - SHEET
shrub - SPIREA, ELDER, ALDER, LILAC, BARETTA, BUSH, LAUREL, SUMAC, PLANT, SENNA
shrub fence - - - - - - - - HEDGE
shrub (low) - - - - - - - - - BUSH
shrub used like tea - - - - - - KAT
shuck - - - - - - - - - - - HUSK
shudder - - - - - TREMBLE, SHIVER
shuffling gait - - - - - - SHAMBLE
shun - AVOID, EVADE, ESCHEW, FLEE
shun (arch.) - - - - - - - - EVITE
shunt - - - - - SWITCH, SIDETRACK
shut - - - - - - - CLOSE, CLOSED
shut close - - - - - - - - - SEAL
shut in - - - - - - - - - - - HEM
shut out from - - - - - - - DEBAR
shut (Prov. Eng.) - - - - - - TEEN
shut up - - - - - - - - - - PENT
shutter - - - - - - - - - - BLIND
shy - TIMID, DEMURE, COY, RECOIL, BASHFUL, SWERVE, WARY, RESERVED, RETIRING, TIMOROUS
shy (colloq.) - - - - - - - - - MIM
shyness - - - TIMIDITY, DIFFIDENCE
shyster - - - - - - - PETTIFOGGER
Siamese - - - - - - - - - - THAI
Siamese coin - - - - - AT, ATT, TICAL
Siamese Island group - - - - - TAI
Siamese measure - - - NIU, RAI, SEN
Siamese race - - - - - - - - - TAI
Siamese river - - - - - - - - - SI
Siamese tribesman - - - - - - TAI
Siamese twin - - - - ENG, CHANG
Siamese weight - - - - - - - - PAI
sib - - - - - - - - - - - - AKIN
Siberian antelope - - - - - - SAIGA
Siberian Mongoloid - - - - - TATAR
Siberian mountains - - - - - ALTAI
Siberian natives - - SAGAI, TATARS
Siberian plains - - - - - - STEPPES
Siberian river - - OB, LENA, AMUR, ONON, OM, TOM, OPUS
Siberian squirrel - - - - - MINIVER
Siberian squirrel skin - - - - CALABAR
sibilant signal - - - - - PST, HIST
sibilant sound - - - - - - - - HISS
Sicilian city - - - - - - PALERMO
Sicilian mountain - - - - - - - ETNA
Sicilian seaport - - - ACI, MARSALA
Sicilian secret society - - - - MAFIA
Sicilian volcano - - - ETNA, AETNA
Sicilian volcano (pert. to) - - ETNEAN
Sicilian whirlpool - - - - CHARYBDIS
sick - - - - - - - - - - AIL, ABED
sick (be) - - - - - - - - - - - AIL
sick person - - - - - - AEGROTANT
sickness - - - - - - - - - - DISEASE
sickness (abbr., med.) - - - - - MAL
side (of the) - - - - - - - LATERAL
side - - PARTY, LATERAL, FACTION, SUPPORT, ASPECT, BORDER, SLOPE, PART, FLANK, PHASE
side away from the wind - - - ALEE
side of book leaf - - - - - - - PAGE
side of building - - - - - - - - WALL
side of coin bearing date - - OBVERSE
side at cricket - - - - - - - ELEVEN
side dish - - - - - - - - - ENTREE
side of doorway - - - - - - - JAMB
side glance - - - - - - - - - OGLE
side piece - - - - - - - - - - - RIB
side piece of window or door - - JAMB
side portion - - - - - - - - RASHER
side post of door - - - - - - JAMB
side road - - - - - - - - - BYWAY
side shoots - - - - - - - LATERALS
side by side - - ABREAST, PARALLEL
side tracked - - - - - - - SHUNTED
side of triangle - - - - - - - - LEG
side view - - - - - - - - - PROFILE
sidelong - - - - - - - - - OBLIQUE
sidelong glance - - - - - LEER, OGLE
sideslip - - - - - - - - - - - SKID
sidestep - - - - - - - AVOID, DUCK
sidetrack - - - - - - - - - - SHUNT
sidewise - - - - - - - - LATERALLY
sidle - - - - - - - - - - - - EDGE
siege - - - - - - BESET, BLOCKADE
sierra - - - - - - - - - - PINTADO
siesta - - - - - - - - - - - - NAP
sieve - - SIFT, SCREEN, STRAINER, FILTER
sift - SCREEN, SIEVE, STRAIN, RIDDLE, BOLT
sift (engr.) - - - - - - - - - - LUE
sifter - - - - - - - - - - - SIEVE
sigh - GROAN, SOB, LAMENT, SUSPIRE
sigh (poet.) - - - - - - - - SUSPIRE
sight - - - - - - - - - - - - EYE
sight (pert. to) - - - - OPTIC, VISUAL
sigil - - - - - - - - - - - - SEAL
sign - - - OMEN, SYMBOL, TOKEN, PORTENT, TRACE, SIGNAL, NOTICE, SHINGLE
sign of addition - - - - - - - PLUS
sign of assent - - - - - - - - NOD
sign of Blue Eagle - - - - - N.R.A.
sign of fire - - - - - - - - SMOKE
sign of future event - - - - - OMEN
sign of infinitive mood - - - - - TO
sign of omission - - - - - - CARET
signal - SIGN, NOTICEABLE, WARNING, ALARM
signal bell - - - - - GONG, CURFEW
signal call - - - - - - - - SENNET
signate - - - - - - - - DESIGNATE
signature of approval - - - - - VISA
signet - - - - - - - - - - - SEAL
significance - - MEANING, IMPORT
significant - - - - - - - IMPORTANT
signification - - - - - - - - SENSE
signify - - DENOTE, MEAN, MATTER, INDICATE
signify agreement - - - - - - NOD
silence - - STILLNESS, GAG, QUIET, STILL, HUSH
silencer - - - - - MUFFLER, GAVEL
silent - - MUM, MUTE, NOISELESS, TACITURN, STILL, TACIT, MUTED

S

silent letter - - - - - - - - MUTE
silent signal - - - - - - - - BECK
silica (kind) - - - - - - - QUARTZ
silicate - - - - - - - - WELLSITE
siliceous rock - - - - - - - - SIAL
silk fabric - ALAMODE, PONGEE, SATIN, SURAH, SAMITE
silk fibers - - - - - - - - - FLOSS
silk filling - - - - - - - - - TRAM
silk (kind) - - - - - - - ERIA, MOIRE
silk net - - - - - - - - - - TULLE
silk thread - - - - - - - TRAM, FLOSS
silk for veils - - - - - - - - TULLE
silk winder - - - - - - - - REELER
silken - - - - - - - SERIC, GLOSSY
silkworm - - - - - - - - - ERI, ERIA
silkworm's envelope - - - - COCOON
silky haired dog - - - - - - SPANIEL
silky haired goat - - - - - - ALPACA
silly - - INANE, ASININE, FATUOUS
silly person - - - - - - SIMPLETON
silly smile - - - - - - - - SIMPER
silt - - - - - - - - - - - - SCUM
silver - - - - - SPLINTER, ARGENT
silver (alch.) - - - - - - - - LUNA
silver (arch.) - - - - - - - - ARGENT
silver (symbol) - - - - - - - - AG.
silver coin - - - - - - - - - DIME
silver coin of India - - - - - - TARA
silver fish - - - - - - - - - SARGO
silver salt - - - - - - - - ARGENTOL
silver white metallic element - - TIN
silverweed - - - - - - - - - TANSY
silvery - - - - - - - - - - ARGENT
simian - - - - - - - - APE, APELIKE
similar - ALIKE, SAME, LIKE, AKIN, SUCH, ANALOGIC
similar qualities (of) - - - - - AKIN
similar things put together - - BUNCH
similarity - - SAMENESS, LIKENESS
simile - - - - - - - - COMPARISON
simmer - - - - - - - - STEW, BOIL
Simon pure - - - - - - - - AMATEUR
simper - - - - - - - - - - SMIRK
simple - MERE, ELEMENTARY, PLAIN, EASY, ELEMENTAL
simple animal - - - AMOEBA, MONAD
simple minded - - - - - - - OAFISH
simple minute organism - - - - MONAD
simple and old fashioned - PRIMITIVE
simple protozoan - - - - - - AMOEBA
simple song - - - - - - BALLAD, LAY
simple sugar - - - - - - - - - OSE
simpleton - IDIOT, OAF, FOOL, ASS, DAW, DOLT, GOOSE, SAPHEAD, SAP, NINNY
simulacre - - - - - - - - LIKENESS
simulate - PRETEND, IMITATE, APE, ACT, FEIGN
simulation - - - - - - - - PRETENSE
simultaneous round of firing - - SALVO
sin - - - - - ERR, EVIL, INIQUITY, TRANSGRESS
Sinbad's bird - - - - - - - - - ROC
since - - - AGO, AS, FOR, BECAUSE
since (arch.) - - - - - - - - - SITH
since (prefix) - - - - - - - - - CIS
since (Scot.) - - - - - - - - - SYNE
sincere - HONEST, GENUINE, HEARTY
sincere good wishes - - - - CORDIALLY
sinew - - - MUSCLE, TENDON, THEW
sinewed - - - - - - - - MUSCULAR
sinewy - - - - - - - - - - - WIRY
sinful - - - - - - - - EVIL, WICKED
sing - CHANT, LILT, CAROL, WARBLE, INTONE, CROON, HUM
sing below pitch (mus.) - - - - FLAT
sing like a bird - - - - - - - TWEET
sing in low tone - - - - - - - - HUM
sing rhythmically - - - - - - - - LILT
sing in shrill voice - - - - - - PIPE
sing in Swiss style - - YODEL, YODLE
Singapore weight - - - - - - - SAGA
singe - - - - - - - - - - - - BURN
singers - - CHOIR, DIVAS, VOCALISTS, TENORS
singing bird - - - - ROBINET, WREN, SHAMA, LARK, VIREO, LINNET, PIPIT, VEERY, REDSTART, BOBOLINK, ORIOLE
singing syllable - - - - - - - - TRA
singing voice - - - - - BASSO, ALTO
single - SPORADIC, LONE, ONE, SOLO
single (comb. form) - - - - MON, UNI
single entry - - - - - - - - - ITEM
single individual - - - - - - - ONE
single masted vessel - - - - - SLOOP
single note - - - - - - - MONOTONE
single thing - - - - - - - - - UNIT
singly - - - - - - - - ALONE, ONCE
singular - - - - - - - - ODD, QUEER
sinister - - - - - - - - UNDERHAND
sink - DRAIN, SETTLE, SAG, MERGE, DESCEND, DIP, DROP, DEBASE, LOWER, EBB
sink intentionally - - - - - SCUTTLE
sink suddenly - - - - - - - - SLUMP
sinner - - PENITENT, TRANSGRESSOR
sinople - - - - - - - - - CINNABAR
sinuous - - - - - - - - - - WINDING
sinus - - - - - - - - - - - - BAY
Siouan Indian - - - - - OSAGE, OTOE
sip - - - - - - - - - - SUP, TASTE
siphon - - - - - - - - - SIPHUNCLE
siphuncle - - - - - - - - - - SIPHON
Sir Walter Scott's friend - - LAIDLAW
Sir Walter Scott hero - - - - IVANHOE
siren - - - ENCHANTRESS, WHISTLE
siri - - - - - - - - - - - - - BETEL
sirup drained from sugar - - TREACLE
sirupy liqueur - - - - - - - - CREME
sister - - - - - - - - - - - - NUN
sit - - ROOST, REST, BROOD, POSE, PERCH
sit astride - - - - - - - - STRADDLE
site - - - - LOCALITY, AREA, SITUS
sitting - - SESSION, SEDENT, SEATED
Sitting Bull's tribe - - - - - SIOUX
situate - LOCATE, LOCATED, PLACE, LIE
situated (is) - - - - - LIES, STANDS
situated at the back - - - POSTERN
situated on membrane of brain - - - - EPIDURAL
situated in the middle - - - - MEDIAL
situation - - SITE, CONDITION, SEAT
situation of perplexity - - - - STRAIT
situs - - - - - - - - - - - - - SITE
six - - - - - - - - - - - - - - VI
six (group of) - - - - SENARY, SEXTET
six line stanza - - - - - - - SESTET
sixth part of a circle - - - - SEXTANT
sixty sixties - - - - - - - SAR, SAROS
sizable - - - - - - - - - - - - BIG
size - - - - - AREA, EXTENT, BULK, MAGNITUDE
size of book - - - - - - - - QUARTO
size of coal - - - - - - - PEA, EGG
size of paper - - ATLAS, DEMY, CAP
size of photograph - - - - - PANEL
size of shot - - - - - - - - - - T.T.
size of type - PICA, AGATE, DIAMOND, GEM
size of writing paper - - - - - - CAP

skeleton - - - FRAME, REMAINS
skeleton part - - - - - - BONE, RIB
skeptic - - - DOUBTER, AGNOSTIC
sketch - - - TRACE, DRAFT, PAINT, DRAWING, LIMN, SKIT, MAP, OUTLINE
sketchy - - - - - - - - - - VAGUE
sketchy poetic study in prose - PASTEL
skew - - - - - - OBLIQUE, TWIST
ski - - - - - - - - - - RUNNER
ski (var.) - - - - - - - - - - SKEE
skid - SLIDE, SLIP, SLUE, SIDESLIP
skiing race and term - - - - SLALOM
skill - - - - - - - - - - - ART
skilled - - - - - APT, ADEPT, VERSED
skilled person - - OPERATOR, ADEPT
skilled shot - - - - - - MARKSMAN
skilled trade - - - - - - MASONRY
skillet - - - - - - - - - - SPIDER
skillful - - - ADEPT, DEFT, CLEVER, ADROIT, APT
skillfully - - - - - - - - - - ABLY
skim - - - - - - - - - - - FLIT
skimpy - - - - - - - - - - SCANT
skin - PEEL, RIND, PELT, FLAY, HIDE
skin (of the) - - - - - - - DERMAL
skin blemish - - - - - - - WART
skin (comb. form) - - DERM, DERMA
skin covering - - - - - - - - FUR
skin disease - PSORA, ACNE, TINEA, RUPIA, HIVES
skin disease of dogs - - - - MANGE
skin elevation - - - - - - BLISTER
skin inflammation - - - - - PAPULA
skin layer - - - - - - - ENDERON
skin mouths or openings - - PORES, STOMA
skin opening and orifice - - - PORE
skin (pert. to) - - - - - CUTANEOUS
skin protuberance - WEN, MOLE, WART, BLISTER
skin of seal - - - - - - - SCULP
skin spots - - - - - - - FRECKLES
skin tumour - - - - - - WEN, WART
skink - - - - - - - - - - LIZARD
skip - - - - - OMIT, TRIP, MISS
skip about - - - - - - - - CAPER
skip along the surface - - - SKITTER
skip over water - - - - - - - DAP
skirmish - - FEUD, MELEE, BATTLE, BRUSH
skirt - - - - - - - - - BORDER
skirt of a suit of armour - - - TASSE
skirt vent - - - - - - - - - SLIT
skit - - PARODY, PLAYLET, SKETCH, LAMPOON
skitter - - - - - - - - SCAMPER
skittle - - - - - - - - - - PIN
skoal - - - - - - - - - - TOAST
skulk - - - - - - - - - HEDGE
skull - - - - - - - - - CRANIUM
skull (pert. to) - - - - - - CRANIAL
skull (wanting a) - - - - - ACRANIAL
skunk - - - - CONEPATE, POLECAT
sky - - - - - FIRMAMENT, WELKIN
sky blue - - - - - - - - - AZURE
sky (poet.) - - - - - - - - - BLUE
slab under column - - - - - PLINTH
slack - - - LOOSE, LAX, CARELESS
slacken - - - - - - RELAX, LOOSEN
slacken speed - - - - - - - SLOW
slackly joined - - - - - - - LOOSE
slag - - - - - - - DROSS, SCORIA
slag from melting metal - - SCORIA
slaggy lava - - - - - - - SCORIA
slake - - - - - - QUENCH, ALLAY
slam - - - - - - - - - - - BANG
slam at cards - - - - - - - VOLE
slander - - DEFAME, ASPERSE, BELIE, LIBEL, CALUMNY, ASPERSION, CALUMNIATE
slanderous report - - - - ASPERSION
slang - - - - - - ARGOT, JARGON
slant - BIAS, SLOPE, CANT, INCLINE, TILT, LEAN, BEVEL, OBLIQUE
slanting - - - ALIST, ATILT, ASKEW
slantways - - - - - - - - SLOPING
slap - - HIT, CUFF, REBUFF, BLOW, STRIKE, INSULT
slash - - - - - - SLIT, CUT, GASH
slat - - - - - - - - - - - - LATH
slate - ROCK, SCHEDULE, REPRIMAND, CENSURE
slate cutter's tool - - - - - - SAX
slate like rock - - - - - - - SHALE
slatted box - - - - - - - - CRATE
slattern - - - - - - - - TROLLOP
slaty - - - - - - - - LAMINATED
slaughter - - - - - - - MASSACRE
slaughter house - - - - - ABATTOIR
slaughter house (Sp.) - - MATADERO
Slav - - - - - - - - SERB, SERBIAN
slave - - - ESNE, SERF, BONDMAN, VASSAL, MINION, THRALL, HELOT, DRUDGE
slave of Sarah (Bib.) - - - - HAGAR
slave ship - - - - - - - - SLAVER
slavery - - - - - - - - BONDAGE
Slavic group - - - - - - SLOVENE
Slavic tribe - - - - - - - - SERB
slavish - - - - - - - - SERVILE
slay - - - - - - - MURDER, KILL
sleazy - - - - - - - - - FLIMSY
sled - - - SLEIGH, SLEDGE, TODE
sled for hauling logs - - - - TODE
sleek - - - - - - GLOSSY, MOLLIFY
sleep - REST, NAP, DOZE, SLUMBER
sleeping - - - - - - - - - - ABED
sleeping car accommodations - BERTH
sleeping lightly - - - - - - - DOZE
sleeping place (Eng. slang) - - DOSS
sleeping sound - - - - - - SNORING
sleepless - - - - - - - WAKEFUL
sleeplessness - - - - - - INSOMNIA
sleeplike state - - - - - - TRANCE
sleepy - - - DROWSY, LETHARGIC
sleeveless garment - - - ABA, CAPE
slender - SLIM, THIN, SVELTE, LANK, FRAIL
slender body of an arrow - - - STELE
slender bristle - - - - - - - AWN
slender finial - - - - - - - - EPI
slender fish - - - - - - - - GAR
slender graceful woman - - - SYLPH
slender prickle - - - - - - - SETA
slender rod - - - - - - - SPINDLE
slender spine - - - - - - - - SETA
slender stick - - - - - - - - WAND
slender streak - - - - - - - LINE
slender thread - - - - - - - FILM
sleuth - - - - - - - - - DETECTIVE
slew - - - - - - - - - - - INLET
slice - - SPLIT, CARVE, CUT, SHAVE, SLAB
slice thin - - - - - - - - SHAVE
sliced cabbage - - - - - - - SLAW
slick - - - - - - - - - - CLEVER
slid - - - - - - - - - - SLIPPED
slide - SKID, SLIP, SLITHER, COAST
slide down hill - - - - - - COAST
slide out of the course - - - - SLUE
sliding compartment - - - - DRAWER
sliding projection - - - - - - CAM

S

slight - - - SNUB, SCANT, TRIVIAL, IGNORE
slight amount - - - - - - - TRACE
slight breeze - - - - - - - BREATH
slight coloring - - - - - - - TINT
slight drink - - - - - - - - SIP
slight error - - - - - - - - LAPSE
slight intentionally - - - - - SNUB
slight knowledge - - - SMATTERING
slight offense - - - - - - - FAULT
slight sound - - - - - - - - PEEP
slight tremulous noise - - - TWITTER
slightest - - - - - - - - LEAST
slighting remark - - - - - - SLUR
slightly opened - - - - - - - AJAR
slightly sour - - - - - - ACIDULOUS
slim - SVELTE, SLENDER, SPARE, THIN
slime - - - - OOZE, MUCK, MUD
slimy sticky mixture - - - - - - MUD
sling - - - - FLING, HURL, SLUE
sling around - - - - - - - SLUE
sling stone - - - - - - - - PELLET
slip - - SLIDE, LAPSE, SKID, ERR, FAULT, GLIDE, ERROR, PETTICOAT
slip away - - - - - ELAPSE, ELOPE
slipped - - - - - - - - - - SLID
slipper - - - - - - MULE, SANDAL
slippery - - - - - - EELY, ELUSIVE
slipshod person - - - - - - SLOVEN
slit - - - - - - - - GASH, SLASH
slit apart - - - - - - - - UNRIP
slog - - - - - - - - - - - PLOD
slogan - - - - - - - - - - MOTTO
slop over - - - - - - - - - SPILL
slope - SLANT, INCLINE, DECLIVITY, SIDE, CANT, BEVEL, GRADIENT, RAMP, DIP
slope upward - - - - - CLIMB, RISE
sloping - - - - - - - - SLANTWAYS
sloping edge - - - - - - - - BEVEL
sloping letter - - - - - - - - ITALIC
sloping walk - - - - - - - - RAMP
slot - - - - - - - - - - GROOVE
sloth - - AI, INDOLENCE, ANIMAL, UNAU
slothfully - - - - - - - - - - IDLY
slouch - - - - - - - - - - DROOP
slough off - - - - - MOULT, MOLT
slovenly woman - - TROLLOP, SLOB, SLATTERN
slow - - - DELIBERATE, SLUGGISH, DILATORY, POKY, GRADUAL, RETARD
slow disintegration - - - - EROSION
slow leak - - - - - - - - - DRIP
slow at learning - - - - - - - DULL
slow lengthened utterance - - DRAWL
slow moving lemur - - - - - LORIS
slow moving person - - - - - SNAIL
slow (mus.) - LENTO, LARGO, RITARD
slow musical movement - - - ADAGIO
slow regular bell ringing - - TOLLING
slowed - - - - - - - - - RETARDED
sludgy - - - - - - - - - - MUDDY
slue - TWIST, SWAMP, VEER, PIVOT, SKID
sluggard - - - - - - - - - DRONE
sluggish - - INERT, LEADEN, SLOW, SUPINE, DULL, IDLE
sluggish inlet - - - - - - - BAYOU
sluggishness - - - - - - - INERTIA
slumber - - - - - - - NAP, SLEEP
slumber music - - - - - - LULLABY
slur - - ASPERSION, TRADUCE, SOIL, INNUENDO, REPROACH
slur over - - - - - - - - - ELIDE
sly - - - FOXY, CUNNING, ROGUISH, FURTIVE, CRAFTY, ARTFUL, ARCH, WILY, SHREWD
sly artifice - - - - - - - - - WILE
sly look - - - - - - - - - - LEER
sly (Scot.) - - - - - - - - - SLEE
smack - - - - - - STRIKE, SAVOR
small - - PETTY, ATOMIC, TRIVIAL, MINIATURE, PALTRY, PETITE, WEE, TINY, MINUTE, LITTLE, FEW, PETIT, LESS
small airship - - - - - - - BLIMP
small amount - TRACE, MITE, BIT, HAIR
small anchor - - - - - - - - KEDGE
small animal - - - INSECT, GENET, ORGANISM
small aquatic animal - - POLYP, NEWT
small arachnids - - - - - - MITES
small area - - - - - AREOLA, PLOT
small banner - BANNERET, BANDEROLE
small barracuda - - - - - - - SPET
small beard - - - - - - - GOATEE
small beetle - - - - - WEEVIL, FLEA
small bird - - TIT, VIREO, SPARROW, WREN, TODY, TOMTIT, FINCH, PEEWEE
small bite - - - - - - - - - - NIP
small boat - DORY, CANOE, CORACLE
small body of land - - - - - - ISLE
small booklet - - - - - - - FOLDER
small bottle - - - - - - - - - VIAL
small boy - - - - - - - - - - TAD
small branch - - - - - SPRIG, TWIG
small brook - RILL, RILLET, RIVULET
small bubble in glass - - - - - SEED
small bullet - - - - - - - - - SLUG
small bunch, as of hay - - - - - WISP
small bush - - - - - - - - - - RISE
small cake - - - - - - - - - - BUN
small candle - - - - - - DIP, TAPER
small carpel - - - - - - - ACHENE
small case - - - - - - - - - ETUI
small cask - - - - - - - - - - TUB
small cavity - - - - - - - - - CELL
small chicken - - - - - - - BANTAM
small child - - - - - - - - - - TAD
small chunk - - - - - - - - - GOB
small city - - - - - - - - - TOWN
small (comb. form) - - MICRO, LEPTO
small convex molding - - - - - REED
small creek - - - - - - - - - COVE
small crevice - - - - - - - - CHINK
small crustacean - - - - - ISOPOD
small cup - - - - - - - PANNIKIN
small dagger - - PONIARD, STILETTO
small deer - - - - - - - - - - ROE
small depression - - DINT, DENT, PIT
small detached piece - - - - - SCRAP
small dog - - - - - - - - - - PUG
small dog (colloq.) - - - - - - PEKE
small draft - - - - - - - - - SIP
small drink - - - DRAM, SIP, NIP
small drums - - - - - - - - TABORS
small drupe (obs.) - - - - - DRUPEL
small enclosure - - - - - PEN, COOP
small engine - - - - - - - - MOTOR
small European tree - - - - LENTISK
small finch - - - - - LINNET, SERIN
small fish - - MINNOW, ID, SHINER, IDE, SARDINE, FRY, DARTER, SMELT, DACE
small fishing vessel - - - - - SMACK
small flag - - - - - - - BANNERET
small flute - - - - - - - - PICCOLO
small fly - - - - - - - - - - GNAT
small fortification - - - - - REDOUBT
small glass bottle - - PHIAL, CRUET
small glass vessel - - - - - AMPULE

small globular body - - - - - BEAD
small graduated glass tube - BURETTE
small groove - - - - - - - STRIA
small handful - - - - - - - WISP
small harbor - - - - - - - COVE
small hat - - - - - - - - TOQUE
small heron - - - - - - - BITTERN
small herring - - - - - - - SPRAT
small hog - - - - - - - - - PIG
small hole in garment - - - EYELET
small horse - BIDET, PONY, NAG, COB
small house - - CABIN, COTTAGE, COT
small iced cake - - - - - - ECLAIR
small inland body of water - - BROOK
small inlet - - - - - - - COVE, RIA
small insect - - - - - MIDGE, APHID
small insectivore - - - - - TENREC
small interstice - - - - - - AREOLA
small iron vessel (Scot.) - - YETLING
small lake - - - - - - - - MERE
small (law) - - - - - - - - PETIT
small light - - - - - - - - TAPER
small loop - - - - - PICOT, TAB
small lunar crater - - - - - - LINNE
small mass - - - LUMP, WAD, PAT
small medal - - - - - - MEDALET
small merganser - - - - - - SMEW
small monkey - - - - - TITI, MONO, MARMOSET
small mug - - - - - - - - NOGGIN
small musical instrument - - OCARINA
small napkin - - - - - - - - DOILY
small number - - - - - - - - FEW
small opening - GAP, CRANNY, EYELET
small ornament - - - - - - BEAD
small part - - - - - - - SNIPPET
small part in performance - - - BIT
small part of whole - - - - - DETAIL
small particle - - - - - - TRINKET
small particle of fire - - - - SPARK
small particle of liquid - - - - DROP
small pavilion - - - - - - - KIOSK
small pebbles - - - - - - - GRAVEL
small perforated disk - - - WASHER
small person - - - - - - - - RUNT
small person or things - - - - - FRY
small piece - CHIP, PARTICLE, MISSEL, SCRAP
small piece of fire - - - - - SPARK
small piece of lumber - - SCANTLING
small piece of paper - - - - - - SLIP
small piece (Scot.) - - - - - - TATE
small pitcher - - - - - - - - TOBY
small plate - - - - - - - - SAUCER
small plot - - - - - - - - - BED
small pocket - - - - - - - - FOB
small point - - - - - - - - - DOT
small pointed process - - - - - AWN
small portion - - - - - TASTE, DAB
small quantity - - - - - - - - IOTA
small quantity of liquor - - - - DRAM
small quarrel - - - - - - SPAT, TIFF
small reed organ - - - - MELODEON
small report - - - - - - - - - POP
small rich cake - - - - - MADELINE
small rill - - - - - - - - - RILLET
small ring - - - - - - - - RINGLET
small river fish - - - - - - - DACE
small room - - - - - - - - - CELL
small root - - - - - - - - RADICEL
small rough house - - - - - SHACK
small Russian sturgeon - - - - STERLET
small (Scot.) - - - - - - - - SMA
small seed - - SEEDLET, CORN, PIP
small share - - - - - - - - MOIETY

small shark - - - - - - - - - TOPE
small shoot - - - - - - - - - SPRIG
small songbird - - - - - - - - VIREO
small spar - - - - - - - - - SPRIT
small speck - - - - - - - - - NIT
small square moulding - - - - LINTEL
small stipule of leaflet - - - - STIPEL
small strait - - - - - - - - - GUT
small stream - - - - - - - RUN, RILL
small sturgeon - - - - - - - STERLET
small surface - - - - - - - - FACET
small swallow - - - - - - - - - SIP
small sweet cake - - - - - CRULLER
small table - - - - - - - - - STAND
small talk - - - - - - - - - CHAT
small tower - - - - - - - - TURRET
small tree - - - - - - - - - MYRTLE
small triangular piece - - - - GUSSET
small and trim - - - - - - - PETITE
small vessel to heat liquids - - ETNA
small village - - - - - - - - DORP
small violin - - - - - - - - - - KIT
small and weak - - - - - - - - PUNY
small weight - - - - - DRAM, MITE
small wood - - - - - - - - - GROVE
small wooden cup - - - - - NOGGIN
smaller - - - - MINOR, LESSER, LESS
smaller particles (of) - - - - - FINER
smaller of two - - - - - - - LESSER
smallest - - - - - - - - - - LEAST
smallest elemental particle - - - ATOM
smallest integer - - - - - - - - ONE
smallest liquid measure - - - - MINIM
smallest particle - - - - - - - WHIT
smallest planet - - - - - - MERCURY
smallest whole number - - - - - UNIT
smallness - - - - - - - - PETTINESS
smart - TRIG, CLEVER, STING, SHREWD, CHIC, DASHING, BRIGHT
smart blow - - - - - - - - - - RAP
smarten - - - - - - - - - - SPRUCE
smartness - - - - - - - CLEVERNESS
smash - - - - - - - CRASH, SHATTER
smear - - DAUB, BEDAUB, SMUDGE, SMIRCH, PLASTER, STAIN, SOIL
smear (var.) - - - - - - - - SPLATCH
smear with fat - - - - - - - - LARD
smell - - - - - OLID, ODOR, SCENT
smile - - - - - - - - - - - - GRIN
smile foolishly - - - - - - - SIMPER
smile superciliously - - - - - - SMIRK
smiling - - - - - - - - - - - RIANT
smirch - - - - - SOIL, SMEAR, STAIN
smirk - - - - - - - - SIMPER, GRIN
smite - - - - - - - - - - - - - HIT
smith's iron block - - - - - - ANVIL
smitten - - - - - - - - - AFFLICTED
smoke - - - - SMUDGE, FUME, REEK
smoke flue - - - - - - FUNNEL, STACK
smoke pipe - - - - - - - - FUNNEL
smoked meat and smoked pork - HAM
smoking leaves - - - - - - TOBACCOS
smokeless powder - - - - - - CORDITE
smokestack - - - - - - - - - FUNNEL
smoldering fragment - - - - - EMBER
smooth - SLEEK, LENE, SAND, LEVEL, EVEN, PLANE, IRON, GLASSY, GREASY, GLIB, PAVE, EASE
smooth, as with beak - - - - PREEN
smooth breathing - - - - - - - LENE
smooth and connected (mus.) - LEGATO
smooth consonant - - - - - - - LENE
smooth and glossy - - - - - - SLEEK
smooth over - - - - - - - - PLASTER
smooth and self-satisfied - - - SMUG

smooth and shining - - - - WAXEN
smooth skinned berry - - - - GRAPE
smooth spoken - - - - - - - GLIB
smoothed - EVENED, IRONED, PAVED, PLANED, MOLLIFIED
smoothing implement - - SADIRON, PLANER, SCRAPER, PLANE
smoothly - - - - - - - - - EASILY
smoothly cut - - - - - - - - SECTILE
smoothly polite - - - - - - SUAVE
smote - - - - - - - - - STRUCK
smother - - - - - - - - - STIFLE
smothered laugh - - - - - SNICKER
smudge - - - BLOT, SMOKE, SMEAR
smug person - - - - - - - GIGMAN
smut - - - - - - - - - - CROOK
Smyrna figs (brand) - - - - ELEME
snag - - - - - - - - - OBSTACLE
snail (soft) - - - - SLUG, DRONE
snailflower - - - - - - - CARACOL
snake - - ASP, RACER, BOA, ADDER, SERPENT, VIPER, REPTILE
snake bird - - - - - - - - DARTER
snake (black) - - - - - - - RACER
snake in the grass - - - - ENEMY
snake which crushes its prey - - BOA
snakelike fish - - - - - - - - EEL
snaky haired spirit - - - - ERINYS
snap - - CRACK, CLIP, WAFER, BITE, FASTENER, COOKY, CRACKLE, FLIP, SNECK
snap with fingers - - - - - - FILLIP
snapper - - - - FASTENER, TURTLE
snappish bark - - - - - - - - YAP
snappy - - - - - - - - - - BRISK
snare - NET, ENTRAP, TRAP, ENTANGLE, PITFALL, SPRINGE, NOOSE, BENET, DRUM, WEB, GIN
snare under a net - - - - - - BENET
snarl - - - TANGLE, GNAR, GROWL
snarly - - - - - - - - - - SURLY
snatch - - - - - NAB, GRAB, WREST
snatch forcibly - - - - - - WREST
snatch (slang) - - - - - - - SWIPE
sneaky - - - - - - - - - FURTIVE
sneck - - - - - - - - - - - SNAP
snee - - - - - - - - - - - DIRK
sneer - GIBE, SCOFF, TAUNT, MOCK, DERIDE
snicker - - - - - - - - - GIGGLE
snide - - - - - - - - MEAN, BASE
sniff - - - - - - - - - - - NOSE
snip - - - CLIP, SHRED, FRAGMENT
snipe - - - - - - - - - - WADER
snood - - - - - - - - - - FILLET
snoop - - - - PRY, PROWL, PEER
snout - - - - PROBOSCIS, MUZZLE
snow - - - - - - - NEVE, WHITEN
snow leopard - - - - - - - OUNCE
snow runner - - - - - - SKI, SKEE
snow runners (var.) - - - - - SKEES
snowshoe (kind) - - - - - - - SKI
snowy - - - - WHITE, SPOTLESS
snub - - - SLIGHT, REBUFF, REBUKE
snub nosed - - - - - - - - - PUG
snuff (pungent) - - - - - - RAPPEE
snuff a candle (Scot.) - - - - SNET
snug - - - - - - - - COSY, COZY
snug retreat - - - - - - DEN, NEST
snug room - - - - - - - - - DEN
snuggle - - - - NESTLE, CUDDLE
so - - - - - - THUS, ERGO, HENCE
so be it - - - - - - - - - - AMEN
so far - - - - - - - - - - THUS
so (Scot.) - - - - - - - - SIC, SAE
soak - - RET, SOP, SOG, DRENCH, SATURATE, STEEP
soak in brine - - - - - - MARINATE
soak flax - - - - - - - - - - RET
soak hide - - - - - - - - - BATE
soak thoroughly - - - - - SATURATE
soaked cracker dish - - - - PANADA
soaked with moisture - - - - SODDEN
soap ingredient - - - - - - - LYE
soap frame part - - - - - - - SESS
soap plant - - - - - - - - AMOLE
soap substitute - - - - - - AMOLE
soapstone - - - - - - - - - TALC
soapy feeling mineral - - - - TALC
soapy frothy water - - - - - - SUDS
soar - - - - - - TOWER, RISE, FLY
sob - - - - - - - - - - - - SIGH
sobeit - - - - - - - - - - - AMEN
sober - - SEDATE, SERIOUS, STAID, GRAVE, SOLEMN, ABSTINENT, DEMURE
sociable - - - NICE, GREGARIOUS
social affair - TEA, RECEPTION, DANCE, PARTY
social class - - - - - - - - CASTE
social division - - - - - - - TRIBE
social error (colloq.) - - - - - BONER
social function - - - - - - - DANCE
social gathering - - - - - PARTY, TEA
social group - - - - - - - - TRIBE
social outcast - - - - LEPER, PARIAH
social position - - - - - - - CASTE
social standing - - - - - - CASTE
social unit - - - CLAN, SEPT, TRIBE, CASTE
society bud (colloq.) - - - - - DEB
society class - - - - - - - CASTE
socks - - - - - - - - - - - HOSE
Socrates' wife - - - - - - XANTIPPE
sod - - SWARD, DIRT, TURF, EARTH, SOIL, GLEBE
sod (poet.) - - - - - - - - - GLEBE
soda - - - - - - - - - - - - POP
soda ash - - - - - - - - - ALKALI
sodden - - - - - - - - - - SOGGY
sodium - - - - - - - - - N.A., SAL
sodium bicarbonate - - - - SALERATUS
sodium carbonate (kind) - - - - TRONA
sodium chloride - - - - - - SALT, SAL
sodium nitrate - - - - - - - NITER
sofa - - - - DIVAN, SETTEE, LOUNGE
soft - TENDER, DOWNY, PLIABLE, LOW, MILD, MELLOW, MALLEABLE, YIELDING
soft candy - - - - - - - - - FUDGE
soft cheese - - - - - - - - - BRIE
soft drink - - - - - - - - SODA, POP
soft fabric - - - - - VELVET, PLUSH
soft feathers - - - - - - - - DOWN
soft food - - - - - - - - - - PAP
soft fruit part - - - - - - - - PULP
soft hat - - - - - - - - FEDORA, CAP
soft hematite - - - - - - - - - ORE
soft leather - - NAPA, SUEDE, ROAN
soft limestone - - - - - - - - CHALK
soft mass - - - - - - - - - - PULP
soft metal - - - - - - - - - - TIN
soft mineral - - - - - - - - - TALC
soft mud - - - - - - - SLUDGE, MIRE
soft murmur - - - - - - - PURR, COO
soft ointment from oil - - - OLEAMEN
soft palate - - - - - - - - - UVULA
soft pedal (mus. abbr.) - - - - - UC
soft resins - - - - - - - - ANIMES
soft roll - - - - - - - - - - - BUN
soft shoe - - - - - - - - MOCCASIN
soft silk thread - - - - - - - FLOSS

soft sticky substance - - - - - SLIME
soft substance - - - - - - - - PAP
soft twilled silk - - - - - - - SURAH
soften - - - RELENT, INTENERATE, MELLOW, MITIGATE, RELENT
soften by soaking - - - - MACERATE
soften in temper - - - - - - - RELENT
soften in tone - - - - - - - - MUTE
softening - - - - - - - MELLOWING
softly - - - - - - - - - - - - LOW
soggy - - - - - - - - - - SODDEN
soggy mass - - - - - - - - - SOP
soil - MESS, DIRT, EARTH, BEGRIME, SMIRCH, COUNTRY, LAND, DEFILE, MOIL, SOD, DIRTY, SULLY, SLUR, TARNISH, MIRE
soil (kind) - - - - MARL, LOAM, CLAY
soil (poet.) - - - - - - - - GLEBE
soil with mud - - - - - - - - MIRE
sojourn - - - - - - - ABIDE, STAY
solace - - - - - COMFORT, CONSOLE
solan - - - - - - - - - - GANNET
solar - - - - - - - - - HELIACAL
solar disc - - - - - - - ATEN, ATON
solar phenomenon - - - - - - CARONA
solar (var.) - - - - - - - - - ATON
solar year excess - - - - - - EPACT
solemn assertion - - - - - - OATH
solder - - - - - - - - - - CEMENT
soldering flux - - - - - - - ROSIN
soldier's bag - - - - - HAVERSACK
soldier - - - - - - - - - WARRIOR
solder's cap - - - - - BERET, SHAKO
soldier's cloak - - - CAPOTE, SAGUM
soldier line - - - - - - - - - FILE
soldier (pert. to) - - - - - MILITARY
soldier in the rank - - - - - PRIVATE
soldiers - - - - - - - - - TROOPS
sole - ONE, ONLY, LONE, INDIVIDUAL
sole of foot - - - - - - - - PLANTAR
sole of plow - - - - - - - - SLADE
solely - - - - - - - - - ALL, ONLY
solemn - - SOBER, GRAVE, SERIOUS, SOMBER
solemn assertion - - - - OATH, VOW
solemn attestation of truth - - - OATH
solemn looking - - - - - - - OWLISH
solemn wonder - - - - - - - - AWE
solicit - BEG, ASK, CANVASS, CANVAS, URGE, COURT, WOO, PETITION, REQUEST, PLEAD
solicit (colloq.) - - - - - - - TOUT
solicitude - - - - - - - - - CARE
solid - HARD, FIRM, COMPACT, RIGID, PRISM, COMPACT
solid (comb. form) - - - - - STEREO
solid figure - - - - - - - - - CONE
solid food - - - - - - - - - MEAT
solid higher alcohols - - - - STEROL
solid mass of matter - - - - - CAKE
solid silver - - - - - - - - STERLING
solidified mass - - - - - - - - CAKE
solidify - - - - - SET, HARDEN, GEL
soliloquy - - - - - - - MONOLOGUE
solitary - - - - - - - LONE, ALONE
solitary (comb. form) - - - - EREMO
solitude - - - - - - - - ISOLATION
solo - - - - - ARIA, LONE, SINGLE
Solomon's son - - - - - - REHOBOAM
solon - - - - - - - - - - - SAGE
solution - - - - - - ANSWER, KEY
solution (abbr.) - - - - - - - - ANS.
solution from ashes - - - - - - LYE
solution in tanning - - - - - - SIG
solve - - - - - - - SEE, EXPLAIN
somber - - SOLEMN, GRAVE, LENTEN
some - - - - - - - ONE, ANY, FEW
some other place - - - ELSEWHERE
some person or thing - - - - - ONE
something added - - - - - - INSERT
something attached - - - - - - TAG
something easy (slang) - - - - - PIE
something found - - - - - - TROVE
something new - - - - - - NOVELTY
something owed - - - - - - - DEBIT
something that injures - - DETRIMENT
something to awaken memory - - - - MEMENTO
sometime - - - - - FORMER, ONCE
sometimes frozen - - - - - - - ASSET
somewhat - - - - - - - - - RATHER
somite - - METAMAERE, METAMERE
Somme city - - - - - - - AMIENS
son - - - - - - - - - - - - SCION
son of (prefix) - - - - - - - - - AP
sonance - - - - - - - - - - SOUND
song - MELODY, BALLAD, DITTY, AIR, LAY, CANTICLE, CAROL, LILT
song bird - - - WREN, VIREO, ROBIN
song of gallantry - - - - - SERENADE
song (gay) - - - - - - LILT, CAROL
song of joy or praise - PAEAN, PAEON
song of joy or praise (var.) - - PEAN
song thrush - - - - - - - - MAVIS
song of triumph - - - - - - PAEAN
song verse - - - - - - - - - LYRIC
sonnet part - - - - - - - - SESTET
Sonoran Indian - - - - - - - - SERI
sonorous - - - - - - - - RESONANT
sonorous body - - - - - - - - BELL
soon - - - ANON, EARLY, SHORTLY, PROMPTLY, ERE
sooner than - - - - - - - - - ERE
soot - - - - - - - CARBON, SMUT
soothe - EASE, ALLAY, PACIFY, CALM, QUIET
soothing - DREAMY, BALMY, ALLAYING
soothing exclamation - - - - - THERE
soothing medicine - - - PAREGORIC, ANODYNE
soothing ointment - - BALM, BALSAM
soothsayer - - SEER, DIVINER, AUGUR
soothsaying - - - - - - - - AUGURY
sooty - - - - - - - - - - BLACKEN
sooty albatross - - - - - - - NELLY
sop - - - - - - STEEP, BRIBE, SOAK
sora - - - - - - - - - - - - RAIL
sorcerer - - - - - - - - - - - MAGI
sorcerer (pl.) - - - - - - - MAGES
sorceress - - - - - - - - - WITCH
sorcery - - - - - - - - - - MAGIC
sordid - - - - - - - - - - - BASE
sore - AFFLICTION, PAINFUL, ANGRY, HURTFUL, DISTRESSING, TENDER
sore (kind) - - - - - - - - - ULCER
sorrow - - - DOLOUR, WOE, REPINE, MOURN, PINE, SADNESS, PENANCE, GRIEVE, GRIEF
sorrow (exclamation of) - - - - ALAS
sorrowful - - SADDEN, MOURNFUL, CONTRITE
sorrowful sinner - - - - - PENITENT
sorrowful state - - - - - - - - WOE
sorrowing for misdeeds - - REPENTING
sorrows for sin - - - - - PENITENCE
sorry - REGRET, PITIABLE, GRIEVED, CONTRITE, REGRETFUL
sorry (be) - - - - - - - - - REPENT
sort - - SIFT, KIND, ILK, VARIETY, MANNER, SEGREGATE, CULL, CLASS,

S

CLASSIFY, TYPE, GRADE
sortie - - - - - - - - - SALLY
sot - - - - - - - TOPER, TIPPLER
soul - - - SPIRIT, ESPRIT, PNEUMA, ESSENCE, PERSON
soul (Fr.) - - - - - - - - - - AME
sound - - - VALID, SONANCE, SANE, NOISE, TONE
sound accompanying breathing - - RALE
sound of auto horn - - - - - HONK
sound of bees on wing - - - - HUM
sound of, or as a bell - - DING, TOLL
sound of bells (rare) - - - - TINK
sound of disapproval - - - - HISS
sound of distress - - - - - - MOAN
sound of dry leaves - - - - RUSTLE
sound to frighten - - - - - - BOO
sound loudly - - - - - - - BLARE
sound of a mule - - - - - - BRAY
sound (pert. to) - - - - - - TONAL
sound resonantly - - - - - - RING
sound smoothly - - - - - - - PUR
sound state - - - - - - - - WEAL
sound of surf - - - - - - - ROTE
sound of trumpet - - - BLARE, BLAST
Sound in Washington - - - - PUGET
sound waves (pert. to) - - - SONIC
soundness - - - - - - - STRENGTH
sounds - - - - - TONES, NOISES
soup - - - POTTAGE, BROTH, PUREE, BISQUE
soup (kind) - - - - - - - - OKRA
soup (thick) - - - - - - - PUREE
soup dish, ladle and vessel - TUREEN
sour - - ACID, ACERB, TART, ACETIC, ACRID, MOROSE, ACETOSE
sour in aspect - - - - - - - DOUR
sour grass - - - - - - - - SORREL
sour substance - - - - - - - ACID
source - ORIGIN, FONT, FOUNT, ROOT, SEED, RISE
source of heat - - - - - - STEAM
source of heat and light - - - - GAS
source of help - - - - - RECOURSE
source of iodine - - - - - - - KELP
source of light - - - - - SUN, LAMP
source of malic acid - - - - - APPLE
source of medicinal oil - - - - ODAL
source of natural indigo - - INDICAN
source of oil - - - - - - - OLIVE
source of ore - - - - - - - MINE
source of perfume - - - - - - MUSK
source of phosphorous compounds - - APATITE
source of potassium salts - - - SALIN
source of power - - - - - - MOTOR
source of splendor - - - - - - SUN
source of sugar - - - - - - - CANE
source of water - - - - - - - WELL
source of wealth - - MINE, GOLCONDA
souse - - SATURATE, PICKLE, DRENCH
South African - - - - - - - - BOER
South African animal - - SURICATE, RATEL
South African antelope - ELAND, GNU
South African country - - - SHEBA
South African district - - - - RAND
South African Dutch - - TAAL, BOER
South African farmer - - - - - BOER
South African fox - - - - ASSE, CAAMA
South African grassland - VELD, VELDT
South African legislative assembly - - RAAD
South African native - KAFIR, BANTU
South African pastureland - - VELDT
South African plateau - - - KAROO
South African province - - TRANSVAAL
South African strips of oxhide - RIEMS
South African thong - - - - - RIEM
South African tribesman - BANTU, ZULU
South African underground stream - AAR
South African village - - - - - KRAAL
South African weaverbird - - - TAHA
South African wooden hammock - KATEL
South American animal - TAPIR, LLAMA, TAYRA
South American arrow poison - CURARE
South American beverage - - - MATE
South American bird - - SCREAMER, SERIEMA, RARA, ARA, TERUTERO, TINAMOU, AGAMI
South American cape - - - - - HORN
South American city - - - - - - ITA
South American dance - - - SAMBA
South American duck - - - - - PATO
South American fish - - - - - AIMARA
South American hare - - - - - TAPETI
South American humming bird - SYLPH
South American Indian - ONA, CARIB, GE, CARIL, MAYAN, INCA
South American laborer - - - - PEON
South American linguistic family - ONAN
South American missile weapon - BOLA
South American mountains - - ANDES, ANDEAN
South American ostrich - - - - RHEA
South American plain - LLANO, PAMPA
South American plain wind - PAMPERO
South American rabbit - - - - TAPETI
South American region - - PATAGONIA
South American republic - - - - PERU
South American river - - APA, PLATA, AMAZON, ORINOCO, ACRE, PARA
South American rodent - PACA, RATEL, TAPIR
South American serpents - - ABOMA, BOAS
South American timber tree - - CAROB
South American tree - MORA, BALSA, CAROB
South American tree snake - - - LORA
South American tuber - - - - - OCA
South American weapon - BOLAS, BOLO
South American wood sorrel - - - OCA
South Dakota capital - - - - PIERRE
southeast wind - - - - - - EURUS
southeast wind of Persian Gulf - - - SHARKI
southern bird - - - - - - - - ANI
southern endearment - - - - - HONEY
South of France - - - - - - - MIDI
South Pacific island - - - PITCAIRN, TAHITI
South Sea canoe - - - - - - PROA
South Sea island - - - BALI, SAMOA
South Sea islander - KANAKA, SAMOAN
southern Slav - - - - - - SLOVENE
southwest wind - - - - - ANER, AFER
southwestern Indian - NAVAHO, HOPIS
souvenir - - - - - MEMENTO, RELIC
sovereign - - - - - RULER, MONARCH
Soviet - - - - - - - - - COUNCIL
sow - PLANT, SEED, SWINE, STREW
spa - - - - - - - SPRING, RESORT
space - - ROOM, AREA, TIME, VOID, DISTANCE
space above door - - - - PEDIMENT
space between bird's eye and bill - - LORAL

space between diverging mouths of river - DELTA
space between net cords - - - - MESH
space between points - - - - DISTANCE
space between two hills - - - - DALE
space devoid of matter - - - - VACUUM
space for goods - - - - - STORAGE
space surrounding castle - - - AMBIT
space theory - - - - - - PLENISM
spaced - - - - - - - SEPARATED
spacious - - ROOMY, BROAD, LARGE
spade - - - - - - - - - SPUD, DIG
spall - - - - - - - - - - - CHIP
span - - - CROSS, REACH, EXTENT, INTERVAL, TEAM, BRIDGE, ARCH
span of horses - - - - - - - - TEAM
spangle - - - - - - - - GLITTER
Spaniard - - - - - - - - IBERIAN
spaniel (kind) - - - - - - SPRINGER
Spanish - - - - - - - - CASTILIAN
Spanish-American cotton cloth - MANTA
Spanish-American farm - - HACIENDA
Spanish-American foreigner - GRINGO
Spanish article - - EL, LA, LAS, LOS
Spanish artist - - - - - - - - GOYA
Spanish building material - - TAPIA
Spanish cathedral city - - - SEVILLE
Spanish channel - - - - - - CANO
Spanish city - IRUN, CADIZ, TOLEDO
Spanish cloth - - - - - - - - LENO
Spanish coin - - - PESETA, PESO, CENTAVO, REAL
Spanish commune - - - - - - IRUN
Spanish conductor - - - - - ITURBI
Spanish conqueror of Mexico - CORTEZ
Spanish cooking pot - - ALLA, OLLA
Spanish dance - BOLERO, JOTA, TANGO
Spanish dance (lively) - - GUARACHA
Spanish dollar - - - - - - - - PESO
Spanish farewell - - - - - - - ADIOS
Spanish feast days - - - - - FIESTAS
Spanish gentleman - CABALLERO, DON
Spanish griddle cake - - - - - AREPA
Spanish hall - - - - - - - - - SALA
Spanish head covering - - MANTILLA
Spanish hero - - - - - - - - - CID
Spanish horse - - - - GENET, JENNET
Spanish house - - - - - - - - CASA
Spanish king's palace - - - ESCORIAL
Spanish lariat - - - REATA, RIATA
Spanish legislature chamber - CAMERA
Spanish mackerel - - - - - BONITA
Spanish measure - - VARA, CANTARA
Spanish nobleman - - - - - HIDALGO
Spanish painter - - - - - - - GOYA
Spanish peninsula - - - - - IBERIA
Spanish priest - - - - CURE, PADRE
Spanish province - - - - - - LERIDA
Spanish river - - EBRO, ORO, MINO
Spanish room - - - - - - - - SALA
Spanish rope - - - - - - - - RIATA
Spanish shawl - - - - SERAPE, MANTA
Spanish title of address - DON, SENOR, SENORA
Spanish war hero - - - - - HOBSON
Spanish weapon - - - - - - BOLAS
Spanish weight - - - - - - ARROBA
spanner - - - - - - - - - WRENCH
spanning - - - - - - - - - ACROSS
spar - - - - MAST, SPRIT, BOX, YARD
spar end - - - - - - - - - - - ARM
spar to extend sail - - - - - - YARD
spar to stow - - - - - - - - STEEVE
spare - - LEAN, DISPOSABLE, SAVE, DESIST, RESERVE, STINT, OMIT, SLIM, EXTRA, TIRE, GAUNT
spare time - - - - - - - - LEISURE
sparing - - - - - - - - - CHARY
spark - - - - - - - FLASH, GALLANT
sparkle - GLISTEN, FLASH, GLITTER, GLEAM
sparkler - - - - - - - - - LIGHTER
sparkling - - - - - - - - - STARRY
sparoid fish - - - - - GAR, SAR, TAI
sparrow hawk - - - - - - - KESTREL
sparse - - - SCANTY, SCARCE, THIN, SCANT
Spartan - STOIC, BRAVE, RIGOROUS, HARDY
Spartan army division - - - - - MORA
Spartan bondsman - - - - - - HELOT
Spartan serf and slave - - - - HELOT
spasm - - - - - - - - - - - - TIC
spasmodic breaths - - - - - - GASPS
spasmodic exhalation - - - - SNEEZE
spasmodic musculc - - - - - - CRICK
spasmodic twitch - - - - - - - - TIC
spat - GAITER, TIFF, ARGUMENT, ROW
spate - - - - - - - FRESHET, FLOOD
spatial - - - - - - - - - - STERIC
spatter - - - - - SPRINKLE, SPLASH
speak - - - - - - - - ORATE, UTTER
speak contemptuously - - - - SNEER
speak covertly - - - - - - WHISPER
speak in defense - - - - - - PLEAD
speak haltingly - - - - - STAMMER
speak imperfectly - - LISP, STUTTER
speak from memory - - - - - RECITE
speak of - - - - - - - - MENTION
speak rhetorically - - - - - DECLAIM
speak from Scriptural text - - PREACH
speak sharply - - - - - - - - SNAP
speak slightingly of - - - - DISPARAGE
speak in slow tone - - - - - - DRAWL
speak softly - - - - - - - - WHISPER
speak stumblingly - - - - - - STUTTER
speak in surly manner - - - - SNARL
speak under the breath - - - - MUTTER
speak with affectation - - - - MINCE
speak with hesitation - - - - - HAW
speak with violence - - - - - - RAGE
speaking imperfectly - - - - - ALISP
speaking many languages - POLYGLOT
spear - - DART, HARPOON, JAVELIN, LANCE, PIKE, ARROW, TRIDENT
spear of grass - - - - - - - - BLADE
special - PARTICULAR, NOTEWORTHY
special causes of legal action - - - - GRAVAMINA, GRAVAMEN
special countenance - - PATRONAGE
special day - - - - - - - - - FEAST
special gift - - - - - - - - TALENT
special writer - - - - - COLUMNIST
specialist in mental disorders - ALIENIST
specie - - - - - - - - - - - CASH
specie (pl.) - - - - - - - - GENRE
species - - - - - - - - - - GENUS
species of banana - - - - PLANTAIN
species of cassia - - - - - - SENNA
species of cedar - - - - - - DEODAR
species of geese - - - - - - BRANT
species of hickory - - - - - - PECAN
species of iris - - - - - - - ORRIS
species of loon - - - - - - - DIVER
species of lyric poem - - - - EPODE
species of pepper - - - - BETEL, KAVA
species of pier (arch.) - - - - ANTA
species of valerian - - - - - - NARD
specific - - CONCRETE, DETERMINATE
specific behaviour - - - - TREATMENT

S

specified epoch - - - - - - - AGE
specify - - - - - NAME, MENTION
specimen - - - - - - - - SAMPLE
specious - - - - - - - PLAUSIBLE
speck - - - DOT, SPOT, MOTE, JOT, BLEMISH, NIT
speck of dust - - - - - - - MOTE
speckle - - - - - - STIPPLE, DOT
spectacle - - - - - PARADE, DISPLAY
spectator - - - - - - - OBSERVER
specter - - - - - - GHOST, SPIRIT
speculate - - - - - - CONJECTURE
speculative undertaking - - VENTURE
speculum - - - - - - - - - MIRROR
speech - - DIALECT, VOICE, ORATION
speech defect - - - - - STUTTERING
speech (long, abusive) - - - TIRADE
speech part - - - ADJECTIVE, NOUN, PREPOSITION
speech (pert. to) - - - - - - VOCAL
speech (slang) - - - - - - - LINGO
speech sound (type of) - - CONSONANT
speechless - - - - - - - - - MUTE
speed - - RACE, HASTE, HIE, PACE, RAPIDITY, RUN, RAN, RUSH
speedily - - - - - - APACE, PRESTO
speedy - - - - - FAST, FLEET, RAPID
spell - - - TRANCE, RELIEVE, CHARM
spell of duty - - - - - - - - TRICK
spelter - - - - - - - - - - ZINC
Spenser character - - - UNA, ENID
spend - - - - - EXHAUST, DISBURSE
spend lavishly - - - - - - - POUR
spend needlessly - - - - - - WASTE
spend time idly - - - - LOITER, LAZE
spender - - - - - - - - - WASTER
spendthrift - - - - - - - - WASTREL
sphagnum bog - - - - - - MUSKEG
sphere - ORB, GLOBE, BALL, ARENA
sphere of action - - - - - - ARENA
sphere extremity - - - - - - - POLE
spherical - - - ROUND, GLOBULAR, ORBICULAR, GLOBATE
spherical body - - - - - - - - ORB
spherical mass - - - - - - - BALL
spherical particle - - - - - GLOBULE
spheroid - - - - - - - - - - BALL
sphinxine - - - - - - MYSTERIOUS
spice - - MACE, GINGER, SEASONING, ZEST
spicy - - - - - - - - - AROMATIC
spider - - - ARACHNID, TARANTULA, SPINNER
spider bugs - - - - - - - EMESA
spiders - - - - - - - - - ARANEIDA
spigot - - - - - - - - - - - TAP
spike - - - - - - - - - - - NAIL
spike in center of shield - - - - UMBO
spike of cereal - - - - - - - - EAR
spike of corn - - - - - - - EAR, COB
spike of flowers - - - - - - AMENT
spike of a fork - - - - - PRONG, TINE
spike-nosed fish - - - - - - - GAR
spikenard - - - - - - - - NA, NARD
spill - - SHED, TUMBLE, DOWNPOUR, SLOP
spin - REEL, TURN, WHILE, ROTATE, TWIRL, WEAVE, WHIRL, REVOLVE
spinal - - - - - - - - VERTEBRAL
spinate - - - - - - - - - THORNY
spindle - - - - - - - - - - AXLE
spindle thread roll - - - - - - COP
spinner - - - - - - - SPIDER, TOP
spinning machine tube - - - - COP
spinning mill - - - - - - SPINNERY
spinning motion - - - - - - SWIRL
spinning toy - - - - - - - - TOP
spinning wheel part - - - - SPINDLE
spiny animal - - - - - - - TENREC
spiral - COIL, HELICAL, COILED, HELIX
spiral ornament - - - - - - HELIX
spiral staircase - - - - - CARACOLE
spirate - - - - - - - - - VOICELESS
spire - - - EPI, STEEPLE, SUMMIT
spirit - - ELAN, DEMON, VIM, SOUL, METTLE, DASH, HEART, GHOST, ELF, ANIMATION, SPECTER
spirit in human form - - - - - FAIRY
spirit in The Tempest - - - - - ARIEL
spirit of the dead - - - - - MANES
spirit of evil - - SATAN, MARA, MORA
spirit lamp - - - - - - - - - ETNA
spirit of nature - - - - - - - GENIE
spirit of the people - - - - - ETHOS
spirit of the water - - - - - - ARIEL
spirited - - - - - - - FIERY, LIVELY
spirited horse - STEED, ARAB, COURSER
spirited opposition (in) - - - - ATILT
spiritless - AMORT, DULL, DEJECTED, VAPID, MOPY
spiritlike - - - - - - - - ETHEREAL
spirits and water mixture - - - GROG
spiritual - - - - - - - - - - AERY
spiritual beings - ESSENCES, ANGELS
spiritual meaning of words - ANAGOGE
spiritual nourishment - - - - MANNA
spiritual overseer - - - - - PASTOR
spiritual session - - - - - - SEANCE
spirituous liquor - - - - - - WINE
spite - - - PIQUE, VENOM, THWART, RANCOR, MALICE
spiteful - - - - - - - - MALICIOUS
spiteful person - - - - - - - WASP
spiteful woman - - - - - - - - CAT
spitefulness - - - - - - - SPLEEN
spittles - - - - - - - - - SALIVAS
splash - - - - - SPLATTER, SPATTER
splash over - - - - - - - - SPILL
splatter - - - - - - - SPLASH, DAB
splay - - - - - - - - - - EXPAND
spleen - - - - - - - - - - - MILT
splendid - - - - - - - - - SUPERB
splendid (Scot.) - - - - - - - BRAW
splendour - - - - - - ECLAT, GLORY
splice - - - - - - - - - - - UNITE
splinter - - - - - - SLIVER, SHIVER
split - - RIVE, RIVET, REND, RIVEN, SLICE, TEAR, CHAP, CLEAVE, DISRUPT
split asunder - - - - - - - - RIVEN
split leather - - - - - - - - SKIVER
split pulse - - - - - - - - - DAL
splotch - - - - - - - - - - BLOT
spoil - - ADDLE, IMPAIR, MAR, ROT, TAINT, VITIATE, PLUNDER, LOOT, BOOTY, PAMPER
spoiled - - - - - - - - - - - BAD
spoiled paper - - - - - - - SALLE
spoils - - - - - - - - - - BOOTY
spoken - - - - - - - - ORAL, PAROL
spokes - - - - - - - - - - RUNGS
spoliate - - - - - - - - - PLUNDER
spoliation - - - - - - - - - RAPINE
sponge - - - - - EXPUNGE, EFFACE
sponges (pert. to) - - - - PORIFERAL
spongy - - - - - - - - - - POROUS
sponsor - - - - - - - - - - BACKER
spontaneous inclination - - - IMPULSE
spook - - - - - - - - - - - GHOST
spool - - BOBBIN, REEL, CYLINDER
spoon (deep) - - - - - - - - LADLE
spore - - - - - - - - - - - SEED
sport - - GAME, PLAY, FUN, FRISK,

FROLIC, PASTIME, DIVERT
sport group - - - - - - - - TEAM
sport official - - - - - - - UMPIRE
sportive - - - - - PLAYFUL, GAY
sports trousers - - - - - - SLACKS
sporty - - - - - - - - - FLASHY
spot - - - STAIN, BLEMISH, BLOT, TARNISH, SPECK, DAPPLE, NOTICE, LOCALITY, MACULATE
spot on playing card or domino - - PIP
spotless - - - - - - CLEAN, SNOWY
spotted animal (poet.) - - - - - PARD
spotted cat - - - CHEETAH, OCELOT
spotted with colors - - - - - - PIED
spotting - - - - - - - - - DAPPLE
spouse - - - MATE, WIFE, CONSORT
spout - - - - - - - - - GUSH, JET
spout to draw sap - - - - - - SPILE
spout oratory - - - - - - - ORATE
spouting hot spring - - - - - GEYSER
sprain - - - - - - - - - - STRAIN
sprawl lazily - - - - - - - - LOLL
spread - - - - SCATTER, UNFURL, DISSEMINATE, TED, BROADEN, DISPERSE, UNFOLD, DIFFUSE, EXTEND, INCREASE
spread by rumour - - - - - - NOISE
spread out in line of battle - - DEPLOY
spread outward - - - - - - - FLARE
spree - - - - - - - - - - FROLIC
spree (slang) - - - - - - - - - BAT
sprig - - - - - - - - - - - TWIG
sprightly - ALIVE, NIMBLE, BUOYANT, AIRY, CHIPPER, PERT
sprightly tune - - - - - - - LILT
spring (Bib.) - - - - - - - - AIN
spring - LEAP, VAULT, BOLT, RAMP, ARISE, SPA
spring back - - - - - - - REBOUND
spring flower - - - CROCUS, VIOLET
spring from - - - - - - - DERIVE
spring of life - - - - - - - PRIME
spring (old word) - - - - - - - VER
spring (pert. to) - - - - - - VERNAL
spring season - - - - - - - - - VER
spring up - - - - - - ARISE, RISE
springe - - - - - - - - - SNARE
springy - - - - - - - - - ELASTIC
sprinkle - - SPATTER, DRIZZLE, WET
sprinkle (Scot.) - - - - - - SPAIRGE
sprinkle water upon - - - - - - WET
sprinkle with flour - - - - - DREDGE
sprint - - - - - - RUN, DASH, RACE
sprite - ELF, IMP, GOBLIN, FAIRY, FAY
sprout - - BUD, CROP, SHOOT, CION, GERMINATE, SCION
sprout from the root - - - RATOON
spruce - - DAPPER, SMARTEN, NEAT, TRIM, NATTY
spruce (black or white) - - EPINETTE
spry - AGILE, ACTIVE, NIMBLE, BRISK
spud - - - - - - - - - - POTATO
spume - - - - - - - FROTH, FOAM
spurn - - DISDAIN, REGRET, REJECT
spurt - - - - - - - - - - - GUSH
sputter - - - - - - - - - JABBER
spun wool - - - - - - - - - YARN
spunk - - - - - - - - - - PLUCK
spur - - - - INCITE, GOAD, URGE, STIMULUS, IMPEL, ROUSE
spurious - SNIDE, BOGUS, FALSE, FAKE
spurn - - - - - - - SCORN, REJECT
spurt - DART, SPOUT, GUSH, BURST, SQUIRT
spy - SCOUT, DISCOVERER, INFORMER, DETECT, DISCERN
spy for a thief (slang) - - - - TOUT
squad - - - - - TEAM, GROUP, GANG
squadron - - - - - - - - - ARMADA
squall - - - - - - - - - - GUST
squander - WASTE, SPEND, DISSIPATE, MISSPEND
square cap - - - - - - - BIRETTA
square column - - - - - - PILASTER
square dance - - - - - - LANCERS
square land measure - - - - - ROOD
square pillar - - - - - - - PILASTER
square of three - - - - - - - - NINE
squash plant - - - - - - - - GOURD
squatter - - - - - - - - - NESTER
squeaking - - - - - - - - - CREAKY
squeeze - - PRESS, CRUSH, PINCH, COMPRESS, HUG
squelch - - - - - - - - SUPPRESS
squib - - - - - - - - - LAMPOON
squire - - - - - - - - - - ESCORT
squirm - - - - - WRING, WRIGGLE
squirming - - - - - - - - WRIGGLY
squirrel - - - - - - - - - GOPHER
squirrel shrew - - - - - - - - TANA
squirt - - - - - - - - - - - SPURT
stab - - - GORE, PIERCE, ATTEMPT, PUNCTURE, PINK
stab with sword - - - - - - - PINK
stabilizer - - - - - - - - - BALLAST
stabilizing cargo - - - - - BALLAST
stable - - - - - BARN, STALL, FIXED
stable compartment - - - - - STALL
stable groom - - - - - - - HOSTLER
stableman - - - - OSTLER, HOSTLER
stack - - - - PILE, HEAP, CHIMNEY
stack of corn - - - - - - - - SHOCK
stack of hay or grain - - - - - RICK
stadium - - - - - - - - - ARENA
staff - POLE, ROD, CUDGEL, FLAGPOLE, WAND
staff of authority - - - - - - MACE
staff of life - - - - - - - - BREAD
staff of office - - - - - - - - MACE
staff officer - - - - - - - - - AIDE
stag - - - - - POLLARD, ELK, HART
stage - - PRODUCE, DEGREE, DAIS, PLATFORM
stage in development - - - - PHASE
stage extra - - - - - - - - - SUPER
stage of frog - - - - - - - TADPOLE
stage hangings - - - - - - - SCENERY
stage immortal - - - - - - - - DUSE
stage of life - - - - - - - - - AGE
stage part - - - - - - - - - ROLE
stage (pert. to) - - - - - - SCENIC
stage players - - - - - - - ACTORS
stage for public speaking - PLATFORM
stage settings - - - - - - - SCENERY
stage show - - - - - - - - REVUE
stage speech and whisper - - ASIDE
stagger - REEL, STUN, TOTTER, WAVER
stagnant - - - - - - MOTIONLESS
staid - - - - - - SEDATE, DEMURE
stain DYE, DISCOLOUR, COLOUR, SPOT, TINGE, BLEMISH, TAX, SOIL, STIGMA, SMEAR, BLOT, SMIRCH
stair - - - - - - - - - - - STEP
stair part - - - - - - RISER, TREAD
stair post - - - - - - - - - NEWEL
stake - - - - POST, WAGER, PICKET, HAZARD, BET, ANTE, RISK, POLE
stake fence - - - - - - - PALISADE
stale - - - - - TRITE, VAPID, OLD, OVERTRAINED, INSIPID
stalk - - - - - - - - - STEM, STIPE
stalk (dry) - - - - - - - - - STRAW

S

stalk of grain - - - - - - - STRAW
stall - - - - STABLE, BOOTH, MANGER
stall in mud - - - - - - - MIRE
stalwart - - - - - - - - STRONG
stamen with pollen (pert. to) - - - - ANTHERAL
stamina - - - - - - - STRENGTH
stammer - - - - - - - - STUTTER
stamp - POSTAGE, BRAND, IMPRESS, PRINT
stamp upon - - - - - - - - TRAMPLE
stamping form - - - - - - - DIE
stance - - - - - - - - POSITION
stanch - - - - - - - - - STEM
stand - - BEAR, ENDURE, POSITION, BOOTH, TOLERATE
stand (let) - - - - - - - - STET
stand against - - - - - - - OPPOSE
stand for - - - - - - - REPRESENT
stand opposite - - - - - - - FACE
stand still - - - - - - - - - HO
stand up - - - - - - - - - RISE
standard - - - FLAG, NORM, IDEAL, NORMAL, TEST, CLASSIC, CRITERION, STREAMER, EMBLEM
standard amount - - - - - - UNIT
standard of comparison - GAGE, GAUGE
standard of conduct - MORAL, NORM, IDEAL
standard of excellence - - - - IDEAL
standard of performance - - - BOGEY
standard of quality and quantity - UNIT
standardize - - - - - - CALIBRATE
standing - - - - - STATUS, GRADE
standing as grain - - - - - - UNCUT
standing (heraldry) - - - - - STATANT
standpoint - - - - - - - - ANGLE
stannum - - - - - - - - - - TIN
stanza - - - - - - VERSE, STROPHE
staple - - - - - - - - - - CHIEF
star - - ASTERISK, FEATURE, NOVA, CELEBRITY, SUN, VEGA, BESPANGLE, GIANSAR, MIRAK
star (comb. form) - - ASTER, ASTERO
star in Cygnus - - - - - - - DENEB
star in Draco - - - - ADIB, ETAMIN
star in Dragon - - - - ADIB, ETAMIN
star flower - - - - - - - - ASTER
star (Fr.) - - - - - - - - - ETOILE
star in Gemini - - - - - - - CASTOR
star in heraldry - - - - - - ETOILE
star in Orion - - - - - - - - RIGEL
star in Perseus - - - - - - - ALGOL
star (pert. to) - - - - - - SIDEREAL
star (resembling a) - - - - STELLATE
star in scorpion - - - - - - ANTARES
star shaped thing - - - - - ASTERISK
star in Virgo - - - - - - - - SPICA
starch - SAGO, ARROWROOT, CASSAVA, FARINA
starch yielding herb - - - - - ARUM
starchlike substance - - - - - INULIN
stare - - GAZE, AGAPE, GAPE, GLARE
stare amorously - - - - - - - OGLE
stargazer - - - - - - ASTROLOGER
staring - - - - - - AGAZE, AGAPE
staring with surprise - - - - - AGAPE
stark - STIFF, RIGID, BARE, ABSOLUTE
starling (var.) - - - - - - - MINO
starry - ASTRAL, SPARKLING, STELLAR
stars (pert. to) - - - - - - STELLAR
start - - - INITIATE, BEGIN, OPEN, COMMENCE, ONSET
start aside suddenly - - - - - - SHY
start a car by hand - - - - - CRANK
starting at - - - - - - - - - FROM
starting line - - - - - - - SCRATCH
startle - SURPRISE, SHOCK, FRIGHTEN, EXCITE, ALARM, SCARE
startling exclamation - - - - - BOO
starve - - - - - - - - - - FAMISH
state - DECLARE, SAY, ASSERT, AVER, CONDITION, NATION, REPUBLIC
state of affairs - - PASS, SITUATION
state of bearing no name - ANONYMITY
state of being annoyed - - DISGUST
state of being disorganized - - ROUT
state of being equal - - - - - - PAR
state of being evil - - - MALIGNITY
state of being precise - - PRIMNESS
state of bliss - - - - - - - - EDEN
state carriage - - - - - - CHARIOT
state (comb. form) - - - - - STATO
state differently - - - - - - REWORD
state of emptiness - - - INANITION
state of enmity - - - - - HOSTILITY
state house - - - - - - - CAPITOL
state of insensibility - - - - - COMA
state by items - - - - - - - ITEMIZE
state of lost soul - - - - - PERDITION
state of mind - - MORALE, SPIRITS, MOOD
state on oath - - - - - - - DEPOSE
state of one who commits offense - - - GUILT
state policeman - - - - - TROOPER
state of quality (suffix) - - - - - CY
state of refinement - - - - ELEGANCE
state of relief - - - - - - EASINESS
state of shaking - - - - - - - AGUE
state treasury - - - - - - - - FISC
state troops - - - - - - - - MILITIA
state without proof - - - - - ALLEGE
state wrongly - - - - - - MISSTATE
stately - - - - - - MAJESTIC, REGAL
stately building - - - - - - EDIFICE
stately ceremony - - - - - - POMP
stately dance - - - - - - - PAVAN
stately house - - - - - - - PALACE
stately market - - - - - - - - FAIR
stately (mus.) - - - - - - - LARGO
statement - - - - ASSERTION, FACT
statement of belief - - CREED, CREDO
statement of merchandise shipped - - INVOICE
station - POST, BASE, DEPOT, DEGREE
station between savagery and civilization BARBARISM
stationary - - - - - - - - LEGER
stationary part - - - - - - STATOR
statue (small) - - - - - - - IMAGE
statue at Thebes - - - - - MEMNON
statue of the Virgin - - - - MADONNA
stature - - - - - - - - - HEIGHT
status - - - - - - STANDING, RANK
statute - - - - - - - - LAW, EDICT
stave - - - - - - - - - - - VERSE
stave off - - - - - - - - - - STALL
stay - REMAIN, WAIT, LINGER, STOP
stay for - - - - - - - AWAIT, WAIT
stead - - - - - AVAIL, PLACE, LIEU
steadfast - - - - - - STAID, TRUE
steadfastness - - - - - - STABILITY
steady - - FIRM, FIXED, INVARIABLE
steady bright flame - - - - - FLARE
steady going - - - - - - - - TROT
steadying rope for a sail - - - VANG
steadying support - - - - - - - GUY
steak - - - - - - - - - - - BEEF
steak (kind) - - - - - - - SIRLOIN
steal - ROB, PURLOIN, PILFER, FILCH
steal (arch.) - - - - - - - - - NIM

steal, as cattle - - - - - - RUSTLE
steal (slang) - - - - - BURGLE, COP
steal in small quantities - - PILFER
stealthy - - - - - - - - - FURTIVE
steam - - - - - - VAPOR, POWER
steam apparatus (dyeing) - - - AGER
steam boiler section - - - - - STRAKE
steamer - - - - - - - - - - LINER
steamer route - - - - - - - LANE
steamship - - - - - - - - - LINER
steed - - - - - - HORSE, CHARGER
steel - - - - - - - - - - HARDEN
steel (kind) - - DAMASK, BESSEMER
steel plating on ships - - - - ARMOR
steep - - - RET, BREW, SOP, IMBUE, HILLY, SOAK, ABRUPT, MACERATE, SHEER
steep acclivity - - - - - - - BANK
steep declivity - - - - - - - SCARP
steep as flax - - - - - - - - RET
steep hill - - - - - - - - -- BUTTE
steep in oil and vinegar - - MARINATE
steep rugged rock - - - - - - CRAG
steep slope - - SCARP, ESCARP, BANK
steep waterfall - - - - - - CASCADE
steeple - - - - - - - SPIRE, EPI
steer - - PILOT, GUIDE, OX, PURSUE, CONTROL, HELM, GLOBE
steer (obs.) - - - - - - - BULLOCK
steer (wild) - - - - - - - YAK, YAW
steerer - - - - - - - - - - PILOT
steering apparatus - HELM, RUDDER, WHEEL
steering arm - - - - - - - TILLER
steering lever - - - - - - - TILLER
steersman - - - - - - - - - PILOT
steeve - - - - - - - - - - STOW
stein - - - - - - - - - - - MUG
stellar - - - - - - ASTRAL, STARRY
stem - PROW, ARREST, STALK, CHECK, PEDUNCLE, PETIOLE, STANCH
stem of an arrow - - - - - - SHAFT
stem of bean plant - - - BEANSTALK
stem from - - - - - - - - DERIVE
stem of palm - - - - - - - RATTAN
stem underground - - - - - - TUBER
stent - - - - - - - - - - - TAX
step - - PACE, STRIDE, RACE, STAIR, GAIT, TREAD, DEGREE, WALK
step heavily - - - - - - TRAMPLE
step of ladder - - - - - - - RUNG
step on - - - - - - - - - - TREAD
step of rope ladder - - - - RATLINE
step for fence crossing - - - STILE
steplike arrangement of troops and planes ECHELON
stereopticon picture - - - - SLIDE
stereotyped - - - - - - - - TRITE
steric - - - - - - - - - SPACIAL
sterile - - - - - - - - - - BARREN
sterling (abbr.) - - - - - - - STG.
stern - - - GRIM, HARSH, SEVERE, RIGOROUS
sterns collectively - - - - STERNAGE
stern of vessel - - - - - - - AFT
stevedore - - - - - LOADER, STOWER
stew - - - RAGOUT, WORRY, BOIL, SEETHE, SIMMER, FRET
stew (colloq.) - - - - - - MULLIGAN
stick - ROD, STALL, ADHERE, COHERE, TRANSFIX, POLE, PASTE, WAND
stick fast, as in mire - - - - STALL
stick three feet in length - YARDWAND
stick tightly - - - - - - - COHERE
sticker - - - - - - - - - PASTER
sticking fast - - - - - - ADHERENT
stickler for perfect English - - PURIST
sticky stuff - - - - - GOO, GLUE, TAR
stiff - RIGID, STARK, FRIGID, FORMAL, STILTED
stiff cloth - - - - - - - - CRINOLINE
stiff hat - - - - - - - - - DERBY
stiffened cloth - - - - - - BUCKRAM
stiffly decorous - - - - - - - PRIM
stiffly proper - - - - - - - - PRIM
stiffness - - - - - - - - - RIGOR
stifle - - - - - SMOTHER, STRANGLE
stigma - - - - - - - BRAND, STAIN
stigmatize - - - - - - - - - BRAND
stiletto - - - - - - - - - DAGGER
still - - YET, SILENT, QUIET, DUMB, SILENCE, IMMOBILE, IMMOVABLE
stillness - - - - - - - SILENCE, HUSH
stilt-like stick - - - - - - - POGO
stilted - - - PEDANTIC, BOMBASTIC, STILL
stimulate - - FAN, STIR, INCITE, JOY, STING, WHET, EXHILARATE, INNERVATE
stimulate curiosity of - - INTRIGUE
stimulating - - - - - - - - BRISK
stimulus - - - - SPUR, INCENTIVE
sting - - BITE, SMART, STIMULATE, GOAD
stinging - - - - - - - - PRICKLY
stinging fish - - - - - - - - - RAY
stinging insect - - - WASP, HORNET
stinging plant - - - - - - NETTLE
stingy - - - - - - MISERLY, MEAN
stint - SCRIMP, TASK, CHORE, SPARE, RESTRICT
stinted - - - - - - - - SPARED
stipe - - - - - - - - - - - STALK
stipend - - - SALARY, WAGES, PAY
stipulate - - - - - - - - PREMISE
stir - MOVE, AROUSE, ROUSE, INSPIRE, EXCITE, MIX, STIMULATE, DISTURB, URGE, BUSTLE, AGITATE, EXCITEMENT
stir the air - - - - - - - - - FAN
stir up - - AGITATE, ROUSE, ROUST, ROIL, PROVOKE, FOMENT
stir up colours - - - - - - - TEER
stirring apparatus to brew - - ROUSER
stitch - - - - - - - - - - - SEW
stitch bird - - - - - - - - - - IHI
stoa - - - - - - - - - - - DOOR
stoat - - - - - - ERMINE, WEASEL
stock - - - - - - - - - - STORE
stock again - - - - - - REPLENISH
stock certificates - - - - - - SCRIP
stock raising establishment - - RANCH
stock soup for white sauces (Fr.) - - - VELOUTE
stock in trade - - - - - - - STAPLE
stodgy - - - - - - - - - - DULL
stogie - - - - - - - - - - CIGAR
stoker - - - - - - - - - FIREMAN
stole - - - - - GARMENT, VESTMENT
stolen goods - - - - - - - MAINOR
stolid - DULL, IMPASSIVE, WOODEN, HEAVY, BRUTISH
stoma - - - - - - - OSTIOLE, PORE
stomach - - - - - - - - - BROOK
stomach of mammal - - - - - - MAW
stomach of ruminant - - - - - TRIPE
stone - LAPIS, AGATE, ROCK, FLINT, LAPIDATE, GEM, JEWEL, PEBBLE, MARBLE
stone carved in relief - - - - CAMEO
stone cutter - - - - - - - - MASON

S

stone cutting tool - - - - - - SAX
stone to death - - - - - - LAPIDATE
stone of drupe - - - - - - NUTLET
stone fruit - - - - - DRUPE, PLUM
stone implement - - - - - - EOLITH
stone jar - - - - - - - - - CROCK
stone (kind) - - - - - AGATE, MARBLE
stone (Latin) - - - - - - - - LAPIS
stone mason's bench - - - - BANKER
stone mug - - - - - - - - - STEIN
stone nodule - - - - - - - - GEODE
stone tablet - - - - - - - - STELE
stone tablet (var.) - - - - - - STELA
stone writing tablet - - - - - SLATE
stonemason's chisel - - - - - TOOLER
stoneworker - - - - - - - - MASON
stony - - - - - ROCKY, UNFEELING
stoolpigeon - - - - - PEACHER, SPY
stoop - BEND, SUBMIT, BOW, PORCH
stop - CEASE, PREVENT, REST, DESIST, HO, CESSATION, STAY, PAUSE, SUSPEND, BAR, ARREST, AVAST, DETER, QUIT, HOLLA
stop, as a hole - - - - - - - - PLUG
stop momentarily - - - - - - PAUSE
stop (naut.) - - - - - - - - AVAST
stop seams of a boat - - - - - CALK
stop temporarily - - - - - - PAUSE
stop unintentionally - - - - - STALL
stop up - - - - - DAM, CLOG, PLUG
stop watch - - - - - - - - - TIMER
stoppage - - - - - - - - - BLOCK
stoppage of trade - - - - - EMBARGO
stopper - - - - - - - PLUG, CORK
storage box - - - - - - - - - BIN
storage compartment - - - - - - BIN
storage crib - - - - - - - - - BIN
storage pit - - - - - - - - - SILO
storage place for arms - - - ARSENAL
storage place for grain - - - - - SILO
storage room - - - - - - - - LOFT
store - MART, FUND, STOCK, PROVIDE, STOW, SUPPLY, SHOP, ACCUMULATE
store attendant - - - - - - CLERK
store fodder - - - - - - - ENSILE
store for safety - - REPOSIT, DEPOSIT
store in a silo - - - - - - ENSILE
store up - - - - - - - - GARNER
storehouse - - - - - DEPOT, ETAPE
storehouse for ammunition - ARSENAL
storekeeper - - - - - - MERCHANT
storeroom - - - - - - - - - GOLA
storied - - - - - - - LEGENDARY
storied temple - - - - - - PAGODA
storing place - - - - - - - CLOSET
storm - - RAVE, RAMPAGE, TEMPEST, WESTER, RAIN, ORAGE, RAGE, BESIEGE, TORNADO
stormy - - - - - INCLEMENT, FOUL
story - - TALE, YARN, NOVEL, FLOOR, FABLE
story with spiritual teaching - PARABLE
stout - - - - - - - - STRONG, BRAVE
stout, of fabric - - - - - WEBBING
stout glove - - - - - - - GAUNTLET
stove - RANGE, ETNA, HEATER, KILN
stove accessory - - - - - - POKER
stove part - - - - - - OVEN, GRATE
stow - - STORE, PACK, BOX, STEEVE, STUFF
stow cargo - - - - - - - - STEEVE
straddle - - - - ASTRIDE, BESTRIDE
straight - - - - - - DIRECT, AROW
straight batted ball - - - - - LINER
straight jacket - - - - - CAMISOLE

straight line (in a) - - - - - LINEAR
straight line cutting a curve - SECANT
straightedge - - - - - - - - RULER
straighten - - ALINE, ALIGN, UNCOIL
straightforward - - - CANDID, DIRECT
strain - - - - TENSION, TAX, SPRAIN, STRIVE, SIFT, STRETCH, FILTER, MELODY, PROGENY, TRACE, HEAVE, EXERT
strain (comb. form) - - - - - TONO
strain forward - - - - - - - PRESS
strained - - - - - TENSE, FILTERED
strainer - - - - - - - SIEVE, SIFTER
strainor for malt - - - - - - STRUM
strait - CHANNEL, NARROW, RIGOROUS
strand - - - - - - - STRING, BREACH
strand of metal - - - - - - - - WIRE
strange - - - - - ODD, ALIEN, NOVEL
strange (comb. form) - - - - - XENO
stranger - ODDER, ALIEN, FOREIGNER
stronger (poet.) - - - - - PUISSANCE
strangle - - - - - - - - - STIFLE
strap - - - - - BELT, THONG, STROP
strap to lead a horse - HALTER, LEASH
strap shaped - - - - - - - LORATE
strata - - - - LAYER, LAYERS, BEDS
stratagem - - - RUSE, WILE, ARTIFICE
stratum - - - - - LAYER, BED, SEAM
Stravinsky - - - - - - - - - IGOR
straw bed - - - - - - - - PALLET
straw hat - - - - - - - - PANAMA
strawberry finch - - - - - AMADAVAT
stray - DIVAGATE, WANDER, DEVIATE, LOSE, ERR
stray from truth - - - - - - - ERR
streak - STRIPE, LINE, VEIN, TRACE, STRIATE, BRINDLE
streaked animal - - - - - - BRINDLE
stream - FRESHET, TORRENT, RIVER, CREEK, POUR, RUN, RILL, FLOW
stream embankment - - - - - LEVEE
stream obstruction to raise water - WEIR
streamer - PENNANT, FLAG, STANDARD
street Arab - - - - - - - - GAMIN
street car device - - - - - - FENDER
street cleaner - - - - - SCAVENGER
street show - - - - - - - - - RAREE
street singer - - - - - SIREN, WAIF
street of squalor - - - - - - - SLUM
street urchin - - - ARAB, WAIF, GAMIN
strength - VIGOR, POWER, SOUNDNESS, STAMINA, VIS
strength of chemical solution - TITER
strength of electric current - AMPERAGE
strengthen - - - - BRACE, FORTIFY, INVIGORATE, PROP
strengthening medicine - - - - TONIC
strengthening piece - - - - - GUSSET
strengthening rim - - - - - FLANGE
stress - STRAIN, ACCENT, PRESSURE, TENSION, COMPULSION, EMPHASIS
stretch - - - - - ELONGATE, STRAIN, PANDICULATE
stretch (Scot.) - - - - - - - STENT
stretch beyond means - - - - STRAIN
stretch forth to - - - - - - REACH
stretch out - EKE, PROLATE, SPRAWL, EXPAND, LIE, SPAN
stretch out one's neck - CRAN, CRANE
stretch over - - - - - - - - - SPAN
stretched - - - - - TAUT, EXTENDED, STRAINED, REACHED
stretched tight - - - - - - - TENSE
stretcher - - - - - - - - - LITTER
stretching muscle - - - - - TENSOR

S

strew - - - SCATTER, DIFFUSE, SOW
striate - - - - STREAK, GROOVED
strict - - STERN, RIGOROUS, RIGID
strict disciplinarian - - - MARTINET
strictness - - - - - - - - RIGOR
stride - - - - - - - - PACE, GAIT
stridence - - - - - - - HARSHNESS
strident - - - - - - - - SHRILL
strife - - FEUD, WAR, CONTENTION, CONTEST
strike - - SLAP, BEAT, RAP, SMITE, CAROME, SWAT. HIT, RAM, SMACK, BANG
strike (arch.) - - - - - - - SMITE
strike, as a bell - - - - - - CHIME
strike breaker - - - - - - - SCAB
strike (colloq.) - - - - - - - LAM
strike gently - - - - PAT, TAP, DAB
strike hard - - - - - - - - - RAM
strike lightly - - - - - - - - PAT
strike out - DELE, ELIDE, FAN, CANCEL, DELETE
strike and rebound - - - - - CAROM
strike together - - - - - - COLLIDE
strike violently - - - - - - - RAM
strike with disaster - - - - - SMITE
strike with palm - - - - - - - SLAP
strike with wonder - - - - - ASTOUND
striking effect - - - - - - - ECLAT
striking part of clock - - - - DETENT
striking success (slang) - - - - WOW
strikingly odd - - - - - - - OUTRE
string - CORD, ROPE, TWINE, STRAND, LINE
string of cars - - - - - - - TRAIN
stringed instrument - - VIOL, VIOLA, REBEC, LUTE, HARP, LYRE, PIANO, CELLO
stringed instrument player - - CELLIST
stringent - - - - - - STRICT, ALUM
stringy - - - - - - - - - - ROPY
strip - - - STRIPE, DIVEST, BAND, DENUDE, PEEL, SHEAR, BARE
strip of cloth - - - - - - - - TAPE
strip covering from - - - - - DENUDE
strip of leather - WELT, STROP, THONG, CLEAT
strip skin from whale - - - - FLENSE
stripe - - - - - - - BAR, STREAK
striped - - - - - - - - - STREAKED
stripling - - - - - - - - - - LAD
stirred up - - - - - - - - AROUSED
stipple - - - - - - - - - SPECKLE
strive - STRAIN, STRUGGLE, ATTEMPT, TRY, CONTEND, VIE, ENDEAVOR, TOIL
strive after - - - - - - - - SEEK
strive to equal - - - - - - EMULATE
strive for superiority - - - - - - VIE
striven - - - - - - - - - FOUGHT
stroke - - - - - - - - - BLOW, PAT
stroke of a bell - - - - - - KNELL
stroke of luck - - - - - - - - - HIT
stroke that needs no repeating (slang) - ONER
stroll - MEANDER, SAUNTER, RAMBLE, ROVE
strong - - - POTENT, STOUT, HALE, ROBUST, STURDY, POWERFUL, STALWART
strong alkaline solution - - - - LYE
strong attachment - - - - - DEVOTION
strong box - - - - - - CHEST, SAFE
strong current - - - - - - TORRENT
strong drink - - - - - - - - - GIN
strong fiber - - - - - - - - - BAST
strong point - - - - - - - - FORTE
strong pull - - - - - - - - - HAUL
strong rope - - - - - - - - - CABLE
strong scented - - - - - - REDOLENT
strong smelling - - - - - - - - OLID
strong tackle (naut.) - - - - - - CAT
strong taste - - - - - - - - TANG
strong thread - - - - - - - - TWINE
strong voiced person - - - - STENTOR
strong white fiber - - - - - - SISAL
stronghold - FORT, FORTRESS, CITADEL
strop - - - - - - - - HONE, STRAP
strophe - - - - - - - - - STANZA
struck - - - - - - - - - - SMOTE
struck with disaster - - - - SMITTEN
struck with wonder - - - - - AGHAST
structural form of language - - IDIOM
structural quality - - - - - TEXTURE
structure - - EDIFICE, SHED, FRAME
studio - - - - - - - - - WORKSHOP
struggle - SCRIMMAGE, COPE, TUSSLE, COMBAT, WRESTLE, STRIVE, CONTEST
struggle against - - - - - - RESIST
strum - - - - - - - - - - THRUM
strut - - BRACE, PEACOCK, SWAGGER
stub - - - - - - STUMP, RECEIPT
stubborn person - - - - - - - MULE
stubborn things - - - - - - - FACTS
stuck - - - - - - - - - - PASTED
stuck in the mud - MIRED, BEMIRED
stud for shoe soles - - - - - HOBNAIL
stud timber - - - - - - - SCANTLE
student - - - - - - SCHOLAR, PUPIL
student at Annapolis - MIDSHIPMAN
student group - - - - - - - CLASS
student of moon - - - - - LUNARIAN
studio - - - - - - - - - - ATELIER
study - - PORE, PERUSE, CON, PON, SCAN, MEDITATE
study of animals - - - - ZOOGRAPHY
study of word origins - - ETYMOLOGY
stuff - PAD, SATE, CRAM, FILL, WAD, RAM, GORGE, STOW
stulm - - - - - - - - - - - - ADIT
stumble - - - - - - - - - - TRIP
stump - - - - - STUB, CHALLENGE
stun - - - - - - - DAZE, ASTOUND
stunt - - - - - FEAT, DWARF, TRICK
stunted child (Scot.) - - - - - - URF
stupefy - STUN, DAZE, DRUG, BESOT
stupid - - - CRASS, DULL, ASININE, INSIPIENT, DUMB, INANE, DOLTISH
stupid fellow - - - - - DOLT, CLOD
stupid person - - DOLT, ASS, DUNCE, LOG, MORON
stupid person (colloq.) - - - - - ASS
stupid play (slang) - - - - - BONER
stupidity - - CRASSITUDE, FATUITY, IDIOCY
stupor - - - - - - COMA, TRANCE
sturdy - - - - - - - - - - STRONG
sturdy tree - - - - - - - - - OAK
stutter - - - - - - - - - STAMMER
sty - - - - - - - - - - - - - PEN
stygian - - - - - - - - - GLOOMY
style - - - - - - - - (See also Type)
style - - MANNER, MODE, FASHION
style of architecture - - DORIC, IONIC
style (Fr.) - - - - - - - - - - TON
style of numeral - - - - - - ROMAN
style of painting - - - - - - GENRE
style of penmanship - - - - - HAND
style of poetry - - - - - - - EPIC

S

style of sewing - - - - - - - SHIRR
style of type - ITALIC, PICA, ITALICA, ROMAN, GOTHIC
style of type (abbr.) - - - - - ITAL.
stylish - - CHIC, ALAMODE, DRESSY
stylish (slang) - CLASSY, NIFTY, TONY
stylus - - - - - - - - - - - PEN
styptic - - - - - - - - - - ALUM
Styx's husband - - - - - - PALLAS
suave - - - - - - - - - - BLAND
subdivision - - - - - - - - ARM
subdivision of defensive position - - - SECTOR
subdue - MASTER, OVERPOWER, TAME
subdued - - - - - - MELLOW, TAME
subdued shade - - - - - - PASTEL
subject - - TOPIC, THEME, VASSAL, TEXT
subject to chemical analysis - - ASSAY
subject for discussion - - - - MATTER
subjected to heat - - FRIED, ROASTED
subjoin - - - - - - - - - - ANNEX
subjugate - - - - - - - - CONQUER
subjugation - - - - - - CONQUEST
sublime - - - - - - EXALTED, NOBLE
submarine worker - - - - - - DIVER
submerge - - SINK, DROWN, IMMERSE
submerged chain of rocks - - - - REEF
submissive - PASSIVE, MEEK, SERVILE
submit - - STOOP, BOW, YIELD, OBEY
submit to - - - - - - - - - ENDURE
subordinate - - MINOR, SECONDARY, UNDERLING
subordinate building - - - - - ANNEX
subordinate part - - - - - - DETAIL
subordinate part of building - - WING
subordinate ship officer - - - BOSUN
subscribe for - - - - - - - TAKE
subsequent selling - - - - - RESALE
subsequently - - - - - LATER, AFTER
subside - - - - - ABATE, EBB, FALL
subsidiary - - - - - - - ACCESSORY
subsidiary building - - - - - ANNEX
subsidise - - - - - BONUS, SUPPORT
subsist - - - - - - - - LIVE, FEED
subspecies - - - - - RACE, VARIETY
substance - MATERIAL, MATTER, GIST, ESSENCE, METAL, PITH
substance causing delirium - DELIRIANT
substance to curdle milk - - RENNET
substance to make chloroform - ACETONE
substance of nervous system - - ALBA
substance on wine casks - - TARTAR
substantial - - - - - - SOLID, REAL
substantive - - - - - - - - - NOUN
substitute - - - ALTERNATE, ERSATZ, VICAR, AGENT
substitute in office - - - - - VICAR
substitution (rhet.) - - - - ENALLAGE
subterfuge - - - EVASION, PRETENSE
subterranean being - - - - - GNOME
subterranean bud - - - - - - BULB
subterranean conduit - - - - - SEWER
subterranean hollow - CAVERN, CAVE
subterranean realm - - - - - HADES
subterranean worker - - - - - MINER
subtle emanation (s.) - - - - - AURA
subtle fluid filling all space - - ETHER
subtle variation - - - - - - NUANCE
subtraction - - - - - - DEDUCTION
subtraction result - - - REMAINDER
suburban detached cottage - - VILLA
subvert - - - - - - - - SUPPLANT
succeed - - - - - - - WIN, ENSUE
succeeding day - - - - - - MORROW
success - - - - - GO, HIT, VICTORY
succession - - - SERIES, ORDINAL
succession of family sovereigns - - - DYNASTY
succession of taps - - - - - PATTER
successive - - - - - - - - - SERIAL
succinct - - - - - - TERSE, SHORT
succor - AID, RELIEF, RESCUE, HELP
succulent - - - - - - - - - - JUICE
succulent fruit - - - - - - - - UVA
succulent fruit part - - - - - - PULP
succulent odorous vegetable - - ONION
succulent plant - - - - - HERB, ALOE
succumb - - - - - - - - - - YIELD
such - - - - - - - - - - SIMILAR
sucking fish - - - - - - - REMORA
suction - - - - - - - - - INTAKE
sudden - - - - - - QUICK, ABRUPT
sudden attack - - - - - - - - RAID
sudden blast of wind - - - - - GUST
sudden effort - - - - - SPURT, SPASM
sudden ejaculation - - - - - - - OH
sudden fear or fright - - STARTLING, PANIC
sudden flood - - - - - - - - SPATE
sudden impulse - - - - - - - START
sudden loud noise - - - - - - BANG
sudden onset - - - - - - - - DASH
sudden outbreak - - - - - ERUPTION
sudden panic rush - - - - STAMPEDE
sudden sensation - - - - - - THRILL
sudden stroke - - - - - - - - CLAP
sudden thrust - - LUNGE, DAB, JAB
sudden toss - - - - - - - - - FLIP
Sudonic language - - - - - - - MO
suds - - - - - - - - - - - FOAM
sue - - - - - - - - - WOO, URGE
suet - - - - - - - - TALLOW, FAT
suffer - AIL, AGONIZE, LET, TOLERATE
suffer loss - - - - - - - - - LOSE
suffer pain - - - - - - - - - ACHE
suffer (Scot.) - - - - - - - - DREE
suffer to be - - - - - - TOLERATE
sufferer - - - - - - - - - MARTYR
suffering - - - - - - AGONY, PAIN
suffice - - - - - - - - DO, AVAIL
sufficient - - - - AMPLE, ADEQUATE
sufficient (be) - - - - - - - - - DO
sufficient (poet.) - - - - - - ENOW
suffix - - - - - - - - - - ER, ES
suffix for words from French - - - OT
suffocate (obs.) - - - - - - SWELT
suffused with red (be) - - - - BLUSH
sugar apparatus - - - GRANULATOR
sugar having 3 oxygen atoms - TRIOSE
sugar (kind) - - - - - TETROSE, OSE, DEXTROSE
sugar plum - - - - - - - BONBON
sugar solution - - - - - - - SYRUP
sugary - - - - - SWEET, HONEYED
suggest - INTIMATE, HINT, PROPOSE
suggest itself - - - - - - - - OCCUR
suggestion - - HINT, TIP, INNUENDO
suggestive look - - - - - - - LEER
suisse (Fr.) - - - - - - - - PORTER
suit - - - PLEASE, SATISFY, ADAPT, BECOME, FIT, PETITION, BEFIT
suit (colloq.) - - - - - - - - - GEE
suit at law - - - - - - - - - CASE
suitable - PAT, BEFITTING, ADAPTED, APT, FIT, MEET
suitable condition - - - - - - TRIM
suitable times - - - - - - SEASONS
suitable to be published - - PRINTABLE

suite - RETINUE, APARTMENT
suited to the occasion - TIMED
suited for song - LYRIC
suitor - BEAU, WOOER
sulk - MOPE, POUT
sullen - MOROSE, DOUR, GLUM
sully - DEFILE, TARNISH, SOIL, BLOT, GRIME
sulphur alloy - NIELLO
sultan's palace - HAREM
sultry - TROPICAL
sum - TOTAL, AMOUNT
sum entered - ITEM
Sumatran chevrotain - NAPU
Sumatran squirrel shrew - TANA
Sumerian deity - ABU
summarize - SUM, EPITOME
summary - EPITOME, PRECIS
summary (pert. to) - EPITOMIC
summary of principles - CREDO
summer (of the) - ESTIVAL
summer clouds - CUMULI
summer (Fr.) - ETE
summit - TIP, APICAL, APEX, CREST, ROOF, TOP, SPIRE, PEAK
summon - BID, CALL, PAGE, CITE
summon forth - EVOKE
summon publicly - PAGE
summon together - MUSTER
summon up - RALLY
sumptuous - RICH
sun - STAR, SOL
sun (of the) - SOLAR
sun (comb. form) - HELIO
sun disk - ATEN
sun dried brick - ADOBE
sun dried brick (colloq.) - DOBE
sun god - RA, APOLLO
sun part - CORONA
sun (pert. to) - HELIACAL
sunburn - TAN
sunburnt - ADUST, TANNED
Sunday - SABBATH
sunder - PART, REND, CUT, RIVE, DIVIDE
sundry - DIVERS
sunfish - BREAM
sunflower - LAREABELL
sung by a choir - CHORAL
sunk fence - HAHA, AHA
sunken part or place - SAG
sunny - CLEAR, BRIGHT, MERRY, CHEERFUL
sun's luminous envelope - CORONO
sunset - SUNDOWN
sunshade - PARASOL
sunshine - BRIGHTNESS
sup - SIP, EAT
superb - SPLENDID
supercilious person - SNOB
superficial - OUTWARD, SHALLOW
superficial cut - SCOTCH
superficial extent - AREA
superficial show - GILT
superfluous article - ODDMENT
superhuman event - MIRACLE
superintend - MANAGE, OVERSEE
superintendent - MANAGER, OVERSEER, BOSS
superior - FINER, UPPER, ABOVE
superior mental endowment - TALENT
superior to - ABOVE
superiority in office - SENIORITY
superiority over a competitor - VANTAGE
superlative suffix - EST
supernal - HEAVENLY
supernatural being - FAIRY
supernatural event - MIRACLE
supersede - REPLACE
supervise an editorial - EDIT
supine - SLUGGISH
supper - TEA
supplant - REPLACE, SUBVERT
supple - PLIABLE, LITHE, LISSOME, COMPLIANT, PLIANT
supplement - EKE, ADD
supplicant - IMPLORER
supplicate - APPEAL, PLEAD, ENTREAT, BEG, IMPLORE, PRAY
supplication - PRAYER, PLEA, ENTREATY, APPEAL
supplied food - MANNA
supplv - AFFORD, STORE, PURVEY, FUND, CATER
supply again - REFIT
supply arranged beforehand - RELAY
supply cattle with pasture - GRAZE
supply food - CATER
supply fully - REPLENISH
supply new front - REFACE
supply (slang) - HEEL
supply what is desired - CATER
supply with air - AERATE
supply with comments - ANNOTATE
supply with food - FEED
supply with fuel - STOKE
supply with men - MAN
supply with resolution - NERVE
supply with thin coat - WASH
support - PROP, BEHALF, ABET, SHORE, SECOND, PEDESTAL, STAY, REST, BRACE, LEG, AID, BEAR, SIDE, GUY, BACK, BOLSTER, HINGE
support for door - HINGE
support for floating bridge - PONTOON
support for furniture - LEG
support for millstone - RYND
support for plaster - LATH
support for rails - TIE
support for rolling stock - RAIL
support for rowing implement - OARLOCK
support for sail - TOPMAST, MAST
support for statue - PEDESTAL
support by timbers - SHORE
support for a vine - TRELLIS
support with enthusiasm - BOOST
sunporter - BOOSTER, ROOTER
supporter of institution - PATRON
supporting beam - SLEEPER
supporting curtain of fire - BARRAGE
supporting dock pillar - STILT
supporting framework - TRESTLE
supporting framework for pictures - EASEL
supporting member - LEG
supporting piece of wood - CLEAT
supporting rod - RIB
supporting structure - FRAME
supporting vitality - STAMINA
supporting wires - GUYS
suppose - PRESUME, OPINE, ASSUME, BELIEVE, DEEM
suppose (arch.) - TROW, WIS
supposed - PUTATIVE
supposition - IF
suppress - SQUELCH, STRANGLE, ELIDE, QUELL
suppress in pronouncing - ELIDE
suppression of a part - ELISION
supremacy - DOMINANCE

S

supreme - - - HIGHEST, GREATEST, PARAMOUNT
supreme ruler - - - - IMPERATOR
supremely good - - - - - - SUPERB
surcease - - - - - - - BALM, END
surd - - - - - - - - - RADICAL
surd consonant (phonet.) - - - ATONIC
sure - CERTAIN, CONFIDENT, POSITIVE
sure thing (slang) - - - - - - PIPE
surely - - - - - - - - - - - YES
surety - - - - - - - BAIL, BACKER
surety for court appearance - - - BAIL
surety (law) - - - - - - - - VAS
surf duck - - - - - - - - - COOT
surface of gem - - - - - - - FACET
surface measurement - - - - AREA
surfeit - SATE, CLOY, GLUT, SATIATE
surfeited with enjoyment - - - BLASE
surge - SWELL, HEAVE, TIDE, BILLOW
surgeon - - - - - - - - - - MAYO
surgical bristle - - - - - - SETON
surgical compress - - - - - STUPE
surgical sewing - - - - - - SUTURE
surgical thread - - - - - SETON
surgical treatment (pert. to) - - - - OPERATIONAL
surging - - - - - - - - BILLOWY
surly - - - CROSS, GRUFF, SNARLY
surly fellow - - - - - - - CHURL
surmise - - - - - - - - GUESS
surmount - OVERCOME, TIDE, HURDLE, TOP
surmounting - - - - - ABOVE, ATOP
surname - - - - - COGNOMEN, DOE
surpass - - - BEAT, EXCEED, BEST, TRANSCEND, TOP, CAP, EXCEL, OUTCLASS
surpassing - - - - - - EGREGIOUS
surpassing quality (of) - - EXQUISITE
surplice (short) - - - - - - COTTA
surplus of profits - - - - - MELON
surprise - - - - - STARTLE, AMAZE, ASTONISHMENT
surrender - - - - - CEDE, CESSION
surreptitious - - - SLY, SNEAKING
surrogate - - - - - - - - DEPUTY
surround - - BESET, HEM, ENCIRCLE, ENVELOP, ENVIRON, ENCLOSE, INCASE, BELAY, MEW, BELT, ENCASE
surround (poet.) - - - - - - ENISLE
surrounded - - - GIRT, ENVIRONED, ENCLOSED, BESET
surrounded by - - AMID, AMONG, MID
surrounded by the ocean - - SEAGIRT
surrounding area - - - - - - AREOLA
survey - - - - - - - - - - REVIEW
surveying instrument - - - ALINER, TRANSIT
surveying instrument part - OMNIMETER
surveyor's nails - - - - - - SPADS
survival of the past - - - - - RELIC
survive - - - - - - OUTLIVE, LIVE
surviving specimen - - - - - - RELIC
suspend - - - - - - - HANG, STOP
suspended - - - - - - - - HANGED
suspenders - - - - - - - - BRACES
suspicious - - MISTRUSTFUL, LEERY
suspicious (slang) - - - - - - LEERY
suspire - - - - - - - - - - SIGH
Sussex land - - - - - - - - LAINE
sustain - STAND, PROP, ENDURE, AID
sustenance - - - - ALIMENT, BREAD
suture - - - - - - - - - - SEAM
svelte - - - SLENDER, SLIM, THIN
swab - - - - - - - - MOP, WIPE
swag - - - - - - - - - - BOOTY
swagger - - - - - - STRUT, ROISTER
swaggering braggart - - - BOBADIL
swain - - - - - - - - - - - LOVER
swallow hurriedly - BOLT, ENGORGE, GULP, ENGULF, ABSORB
swallow (kind) - - - - MARTIN, TERN
swallow a liquid - - - - - - DRINK
swallow of liquid - - - - - - - SIP
swallow spasmodically - - - - - GULP
swallow up - - - - - - - - ENGULF
swallowlike bird (Scot.) - - - - CRAN
swamp - BOG, FIN, MARSH, EVERGLADE, MORASS, POCOSIN, SLUE, OVERWHELM
swamp rabbit - - - - - - - TAPETI
swan - - - - - - LEDA, TRUMPETER
swan (male) - - - - - - - - - COB
swap - - - - - - - - - - TRADE
sward - - - - - SOD, TURF, GRASS
swarm - TEEM, HORDE, CONGREGATE
swarm of bees - - - - - - - HIVE
swarm of bees (Scot.) - - BYKE, BIKE
swarming - - - - - - - - - ALIVE
swart - - - - - - - - - - TAWNY
swarthy - - - - - - - - - - DUN
swat - - - - - - - - - - - - HIT
swathe - - - - - - - - - - WRAP
sway - - - - TOTTER, ROCK, REEL, TEETER, FLUCTUATE, NOD, WAG
sway from side to side - - - CAREEN
sway from side to side (naut.) - RACK
swaying movement - - - - - LURCH
swear - - - - - - - - - - - - VOW
swear falsely - - - - - - - PERJURE
sweat - - - - - - - - PERSPIRE
Swedish chemist - - - - - - NOBEL
Swedish coin - - ORE, KRONE, KRONA
Swedish explorer - - - - - - HEDIN
Swedish measure - - - - - AMAR (pl.)
Swedish nightingale - - - - - LIND
Swedish physicist - - - - - - NOBEL
Swedish province - - - - - - LAEN
Swedish river - - - - - - - KLAR
Swedish tribe - - - - - - - GEATAS
sweep - - - - - - - - - - RANGE
sweep away - - - - - - - - SCOUR
sweet - SUGARY, SACCHARINE, CANDY
sweet biscuit - - - - - - - - BUN
sweet cake - - - - - - - CRULLER
sweet clover - - - - - - - MELILOT
sweet drink - - - - - - - NECTAR
sweet flag - - - - - - - - SEDGE
sweet liquid - - - - - - - SYRUP
sweet pepper - - - - - - PIMIENTO
sweet potato - - - - - - - - YAM
sweet singer - - - - - - - - SIREN
sweet sound - - - - - - - MUSIC
sweet tone - - - - - - - - DULCET
sweet viscid material - - - - HONEY
sweetbrier - - - - - - - EGLANTINE
sweeten - - - - - - - - - - SUGAR
sweetened brandy with mint - - JULEP
sweetened sherry drink - - - - NEGUS
sweetheart - - LOVER, INAMORATA, LEMAN, AMORET
sweetheart (Anglo. Ir.) - - - - - GRA
sweetheart (arch.) - - - - - LEMAN
sweetheart (Scot.) - - - - - - - JO
sweetmeat - - - - - CANDY, NOUGAT
sweetsop - - - - - - - - ATES, ATTA
swell - DILATE, BULB, SURGE, EXPAND, DISTEND
swell of water - - - - - SURGE, SEA
swelling - - - - - - - - - - NODE

swelling wave - - - - - - - ROLLER
swerve - VEER, SHEER, CAREEN, SHY, DEVIATE
swift - RAPID, FLEET, FAST, MERCURIAL
swift Malaysian vessel - - - - - PROA
swiftly - - - - - - - - - - APACE
swiftness - - - - - CELERITY, SPEED
swimming - - - - - - - - NATANT
swimming (art of) - - - - - NATATION
swimming bird - - LOON, GREBE, AUK
swimming organ - - - - - FINS, FIN
swindle - - WANGLE, DUPE, FRAUD, BILK, FLEECE, CHEAT, GIP, GYP
swindle (slang) - - GIP, GYP, SHARK
swindler - - - - - - - - - CHEAT
swindler (var.) - - - - - - - - GIP
swine - - PORCINE, TAPIR, SOW, HOG
swine (female) - - - - - - - SOW
swine (male) - - - - - - - - BOAR
swinelike animal - - - - - - TAPIR
swing - - - - - - SWAY, BRANDISH
swing about a fixed point - - - SLUE
swinge - - - - - - - - - - BEAT
swinging barrier - - - - - - - GATE
swinging support - - - - - - HINGE
swirl - - - - - - - EDDY, WHIRL
Swiss canton - - - - - URI, AARGAU
Swiss capital - - - - - BERN, BERNE
Swiss city - - BASLE, SION, BASEL, AARAU
Swiss commune - - - - - - - SION
Swiss cottage - - - - - - - CHALET
Swiss dialect - - - - - - - LADIN
Swiss-French river - - - - - RHONE
Swiss lake - URI, LUCERNE, CONSTANCE
Swiss measure - - - - - STAAB, ELLE
Swiss mountain - - - - - - - RIGI
Swiss mountaineer's song - - YODEL
Swiss patriot - - - - - - - - TELL
Swiss poet - - - - - - - - AMIEL
Swiss river - - - - - - - - - AAR
Swiss school - - - - - - - DADA
Swiss song - - - - - - - - YODEL
Swiss wind - - - - - - - - - BISE
switch - - - - - - - - - - SHUNT
switchboard section - - - - - PANEL
swollen - - - - - - - - - TUMID
swoon - - - - - - - FAINT, TRANCE
sword - SABER, EPEE, RAPIER, SABRE, TOLEDO
sword handle - - - - - HILT, HAFT
sword shaped - - ENSATE, ENSIFORM
swordsmen's dummystake - PELS, PEL
sworn statement - - - - - - - OATH
sycophant - - - PARASITE, TOADY
syllabic sound - - - - - - SONANT
syllable of hestitation - - - - - - ER
syllable stress - - - - - - - TONE
sylvan - - - - - - WOODED, RUSTIC
sylvan deity - - - - - - - - SATYR
symbol - - - - - - SIGN, EMBLEM
symbol of bondage - - - - - - YOKE
symbol of dead - - - - - - ORANT
symbol of indebtedness (colloq.) - - - I.O.U.
symbol of mourning - - - - - CREPE
symbol of office - - - - - - - MACE
symbol of peace - - - - - - DOVE
symbol of power - - - - - - SWORD
symbol of quick death - - - - - ASP
symbol of victory - - - - - - PALM
symbol of wedlock - - - - - - RING
symmetrical - - - - - - - REGULAR
symmetry - - - - - SHAPELINESS
sympathiser - - - - - CONDOLER
symptom of cold - - - - - SNEEZE
synopsis - OUTLINE, TABLE, EPITOME
synthetic fabric - - - - - RAYON
Syriac - - - - - - - - - SYRIAN
Syrian - - - - - - - - - - SYRIAC
Syrian antelope - - - - - - ADDAX
Syrian city - - - - - - - - ALEPPO
Syrian deity - - - - - - - - - EL
Syrian garment - - - - - - - ABA
Syrian native - - - - - - - SYRIAN
Syro-Phoenecian god - - - - - BAAL
syrt - - - - - - - - - - - BOG
system - - - - ORDER, METHOD, ARRANGEMENT
system of management - - - - REGIME
system of religious observances - CULT
system of rules - - - - CODE, LAWS
system of signals - - - - - - CODE
system of voting - - - - - - BALLOT
system of weaving - - - - - - TWILL
system of weights - - - - - - TROY
system of worship - - - - - - CULT
systematic course of living - REGIMEN
systematic instruction - - - TRAINING
systematic pile - - - - - - - STACK
systematize - - - - - - ORGANIZE
systematized body of law - - - CODE

T

tab - FLAP, LABEL, TALLY, ACCOUNT, MARK
table - - - - - SCHEDULE, STAND
table centerpiece - - - - - EPERGNE
table dish - - - - - - - - PLATTER
table linen - - - - - - - - NAPERY
table (small) - - - - - - - - STAND
table utensil - - - - - - - - DISH
table vessel - - - - - - - - TUREEN
tableland - - - - - MESA, PLATEAU
tableland of South Africa - - KAROO
tablet - - - - - - - - PAD, TROCHE
tablet of stone - - - - - - - STELE
tableware - - - - - - - - DISHES
tabor - - - - - TABOURET, TIMBREL
tabouret - - - - - - - - - TABOR
tabulation of the year - - CALENDAR
tacit - - - - - - IMPLIED, SILENT
taciturn - - - - - SILENT, RETICENT
taciturnity - - - - - - RETICENCE
tack - - - - - - BRAD, BASTE, GEAR
tackle - - - - - - - - - - GEAR
tactical trap - - - - - - - AMBUSH
tad - - - - - URCHIN, ARAB, GAMIN
tadpole - - - - - - - - POLLIWOG
tag - - - - - - - - - LABEL, LAMB
Tagalog term - - - - - - - - ITA
Tai race (branch) - - - - - - - LAO
tail - - - - - - - - - - - TRACE
tail end - - - - - - - - - - RUMP
tailless amphibian - - - - - - TOAD
tailor - - - - - - - - - - SARTOR
tailor's iron - - - - - - - - GOOSE
taint - - POLLUTE, POISON, INFECT, DEFILE, BLEMISH, CORRUPT, VITIATE
Taj Mahal city - - - - - - - - AGRA
take - - - SEIZE, ACCEPT, RECEIVE, CAPTURE, GRASP, ADOPT
take as one's own - - - - - - ADOPT
take away - ADEEM, DEDUCT, DETRACT, REMOVE
take away from - - - - - - DEPRIVE
take away (law) - - - - - - ADEEM

T

take back - - - RESCIND, RETRACT, RECANT
take back publicly - - - - - RECANT
take beforehand - - - - - PREEMPT
take care - - BEWARE, TEND, MIND
take care (arch.) - - - - - - RECK
take care of horse - - - - - GROOM
take on cargo - - - - - - - LADE
take charge - - - PRESIDE, ATTEND
take cognizance of - - - - - NOTICE
take courage - - - - - - HEARTEN
take credit - - - - - - - - PRIDE
take delight - - - - - - - REVEL
take ease - - - - - - - - - REST
take evening meal - - - - SUP, DINE
take exception - - - - - - - DEMUR
take food by violence - - - - - PREY
take from - - - - - - - - WREST
take for granted - ASSUME, PRESUME
take great delight - - - - - - REVEL
take heed of - - - - - RECK, WARE
take illegally - - - - - STEAL, POACH
take impressions from type - - PRINT
take the initiative - - - - - - LEAD
take into custody - - - - - - ARREST
take into stomach - - - - - - INGEST
take liberties - - - - - - PRESUME
take medicine - - - - - - - DOSE
take movie - - - - - - - - FILM
take oath - - - - - - - - - SWEAR
take off - - - - - - DOFF, DEPART
take off weight - - - - - - REDUCE
take offense at - - - - - - RESENT
take one's way - - - - - - - WEND
take out - - - - - - DELE, DELETE
take part in contest or game - COMPETE, PLAY
take part of - - - - - - - - SIDE
take picture - - - - - PHOTOGRAPH
take place - - - - - - - - HAPPEN
take place again - - - - - - RECUR
take place of - - - - - - SUPPLANT
take pleasure in - - - - - - ENJOY
take position - - - - - - - - STAND
take possession of (arch.) - - SEISE
take possession of by force - - USURP
take precedence - - - - - - - RANK
take prominent part - - - - - FIGURE
take a recess - - - - - - - - REST
take in sail - - - - - - - - REEF
take satisfaction - - - - - - AVENGE
take turns - - - ALTERNATE, ROTATE
take umbrage - - - - - - - RESENT
take unawares - - - - - - SURPRISE
take up again - - - - - - RESUME
taken - - - - - - - - RESERVED
taken by two's - - - - - - - DUPLE
taking in - - - - - - - - INTAKE
Tai race - - - - - - - - - LAO
talar - - - - - - - - - - ROBE
talc (kind) - - - - - - - AGALITE
tale - FALSEHOOD, STORY, ANECDOTE, LEGEND
tale of adventure - - - - - - GEST
talebearer - - - - - - - TATTLER
talent - - - GIFT, APTITUDE, FLAIR
talisman - - - - - - - - - AMULET
talisman (former spelling) - - TALESM
talk - - - CHAT, CONVERSE, ORATE, ADDRESS
talk bombastically - - - - - - RANT
talk childishly - - - - - - PRATTLE
talk (colloq.) - - - - - - - SPIEL
talk dogmatically - - - - - LECTURE
talk effusively - - - - - - - GUSH
talk foolishly - - - - DRIVEL, PRATE
talk glibly - - - - - PRATE, PATTER
talk hypocritically - - - - - - CANT
talk idly - - PRATE, GAB, CHATTER, TATTLE
talk imperfectly - - - - - - - LISP
talk incoherently and irrationally - RAVE
talk informally - - - - - - - CHAT
talk (slang) - SPIEL, GAB, CHATTER, JABBER
talk superficially - - - - - SMATTER
talk tediously - - - - - - - PROSE
talk unintelligibly - - - - - JABBER
talk vainly - - - - - - - - - PRATE
talk vehemently - - - - - - - DING
talk volubly - - - - - CHIN, PATTER
talk wildly or with enthusiasm - RAVE, RANT
talkative - - - - - - - - - CHATTY
talkativeness - - - - - - LOQUACITY
talking bird - - - - - - - PARROT
tall - - - - - - LONG, HIGH, LOFTY
tall building - - - - - - - - TOWER
tall and thin - - - - - - LEAN, LANK
tall timber - - - - - - - - - TEAK
tallow - - - - - - - - - - - SUET
tally - - - SCORE, COUNT, RECKON, REGISTER, CORRESPOND, MATCH
tally (colloq.) - - - - - - - - TAB
talon - - - - - - - - - - - CLAW
talus - - - - - - - - - - ANKLE
tamarack - - - - - - - - - LARCH
tamarin - - - MONKEY, MARMOSET
tamarisk salt tree - ATLEE, ATLE, ATLI
tambour - - - - - - - - - - DRUM
tame - - SUBDUE, DOCILE, GENTLE, TRACTABLE, MILD, CONQUER, MEEK, FLAT, SUBDUED
tame animal - - - - - - - - - PET
tamp - - - - - - - - - - - - RAM
tamp with clay - - - - - - - PUG
tamper - - - - - - MEDDLE, TINKER
Tampico fiber - - - - - - - ISTLE
tan - - - - ECRU, SUNBURN, BRONZE
tang - - - - - - - - TASTE, TRACE
tangent - - - - - - - - TOUCHING
tangible - - - - TACTILE, PALPABLE
tangle - SNARL, MAT, RAVEL, ENMESH, ENSNARE
tangled mass - - MOP, SHAG, RAVEL
tank - - - - - - - - - - CISTERN
tanned - - - - - - - - - - TAWNY
tanned hide - - - - - - - LEATHER
tanning material - - - - - - SUMAC
Tannhauser's composer - - - WAGNER
tantalize - - - - - - TAUNT, TEASE
Tantalus' daughter - - - - - NIOBE
tantrum - - - - - - - - - - RAGE
tap - - - - - - - - - PAT, SPIGOT
tape - - - - - - - - - - - - BIND
taper - - - - - CANDLE, DIMINISH
taper a timber in shipbuilding - SNAPE
tapered slip of wood - - - - - SHIM
tapering - - - - - - - - - TERETE
tapering piece - SHIM, GORE, GUSSET
tapering solid - - - - - - - - CONE
tapestry - - - - - - ARRAS, TAPIS
tapir - - - - - - - - - - DANTA
Tapuyan Indian - - - - - - - - GES
tar - - - - - - - - - - - SAILOR
tardy - - - - - BELATED, SLOW, LATE
tare - - - - - - - - WEED, VETCH
targe - - - - - - - - - - SHIELD
target - AIM, MARK, GOAL, OBJECT, AMBITION, BUTT

tariff - - - - - - - - - - - DUTY
tarnish - SULLIED, MARRED, DULLED, SOILED, SPOTTED
taro paste - - - - - - - - - - POI
taro roots - - - EDDOES, EDDO (s.)
tarry - WAIT, REMAIN, BIDE, LINGER, LOITER, LAG, ABIDE
tarsus - - - - - - - - - - ANKLE
tart - - ACUTE, ACID, SOUR, ACRID, SHARP, CAUSTIC
tartan - - - - - - - - - - PLAID
Tartar - - - - - - - - - - TURK
Tartar militiaman (var.) - - - ULAN
tartness - - - - - - - - ACERBITY
task - - CHORE, STINT, STENT, JOB, DUTY, TAX
taskmaster - - - - - - - OVERSEER
taste - RELISH, PENCHANT, SAVOR, SIP, FLAVOUR, PALATE, SAPOR, TANG
taste (strong) - - - - - - - TANG
tasteful - - - - - - - - - - NEAT
tastefully executed - - - - ARTISTIC
tasteless - - - - - - PALL, VAPID
tasty - - - - - - - SAVORY, SAPID
tatter - - - RAG, SHRED, FRAGMENT
tatter (Scot.) - - - - - - - TAVER
tattered - - - - - - - - RAGGEDY
tattle - - - - - - GOSSIP, BLAB
taunt - - SNEER, PLAGUE, CENSURE, TWIT, GIBE, REPROACH, MOCK, JIBE
taurus - - - - - - - - - - BULL
taut - - - - - - - TENSE, TIGHT
tavern - - - - - - - INN, CABARET
tavern (slang) - - - - - - - - PUB
taw - - - - - - - - - - MARBLE
tawdry - - - CHEAP, TINSEL, GAUDY
tawny - - - SWART, TANNED, OLIVE
tax - - STENT, ASSESS, LEVY, TOLL, DUTY, SCOT, TRIBUTE, TARIFF, STRAIN, ASSESSMENT, EXACTION, CESS, EXCISE, IMPOST, TASK
tax (kind) - - - - - - - - - POLL
tax levied by the king - - - TAILLE
taxi - - - - - - - - - - - CAB
tea - - - - - - - - - - - - CHA
tea (kind) - - - - - - - - OOLONG
tea tester - - - - - - - - TASTER
tea urn - - - - - - - - SAMOVAR
teacake - - - - - - - - - - SCONE
teach - - - - - INSTRUCT, TRAIN
teacher - - - EDUCATOR, TRAINER, INSTRUCTOR
teacher of the deaf - - - - ORALIST
teaching - - - MORAL, INSTRUCTION
teak tree - - - - - - - - - TECA
team - - - - CREW, YOKE, SQUAD, OVERFLOW, BROOD, GROUP, SPAN
team drivers - - - - - - TEAMSTERS
team harnessed one before the other - - TANDEM
team of horses - - - - - - - SPAN
team partisan (slang) - - - ROOTER
teamster - - - - - - - - - CARTER
teamster's command - - - HAW, GEE
tear - RIP, REND, LACERATE, CLEAVE, SEVER, SPLIT
tear apart - - - TATTER, REND, RIP
tear asunder - - - - - - - - SPLIT
tear down - - RASE, DEMOLISH, RAZE
tear into strips - - - SHRED, TATTER
tears (Phil. Isl.) - - - - - - LOHA
tease - - PLAGUE, ANNOY, MOLEST, TANTALIZE, PESTER, COAX, NAG, IMPORTUNE
tease (slang) - - - - - - - - RAG

teasing propensity - - - - - - ITCH
Tibetan antelope - - - - - - - SUS
technique - - - - - - - METHOD
techy - - - - - - - - - - PEEVISH
tedious - PROSE, IRKSOME, TIRESOME, FATIGUING
tedious discourse - - - - - - PROSE
tedium - - - - - - - - - - ENNUI
tee - - - - - - - - - - - MOUND
teem - - - - - - - - - - ABOUND
teepee - - - - - - - - - WIGWAM
teeter - - - SEESAW, JIGGLE, SWAY, VACILLATE
teeth - - - - - - - - - - FANGS
teeth coating - - - - - - - ENAMEL
teeth incrustation - - - - - TARTAR
teeth (pert. to) - - - - - - DENTAL
teeth on wheel - - - - SPROCKETS
teetotaler - - - - - - - ABSTAINER
tela - - - - - - - - - WEB, TISSUE
Telamon's son - - - - - - - - AJAX
telar - - - - - - - - - - WEBLIKE
telegram - - - - - - - - - - WIRE
telegraph - - - SEMAPHORE, WIRE
telegraph code - - - - - - MORSE
teleost fish - - - - - - - - - EEL
tell - - RELATE, NARRATE, IMPART, RECOUNT, INFORM, DISCLOSE
tell an adventure story (colloq.) - YARN
tell revelatory facts abount - DEBUNK
tell secrets - - - - - - BLAB, SPILL
tell tales - - - - - - BLAB, TATTLE
tell thoughtlessly - - - - BLAB, BLAT
teller's office - - - - - - - CAGE
temper - - ANNEAL, MEDDLE, TONE, QUALIFY, TANTRUM, MITIGATE
temper glass - - - - - - - ANNEAL
temper by heat - - - - - - ANNEAL
temperament - - - - MIEN, HUMOR
temperance - - - - - MODERATION
temperate - - MODERATE, ABSTINENT
temperature below freezing - - FROST
tempest - - STORM, TUMULT, ORAGE
"The Tempest" character - - CALIBAN
"The Tempest" spirit - - - - - ARIEL
tempestuous - - - STORMY, VIOLENT
temple (arch.) - - - - - - - - FANE
tempo - - - TIME, METER, RHYTHM
temporal - - - - - - TRANSITORY
temporarily - - - - - - - - NONCE
temporarily brilliant star - - - NOVA
temporary - - - - - - - TRANSIENT
temporary abode - - - - - - LODGE
temporary cessation - - PAUSE, LULL
temporary expedient - - - STOPGAP
temporary fashion - - - - - - FAD
temporary grant - - - - - - LOAN
temporary headquarters - - - CAMP
temporary inaction - - - - - PAUSE
temporary stop - - - - - - - DELAY
temporary stopping place - REPOSOIR
temporary use (naut.) - - - - - JURY
tempt - - - ALLURE, LURE, ENTICE
temptation - - - - - - ALLUREMENT
tempter - - - - - - - - - - SATAN
ten (suffix) - - - - - - - - - TEEN
ten - - - - - - - DECADE, DENARY
ten (comb. form) - - - - - - - DECA
ten decibels - - - - - - - - - BEL
ten dollar bill (slang) - - - - TENNER
ten dollar gold piece - - - - - EAGLE
ten thousand things - - - - MYRIAD
ten years - - - - - - - - - DECADE
tenacious - - - - - - - - - CLINGY
tenacious viscid - - - - - - - GLUE

T

T

tenant - - - - - - LESSEE, RENTER
tend - - - - - CARE, MIND, TREND, CONTRIBUTE, TREAT, GUARD, INCLINE, CONDUCE
tend to rise - - - - - - - LEVITATE
tend to wear away - ABRASIVE, EROSIVE
tendency - - - - - - TREND, BENT
tendency to go astray - - - ERRANCY
tender (to) - - - - - - - - OFFER
tender - - - - SORE, SOFT, GENTLE, PROFFER, OFFER, SENSITIVE, KIND
tender feeling - - - - - SENTIMENT
tender (It.) - - - - - - AMOROSO
tenderness - - - - - LOVE, KINDNESS
tending to obstruct - - - - OCCLUSIVE
tending to produce sleep - - HYPNOTIC
tendon - - - - - - - - - - SINEW
tendon (comb. form) - - - - - TENO
tenebrous - - - - - - - - GLOOMY
tenement - - - - - FLAT, DWELLING
tenet - BELIEF, MAXIM, PRINCIPLE, CREED, DOCTRINE, DOGMA
tenfold - - - - - - - - - DENARY
tennis point - - - - - - - - - ACE
tennis score - - - - SET, ALL, DEUCE, LOVE
tennis stroke - - - - - - LOB, CHOP
Tennyson hero - - - - - - - ARDEN
Tennyson heroine - - - - ENID, ELAINE
Tennyson poem - - - - - - - MAUD
tenon receiver - - - - - - MORTISE
tenor - - TREND, COURSE, PURPORT, DRIFT
tenor violin - - - - - - ALTO, VIOLA
tenpin ball - - - - - - - - BOWL
tense - - - - RIGID, TAUT, STRAINED
tensile - - - - - - - - DUCTILE
tension - - - - - - STRAIN, STRESS
tent - - - - - - - ENCAMP, TEPEE
tent dweller - - - - - ARAB, CAMPER
tentacle - - - - - - - - - FEELER
tented down - - - - - - - - - CAMP
tenth - - - - - - - - - - TITHE
tenth muse - - - - - - - SAPPHO
tenth part - - - - - - - - - TITHE
tenth (prefix) - - - - - - - - DECI
tenuous - - - - - - - - - - RARE
tenure - - - - LEASE, HOLDING, TERM
tepee - - - - - - - - - - WIGWAM
tepid - - - - - - - - - - WARM
terebrate - - - - - - - PERFORATE
terella - - - - - - - - - EARTHKIN
tergal - - - - - - - - - - DORSAL
term - WORD, CALL, LIMIT, TENURE, DURATION
term of holding - - - - - - TENURE
term in Tagalog - - - - - - - ITA
termagant - - - - - - - - SHREW
terminal - - - - END, CONCLUDING
termination - ENDING, LIMIT, FINALE
termination of a disease - - - - LYSIS
termination of feminine nouns - ESS
terminus - - - - - - - - BOUNDARY
tern-like bird - - - - - - SKIMMER
ternary - - - - - - - - - - TRIAD
terpsichoreans - - - - - - DANCERS
terra - - - - - - - - - - EARTH
terrace - - - - - - - - - BALCONY
terrain - - - - - - - - - REGION
terrapin - - - - - - - - - TURTLE
terrene - - - - - - - - - WORLDLY
terrestrial - - - - - TERRENE, EARTHY
terrible - - - - DIRE, AWFUL, TRAGIC, DREADFUL, GRIM
terrier (kind) - - - - - - - - SKYE
terrified - - - - - - - - - AGHAST
terrify - - - - - - - - - - DISMAY
terrifying person - - - - - GORGON
territorial division - - - - - CANTON
territory - - - - - - - - - REGION
territory governed by a ban - - BANAT
terror - DREAD, FRIGHT, FEAR, HORROR
terse - - LACONIC, CONCISE, PITHY, COMPACT, BRIEF
test - - TRIAL, TRY, TRYOUT, ESSAY, CHECK, EXAMINE, PROVE, STANDARD, ASSAY, CRITERION
test ore - - - - - - - - - - ASSAY
test print - - - - - - - - - PROOF
testa - - - - - - - - - - - SEED
testament - - - - - COVENANT, WILL
testator - - - - - - - BEQUEATHER
tested eggs - - - - - - - CANDLED
testify - AVER, DEPONE, AVOW, ATTEST
testify under oath - - - - - DEPONE
testimony - - - - - - - - EVIDENCE
testy - - - - - - - PEEVISH, TOUCHY
tether - FASTEN, RESTRAIN, CONFINE, TRY, TIE
Teutonic alphabet character - - - RUNE
Teutonic deity - - ER, FREA, WODEN
Teutonic demi-goddess of fate - NORN
Teutonic god - AESIR, ODIN, TYR, ER
Teutonic mythological character - FREA
Texas city - WACO, LAREDO, PALESTINE
Texas county - - - - - - - - NOLAN
Texas mission - - - - - - - ALAMO
text - - - - - - - TOPIC, SUBJECT
textbook - - - - - MANUAL, PRIMER
textile fabric - - - - - - - - - WEB
texture - - - - - - - - WALE, WEB
texture of threads - - - - - - WEB
Thai - - - - - - - - - - SIAMESE
Thailand - - - - - - - - - - - SIAM
thane - - - - - - - CHURL, CEORL
thankfulness - - - - - - GRATITUDE
thankless person - - - - - INGRATE
thanks - - - - - - - - GRATITUDE
that - - - - - - - - - - - - YON
that (arch.) - - - - - - - - - YON
that is (abbr.) - - - - - - - IE, EG
that is to say - - - - - - NAMELY
that may be readily moved - PORTABLE
that may be repeated - - - ITERANT
that in particular - - - - - - - THE
that which attracts - - - - MAGNET
that which binds - - - - - - GIRDER
that which comes in - - - RECEIPTS
that which cures - - - PALLIATIVE
that which erodes - - - - - WEARER
that which gives stability - - BALLAST
that which gives zest - - - - - SPICE
that which is kept - - - - - RETENT
that which lacerates - - - - TEARER
that which is left - - - - - REMNANT
that which one thinks - - - OPINION
that which produces - - - - - PARENT
that which produces added weight - - FATTENER
that which is retained - - - - RETENT
that for which something can be bought - PRICE
that which is taught - - - DOCTRINE
that which uncovers - - - - - OPENER
that which will counteract - ANTIDOTE
thaw - - - - - - - - - - - - MELT
the (Scot.) - - - - - - - - - - - TA
theatre - - - - - - - - PLAYHOUSE

T

theater group - - - - - - - ANTA
theatrical - - - - - - - - STAGY
theatrical exhibition - - - PAGEANT
theatrical profession - - - - STAGE
theatrical success (slang) - - - HIT
them (of) - - - - - - - - THEIR
theme - TOPIC, SUBJECT, MOTIF, ESSAY
theodolite - - - - - - - ALIDADE
theological authority - - - - IMAM
theological degree - - - - - D.D.
theoretical force - - - - - - OD
theory - - - - - - - - - IDEA
theory that space is filled with matter - PLENISM
therefore - ERGO, HENSE, SO, THUS, HENCE
thermometer (kind) - - CENTIGRADE
thespian - - - - - - - - ACTOR
Thessaly mountain - - - - - OSSA
thew - - - - - - - - - SINEW
thick - - - - DENSE, FAT, COARSE
thick board - - - - - - - PLANK
thick flat slice - - - - - - SLAB
thick ointment - - - SALVE, CERATE
thick piece - - - - - - - - SLAG
thick set - - - - - - - - STOUT
thick soup - - - - PUREE, BISQUE
thick soup (arch.) - - - - POTTAGE
thicken - - - - - - - DEEPEN, GEL
thicket - - - BUSH, BRAKE, HEDGE, COVERT, COPSE, BOSK
thicket (dense) - - - - CHAPARRAL
thickness - - - - - - PLY, LAYER
thief - - ROBBER, LOOTER, BURGLAR
thieve - - - - - - - PILFER, ROB
thieves' slang (Fr.) - - - - ARGOT
thin - - SLENDER, RAREFIED, LEAN, SPARSE, FINE, SHEER, DILUTE, WATERY, SLIM, BONY, SVELTE, DILUTED, GAUNT, LANK
thin bark - - - - - - - - - RIND
thin batter cake - - - - - PANCAKE
thin cake - - - - - - - - WAFER
thin coating - - - - FILM, VENEER
thin cotton fabric - - - - - JACONET
thin covering - - - - - - - VENEER
thin dress material - - - - - VOILE
thin facing of superior wood - VENEER
thin fogs - - - - - - - - MISTS
thin gauzy material - - - - CHIFFON
thin layer - - - - - - - LAMELLA
thin layer over inferior one - - VENEER
thin leaf - - - - - - - - BLADE
thin and light - - - - - - PAPERY
thin metal band - - - - - - STRAP
thin metal disk - - - PATEN, PATINA
thin muslin - - - - - - TARLATAN
thin nail - - - - - - - - - BRAD
thin narrow board - - - LATH, SLAT
thin net for veils - - - - - TULLE
thin oatmeal griddle cake - - SCONE
thin out - - - - - - - - - PETER
thin paper - - - - - - - TISSUE
thin pencil mark - - - - - - LINE
thin piece of stone - - - - - SLAB
thin piece of wood - - - - SLIVER
thin plate - LAMINA, LAMELLA, DISC
thin porridge - - - - - - - GRUEL
thin rain - - - - - - - - - MIST
thin scale - - - - - - - LAMINA
thin and sharp in tone - - - REEDY
thin sheet material - - - - - VENEER
thin sheets of metal - - - - FOIL
thin slice - - - - - - - - - SLAB
thin soup - - - - - - - - BROTH
thin strip of wood - - LATH, SPLINT
thin and vibrant - - - - - - REEDY
thing - - - - - - - - - - MATTER
things American - - - AMERICANA
things done - - ACTA (pl.), ACTUM (s.)
things found - - - - - - - TROVE
things to be added - - - ADDENDA
things to be done - - - - - AGENDA
thing being so - - - - - - - NOW
things differing from others - VARIANT
things difficult to bear - - HARDSHIPS
things to do - - - - - - - AGENDA
things in law - - - - - RES, LES, RE
things lost - - - - - - - LOSSES
things obtained from other things - - DERIVATIVES
things owned - - - - - - PROPERTY
things past - - - - - - - BYGONES
things to see - - - - - - - SIGHTS
things of small value - - - TRIFLES
things which existed - - - REALITIES
think - - OPINE, PONDER, COGITATE, BELIEVE, DEEM, CEREBRATE, CONSIDER
think alike - - - - - - - - AGREE
think (arch.) - - - TROW, WEEN, WIS
think logically - - - - - - REASON
think moodily - - - - - - - BROOD
thinly clinking - - - - - - TINKLY
thinly diffused - - - - - - SPARSE
thinly scattered - - - - - - SPARSE
thinner - - - - - - - - - FINER
third in degree - - - - - - TERTIARY
third (musical) - - - - - - TIERCE
third power - - - - - - - - CUBE
thirsty - - - - - - DRY, PARCHED
this evening - - - - - - - TONIGHT
this place - - - - - - - - - HERE
this springs eternal - - - - - - HOPE
this time - - - - - - - - - - NOW
thistle plant - - - - - - - ASTER
thong - - - STRAP, LASSO, AMENTA
thong by which javelin was thrown - - AMENTA
thorax - - - - - - - - - CHEST
thorn - BRIAR, BRIER, SPINE, SETA
thorny - SPINOSE, BRAMBLY, SPINATE
thorny bush - - - - - - - BRIAR
thorny shrub - - - - ACACIA, BRIER
thoroughly - - - - - - - - - ALL
those against - - - - - - - ANTIS
those born in a place - - - NATIVES
those in a foray - - - - RAIDERS
those impervious to pain or pleasure - - STOICS
those in the know - - - - INSIDERS
those in office - - - - - - - INS
those there (arch.) - - - - - - YON
those things - - - - - - - THEM
those who ask alms - - - BEGGARS
those who sell - - - - - SALESMEN
though - - - - - - - - - - YET
thought - - OPINION, IDEA, OPINED
thoughtful - - PENSIVE, CONSIDERATE
thoughtful person - - - - - THINKER
thousand - - - - - - - - CHILIAD
thousand (comb. form) - KILO, MILLE
thrall - - - SLAVE, SERF, BONDMAN
thrash - - - BEAT, BELABOR, DRUB, WHIPLASH
thrash (slang) - - - - - - - LAM
thread - LACE, TWINE, LISLE, FIBER, REEVE, FILAMENT
thread fabric - - - - - - - - LACE
thread (kind) - LINEN, LISLE, COTTON, SILK

T

thread of metal - - - - - - - WIRE
thread network - - - - - - - LACE
thread of silk forming cocoon - BAVE
thread of a story - - - - - CLUE
thread of wool or silk - - ARRASENE
threaded fastener - - - - - - - NUT
threadlike - - FILOSE, FILAR, LINEAR
threadlike filament - - - - - FIBER
threadlike line - - - - - - - STRIA
threadlike ridge on shells - - - LIRA
threadlike tissue - - - - - - FIBER
threat - - - - - - - - MENACE
threatened - - IMPENDED, MENACED
threatening - - - - - - - LOWERY
three - - - - - - - TRIAD, TRIO
three (musical) - - - - - - - - TER
three (prefix) - - - - - - - - TRI
three-corner - - - - - - TRIGONOUS
three-cornered sail - - - - - LATEEN
three dimensional - - - - - - CUBIC
three goddesses of destiny - - FATES
three in one - - - - - - - TRIUNE
three joints - - - - - - - TRINODAL
three-legged chair - - - - - - STOOL
three-legged stand - TRIPOD, TRIVET, TEAPOY
three-masted vessel - - - - - BARK
three part composition - - - - TRIO
three points in Rugby football - TRY
three pronged weapon - - - TRIDENT
three Roman Fates - - - - - PARCAE
three score and ten - - - - SEVENTY
three-sided figure - - - - TRIANGLE
three spotted dominoes - - - - TREYS
three stringed musical instrument - - REBEC
three-toed sloth - - - - - - - - AI
three toned musical chord - - TRIAD
threefold - TRINE, TREBLE, TRINAL, TRIPLE
threshing implement - - - - - FLAIL
threshold - - - - - - - - - - SILL
threw (poet.) - - - - - - ELANCED
thrice (prefix) - - - - TER, TRI, TRO
thrifty - - - - - PROVIDENT, FRUGAL
thrill - - - - - - - - - - TINGLE
thrive - - PROSPER, BATTEN, GROW
throat disease - - - - - - - CROUP
throat lozenge - - - - - - - PASTIL
throat part - - - - TONSIL, GLOTTIS
throat (pert. to) - - - - - - GULAR
throat swelling - - - - - - GOITER
throb - - - - BEAT, PANT, PULSE
throe - - - - - - - - - - PANG
throne - - - - - - - - - - ASANA
throng - MASS, HORDE, CROWD, HORD, ROUT
thronged - - - - - - - - ALIVE
through - - - - - - PER, DIA, BY
through the mouth - - - - - PERORAL
throve - - - - - - - PROSPERED
throw - HURL, TOSS, CAST, HEAVE, FLING, PITCH, PELT
throw away - - - - - - - DISCARD
throw back - - - - - - - - - REPEL
throw into confusion - - DISTURB, PIE
throw of dice - - - - - - - - MAIN
throw into disorder - DERANGE, PIE, CLUTTER
throw light on - - - - - - ILLUME
throw lightly - - - - - - - - TOSS
throw off - - - - - - - SHED, EMIT
throw off the track - - - - DERAIL
throw out - - - - - - - - - EJECT
throw over - - - - - - - - - JILT
throw (poet.) - - - - - - - ELANCE
throw of six at dice - - - - - SISE
throw up - - - - - - - - - RETCH
thrown into ecstasy - - - - - ENRAPT
thrum - - - - - - - - - - - STRUM
thrush - - MAVIS, MISSEL, ROBIN, VEERY
thrust - POKE, LUNGE, STAB, PROD, SHOVE
thrust back - - - - - - - - - REPEL
thrust, as a lance - - - - - - TILT
thrusting weapon - - - - - - LANCE
thud - - - - - - - - - - - - BEAT
thump - BANG, BUMP, BLOW, POUND
thumping - - - - - - - - - TATTOO
thunder - - - - - - - - - - - PEAL
thunder and lightning (pert. to) - - - CERAUNIC
thurible - - - - - - - - - CENSER
thus - - SIC, THEREFORE, SO, HENCE
thus far - - - - - - - - - - - YET
thus (Latin) - - - - - - - - - SIC
thus (Scot.) - - - - - - - - - SAE
thwart - - SPITE, FRUSTRATE, BRAIN
tiara - CORONET, DIADEM, FRONTLET
Tibetan capital - - - - - - - LASSA
Tibetan gazelle - - - - - - - GOA
Tibetan monk - - - - - - - - LAMA
Tibetan mountain ruminant - - TAKIN
Tibetan ox - - - - - - - - - - YAK
Tibetan priest - - - - - - - LAMA
tick - - - - - - - - MITE, ACARID
tick stuffed with hair - - MATTRESS
ticklish - - - - - - - - UNSTABLE
tidal flood and wave - - - - - EAGRE
tide - - CURRENT, SEASON, SURGE, BEFALL, NEAP
tide (kind) - - - - - - - RIP, NEAP
tidings - - - - - - - WORD, NEWS
tidy - - - - - - TRIM, NEAT, TRIG
tie - - DRAW, KNOT, BOND, CRAVAT, LACE, BIND, EQUAL, LASH, UNITE, LINK, SCARF, TETHER, FASTEN
tie an animal - - - - - - - TETHER
tie game - - - - - - - - - - DRAW
tier - ROW, LAYER, DEN, RANK, BANK
tierce - - - - - - - - - - - CASK
Tierra del Fuego Indian - - - - - ONA
tiff - - - - - - - - - - - - SPAT
tight - - - - - - - - TAUT, TENSE
tight fitting - - - - - - - - - SNUG
tight fitting cap - - - - - - - COIF
tighten the cords of a drum - - FRAP
tightwad (colloq.) - - - - - - PIKER
til - - - - - - - - - - - - SESAME
tile - - - - - - - - DOMINO, SLATE
tile factory - - - - - - - - TILERY
tiles (of) - - - - - - - - TEGULAR
till - PLOW, FARM, CULTIVATE, HOE
tillable - - - - - - - - - - ARABLE
tilled land - - - - - ARADA, ARADO
tiller - - - - - - - - - - - HELM
tilt - - - - TIP, LEAN, INCLINE, CANT, SLANT, NAME, JOUST
timber - - WOOD, ASH, OAK, CEDAR, LUMBER
timber bend - - - - - - - - - SNY
timber for flooring - - - - - BATTEN
timber projecting piece - - - - TENON
timber to secure hawsers - - - - BITT
timberwolf (western) - - - - - LOBO
timbrel - - - - - - - - - - TABOR
time - - - TEMPO, ERA, SCHEDULE, LEISURE, PERIOD, DURATION, OCCASION

time being - - - - - - - - NONCE
time free from employment - LEISURE
time (Fr.) - - - - - - - - FOIS
time gone by - - - - - - PAST, AGO
time of greatest depression - - NADIR
time of greatest vigor - - - HEYDAY
time honored - - - - - - - - OLD
time immediately before - - - - EVE
time intervening - - - - - INTERIM
time long ago - - - - - - - YORE
time preceding event - - - - - EVE
time (Scot.) - - - - - - - - TID
time when (to the) - - - - - UNTIL
time of year - - - - - - SOLSTICE
timeless - - - - AGELESS, ETERNAL
timely - - - OPPORTUNE, PAT, APT
timepiece - - - - - - - - - CLOCK
times ten (suffix) - - - - - - - TY
timid - - - - - - - - - - SHY
timidity - - - - - - - - SHYNESS
Timor coin - - - - - - - - - AVO
timorous - - - AFRAID, TREPID, SHY
tin - - - - - - - STANNUM, CAN
tin container - - - - - - CANNISTER
tin foil for mirrors - - - - - - TAIN
tin and lead alloy - - - - - - TERNE
tin (symbol) - - - - - - - - SN.
tincture - - MODICUM, IMBUE, TINT
tincture employed in heraldry - - FUR
tincture of opium - - - PAREGORIC
tine - - - - - - - PRONG, SPIKE
tinge - TINT, IMBUE, STAIN, TRACE, SHADE, HUE
tinged with rose - - - - ROSEATE
tingle - - - - - THRILL, PRICKLE
tinker - - - - - - - - - TAMPER
tinkle - - - - - - DINGLE, CLINK
tinkling sound - - - - - - - CLINK
tinsel - - - - - - - - - TAWDRY
tint - - - HUE, TINGE, DYE, SHADE, TINCTURE
tiny - - - - - - - SMALL, ATOMIC
tip - POINT, APICAL, CAREEN, CUE, OVERTURN, TILT, LEAN, HINT, END
tip of fox's tail - - - - - - - TAG
tip to one side - CAREEN, TILT, LIST
tip over - - - - - - OVERSET, CANT
tip of a pen - - - - - - - - NEB
typify - - - - - - - - REPRESENT
tippet - - - - - - - FUR, SCARF
tipping - - - - - - - - - ATILT
tipping to one side - ALIST, CAREENING
tippler - - - TOPER, SOT, DRINKER
tipster - - - - - - - - - - TOUT
tipsy - - - - - - - - - FUDDLED
tipsy (slang) - - - - - - - LOADED
tiptoe - - - - - - - - - - ATIP
tirade - - - SCREED, OUTPOURING, PHILIPPIC
tire - - - - - FAG, EXHAUST, WEARY
tired - - JADED, FATIGUED, BORED, WEARY
tired (poet.) - - - - - - AWEARIED
tireless - - - - - - - - UNWEARIED
tiresome - DREARY, TEDIOUS, BORING
tiresome person - - - - - BORE, PILL
tiresome thing - - - - - - - BORE
tissue - - - - - - TELO, TELA, TECA
titan - - - - - - - - - - GIANT
Titania's husband - - - - - OBERON
titanic - - - - - - - - - GIGANTIC
tithe - - - - - - - - - - TENTH
title - NAME, SIR, CLAIM, OWNERSHIP, HEADING

title of ancient kings of Peru - - INCA
title of Athena - - - - - - - ALEA
title of baronet - - - - - - - SIR
title of clergyman - - - - REVEREND
title of distinction (abbr.) - - HON.
title of monk - - - - - - - - FRA
title of nobility - - - - - - - LORD
title of prelate - - - - MONSIGNOR
titled ecclesiastic - - - - PRELATE
titled men - - - - - PEERS, LORDS
titled woman - - - - - - - DAME
titmouse - - - - - - - - TOMTIT
titter - - - - - - - - - - GIGGLE
tittle - - - - - - - - - - - JOT
to - UNTO, FORWARD, INTO, TOWARD, UNTIL, FOR
to any point - - - - - - ANYWHERE
to be (Fr.) - - - - - - - - ETRE
to do - - - - - - - - - - - ACT
to be expected - - - - - - NATURAL
to a higher point - - - - - - - UP
to an inner point - - - - - - INTO
to lee side - - - - - - - - ALEE
to the left - - - - - - - - APORT
to no extent - - - - - - - - NOT
to one side - - - - - - - - ASIDE
to other side - - - - - - - OVER
to a point on - - - - - - - ONTO
to (prefix) - - - - - - - - - AC
to same degree - - - - - - - - AS
to (Scot.) - - - - - - - - - TAE
to such degree - - - - - - SO, EVEN
to such an extent - - - - - - EVEN
to that extent - - - - - - - - SO
to the third power - - - - - CUBED
to this - - - - - - - - - HERETO
to the time that - - - - TILL, UNTIL
to be of use - - - - - - - - AVAIL
to your health - - - - - - PROSIT
toad (Scot.) - - - - - - - - TADE
toads - - - AGUA, ANURANS, ANURA
toady - - - - - - - - - TRUCKLE
toast - - - SCORCH, WARM, PROSIT, BROWN, SKOAL
tobacco box - - - - - - HUMIDOR
tobacco (kind) - - - CAPA, CAPOREL, CAPORAL, SNUFF, LATAKIA
tobacco pipe (short) - - - - DUDEEN
tobacco roll - - - - - - - - CIGAR
tobacco roll (var.) - - - - - SEGAR
tod - - - - - - - - - - - BUSH
toddle - - - - - - - - - - TOTTER
toddler - - - - - - - - - - - TOT
tog - - - - - - - - - - - OUTFIT
together - - - - - - - - ALONG
together (prefix) - - - - - - - CO
together with - - - - - - - - AND
toggery - - - - - - - - CLOTHES
toil - - - - LABOUR, RING, MOIL
toil wearisomely - - - - - - MOIL
toilsome - - - - - - - LABORIOUS
token - SIGN, RELIC, PLEDGE, BADGE
token of affection - - - - - - KISS
tolerable - - - - - SOSO, PASSABLE
tolerably - - - - - - - - PRETTY
tolerant - - - PATIENT, INDULGENT
tolerate - - ENDURE, STAND, BIDE, DIGEST
toll - - DUE, TAX, IMPOST, STRIVE, RESOUND, RING, PEAL, KNELL
toll (poet.) - - - - - - - - KNELL
tomato sauce (var.) - - - - - CATSUP
tomb of a saint - - - - - - SHRINE
tomboy - - - - - - - - - HOYDEN
tomcat - - - - - - - - - - - GIB

T

tomorrow (Sp.) - - - - - - MANANA
tonal quality - - - - - - TONALITY
tone - - - - SOUND, ACCENT, AIR
tone colour - - - - - - - - TIMBRE
tone down - - - - - - - - SOFTEN
tone succession - - - - - - MELOS
tongue - - - - - - - - - LANGUAGE
tongue (pert. to) - - - - - GLOSSAL
tongue of shoe - - - - - - - TAB
tonic - - - - - - BRACER, BRACING
too - - - - - - - - - - - OVERLY
too bad - - - - - - - - - ALAS
too late - - - - - - - - BELATED
tool - - - UTENSIL, CHASER, DUPE, IMPLEMENT
tool to enlarge holes - - - - REAMER
tool to flesh hides - - - - - SLATER
tool handle - - - - - - - - HELVE
tool to smooth lumber - - - - PLANE
tool to trim slate - - - - - ZAX, SAX
toot lightly - - - - - - - TOOTLE
tooth - - - - MOLAR, COG, FANG
tooth of a comb - - - - - - DENT
tooth (comb. form) - - - - - DENTI
tooth decay - - - - - - - CARIES
tooth of gear wheel - - - - COG, DENT
tooth point - - - - - - - - CUSP
tooth socket - - - - - - - ALVEOLUS
tooth substance - - - - - - DENTINE
tooth wheel - - SPROCKET, GEAR, COG
toothed - SERRATE, DENTATE, CEROSE
toothed instrument - - - - SAW, COMB
toothed irregularly - - - - - EROSE
toothed wheel - - - - - ROWEL, GEAR
toothless - - - - - - - - EDENTATE
toothless animal - - - - - EDENTATE
toothlike ornament - - - - - DENTIL
top - - VERTICE, CREST, ACE, APEX, HEAD, CAP, EXCEL, SURPASS, TIP, LID, SURMOUNT, ACME, SUMMIT
top of altar - - - - - - -....MENSA
top piece of doorway - - - - - LINTEL
topaz humming bird - - - - - - AVA
toper - - - - - - - - SOT, DRINKER
topic - - - TEXT, THEME, SUBJECT
topic of discourse - - - - - THEME
topple - - - - - - - - - - UPSET
Topsy's friend - - - - - - - - EVA
tor - - - - - - - - - - - - CRAG
torch - - - - - - LAMP, FLAMBEAU
tore (pert. to) - - - - - - TOROIDAL
torment - - BAIT, TORTURE, PLAGUE, TEASE, RACK, TAUNT
torn - - - - - - - - - - - - RENT
tornado - - - - - - - - - TWISTER
toro - - - - - - - - - - COWFISH
torpid - - - - - - INERT, DORMANT
torpor - - - - - - COMA, NUMBNESS
torrent - - - - - - - - - - FLOOD
torrid - - - - - - - TROPICAL, HOT
tortion - - - - - - - - - TWISTING
tortile - - - - - - - - - TWISTED
tortoise - - - - - - - - - TURTLE
torture - - - - - - - - - TORMENT
Tory - - - - - - - - - - LOYALIST
toss - - HURL, PITCH, FLIP, BUFFET
toss about loosely - - - - - - FLOP
tossing - - - - - - - - - RESTLESS
tot - - - - - - - - - - - - CHILD
total - . - ADD, SUM, WHOLE, ENTIRE, COMPLETE, TOT, UTTER, ABSOLUTE, ALL
total abstainer - - - - - TEETOTALER
total of bets at stake - - - - - POT
total surface - - - - - - - - - AREA
totality - - - - - - - - - - - ALL

tote - - - - - - - - - - - - CARRY
toter - - - - - - - - - - - CARRIER
totter - - STAGGER, WAVER, TODDLE, ROCK
touch - - - CONTACT, FEEL, FINGER, ADJOIN
touch at boundary line - - - - - ABUT
touch lightly - - - - - - - PAT, DAB
touch at one point - - - - - TANGENT
touch, with elbow - - - - - - NUDGE
touching - - - - - - - - - TANGENT
touching at the boundary - BORDERING
touchwood - - - - - - - - - - PUNK
touchy - - - - - IRASCIBLE, TESTY
tough - - - - - - - - - - - - WIRY
toughwood - - - - - - - - - - ELM
toupee - - - - - - - - - - - - WIG
tour - - - - - - - - - SHIFT, TRIP
tourist - - - - - - - - - TRAVELLER
tousle - - - - - RUMPLE, DISHEVEL
tout - - - - - - - - - - - TIPSTER
tow - - DRAG, DRAW, PULL, BARGE
toward - - - - - - - TO, AT, FACING
toward the center - - - ENTAD, ORAD
toward the east - - - - - - EASTERLY
toward end of action - - - - - - TO
toward the inside - - - INTO, INWARD
toward the left side - - - - - APORT
toward the mouth - - - ORAD, ENTAD
toward (prefix) - - - - - - - IN, OB
toward the rear of ship - ASTERN, AFT
toward the rising sun - - EASTWARD
toward (Scot.) - - - - - - - - TAE
toward the stern - - - - AFT, ABAFT
toward the top - - - - - - - - UP
towel cloth - - - - - - - - - TERRY
tower - - - - TURRET, SOAR, PYLON, CITADEL
tower for cables - - - - - - - PYLON
towerlike structure - - - - - PAGODA
town - - - - - - - - - - - VILLAGE
town (colloq.) - - - - - - - - BURG
town near Cannes - - - - - GRASSE
town (pert. to) - - - - - - OPPIDAN
town (prefix) - - - - - - - - - TRE
town (small) - - - - - - - - HAMLET
toy - - - - DALLY, TRIFLE, PLAY
trace - - TRACK, SIGN, FOOTPRINT, TINGE, TAIL, VESTIGE, MARK, STREAK, FOLLOW, TANG, DERIVE
tracery - - - - - - - - - LACEWORK
track - - TRAIL, RAIL, TRACE, PATH, MARK, FOOTPRINT
track game - - - - - - - - - TRAIL
track for sliding door - - GUIDERAIL
track worn by a wheel - - - - - RUT
tract - - TREATISE, REGION, EXPANSE, AREA
tract drained by river - - - - - BASIN
tract of grassy land - - - - - PRAIRIE
tract of ground for game - - - - PARK
tract of land - - - - - - - TERRITORY
tract of land between two rivers - DOAB
tract of land for public recreation - - PARK
tract of open upland - - - - - DOWNS
tractable - - - - DOCILE, TAME, EASY
track official - - - - - - - STARTER
trade - - BARTER, SELL, EXCHANGE, CRAFT, DEAL, SWAP, TRAFFIC, STRAIN, COMMERCE, BUSINESS
trade agreement - - - - - - CARTEL
trader - - - - - DEALER, MERCHANT

tradesman - - - - - - - - SELLER
trading place - - - - - - - STORE
traditional tale - - - SAGA, LEGEND, FOLKLORE
traduce - - DEBASE, SLUR, REVILE, ASPERSE
traducers - REVILERS, CALUMNIATORS
Trafalgar victor - - - - - - NELSON
traffic - - - - - - TRADE, BARTER
traffic by exchange - - - - - BARTER
tragacanth - - - - - - - - GUM
tragic - - TERRIBLE, CALAMITOUS
trail - - PATH, TRACK, ROUTE, WAY, COURSE, LAG, FOLLOW, DRAG, HUNT
trail (slang) - - - - - - - - TAIL
trail of wild animal - - - - - SPOOR
trailing branch that takes root - - - STOLON
train - - EDUCATE, SCHOOL, TAME, INSTRUCT, DRILL, TEACH, RETINUE, COACH
train of attendants - - - - CORTEGE
train making all stops - - - LOCAL
train the mind - - - - - - EDUCATE
train not on regular schedule - SPECIAL
train of wives - - - - - - HAREM
trainer - - - - - - - - COACH
trainer of gladiators - - - - LANISTA
training - - - - - - - EDUCATION
traitor - - - BETRAYOR, RENEGADE
trammel - - - - - - - - - HAMPER
tramp - - - - HIKE, SLOG, HOBO, VAGRANT, TREAD
trample - - - - - - TREAD, CRUSH
trampled - - - - - TRODDEN, TROD
trance - - - SPELL, STUPOR, DAZE, SWOON
tranquil - SERENE, SEDATE, REPOSED, CALM
tranquility - - - - - - - - PEACE
tranquilize - - - - - CALM, SERENE
transact - - - NEGOTIATE, CONDUCT
transaction - DEAL, SALE, ACT, DEED
transcend - - - SURPASS, OVERTOP, OVERPASS
transcribe - - - - - - COPY, WRITE
transfer - - - TRANSMIT, CONVEY, TRANSPOSE
transfer to another container - REPOT
transfer (law) - - - - - - ATTORN
transfer of property - - - - ALIENER
transfer rents - - - - - - - ATTORN
transfix - - - - - - - - PIN, STICK
transform - - - - - - - TRANSMUTE
transgress - VIOLATE, OVERSTEP, ERR, SIN
transgression - - - - - - - - SIN
transient - - - MOVING, TEMPORARY
transient illumination - - - - GLEAM
transition - - - - - - - METABASIS
transistory - - - TEMPORAL, BRIEF
translate - - - - RENDER, DECODE, CONSTRUE
translate from cipher - - - DECODE
translation - - VERSION, RENDITION
transmission gear wheel - - - IDLER
transmit - RENDER, SEND, TRANSFER, FORWARD
transmute - - TRANSFORM, CONVERT
transparent - CRYSTAL, SHEER, CLEAR
transparent mineral - - - - - MICA
transparent quartz - - - - CRYSTAL
transport - CONVEY, CART, ENTRANCE, FERRY
transport over a river - - - FERRY
transportation charge - - - - FARE
transportation line (abbr.) - - R.R.
transportation service bonds - - - - TRACTIONS
transported - - - - - - - - RAPT
transporting device - - - BARROW
transpose - - - REVERSE, INVERT, TRANSFER
transposition - - - - - - REVERSAL
transposition of one word into another - ANAGRAM
trap - GIN, SNARE, TREE, ENSNARE, PITFALL,WEB, NET, AMBUSH, PAT, GRAB, NAB
trap door - - - - - - - - - DROP
trapper - - - - - - - - - SNARER
trappings - - - - - - - - - GEAR
trapshooting - - - - - - - - SKEET
trash - - - RUBBISH, DIRT, REFUSE
trashy - - - - - - - - - WORTHLESS
travail - - - - - - - - - ANGUISH
travel - TOUR, WEND, RIDE, JOURNEY
travel by car - - - - - - - - MOTOR
travel by ox wagon - - - - - TREK
traveller - - - - TOURIST, VIATOR, PASSENGER, WAYFARER
traveling company - - - - - CARAVAN
traverse - - - -CROSS, RUN, SCOUR
traversity - - - - - - - - PARODY
travesty - - MIME, SATIRE, PARODY
trawl - - - - - - - - - DRAGNET
tray - - - - - - SERVER, SALVER
treacherous - - - - - - ..INSIDIOUS
tread heavily - - - - - - - CLAMP
treacherous murderer - - - ASSASSIN
treachery - - - - - - - - TREASON
treacle - - - - - - - - MOLASSES
tread - STEP, TRAMPLE, WALK, TRAMP
tread underfoot - - - - - TRAMPLE
treader - - - - - - - - - STAMPER
treasure - - WEALTH, PRIZE, VALUE
treasurer - - - - - - - - BURSAR
treat - USE, REGALE, TEND, HANDLE, NEGOTIATE
treat carelessly (obs.) - - - DANDLE
treat indulgently - - - - - PAMPER
treat maliciously - - - - - - SPITE
treat remedially - - - - - MEDICATE
treat slightingly - - - - - MINIMIZE
treat surgically - - - - - - OPERATE
treat tenderly - - - - - - SPARE
treat unkindly - - - - - - MISTREAT
treat with borax - - - - - BORATE
treat with deference - - - - KOWTOW
treat with great rudeness - - INSULT
treat with hot water - - - - ..SCALD
treatise - - - - - TRACT, DISCOURSE
treatment - - - - - - - HANDLING
treaty - - - - - - PACT, ALLIANCE
tree - - CATALPA, YEW, TAMARACK, CORNER, ULE, RACK, ASPEN, MYRTLE, ARAR
tree of antiquity - - - - - - OLIVE
tree character in given region - - - SILVANITY
tree of chocolate family - - - COLA
tree covering - - - - - - - ..BARK
tree exudation - ROSIN, RESIN, GUM
tree frog (young) - - - - - PEEPER
tree furnishing resin - - - - - ARAR
tree of life site - - - - - - - EDEN
tree in a river - - - - - - - SNAG
tree roots - - - - - - - - WATAP
tree snake - - - - - LORA, LEROT
tree stock - - - - - - - - - STEM

tree stump - - - - - - - - STUB
tree trunk - - - - - - BOLE, LOG
tree with needlelike leaves - - -FIR
tree with quivering leaves - - ASPEN
tree yielding caucho - - - - - - ULE
tree yielding chicle - - - - - BALATA
treeless plains - - PAMPAS, TUNDRAS
treenail - - - - - - - - - - NOG
trees - - - - - - - - - - FOREST
trees (pert. to) - - - - - ARBOREAL
trellis - - - - - LATTICE, ESPALIER
tremble - DITHER, QUIVER, DODDER, SHAKE, SHIVER, QUAKE
trembler - - - - - - - - - QUAKER
trembling - - - - - - - - TREMOR
tremor - - QUAKE, SHAKE, SHIVER, SHAKING
tremulous - - - - - - - - - ASPEN
trench - - - - - - - DITCH, MOAT
trenchant humour - - - - - - SATIRE
trend - TENDENCY, MOVEMENT, TEND, TENOR, INCLINE, DRIFT, BENT
trepan - - - - - - - - - - ENTRAP
trepid - - - - - - - - - TIMOROUS
trepidation - - - - - - - - - FEAR
trespass - - - ENCROACH, POACH, VENTURE, INTRUDE
tress - BRAID, LOCK, RINGLET, CURL
tress of hair - - - - RINGLET, LOCK
trestle - - - - - - - - - VIADUCT
triacid - - - - - - - - - - CITRIC
triad - - TRINE, TRIVALENT, TERNARY
trial - - TEST, ORDEAL, ATTEMPT, HARDSHIP
trial impression - - - - - - PROOF
triangle with unequal sides - SCALENE
triangular flag - PENNON, PENNANT
triangular inset - - - - - - - GORE
triangular piece - - GORE, GUSSET
triangular sail - - - - - - - - - JIB
tribal group - - - - - - - - CLAN
tribal sign - - - - - - - - TOTEM
tribe - - - - - - - - CLAN, GENS
tribe near Annam - - - - - - - MOI
tribe subdivision - - - - - - - GENS
tribulation - - - - - - - TRIAL, WOE
tribunal - - - - - - - - - - BAR
tributary - - - - - - - - - FEEDER
tributary of the Amazon - - - - NAPO
tributary of the Colorado - - - - ..GILA
tributary of the Elbe - - - - - ISER
tributary of the Missouri River - OSAGE, PLATTE
tributary of the Ohio River - - WABASH
tributary to the Order - - - - WARTA
tributary of the Seine - - - - - OISE
tributary of Somme - - - - - ANCRE
tribute - - TAX, PRAISE, OFFERING
tricar - - - - - - - - - - TRICYCLE
trice - - - - - - - MOMENT, INSTANT
triceps - - - - - - - - - - MUSCLE
trick - - STUNT, PRANK, JAPE, FEINT, DELUDE, RUSE, ANTIC, DEFRAUD, PALTER, WILE, DECEIT, FRAUD
trick (colloq.) - - - - - - - - - DO
trick (slang) - - - - - - - - - FOX
trick in war - - - - - - STRATAGEM
trickery - - DECEIT, ARTIFICE, FRAUD
trickle - - - - - - - - - - - DRIP
tricky (slang) - - - - - - - - SNIDE
triclinic feldspar - - - - - - ALBITE
tricycle - - - - - - - - - - TRICAR
Trieste measure of wine - ORNA (s.), ORNE (pl.)
trifle - - DALLY, TOY, PETTY, STRAW
trifling - - - - - - - - - - PETTY
trifling objection - - - - - - CAVIL
trig - - TRIM, NEAT, TIDY, SPRUCE, SMART
trigonometric function, ratio or figure - SINE, SECANT, COSINE
trigonometric ratio - - - - - COSINE
trill - - - - - - - WARBLE, ROLL
triller - - - - - - - - - - - PIPER
trim - - DECORATE, ADORN, PRUNE, TRIG, SPRUCE, NEAT, PREEN, LOP
trim and simple - - - - - TAILORED
trim with the beak - - - - - PREEN
trim with loose threads - - - - TASSEL
trimming - - - - - RUCHE, EDGING
trine - - - - - - - - - - - TRIAD
trinitrotoluene - - - - - - - - TNT
trinity - - - - - - - - - - - TRINE
trinity (theol.) - - - - - - - - TRIAS
trip - - STUMBLE, MISSTEP, JAUNT, TOUR
trip to discharge business - - ERRAND
triple - - - - - TRINE, THREEFOLD
triple crown - - - - - - - - - TIARA
Tripoli measure - - - - - - - - DRA
Tripoli ruler - - - - - - - - - DEY
Tristan's love - - - -- - ISOLDE
triste - - DEPRESSED, SAD, DISMAL
trite - - BANAL, THREADBARE, STALE
trite phrase - - - - - - - - CLICHE
trite remark - - - - - - PLATITUDE
triton - - - - - NEWT, SALAMANDER
triumph - - WIN, PREVAIL, VICTORY
triumphant - - - - - - - - JUBILANT
trivalent - - - - - - - - - - TRIAD
trivial - - - SMALL, SLIGHT, BANAL
trod heavily - - - - - - - - TRAMP
trod (poet.) - - - - - - - - STEPT
trod under foot - - - - - TRAMPLED
Trojan hero and defender - - ENEAS, AENEAS
Trojan prince - - - - - - - AENEAS
Trojan soothsayer - - - - - HELENUS
Trojan war chieftain - - - - ULYSSES
Trojan warrior - - - - - - AGENOR
troll - - - - - - - - - - - - REEL
trollop - - - - - - - - - SLATTERN
troop - - - - - - BAND, COMPANY
troop sallies - - - - - - - - SORTIES
troops in close order - - - - PHALANX
tropical - - TORRID, SULTRY, WARM
tropical American fruit - - - - PAPAYA
tropical American mallow - - - ALTEA
tropical American plant - - - - - PIPI
tropical American skunk - - CONEPATE
tropical American tree - DALI, GUAVA, ICICA
tropical American wildcat - - OCELOT
tropical animal - - COATI, ANTEATER
tropical bird - ANI, TOUCAN, PARROT
tropical carnivore - - - - - - RATEL
tropical creeping plant - - - - IPECAC
tropical fiber - - - - - - - - ISTLE
tropical fish - - - - - - - - REMORA
tropical food plant - - - - - - TARO
tropical fruit - - - - PAWPAW, DATE, BANANA, GUAVA, MANGO, PAPAYA
tropical herb - - - - - - - - - SIDA
tropical mammal - - - - - - - TAPIR
tropical plant - - ALOE, IPECAC, TARO
tropical plant of arum family - - TARO
tropical rodent - - - - - - - - PACA
tropical tree - - - - PALM, TAMARIND, MABI, ZORRO, GUAVA
trot - - - - - - - - - - - - - JOG

troth - - - - - - - - - - - FAITH
trouble - - - BOTHER, AID, AGITATE, MOLEST, ADO, AIL, SORE, WOE
troublemaker - - - - - - AGITATOR
troublesome - - - FUSSY, PESTILENT
troublesome business - - - - ADO
trough to cool ingots - - - - BOSH
trounce - - - - - - - - - FLOG
trousers - - - - - SLACKS, PANTS
Troy defender - - - - - - - ENEAS
Troy (story of) - - - - - - - ILIAD
truant - - - - - - - - SHIRKER
truce - - - - ARMISTICE, RESPITE
truck - - - - BARTER, VAN, LORRY
truckle - - - - - - - - - TOADY
trudge - - - - - - - - - PLOD
trudge (colloq.) - - - - - - TRAIPSE
true - - HONEST, LOYAL, FAITHFUL, ACCURATE
true to fact - - - - - - - LITERAL
true hearted - - - - - - - - LEAL
truly - - - - INDEED. YES, VERILY, VERITABLY, YEA
truly (arch.) - - - - - - - SOOTH
Truman's birthplace - - - - LAMAR
trump - - - - - - - RUFF, OUTDO
trumpet creeper - - - - - - TECOMA
trumpet (small) - - - - - CLARION
trumpet sound - - - BLARE, BLAST
trumpeter bird - - - - - - AGAMI
truncate - - - - - - - - STUMP, LAP
trunk of cut tree - - - - - - - LOG
trunk of human body - - - - TORSO
trunk of palm - - - - - - CAUDEX
trunk of statue - - - - - - TORSO
trunkfish - - - - - - - - - TORO
truss - - - - - - - - - - - BIND
trust - - MONOPOLY, CREDIT, RELY, CONFIDE, BELIEVE, HOPE, LEAN, MERGER, FAITH, RELIANCE, DEPEND, BELIEF
trustworthy - SAFE, HONEST, RELIABLE
trustworthy convicts - - - TRUSTIES
trusty - - - - - - - - - RELIABLE
truth - - VERITY, VERACITY, FACT, REALITY
truth (arch.) - - - - - - - SOOTH
truthful - - - - - - - - HONEST
try - - - TEST, SAMPLE, ENDEAVOR, ESSAY, STRIVE, ATTEMPT, TETHER, UNDERTAKE, TRIAL
try experimentally - - - - HANDSEL
try out - - - - - - - - REND, TEST
trying experience - - - - - ORDEAL
tryout - - - - - - TEST, AUDITION
tryst - - - APPOINTMENT, MEETING
tsar's wife - - - - - - - TSARINA
tub - - - - - - KEEVE, CASK, VAT
tub (large) - - - - - - - - - VAT
tube - - - - - - - - - - - PIPE
tube on which silk is wound - - - COP
tuber - - - - - - - - - - POTATO
tuft - - - - BUNCH, CLUMP, CREST
tuft of feathers - - - CREST, AIGRET
tug - - - - - - - - - - - HAUL
tumble - - - - - - SPILL, WILTER
tumble over - - - - - - - - FLOP
tumeric - - - - - - - - - - REA
tumid - - - - - - - - SWOLLEN
tumor - - - - - - - - - - - WEN
tumult - BEDLAM, RIOT, DIN, TEMPEST, HUBBUB
tumultuous language or flow - TORRENT
tumultuous mob movement - STAMPEDE

tun - - - - - - - - - - - CASK
tune - - ARIA, AIR, MELODY, ADAPT
tune writer - - - - - - MELODIST
tuneful - - - MELODIC, MELODIOUS
tungsten ore - - - - - - - - - CAL
Tunisia capital - - - - - - - TUNIS
Tunisia city - - - - - - - - SFAX
Tunisia measure - - - - - SAA, SAAH
Tunisia pasha - - - - - - - - DEY
Tunisia ruler - - - - - - BEY, DEY
tup - - - - - - - - - - - - RAM
turban hat - - - - - - - - MOAB
turbid - - - - - - - - - - ROILY
turbot - - - - - - - - - - BRET
turbulent steam - - - - - - TORRENT
turf - - - - - - - - SOD, SWARD
turf in golf - - - - - - - - DIVOT
turf (poet.) - - - - - - - - GLEBE
turf used for fuel - - - - - - PEAT
Turk - - TATAR, OTTOMAN, TARTAR
Turkestan salt lake - - - - - SHOR
turkey buzzard - - - - - - - AURA
turkey (male) - - - - - - - - TOM
Turkey part - - - - - - - ANADOLU
Turkish - - - - - - - - OTTOMAN
Turkish bath - - - - - - HAMMAM
Turkish capital - - - - - - ANKARA
Turkish city - - - - ADANA, AINTAB
Turkish coin - - - - - ASPER, PARA
Turkish commander - - - - - - AGA
Turkish decree - - - - - - - IRADE
Turkish district governor - - - BEY
Turkish flag - - - - - - - - ALEM
Turkish government - - - - - PORTE
Turkish governor - - - BEY, PASHA
Turkish hat - - - - - - - - - FEZ
Turkish headdress - - - - - - - FEZ
Turkish imperial standard - - ALEM
Turkish inn - - - - - - - IMARET
Turkish judge - - - - - CADI, AGA
Turkish magistrate - - - CADI, AGA
Turkish measure of length - ARSHIN
Turkish monetary unit - - - - ASPER
Turkish money - - - - - - - ASPER
Turkish mountain range - - - ALAI
Turkish name - - - - - - ALA, ALI
Turkish officer - - EMIR, AGA, PASHA
Turkish official (var.) - - - EMEER
Turkish prince - - - - - - AMEER
Turkish province - - ANGORA, EYALET
Turkish regiment - - - - - - ALAI
Turkish ruler - - - - SULTAN, BEY
Turkish sailing vessel - - - - SAIC
Turkish slave - - - - - MAMELUKE
Turkish soldier - - - - - - NIZAM
Turkish standard device - - CRESCENT
Turkish sultan - - - - - - - SELIM
Turkish title - AGA, EMIR, PASHA, BEY
Turkish title (var.) - - - - - AMIR
Turkish town - - - - - - - - - BIR
Turkish tribesman - - - TATIR, TATAR
Turkish unit - - - - - - - - ASPER
Turkish vilayet - - - - - - - ADANA
Turkish weight - - - - - - - - OKA
Turkish women's costume - CHARSHAF
turmoil - - - - - - - - - - RUST
turn - TWIST, ROTATE, BEND, REVOLVE, PIVOT, WHIRL, VEER
turn about fixed point - SLUE, ROTATE
turn around rapidly - - - - - WHIRL
turn aside - SHUNT, DEVIATE, DETER, DIVERT, SWERVE, WRY, AVERT
turn away - - - - - - - - - - SHY
turn back - REPEL, REVERT, REPULSE
turn back (botanical) - - - EVOLUTE

T

turn down - REJECT, VETO
turn the front wheels - CRAMP
turn for help - RESORT
turn inside out - EVERT
turn into money - CASH
turn inward - INTROVERT
turn to left - HAW
turn off - DIVERGE
turn out to be - PROVE
turn outward - EXTROVERT, EVERT
turn over - KEEL
turn over new leaf - REFORM
turn pages of - LEAF
turn on pivot - SLUE, SWIVEL
turn to right - GEE
turn round - GYRE
turn the soil - SPADE
turn toward the axis - INTRORSE
turn upside down - INVERT
turn white - PALE
turner - GYMNAST
turning - ROTARY
turning joint - HINGE
turning machine - LATHE
turning muscle - ROTATOR
turning point - PIVOT, CRISIS
turning post for Roman racers - META
turning round like a wheel - ROTARY
turning sour - ACESCENT
turning stem of plant - BINE
turning support - HINGE
turpentine tree - TARATA
turret - TOWER, CUPOLA
turtle - TERRAPIN, SNAPPER, TORTOISE
turtle plastron - PEE
turtle shell - CARAPACE
Tuscany island - ELBA
tusk - TOOTH
tussle - STRUGGLE
tutelar - PROTECTING
Tutelary gods - LARES
tutor - SCHOOL, TEACH, TRAIN
twaddle - NONSENSE
twain - TWO, DOUBLE
tweak - TWITCH
tweet - CHIRP
twelve - DOZEN
twelve dozen - GROSS
twelve month - YEAR
twelve patriarchs (one of) - LEVI
twenty-fourth part - CARAT
twenty quires - REAM
twice - BIS, DOUBLY
twice (prefix) - DI, BI
twig - SPRIG, ROD, CION
twig broom - BARSOM
twilight - DUSK, EVE
twilled fabric - SERGE, SILESIA, DENIM, COVERT, SURAH, REP
twin - MATCH, DOUBLE, GEMEL
twin crystal - MACLE
twine - WIND, TWIST, COIL, MEANDER, ENCURL, CORD, STRING, WREATH
twinge - TWITCH
twining plant - SMILAX, WINDER, VINE
twining plant part - TENDRIL
twining stem of plant - BINE
twinkle - WINK
The Twins - GEMINI
twirl - TURN, SPIN
twist - CONTORT, WRITHE, WRAP, BEND, TURN, COIL, TWINE, SLUE, SPIRAL, WRENCH, QUIRK, GNARL, SKEW, WRING, SCREW, WRY
twist around - SLUE, SLEW
twist out of shape - WARP, CONTORT, DISTORT
twist violently - WRITHE
twisted - WRY, TORTILE
twisted cotton thread - LISLE
twisted roll of wool - SLUB
twisted silk - SLEAVE
twisted (var.) - SLEWED
twister - TORNADO
twisting - TORSION
twit - TAUNT, UPBRAID, RIDICULE
twitch - TWEAK, TWINGE
twitching - TIC
twitter - CHIRP, CHIRRUP
two - PAIR, BOTH, COUPLE
two edged - ANCIPITAL
two faced deity - JANUS
two feet (having) - BIPEDAL, DIPODE
two footed animal - BIPED
two halves - ONE
two headed deity - JANUS
two hulled boat - CATAMARAN
two of a kind - PAIR
two leaves or folds - DIPTYCH
two legged animal - BIPED
two legged dragon - WYVERN
two lined stanza - DISTICH
two masted craft of the Levant - BUM
two masted square ship - BRIG
two part composition - DUET
two pointed tack - STAPLE
two poles (having) - BIPOLAR
two (prefix) - DI, BI
two pronged instrument - BIDENT
two (Scot.) - TWA
two seated carriage - TANDEM
two sided - BILATERAL
two toed sloth - UNAU
two together - BOTH
two wheeled cab - HANSOM
two wheeled chariot - ESSED, ESSEDE
two wheeled conveyance - BIKE, GIG, CART
two wheeled vehicle - GIG, CART
two winged fly - GNAT
two year occurrence - BIENNIAL
twofold - DUAL, TWIN
Tyderis' son - DIOMED
type - (See also Style)
type - VARIETY, SORT, KIND, MODEL, NATURE, NORM, EMBLEM, GENRE, STYLE
type of architecture - IONIC, DORIC
type of excellence - PARAGON
type of football game - SOCCER
type (kind) - ITALIC
type of lens - TORIC
type of measure - EM, EN
type metal used for spacing - QUAD
type of molding - TORUS
type of perfection - PARAGON
type of piano - GRAND
type of plant - EXOGEN
type of song - CAROL
type square - EM
type (style of) - ROMAN
typesetter - COMPOSITOR
typewriter bar - SPACER
typewriter roller - PLATEN
typical example - NORM
typical portion - SAMPLE
typographer - PRINTER
typographical error - MISPRINT
typography - PRINTING
tyranny - DESPOTISM
tyrant - DESPOT
tyrian - PURPLE

tyro - - - - - - - - - NOVICE
Tyrol river - - - - - - - - ISAR

U

ugly - - - - - - - - - HIDEOUS
ugly old woman - - - - - CRONE, HAG
ugly sprite - - - - - - - GOBLIN
ulcer - - - - - - - - - - SORE
ulna (of the) - - - - - - CUBITAL
ulterior - - - - - - UNDISCLOSED, UNDISCOVERED
ultimate - - EVENTUAL, LAST, FINAL
ultimate peduncle - - - - - PEDICEL
ultra - - - - - - - - - EXTREME
ululant - - - - - - - - - HOWLING
Ulysses' friend - - - - - - MENTOR
umbrella (colloq.) - - - - - - GAMP
umbrella part - - - - - - - - RIB
umpire - - - - - REFEREE, ARBITER
unable to tell pitch - - - - TONE DEAF
unaccented - - - - - - - - ATONIC
unaccented vowel sound - - - - SCHWA
unaccompanied - ALONE, SOLE, LONE
unaccustomed - - - - - - - - NEW
unadorned - - - - BARE, STARK, BALD
unadulterated - - - - - - - PURE
unaffected - - - - - - - - NATURAL
unalloyed joy - - - - - - - BLISS
unaspirated - - - - - - - - LENE
unassumed - - - - - - - - NATURAL
unassuming - - - - - - - - MODEST
unattached - - - - - - LOOSE, FREE
unattended - - - - - - - - - ALONE
unaware - IGNORANT, UNCONSCIOUS
unbalanced - - DERANGED, ONESIDED
unbend - - - - - - THAW, RELAX
unbiased - - - - - - - IMPARTIAL
unbind - - - - - - UNTIE, RELEASE
unbleached - - - - - - - - - ECRU
unblemished - - - - - - - - CLEAN
unbound - - - - - - - - - LOOSE
unbounded - - - - - - - LIMITLESS
unbranded calf - - - - - MAVERICK
unbridled - - - - - - - - - - FREE
unbroken - - - - - - - - - INTACT
uncanny (var.) - - - - - EERY, EERIE
unceasing - - PERENNIAL, PERPETUAL, ENDLESS
unceremonious - - - - - - ABRUPT
unceremonious attire - - - - NEGLIGEE
uncertain - - - - - - ASEA, UNSURE
uncertain (be) - - - - - - WONDER
uncertainty - - - - - - - - DOUBT
unchanging - - UNIFORM, UNVARYING
unchaste - - - - - - - - OBSCENE
unchecked - - - - - RAMPANT, FREE
uncivil - - - - - - - - - - RUDE
uncivilized - - - - - - - - SAVAGE
unclasp - - - - - - - - - - UNDO
Uncle Remus creator - - - - - HARRIS
uncle (Scot.) - - - - - - - - - EME
Uncle Tom's Cabin character - LEGREE, SIMON
unclean - - - - - - - - - - VILE
unclose - - - - - - - - OPEN, OPE
unclouded - - - - - - - - - CLEAR
uncoil - - - - - - - - - UNWIND
uncoined gold or silver - - BULLION
uncomely - - - - - - - - - UGLY
uncommon - - SINGULAR, UNUSUAL, RARE, ODD
uncompromising - - - - - - STERN
unconcealed - - - - - - - - OPEN
unconfined - - - - - - - - - FREE
unconfirmed report - - - - - RUMOR
unconnected - - - - - - SEPARATE
unconscious - - - - - - UNAWARE
uncorked - - - - - RAW, UNSTOPPED
uncouth - - - - - - - - - - RUDE
uncouth fellow - - - - - - - CODGER
uncovered - BARE, OPEN, UNEARTHED, LIDLESS
unctuous - - - - - - - - - - OILY
unctuous substance - - - - - CERATE
uncultivated - - WILD, UNREFINED, FALLOW
uncultivated tract of land - - - HEATH
uncultured - - - - - - UNREFINED
uncurbed - - - - - - - - - - FREE
uncut glove leather - - - - - TRANK
uncut lumber - - - - - - - - - LOG
undamaged - - - - - - - UNHARMED
undaunted - - - - - - - - SPARTAN
undecided - - - - - PEND, WAVERING
undecorated - - - - - - - - PLAIN
under - - BENEATH, BELOW, NETHER
under a ban - - - - - - - - TABU
under (It.) - - - - - - - - - SOTTO
under obligation - - - - - INDEBTED
under part of auto - - - - - CHASSIS
under (poet.) - - - - - - - - NEATH
under (prefix) - - - - - - - - - SUB
under severe strain - - - - - TENSE
under surface of foot - - - - - SOLE
underdone - - - - - - - - - RARE
undergird (naut.) - - - - - - FRAP
undergo - - - - - - - EXPERIENCE
undergo cell destruction - - - - LYSE
undergo a decline - - - - - - SLUMP
underground bud - - - - - - - BULB
underground cavity - - - - - - CAVE
underground chamber - CAVERN, CAVE
underground excavation (mining) - - - STOPE
underground goblin - - - - - GNOME
underground passageway - - TUNNEL
underground river - - - - - - - STYX
underground stem - - - - - - TUBER
underground room - - - - - CELLAR
underground tram - - - - - - TUBE
underground worker - - - - - MINER
underhand - - - - - - - - SINISTER
underhanded - - - - - - - - - SLY
underhanded person - - - - - SNEAK
underlings - - - - - SLAVES, SERFS
undermine - - - - - - - - - - SAP
underneath - - - - - - - - BELOW
undersea dweller - - - - - MERMAN
understand - - REALIZE, SEE, KNOW, COMPREHEND
understand (I) (mil.) - - - - - ROGER
understanding - - REASON, ENTENTE, SENSE
understood - - - - - - - - - TACIT
undertake - - - - - ENDEAVOR, TRY
undertaking - - - - - - - - VENTURE
underwater ridge - - - - - - - REEF
underwater worker - - - - - - DIVER
underworld - - - - - - - - HADES
underwrite - - - - - - - - INSURE
undetached statue piece - - - - TENON
undetermined article - - SOMETHING
undeveloped - - - - - - - - LATENT
undiluted - - - - - - - - - SHEER
undisclosed - - - - - - - ULTERIOR
undiscovered - UNESPIED, ULTERIOR
undisguised - - - - - - - - - BARE
undivided - - ONE, ENTIRE, WHOLE, TOTAL
undivided whole - - - - - - - - UNIT

U

undo - - RELEASE, NEGLECT, OFFSET, ANNUL, RUIN, UNCLASP, UNTIE
undo (poet.) - - - - - - - - OPE
undoing - - - - - - - - - RUIN
undomesticated - - - - FERAL, WILD
undressed calk skin - - - - - - KIP
undressed fur skin - - - - - - PELT
undressed hide - - - - - - - KIP
undressed kid - - - - - - - SUEDE
undulate - - - - - - WAVE, ROLL
undulation - - - - CRIMP, WAVE
unduly dainty - - - - - - FINICAL
unearth - - - UNCOVER, DISCLOSE
unearthly - - - - - - - - - EERIE
unease - - - - - - - - - DISQUIET
uneasiness - - - - - - - UNREST
uneasy - RESTIVE, RESTLESS, NERVOUS
unelevated - - - - - - - - LOW
unembellished - - - - - - - PROSE
unemployed - - - - - - - - IDLE
unenclosed - - - - - - FENCELESS
unencumbered - - - - - - - FREE
unending - CEASELESS, EVERLASTING
unending existence - - - - ETERNITY
unenlightened - - - - - - - DARK
unenthusiastic - - - - - - - COOL
unequalled - - - - - - - PEERLESS
uneven - - - - - - - EROSE, ODD
uneven in color - - - - - - STREAKY
unexciting - - - - - - - - TAME
unexpected - - - - - - - - ABRUPT
unexpected difficulty - - - - - SNAG
unexpected pleasure - - - - - TREAT
unexpected result - - - - - - UPSET
unexpected stratagem - - - - - COUP
unexplosive shell - - - - - - DUD
unfailing - - - - - - - - - SURE
unfair - - - - - - - - - FOUL
unfamiliar - STRANGE, UNKNOWN, NEW
unfastened - RIPPED, LOOSE, UNDID, UNTIED, UNTETHERED
unfavourable - - - AVERSE, BAD, ILL
unfeeling - - - STONY, INSENSATE, MARBLE, NUMB
unfeigned - - - - - - - - SINCERE
unfettered - - - - - - - - - FREE
unfilled cavity - - - - - - - VUG
unfledged - - - - - - - - CALLOW
unfold - - - OPEN, SPREAD, DEPLOY
unfold gradually - - - - - DEVELOP
unforested plain - - - - - - STEPPE
unforged metal - - - - - - - PIG
unfortunate - - - - - - LUCKLESS
unfounded - - - - - - - - - IDLE
unfriendly - - - - - - - INIMICAL
unfruitful - - - - - - - - STERILE
unfurl - - - - - - SPREAD, OPEN
ungainly - - - - - - - - AWKWARD
ungentlemanly person - - - - - CAD
ungrateful person - - - - - INGRATE
ungulate animal - - - DAMAN, TAPIR
unharmed - - - - - - - UNDAMAGED
unhealthy - - - - - - - DISEASED
unheeding - - - - - - - - - DEAF
unhorse - - - - - - - - UNSEAT
unhurried - - - - - - - - - EASY
unicorn - - - - - - - - REEM, URUS
uniform - - - - EVEN, UNCHANGING, CONSISTENT
uniformly (poetic) - - - - - - EEN
unimaginative - - - - - - - LITERAL
unimaginative discourse - - - - PROSE
unimpaired - - - - - - - - INTACT
unimportant - - - - - - - TRIVIAL
unimportant matters - - - - TRIFLES
uninhabited - - DESERTED, DESOLATE
uninjured - - - - - - - - - INTACT
unintentional aperture - - - - - LEAK
uninteresting - - - - - - DRY, DULL
uninterrupted - - - - - - STRAIGHT
uninvited participant - - - - MEDDLER
union - - - - JUNCTION, COALITION, FUSION, LEAGUE, MERGER, MARRIAGE, JUNCTURE, ALLIANCE
union of three in one - - - - TRINITY
unique - - - - - ODD, RARE, ALONE
unique person - - - - - - - - ONER
unison - - - HARMONY, AGREEMENT, ACCORD, CONCORD
unit - - - - - - (See also Measure)
unit - - - - - - - ACE, ONE, ITEM
unit of acoustics - - - - - - - BEL
unit of apothecaries' weight - - DRAM
unit of capacity - - - - - - - - PINT
unit of capacity for ships - - - - TON
unit of conductance - - - - - - MHO
unit of discourse - - - - - - - WORD
unit of dry measure - - - - - - PECK
unit of electric capacity - - - - FARAD
unit of electric current - - - - AMPERE
unit of electrical intensity - - AMPERE
unit of electrical power - - - - WATT
unit of electrical reluctance - - - REL
unit of electrical resistance - - - OHM
unit of electricity - - - - - - - VOLT
unit of electrolysis - - - - - - - ION
unit of energy - - - - - - - - ERG
unit in engineering - - - - - - - BEL
unit of force - - - - - - DENE, DYNE
unit of germ plasm - - - - - IDS, ID
unit of heat - - - - CALORIE, THERM
unit of heavyweight - - - - - - TON
unit of illumination - - - - - - PHOT
unit of inductance (elect.) - - HENRY
unit of length - - - - - MIL, METER
unit of light - - - - - - - - LUMEN
unit of light intensity - - - - - PYR
unit of liquid measure - - - - LITER
unit of measure - - - - - - - - MIL
unit of measure for interstellar space - PARSEC
unit of metric system - - DECIMETER
unit of pressure - - - - - - BARAD
unit of quantity of electricity - - - ES
unit of square measure - - ACRE, ROD
unit of time - - - - - MONTH, DAY
unit of score at bridge - - - - TRICK
unit of velocity - - - - - KINE, KIN
unit of weight - CARAT, GRAM, TON, GRAIN
unit of wire measure - - - - - - MIL
unit of work - - - - - - ERG, KILERG
unit of work (pert. to) - - - - ERGAL
unite - COALESCE, LINK, TIE, UNIFY, MERGE, CEMENT, ADD, BAND, CONNECT, ALLY, KNIT, CONSOLIDATE, COMBINE, SPLICE
unite closely - - - - ALLY, WELD, FAY
unite firmly - - - - - - - - CEMENT
unite by fusing - - - - - - - WELD
unite by weaving - - - - - - SPLICE
united - - ONE, BANDED, COMBINED
united group - - - - - - - - BAND
United Kingdom part - - - - - WALES
united in opinion - - - - - AGREED, UNANIMOUS
United States capitalist - - RASKOB
United States citizen - - AMERICAN
United States monetary unit - DOLLAR
United States plant - - - - - BLUET
unity - ONE, ONENESS, AGREEMENT
universal - - - - - PUBLIC, GENERAL

universal remedy - - - - PANACEA
universe - - - NATURE, CREATION
universe (pert. to) - - - - COSMIC
university lecturer - - - PRELECTOR
university session - SEMINAR, TERM, SEMESTER
unkeeled - - - - - - - - RATITE
unkind - - - - - - - ILL, CRUEL
unknown god - - - - - - - - KA
unknown person - - - - STRANGER
unlawful outbreak - - - - - RIOT
unlearned - - - - - - - IGNORANT
unless - - - - - - - - - EXCEPT
unless (Latin) - - - - - - NISI
unlighted - - - - - - - - DARK
unlike - - - - - - - - DIVERSE
unlimited authority - - AUTOCRACY
unlock - - - - - - - - - OPEN
unlucky (obs.) - - - - - - - FEY
unmannered - - - - - - - RUDE
unmannerly person - - - - CAD
unmarried - - - - - - - CELIBATE
unmarried girl - - MAID, SPINSTER
unmatched - - - - - - - - ODD
unmated - - - - - - - - - ODD
unmelodious - - - - - TUNELESS
unmethodical - - - - - CURSORY
unmistakable - - - - - DECISIVE
unmitigated - - - ARRANT, SHEER
unmixed - - - - - - - - - PURE
unnaturally white - - - - ALBINO
unnecessary - - - - - NEEDLESS
unnecessary activity - - - - - ADO
unnerve - - - - - - - - WEAKEN
unoccupied - - - - IDLE, VACANT
unoccupied place - - - - VACANCY
unpaid debt - - - - - - - ARREAR
unparalleled - - - - - - ALONE
unplayed golf holes - - - - - BYE
unpleasant - - - - - - IRKSOME
unpolished - - RUDE, RUSTIC, DULL
unprepared - - - - - - - - RAW
unproductive - - - BARREN, STERILE
unprogressive - - - - BACKWARD
unpropitious - - ADVERSE, HOSTILE
unqualified - - - - MERE, SHEER
unravel - - UNFOLD, DISENTANGLE
unreadable - - - - - - ILLEGIBLE
unreal - - - - - - - - VISIONARY
unrefined - - - - - - CRUDE, WILD, UNCULTIVATED, INELEGANT, UNCULTURED, RAW
unrelenting - - - IRON, INEXORABLE
unreliable - - - - - - - - UNSAFE
unremembered - - - - FORGOTTEN
unreservedly - - - - - FRANKLY
unresponsive - - - COLD, PASSIVE
unrestrained - - - RAMPANT, FREE
unripe - - - - - - - - IMMATURE
unroll - - - - - - - - - UNFURL
unruffled - - SERENE, CALM, COOL
unruly - - - - RESTIVE, LAWLESS, DISORDERLY
unruly child - - - - - - - - BRAT
unruly lock of hair - - - - COWLICK
unruly person - - - - - - - REBEL
unsafe - - - - - - - - INSECURE
unsatisfactory - - - - - - LAME
unseal - - - - - - - - - - OPEN
unsealing device - - - - - - OPENER
unseat - - - - - - - - UNHORSE
unseeable - - - - - - - INVISIBLE
unserviceable - - - - - - USELESS
unsettle - - - - - - - - DISTURB
unsewed glove - - - - - - TRANK
unshackled - - - - - - - - - FREE
unshadowed - - - - - - - - CLEAR
unshaped piece of metal - - - SLUG
unsightly - - - - - - - - - UGLY
unskilled - - - - - - - - - INEPT
unskilled workman - - - - - LABORER
unsoiled - - - - - - - - - CLEAN
unsophisticated - - - - - - CALLOW
unsophisticated person - - - - RUBE
unsorted wheaten flour - - - - ATTA
unspoiled - - - - - - RACY, FRESH
unspoken - - - - - - - - - TACIT
unstable - - - - ERRATIC, TICKLISH
unsteady glare - - - - - - - FLARE
unstitched glove - - - - - - TRANK
unstopped - - - OPEN, UNCORKED
unsubstantial - - AIRY, AERY, FLIMSY
unsubstantial building - - - - HUT
unsuccessful - - - - - - - FAILED
unsuitable - - - - - - INEPT, UNAPT
unsure - - - - - - - - UNCERTAIN
unsympathetic - - - - - - UNKIND
untamed - - - - - - - WILD, FERAL
untanned skin - - - - - - - PELT
untended - - - - - - - NEGLECTED
untether - - - - - - - UNFASTEN
untidy - - - - - - MESSY, MUSSY
untidy person - - SLOVEN, SLATTERN
untie - - - - - LOOSEN, UNFASTEN
until - - - - - - - - - UNTO, TO
until (poet.) - - - - - - - - TIL
unto - - - - - - - - - UNTIL, TO
untouchable - - - - - - - LEPER
untouched - - - - - - - PRISTINE
untoward - - - - - - - VEXATIOUS
untrained - - - - - - - - - - RAW
untrained for hardship - - - - SOFT
untrammeled - - - - - - - - FREE
untried - - - - - - - - - - NEW
untroubled - - - - - - - - - EASY
untrue - - - - - - - - - - FALSE
untruth - - - - - - - - - - - FIB
untruthfulness - - - - - MENDACITY
untwist - - - - - - - - - - RAVEL
untwisted silk - - - - - - - SLEAVE
unused - - - - - - - UNTRIED, NEW
unusual - - - RARE, ODD, NOVEL, UNCOMMON
unusual performance - - - - - STUNT
unvaried - - - - - - - - - - EVEN
unvarying - - - - - - - - - EVEN
unvarying sound - - - - - MONOTONE
unweave - - - - - - - - - RAVEL
unwell - - - - - - - - - - - ILL
unwholesome - - - - - - - - - ILL
unwilling - - - - - - - - - AVERSE
unwind - - - - - - - - - - UNCOIL
unwise - - - - IMPOLITIC, FOOLISH
unwoven cloth (kind) - - - - - FELT
unwritten - - - - - - - ORAL, PAROL
unwrought - - - - - - - - - - RAW
unyielding - - - - GRIM, SET, STERN, OBDURATE, HARD, ADAMANT, RIGID
up - ALOFT, ABOVE, HIGHER, UPON, ATOP
up above - - - - - - - - - ATOP
up (prefix) - - - - - - - - - ANA
up to - - - - - - - - - - UNTIL
upbraid - - - - - REPROACH, TWIT
upbraid (slang) - - - - - - - - JAW
upbuilding - - - - - - EDIFICATION
uphold - - - - SUSTAIN, ABET, BACK
uplift - - - - RAISE, INSPIRE, ERECT
uplifted - - - - - - - - - - ERECT
upon - ATOP, ONTO, ON, UP, ABOVE

U

V

upon (poet.) - - - - - - - - OER
upon (prefix) - - - - - - - EPI, EP
upper - - HIGH, HIGHER, SUPERIOR, TOP
upper air - - - - - - - - ETHER
upper brack to enclose flowers - PALEA
upper end of ulna - - - - - ANSON
upper house - - - - - - - SENATE
upper house of French Parliament - - SENAT
upper member of a pilaster - - CAP
upper part - - - - - - - - - TOP
upper part of high mountain - - CONE
upper partial vibration - - - OVERTONE
upper regions - - - - - - - ETHER
upper room - - - - - - - - LOFT
upper story - - - - - - - - LOFT
upper throat (zool.) - - - - - GULA
uppermost part - - - - - - - TOP
upright - ERECT, HONEST, VERTICAL
upright part of stairs - - - RISERS
upright piece in a doorway - - JAMB
upright pole and spar - - - - MAST
upright surface that bounds any opening - JAMB
uprightness - - - VIRTUE, HONESTY
uprising - - - - - - - - REVOLT
uproar - TUMULT, RIOT, DIN, HUBBUB
uproot - - - - - - - ERADICATE
upset - - TOPPLE, KEEL, OVERTHROW, COUP, DISCONCERT, DISCOMPOSE
upshot - RESULT, SEQUEL, CONCLUSION
upstart - - - - - - PARVENU, SNOB
upturned nose - - - - - - - PUG
upward (comb. form) - - - - - ANO
upward bend in timber (naut.) - SNY
upward movement of ship - - SCEND
upward (prefix) - - - - - - - ANO
upward turn - - - - - - - - COCK
uranic - - - - - - - - CELESTIAL
Uranus' daughter - - - - - - RHEA
Uranus' mother - - - - - - - GE
Uranus' satellite - - - - - - ARIEL
urbane - - - - - - SUAVE, POLITE
urchin - - TAD, ELFIN, ARAB, GAMIN
uredo - - - - - - - - - HIVES
urge - - EGG, PRESS, SPUR, INSIST, PROD, STIR, INCITE, FLAGITATE, IMPEL, QUICKEN, ACTUATE, SUE, SOLICIT, PERSUADE, PUSH, DRIVE, GOAD, DUN
urge forward - - - - - - - GOAD
urge importunately - - - - - - DUN
urge by iteration (colloq.) - - - DING
urge on - ABET, HURRY, INCITE, SPUR, EGG
urgency - - - - PRESSURE, PRESS
urgent - - PRESSING, IMPERATIVE, INSISTENT
urial - - - - - - - - - - SHA
Urgian tribesman - - - - - - AVAR
urn-like vessel - - - - - - - VASE
usage - - HABIT, MANNERS, CUSTOM
use - EXERCISE, WORTH, PRACTICE, AVAIL, EMPLOY, UTILITY, CUSTOM, TREAT, SERVICE, MANIPULATE, OCCUPY, INURE
use diligently - - - - - - - - PLY
use to fasten shoe - - - - - - LACE
use frugally - - - - - - - SPARE
use (Latin) - - - - - - - - UTOR
use a lever - - - - - - PRY, PRIES
use of new word - - - - - NEOLOGY
use (suffix) - - - - - - - - IZE
use trickery - - - - - - - PALTER
use up - - - - - - - - CONSUME
used - - - - - - - SECONDHAND
used in flight - - - - - - - VOLAR
used to be - - - - - - - - - WAS
useful - - - - - - - - - - UTILE
usefulness - - - - - - - UTILITY
useless - IDLE, INUTILE, FUTILE, VAIN, FRUITLESS, NEEDLESS
user - - - - - - - - - CONSUMER
usher - - - - - ESCORT, INTRODUCE, FORERUN, FOREARM
usual - - - - - COMMON, AVERAGE, CUSTOMARY
Utah river - - - - - - - - - WEBER
Utah state flower - - - - - - SEGO
utensil - - - - TOOL, IMPLEMENT
utile - - - - - USEFUL, PRACTICAL
utility - - - - - - - - - - - USE
utilizer - - - - - - - - - - USER
utmost - - - - - - - - - - BEST
utmost degrees - - - - - - - TOPS
utmost limit - - - - - - EXTREME
utopian - - - - - - - - - IDEAL
utter - - STATE, SPEAK, ABSOLUTE, STARK, TOTAL, VOICE, PRONOUNCE, SAY
utter boisterously - - - - - BLUSTER
utter chaos - - - - - - - TOPHET
utter confusedly - - - - - - STUTTER
utter in high key - - - - - - PIPE
utter impulsively - - - - - - BLURT
utter prayers - - - - - - - PRAY
utter raucously - - - - - - - BLAT
utter shrilly - - - - - - PIPE, SKIRL
utter slight sound - - - - - - PEEP
utter sonorously - - - - - - - ROLL
utter suddenly - - - - - - - BLURT
utter vehemently - - - - - THUNDER
utter vibratorily - - - - - - TRILL
utterly - - - - - - - DIAMETRALLY
uva - - - - - - - - - - - GRAPE

V

V-shaped indentation - - - - NOTCH
V-shaped piece - - - - - - WEDGE
vacant - - - HOLLOW, IDLE, EMPTY
vacate - - - - - - EVACUATE, QUIT
vacation - - - - - - - HOLIDAYS
vacillate - - WAVER, TEETER, WOBBLE
vacillation - - - - - - - - SEESAW
vacuity - - - - - - - - - - INANE
vacuum tube - - - - - - - DIODE
vagabond - - BUM, VAGRANT, TRAMP, HOBO
vagary - - - - - - FANCY, CAPRICE
vagrant - - VAGABOND, BUM, TRAMP
vagrant (slang) - - - - - - - VAG
vague - SKETCHY, HAZY, INDEFINITE
vain - - - EMPTY, IDLE, USELESS, CONCEITED
vain fellow - - - - - - - - - FOP
vainglory - - - - - - - - - PRIDE
vale - - - GLEN, DALE, CHANNEL
valiant - - - - - - - BRAVE, HEROIC
valiant man - - - - - - - - HERO
valid - - - SOUND, COGENT, LEGAL
valise - - - GRIP, BAG, HANDBAG, SATCHEL
valley - - DALE, VALE, GLEN, DELL, DINGLE, CANYON
valley (poet.) - - - - - VALE, DALE

V

valor - - - - COURAGE, HEROISM
valorous person - - - - - - HERO
valuable - - - - - - - - COSTLY
valuable metal - - - - - - URANIUM
valuable ore - - - - - - SIDERITIC
value - PRIZE, PRICE, WORTH, RATE, ESTEEM, APPRAISE, APPRECIATE, TREASURE
value highly - - - - - - - ENDEAR
valve - - - - - - - - - - PISTON
vamp - - - - - - - - - - PATCH
van - - - - - - - - - - - TRUCK
Vandal - - - - - - - - - - - HUN
vanish - - FLEE, FADE, DISAPPEAR
vanity - - - - - - - - - - PRIDE
vanquish - DEFEAT, CONQUER, WORST, BEAT
vapid - - - STALE, DULL, INSIPID, SPIRITLESS, FLAT, TASTELESS
vapidity - - - - - - - DULLNESS
vapour - - - GAS, STEAM, AIR, MIST
vapour in the air - - - - - - - HAZE
vapour (dense) - - - - - - - - FOG
vapourous - - - - - - - - - MISTY
vaqueros - - - - - - - - COWBOYS
veracity - - - - - - - - - - TRUTH
Varanglans - - - - - - - - - - ROS
variable - - - - - - - - PROTEAN
variable star - - - - - MIRA, NOVA
variable star in Cetus - - - - - MIRA
variable star in Perseus - - - - ALGOL
variant - - - - - - - - DIFFERENT
variation - - - - - - - - CHANGE
variation in color - - - - - NUANCE
variegated - PIED, TISSUED, DAPPLED, STRIPED
variety - SPECIE, SORT, CLASS, FORM, DIVERSITY, TYPE, GENUS
variety of cabbage - - - - - - KALE
variety of chalcedon - - SARD, CHERT
variety of china - - - - - - - SPODE
variety of corundum - - - - - EMERY
variety of hematite - - - - - - ORE
variety of lettuce - - COS, ROMAINE
variety of mint - - - - - MARJORAM
variety of peach - - - - - NECTARINE
variety of quartz - - - - SARD, ONYX
variety of quartz (Braz.) - - - - CACO
variety of silk - - - - - - - MOIRE
variety of talc - - - - - - STEATITE
variety of terrier - - - - - AIREDALE
variety of turtle - - - - - SNAPPER
variety of velvet - - - - - - PANNE
variety of wheat - - - - - - SPELT
variety of zoophyte - - - - RETEPORE
various - - - - - - MANY, DIVERSE
varlet - SCOUNDREL, KNAVE, MENIAL
varnish - - - - - - LAC, SHELLAC
varnish ingredient - - - - RESIN, LAC
vary - - CHANGE, ALTER, DIVERGE
vary from normal - - - - - DIVERGE
varying weight (Ind.) - - - - - SER
vas - - - - - - - - DUCT, VESSEL
vase - - - - - - - - - - - - URN
vassal - - - SUBJECT, SLAVE, SERF, BONDMAN, LIEGE
vast - - - IMMENSE, HUGE, GREAT
vast age - - - - - - - - - - EON
vast amount - - - - - - - - MINT
vast assemblage - - - - - - - HOST
vast horde - - - - - - - LEGION
vast number - - - - - - - BILLION
vast (poet.) - - - - - - - ENORME
vat - - TUB, KEEVE, BAC, CISTERN
vault - - - - - - - - LEAP, CRYPT
vaunt - - - - - - - - - - - BOAST
vaunting - - - - - - - - BOASTFUL
Vedic Aryan dialect - - - - - - PALI
Vedic fire god - - - - - - - - AGNI
Vedic god of storms - - - - - RUDRA
veer - - - - - SHIFT, SLUE, FICKLE, FLUCTUATE, TURN
vegetable - - - - - LEEK, KOHLRABI
vegetable caterpillar - - - - - AWETO
vegetable exudation - - - - - RESIN
vegetable organism - - PLANT, TREE
vegetation - - - - - - - VERDURE
vehemence - ARDOR, FURY, RAGE, HEAT
vehement - - - - - FERVENT, ARDENT
vehement scolding - - - - - TIRADE
vehemently - - - - - - - - AMAIN
vehicle - - - LANDAU, LORRY, AUTO
vehicle carrying a display - - FLOAT
vehicle for heavy loads - LORRY, DRAY
vehicle on runners - - CUTTER, SLED
veil - CURTAIN, DISGUISE, CONCEAL, HIDE
veil (silk) - - - - - - - - - ORALE
veil (having a) - - - - - - - VELATE
veiling-like material - - - - - VOILE
vein - - - - - - RIB, VENA, STREAK
vein of character - - - - - - STREAK
vein of coal - - - - - - - - STREAK
vein of leaf - - - - - - - - - - RIB
velar - - - - - GUTTURAL, PALATAL
velation - - - - - - - - - SECRECY
velocity - - - - - - - - - - - SPEED
velvet - - - - - - - - - - - VELOUR
velvet (variety of) - - - - - - PANNE
velvetlike fabric - - PANNE, VELOUR
venal - - - - - - - - - MERCENARY
vend - - - - - - - - - - - - - SELL
vender - - - - - - - - MERCHANT
vendition - - - - - - - - - - - SALE
veneering form - - - - - - - CAMUL
venerable - - - - - - AUGUST, AGED
venerable old man - - - - PATRIARCH
venerate - - REVERE, HONOUR, ADORE. WORSHIP, REVERENCE
veneration - - - - - AWE, REVERENCE
venerator - - - - - - - - - ADORER
Venetian boat song - - - - BARCAROLE
Venetian bridge - - - - - - - RIALTO
Venetian magistrate - - - - - - DOGE
Venetian painter - - - - - - - TITIAN
Venetian red - - - - - - - - SIENA
Venetian traveler - - - - - - - POLO
Venezuela capital - - - - - CARACAS
Venezuelan coin - - - - - - BOLIVAR
Venezuela river - - - - - ORINOCO
Venezuelan state - - - - - - - LARA
Venezuelan town - - - - - - - AROA
Venezuelan tree snake - - - - - LORA
vengeance - - - - NEMESIS, REVENGE
venom - - - - - - - - SPITE, VIRUS
venomous - - POISONOUS, VIPERINE
venomous serpent - - - - - - - ASP
venous - - - - - - - - - - - VEINY
vent - OUTLET, OPENING, APERTURE, BREACH, GAP
vent in earth's crust - - - - VOLCANO
vent (zool.) - - - - - - - - OSCULE
ventilating device - FANNER, BLOWER
ventilating shaft - - - - - - UPCAST
venture - - DARE, PRESUME, RISK, ENTERPRISE, TRESPASS, UNDERTAKING
ventured - - - - - - - - - - DURST
venturesome - - - - - DARING, BOLD
Venus as evening star - - - - HESPER

V

Venus' lover - - - - - - - ADONIS
Venus' son - - - - - - - - CUPID
veracity - - - - - - - - TRUTH
veranda - - - - - - PORCH, PIAZZA
verb form - - - - - - - - - TENSE
verb of future time - - - - - SHALL
verbal - - - - - - - - - - ORAL
verbal examination - - - - - - ORAL
verbal noun - - - - - - - - GERUND
verdant - - - - - - - - - GREEN
Verdi's opera - - - - - - - AIDA
verdict - - - - - - - - JUDGMENT
verdure - - VEGETATION, GREENERY
verge - - - BRINK, BORDER, EDGE, MARGIN, APPROACH
Vergil's epic - - - - - - - ENEID
Vergil's hero - - - - - - - ENEAS
Vergil's poem - - - - - - - AENEID
verification - - - - - TRIAL, PROOF
verify - - - AVER, COLLATE, PROVE
verily - INDEED, AMEN, YEA, TRULY
verisimilar - - - - - - - - LIKELY
verisimilitudinous - - - - - - TRUE
veritable - - - - - - - - - REAL
veritably - - - - - - - - - TRULY
verity - - - - - - - - - TRUTH
vermilion - - - - - - - - - - RED
Vermont town - - - - - - - BARRE
vernacular - - - - - - - IDIOMATIC
verse - RIME, POEM, POETRY, CANTO, STANZA, STAVE
verse form - TERCET, POEM, TRIOLET, SONNET
verse pattern - - - - - - - METER
verse of two feet - - - - - DIMETER
versed - - - PROFICIENT, SKILLED
versed in many languages - POLYGLOT
version of the Scriptures - - VULGATE
verso (abbr.) - - - - - - - - VO
versus - - - - - - - - - AGAINST
vertebral - - - - - - - - SPINAL
vertebrate of birds - - - - - AVES
vertex - - - - - - - - - - APEX
vertical - - - - - - - - UPRIGHT
vertical (naut.) - - - - - - - APEAK
vertical pipe - - - - - - - STACK
vertical support - - - - - - PILLAR
vertical timber - - - - - BITT, MAST
verve - - - - - - ELAN, ARDOR, PEP
very cold - - - - - - - - - - ICY
very (comb. form) - - - - - - - ERI
very hard - - - - - - - - - IRON
very large (poet.) - - - - - ENORM
very loud (mus. abbr.) - - - - - FF
very much - - - - - - - - - - FAR
very much (prefix) - - - - - - ERI
very (Scot.) - - - - - - - - VERA
very soft (mus. abbr.) - - - - - PP
vespers - - - - - - - - EVENSONG
vessel - BASIN, CRAFT, LINER, SETTEE, POT, VAS, SHIP, SLOOP, TUG, CAN, YAWL, BOAT, BARQUE, PAN, TUB, URN
vessel (abbr.) - - - - - - - - S.S.
vessel for ashes of dead - - - - URN
vessel to carry liquids - - - - - CAN
vessel curved planking - - - - - SNY
vessel to heat liquid - - - - - ETNA
vessel to hold liquid - CRUSE, TEAPOT, VIAL
vessel to hold oil, etc. - - - - CRUSE
vessel of known capacity - - MEASURE
vessel (large, deep) - TUREEN, VAT, TANKARD
vessel (large, open) - - - - POT, PAN
vessel for liquids - - - - - - VIAL
vessel for liquors - - FLAGON, FLASK
vessel of logs - - - - - - - - RAFT
vessel (long and narrow) - - TROUGH
vessel's personnel - - - - - - CREW
vessel (poet.) - - - - - - - - BARK
vessel (shallow) - - - - - - - BASIN
vessel for vinegar - - - - - - CRUET
vessel which raids - - - - - RAIDER
vest - - - - - - - - INVEST, ENDOW
Vesta handmaidens - - - - - VESTALS
vestal - - - - - - - - - - - PURE
vestibule - - - ENTRY, HALL, LOBBY
vestige - - - - - - - - TRACE, RELIC
vestment - - - - - COPE, ALB, STOLE
vestry - - - - - - - - - - - CHAPEL
vetch - - - - - - - - - - - - TARE
vetch seed - - - - - - - - - - TARE
veto - - - - - - - PROHIBIT, FORBID
vex - - ROIL, IRK, IRRITATE, TEASE, HARASS, PEEVE, AGITATE, FRET, ANNOY
vex (colloq.) - - - - - - - - - RILE
vexation - - PEST, PIQUE, CHAGRIN
vexatious - - - - - - - - UNTOWARD
vexatious (colloq.) - - - - - - PESKY
via - - - - - - - - - - - - - - BY
viaduct - - - - - - - - - TRESTLE
vial - - - - - - - - - - - PHIAL
viands - - - - - - - - - - EDIBLES
viator - - - - - - - - - TRAVELLER
vibrate - - - - - - - - - - ROCK
vibration - - - - - - - - - TREMOR
vibrationless point - - - - - - NODE
vibratory motion - - - - - - TREMOR
vicar's assistant - - - - - - CURATE
vicarage - - - - - - - - - - MANSE
vice - - - - - EVIL, SIN, INIQUITY
vicinity (in the) - - - - - - AROUND
vicious - - - - - - - - CRUEL, MEAN
vicissitude - - - - - - - REVERSE
victim - - - - - - - - PREY, DUPE
victimize - - - - - - - - - - DUPE
victor - - - - WINNER, CONQUEROR
victor's crown - - - - - - - - BAY
Victorian vehicle - - - - - - CALASH
victorious (be) - - - - - - PREVAIL
victory - - - - - TRIUMPH, SUCCESS, CONQUEST
victory trophy (Amer. Indian) - SCALP
victual - - - - - - - - - - - MEAT
vie - CONTEND, EMULATE, CONTEST, STRIVE
view - - - - - - SCENE, VISTA, EYE
viewpoint - - - - - OPINION, SIDE
vigil - - - - - - - - - - - WATCH
viligance - - - - - - - - - - CARE
vigilant - - ALERT, AWARE, AWAKE, WATCHFUL
vigour - PEP, VIM, ENERGY, STRENGTH, POWER, VIS
vigorous - - - ENERGETIC, STURDY ROBUST, HALE, FORCIBLE, ANIMATED, VIRILE, LUSTY
vigorously - - - - - - - - LUSTILY
vile - - FILTHY, VULGAR, UNCLEAN, BASE
vilify - - ASPERSE, REVILE, SLANDER, DEFAME
village - - - - HAMLET, TOWN, DORP
villain - MISCREANT, ROGUE, FIEND
villainy - - - - - - - - - - CRIME
villein - - - - - - - - - - - SERF
villification - - - - - - - - ABUSE
vim - - PEP, VIGOR, ENERGY, FORCE

vim (colloq.) - - - - - - - - ZIP
vindicate - - - JUSTIFY, MAINTAIN, EXCULPATE
vindictive retaliation - - - REVENGE
vindictiveness - - - - - - - SPITE
vine - IVY, WISTERIA, CREEPER, PEA, HOP
vinegar bottle - - - - - - - CRUET
vinegar made from ale - - - - ALEGAR
vinegar (obs.) - - - - - - - EISEL
vinegar (pert. to) - - - - - - ACETIC
vineyard - - - - - - - - - CRU
violate - - - - - - - - DISTURB
violation - - - - - - - INFRACTION
violation of allegiance - - - TREASON
violation of confidence - - BETRAYAL
violence - - - FURY, RAGE, FORCE
violent - - - RABID, TEMPESTUOUS
violent blast of wind - - - - GUST
violent effort - - - - - - STRUGGLE
violent speech - - - - - - TIRADE
violent storm - - - - - - TORNADO
violent windstorm - - - - - TEMPEST
violent woman - - - - - - VIRAGO
violently - - - - - - HARD, AMAIN
violet - - - - - - - - WISTERIA
violet blue - - - - - - - - INDIGO
violin (colloq.) - - - STRAD, FIDDLE
violin instrument of India - - RUANA
violin maker - - - - - - - AMATI
violin (old) - CREMONA, AMATI, REBEC
violin (small) - - - - - - - - KIT
violinist's implement - - - - BOW
viper - - - - ADDER, SNAKE, ASP
Virgil's hero - - - - - - - ENEAS
Virgil's poem - - - - - - AENEID
virile - - - - VIGOROUS, MANLY
virtue - EXCELLENCE, DUTY, CHASTITY
virtuous - - - - - - - - MORAL
virulent - - - - - - - - BITTER
virulent epidemic - - - - - - PEST
virus - - - - - - POISON, VENOM
vis - - - - - - - - - - - POWER
visage - - - - - - - COUNTENANCE
viscous - - - - - - - - - ROPY
viscous liquid - - - - - - - - TAR
viscous substance - GLUE, SEMISOLID, GREASE, TAR
vise part - - - - - - - - - JAW
Vishnu's incarnation - - - - - RAMA
visible trace - - - - - - - - MARK
visible vapor - - - - - - - STEAM
vision - - - - - - - DREAM, EYE
vision (pert. to) - - VISIVE, OPTICAL, OPTIC
visionary - DREAMER, IDEALIST, IDEAL, AERY. UTOPIAN, UNREAL
visionary scheme - - - - - - BABEL
visionary zealot - - - - - - FANATIC
visit - - - - - - SEE, HAUNT, CALL
visit stores - - - - - - - - SHOP
visitant - - - - - - - - - GUEST
visitor - - - - - - GUEST, CALLER
vista - - - VIEW, OUTLOOK, SCENE, PROSPECT
visual - - - - - - - - - OCULAR
visualize when absent - - - IDEATE
vital - - - - - - - - NECESSARY
vital organ - - - - - - - - HEART
vital principle - - - - - - - LIFE
vitality - - - - - SAP, PEP STAMINA
vitiate - - - DEPRAVE, TAINT, SPOIL
vitreous material - - - - - ENAMEL
vitrify by heat - - - - - - - BAKE
vivacious - - GAY, ANIMATED, BRISK, AIRY
vivacity - - - GAIETY, ANIMATION
vivacity (mus.) - - - - - - - BRIO
vivid - - - - - - - - - GRAPHIC
vixen - - - - - - - - - - SHREW
Vladimir Ilyitch Ulyanoff - - LENIN
vocabulary of a language (pert. to) - - LEXICAL
vocal - - - - - - - - - - ORAL
vocal composition - - - - - - SONG
vocal inflection - - - - - - - TONE
vocal solo - - - - - - - - ARIOSO
vocal sound - - - - - - - - TONE
vocalist - - - - - - - - - SINGER
vocation - - CALLING, PROFESSION, CAREER, TRADE
vocation of a knight errant - CHIVALRY
vociferated - - CLAMORED, ROARED, YELLED
vociferous - - - - - - - BLATANT
vociferous cry - - - - - - - - HUE
vogue - - - - - - - - - FASHION
vogue (is in) - - - - - - PREVAILS
the vogue - - - - - - - - - - TON
voice - EMIT, DIVULGE, SAY, SPEECH, EXPRESS, UTTER
voice objection - - - - - - PROTEST
voice (pert. to) - - VOCAL, PHONETIC
voiced - - - - - - - - - UTTERED
voiceless - - - - - SPIRATE, SURD
void - SPACE, ANNUL, EMPTY, NULL
void space - - - - - - - - INANITY
voided escutcheon - - - - - - ORLE
voided law trial - - - - - MISTRIAL
volatile - - - - - - - - EVAPORABLE
volatile compound - - - - - - ETHER
volatile liquid - - - ALCOHOL, ETHER
volcanic cinder - - - - - - SCORIA
volcanic deposit - - - - - - TRASS
volcanic earth - - - - - - - TRASS
volcanic glass froth - - - - PUMICE
volcanic island - - - - - - LIPARI
volcanic lava - - - - - - - - SLAG
volcanic matter - - - - - - - LAVA
volcanic rock - - BASALT, TEPHRITE, OBSIDIAN, TRASS
volcano - - - - - - - ETNA, PELEE
volcano island - - - - - - - - IWO
volcano mouth - - - - - - CRATER
volcano in Sicily - - - - - - ETNA
Voltaire play - - - - - - - ZOIRE
volume (large) - - - - - - - TOME
voluntary forebearance - ABSTINENCE
volunteer - - - - - - - - OFFER
volution - - - - - - - - WHORL
voracious - - - EDACIOUS, GREEDY
voracious animal - - - GOAT, HOG
vortex - - - - - - - - EDDY, GYRE
vote - - - - BALLOT, POLL, ELECT
voter - - - - - - - - - ELECTOR
voting ticket - - - - - - - BALLOT
vouch for - - - SPONSOR, ATTEST, ASSURE, AVER
voucher acknowledging a debt - - - - DEBENTURE, CHIT
vouchsafe - - - - - - - - DEIGN
vow - - - - - - - OATH, PLEDGE
vowel mutation - - - - - - UMLAUT
voyage - - - - - - SAIL, PASSAGE
vulgar - - - - - - - VILE, COARSE
vulgar fellow - - - - - - - - CAD
vulnerable - - - - - - UNTENABLE
vulture (large) - - - - - - CONDOR

W W

wad - - - - - - - STUFF, CRAM
wade - - - - - - - - - - - FORD
wader - - - - - - - - - - SNIPE
wading bird - - STILT, HERON, RAIL, CRANE, JABIRU, BOATBILL, IBIS, STORK, SORA, FLAMINGO
wafer - - - - - - - - - - - - SNAP
waft - - - PUFF, WAVE, GUST, FLOAT
wag - - WIT, JOKER, SHAKE, SWAY
wage - - - - - - - - - - PAY, LEVY
wager - ANTE, BET, STAKE, PARLAY, WIT
wagerer - - - - - - - - - BETTOR
wages - - - SALARY, PAY, STIPEND
waggery - - - - - - - - - - WIT
waggish - - - - - - - - - - ARCH
Wagnerian character - - HAGEN, ERDA
Wagnerian heroine - - ELSA, SENTA
Wagner's wife - - - - - - COSIMA
wagon - WAIN, CART, LORRY, TRAM
wagon (heavy) - - - - DRAY, TRUCK
wagon track - - - - - - - - - RUT
wail - - - HOWL, LAMENT, MOAN, BEMOAN
wain - - - - - - - - - - - WAGON
wainscot - - - - - - - - - - CEIL
waist - - - - - - - - - - BODICE
waistcoat - - - - - - - - - - VEST
wait - STAY, LINGER, TARRY, DELAY, ATTEND, BIDE
wait in ambush for - - - - - WAYLAY
wait expectantly - - - - - - - BIDE
wait for - - - - - - - - - - - BIDE
wait on - - - ATTEND, SERVE, TEND, CLERK, CATER
waiting line - - - - - - - - QUEUE
waive - - - - DISREGARD, FOREGO, RENOUNCE
wakeful - - - - - - - - SLEEPLESS
waken - - - - - - - - - - - ROUSE
wale - - - - - - - - TEXTURE, WELT
walk - STEP, TREAD, STRIDE, PACE, HIKE, AMBULATE, TRAMP
walk about - - - - - - - - AMBULATE
walk feebly - - - - - - - - TOTTER
walk heavily - - - - - TRAMP, PLOD
walk lamely - - - - - - - - - LIMP
walk leisurely - - - - - - - STROLL
walk on - - - - - - - - - - TREAD
walk pompously - - - - STRUT, STALK
walk proudly - - - - - - - - PRANCE
walk unsteadily - - STAGGER, TODDLE, TOTTER
walk wearily - TRUDGE, PLOD, TRAIL
walk with affected gait - - - - MINCE
walk with high steps - - - - PRANCE
walk with long steps - - - - - STRIDE
walking - - - - - - - - - GRADIENT
walking stick - CANE, RATTAN, STAFF, STILT, POGO
walking trip - - - - - TRAMP, HIKE
wall - - - - - - - OGEE, PARTITION
wall border - - - - - - - OGEE, DADO
wall coating - - - - - - - PLASTER
wall column - - - - - - - PILASTER
wall like - - - - - - - - - MURAL
wall painting - - - - - - - - MURAL
wall (pert. to) - - MURAL, PARIENTAL
wall projecting into sea - - - - PIER
wall section - - - - - - - - PANEL
wall of separation in mine - BRATTICE
Wallaba - - - - - - - - - - - APA
walled city - - - - - - - - CHESTER
wallflower - - - - - - - - - CHEIR
walrus collection - - - - - - - POD
wampum - - - - - - - - - - - PEAG
wan - - PALE, PALLID, COLORLESS, ASHY, LANGUID
wand - POLE, ROD, SCEPTER, OSIER, STAFF
wander - ERR, ROAM, STRAY, ROVE, STROLL, TRAIPSE, RAMBLE, DIGRESS, GAD, MEANDER, DIVAGATE
wander over - - - - - - - TRAVERSE
wanderer - - - - - ROVER, NOMAD, MEANDERER, STRAY
wandering - - - - ERRANT, VAGRANT, ABERRANT, NOMADIC, ERRING, ASTRAY
wandering domestic animal - - ESTRAY
wandering race - - - - - - - GYPSY
wane - - - - EBB, FADE, DECREASE, SHRINK
wangle - - - - - - - - - - WRIGGLE
want - NEED, LACK, POVERTY, DESIRE, WISH, SCARCITY, DEFICIENCY
want of success - - - - - - FAILURE
wanting a skull - - - - - ACRANIAL
wanton destroyer - - - - - - - VANDAL
wapiti - - - - - - - - - - - - ELK
war - - CONFLICT, STRIFE, BATTLE
war fleet - - - - - - - - ARMADA
war horse - - - - - - - - - - STEED
war (pert. to) - - - - - - - MARTIAL
war vessel - - DESTROYER, MONITOR, NAVY
warble - YODEL, SING, TRILL, CAROL
ward off - - AVERT, FEND, PREVENT, PARRY, REPEL, STAVE
warden - - - - - KEEPER, GUARDIAN
warder - - - - - - - - - SENTINEL
warehouse - - - - STORE, ENTREPOT
wares - - - - - - - - - - - GOODS
wariness - - - - - - - - - CAUTION
warlike - - - - - - - - - - MARTIAL
warlike Indian - - - - - ARAPAHOE
warm - - THERMAL, TOASTY, TEPID, TROPICAL, TOAST, FERVENT
warm and balmy - - - - - SUMMERY
warm compresses - - - - - STUPES
warm covering - - - - - - BLANKET
warm drink - - - - - - - - CAUDLE
warm thoroughly - - - - - - TOAST
warmth - - - - - - - - - - - HEAT
warmth of feeling - - - - - - ARDOR
warn - - - - - - - - - - CAUTION
warning - - NOTICE, ALERT, CAVEAT, SIGNAL
warning of danger - - - - - ALARM
warning (old form) - - - - - ALARUM
warning signal - - - TOCSIN, SIREN, ALARUM, ALERT, ALARM
warp - - - - - - - - - - CONTORT
warp yarn - - - - - - - - - - - ABB
warped - - - - - - - - - - - - WRY
warrant - - - - - - - - - - MERIT
warranty - - - SECURITY, GUARANTY
warriors - - - COHORTS, SOLDIERS, FIGHTERS
warrior's headpiece - - - - - HELMET
warship's defensive plating - - ARMOR
warship's part - - - - - - - TURRET
wary - - SHY, CAUTIOUS, WATCHFUL
wary (colloq.) - - - - - - - - LEERY
wash - - - LAVE, BATHE, LAUNDER, RINSE
wash in clear water - - - - - RINSE
washing preparation - - - - - SOAP

Washington city - - - - SPOKANE
Washington Irving character - - - RIP
wasp - - - - - - - - - - HORNET
waste - EMACIATE, REFUSE, SQUANDER, LOSE, FRITTER, EXHAUST, DROSS
waste allowance - - - - - - TARE
waste away - - - - - - REPINE
waste land - - - - HEATH, DESERT
waste land (Eng.) - - - - - - MOOR
waste matter - - - - - - DROSS
waste pipe - - - - - - - SEWER
waste silk fibers - - - - - FLOSS
waste silk (piece) - - - - - NOIL
waste time - - - - - DALLY, IDLE
wasteful - - - - - - - PRODIGAL
waster - - - - - - - - SPENDER
wasting - - - - - - - - AWASTE
wasting with disease - - - - TABID
wastrel - - - - - - SPENDTHRIFT
watch - - PATROL, EYE, VIGIL, TEND
watch accessory - - - - - - FOB
watch chain - - - - - - - FOB
watch closely - - - - - - - EYE
watch dog - - - - - - MASTIFF
water jug - - - - - - - - OLLA
watch narrowly - - - - - - - EYE
watch over - - - - - - - - TEND
watch pocket - - - - - - - FOB
watch secretly - - - - - - SPY
watch with satisfaction - - - GLOAT
watchful - - ALERT, VIGILANT, WARY
watchful person - - - - - ARGUS
watchman - - - - - - - SENTINEL
water - IRRIGATE, AQUA, EAU, DILUTE
water around castle - - - - MOAT
water barrier - - - - - - - DAM
water bird - - - - - COOT, SWAN
water bottle - - - - - - - CARAFE
water buffalo (female) - - - ARNEE
water conveyor from a roof - - GUTTER
water craft - - - - - - - - BOAT
water duct from eaves - - - LEADER
water excursion - - - - - - - SAIL
water flying in small drops - - SPRAY
water fowl - - - - BRANT, EGRET
water (Fr.) - - - - - - - - EAU
water glass - - - - - - TUMBLER
water jar - - - - - - - HYDRIA
water jug - - - - - - EWER, OLLA
water lily - - - - - - - - LOTUS
water lily leaf - - - - - - - PAD
water passage - - - SOUND, STRAIT
water pipe (large) - - - - - MAIN
water plant - - - - - - - LOTUS
water of the sea - - - - - BRINE
water spirit - - - - UNDINE, ARIEL
water sprites - - - KELPIES, NIXES
water stream obstruction - - - WEIR
water wheel - - - - - - - NORIA
watercourse - - - - - - - STREAM
watercourse (Sp.) - - - - - ARROYO
watercress (dial.) - - - - - EKERS
watered appearance on silk - - MOIRE
waterfall - CATARACT, LINN, CASCADE, LIN
waterfall (rare) - - - - - - LIN
waterfall (Scot.) - - - - - - LIN
watering place - - - - SPA, OASIS
watering place on Isle of Wight - RYDE
waterless - - - - - - - ARID, DRY
waterproof garment - - - GOSSAMER
waterway - - - - CHANNEL, STREAM
waterwheel flatboard - - - - LADLE
watery - - - - WET, THIN, SEROUS, BRIMMING
watery vapor condensation - - MIST
wave - SEA, COMBER, SURF, BREAKER, FLUTTER, CRIMP, UNDULATE, SURGE, ROLLER, WAFT
wave (heraldry) - - - - - - ONDE
wave back and forth - - - - - WAG
wave of surf - - - - - - BREAKER
wave to and fro - - - - - FLAP, WAG
wavelet - - - - - - - - RIPPLE
waver - FALTER, STAGGER, FLUCTUATE, TOTTER, REEL, HESITATE, FLICKER
wavering - - - - - - - UNDECIDED
wavering sound - - - - - TREMOLO
Waverly author - - - - - - - SCOTT
wax - CERE, GROW, INCREASE, CERATE
wax candle - - - - - - - - TAPER
wax match - - - - - - - - VESTA
wax (obs.) - - - - - - - - CERE
wax ointment - - - - - - - CERATE
wax (pert. to) - - - - - - - CERAL
waxy substance (bot.) - - - - CUTIN
waxy substance from sperm whale - - AMBERGRIS
way - - MANNER, ROUTE, METHOD, PATH, PASSAGE, COURSE, ROAD, LANE
way of putting - - - PRESENTATION
way through - - - - - - PASSAGE
wayfarer - - - PILGRIM, TRAVELLER
weak - PUNY, FRAIL, FEEBLE, FAINT
weak (arch.) - - - - - - - SEELY
weak minded - - - - - - - - DAFT
weak spot - - - - - - - - GALL
weaken - - SAP, ENERVATE, DILUTE, UNNERVE, DEBILITATE, ATTENUATE
weakness - - - - - - - - FOIBLE
weal - - - - - - - - PROSPERITY
wealth - - - TREASURE, AFFLUENCE, MAMMON, MEANS, OPULENCE
wealthy - - - - - RICH, AFFLUENT
wealthy person - - - NABOB, MIDAS
wean - - - - - - - - ALIENATE
weapon - - BOMBER, GUN, SPEAR, SWORD, PISTOL, ARMS, DAGGER, FIREARM
weapon to expel stones - - SLINGSHOT
wear - - - - - EXHIBIT, DISPLAY
wear away - - ERODE, ABRADE, EAT, FRAY
wear away (tending to) - - - EROSIVE
wear at the edge - - - - - FRAY
wear by friction - - - - - - - RUB
wear into shreds - - - - - - FRAY
wear ostentatiously - - - - - SPORT
wearing away - - - - - - EROSION
wearisome - - - - - - - TOILSOME
wearisome person - - - - - - BORE
wearisomeness - - - - - - TEDIUM
weary - TIRE, BORE, IRK, FATIGUE, FAG
weary (colloq.) - - - - - - - FAG
weasel - - ERMINE, STOAT, OTTER, FERRET, SABLE, MARTEN
weasel-like - - - - - - MUSTELINE
weather - - - - - - - - SEASON
weathercock - - - - - - - - VANE
weather conditions - - - - - CLIMATE
weave - - - SPIN, REEVE, INTERLACE
weave together - RADDLE, BRAID, KNIT
weaver's reed - - - - - - - SLEY
weaving harness - - - - - - HEALD
weaving machine - - - - - - LOOM
web - - NETWORK, FABRIC, TRAP,

TEXTURE, SNARE, PLY, TELA

web, as of cloth - - - PLY
web-footed bird - - - SWAN, GOOSE, AVOCET, PENGUIN, GANNET
web-footed carnivore - - - OTTER
web-footed rodent - - - MUSKRAT
web-like - - - TELAR
web-like membrane - - - TELA, TELAE
wedge - - - CLEAT
wedge in - - - JAM
wedge shaped - - - CUNEATED
wedge shaped piece - - - VEE
wedge shaped support - - - CLEAT
wedlock - - - MARRIAGE, MATRIMONY
wee - - - SMALL
weed - - - TARE
weeding implement - - - HOE
weedy - - - OVERGROWN
weekly - - - AWEEK
ween - - - CONJECTURE
weep - - - MOAN, SOB, CRY, BOOHOO
weeping - - - TEARFUL
weepy - - - TEARY
weigh heavily upon - - - OPPRESS
weighing device - - - STEELYARDS
weight - - - DRAM, TON, PRESSURE, HEFT, ONUS, TROY, CARAT, POUND, IMPORT, MITE
weight allowance - - - TARE
weight of Eastern Asia - - - TAEL
weight on fishlines - - - SINKERS
weight of India - - - SERS, TOLA, SER
weight of Libya - - - KELE
weight in pile driver - - - RAM
weight for wool - - - TOD
weighted down - - - LADEN
weights (system of) - - - TROY
weighty - - - MOMENTOUS
weir - - - DAM
welcome - - - GREET, PLEASING
welkin - - - SKY, AIR
well - - - FOUNTAIN, FIT, HEALTHY, HARDY
well assured - - - CONFIDENT
well behaved - - - GOOD
well bred - - - GENTEEL
well bred woman - - - LADY
well done - - - BULLY
well grounded - - - VALID
well known - - - FAMILIAR
well lining - - - STEEN
well timed - - - OPPORTUNE
Welsh - - - CYMRIC
Welsh astronomer - - - MEE
Welsh onion - - - CIBOL
welt - - - WHEAL, WALE
welter - - - TUMBLE
wen - - - CYST, TUMOR
went first - - - LED
West African baboon - - - MANDRILL, MANDRIL
West African seaport - - - DAKAR
West Coast Indian - - - SERI
West Indian bird - - - TODY
West Indian fish - - - PELON, PEGA
West Indian fruit - - - GENIPAP
West Indian island - - - ANTILLES, BAHAMAS, HAITI, CUBA, NEVIS
West Indian lizard - - - ARBALO
West Indian plant - - - ANIL
West Indian rodent - - - HUTIA
West Indian shark - - - GATA
West Indian shrub - - - ANIL
West Indian sorcery - - - OBI
West Indian tree - - - ARALIE, GENIP
West Indian vessel - - - DROGER
West Point freshman - - - PLEB, PLEBE
West Point sophomore - - - YEARLING
West Saxon king - - - INE
western hemisphere - - - AMERICA
wet - - - MOIST, WATERY, RAINY, HUMID, DAMP, DAMPEN
wet earth - - - MUD
wet (Scot.) - - - WAT
wet thoroughly - - - SOUSE, SOAK
wet with condensed moisture - - - DEW
whale - - - CETE, SPERM, ORC
whale (pert. to) - - - CETIC
whale school - - - GAM
whale skin - - - RIND
whaleboat - - - WHALER
whalebone - - - BALEEN
whaleman's spear - - - LANCE
wharf - - - PIER, LAND, KEY, QUAY
wharf loader or loafer - - - RAT
wharf (var.) - - - QUAI
what - - - EH
what one believes - - - CREDO
what person - - - WHO
whatnot - - - ETAGERE
wheedle - - - CAJOLE
wheel bar - - - AXLE
wheel braker - - - SPRAD
wheel of caster - - - ROLLER
wheel covering - - - TYRE
wheel groove - - - RUT
wheel hub - - - NAVE
wheel mounting - - - AXLE
wheel nave - - - HOB
wheel, as ore - - - RULL
wheel part - - - CAM, SPOKE, RIM, TYRE
wheel (pert. to) - - - ROTAL
wheel shaft - - - AXLE
wheel (small) - - - CASTER
wheel of spur - - - ROWEL
wheel tooth - - - COG
wheel track - - - RUT
wheeled vehicle - - - WAGON
whelm - - - ENGULF
whelp - - - PUPPY
When We Were Very Young author - - - MILNE
where (Latin) - - - UBI
wherewithal - - - MEANS
whet - - - STIMULATE, SHARPEN
whether - - - IF
whetstone - - - HONE
whey of milk - - - SERUM
while - - - YET, AS
whilom - - - FORMER
whim - - - FAD, CAPRICE, HUMOR, NOTION
whimper - - - MEWL, PULE
whimsical - - - DROLL, QUAINT
whimsy - - - CAPRICE
whine - - - COMPLAIN
whine and cry - - - SNIVEL
whinny - - - NEIGH
whip - - - KNOUT, SCOURGE
whip (to) - - - BEAT, FLAY, DEFEAT, SCOURGE, CANE, LASH, FLOG, KNOUT
whip handle - - - CROP
whip of untanned skins - - - RAWHIDE
whiplash - - - THRASH
whirl - - - SPU, SPIN, SWIRL, TWIRL, REEL, EDDY, REVOLVE
whirling - - - SPIN
whirling motion - - - SWIRL

whirlpool - - - - - EDDY, VORTEX
whirlpool (arch.) - - - - - - GURGE
whirlwinds - - - - - - TORNADOES
Whirlwind of Faroe Islands - - - OE
whisk broom - - - - - - - - WISP
whisper - - - - - - - - - - LISP
whistle - - - - - - - PIPE, SIREN
whit - - - - - - DOIT, JOT, IOTA
white - - PALE, HOAR, ASHY, SNOWY
white animal - - - - - - - ALBINO
white bony substance - - - - IVORY
White Cliffs site - - - - - - DOVER
white crystalline acid (designating) - - TEREBIC
white crystalline compound - - BORAX
white of egg - - - ALBUMEN, GLAIR
white fiber - - - - - - - - SISAL
white frost - - - - - - - - - RIME
white grapes - - - - - - MALAGAS
white hair (poet.) - - - - - SNOW
white man - - - - - - - - PALEFACE
white metal - - - - - - - - - TIN
white mountains - - - - - TREMONT
white poplar - - - - - - - ABELE
white silk veil - - - - - - - ORALE
white spruce - - - - - - EPINETTE
white substance - - - - - - IVORY
white substance of nervous system - - ALBA
white vestment - - - - - ALB, AMICE
white wine - - - - - - - - MALAGA
white yam - - - - - - - - - UBE
Whitefriars, London - - - - - ALSATIS
whiten - - BLANCH, SNOW, BLEACH
whitewash - - - - - - - - PARGET
whither - - - - - - - - - WHERE
whitish - - - - - - - - - CHALKY
whittle - - - - - - - - - - - CUT
whole - - ALL, ENTIRE, COMPLETE, AGGREGATE, TOTAL, ENSEMBLE, UNDIVIDED
whole number - - - - - - INTEGER
wholesome - - - - - - - - SALUTARY
wholly - - - - - - - - - - - ALL
wholly occupied - - - - - - RAPT
whoop - - - - - - - - - - HOOP
whorl - - - - - - - - - VOLUTION
why - - - - - - - - - WHEREFORE
wicked - - - - - - - - EVIL, SINFUL
wicked person - - - FIEND, CAITIFF
wickedness - - EVIL, SIN, DEPRAVITY
wicker basket - - - - - - PANNIER
wickerwork hamper - - CRATE, CREEL
wide - - - - - - - - - - BROAD
wide awake - - - - - - - - ALERT
wide mouth jar or jug - - OLLA, EWER, OLA
widen - - - - - - - - - AMPLIFY
widespread - - - PREVALENT, RIFE
widespread fear - - - - - - PANIC
widgeon - - - - - - - - - - SMEE
widow - - - - - - - - - - RELICT
widow's coin - - - - - - - - - MITE
widow's dower (law) - - - - - TERCE
widow's income - - - - - - DOWER
wield - - - MANAGE, PLY, HANDLE
wield diligently - - - PLY, HANDLE
wierd - - - - - - - EERY, EERIE
wife - - - - - - - - - - SPOUSE
wig - - - - TETE, TOUPEE, PERUKE
wigwam - - - - - - TEPEE, TEEPEE
wild - - FEROCIOUS, FERAL, FERINE, FIERCE
wild animal - BEAST, POLECAT, ELK, FOX, TIGER, LION, LYNX, MOOSE
wild apple - - - - - - - CREEPER
wild ass of Asia - - - - - - ONAGER
wild buffalo of India (female) - ARNEE
wild buffalo of India (male) - - ARNA
wild cat - - - - EYRA, LYNX, OCELOT
wild celery - - - - - - - SMALLAGE
wild cherry - - - - - - - - - GEAN
wild cranberry - - - - - - PEMBINA
wild cry - - - - - - - - - - EVOE
wild dog of India - - - - - - DHOLE
wild duck - - - - - - - MALLARD
wild flower - - - - ASTER, ARBUTUS
wild geese (var.) - - - - - - BRENTS
wild goat - - - - - - - - - - IBEX
wild goose - - - BRANT, BARNACLE
wild hog - - - - - - - - - - BOAR
wild ox - - - - - - - - ANOA, URUS
wild ox (extinct) - - - - - - URUS
wild ox of Malayan peninsula - BANTENG
wild pig - - - - - - - - - - BOAR
wild plant - - - - - - - - - WEED
wild plum - - - - - - - - - SLOE
wild revelry - - - - - - - - ORGY
wild sheep - - - SHA, ARGALI, URIAL
wild sheep of India - - - - - URIAL
wild shrub - - - - - - - - GORSE
wild swine - - - - - - - - - BOAR
wild tract of land - - - - - - HEATH
wildcat - - - - EYRA, LYNX, OCELOT
wildly moved - - - - - - FRANTIC
wile - - - - - - - - - TRICK, ART
will - - - - - - BEQUEATH, DECREE
will left and made - - - - - TESTATE
willing - - - - - - - - LIEVE, READY
willing (more) - - - - - - RATHER
willing (obs. form) - - - - - LIEVE
willingly - - - - - - - - - - - LIEF
willow - - - - - OSIER, ITEA, SALIX
willow twig - - - - - - - - - OSIER
willowy - - - - - - - - - FLEXIBLE
wilt - - - - - - - - - - - - DROOP
wily - - - - - - SLY, FOXY, ARTFUL
win - - - - GAIN, ACQUIRE, ENTICE, PREVAIL, EARN, TRIUMPH, GET, OBTAIN
win advantage over - - - - - - BEST
win over - - - - DEFEAT, PERSUADE
win through effort - - - - - - EARN
wince - - - - - - - - - - FLINCH
winch - - - - - - HOIST, WINDLASS
wind - - - - - GALE, BREATH, COIL
wind blast - - - - - - - - - GUST
wind of France - - - - - - - - BISE
wind gauge - - - - - ANEMOMETER
wind into a hank - - - - - - SKEIN
wind indicator - - - - - - - - VANE
wind instrument - - - - REED, HORN, CLARINET, TUBA, ORGAN, BAGPIPE, FLUTE, BUGLE, ACCORDION
wind instrument of Mexico - - CLARIN
wind player - - - - - - - - PIPER
wind (pert. to) - - - - - - EOLIAN
wind of Spanish coast - - - - SOLANO
wind (to) - - - - - - - - - - COIL
wind spirally - - - - - - - - COIL
windflower - - - - - - - ANEMONE
winding - - - - - SPIRAL, SINUOUS
winding twin - - - - - - - WIMPLE
windlass - - - - - CAPSTAN, WINCH
windmill arm - - - - - - - - VANE
window above a door - - - TRANSOM
window compartment - - - - - PANE

W

window cover - - - - - SHUTTER
wing - - - ALA, PINION, ALAE (pl.)
wing of building - - - - - - ANNEX
wing footed - - - - - - - ALIPED
wing of house - - - - - - - - ELL
wing membrane of bat - - PATAGIUM
wing shaped - - ALARY, ALAR, ALATE
winged - - - ALATE, FLEW, ALATED
winged, as birds (her.) - - - - AILE
winged hat of Mercury - - PETASUS
winged insect - - - - - WASP, MOTH
winged sandals of Mercury - - TALARIA
winged serpent - - - - - - DRAGON
winged steed - - - - - - PEGASUS
wingless - - - - - - - - APTERAL
winglike - - - - - - - ALAR, ALARY
wings (pert. to) - - - - - - - ALAR
wink - NICTATE, NICTITATE, TWINKLE
winner - - - - - - - - - - VICTOR
winnow - - - - - - - - - - FAN
winnowing machine - - - - - - FAN
winter fodder - - - - - - - - HAY
winter (pert. to) - - - - - - HIEMAL
winter resort - - - - - - - MIAMI
winter vehicle - - - SLEDGE, SLED
wipe - - - - - MOP, CLEAN, SWAB
wipe out - - - - - - - - ERASE
wire - - - - - - - - TELEGRAPH
wire coil - - - - - - - - SPRING
wire measure - - - - - - - - MIL
wire pen - - - - - - - - - CAGE
wire rope - - - - - - - - CABLE
wire-toothed brush - - - - - - CARD
wireless - - - - - - - - - RADIO
wireless antenna - - - - - - AERIAL
wireman - - - - - - - - - WIRER
wiry - - - - - - - - - - SINEWY
Wisconsin city - - - - - - RACINE
wisdom - LORE, GNOSIS, ERUDITION, KNOWLEDGE
wise - - SAGE, LEARNED, ERUDITE, PRUDENT, KNOWING, SANE
wise answers - - - - - - ORACLES
wise counsellor - - NESTOR, MENTOR
wise men - SAGES, MAGI, SOLOMONS, SOLONS, NESTORS
wise saying - - - - - ADAGE, ORACLE
wise scholar - - - - - - - SAVANT
wisely - - - - - - - - - SAGELY
wish - - HOPE, DESIRE, WANT, COVET
wisp - - - - - - - - - - SHRED
wisp of hair (Scot.) - - - - - TATE
wisp of smoke - - - - - - - FLOC
wisteria - - - - - - - - VIOLET
wistful - - - - - - - - - YEARNING
wit HOUMOUR, SENSE, SATIRE, BANTER, WAGGERY, CLEVERNESS, AS, WAG, INGENUITY
witch - - - - - - HEX, LAMIA, HAG
witchcraft - - - - - - - SORCERY
with the bow (mus.) - - - - - ARCO
with difficulty - - - - - EDGEWISE
with the end first - - - - - ENDWAYS
with full force - - - - - - AMAIN
with great ability - - - - - - ABLY
with hand on hip - - - - - AKIMBO
with might - - - - - - - - AMAIN
with (prefix) - - - SYN, CON, COM
with (Scot.) - - - - - - - - - WI
with this - - - - - - - HEREWITH
withal - - - - - - - - - - ALSO
withdraw - RETREAT, RETRACT, RETIRE, SECEDE, SECLUDE, RECEDE, DETRACT
withdrawal - RECESSION, DEPARTURE
wither - SERE, SEAR, SHRINK, WILT, DRY, DROOP, SHRIVEL
withered old woman - - - - - CRONE
withhold - - - KEEP, DENY, DETAIN
withhold business from - - BOYCOTT
withhold food from - - - - - STARVE
withhold from - - - - - - - SPARE
within - - INTO, INSIDE, INNER, IN
within (comb. form) - - ESO, ENDO
within (prefix) - - - - - - INTRA
without anxiety - - - - - CARELESS
without a center - - - - - ACENTRIC
without charge - - - - - - - FREE
without (comb. form) - - - - - ECTO
without company - - - - - - LONELY
without discomfort - - - - - PAINLESS
without elevation - - - - - - FLAT
without end - - - - - - - - EVER
without feeling - - - - - - - NUMB
without feet - - - - - - - - APOD
without foliage - - - - - LEAFLESS
without (Fr.) - - - - - - - SANS
without friends - - - - - - - LORN
without gentlemanly instincts - - CAD
without large plants - - - TREELESS
without (Latin) - - - - - - - SINE
without life - - - - - - - AMORT
without limits of duration - - AGELESS
without luster - - - - - - - - MAT
without mate - - - - - - - - ODD
without (prefix) - - - - - - - - IN
without purpose - - - - - AIMLESS
without reason - - - - - INSENSATE
without reserve - - - - - - FREELY
without result - - - - - - - BLANK
without a saddle - - - - - BAREBACK
without small leaves below calyx - - - BRACTLESS
without sound - - - - - - TONELESS
without purpose - - - - - - - IDLY
without teeth - - - - - - EDENTATE
without title - - - - - - NAMELESS
withstand - RESIST, OPPOSE, ENDURE
withstand use - - - - - WEARS, WEAR
witness - - - - - - - ATTEST, SEE
witnessed - - - - - - - - - SEEN
witnessing clause of a writ - - TESTE
witticism - - - - MOT, JOKE, SALLY
witty - - - - - - - - - FACETIOUS
witty person - - - - - WAG, PUNSTER
witty reply - - - - - - - REPARTEE
witty sally - - - - - - - - - QUIP
witty saying - - - - - - - - - MOT
wizard - - - - - - - - - - MAGE
wizen - - - - - - - - - - SHRIVEL
wobble - - - - - - - - VACILLATE
woe - - - - - ILL, DISASTER, BANE
woebegone - - - - - - - DESOLATE
woeful - - - - - - - - - - - SAD
wolf's foot - - - - - - - - PAD
wolfhound - - - - - - - - - ALAN
wolframite - - - - - - - - - CAL
woman's cloak - - - - - - DOLMAN
woman's club - - - - - - SOROSIS
woman's garment - - - - - - JUPON
woman's marriage (pert. to) (or portion) DOTAL
woman's part of Mohammedan house - - HAREM
woman's shoulder cape - - - BERTHA
woman's station - - - - - - DAME
woman's suffrage leader - - ANTHONY
woman under religious vows - - NUN
woman who makes and leaves a will - - TESTATRIX
womanish - - - - - - EFFEMINATE

won through effort - - - - EARNED
wonder - - - - - - MARVEL, AWE
wonderful - - - - - - MARVELOUS
wondering fear - - - - - - - AWE
wont - - - - - - CUSTOM, HABIT
woo - - - - - SUE, COURT, SOLICIT
woo (Scot.) - - - - - - - - SPLUNT
wood - EBONY, TEAK, GROVE, TIMBER, WALNUT, OAK, FIR, BALSA, POPLAR
wood ash substance - - - - - POTASH
wood check wheel motion - - SPRAG
wood (comb. form) - - - - - - HYL
wood deity - - - - - - - - - FAUN
wood of East Indian tree - - - ENG
wood eating insect - - - - - TERMITE
wood fastening strip - - - - BATTEN
wood hyacinths - - - - - HAREBELLS
wood (light) - - - - - - - - BALSA
wood louse - - - - - - - - SLATER
wood nymph - SPRITE, DRYAS, DRYAD
wood of sandarac tree - - - - ALERCE
wood (small) - - - - - - - - GROVE
wood sorrel - - - - - OCA, OXALIS
wood used as a break - - - - SPRAG
woodbine green - - - - - - PERIDOT
woodchuck - - - - - - - - MARMOT
woodcutter - - - - - - - - SAWYER
wooded - - - - - - - - - SYLVAN
wooded hill - - - - - - - - - HOLT
wooden - - - - - - - - - STOLID
wooden bench - - - - - - - SETTEE
wooden container - - - - CRATE, BOX, BARREL, CASE
wooden cup - - - - - - - - NOGGIN
wooden golf club - - DRIVER, SPOON
wooden head hammer - - - - MALLET
wooden joint - - - - - - - - TENON
wooden peg - - - - - - - - - - NOG
wooden pin - DOWEL, FID, TRENAIL, PEG, NOG
wooden pole - - - - - - STAFF, ROD
wooden shoe - - - - - - - - SABOT
woodland - - - - - - - - - FOREST
woodland bird - - - - - - TANAGER
woodland clear space - - - - - GLADE
woodland deity - - SATYR, PAN, FAUN
woodland plant - - - - - MANDRAKE
woods - - - - - - - TREES, FOREST
woodwind instrument - - - - - OBOE
woodworker - - - - - - - CARPENTER
woodworking tool - - - - - - ADZE
woody corn spike - - - - - - - COB
woody fiber - - - - - - - - - BAST
woody grass stem - - - - - - REED
woody tissue of a plant - - - XYLEM
woody twig - - - - - - - - - ROD
wool - - - - - - - - - - - - LANA
wool coloured - - - - - - - BEIGE
wool (kind) - - - MERINO, CHALLIS, ALPACA
woolen cluster - - - - - - - - NEP
woolen fabric - TAMIS, TAMINE, SERGE, MOREEN, DELAINE, BEIGE, RATINE, CHALLIS, TWEED
woolen shawl - - - - - - - PAISLEY
woolen surface of cloth - - - - - NAP
wooly - - - - - - LANATE, FLEECY
wooly hair - - - - - - - - - SHAG
wooly surface of cloth - - - - - NAP
word - - MESSAGE, TERM, TIDINGS, PROMISE
word of affirmation - - - - - AMEN
word of assent - - - - - - - AMEN
word to call cows - - - - - - BOS
word of commiseration - - - - ALAS
word of consent - - - - - YES, AMEN
word game - - - - - - - - CRAMBO
word of honour - - - - - - PAROLE
word of lamentation - - - - - ALAS
word of mouth - - - - - - - PAROL
word of negation - - - - - NOT, NO
word opposed in meaning to another - - ANTONYM
word of promise - - - - - - PAROLE
word puzzle - - - - - - - ANAGRAM
word of similar meaning - - SYNONYM
word square - - - - - PALINDROME
word for word - - - - - - LITERAL
wordbook - - - - - - - - LEXICON
words of play - - - - - - - - LINES
work - - OPERATE, OPUS, REMARK, TOIL
work aimlessly - - - - - - - PUTTER
work appearing in successive parts - - SERIAL
work at - - - - - - - - - - - - DO
work of art - - ETCHING, PAINTING
work drudgingly - - - - - SCRABBLE
work for - - - - - - - - - SERVE
work group - - - - - - - - - GANG
work hard - MOIL, PLY, DRUDGE, TOIL
work hard (Scot.) - - - - - - TEW
work inefficiently - - - - - POTTER
work out - - - - SOLVE, ELABORATE
work out in detail - - - - ELABORATE
work over - REHASH, REVAMP, REWORK
work over to new form - - - - RECAST
work party - - - - - - - - - - BEE
work and press into a mass - - KNEAD
work at steadily - - - - - - - PLY
work in superficial manner - DABBLE
work too hard - - - - - - OVERDO
work wearisomely - - - - - - MOIL
work with hands - - - - - - KNEAD
work with a loom - - - - - - WEAVE
workaday - - - - - - - - PROSAIC
worked at - - - - - - - - - PLIED
worker - - - - - - - - - - TOILER
worker in alloys - - - - - PEWTERER
worker in rattan - - - - - - CANER
working agreement - - - - - - CODE
working automaton - - - - - ROBOT
workman - - - - - - - - LABORER
workshop - - ATELIER, STUDIO, LAB
workshop (colloq.) - - - - - - LAB
world - - - - - - - - - - EARTH
world fair - - - - - - EXPOSITION
World War I battle - - - - - MARNE
world wide - - - - - - - - GLOBAL
worldly - - - - - - - - - TERRENE
worm - ASP, CADEW, ESS, EIS, LOA, ANNELID
wormlike form of insect - - - - LARVA
worn garment (colloq.) - - - - - DUD
worn out - - EFFETE, DETERIORATED, PASSE, SPENT, OLD
worn into shreds - - - - - - FRAYED
worry - FRET, CARE, HARASS, STEW, BAIT
worry (colloq.) - - - - - - - - STEW
worse - - - - - INFERIOR, POORER
worship - IDOLIZE, REVERE, VENERATE, ADORATION
worshipers of false gods - IDOLATORS
worshipful - - - - - - - REVERENT
worshipped animal - - - - - - TOTEM
worst - - - BEAT, POOREST, DEFEAT
worsted - - - - - - - - - - WOOL
worsted cloth - - - - - - - SERGE
worsted yarn - - - - - - - CADDIS

worsts (colloq.) - - - - - - BESTS
worth - - - - VALUE, MERIT, USE, DESERVING
worth having - - - - - - DESIRABLE
worthless - - - BAD, TRASHY, RACA
worthless (Bib.) - - - - - - - RACA
worthless (colloq.) - - - - - - N.G.
worthless dog - - - - - - - CUR
worthless fellow - - - BUM, LOSER
worthless hand at cards - - - BUST
worthless leaving - - - - - - - ORT
worthless matter - - - - - - DREGS
worthless thing (slang) - - - TRIPE
worthy of (be) - DESERVE, DESERVING
wound mark - - - - - - SCAR, SCAB
wound with a horn - - - - - - GORE
woven cloth - - - - - - - FABRIC
woven fabric - - - TISSUE, TEXTURE, BLANKET, WEB
woven in meshes - - - - - - NETS
wrangle - - BICKER, DISPUTE, SPAR
wrap - - CERE, ENVELOP, ENSWATH, SHAWL, ENFOLD, SWATHE
wrap a dead body - - - - - - CERE
wrap round and round - - - - - ROLL
wrath - - ANGER, IRE, FURY, RAGE
wrathful - - - - - - - - IRATE
wreak - - INFLICT, EXACT, GRATIFY
wreath - TWINE, ANADEM, GARLAND, LEI, GREEN, CIRCLET
wreath bearing a knight's crest - ORLE
wreath of olive - - - - - - IRESINE
wreath (poet.) - - - - - - ANADEM
wreck - - - - - - - - - - RUIN
wrench - - SPANNER, WREST, TWIST
wrench out of shape - - - DISTORT
wrest - - WRENCH, WRING, SNATCH
wrest illegally - - - - - - EXTORT
wrestle - - - - TUSSLE, STRUGGLE
wrestlers's cushion - - - - - - MAT
wretched - MISERABLE, ILL, FORLORN
wriggle - - - - - SQUIRM, WANGLE
wriggly - - - - - - - - - - EELY
wring - - - EXTRACT, WREST, TWIST
wrinkled - - - - - - - - RUGATE
wrinkles - - CREASES, RUGAE, CRIMP, FOLD, RUGAS, RIMPLES, CRINKLES, CRIMPS
wrist - - - - - - - - - CARPUS
writ summoning a jury - - - VENIRE
write - - TRANSCRIBE, PEN, INDITE, COMPOSE, INSCRIBE, SCRIBE
write carelessly - - - - - SCRAWL
write one's name - - - - - - SIGN
write poorly - - - - - - - SCRAWL
writer - - AUTHOR, SCRIBE, PENMAN
writer of prose - - - - - PROSAIST
writer of verse - - POET, SONGSTER
writing character - - - - - - WEDGE
writing flourish - - - - - CURLICUE
writing implement - - - - - CHALK
writing instrument - - - - - STYLUS
writing material - - - - - - PAPER
writing table - - - - - - - DESK
written agreement - - - - - CARTEL
written communication - - - LETTER
written discourse - - - - - - PAPER
written engagement on bill of exchange - AVAL
written exposition - - - - TREATISE
written instrument - - - - - - DEED
written legal orders for writs - PRECIPES
written promise to pay - - - - NOTE
wrong - AMISS, FAULTY, INJURE, ERR
wrong (be) - - - - - - - - - ERR
wrong (do) - - - - - - - - MISDO
wrong act - - - - - - - - MISDEED
wrong (colloq.) - - - - - - - OFF
wrong move - - - - - - - MISSTEP
wrong name - - - - - - MISNOMER
wrong (prefix)- - - - - - MAL, MIS
wrongdoing - - - - SIN, EVIL, CRIME
wrongful act - - - - - - - - - TORT
wrongful dispossession - - - - OUSTER
wrongs - - - - - - - - - - MALA
wroth - - - - - - - - - - IRATE
wry - - TWISTED, TWIST, COMFORT, WARPED
Wyoming mountain - - MORAN, TETON

X

xanthic - - - - - - - - - YELLOW

Y

yak - - - - - - - - - - SARLAK
Yale - - - - - - - - - - - - ELI
yam - - - - - - - - - UVE, UBE
yank - - - - - - - - - - - JERK
yap - - - - - - - - - - - YELP
yap stone money - - - - - - - FEI
yarn - - - - TALE, CLEW, CREWEL
yarn fibers - - - - - - - STRANDS
yawn - - - - - - - - - - - GAPE
yawning - - - - - - - - GAPING
yawning hollow - - - - - - CHASM
year - - - - - - - - - - ANNUM
year's record - - - - - - - ANNAL
year of the reign - - - - - - A.R.
yearbook - - - - - - - ALMANAC
yearling sheep - - - - - - - TAG
yearn - - LONG, DESIRE, PANT, PINE
yearning - - - - - - - - WISTFUL
years of one's life - - - - - - AGE
yeast - - LEAVEN, FROTH, FERMENT
yeast on brewing liquor - - - - BARM
yell - - - - - - - SHOUT, ROAR
yellow - - - XANTHIC, JAUNDICED
yellow brown - - - - - - - SORREL
yellow bugle - - - - - - - - IVA
yellow gray colour - - - - - - DRAB
yellow like gold - - - - - - - GILT
yellow ocher - - - - - - - - SIL
yellow pigment - - CHROME, ETIOLIN
yellow pond lily - - - - - - NUPHAR
yellow toadflax - - - - - RANSTEAD
yellow brown - - - - - - - - - DUN
yellow green mineral - - - - EPIDOTE
yellow red - - - - - - - - - CORAL
yellowish - - - SALLOW, XANTHIC, ICTERINE
yelp - - - - - - - - - YAP, YIP
yen - - - - - - - - - - DESIRE
yeoman - - - - - - - FREEHOLDER
yes - - - - - - - - YEA, AY, AYE
yes (German) - - - - - - - - - JA
yes (Italian) - - - - - - - - - - SI
yet - BESIDES, THOUGH, BUT, WHILE, HOWEVER, FURTHER, STILL
yield - - OBEY, CEDE, RETURN, BOW, SUCCUMB, NET, CONCEDE, RELENT, SUBMIT, PRODUCE, GIVE

yield precious metals - - - - - PAN
yield under pressure - - - - - GIVE
yielding - - - - - - - - - - SOFT
yodel - - - - - - - - - - WARBLE
yogi - - - - - - - FAKIR, ASCETIC
yoke - - - SERVITUDE, LINK, TEAM, COUPLE, JOIN, HARNESS
yoke of beasts - - - - - - - - SPAN
yon - - - - - - - DISTANT, THAT
yonder - - - - - - - - - - - - YON
you (arch.) - - - YE, THOU, THEE
you people - - - - - - - - - - YE
young - - - - - - - - JUVENILE
young antelope - - - - - - - KID
young barracuda - - - - - - SPET
young bird - - - - - - - NESTLING
young bird of prey - - - - - EAGLET
young bluefish - - - - - - SNAPPER
young branch - - - - - - - SHOOT
young cat - - - - - - KITTEN, KIT
young chicken - - - - - - - FRYER
young child - - - - - - - - - TAD
young cod - - - - - - - - - SCROD
young deer - - - - - - - - - FAWN
young dog - - - - - - - - - PUP
young eel - - - - - - - - - ELVER
young fish - - - - - - - - - FRY
young fowl - - - - - - - - - BIRD
young fox - - - - - - - - - - CUB
young frog - - - - - - - TADPOLE
young girl - - - - - - - MAIDEN
young goat - - - - - - - - KID
young hare - - - - - - - LEVERET
young hawk - - - - - - - - EYAS
young hen - - - PULLET, CHICKEN
young herring - - - BRIT, SARDINE
young hog - - - - SHOAT, SHOTE
young horse - - - - - - COLT, FOAL
young lady - - - - - - - - BELLE
young lion - - - - - - - - LIONET
young man - - - - - - - - - BOY
young man (Scot.) - - - - - LADDY
young of animals - - - - - - BROOD
young onion - - - - - - - SCALLION
young owl - - - - - - - - - OWLET
young oyster - - - - - - - - SPAT
young pig (dial.) - - - - - - - ELT
young plant - - - - - - SEEDLING
young rowdy - - - - - - HOODLUM
young salmon - - - - - - - PARR
young screen star - - - - - STARLET
young seal - - - - - - - - - PUP
young sheep - - - - - - - - LAMB
young swan - - - - - - - CYGNET
young swine - - - - - - - - PIG
young tree frog - - - - - - PEEPER
young woman - - - MAIDEN, GIRL
younger - - - - - - - TOT, JUNIOR
youngest son - - - - - - - CADET
youngster - - LAD, TOT, TAD, SHAVER
your (arch.) - - - - - - - - - THY
yours (arch.) - - - - - - - - THINE
youth - - LAD, STRIPLING, BOYHOOD
youthful - - - - - YOUNG, JUVENILE
Yucatan Indian - - - - - - - - MAYA
Yucca-like plant - - - SOTOE, SOTOL
Yugoslav - - - - - - - - - - - SERB
Yugoslav coin - - - - - - - - DINAR
Yugoslav commune - - - - - VELES
Yugoslav partisan leader - - - - - - MIKHAILOVITCH
Yugoslav partriot and leader - - TITO
Yugoslav premier - - - - - - TITO
Yukon mountain peak - - - - LOGAN
Yuman Indian - - - - - - - MOHAVE

Z

Z (English form) - - - - - - - - ZED
zeal - - - ARDOR, ELAN, FERVOR, INTEREST
zealot - - - FANATIC, ENTHUSIAST
zealous - - - - ARDENT, EARNEST
zenith - - - TOP, MERIDIAN, ACME
Zeno's followers - - - - - - STOICS
zero - - NOTHING, NAUGHT, CIPHER, NOUGHT
zest - - - - - - - - - - - - SPICE
zesty - - - - - - - - - - PIQUANT
Zeus - - - - - - - - - - - JUPITER
Zeus' brother - - - - - - - HADES
Zeus changed to stone - - - - NIOBE
Zeus' daughter - - - - - - - - IRENE
Zeus' first wife - - - - - - - METIS
Zeus' love - - - - - - - - - - IO
Zeus' mother - - - - - - - - RHEA
Zeus' sister - - - - - - - - - HERA
Zeus' son - - ARES, HERMES, ARGUS
Zeus' wife - - - - - - - - - HERA
zigzag ski race - - - - - - SLALOM
zinc - - - - - SPELTER, GALVANIZE
zinc ore - - - - - - - - - BLENDE
Zodiac's fifth sign - - - - - - LEO
Zodiac's sign - - ARIES, LEO, LIBRA, VIRGO
Zodiac's second sign - - - - TAURUS
Zodiac's third sign - - - - - GEMINI
Zola's novel - - - - - - - - NANA
zonal - - - - - - - - - REGIONAL
zone - BELT, AREA, REGION, ENGIRDLE, GIRDLE
zone of contention for vegetable mastery ECOTONE
zoo - - - - - - - - - MENAGERIE
zool with spiny tip - - - - ARISTATE
zoroastrian - - - - - - - - PARSEE
zoroastrian bible - - - - - - AVESTA
zoroastrian of India - - - - - PARSI

MEASUREMENTS

1/6 drachma	OBOL
1/8 mile	FURLONG
1/10 of an ephah	OMER
1/10 of a meter	DECIMETER
1/16 of an ounce	DRAM
1/16 of a yard	NAIL
.025 acre	ARE
1 cubic meter	STERE
2 ens	EM
2 quarts	FLAGON
3 miles	LEAGUE
4 inches	HAND
5 centimes	SOU
5 (comb. form)	TENT, PENT
5½ yards	ROD
6 (prefix)	HEX
9 inches	SPAN
10	X
12	DOZEN
12 dozen	GROSS
16 annas	RUPEE
16½ feet	ROD
20	SCORE
20 cwt.	TON
20 quires	REAM
26 mile race	MARATHON
39.37 inches	METER
40	XL
49	IL
50	L
51	LI
55	LV
60 grains	DRAM
90	XC
99	IC
100	C
100 cubic feet	TON
100 make a yen	SEN
100 sen	YEN
100 square meters	AR, ARE
110	CX
119.6 square yards	ARE, AR
120 yards of silk	LEA
144 units	GROSS
150	CL
160 square rods	ACRE
200 milligrams	CARAT
220 yards	FURLONG
300 yards of linen	LEA
320 rods	MILE
433rd asteroid	EROS
451	CDLI
480 sheets	REAM
501	DI
550	DL
600	DC
900	CM
1000	M
1000 square meters	DECARE
1001	MI
1050	ML
1100	MC
1760 yards	MILE
2000	MM
2000 pounds	TON
4047 square meters	ACRE
4840 square yards	ACRE
3.1416	PI
100,000 rupees	LAC